THE GOVERNOR

THE GOVERNOR

The Life and Legacy
of
Leland Stanford

A California Colossus

There were Giants on the Earth in those Days. —*Genesis 6:4*

VOLUME TWO

by
Norman E. Tutorow

With the Special Research and Editorial Assistance of
Evelyn "Evie" LaNora Tutorow
Foreword by Governor George Deukmejian

THE ARTHUR H. CLARK COMPANY
Spokane, Washington
2004

THE ARTHUR H. CLARK COMPANY
P.O. Box 14707
Spokane, WA 99214

ISBN 0-87062-326-5

Library of Congress Cataloging-in-Publication Data

Tutorow, Norman E.
 The governor : the life and legacy of Leland Stanford, a California
colossus / by Norman E. Tutorow.
    p. cm.
Includes bibliographical references (p.) and index.
 ISBN 0-87062-326-5 (hardcover : alk. paper)
 1. Stanford, Leland, 1824-1893. 2. Governors—California—Biography.
3. Businesspeople—California—Biography. 4. Legislators—United
States—Biography. 5. United States. Congress. Senate—Biography. 6.
California—Politics and government—1850-1950. I. Title.
E664.S78T77 2004
979.4'04'092—dc22
                        2003023058

Dedicated to
Evie
and to the
loving memory of
Miss Lizzie Hull

Contents

ILLUSTRATIONS

ABBREVIATIONS

Abbreviated entries in the notes are given in full in the bibliography.

A & D	Agnew & Deffebach
A & PRR	Atlantic & Pacific Railroad
AAC	Alfred A. Cohen
AAK	Alfred A. Knopf
AAS	Aaron A. Sargent
AB	Assembly Bill
Abb.	Abbreviated
ABC	Alley, Bowen & Co.
ABNC	American Bank Note Co.
AC	Amador County
ACAS	A.C. Armstrong and Son
ACBD	Albany County Book of Deeds
ACC	Appleton-Century-Crofts
Acct.	Accountant
ACD	*Albany City Directory*
ACHAR	*Albany County Historical Association Record*
ACPH	Alta California Printing House
ACR	Alameda County Records
ACSAJ	*Appendix to the California Senate and Assembly Journals*
ACSC	Automobile Club of Southern California
Ad.	Advertisement
AD	Albert Dressler
ADB	*Australian Dictionary of Biography*
Add.	Address
ADHBS	Administration du Dictionnaire Historique et Biographique de la Suisse
Admin.	Administration
AdP	Adobe Press
AH	*American Heritage*
AHC	A. H. Cawston
AHCC	Arthur H. Clark Co.
AHS	Arizona Historical Society
AJJ	Alfred J. Johnston, California Superintendent of State Printing
AL	Abraham Lincoln
ALBC	A. L. Bancroft and Co.
ALGB	Ancienne Librairie Germer Bailliére
ALS	Autograph Letter Signed
A.m.	ante meridian
AM	*Atlantic Monthly*

Amal.	Amalgamation
AmHC	American Heritage Center
AMR	*Arizona Mining Record*
AMRob	A. M. Robertson
AMS	*American Men of Science*
AN	*American Neptune*
ANC	American News Co.
Ann.	Annual
Anon.	Anonymous
ANT	Alban Nelson Towne
AP	Arno Press
APr	Adams Press
APHSSC	*Annual Publications of the Historical Society of Southern California*
App.	Approved/Appendix
Approx.	Approximately
APS	Asa Phillips (Phil) Stanford
AQ	*Academic Questions*
ARG	Architectural Resources Group
Ariz.	Arizona
AR, CPRR	*Annual Report, Central Pacific Railroad*
AR, SPC	*Annual Report, Southern Pacific Co.*
AR, SPRR	*Annual Report, Southern Pacific Railroad*
Art(s).	Article(s)
ASCE	American Society of Civil Engineers
ASCET	*American Society of Civil Engineers Transactions*
Assn.	Association
Assoc.	Associate
Asst.	Assistant
Assy.	Assembly
Assy/man	Assemblyman
AT	*Adobe Trails*
ATSF	Atchison, Topeka and Santa Fe Railway Co.
Att.	Attorney
AUA	American Unitarian Association
Ave.	Avenue
AWM	*American Wine Merchant*
AWPC	American West Publishing Co.
BaB	Ballantine Books

BB	Bertha Berner	CB	Chronicle Books
BBHS	*Bulletin of the Business Historical Society*	CC	Charles Crocker
BBR	Berkeley Branch Railroad	CCA	Centre Canadien d'Architecture
BC	Bancroft Co.	CCCC	Charles C. Chapman Co.
B & C	Bacon and Co.	CCH	Charles C. Hoag
BCC	Book Club of California	*CCom*	*California Commerce*
BCCQN	*Book Club of California Quarterly Newsletter*	CCRR	California Central Rail Road
		CCSF	City and County of San Francisco
BCl	Belford, Clarke	*CDI*	*California Death Index*
BCR	Butte County Records	CDPR	California Department of Parks & Recreation
BDAC	*Biographical Directory of the American Congress*		
		CED	California Executive Department
BEMSSC	Board of Examiners of the Medical Society of the State of California	CER	California Executive Records
		Cert.	Certificate
BGC	Baker, Godwin & Co.	*CF*	*California Freemason*
BGT	B[enedikt] G[otthelf] Teubner	CFC	Charles Frederick Crocker
BHB	Berkeley Hills Books	C & FC	Contract and Finance Co.
BI	Brookings Institution	CG	Coast Guard
Biblio.	Bibliography, bibliographical	*CH*	*California History* (1978–present)
Bio.	Biography, biographical	Chap.	Chapter
BL	Bancroft Library	CHC	Century History Co.
BMC	Bender-Moss Co.	ChH	Chapel Hill
BMuC	Blair-Murdock Co.	CLB	Cooke & LeCount, Booksellers
BMJ	*British Medical Journal*	CHL	Chadwyck-Healey Ltd
BoB	Bonanza Books	CHP	Chadwick House Publishers
BP	Boxwood Press	*CHQ*	*California Historical Quarterly* (1972–1977)
BPC	Burke Publishing Co.		
BPI	Beekman Publishers, Inc.	CHS	California Historical Society
BR	Britton & Rey	CHSoc	Clinton Historical Society
Brig.	Brigadier	*CHSQ*	*California Historical Society Quarterly* (1923–1971)
BS	Biographical Society		
BSFC	Brown, Son & Ferguson Co.	CIF	California Information File
BSMFW	*Bulletin of the Society of Medical Friends of Wine*	CINMS/CINP	Channel Island National Marine Sanctuary and Channel Island National Park
BuC	Butte County		
BUL	Brown University Library	CLB	Cooke and LeCount Booksellers
Bur.	Bureau	CLE	Custom & Limited Editions
Bus.	Business	CLI	Clinton Liberal Institute
BUW	*Bulletin of the University of Wisconsin*	CLMP	Cypress Lawn Memorial Park
		ClP	Clarendon Press
CAA	California Alumni Association	*CMB*	*California Mail Bag*
CAJ	*California Assembly Journal*	CMC	Coward-McCann
Calif.	California	*CMP*	*California Magazine of the Pacific*
Calif. Assy.	California Assembly	CMSBC	C.M. Saxton, Barker & Co.
Calif. Com.	California Commandery	Co.	Company
Calif. Sen.	California Senate	Col.	Colonel
Calif Stats	*California Statutes*	Coll.	Collection
CAM	Crocker Art Museum	Colo.	Colorado
CAS	California Academy of Sciences	Com.	Commerce
C & H	Chapman & Hall	Comm.	Committee, commission
C & O	California and Oregon Railroad	Comp.	Compiler/compiled
C & W	Cottle & Wright	Cong.	Congress/Congressional
CaUP	Cambridge University Press	Conn.	Connecticut

Consol.	Consolidation		DCS	DeWitt Clinton Stanford
Conv.	Convention		DCUS	District Court of the United States
COP	College of the Pacific		*DDAP*	*Directory of Deceased American Physicians*
CoPC	Cosmopolitan Publishing Co.			
CoPH	Commercial Printing House		DDC	David Douty Colton
Corp(s).	Corporation(s)/corporate		Dec	December
Corres.	Correspondence, correspondent		Del.	Delaware
CP	Caxton Printers		Dem.	Democrat/Democratic
CPA	Central Pacific Associates		Dep.	Deposition
CPC	Chapman Publishing Co.		DePC	Dell Publishing Co.
CPH	Collis Potter Huntington		Dept.	Department
CPubH	Christopher Publishing House		Dir.	Director/directory
CPr	Courier Print		Diss.	Dissertation
CPacRR	California Pacific Railroad		Dist.	District
CPRR	Central Pacific Railroad Co.		DistC	District Court
CR	*Campus Report* [Stanford Univ.]		Div.	Division
CRC	California Railroad Commission		DJC	D[avid] Johnston and Co.
CRD	California Railroad Documents		DJS	D. J. Stewart
CRec	*Carnival Record*		DMC	Dodd, Mead & Co.
CRMM	Columbia River Maritime Museum		Doc.	Document, Documentation, documented
CrP	Crown Publishers			
CS	Charles Stanford		DOI	Department of the Interior
CSA	California State Archives		DP	Dover Publications
CSC	California Supreme Court		DPC	Doubleday, Page & Co.
CSCHSY	*California Supreme Court Historical Society Yearbook*		DPD	Division of Beaches and Parks
			DPE	Delta Printing Establishment
CSCR	*California Supreme Court Reports*		DPP	Dave's Printing and Publishing
CSH	Charles S. Hamilton & Co.		DPR	Department of Parks and Recreation
CSJ	*California Senate Journal*		DPr	Dorset Press
CSL	California State Library		DSC	Department of Special Collections
CSLF	California State Library Foundation		DSJ	David Starr Jordan
CSMB	California State Mining Bureau		DSJO	Democratic State Journal Office
CSMRC	California State Museum Resource Center		*DTQ*	*Dogtown Territorial Quarterly*
			DVN	D. Van Nostrand
CSNC	California Steam Navigation Co.		DWS	Daniel W. Strong
CSPC	California State Park Commission		DZY	Daniel Z. Yost
CSR	California Southern Railroad			
CSRM(L)	California State Railroad Museum (Library)		E.	Encyclopedia
			EA	*Encyclopedia Americana*
CSS	California Secretary of State		*EB*	*Encyclopaedia Britannica*
CT	California Traveler		EBC	Edwin Bryant Crocker
CUP	Columbia University Press		EBCh	E. B. Child
CWJ	Charles W. Johnson		ECV	E Clampus Vitus
			Ed.	Editor/edition/edited
D	Democrat		EDC	El Dorado County
D & C	Doubleday & Co.		E.g.	For example
DAB	*Dictionary of American Biography*		EHM, Jr.	Edward H. Miller, Jr.
DAC	D. Appleton & Co.		EJC	Éditions Jacqueline Chambon
DAR	Daughters of the American Revolution		ELT	Evelyn "Evie" L. Tutorow
			Eng.	Engineer
DBP	Division of Beaches and Parks		EPD	E. P. Dutton
DBS	Dawson's Book Shop		EPSP	Evening Post Steam Presses
DC	District of Columbia		ERA	Edwin Raymond Anderson

EUSA	*Encyclopedia USA—The Encyclopedia of the United States of America—Past and Present*
FAB	F[riedrich] A[rnold] Brockhaus
F & R	Farrar & Rinehart
F & S	Fariss & [Clarence L.] Smith
FARC	Federal Archives and Records Center
FFC	Follett, Foster and Co.
FLIN	*Frank Leslie's Illustrated Newspaper*
FMP	Frank Morrison Pixley
FP	Fearon Publishers
FPC	Fukuin Printing Co.
FR	*Federal Register*
FRep	*Federal Reporter*
FRo	Fred Rosenstock
FT	*Frontier Times*
FVC	Francis, Valentine & Co.
FWC	Frederick Warne and Co.
GAR	Grand Army of the Republic
GAU	George, Allen & Unwin
GB	*Grizzly Bear*
GDC	Gould Directory Co.
Gen.	General
GFG	Grafiche Francesco Ghezzi
GHDC	George H. Dean Co.
GhP	Grabhorn Press
GHS	G. H. Springer
GLD	Guy L. Dunscomb
GLO	General Land Office
GM	G. Masson
Gov.	Governor
Govt.	Government
GP	Grossman Publishers
GPI	Garland Publishing, Inc.
GPO	Government Printing Office
GPPS	G. P. Putnam's Sons
GPr	Greenwood Press (with variations)
GRC	Gale Research Co.
GRCo	Genealogical Records Committee
GRP	Gilbert Richards Publications
GTB	G[rafton] T[yler] Brown & Co.
GTC	George Thomas Clark
GTP	Ghost Town Publications
GWB	Golden West Books
GrWB	Great West Books
H & B	Harper and Brothers
HB	House Bill
HBC	Holmes Book Co.
HiBC	Higginson Book Co.
HBe	*Hoof Beats*
HBPC	Henry Bill Publishing Co.
HBr	Hubbard Brothers
HBW	Harcourt, Brace & World
HC	Hachette et Cⁱᵉ
HCM	*Hutchings' California Magazine*
HCN	Herbert Charles Nash
HD	House Document
HED	*House Executive Document*
HEI	*Historical Encyclopedia of Illinois*
HHB	Hubert Howe Bancroft
HHC	Henry Holt & Co.
HiC	History Co.
Hist.	History/historical
HL	Huntington Library
HLQ	*Huntington Library Quarterly*
HMC	Houghton Mifflin Co.
HNA	Harry N. Abrams
HNB	Howell-North Books
HNP	Howell-North Press
HNMM	*Harper's New Monthly Magazine*
HP	Heritage Press
HPo	Harry Polkinhorn
HR	*House Report*
HRep	House of Representatives
HRC	Historic Record Co.
HRM	Henry R. Miguels
HRW	Holt, Rinehart and Winston
HS	*Historical Studies*
HSCC	H[enry] S[mith] Crocker & Co.
HSJ	History San José
HSSCQ	*Historical Society of Southern California Quarterly*
HUP	Harvard University Press
HVP & HWP	Henry Varnum Poor and Henry William Poor
HWPC	Harr Wagner Publishing Co.
IDMB	*International Dictionary of Medicine and Biology*
Ill.	Illinois
ICC	Interstate Commerce Commission
Inc.	Incorporation/incorporated
Ind.	Industry/Indiana
Indep.	Independent
Ind'pls	Indianapolis
Info.	Information
Infra	See below
Ins.	Insurance
Int.	Interior
Inter.	Interview
Intro.	Introduction, introduce(d)

IP	Index Publishing		LLA	Librairie Letouzey et Ané
ISHL	Illinois State Historical Library		L M	Langley and Morison
			LO	Lewis Osborne
ISLA	*Imprint of the Stanford Library Associates*		Long.	Longitude
IU	Indiana University		*LP*	*La Peninsula*
			LPC	Lewis Publishing Co.
JAC	James Anthony & Co.		LS	Leland Stanford
JAH	*Journal of American History*		LSJ	Leland Stanford Junior
JAMA	*Journal of the American Medical Association*		LSJM	Leland Stanford Junior Museum
			LSJU	Leland Stanford Junior University
JBLC	J. B. Lippincott & Co.		*LSJUP*	*Leland Stanford Junior University Publications*
JBS	Jerome Bonaparte Stanford			
JCSP	John Church, State Printer		*LSSM*	*The Land of Sunshine, A Southwestern Magazine*
JD	Juris Doctor			
JDBS	Jacob Davis Babcock Stillman		LSUP	Louisiana State University Press
JDY	J. D. Young			
JHBC	James H. Barry Co.		M.A.	Master of Arts
JHCCP	J. H. Carmany & Co., Printers		Mac.	Macmillan Publishing Co.
JHN	John Henry Nash		Mass.	Massachusetts
JHS	James Harvey Strobridge		MB	McLoughlin Brothers
JLS	Jane Lathrop Stanford		MBC	Moorhead, Bond & Co.
JM	Joel Munsell		MCA	Microfilming Corporation of America
JM/JS	John Miller (H. H. Bancroft) interview with Josiah Stanford		*MCH*	*Military Collector & Historian*
			MCHSB	*Marin County Historical Society Bulletin*
Jour(s).	Journal(s)		*MD*	*Marine Digest*
JP	Justice of the Peace		Mess.	Message
JR	Joint Resolution		Mex.	Mexican
JRC	James Russell Crocker		Mfilm	Microfilm
JROC	J. R. Osgood and Co.		MGH	McGraw-Hill
JS	Josiah Stanford, Jr.		MH	Mark Hopkins
JTRS	James T. Robinson & Son		MHIC	Mark Hopkins Inter-Continental
JTTP	John T. Towers, Printer		MHP	Midland House, Publishers
JTWC	James T. White & Co.		Mich.	Michigan
JW	*Journal of the West*		Milw.	Milwaukee
JWCI	*Journal of the Warburg and Courtauld Institute*		ML	Modern Library
			MMC	Mathis-Mets Co.
JW & S	John Wiley & Sons		MP	Menlo Park [California]
JWS	Josiah Winslow Stanford		MPC	Monarch Printing Co.
			MarWW	*Marquis Who's Who*
Kan.	Kansas		MPCo	Marvin Publishing Co.
KC	Kern County		MPHA	Menlo Park Historical Association
KRI	Kellogg Research Incorporated		MRRC	Marysville Railroad Co.
			Ms(s).	Manuscript(s)
LA	Los Angeles		MSA	Massachusetts State Archives
LA & SP	Los Angeles and San Pedro Railroad		MSL	Michigan State Library
LAI	L[uther] A. Ingersoll		MSM	Mackay School of Mines
LAB	Lea and Blanchard		MV	Mosaik Verlag
Lat.	Latitude		*MVHAP*	*Mississippi Valley Historical Association Proceedings*
LBC	Little, Brown, and Co.			
LC	Library of Congress		*MVHR*	*Mississippi Valley Historical Review (JAH after 1964)*
Leg.	Legislature/legislative			
LHP	Lymanhouse Publishers		MWW	M[yron] W. Wood
Lib.	Library/librarian			

NA	National Archives
NAL	New American Library
NARA	National Archives and Records Administration
NC	North Carolina
n.c.	no city [of publication] given
NCAB	*National Cyclopedia of American Biography*
NCE	*New Columbia Encyclopedia*
NCSHPO	National Conference of State Historic Preservation Officers
NDBI	Nevada Department of Business and Industry
n.d.	no date [of publication] given
NE	Northeast
NEB	*New Encyclopedia Britannica*
NET	Norman E. Tutorow
Nev.	Nevada
Nev. Stats.	*Nevada Statutes*
NHS	Nevada Historical Society
NHSQ	*Nevada Historical Society Quarterly*
nitro.	nitroglycerin
NJ	New Jersey
NJSC	N[athan] J. Stone & Co.
NM	New Mexico
NMHR	*New Mexico Historical Review*
NMMA	National Maritime Museum Association
no.	number
NO	New Orleans
n.p.	no publisher given
NP	Nelson and Phillips
NPC	Neale Publishing Co.
NPS	National Park Service
NRC	Northern Railway Co.
NSA	Nevada State Archives
NSHC	National Statuary Hall Collection
NSHS	Nebraska State Historical Society
NSJ	*Nevada Senate Journal*
NSLA	Nevada State Library and Archives
NTS	Nicholas T. Smith
NY & HPC	NY and Hartford Publishing Co.
NvSHS	Nevada State Historical Society
NSRM	Nevada State Railroad Museum
NVR	Napa Valley Railroad
NW	Northwest
NY	New York
NYC	New York City
NY CFCHMM	*NY Commercial and Financial Chronicle and Hunt's Merchant's Magazine*
NYH	*New York History*
NYSL	New York State Library
NZZ	*Neue Zürcher Zeitung*

O & C	Oregon and California Rail Road Co.
O & O	Occidental and Oriental Steamship Co.
Obit.	Obituary
OCD	*Oakland City Directory*
OCHS	Ozaukee County Historical Society
OCRC	Oregon Central Railroad Co.
OCT	Oak Cliff Typesetting
OG	Otto Gritschneder
OGUSPO	*Official Gazette of the United States Patent Office*
OHP	Office of Historic Preservation
OHS	Oregon Historical Society
OM	*Overland Monthly*
OMA	Oakland Military Academy
OMC	O[rlando] M. Clayes
OP	Orion Press
OPL	Oakland Public Library
Ore.	Oregon
OREGR	*Official Railway Equipment Guide Register* (title varies)
Orig.	Original
OSAHS	Ohio State Archeological and Historical Society
OSC	Oceanic Steamship Co.
OUP	Oxford University Press
OWFC	Oakland Water Front Co.
OWPC	Old West Publishing Co.
P	Populist
p.	page
PA	Palo Alto
Pac.	Pacific
PACL	Palo Alto City Library
PAHA	Palo Alta Historical Association
pam.	pamphlet
P & SV	Placerville and Sacramento Valley Rail Road
PASF	Palo Alto Stock Farm
PBSA	*Papers of the Bibliographical Society of America*
PC	Placer County
PCA	Placer County Archives
PCD	*Placerville City Directory*
PCLB	Pacific Coast Land Bureau
PCNS	Pacific Coast Numismatic Society
PCR	Pamphlets on California Railroads
PDR	Pacific Data Resources
PEC	Pacific Express Co.
Penn.	Pennsylvania
PFCS	P. F. Collier & Son
Ph.D.	Doctor of Philosophy

Phil.	Philadelphia		Reg.	Regular
PHMECS	Publishing House of the Methodist Episcopal Church, South		Rep.	Republic, Republican, representative
PHPC	Pioneer Historical Publishing Co.		Repr.	Reprint/reprinted
PHR	*Pacific Historical Review*		Res.	Residence
PIC	Pacific Improvement Co.		*ResC*	*Resources of California*
PiP	Pioneer Press		Rev.	Revised
PJ	*Police Journal*		RFL	Rocklin Friends of the Library
PL	*Peninsula Living*		RFS	Richard F. Stevens
PLP	Peter Lang Publishing		RG	Record Group of the National Archives
P.M.	post meridian			
PMLICC	Pacific Mutual Life Insurance Co. of California		RGB	R. G. Badger
			RIHS	Rhode Island Historical Society
PMSC	Pacific Mail Steamship Co.		RP	Rather Press
PMSJ	*Pacific Medical and Surgical Journal*		RiP	Riverside Press
PP	Publishers Press		RPC	Ronald Press Co.
PPub	Peregrin Publishers		*RR*	*Review of Reviews*
PPCBAHA	*Proceedings* of the Pacific Coast Branch of the American Historical Association		RRDS	R. R. Donnelley & Sons
			RRH	R. R. Hill
			RRP	Railroad Pamphlets
PPPC	Pacific Press Publishing Co.		RUP	Rutgers University Press
PPPH/OPC	Pacific Press Publishing House and Occidental Publishing Co.		*RUSPRC*	*Report of the United States Pacific Railway Commission*
PR	Public Relations			
Pres.	President, presidency, presidential		*SA*	*Stanford Alumnus*, 1899–1917, title varies; *Stanford Illustrated Review*, 1916–1941; *Stanford Alumni Review*, 1940–1951; *Stanford Review*, 1951–1967; *Stanford Magazine*, 1967–
PRJ	*Pacific Railway Journal*			
Priv.	Private			
PRJ	*Pacific Railway Journal*			
Prof.	Professor			
Prop.	Property			
PrP	Presidio Press		SAA	Stanford Alumni Association
PRR	Panama Railroad		Sac	Sacramento
PS	Paolo Sioli		SacHS	Sacramento Historical Society
PSEH	Publication Service, Encina Hall		*SAM*	*Stanford Alumnus Magazine*
PSM	*Popular Science Monthly*		S & C	Stanley & Co.
PSR	Pacific School of Religion		SageB	Sage Books
Pub.	Published/publisher		SanD	San Diego
Punc.	Punctuation		S & M	Smith & McKay
PVBC	Packard, Van Benthuysen and Co., Printers		SCA & MCC	Sacramento City Archives and Museum Collection Center
PVGS	Pomona Valley Genealogical Society		S & S	Simon and Schuster
PW	Port Washington		*S &T*	*Sandstone & Tile*
PWo	*Petroleum World*		*SAR*	*Stanford Alumni Review*
PWSR	*Pacific Wine and Spirit Review*		*SAS*	*Scientific American Supplement*
			Sat.	Saturday
R	Republican		SB	Senate Bill
RA	*Railway Age*		S-B	Simmons-Boardman
RB	Red Bluff		SBar	Santa Barbara
RC	Redwood City		SBC	Slocum, Bowen, & Co.
Reg.	Regiment		SBCC	Sacramento Book Collectors Club
RCLL	Robert Crown Law Library		SBCR	Santa Barbara County Records
Rec.	Record/recorded		*SBMMC*	*Santa Barbara Maritime Museum Currents*
Ref.	Reference			

SC & PV	Santa Clara and Pajaro Valley Rail Road		*SFDR*	*San Francisco Daily Report*
SC	Santa Cruz		*SFGR*	*San Francisco Great Register*
SCa	San Carlos		SFHR	San Francisco Historical Records
ScA	Scottwall Associates		SFNC	San Francisco News Co.
SCon	S. Converse		*SF News-Letter*	*San Francisco News-Letter and California Advertiser*
SCB	*Sierra Club Bulletin*		*SFOSB*	*San Francisco Our Society Bluebook*
SCC	Santa Clara County		SFP	Stanford Family Papers
SCCHS	Santa Clara County Historical Society		SFS	Stanford Family Scrapbooks
			SFWI	San Francisco Wine Institute
SCCR	Santa Clara County Records		*SH*	*Sagebrush Headlight*
SCrCR	Santa Cruz County Records		SHS	Stanford Historical Society
SCD	*Sacramento City Directory*		*SHSN*	*Stanford Historical Society Newsletter*
SCGC	S. C. Griggs and Co.		SHSW	State Historical Society of Wisconsin
SCHSHMC	Sacramento County Historical Society and Heritage Media Corporation		*SIR*	*Stanford Illustrated Review*
			SJ	San José
SCP	Society of California Pioneers		SJC	San Joaquin County
SCR	Sacramento County Records		SJCPC	S. J. Clarke Publishing Co.
SCVHS	Santa Clarita Valley Historical Society		*SJMH*	*San José Mercury Herald*
			SJPL	San José Public Library
SD	*Senate Document*		*SJS*	*San Jose Studies*
sem.	seminary		SJV	San Joaquin Valley Railroad
Sheb.	Sheboygan		SL	S. Levinson
SDA	Stanford Department of Art		SL & SF	St. Louis & San Francisco Railway (Railroad) Co.
SDC	Southern Development Co.			
SDM	*Stanford Daily Magazine*		SLC	Salt Lake City
SE	Southeast		SLCC	Salt Lake Commercial Club
Sec.	Secretary		*SLCD*	[*Gould's*] *St. Louis City Directory*
Sect(s).	Section(s)		SLDA	Stanford Lands: Deeds & Abstracts
SED	*Senate Executive Document*		SLNSW	State Library of New South Wales
Sen.	Senate		*SM*	*Stanford Magazine*
Sess.	Session(s)		SMC	San Mateo County
SF	San Francisco		SMCHS	San Mateo County Historical Society
SF & A	San Francisco & Alameda Railroad		SMCR	San Mateo County Records
SF & O	San Francisco and Oakland Railroad		*SMD*	*Senate Miscellaneous Document*
SFB & BPC	San Francisco Bench and Bar Publishing Co.		*SMDic*	*Stedman's Medical Dictionary*
			SMFW	Society of Medical Friends of Wine
SF, O & A	San Francisco, Oakland, & Alameda Railroad		SMJC	San Mateo Junior College
			SMu	*Stanford Museum*
SFBRR	San Francisco Bay Railroad		SNPC	Saturday Night Publishing Co.
SFCC	San Francisco City and County		SO	State Office
SFCCR	San Francisco City and County Records		SoC	Sonoma County
			Soc.	Society
SFCD	*San Francisco City Directory*		SP	Scarecrow Press
SF CFJUS	[*SF*] *California Farmer and Journal of useful Sciences*		*SPB*	*Southern Pacific Bulletin*
			SPB	Southern Pacific Branch Railroad
SF & SJ	San Francisco and San José Railroad		SPC	Southern Pacific Company
SF CSTUJ	*San Francisco California Spirit of the Times, 1857–1859; title varies, merged with Fireman's Journal, 1859–1870; California Spirit of the Times and Underwriter's Journal, 1870–1892*		SPCR	South Pacific Coast Railroad
			SPD	Stanford Planning Department
			Spec.	Special
			SPO	State Printing Office
			SPP	SP Press
			SPPEC	Sunset Press and Photo Engraving Co.

SPr	State Printer		TCR	Tehama County Records
SPRC	State Park and Recreation Commission		TD	The Depot
			TDJ	Theodore DeHone Judah
SPRR	Southern Pacific Railroad Co.		Terr.	Territory
SPSNCM	*Seabreezes, the P[acific] S[hip] N[avigation] C[ompany] Magazine*		Test.	Testimony
			TF	Twin Falls [Idaho]
SPub	Sutton Publishing		THC	The History Co.
SQ	*Stanford Quad*		TNH	Timothy Nolan Hopkins
SR	*Senate Report*		THT	Thomas H. Thompson
SRev	*Stanford Review*		TM & C	Thomas McGill & Co.
SRL & MT	Save-the-Redwoods League and the Menninger Tradition		TP	Torch Press
			TaP	Talisman Press
S & S	Simon & Schuster		TPC	Times Publishing Co.
S & Sons	Scribner & Sons		*TPM*	*The Pacific Monthly*
SS	*Stanford Sequoia*		TPP	The Pilgrim Press
SsM	*Sunset Magazine*		TPRC	Texas Pacific Railroad Co. (until 1872)
SSN	Serial Set Number			
SSR	Sidney S. Rider		Treas.	Treasurer/Treasury
St.	Street/state		TR (TCP)	Terminal Railway
ST	S. Tuttle		*TRG*	*The Railroad Gazette*
Stan.	Stanford		TriP	Trinity Parish
Stats	Statistics		TrPC	Tribune Publishing Co.
STPC	Sierra-Tahoe Publishing Co.		TSHA	Texas State Historical Association
SUA	Stanford University Archives		TSPH	Thomas' Steam Printing House
SUL	Stanford University Library		TTD	The Tentacled Press
SUM	Stanford University Museum		TTP	Town Talk Press
SUMA	Stanford University Museum of Art		TTUP	Texas Tech University Press
SUNS	Stanford University News Service		*TWR*	*The Western Railroader*
SupC	Superior Court		TWS	Thomas Welton Stanford
SUP	Stanford University Press		TYCC	Thomas Y. Crowell & Co.
Supra	See above			
Supt.	Superintendent		U	Unionist
SUR	Stanford University Register		UAP	University of Arizona Press
SV	Süddeutscher Verlag		UC	University of California
SVRR	Sacramento Valley Railroad		UCB	University of California at Berkeley
SW	Southwest		*UCC*	*University of California Chronicle*
SWP	South-Western Publishing Co.		UChP	University of Chicago Press
SyUP	Syracuse University Press		UCP	University of California Press
			UHQ	*Utah Historical Quarterly*
TA	[NY] Tribune Association		UIP	University of Illinois Press
TA & MUP	Texas A & M University Press		UKP	University of Kansas Press
T & B	Towne & Bacon		UM	University Microfilms
T & NO	Texas and New Orleans Railroad		UML	University of Michigan Library
T & PRC	Texas & Pacific Railway Co. (after 1872)		UNC	Unidentified Newspaper Clipping
			UNCP	University of North Carolina Press
T & W	[Thomas H.] Thompson and [Albert A.] West		Undoc.	Undocumented
			Unit.	Unitarian
TBMA	*The Bankers' Magazine of Australasia*		Univ.	University
TBMJ	*The British Medical Journal*		UNP	University of Nebraska Press
TBP	Towne and Bacon, Printers		UNvP	University of Nevada Press
TC	Tehama County		UOP	University of Oklahoma Press
TCHC	The [Carnall-Hopkins] Co.		UP	University of Pennsylvania
TCP	Terminal Central Pacific Railway		UPC	Union Publishing Co.

UPP	University of Pennsylvania Press		WARS	Western Association of Railway Surgeons
UPRR	Union Pacific Railroad			geons
UPK	University Press of Kansas		Wash.	Washington, D.C.
U.S.	United States		WB	World Book
USACE	U.S. Army Corps of Engineers		WBS	William Blackwood and Sons
USAG	U.S. Attorney General		WC	Washington County
USBC	U.S. Bureau of Customs		WDC	Western Development Co.
USBGN	U.S. Board on Geographic Names		WDE	William D. Edson
USC	University of Southern California		WDP	Word Dancer Press
USCarP	University of South Carolina Press		WE	Western Epics
USCC	United States Circuit Court		WeP	Westernlore Press
USCCA	United States Circuit Court of		*WF*	*Wisconsin Freemason*
	Appeals		*WH*	*Western Horseman*
USCG	*U.S. Congressional Globe*		WHa	William Halley
USCR	*U.S. Congressional Record*		WHC	Western Historical Co.
USDC	U.S. Department of Commerce		WHPC	Western Historical and Publishing
USGS	U.S. Geological Survey			Co.
USNA	U.S. Naval Academy		WHo	Warren Holt
USPRC	U.S. Pacific Railway Commission		Wisc.	Wisconsin
USSCR	U.S. Supreme Court Reports		WLC	Wertheimer, Lea and Co.
US Stats	*U.S. Statutes at Large*		*WMH*	*Wisconsin Magazine of History*
USWD	United States War Department		WNF	Walter N. Frickstad
UT	Utah Territory		WP	White Pine
UTEP	University of Texas at El Paso		WPPC	Wright and Potter Printing Co.
UU	University of Utah		WPr	Wilderness Press
UV	University of Virginia		WPRR	Western Pacific Railroad
UW	University of Wisconsin		WRP	Ward Ritchie Press
UWa	University of Washington		WTC	W. Thacker & Co.
UWy	University of Wyoming		*WV*	*Wines and Vines*
			WW	*Wagon Wheels*
V & T	Virginia & Truckee Railroad		WWMC	W. W. Munsell & Co.
Va.	Virginia		WWN	W. W. Norton
VI	Visalia Incorporated			
Vol(s).	Volume(s)		YC	Yuba County
VP	Vice president		YC & MP	Yarnell, Caystile & Mathes, Printers
VUP	Vanderbilt University Press		YCHS	Yuma County Historical Society
			YHVS	Yolo Hills Viticultural Society
W & AM	W. & A. McPherson		*YNN*	*Yosemite Nature Notes*
W & B	White & Bauer		YRR	Yuba Railroad Co.
W & N	Weidenfield and Nicolson		YUP	Yale University Press
W & W	Williams & Wilkins			

CHAPTER 13

CALIFORNIA STATE
RAILROAD REGULATION
1864–1887

A Competing Railroad Was the Dream of the Opposition[1]

. . . you'll wake this State of California up some of these days by going just a little bit too far, and there'll be an election of railroad commissioners of, by, and for the people, that'll get a twist of you, my bunco-steering friend—you and your backers and cappers and swindlers and thimble-riggers, and smash you, lock, stock, and barrel.
—Frank Norris[2]

I feel deeply on this subject, Mr. Speaker, because what is called the Southern Pacific Railroad was intended in a few months to connect with the city of Los Angeles; and I do fear, I dread, if an Act of this kind [the Archer Bill] should pass, that the road will not be completed, according to the present programme. There is now a gap of 100 miles to fill, but in addition to that, that same company is engaged in extending the road eastward through the San Gorgonio Pass to the Territory of Arizona, and are making rapid progress.
—Los Angeles assemblyman John R. McConnell[3]

EARLY STATE RAILROAD REGULATION

Since its earliest years the Golden State had permitted relatively high railroad rates for passengers and freight in order to encourage railroad construction. The first bill to create a railroad in California was presented just three years after statehood.

On February 15, 1853, Democratic senator James W. Coffroth stood up in the state Senate—then meeting in Benicia—and announced that he was planning to introduce a bill for an "Act to provide for the incorporation of Railroad companies."[4] He did so on the following day and the bill was referred to the Judiciary Commit-

---

[1] Evans, *Huntington*, I, 307.
[2] Benjamin Franklin ("Frank") Norris, *The Octopus: A Story of California* (NY: NAL, [1901] 1964), 142.
[3] *Sac Record-Union*, Mar 6, 1876.   [4] *CSJ*, 4th Sess., 114 (May 11, 1853).

tee.[5] Somehow the Corporations Committee ended up with his bill and reported back on March 16, recommending passage of it, with slight amendments.[6] The bill was debated in the upper house until March 25, 1853, and then was passed.[7]

Three days later the Coffroth Bill was introduced into the assembly, where it was examined carefully and amended.[8] The assembly passed its amended version on April 9.[9] The senate concurred with the assembly amendments and on April 21 the bill was sent to Democratic governor John Bigler, who signed the bill into law on the following day.[10]

Railroad rates were so high as provided by this law—twenty cents per mile for passengers and sixty cents per mile per ton of freight—that there was in effect *no* regulation.[11] This changed only slightly in the following years when the 1853 law was modified.

On March 21, 1854, Democratic assemblyman Charles W. Dannels of Yuba introduced a bill (AB 188) into the lower house of the California legislature calling for an amendment to the April 22, 1853, statute.[12] This act was an amendment to several aspects of the earlier law but the relevant portion simply lowered rates to ten and fifteen cents per mile respectively for passengers and freight. The assembly made minor amendments to Dannels' bill, incorporated other similar bills into it, and then passed it.[13] The senate passed it on May 13 and Governor Bigler signed it into law on May 15, 1854.[14]

Though this law reduced passenger and freight rates, they were still considered exorbitantly high. Nationwide movements to bring railroad rates under state regulation surfaced later in California as post-Civil War reformers united in a campaign to reduce rates.

Movements for lower rates prompted the Central Pacific Associates to press for rate regulation in the form of a binding contract that could not be tampered with by subsequent state legislation. They supported a bill that would have lowered maxi-

---

[5]Ibid., 118 (Feb 16, 1853).   [6]Ibid., 221 (Mar 16, 1853).

[7]Ibid., 228–229 (Mar 17, 1853), 234–235 (Mar 18), 237 (Mar 19), 256 and 260, passed (Mar 25).

[8]*CAJ*, 4th Sess., 344 (Mar 28, 1853), 385 (Apr 6), 389 (Apr 7), 400 (Apr 9), 418 (Apr 15), 456 (Apr 21), 466 (Apr 22), 609 (May 12), and 656 (May 17).

[9]*CSJ*, 4th Sess., 329 (Apr 12, 1853); *CAJ*, 4th Sess., 400 (Apr 9).

[10]*CSJ*, 4th Sess., 337 (Apr 12, 1853), 381 (Apr 21), and 401 (Apr 23); *Calif Stats*, 4th Sess., 99–114 (Jan 3–May 19, 1853), Chap. 72, "An Act to Provide for the Incorporation of Railroad Companies."

[11]On lack of effective regulation, see Evander Berry Willis and Philip Keagy Stockton, official stenographers, *Debates and Proceedings of the Constitutional Convention of the State of California, convened at the City of Sacramento, Saturday, Sep 28, 1878* (3 vols., Sac: JDY, 1880), I, 574; also, Gov. John Bigler's speech of Apr 8, reported in the *SF Alta California*, Apr 10, 1854.   [12]*CAJ*, 5th Sess., 233 (Mar 13, 1854), 273 (Mar 21).

[13]Ibid., 316 (Apr 1, 1854), 413 (Apr 27), and 421–422 (Apr 28).

[14]*CSJ*, 5th Sess., 573, intro. (May 9, 1854), 585, passage recommended (May 11), and 614, passed (May 13); signed into law, *CAJ*, 5th Sess., 579 (May 15); *Calif Stats*, 5th Sess., 170–176 (Jan 2–May 15), Chap. 105, *Amendatory of an Act entitled "An Act to Provide for the Incorporation of Railroad Companies," approved April twenty-second, eighteen hundred and fifty-three*. App. May 15, 1854, by Gov. John Bigler (D).

mum rates at sea level and raised them in mountain areas. On January 12, 1866, Union (formerly Republican) senator Joseph Kutz of Nevada City introduced a bill (SB 103) to amend the statute of record—the act of May 2, 1861—pertaining to the incorporation and management of railroad companies in California.[15] After modification by the Committee on Corporations, a substitute for the Kutz Bill passed the senate on March 14.[16] Five days later the substitute Senate Bill 103 was read in the assembly and referred to the Committee on Corporations of the lower house.[17] On March 23 the assembly received a favorable recommendation from this committee and on March 30 it was passed.[18]

Though passed by the legislature, Senate Bill 103 was vetoed by Gov. Frederick Low. His veto message to the senate on April 2, 1866, gave his reason: "This bill, were it to become law, would clearly create a contract that no subsequent legislature could repeal or impair."[19]

Undaunted by this reversal, on November 26, 1867, Huntington wrote to Crocker: "I am sorry to notice that there is a movement in Cal. [sic] to reduce fares on the C.P.R.R., but I suppose you can take care of the Sargent crowd without much trouble. If we could get the rates fixed so that the Legislature could not change them, at about the present rates it would be a great thing."[20] (This telling comment reveals the possibility that Aaron Sargent's loyalty to the railroad was to be questioned.)

Politicians, who were frequent users of the railroads, and reformers agreed in wanting lower railroad rates, but there is no evidence that the *majority* of Californians had any interest in stringent control of these rates, primarily because railroads had not yet been constructed in many areas where they were needed; people in those areas felt that legislative controls might deprive them forever of this much-needed means of transportation.

It was Stanford's duty to watch out for Central Pacific interests in the state legislature. He swore under oath that he had never used his wealth or railroad money to corrupt a member of the legislature.[21] However, some railroad historians argue that circumstantial evidence points to the fact that he did.[22] Unfortunately for their case, circumstantial evidence in historical analysis has no more weight than in a court of law—other than implied or imagined guilt by innuendo.

[15]*CSJ*, 16th Sess., 152 (Jan 12, 1866).

[16]After modification by the Committee on Corps., a substitute for the Kutz Bill passed the Calif. Sen. on Mar 15, *CSJ*, 16th Sess., 473 (Mar 14, 1866), passed Calif. Assy., in *CAJ*, 16th Sess., 769 (Mar 30, 1866).

[17]*CAJ*, 16th Sess., 609 (Mar 19, 1866).

[18]Ibid., 665, passage recommended (Mar 23, 1866), 769, passed (Mar 30).

[19]*CSJ*, 16th Sess., 734–735 (Apr 2, 1866).

[20]CPH, *Letters from Collis P. Huntington to Mark Hopkins, Leland Stanford, Charles Crocker, E.B. Crocker, Charles F. Crocker, and David D. Colton* (NY: [n.p.], 1892–1894), I, 63; in *Huntington Papers, 1856–1901. A Guide to the Microfilm Collection* (NY: MCA, 1979), Series IV, 90A, Reel 2, No. 62.   [21]LS test., *USPRC*, VI, 3170–3172 and 3180.

[22]Ward M. McAfee, *California's Railroad Era 1850–1911* (San Marino: GWB, 1973), 146. This book is an extensive revision and expansion of McAfee's Ph.D. diss. (Stanford, 1965), "Local Interests and Railroad Regulation in Nineteenth Century California."

STATE LAWS TO REGULATE THE CENTRAL PACIFIC RAILROAD

On July 29, 1887, at the Palace Hotel in San Francisco Stanford had to respond in detail to Pacific Railroad Commissioners' questions about opposition to the Central Pacific Railroad. First, he pointed out that widespread opposition since the original construction of the transcontinental railroad was based entirely upon economic or competitive considerations. To begin with, since Congress required that the transcontinental build a parallel telegraph line, he and his partners had to face the opposition of existing telegraph companies.[23] Because the railroad was to extend to San Francisco, they encountered opposition from the competing Steam Navigation Company and Pacific Mail Steamship Company. And since they had to build across the mountains, they antagonized the Sacramento Valley Rail Road Company, which operated a railroad eastward about forty miles from Sacramento. The line across the continent itself aggravated existing stage and express companies, including the short-lived Pony Express.

As a further consequence of economic motives and jealousies, Stanford explained: "Hostile legislation has been proposed at every session of the legislature since the commencement of the road. It has assumed various forms, and often of so serious a character that if successful it would have been impossible to operate the road under its restrictions."[24]

In its regular meeting on November 11, 1873, the San Francisco Chamber of Commerce had drawn up a bill on railroad rates and fares that it intended to support in the legislature.[25] Caspar T. Hopkins (no relation to Mark) was appointed chairman of a five-man committee to pursue the proposed legislative bill. Hopkins sent questions on related railroad topics to Stanford requesting his ideas on them. He also wanted to know what objections Stanford—or the Central Pacific—might have to Chamber of Commerce policies on rates.[26]

Stanford's opening in his reply shows clearly how he felt about state regulation of railroads: "To me it seems that the only proper legislation on this subject is that of the total abolition of any fixed rates by law."[27] In an expression of the classical doctrine of laissez faire, he argued that the free market was the best regulatory device: excess profits would attract competition and competition would lower profits. He warned the committee that the end result of control was ownership; the two were inseparable. He denied that the state had the power to destroy the value of property by regulatory legislation. Furthermore, he attributed the great nationwide depres-

[23]LS test., *USPRC*, V, 2535.   [24]Ibid.

[25]*Extracts from Report of the Committee appointed Nov 11, 1873, by the Chamber of Commerce of San Francisco, to Prepare Bills for Legislative Action on the Subject of Fares and Freights* (SF: [n.p.], 1874). Pub. as Pam. 3, *In the District Court of the Fourth Judicial District of the State of California*.

[26]Caspar T. Hopkins to LS, signed by all five members of the comm., Nov 11, 1873, repr., ibid., 18—19.

[27]LS to Caspar T. Hopkins, Dec 1, 1873, repr., ibid., 30.

sion of 1873 to loss of foreign confidence in the integrity of the American market, caused by "injudicious agitation" in and out of legislatures about railroads. If legislatures would mind their proper business, he admonished, prosperity would return to the state and the nation.

Stanford offered one legal argument that the committee rejected in its report to the Chamber of Commerce: the Central Pacific Railroad was created by a federal law, so the state of California had no jurisdiction over its operation, management, or rate schedules. To make his point clear, he added a postscript: "Congress having the sole right to regulate the Traffic on the Central Pacific Railroad, I hope in any bill recommended by your Committee on the subject, this fact, so far as affecting that road, may not be lost sight of." Here Stanford was citing and relying on an argument researched and argued cogently in a fifty-two-page document by Silas Woodruff Sanderson, Judge Crocker's successor as head of the railroad's legal department.[28] Sanderson was by no means a railroad lackey; he had been an assemblyman in the fourteenth session of the legislature and chief justice of California from 1864 to 1870.[29]

Sanderson argued that since Congress had established the "Central Pacific Railroad as a national highway for postal, military and commercial purposes," the state of California lacked jurisdiction in the regulation of the railroad's affairs.[30] In its report to the full Senate, the committee rejected the Sanderson-Stanford argument on the basis of the fact that unlike the Union Pacific, which had been incorporated under federal law, the Central Pacific Railroad had been incorporated in California under California law and therefore was subject to California regulations on rates and fares.[31]

ASSEMBLYMAN FRANK S. FREEMAN BILL (ASSEMBLY BILL 2)— JANUARY 29, 1874

Republican assemblyman Frank Freeman had long been determined to get a piece of railroad restriction legislation through under his name. As early as December 7, 1871, he had introduced a bill with this intention in mind.[32] The Committee on Corporations in the California Assembly held a hearing on Freeman's Bill in January 1872. In the 120 pages of testimony, Stanford annihilated the proponents of stringent regulation by his superior knowledge of railroad practices, railroad expenses, railroad profits and losses, and the geography and topography of the state

---

[28]Shay, "A Lifetime in California," 222.   [29]Driscoll and White, *List of Constitutional Officers*, 59 and 148.

[30]Silas Woodruff Sanderson, *An Argument against the Power of the Legislature of the State of California to regulate Fares and Freights on the Central Pacific Railroad* (Sac: HSCC, 1872). Repr. as Pam. 2, *In the District Court of the Fourth Judicial District of the State of California*.

[31]*Extracts from Report of the Committee appointed Nov. 11, 1873, by the Chamber of Commerce of San Francisco*, 7 and 9.

[32]*CAJ*, 19th Sess., 114 (Dec 7, 1871).

of California.[33] In answer to questions from the chairman of the committee and from Stanford, a barrage of responses from witnesses ran:

> "I don't know,"
> "I had not thought of that,"
> "That is a problem that did not occur to me,"
> "That is a question I have never examined,"
> "I don't know the grade of the roadway,"
> " I do not understand the matter,"
> "I don't know the distance the railroads run,"
> "I don't know the cost per ton'per mile or how it varies with grade,"
> "I do not know, but I believe . . . ,"
> "I know nothing about the costs of mountain grades,"
> "I am not prepared to answer that question,"

and a variety of similar evasions, vacillations, and gargantuan displays of ignorance about the matter at hand, namely, the Freeman Bill then before the assembly.

Nothing came of Freeman's Bill.

On the 29th of January 1874 the lower house of the state legislature finally adopted a different regulatory bill introduced by Freeman—"An Act to regulate fares and freights on the railroads in the State of California"—Assembly Bill 2. The bill was adopted at once by the lopsided vote of 68 to 8.[34] Assemblymen of all parties supported the bill. Of those voting, 31 Independents (97 percent), 23 Democrats (89 percent), and 14 Republicans (70 percent) cast their ballots with Freeman in support of it.[35]

On January 30 the Assembly bill was introduced into the Senate and was referred to the Committee on Corporations.[36] Sen. William Irwin was a member of this committee.[37]

Stanford obviously had gotten wind of the proposed legislation. On January 22, 1874, even before Assembly Bill 2 had been presented to the assembly, he wrote an open letter to the California Senate Committee on Corporations explaining his view of the adverse effects of the proposed measures, arguing that present railroad policy and rates were beneficial to the people of California and that any change in the laws regulating fares or rates would be detrimental to them as well as to the railroad.[38] He argued that the people of the state were saving over $15 million per year by using railroad service rather than another form of transportation.

---

[33]*ACSAJ*, 19th Sess. (1871–1872), 4 vols., Vol. I: *Appendix to the Report of the Committee on Corporations of the Assembly, upon Railroad Freights and Fares*. Pub. as Pam. 8 of *Business Regulation Pamphlets*, in RCLL, LSJU.

[34]*CAJ*, 20th Sess., 506 (Jan 29, 1874).   [35]Ibid.

[36]*CSJ*, 20th Sess., 375–376 (Jan 30, 1874).   [37]Ibid., 167 (Dec 10, 1873).

[38]LS to Calif. Sen. Comm. on Corps., Jan 22, 1874, in *SF Bulletin*, Jan 23, 1874; printed as Communication from LS to the Comm. on Corps. of the Calif. Sen., Jan 22, 1874, the last 2 pp. of Calif. Sen., Comm. on Corps., *Report on The Testimony and Proceedings had before the Senate Committee on Corporations having under Consideration the Subject of Fares and Freights*, in *Corporations Fares and Freights*; also in *ACSAJ*, 20th Sess., IV, Doc. 12, LS test., 9–55 (Feb 9, 1874).

Stanford argued another point: the railroad's huge bonded indebtedness to the government was evidence that it was not reaping the wild profits imagined by its enemies. This indebtedness was incurred, he insisted, upon the railroad's belief that the laws that brought the company into existence should not be altered to its detriment. Passage of the proposed regulatory legislation would deprive investors of part of the money they had placed in railroad securities. If the money of investors could be confiscated in this way, other investors would be scared off. There would then be no more lines built unless the state assumed both ownership and construction costs of all the railroads in the state.

Stanford continued: California railroad rates were the lowest in the world. Because of this, many railroads in the state were not yet profitable; even fewer were paying dividends. These roads would be the ones hurt most by regulatory legislation; the main railroad in the state and almost the only one showing a profit was the Central Pacific, to which state legislation would not apply. He then repeated his old argument that the Central Pacific Railroad had been created by federal, not state, law. He asserted that a thorough investigation would show that the alleged abuses of the railroads in California were imaginary.

The senate Committee on Corporations convened in Sacramento on February 9, 1874. There followed an intense investigation of every aspect of railroad rates, fares, management, fraud—anything conscientious senators knew they were expected to question. The hearing lasted until March 11, with several volumes of testimony from more than two dozen witnesses.

The senate committee first invited Stanford to appear and give his reasons in person for opposing the assembly bill. Stanford's testimony, along with questions posed by the committee and Stanford's answers, filled forty-five pages, in addition to the extensive and impressive documentation he brought along.[39]

Stanford's opening statement—more a salvo—left no doubt about his position: "I beg leave to state that an examination of the bill which is under consideration, reveals what appears to me to be radical defects, calculated, should the bill become a law, to inflict most disastrous injury upon the productive interests of the State, and the necessaries of life."[40] His analysis suggested unmistakably the partisan character of the Freeman Bill, particularly when he referred to it as another example of the "biennial attacks upon the railroad system and management of the State."[41] He reminded the committee that just two years before, when it had examined similar charges against the management of the railroads, the state had found the charges to be wholly without foundation in fact.

To show that legislative controls revealed ignorance of the facts of the railroad

---

[39]*ACSAJ*, 20th Sess., Calif. Sen. Comm. on Corps., IV, 9ff (Feb 9, 1874), *Report of the Testimony and Proceedings had before the Senate Committee on Corporations having under Consideration the subject of Fares and Freights* (Feb 9, 1874).

[40]Ibid., 9.   [41]Ibid., 10.

business, Stanford cited a magazine article he had just read on the subject of railroad regulation, which drew a parallel between public authorities' regulating railroads and Voltaire's doctors, "who put drugs of which they knew little into bodies
of which they knew nothing."[42] Stanford's argument, that drafters of regulatory
bills knew nothing of which they spoke or wrote, was borne out many times in his
appearances before California State Senate committees. He spelled out his position
in no uncertain terms: "A careful reading of that essay must convince any one that
the subject is one that no uneducated mind can successfully master."[43] Stanford
overwhelmed the committee with case studies and statistics of regulation in other
states; these pointed out the mistakes that had been made and the deleterious
effects such regulation had upon the business and prosperity of those states.

In its report to the senate, the Committee on Corporations recommended
against passing the Freeman Bill and offered an alternative measure.[44] The committee underscored its belief that railroad fares and rates were subject to legislative
control, but the passage of this particular act would "prove a public calamity" to
California.[45] The committee argued that if Assembly Bill 2 were enacted, California
producers would not be able to get their goods to market at any lower rate than
they were now paying. In a devastating blow to the bill's Assembly supporters and
to reformers in general who wanted rates lowered, the report closed with reference to a substitute bill of its own (with higher rates than AB 2 provided for) with
rates fixed "probably as low as they ought to be."[46]

Just after the introduction of the Freeman Bill, eighty-seven prominent San
Franciscans affixed their signatures to an undated petition to the state legislature
regarding the exercise of arbitrary monopolistic practices of California railroads—
without naming any in particular.[47] They proposed, among other ways of correcting
the ills resulting from "arbitrary exactions and injustices of railroad companies,"
regulatory legislation and a railroad commission to be appointed by the governor.
They argued that the Freeman Bill was "crude and unsatisfactory," based on lack of
correct information on the part of the man who drafted it.

More clearly and more directly addressed in opposition to the Freeman Bill was
a remonstrance to the legislature signed by seventy-three of Sacramento's leading
citizens and businessmen representing a wide variety of commercial fields.[48] Hav-

---

[42]William Mason Grosvenor, "The Railroads and the Farms," *AM* 1873 32 (193): 604.

[43]*Report of the Testimony and Proceedings had before the Senate Committee on Corporations*, Feb 9, 1874, 11.

[44]Calif. Sen., *Preliminary Report of the Committee on Corporations*, 3. Printed in *Business Regulation Pamphlets*, VII, Pam.
4, RCLL, LSJU; *CSJ*, 20th Sess. (Mar 14, 1874), 657.

[45]Calif. Sen., *Preliminary Report of the Committee on Corporations*, 3.   [46]Ibid., 20.

[47]*ACSAJ*, 20th Sess., IV, 3–5, *Petitions of Citizens of San Francisco relative to Arbitrary Exactions and Injustices of Railroad
Companies*; also printed in *Business Regulation Pamphlets*, VII, Pam. 7, RCLL, LSJU.

[48]*ACSAJ*, 20th Sess., V, 1–5, *Remonstrance from Citizens and Residents of the City of Sacramento against the Passage of Freeman's Freight and Far Bill.*

ing studied the terms of the bill, these petitioners came to the conclusion that its passage would work "incalculable injury to the mercantile and business interests of California."[49] They began with a theoretical argument—that the less trade and commerce are "trammeled by positive and arbitrary laws, the better"—and moved on to very practical objections: "Rules, which to-day may be eminently proper, might, a few months hence, operate most injuriously, and rates and fares which would be abundantly remunerative in other places, and in different circumstances, would be totally inadequate in California."[50] They underlined their confidence in the men presently running California railroads—men thoroughly familiar with the needs of trade and men whose integrity and business qualifications were above reproach. With a direct swipe at Freeman, they concluded: "To us it seems to be more wise to leave the regulations of these matters to men of intelligence, who have made it their study for years, than to those who, from the nature of their habits and pursuits, can have but a very limited knowledge of the subject."[51]

SEN. WILLIAM IRWIN BILL (SENATE BILL 449)— MARCH 14, 1874

After weeks of working on an alternative to the Freeman Bill, on March 14, Senator Irwin came up with a Fare and Freight bill that was approved unanimously by the Senate Committee on Corporations.[52] The terms of this bill were published in all the San Francisco newspapers and were discussed widely across the state. It was hailed by supporters as a much more sensible scheme than was Freeman's, fair to all parties concerned, and one that dealt with a broad range of passenger and freight rates, particularly rates on the transport of grains. For example, the freight charges for wheat shipments over sixty miles were considerably lower than provided for in the Freeman Bill. It was predicted that this bill would be assailed from all sides.[53] Divided opinion on the bill across the state was symbolized by the *Chronicle*'s assessment that the railroads would not like it, while the *Morning Call*, on the other hand, was sure that David Colton had helped Irwin write the bill and that "no better bill for the Railroad could have been drawn."[54]

The *Chronicle* writer was right on one point: as a compromise measure, which it was, the Irwin bill would not please the radicals on either side of the issue.[55] As it turned out, neither the Freeman nor the Irwin bill was passed by the legislature.

---

[49]Ibid., 3.   [50]Ibid.   [51]Ibid.

[52]*CSJ*, 20th Sess., 657 (Mar 14, 1874), and 1123 (Index), "An Act Prescribing the maximum rates which may be charged for the transportation of passengers and freights on the railroads of this State." *SF Chronicle*, Mar 15, 1874; *SF Morning Call*, Mar 15, 1874.   [53]*SF Chronicle*, Mar 15, 1874.

[54]Ibid.; *SF Morning Call*, Mar 16, 1874.   [55]*SF Chronicle*, Mar 17, 1874.

An Interview with "The Railroad King"

On May 18, 1875, a reporter for the *San Francisco Chronicle* was ushered into Stanford's office at Fourth and Townsend for an extensive interview.[56] During the course of the interview—which he titled for publication "The Railroad King"—the subject turned from immigration into California and railroad development, the nominal subjects of the meeting, to Stanford and politics. Stanford explained very simply: he was so absorbed in business affairs that he was no longer interested in politics of any kind. Even if he had been, he did not have the time. When Stanford was asked to comment on the allegation that he controlled the politics of the state, he denied the charge, admitting that when the railroad was young he and his Associates had had to demand protective legislation. Since that necessity no longer existed, however, they wanted only justice—their legal rights—with no special favors. When asked if he were indifferent to politics, especially to an upcoming election, he pointed out that he was a Republican. Then he quickly added: "I have no personal preferences; I am taking no part in the election. I never talk politics and I seldom think about them." In a closing grandiloquence, he stated: "I will vote the Republican ticket, and I will do all in my power to advance its interests, but I will not burden my mind or employ my time in an attempt to influence or manage party politics."

Sen. Miles P. O'Connor Bill—January 4, 1876

Coinciding with legislative attempts to control the costs of passenger and freight travel was another form of railroad control—that of creating state commissioners with the power to regulate even more than rates.

State investigations were expensive and annoying, but they presented little danger to the railroads. In 1874, for example, an assembly committee, in an investigation into the charge that public officials were not getting the railroad passes they were entitled to, used it as an occasion for a "fishing trip" into railroad practices, even inquiring into details of the organization of the Central Pacific system.[57] Nothing came of this.

The California legislature had failed on two occasions to adopt regulatory measures—the Freeman and Irwin bills. However, a regulatory bill introduced by Democratic senator Miles P. O'Connor of Nevada City *did* pass—over the opposition of Stanford. This bill was designed to create a State Board of Transportation Commissioners empowered to function as a regulatory body by investigating alleged discriminations and prohibiting such practices.

O'Connor introduced his bill—"An Act to provide for the appointment of a Commissioner of Transportation, and prevent extortion and discrimination in fares and

---

[56]Ibid., May 19, 1875.

[57]*Sac Record*, Mar 31, 1874; LS test., in *ACSAJ*, 20th Sess., VI, 10–14 (Mar 5, 1874), and 24–34 (Mar 10), "Testimony Taken by the Special Committee on Central Pacific Railroad Matters."

freight rates on railroads within this State"—on January 4, 1876.[58] It was referred to the Committee on Corporations. Numbered Senate Bill 134, this measure called for mild regulations that offended no one in particular, but it contained one provision that was anathema to railroad men everywhere—the creation of a three-man railroad commission that would investigate railroad conditions in the state and then make recommendations to the legislature about the kind of legislation the state needed.

After several proposed amendments were rejected by the senate, and after the Irwin Bill was incorporated into Senate Bill 134, the O'Connor Bill passed the Senate on March 22 by a vote of 30 to 9, with one member not voting.[59] It was supported by 89.5 percent of Democrats in the senate, 85.7 percent of Republicans, 66.7 percent of Independent Democrats, and 45.5 percent of Independents; opposed were 45.5 percent of Independents, 33.3 percent of Independent Democrats, 14.3 percent of Republicans, and 10.5 percent of Democrats.

The O'Connor Bill was presented to the assembly on March 24, and after making several amendments, the assembly passed it unanimously, 76 to 0, on the same day.[60] The amended bill was returned to the Senate the following day; one assembly amendment was rejected and the others accepted.[61] The assembly continued to insist upon its remaining amendment and on March 28 a conference committee was appointed.[62] After a committee conference, the senate refused again to accept the assembly amendment. The lower house withdrew its amendment on March 30, 1876, and the bill was sent to the governor for approval.[63]

Gov. William Irwin signed the disputed and innocuous O'Connor Bill into law on April 3, 1876.[64]

Under its terms, the position of railroad commissioner could be held only by someone who was not a stockholder in *any* railroad company or *any* express or freight company doing business with *any* railroad in the country. The three-man railroad commission, which at first the railroad men had feared, was subsequently appointed and proved ineffective. In 1878, after only two years, the O'Connor Act was replaced by the Hart Act, named for Democratic assemblyman Thomas J. Hart, its sponsor.[65] This law, which provided for an emasculated one-man commission, and which had the support of the Central Pacific Railroad, proved as much a failure as its predecessor.

---

[58]*CSJ*, 21st Sess. (1875–1876), 85.   [59]Ibid., 476.

[60]*CAJ*, 21st Sess., 562 intro. and 564 passed (Mar 24, 1876).   [61]*CSJ*, 21st Sess., 515 (Mar 25, 1876), and 541 (Mar 28).

[62]*CAJ*, 21st Sess., 600 (Mar 28, 1876); *CSJ*, 21st Sess., 546 (Mar 28).

[63]*CAJ*, 21st Sess., 636 (Mar 30, 1876); *CSJ*, 21st Sess., 572 and 580 (Mar 30).

[64]*CSJ*, 21st Sess., 632 (Apr 3, 1876); *Calif Stats*, 21st Sess., 783–791 (Dec 6, 1875–Apr 3, 1876), Chap. 515, *An Act to provide for the appointment of Commissioners of Transportation, to fix the maximum charges for freights and fares, and to prevent extortion and discrimination on railroads in this State*. App. Apr 3, 1876, by Gov. William Irwin (D).

[65]*Calif Stats*, 22nd Sess., 969–986 (Dec 3, 1877–Apr 1, 1878), Chap. 641, *An Act to create the office of Commissioner of Transportation, and to define its powers and duties; to fix the maximum charges for transporting passengers and freights on certain railroads, and to prevent extortion and unjust discrimination thereon*. App. Apr 1, 1878, by Gov. William Irwin (D).

Assemblyman Lawrence Archer Bill (Assembly Bill 182)—
January 11, 1876

Stanford was shaken out of his indifference to political affairs when Santa Clara County Democratic assemblyman Lawrence Archer introduced a bill to the Assembly that would have imposed stringent regulations upon the Central Pacific Railroad. Assembly Bill 182, known as the Archer Bill, was introduced to the assembly on January 11, 1876.[66] The awkward and elliptical title, *An Act to amend an Act to amend an Act to provide for the incorporation of railroad companies and the management of the affairs thereof, and other matters relating thereto, approved May twentieth,* A.D. *eighteen hundred and sixty-one, approved May fourteenth, eighteen hundred and sixty-two*, did not clearly reflect the purpose of the act: it was designed to prescribe the *maximum* rates that might be charged for transportation of passengers and freight on California railroads.[67]

Stanford sent lengthy communications to the committees on corporations of both houses of the state legislature in January 1876, listing his reasons for opposing regulatory legislation of any kind.[68] In his ten-page letter to the assembly he reminded members of the lower house of the prolonged and intense investigations of 1872 and 1874, when the state Senate had concluded that there was nothing amiss in Central Pacific Railroad rates, fares, management, and policies. Now, he had nothing significant to add to his earlier explanations because the proposed 1876 regulatory legislation was little different from that of earlier sessions. Following Stanford's lecture on the essence of good government and its purposes, particularly those purposes that related to the creation of corporations and the right of free capital to operate unmolested through these corporations, he wrote: "The right granted to the railroad is a privilege—or necessity—for which the company makes ample recompense, in obedience to the law."[69] The legislation before the assembly amounted to condemnation of property without due compensation. Rather than restricting the railroads of California, at a time when the railroad system had not yet been completed, Stanford enjoined the assembly to encourage the growth of the Southern Pacific in order to bring the commerce of Arizona and New Mexico within reach of California. He summarized his ideas on the subject:

1. The benefits accruing to California by the construction of railroads far exceed any advantages the companies derive from the creation of wealth.
2. It is not in the interest of the state to restrict the use of capital.
3. There are enterprises indispensable to the material interests of the state that can be carried out only with the use and aggregation of large sums of money.

---

[66]*CAJ*, 21st Sess., 133 (Jan 11, 1876). For a detailed description of the Archer bill, see *SF Bulletin*, Feb 28, 1876.
[67]*CAJ*, 21st Sess., 134 (Jan 11, 1876).
[68]LS to Calif. Assy. Comm. on Corps., Jan [n.d.], 1876, *In the District Court of the Fourth Judicial District of the State of California*, 1–10.   [69]Ibid., 6.

4. The legislature in the past has recognized this and has allowed the creation of ancillary corporations.

5. The state in recognition of the value of railroads has allowed railroads to condemn private property for railroad use—with just compensation.

6. The railroads must serve the best interests of the people in order to serve their own best interests—and this can be done without legislative interference.

7. California railroads are no more costly than the roads of other states.

8. Present cost of railroad transportation in California is already 11.34 cents per ton per mile less than allowed by present legislation.

9. The Central Pacific Railroad by policy has discriminated in favor of the mineral, agricultural, and mechanical products of the Pacific Coast.

10. The proposed legislation could result in the suspension of the railroad business in California.[70]

Alban Towne—general superintendent of the Central Pacific and later third vice president and general manager of the Southern Pacific—said that at least three divisions of the Central Pacific could not afford to operate under the provisions of the Archer Bill.[71] A San Francisco newspaper editor warned that the Archer Bill would be calamitous to the state's prosperity and would suspend operation of a number of short railroads.[72] He reminded his readers that the Central Pacific had been one of California's greatest bonanzas and that the Central Pacific Associates— the greatest railroad builders of the age—had rendered incalculable service to California and the nation.[73]

The Associates, meanwhile, were not going to stand by idly and let this bill be passed without a show of resistance. They treated a number of Assemblymen and their friends to a trip from the capital city to Truckee. The honored guests traveled in the best railroad cars available, including the personal cars of Stanford and his partners. Food, drink, and after-dinner cigars of the finest quality were free to all. After a sleigh ride to a small lake and a day of ice skating, the merrymakers returned home.[74] Despite this treatment, the Assembly passed the Archer Bill.

On January 11 Archer's bill was referred to the Committee on Corporations.[75] Obviously the members of the committee had paid attention to Stanford's letter. After quoting him directly, the chairman of the committee—Archer himself— said: "After a careful investigation of this subject, your committee are [sic] led to believe that the main line of railroads in this State can be and are operated as cheap or even cheaper, per mile, than the great railroads of the Atlantic States."[76] Chairman Archer, no longer as sure of himself after examining the facts, still demanded

[70]Ibid., 8–10.

[71]*SF Chronicle*, Mar 7, 1876.

[72]*SF Alta California*, Mar 5, 1876.

[73]Ibid., Aug 29, 1876.

[74]See *Sac Record-Union*, Feb 21, 1876.

[75]*CAJ*, 21st Sess., 134 (Jan 11, 1876).

[76]Calif. Assy. Comm. on Corps., *Minority Report of the Assembly Committee on Corporations on Assembly Bill No. 182,* in *Business Evaluation Pamphlets*, VII, Pam. 6, 1–14, p. 8 quoted.

the passage of some kind of regulatory bill and then substituted a modified bill in place of his original.

The bill again came before the assembly on February 29, 1876, and was passed by the overwhelming vote of 66 to 8.[77] The twenty-first session of the California Assembly was made up of 64 Democrats (80 percent), 12 Republicans (15 percent), and 4 Independents (5 percent).[78]

The party breakdown of support and opposition to the Democratic Archer Bill in the assembly is surprising, with all four Independents (100 percent) supporting it, as did 11 of 12 Republicans (100 percent, with one abstention), compared to 51 of 64 Democrats (79.2 percent). All eight voting against the bill were Democrats; there were five abstentions.[79] Still, support was overwhelming by Assemblymen of all parties.

On February 7, 1876, Independent senator Tipton Lindsey, representing Fresno, Kern, and Tulare counties, introduced to the state's upper house *An Act Prescribing the maximum rates which may be charged for the transportation of passengers and freight on railroads of this State*.[80] Numbered Senate Bill 332, it was referred to the Committee on Corporations.

As mentioned, Stanford sent a letter to the senate Committee on Corporations and to the assembly on the same day.[81] The assembly passed the Archer Bill; the Central Pacific partners then turned their attention to the state Senate—and there the bill was killed.

Once Assembly Bill 182 had been adopted in the lower house, it was sent to the state Senate. There it was introduced on March 1, 1876, under the more accurate and telling title: *An Act prescribing the maximum rate which may be charged for the transportation of passengers and freight on the railroads in this State*.[82] On that day it and Senate Bill 332 were referred to the Committee on Corporations.

On March 22 these bills came up for consideration, along with still a third—Senate Bill 319, *An Act to Amend the Civil Code*—which had been introduced on February 3 by Samuel G. Hilborn, a Republican from Solano.[83] Democratic senator Edward J. Lewis moved that all three of these so-called "special order" bills be tabled. By a vote of 20 to 19, with one abstention, this was done.[84]

As in 1874 when it investigated the Freeman Bill, the California Senate Committee on Corporations took its investigation seriously. Close to a dozen expert witnesses were summoned, many of them Central Pacific Railroad officers—but not Stanford. In its report to the full Senate, the committee recommended the following:

---

[77]*CAJ*, 21st Sess., 381 (1875–1876).   [78]Driscoll and White, *List of Constitutional Officers*, 139.

[79]*CAJ*, 21st Sess., 381 (Feb 29, 1876).   [80]*CSJ*, 21st Sess., 223 (Feb 7, 1876).

[81]LS to Calif. Sen. Comm. on Corps., Jan [n.d.], 1876, *In the District Court of the Fourth Judicial District of the State of California*, 11–16.   [82]*CSJ*, 21st Sess., 339 (Mar 1, 1876).

[83]*ACSAJ*, 21st Sess., 213 (Mar 3, 1876), and 474 (Mar 22).   [84]Ibid., 476.

1. That Senate Bill 332 (Lindsey Bill) and Assembly Bill 182 (Archer Bill) be rejected.
2. That Senate Bill 134 (O'Connor Bill) be amended and passed.
3. That Senate Bill 319 (Hilborn Bill) not be accepted, on the ground that its provisions had all been incorporated into Senate Bill 134.[85]

The twenty-first session of the California Senate was made up of 19 Democrats (47.5 percent), 11 Independents (27.5 percent), 7 Republicans (17.5 percent), and 3 independent Democrats (7.5 percent).[86] The vote to table, which was a vote against all three regulatory bills, was 20 (51.3 percent) to 19 (48.7 percent). Had the only abstention, Independent Creed Haymond—for years Stanford's friend and attorney—voted for the bill, the vote would have resulted in a tie, to be broken by Democratic lieutenant governor James A. Johnson.

In the final analysis, the party breakdown on these bills themselves—rather than on the confusing negative motion to table—was 10 (52.6 percent) Democrats *for,* 9 (47.4 percent) *opposed;* 6 of 10 (60 percent) voting Independents *for,* 4 (40 percent) *against;* 2 Republicans (28.6 percent) *for,* 5 (71.4 percent) *against;* of Independent Democrats 1 (33.3 percent) *for,* 2 (66.7 percent) *against.*[87]

Thus the Archer Bill—our major concern here rather than the two senate bills—came to an ignominious end by being dropped. Ignoring the votes of the Republicans and Independents, who had no compelling partisan reason to support the bill, there is the surprising spectacle of a Democratic bill—in a state with a Democratic governor, a Democratic lieutenant governor, 80 percent of the assemblymen Democrats, and 55 percent of the senators (including Independent Democrats)—going down to a one-vote defeat with the connivance of nine fellow Democrats. A change of only one of their votes could have reversed the results. The Democratic senators voting as a bloc possessed the numerical strength necessary to pass it in the upper house.

The reasons for the senate vote are easy to understand. Senators from counties without railroads—in hopes that railroads would soon grace their constituencies—opposed the Archer Bill. Other senators, from counties where railroad construction was currently underway, feared that the passage of the Freeman measure would halt this construction. Moreover, opposition to strict railroad regulation in San Francisco, whose merchants enjoyed the lowest intrastate rates offered by the Central Pacific Railroad, feared that overall rate reduction might in fact *raise* theirs![88]

---

[85]Ibid., Calif. Sen. Comm. on Corps., *Railroad Fares and Freights. Report of the Senate Committee on Corporations on Senate Bills Nos. 332, 319, and 334, and Assembly Bill No. 182.* Repr. as Pam. 6, *In the District Court of the Fourth Judicial District of the State of California.* See also Railroad Fares and Freights. Report of the Sen. Comm. on Corps. on Sen. Bills Nos. 332, 319, and 334, and Assy. Bill No. 182. Bound as Pam. 9 in *Business Regulation Pamphlets,* pp. 3–66. RCLL, LSJU, CN H7.

[86]The list in Driscoll and White, *List of Constitutional Officers,* 139, overlooked one Rep. and gives the statistics as 20 Dems., 11 Indeps., 6 Reps., and 3 Indep. Dems.   [87]*CSJ,* 21st Sess., 476 (Mar 22, 1876).

[88]See McAfee, *California's Railroads,* 147–158, on statewide opposition to rate regulation in general and to the Freeman act in particular.

There is nothing to suggest that Stanford employed any unusual or illegal influence in the state's upper house to lead to the bill's rejection. There was a tantalizing hint of bribery in the following legislature, however; in a December 1877 letter David Colton wrote Huntington: "I do not think this legislature will hurt us very much, for we looked at these matters in advance, but if we had not looked after the Senate, they would try to steal all we have before their adjournment."[89]

Less tantalizing, but more to the point, in 1876 Tom Scott, president of the Texas Pacific, was doing everything within his power to drive a second transcontinental across the southern United States; his road could have spelled disaster for the Southern Pacific of California. If Scott gained control of California's railways, the advantageous position of San Francisco merchants would have been lost, resulting in increased rates. For this reason seven of San Francisco's ten state senators opposed the Archer Bill.[90]

Charles Crocker would say later, "We have been two or three times within a few votes of being entirely ruined by legislation that was proposed in the state legislature."[91]

Railroad Regulation by Constitutional Reform

More and more people disillusioned by legislative control of railroads—with legislatures and railroad commissioners bought by political favor, as they saw it—looking to the reform of the state constitution as the only means of creating effective control of railroads.

On January 10, 1874, Independent assemblyman Paschal Coggins of Sacramento introduced Joint Resolution 18, whereby the senate called for a seven-man committee—three from the senate and four from the assembly—to study the need for a constitutional convention to bring about a thorough revision of the state's constitution. It was adopted by the assembly at once.[92] The senate adopted it two days later.[93] On February 25, a report signed by all seven committee members called for a constitutional convention.[94]

A statewide popular referendum calling for a complete overhaul of their state constitution was passed by the voters of California on September 5, 1877. It was

---

[89]DCC to CPH, Dec 22, 1877, in SupC of the State of Calif. in and for the County of Sonoma, 1883, *Ellen M. Colton Plaintiff, vs. Leland Stanford, C.P. Huntington, Charles Crocker, and Wells, Fargo & Company, 1883. Ellen M. Colton, Leland Stanford*, et al., Defendants, XV, 7540–7542. Cited hereafter as *Colton Case*. Contains 18 vols. plus 3 vols. of depositions.

[90]*Sac Record-Union*, Mar 23, 1876; see McAfee, *California's Railroad Era*, 150–151, for the argument of how a second transcontinental controlled by Scott would have affected Calif.'s railway system.

[91]CC Papers, BL. The main bio. record in these papers is the account of a HHB researcher inter. of CC.

[92]*CAJ*, 20th Sess., 394 (Jan 10, 1874).   [93]*CSJ*, 20th Sess., 301–302 (Jan 12, 1874).

[94]*ACSAJ*, 20th Sess., V, 1–4, *Report of Joint Committee on propriety of calling a Constitutional Convention*. Report dated Feb 25, 1874.

passed over the protest of many significant voices, among them the editor of the *San Francisco Chronicle*, who warned that the proposed constitution would amount to nothing but what the "capitalists and monopolists" would force upon the constitutional convention.[95]

The twenty-second session of the California legislature (1877–1878) passed the enabling act to write the new document.[96] This act provided for the election of a constitutional convention in June 1878. A body of 152 delegates assembled for business in late September and sat for fifty-six working days.[97] Its political composition reflected the mood of the times: there were 85 nonpartisan delegates, 50 from the Workingmen's Party of California, 9 Republicans, and only 8 Democrats.[98] Under no circumstances could effective railroad influence have been brought to bear on a group this large, particularly on the 50 Workingmen delegates who had agreed ahead of time to operate as a unit—a *radical* unit by the standards of the day. Perhaps the prevailing mood of the Central Pacific Associates ought to have been one of depression, but quite to the contrary, they had no troubling facing up to the test of political reality. Stanford wrote Huntington a letter both hopefully optimistic—a matter of wishful thinking?—and also realistic about the convention's work and how the people of the state would react to it:

> I don't know how the Constitutional Convention will act as to RR matters. But there is a bad disposition there, I have done what I could to counteract it. They are now debating the subject of corporations. Very likely I shall have to go to Sac again before the debate is concluded. It is the general opinion that what the Convention will submit to the people will not be adopted.[99]

Still, Stanford regarded the convention as a dangerous body that would not do the railroad any good.[100]

The self-appointed watchdogs of railroad morality did not give up easily. The delegates discussed several possibilities for controlling and regulating the railroads and decided that a railroad commission would be the best way to do it. The new state constitution as written provided for three railroad commissioners, each

---

[95]*SF Chronicle*, Sep 5, 1877; see *SF Alta California*, Sep 6, 1877, for an analysis of the election results.

[96]*CAJ*, 22nd Sess., intro. of AB 436, to implement the constitutional referendum, 340 (Feb 11, 1878), passed the Calif. Assy., 416 (Feb 21), passed the Calif. Sen., 510 (Mar 5); *Calif Stats*, 22nd Sess., 759–765 (Dec 3, 1877–Apr 1, 1878), Chap. 489, *An Act to Provide for a Convention to frame a new Constitution for the State of California*. App. Mar 30, 1878, by Gov. William Irwin (D).

[97]McAfee, *California's Railroads*, 163–168; Frank M. Fahey, "The Legislative Background of the Constitutional Convention of 1879," MA thesis (LSJU, 1947), 90; *Sac Record-Union*, Apr 9, 1878. For a record of the conv., see Willis and Stockton, *Debates and Proceedings of the Constitutional Convention of California*.

[98]*SF Alta California*, Jun 26, 27, 1879; *SF Chronicle*, Jun 27, 1879. The Workingmen's Party of Calif. is not to be confused with the Workingmen's Party of the U.S., a Marxist organization created in NY and Chicago, which later changed its name to the Socialist Labor Party. The Calif. organization came into existence sometime between Aug and Oct of 1877 with Denis Kearney as sec. and soon thereafter as pres.   [99]LS to CPH, Nov 13, 1878.

[100]Ibid., Dec 5, 1878.

Denis Kearney

was a thirty-one-year-old Irish-born teamster who agitated labor leaders in a series of sandlot meetings in which he harangued workers with incendiary speeches calling for the creation of a "workers militia" to oversee the hanging of corrupt officials, oppressive capitalists, and the "heathen Chinese."[a] In 1878 Marcus Boruck's *Spirit of the Times and Underwriters' Journal* carried a lengthy editorial on Kearney titled "California's Traveling Disgrace." The editor wrote, in part: "A low, brutal blackguard; a coarse, profane ruffian; a miserable and irresponsible fanatic, under the name of Denis Kearney is representing California, at the East today. In charge of two men who were residents of this city, and who daily stuff him with obscenity, ribaldry and blasphemy, he assails the good sense, peace, quiet and order of the communities in which he condescends to speak, in the name of the workingmen and as the representative of California. For months he was permitted, through the abject fear and cowardice of our city officials and authorities to insult the people of this city and State, and by his threats and intimidation he succeeded in driving capital from this coast, reducing the wages of the laboring man, stagnating all business and rendering the name of California a by-word and reproach. Since the cowardly cur left these shores and proceeded on his eastern trip a better feeling has pervaded the community, the blight of his infamous tirades of brutality and abuse, has in a measure died out, confidence has been measurably restored, business has improved, building has been going on, enterprises have been entered into, the laborers and workingmen have been employed, and a most decided change has taken place. The people demand that this state of affairs shall continue and increase, and not be lessened or stopped altogether. And they demand of Mayor Bryant and those in authority with him, that ruffianism, obscenity and infamy on the sand lots shall cease to be a Sunday pastime in San Francisco. Kearney will shortly return to California, and basing a further lease of power upon lying telegraphic dispatches, sent here to 'tickle the ears of the groundlings,' he will again erect his power-house in San Francisco, keeping the people

elected from a different district within the state.[101] Other states had created railroad commissions to set maximum rates, but California was the first state to provide for such a commission in its state constitution.[102] Thus when state legislators passed laws regulating the railroads, they would be required to consider the recommendations of the commission. In later years constitutional reform would stymie reformers, because changes needed to keep up with the times could be made only by the cumbersome process of constitutional amendment.

The Constitutional Convention's task was massive. When completed, the three-

---

[101]The editor of the *Sac Record-Union* took a strong stand against the creation of the state railroad commission, arguing that it was illegal, but once it was ratified as a part of the state's constitution, the argument was moot. Cited in *SF Argonaut*, Dec 11, 1880.

[102]McAfee, *California's Railroads*, 166–167.

in suspense as to the precise time when he will light the match that will lead to its explosion. We tell Mayor BRYANT and the other officials of this city that they will be held to a strict accountability for the future progress and business prosperity of San Francisco, so far as DENIS KEARNEY can have any bearing upon the matter. Politically, we are well assured that DENIS KEARNEY is dead. In that respect we have no fear of him. As a blatant nuisance, as an incendiary, as a criminal before and after the fact, without courage to commit the crime, we look upon him as one that should be suppressed at all hazards; and his progress so far as San Francisco and California is concerned, should be checked the moment he sets foot on this soil again."[b]

In 1886, the editor of the *San Francisco Wasp* wrote of Kearney in much the same vein: "Denis Kearney making protrusion of his moldy pow from the political tomb and announcing his 'acceptance' of a candidacy not offered him is a spectacle for which we are probably indebted to the nomination of Mr. Swift. Kearney is everybody's blackguard, but he is nobody's fool: he has a nose for corruption, and when it is in the air he comes out of his hole. If a Swift is to be taken seriously as an aspirant for Governor, where is the humor of a Kearney's ambition to be Sheriff. If the public stomach is strong enough to retain the one, it can keep down the other. Debauched by Swift, the political situation naturally conceives Kearney. That the latter has no chance of election let not those who support the former be too quick to affirm: Kearney is gifted by nature with the rarest and most valuable of political instincts, the sense of opportunity. He doesn't go out when it is going to rain; when hunted he stands behind a tree. The fact that he is 'abroad in the land'—prevalent, epidemic, imminent—proves the presence of congenial conditions. Bats do not fly by day; buzzards do not follow the militia nor snap their beaks above a Quaker picnic. In Kearney's candidacy Republicans may discern a ray of hope for Swift's. The golden drayman's every boast is a benediction upon the no head of the acephalous ticket."[c]

[a]Perley Orman Ray, "Denis Kearney," *DAB*, V, Part 2, 268–269. [b]*SF CSTF/UJ*, Sep 7, 1878.
[c]*SF Wasp*, Sep 25, 1886.

volume *Debates and Proceedings of the Constitutional Convention of the State of California* filled 1,578 pages.

The convention sent the proposed constitution to the people of California at a time when the Central Pacific was least prepared to fight it. Mark Hopkins, as seen, had died during a health-cure in the desert in Yuma, Arizona Territory, on March 29, 1878, while inspecting the Southern Pacific's progress. It was just a few months later, on October 9, that the Associates lost another of their big guns, when forty-six-year-old David Colton died.

Leland Stanford was too ill from January through June of 1879 to work effectively against it, and Huntington, as usual, was too preoccupied with railroad business in the East to put up much of a fight by himself. This left only Charles Crocker to oppose the new constitution—and *he* was certainly not the man for the task.

THE *SAN FRANCISCO ARGONAUT* AND THE SOUTHERN PACIFIC'S TRANSCONTINENTAL RAILROAD

But the Southern Pacific Associates did not have to fight alone. They had the support of Frank Pixley's mighty *Argonaut*. For months before the adoption of a new state constitution, this journal regularly attacked the reformers in print for their ignorance, laziness, political opportunism, and public immorality.

On May 7, 1879, California voters adopted the new constitution.[103] Reform-minded San Franciscans rejected it, but agricultural interests of the state gave it a statewide edge of 10,820 out of a total vote of 145,088.[104] It went into effect at noon on July 4, 1879. All laws of the state inconsistent with its terms were repealed on January 1, 1880.

It is difficult to improve upon Bancroft's assessment: "So far, as its practical workings are concerned, it has achieved nothing which a few amendments would not have done."[105]

THE FIRST THREE RAILROAD COMMISSIONERS UNDER THE NEW STATE CONSTITUTION

The state's first three railroad commissioners elected under the new California state constitution were Joseph Spencer Cone, a Republican, elected from the northern part of the state, Charles J. Beerstecher, a radical Workingmen's delegate to the constitutional convention, elected to represent San Francisco, and Democrat Gen. George B. Stoneman, elected from southern California. Stoneman was a West Point graduate and served during the Mexican War as a quartermaster in the Mormon Battalion.[106] During the Civil War he was brevetted a major general in the regular army in 1865 and was given a disability retirement in August 1871. In 1883 he resigned his army rank to be nominated for the governorship of California, but throughout his political career was always known as "General Stoneman."

Not one of the three railroad commissioners paid much attention to the problem of regulating railroads. Cone, a long-time friend of Stanford (as reflected earlier in his land sales at Vina) and of many other railroad men, soon emerged as the dominating force on the commission, to the chagrin of reformers across the state. As for Beerstecher, he "easily made the transition from sand-lot agitator to pro-railroad commissioner"—and not a very effective one at that.[107] Stoneman was easily held in check by the majority vote of Cone and Beerstecher. It was never proven that any of these commissioners ever received direct bribes from the railroad. Neverthe-

---

[103]*SF Alta California*, May 8, 1879.   [104]HHB, *History of California*, VII, 400.

[105]Ibid., 403–404.   [106]Oliver L. Spaulding, Jr., "George Stoneman," *DAB*, XI, Part 2, 92–93.

[107]McAfee, *California's Railroads*, 175.

less, they accepted favors from the Associates, leaving little doubt in the minds of some that it was bribery in all but name.[108]

On January 12, 1883, Democratic assemblyman Lewis C. Granger introduced a resolution (Assembly Resolution 4) to the twenty-fifth session of the assembly calling for the investigation of the official, business, and personal activities of the three railroad commissioners.[109] The resolution was adopted immediately.

The investigation took a total of nine days between January 17 and February 9. The investigation involved the commissioners' real estate activities, whether railroad rates in the state had been reduced as a result of any action taken by them, whether any of them was guilty of dereliction of official duty, whether they showed incompetence or evidenced any corruption while in office, and whether the state of California suffered any damages or losses as a result of any of their actions.

Twelve exhibits were presented to the investigating committee, many of which proved embarrassing to Cone and Beerstecher.[110] Exhibit 2 showed real property acquired by Cone in Tehama County after January 1, 1880.[111] Exhibits 10 and 11 contained similar information on Beerstecher's real estate acquisitions in San Francisco and his bank account activity.[112]

During Gov. George Stoneman's testimony—he had become governor of California on January 10, 1883—it was brought out that a lowering of railroad rates prepared by Stoneman could not be implemented until Stanford returned from Europe. Thus the lower rates were adopted but never put into effect.[113]

Q. The action of the Commission was to wait the return of Mr. Stanford?
A. Yes, sir.
Q. Was that publicly stated and recorded or only private?
A. Private.
Q. Was action taken after the return of Mr. Stanford?
A. Action never was taken. The schedule never went into force.[114]

On one occasion, Cone actually negotiated with Alban Towne, long-time general manager of the Central Pacific and Southern Pacific, about the terms of a proposed passenger and freight schedule, rather than enforcing the new rates.[115] Cone testified, however, that he had inquired of railroad leaders about fares because he knew they were an interested party and he was simply offering them a chance to explain why lower rates should not go into effect.[116] His invitation called upon them to appear and show cause.[117] Cone conceded that he had an agreement with Stan-

---

[108]Daggett, *Chapters on the History of the Southern Pacific*, 194–196.

[109]*ACSAJ*, 25th Sess. (Jan 8–Mar 13, 1883), Hearings (Jan 17–Feb 9, 1883), III, 1-176, Doc. 4, Comm. on Corps., *Report on the Committee on Corporations of the Assembly of California.*

[110]Ibid., 153–176.   [111]Ibid., 159–164.   [112]Ibid., 172–175.

[113]Ibid., 9.   [114]Ibid.   [115]Ibid., 14.

[116]Ibid., 73.   [117]Ibid., 74.

THE *SAN FRANCISCO ARGONAUT* ON THE CONSTITUTIONAL CONVENTION

"It surprises us that any reflecting and intelligent person should question the propriety of united non-partisan action in selecting delegates to a Constitutional Convention. . . . There is a need of reform, and a demand for it. If intelligence and property does not concede it peacefully, the ignorant and the destitute will endeavor to accomplish it by brute force. The First Ward Club met on Wednesday night and nominated as delegates to the Constitutional Convention . . . nearly all unknown, except through their offenses against society; nearly every one ignorant, uneducated, and unmannerly—destitute not only of intelligence and morals, but of property and honest purpose; scarce one in any employment save that of political agitation. And yet while this class of rogues and adventurers conspire [sic] to form a Convention to give to the State its organic law, such men as Governor Haight and Governor Stanford, Senator Cole and Senator Casserly, Judge Wallace and Judge Lorenzo Sawyer, Mayor Bryant and Mayor Alvord, D. O. Mills and Mr. Flood, Mr. Fitch and Mr. Pen Johnson, Mr. William T. Coleman and Mr. William F. Babcock, cannot agree to sit together in Convention to frame for the State a Constitution, because they are not members of the same political party. It is not creditable to our intelligence that such a question as this should have two sides."[a]

"More than half of the electors of San Francisco are adventurers from other lands . . . a very large percentage are of the poor and ignorant class . . . and, owing to dissensions among the intelligent and native born, it has sent a compact delegation to the Constitutional Convention composed mostly of ignorant, propertyless, foreign adventurers."[b]

"And yet the Constitutional Convention, now engaged in the preparation of an organic law, . . . this mob-fearing body of wisdom seriously proposes to give over the absolute control of the Southern Pacific Railroad to three politicians elected by the people—who 'shall have the sole control to fix the rates of freight and passage;' a railroad built without subsidy through an unsettled part of the State, reaching out to the Rio Grande in Texas in order to grasp and bring to San Francisco the vast future trade of the great Arizona and the valley of Mexico, and whose prospects of ultimate profit is in a distant future. This Southern Pacific Railroad enterprise is doing for our city, more than all the rich men, corporations, merchants, and business men of the State beside. It is extending the jurisdiction, the businesses, and the commercial area of the city, to a great, productive, and unoccupied country. It is opening up to us a future business, the extent and value of which the unthinking city trader has no conception or appreciation of. It is giving us a grasp upon a valuable trade, and is inviting to our port a business that in the future will be of inestimable value. The Southern Pacific corporation has no subsidy, no lands, and is asking no aid, yet in San Francisco there is an ignorant, mean, and

ford to hold off the lowering of some rates until Stanford returned from Europe, though at the time he expected Stanford's stay to be much shorter than it was.[118]

Some of the questions put to Cone made it clear that the committee was investigating *Stanford* more than it was the railroad commissioners. One question put to Cone was:

---

[118]Ibid., 76–77.

jealous prejudice against it difficult to understand. Half the press are continually denouncing it; all the politicians are making capital in abuse of it; a Constitutional Convention threatens to go to the voting masses with propositions to confiscate it; the sand-lot mob meet before the dwellings of its promoters, and with bonfires, blasphemy, and threats of personal violence seek to intimidate the men who are building it, and who are giving labor to honest workers. Such narrow-minded ignorance, such mean and jealous stupidity, we never saw before in any community. If this road is built to the Gulf of Mexico—which is its objective point—it will bring to our city all the trade of that great empire of undeveloped wealth. If the system of California railroads, now being carried out by Governor Stanford and his associates, is left to be developed, without needless interference, the Rocky Mountains will bound our commercial jurisdiction on the east, and it will bring to our port the splendid commerce of Asia and the islands of the Pacific. If the narrow-minded political newspaper and sand-lot bigots are permitted to arrest the development of this enterprise, the Sierra Nevada hills will bound our trade eastward, and we shall find ourselves, like Portugal, locked in between the ocean and the Sierra, with a limited trade and a limited political influence. It seems a pity that San Francisco can not produce one man who has breadth of statesmanship enough to recognize this fact, and boldness enough to give the fact utterance. It is shameful that the press is cowardly, mercenary, selfish, and stupid; that it is left to an 'obscure literary paper of limited circulation' to announce what everyone ought to know; and the most absurd thing of all is the howling of the jackass mob at the only concern that gives labor and the only men who spend money generously. If the community—of course we mean that portion of it that is disinterested and intelligent—would consider this work that the Southern Pacific Railroad Company is now doing, and its relation to the future prosperity of San Francisco; would contemplate in all its bearings the effect of a new southern transcontinental road, owned and operated in the interest of this city, it would be convinced that it is the most important enterprise ever undertaken upon this coast. If Tom Scott could be permitted to accomplish the building of a road to San Diego, to be controlled by him in the interest of eastern capital, it would strike a most serious blow at San Francisco. Thanks to the enterprises of Governor Stanford and his associated railroad builders, this danger is now indefinitely postponed. The time will come when our citizens will understand and appreciate this contest for railroad supremacy; when they do, they will do justice to the railroad men of this coast and give them a credit well deserved, but now withheld, under the influence of demagogy in politics; bigotry in journalism, jealously in business circles, and ignorance among the masses."[c]

^a*SF Argonaut*, Apr 27, 1878.   ^bIbid., Jun 29, 1878.   ^cIbid., Nov 16, 1878.

Has the railroad corporation known as the Central Pacific Railroad Corporation, or the railroad corporation known as the Southern Pacific Railroad Corporation, or any officer of either of such railroad corporations . . . attempted to influence your conduct as a Railroad Commissioner during your term of office as a Railroad Commissioner?[119]

---

[119]Ibid., 108.

Cone's answer was straightforward: "Well, Governor Stanford has talked to me and tried to influence me by persuasion, but no other way."[120]

> Q. Has he ever held out any inducement of any character to you; promises?
> A. No, not at all; he has in a friendly way tried to persuade me not to do certain things, but in no other way.
> Q. Have the friendly offices of Governor Stanford, or your feeling of friendship for him, influenced your conduct as a Railroad Commissioner?
> A. I think not.[121]

The committee was relentless in its examination of Cone on the Gerke property transaction.[122] Cone denied that *he* was to benefit in any way from the unusual property transaction to Nick Smith and then to Leland Stanford. He denied, further, that he had any knowledge that Smith was holding the property for Stanford or that *he himself* (Cone) was acting as an agent for Stanford in buying and selling the property to Smith.[123]

The committee was not convinced! Nor, it must be added, was it "convincible."

The investigating committee concluded that a very small portion of the railroad commissioners' time had actually been spent in performing the duties of their office.[124] For more than a year after his appointment, Commissioner Beerstecher had pursued his own professional interests. The brunt of the condemnation by the committee was leveled at Cone: he had continued in many of his own business interests, and had greatly increased his material wealth while serving as a commissioner, "largely due to extraordinary and unusual facilities afforded by the railroad officers." In particular the profit of $100,000 from his purchase and sale of the Gerke Ranch to N. T. Smith was cited as "giving rise to the suspicion that more was contemplated in the purchase and sale than appears on the face of the transaction."[125] Most damaging of all to Leland Stanford, the committee reported to the California State Assembly that "Commissioner Cone sacrificed the best interests of the State through personal friendship for Governor Stanford, and in return therefore received favors from him."[126] Lumping Cone and Beerstecher together, the committee report went on: "Commissioner Beerstecher's conduct admits of no other explanation than that

GEN.—LATER CALIFORNIA GOVERNOR—
GEORGE STONEMAN'S

detractors rarely questioned his basic honestly, but one at least—Ambrose Bierce—doubted even his mental powers; in an epitaph written eight years in advance of Stoneman's death, Bierce poured his premature vitriol over Governor Stoneman in the following verse: "Here lie, in sum and substance, his remains: Blood, bones, flesh, gristle—everything but brains."*

*SF Wasp, Aug 21, 1886.

[120]Ibid.
[123]Ibid., 144.
[126]Ibid., 5.

[121]Ibid., 108–109.
[124]Ibid., 4.

[122]Ibid., 142–151.
[125]Ibid., 4–5.

he was bribed, and that in the opinion of this committee, Commissioners Cone and Beerstecher acted in the interests of the railroad corporations rather than of the people."[127] General Stoneman, the committee reported, "devoted most of his time to the management of his ranch near Los Angeles."[128]

One result of this investigation and the committee's subsequent exposé was that subsequently, when the Central or Southern Pacific railroads were not sufficiently controlled by the state, it was believed that they owned the railroad commissioners. This allegation was easier to maintain than that they owned the legislature or controlled the state's political conventions.

Stanford Returns Home Alone from Europe—July 8, 1880

The battle over regulation, the threat to the Associates' system posed by attempts made by other railroads to build a second and competing southern transcontinental, and the aftermath of a bloody confrontation in the Central Valley called the Mussel Slough tragedy, made it impossible for Stanford to continue his 1880 European tour.

Stanford sailed from Liverpool on July 8 on the White Star Line's 5,008-ton *Germanic*.[129] (The White Star Line ended almost all its ships' names in "-ic," including the best known of all—the *Titanic*.) Stanford arrived in New York on July 18.[130] He remained there almost a week before leaving for home. He arrived in Oakland on August 3, where Alban Towne, Fred Crocker, and other railroad officials met him.[131]

Hotel del Monte

Having taken "a new lease of life," as the *Argonaut* reported it, Stanford recovered from the fatigue of his brief foreign travels, two transoceanic trips within just over a month, and a hurried train trip across the American continent by resting at the Hotel del Monte in Monterey. There, he indulged in "occasional buffets" while enjoying the company of many old friends, among them James Ben Ali Haggin and Charley Crocker, who was reportedly "full of enthusiasm over the place." [132]

During the 1870s the Central Pacific Associates, under the aegis of their Pacific Improvement Company, had purchased 7,000 acres of choice real estate that eventually included Pebble Beach, part of the Seventeen-Mile Drive, 150 miles of forested bridle trails, and the site of the magnificent Hotel del Monte.[133] The Associates built the hotel on the south shore of Monterey Bay about a half-mile from the

---

[127]Ibid.   [128]Ibid., 4.

[129]*Times* (of London), Jul 9, 1880.   [130]*NY Times*, Jul 19, 1880.

[131]*SF Argonaut*, Aug 7, 1880.   [132]Ibid., Aug 28, 1880.

[133]Randall A. Reinstadt, *Incredible Ghosts of old Monterey's Hotel Del Monte* (Carmel: GTP, 1980), 8–9.

center of town. It was built at a cost of $1 million in just one hundred days, with the formal opening on June 3, 1880.[134] This "Queen of American Watering Places" was three and a half hours from San Francisco by rail and had its own private sidings for those who chose to travel in their own cars. The 120-acre park-like grounds boasted 1,200 trees, croquet courts, archery ranges, a 15-acre lake, a stable and carriage house, a ladies' billiard parlor—which Jane Stanford must have loved!—smoking and game rooms for the men, a bowling alley, and a bath house with several pools heated to different temperatures. Each of the guestrooms was heated with gas, had hot and cold running water, and contained its own telephone.[135]

In "Hebe's" columns in the *Argonaut* we find the following testimonial to the beauty of the nation's "prettiest, breeziest-looking, and most handsomely furnished watering-place:"

> It is situated so delightfully, too, in a grove of pine and oak; and the sun shines so gloriously into every part of it; and the atmosphere is so pure, and soft, and elastic; and there are so many walks and drives, and other means of recreation and enjoyment, that I doubt not, when its superior attractions are widely known, and the unrivaled equability of temperature of the location is made apparent to the Eastern valetudinarian, this hotel will be a winter Mecca as well as a summer resort, and fashion and frolic, good living and good cheer, will here hold, high carnival from January to December. Standing upon the veranda of the new hotel Saturday night last, the delicious evening air impregnated with the breath of harvest and of aromatic shrub, my mind wandered back to those periods more than a century ago, when, upon the decline of some fair day, Father Junipero Serra strayed, with violin in hand, among the very trees through which the bewitching diminuendos of Ballenberg's rendition of the ecstatic "Beautiful Blue Danube" now chase each other like lights and shadows for mastery. The ball-room is spacious, being thirty-six by seventy-two feet, and will only be used for dancing; it lights up very beautifully, and is nicely ventilated. There will be no liquors sold on the premises, a place for that purpose having been erected at a convenient but proper distance from the hotel. A stable that will house sixty horses and as many carriages is in close proximity.[136]

On April 1, 1887, the entirely wooden Hotel del Monte burned to the ground.[137] Between two and three hundred guests were left on the grounds with all of their possessions destroyed except what they were wearing, but no one was killed. On April 23, E. T. M. Simmons, the manager of the hotel, was arrested for arson.[138] The

---

[134] *SF Argonaut*, Jun 12, 1880.

[135] Reinstadt, *Incredible Ghosts of old Monterey's Hotel Del Monte*, 10.

[136] *SF Argonaut*, Jun 12, 1880. Ben C. Truman of *Del Monte Wave* fame and other literary works wrote arts. for the *SF Argonaut* under the *noms de plume* Hebe and Bella. *SF Argonaut*, Mar 13, 1883.

[137] *SF Call*, Apr 2, 1887.

[138] His trial began on Jun 20, *SF Chronicle*, Jun 21, 1887. For the story of the fire and the trial, see Elmer Lagorio, "Burning Questions, Mysteries revealed as Man stands trial for Hotel Del Monte fire," *Alta Vista Magazine* (Sunday supplement to the *Monterey Herald*), Jul 26, 1992.

five-day trial ended on June 25 when, after only seven minutes of deliberation, the jury returned a verdict of not guilty.[139]

Arson or accident, within less than a year the hotel was replaced by an even more impressive structure, having room now for seven hundred guests, rather than only four hundred that the original hotel accommodated.[140]

STANFORD ENTERTAINS PRESIDENT RUTHERFORD B. HAYES—SEPTEMBER 1880

On September 15, 1880, Stanford outdid himself in extravagant hospitality, fêting Rutherford B. Hayes, the first U.S. president to visit California while still in office. Frank Pixley's *Argonaut* best describes the occasion:

> Monterey has been on the tip-toe of expectation for a week past. Good President Hayes and party were coming to honor us with their presence. The Hotel del Monte was being transformed into a fairy place; and a couple of hundred of California's fairest women and most distinguished men were summoned as the guests of Governor Stanford, to greet the greatest man of the greatest republic of the greatest inhabited sphere within mortal ken. A perceptible thrill ran through all things, animate and inanimate. Houses and stores—ancient adobe and modern frame—were swathed in bunting, Spanish shawls of rare embroidery, and garlands of gay flowers. The inhabitants, foreign and native-born, from the plump and round-eyed infant to the scrawny and wrinkled señora—placarded "104 years old"—donned their festive garbs for the occasion, and from early morn to set of sun, on the never-to-be-forgotten 15th of September, filled the hotel grounds, eagerly awaiting the arrivals and inspecting the decorations. At 5:30 P.M., the special train bearing the distinguished visitors arrived. The usual amount of speculation was indulged in as each carriage drove up to the hotel steps and the occupants descended therefrom. Mrs. Hayes was easily distinguished by simple and old-style arrangement of her hair, and her resemblance to her portraits. Governor Stanford accompanied Mrs. Hayes, and was mistaken for the President by a few of the spectators, as was also Captain Oliver Eldridge and one or two others. President Hayes preferred to walk from the depot, and escorted Mrs. Hunt, arriving very shortly after the first carriages, and before the rush of invited guests.[141]

The guest list was a catalog of San Francisco's greatest and wealthiest, including judges, business directors and managers, celebrities of all sorts, the leading ladies and debutantes of the city. And, of course, as Pixley mentioned, there was Mrs. Hayes, the president's childhood sweetheart, Lucy, née Webb, whose attractiveness, shrewdness, and poise contributed much to his *own* later success.[142]

---

[139]*SF Chronicle*, Jun 26, 1887.   [140]See Chap. 26, "Epilogue and Legacy," for subsequent hist. of the hotel.
[141]*SF Argonaut*, Sep 18, 1880.
[142]Allan Nevins, "Rutherford Birchard Hayes," *DAB*, IV, Part 2, 447.

97. President Rutherford B. Hayes and party visit the Palo Alto farm
in September 1880. *Stanford University Archives.*

Representatives of the city of Monterey, General Sherman, and the president all made public addresses.

This was but the beginning of the Stanford largess lavished upon the presidential party. Many of the merrymakers hurried to the capital city to join Sacramentans in honoring the Chief Executive and entourage. Hayes was the highest-ranking guest entertained at the Stanford's Sacramento mansion. Accompanied now by Secretary of War Alexander Ramsey, who either was not in Monterey or was not mentioned by the *Argonaut*, the Hayes procession was given a military escort from the railroad station to J Street, up J to Tenth, down Tenth to N, down N to Eighth; then the procession proceeded past a regiment of soldiers at present arms, and turned into the Stanford residence. The streets in all directions were thronged with people cheering Hayes and Sherman. The host met their carriage at the front entrance, led Mrs. Hayes upstairs, and installed her as hostess, in the absence of his wife Jane, who was then in Europe.[143] We have it on the sole and dubious authority of H. H. Bancroft that Stanford made such a favorable impression upon the chief executive that he remarked to his host, "I wish I had known you earlier, I would have been glad to have

---

[143] *Sac Record-Union*, Sep 22, 1880.

had you in my cabinet."[144] Hayes later wrote to Stanford: "Mrs. Hayes and myself will always remember gratefully your abundant kindness to us in the most enjoyable journey of our lives, our California trip in 1880."[145]

While at home without his family, Stanford was no more a social recluse than when his family was there. When on February 15, 1881, Hattie Crocker gave a "German" (the name for a popular dance and social event in San Francisco society)—described as the "most pretentious society circumstance of the present week"—Stanford walked the two blocks up California Street to Charley Crocker's and visited with many old friends who were entertained royally in the art gallery by Nathan Ballenberg's band. The German was concluded a little before twelve o'clock, when the guests were summoned to an elegant supper. Afterward, they returned to the art gallery and enjoyed a waltz or two before taking to their carriages and to their homes. Among those present were Governor Stanford, Col. and Mrs. Fred Crocker, Mrs. Judge Silas W. Sanderson, Gov. and Mrs. Frederick Low, and "Joe" Grant.[146]

STANFORD ON GOVERNMENT REGULATION

Stanford did not avoid politics when they were specific threats to the railroad empire that he and his Associates had built. An example was in 1878–1879, when the new state constitution required that railroads operating in more than one county in the state pay higher taxes than short lines operating entirely within one county. As a result, from 1880 to 1888 the Associates paid taxes of $100 per mile above the average tax base in fifteen other states (they paid $250 per mile, while the others averaged $151 per mile).[147]

In 1878, when the legislature was still considering the matter of regulatory legislation, Stanford wrote an open letter to the *San Francisco Call* again spelling out his views on the regulation of corporations. This letter was more than a rationalization of Stanford's railroad position: it was a well-reasoned, well-thought-out statement of his economic philosophy. To Stanford regulation of corporations was a serious break with America's traditional respect for the property rights of the individual, especially the little man who needed to cooperate with others in his class to give him the economic leverage needed to protect himself from the wealthy.

Stanford characterized the modern corporation as the most effective economic institution for allowing common people to cooperate in enterprises too big to take on alone. It constituted "the poor man's absolute defense against the monopoly of

---

[144]HHB, *Stanford*, 194. This statement is not found in any Hayes writings.

[145]Rutherford B. Hayes to LS, Dec 12, 1885, in Charles Richard Williams, ed., *Diary and Letters of Rutherford Birchard Hayes, Nineteenth President of the United States* (4 vols., Columbus: OSAHS, 1925), IV, 255.

[146]*SF Argonaut*, Feb 19, 1881.   [147]HHB, *Stanford*, 48, based on an analysis of the 1880 census.

the rich." He again went to great lengths to explain that corporate ownership was a matter of individual ownership of a small part of a big business. Since it was the same as a partnership, except for its greater number of partners, a wrong done to a corporation was a wrong done to individuals. Stanford felt that the attacks against corporations throughout the country, especially in California, amounted to attacks against private initiative and individualism; they were repugnant to the individualism that had made the American republic great. When the individual is safe, he asserted, "the many cannot be otherwise." In fact, he added, the very basis of civilization was the right of property and the protection of individuals in the fruit of their industry. Stanford rejected legal regulation of railroads as superfluous—entirely unnecessary—since competition would keep rates as low as possible without government intervention. Repeating one of his favorite doctrines, he warned that state regulation would lead ultimately to state ownership.[148]

The *Argonaut* praised Stanford's long overdue end to his "long silence in reference to railroad affairs." Pixley's journal described Stanford's letter as a "well matured paper," containing an able argument that would "challenge the best reasoning of its opponents to answer."[149]

The *Argonaut*'s assessment was proven accurate by the *San Francisco Chronicle*'s efforts to dispute Stanford's argument in a diatribe titled "Mr. STANFORD'S LETTER. HIS SOPHISTRIES CONFRONTED WITH INDISPUTABLE FACTS."[150]

In Stanford's annual presidential report to the stockholders of the Central Pacific Railroad—dated July 22, 1879—for the year ending July 1, 1879, he addressed himself to the subject of federal regulation.[151] Not only did he give the stockholders a clear and lucid statement on the affairs of the company, but he challenged those who would regulate the railroads out of business: he insisted that there was no good reason for attempts by either the federal or state government to control the railroads of California.[152] He elaborated upon his earlier assertion that free enterprise, private wealth, individualism, and the rights of labor were threatened by state regulation of the nation's railroads. Realizing that most of the California opposition to his railroad centered in San Francisco, he focused on that city's benefits derived from railroad transportation.[153] Of all the important cities in California, San Francisco was the least likely to be injured by any so-called railroad monopoly. The city's location gave merchants the option to ship and receive via either the Isthmus of Panama or Cape Horn, which allowed them to dictate the rates they would pay for transcontinental service.

---

[148]*SF Morning Call*, Nov 3, 1878.   [149]*SF Argonaut*, Nov 9, 1878.

[150]*SF Chronicle*, Nov 18, 1878.

[151]CPRR, *Annual Report of the Board of Directors of the Central Pacific Railroad Co. to the Stockholders for the Year Ending December 31st, 1878* (SF: HSCC, 1879).   [152]Ibid., 5.   [153]Ibid., 7–8.

Stanford told the stockholders of the Central Pacific Railroad that if the state regulated profits, it should also guarantee against loss resulting from such regulation.[154] He then reminded them of a little-appreciated side effect of that article in the new constitution—the creation of a Board of Railroad Commissioners, a body invested, he said, with many arbitrary powers. The existing roads in the state were given the right to regulate their own rates by the railroad act of 1862. If the state moved against this prerogative, he warned, there would be no more railroad construction within the state; there were no capitalists so reckless as to make investments where the gross proceeds were regulated by somebody *other* than those who made the investment. Furthermore, those moving against the railroads would probably bring about a state of affairs exactly opposite to what they intended; since the proposed legislation would discourage the building of new roads, it would indirectly benefit the old roads by scaring off competition.

Stanford's remarks on railroad regulation reflected a deep-seated aversion to pure democracy. "Unfortunately," he said, "scarcely was the [United States] constitution adopted when came the declaration that the majority should rule, intensified afterwards in its application by that calamitous declaration that to the victors belonged the spoils." Like the property-oriented conservatives of all ages, Stanford was fearful that democracy meant the end of personal property and effective government. He rejected majority rule and endorsed instead a system in which the majority administered but the Constitution ruled. He complained that the Constitution was gradually being eroded by the Granger cases, various railroad decisions adverse to the railroads, and the Thurman Act, which required that a fund be set aside for retiring the railroad's debt to the central government. In the words of one critic, the controversial Thurman Act of May 7, 1878,

> deliberately undertook to override the decision of the Supreme Court [in 1875], and to seize and withhold a much larger sum than the whole of the charges for Government transportation and the five percent of net earnings, under the pretense of establishing a sinking fund out of the earnings of the Companies, for the purpose of retiring their bonds at their maturity.[155]

The Thurman Act was barely passed when the Central Pacific and Union Pacific railroads brought suits to test its constitutionality. Albert Gallatin, the owner of five

---

[154]CPRR, *Annual Report of the Board of Directors of the Central Pacific Railroad Co. to the Stockholders for the Year Ending Dec 31st, 1878*. SF: HSCC, 1879; the entire report, without tables and figures, was repr. in the *SF Argonaut*, Oct 4, 1879.

[155]Poor, *The Pacific Railroads and the Relations existing between them and the Government of the United States*, 12. Thurman Act, 20 *US Stats* 56–61, 45th Cong., 2nd Sess. (Dec 3, 1877–Jun 20, 1878). Chap. 96, *An Act to alter and amend the act entitled "An act to aid in the construction of a railroad and telegraph line from the Missouri River to the Pacific Ocean, and to secure to the Government the use of the same for postal, military and other purposes"*, [sic] approved *July first eighteen hundred and sixty-two, and also to alter and amend the act of Congress approved July second, Eighteen hundred and sixty-four, in amendment of said first-named act*. App. May 7, 1878.

shares of Central Pacific stock, brought suit against the company—no doubt at the instance of the Central Pacific directors—in such a way as to question the constitutionality of the Thurman law.[156] A six-to-three majority of the Supreme Court justices upheld the law. Justice Stephen Field wrote a minority opinion "unanswerable in its logic, and altogether sound in its legal conclusions."[157]

All this, Stanford argued, was leading to two conditions repugnant to American political traditions: first, a communistic distribution of property; second, an absolute control by the majority. This kind of absolutism, he said, with no guarantees of the rights of minorities, had at times been more tyrannical under republican governments than under monarchies. He challenged statesmen to scrutinize carefully the present tendencies towards absolutism and to return to the civilized government of their political fathers.[158]

ALL THE PROVISIONS OF THE THURMAN ACT, as a Senate Report from the Committee on Railroads made in 1896 pointed out, were "complied with by both the Union and Central Pacific railroad companies." The government then invested these paid-in funds in its own bonds and lost money on them! Not until 1887, when the paid-in funds were invested in Union and Central Pacific first-mortgage bonds, did the government make money on the collected funds!*

*U.S. Senate, 54th Cong., 1st Sess., Report No. 778, to accompany S.B. 2894, Part 2, Vol. 4 (Feb 20, 1896), 298 pp. (citation from 3). SSN 3365.

Stanford's clear reasoning, his masterful grasp of the entire national railroad picture, and his unmatched comprehension of the details of railroad operations led the editor of the *Argonaut* to write: "There is no man in America who has more thorough and complete knowledge of railroad affairs than Governor Stanford."[159] The 1879 stockholders' report demonstrated this once again.

In August of 1880 the Committee on Railroad Transportation of the New York Chamber of Commerce sent a circular to several prominent men throughout the country asking them to comment on some of the chief problems of railroad transportation. The circular posed a number of questions, among them the following:

1. How can the prevailing discriminations against individuals and communities be prevented?
2. Is it safe to allow railroad managers to follow their new theory of charging "all the traffic will bear?"
3. Ought not the companies to be supervised in the public interest, as banks and insurance companies are?

---

[156]Carl Brent Swisher, *Stephen J. Field: Craftsman of the Law* (Wash.: BI, 1930), 247.

[157]USSCR, Vol. 99, *Cases Argued and Adjudged in the Supreme Court of the United States. Oct Term, 1878*. Sinking-Fund Cases. *Union Pacific Railroad Company v. United States and Central Pacific Railroad Company v. Gallatin*. Cases to test the constitutionality of the Thurman Act. The report covers pp. 700–769; there were three dissenting opinions, with that of Justice Field covering pp. 750–769; Field's report was repr. in the *SF Argonaut*, Nov 15, 1879.

[158]Quoted in HHB; *Stanford*, 54.   [159]*SF Argonaut*, Oct 4, 1879.

4. What do you think of companies and managers contributing large sums of money to election expenses or to influence legislation?

5. Is it right to water stock through any means by which fictitious bases of value are established?

6. Is a law which limits passenger rates just, and if so should not the principle be extended to freight charges?

7. What do you think of $4 per hundred pounds from New York to Salt Lake City, and only $2.50 from New York to San Francisco?[160]

The members of the Chamber of Commerce chose the recipients of its questionnaire with great care. It knew the answers it wanted to its questions (two of them posed as though they were only a single interrogative), and it selected opinions from men whose opinions they already knew, opinions they expected to help make their case for railroad regulation.

The prime example of their selective choosing of public figures was Judge Jeremiah Sullivan Black, a distinguished and, it must be said, eccentric public servant of towering ability.[161] Black had a reputation for idiosyncratic and intemperate attacks on men whose ideas he opposed. In writing a minority opinion on one case before the Pennsylvania Supreme Court he was so critical of his colleagues and stinging in his satire of them it was reported that the other judges discussed the propriety of holding him in contempt of the very court of which he was a member.[162]

Black served on the Pennsylvania Supreme Court from 1851 to 1857, when he resigned to accept the post of attorney general in President James Buchanan's cabinet. In 1860 he was appointed to replace Lewis Cass when Cass resigned as secretary of state. Black was expecting an appointment to the U.S. Supreme Court, but the coming of secession in the last days of Buchanan's administration dashed these hopes.

For years Black had argued for strict and uncompromising control of railroads and other corporations by all levels of government. In this position he won the enmity of corporation leaders at all levels. In 1881 various statements by Black had spread his ideas again throughout the press of the country.

When on November 16, 1880, Black addressed a letter to the "Committee on Railroad Transportation of the New York Chamber of Commerce," the gentlemen comprising this committee had found the letter they wished to publish.[163] They regarded Judge Black's commentary as "a most valuable contribution toward the solution of the railroad problem."

---

[160]*NY Times*, Jan 23, 1881.

[161]William Norwood Brigance, *Jeremiah Sullivan Black, A Defender of the Constitution and the Ten Commandments* (Phil.: UPP, 1934); Chauncey F. Black, ed., *Essays and Speeches of Jeremiah S[ullivan] Black. With a Biographical Sketch* (NY: DAC, 1885); Roy F. Nichols, "Jeremiah Sullivan Black," *DAB*, I, Part 2, 310–313.

[162]Brigance, *Jeremiah Sullivan Black*, 34.   [163]*NY Times*, Dec 2, 1880.

Black argued again, as he had for years, that railroads were public highways, constructed for the states, and that the taxes imposed upon them were the way that the state had for reimbursing itself for the expenses of the builders and operators. And the amount of that tax, he insisted, was to be fixed by public authority with no consideration for the bargaining of shippers or corporations. The doctrine that the so-called "owners" of the railroads could charge for their services whatever the traffic would allow he denounced as "the most enormous, oppressive, and unjust tax that was ever laid upon the industry of any people under the sun," and, he argued further, the states had a "clear and indefeasible right to protect their people" against such wrongs.

Black's argument began with the assertion that railroad men either believe or pretend to believe that railroads are the property of the companies authorized to run them. His opposition to this he summarized in one simple statement: "A public highway cannot be public property, and a railroad laid out and built by the authority of the State for the purpose of commerce is as much a public highway as a turnpike road, canal, or navigable river."[164] Judge Black declared war on the Central Pacific Railroad with his concluding statement on what he thought were the chances of regulating the railroad by means of a board of railroad commissioners: "In England I believe that plan has been a complete success; in California I understand it is a dead failure."

Judge Black had torn asunder a veritable hornet's nest.

Prominent New York and Washington, D.C., attorney George Ticknor Curtis was one of the first to respond to Black's peroration in print, in a public letter to Pres. Hugh Judge Jewett of the New York, Lake Erie & Western Railroad Company.[165]

Curtis denied both of Black's premises, namely that railroads were public highways and that railroad property was public property. He cited the decision of the U.S. Supreme Court in the Dartmouth College cases in support of his position. This decision recognized (1) that the grant of a charter of incorporation is a contract between the sovereign power and the grantee, and (2) that the obligations under this contact are under the protection of that clause of the Constitution of the United States that prohibits passage of laws impairing them. It follows, Curtis argued:

> If a State Legislature has once granted to a railroad corporation a power to make its own contracts, without any reservation of a right to control the exercise of that power, it cannot subsequently control or resume it: and, second, that private property remains private property, although held by a corporation, and held by the terms

[164]Ibid.   [165]*NY Times*, Dec 16, 1880.

98. Cartoon depicting forces trying to break the back of the
Central Pacific Railroad. *San Francisco Argus.*

of the charter for the use of any individual of the public who may desire to enjoy its
benefits complying with the conditions on which its use is offered. In regard to the
scope of the commercial power of Congress, Curtis quotes Justice Field's opinion
that "the power to regulate commerce among the several States was vested in Congress in order to secure equality and freedom in commercial intercourse against dis-
criminating State legislation; it was never intended that the power should be
exercised so as to interfere with private contracts not designed at the time they were
made to create impediments to such intercourse."[166]

[166]Ibid.

GEORGE TICKNOR CURTIS

was the brother of Benjamin R. Curtis, justice of the U.S. Supreme Court from 1851 to 1867; he was married to Mary Oliver Story, the daughter of Chief Justice Joseph Story.*

Curtis was a Harvard alumnus who studied law at Harvard and in a Boston law office. He later maintained law offices in New York and Washington, D.C., where much of his practice was before the U.S. Supreme Court. He soon turned to a career of writing books that covered a wide field of legal case studies. In 1839 the twenty-six-year-old Curtis published his *Digest of Cases Adjudicated in the Courts of Admiralty of the United States, and in the High Court of Admiralty in England*. Following a number of other works on legal cases, in 1854 and 1858 he published two volumes of *Commentaries on the Jurisdiction, Practice, and the Peculiar Jurisprudence of the Courts of the United States*.

It is generally agreed that Curtis' reputation rests primarily on his studies of the history of the Constitution of the United States.

*Carl Russell Fish, "George Ticknor Curtis," *DAB*, II, Part 2, 613–614.

In early 1881, the *Chicago Tribune* and other newspapers across the country published an editorial titled "THE RAILROAD PROBLEM." It consisted of a January 12 report by the Committee of the New York Board of Trade and Transportation, whose findings gave the cited article its bold subtitle:

The New York Board of Trade and Transportation Informed by Its Committee that Railroads Charge Unreasonable Rates, Discriminate, Water Stock, and Take a Hand in politics. [167]

This report was directed primarily at the system as it existed in the state of New York, but its repercussions were national in scope. In essence, the report was just another step in the anti-railroad campaign to which Justice Black had lent his support.

The most comprehensive expression of Stanford's economic and political philosophy was published in his January 21, 1881, letter to the New York Chamber of Commerce in which he responded to the questionnaire sent to him and others by the New York Board of Trade. His letter was published by newspapers all over the country. [168]

Stanford's statement was published in the *Tribune* under the subtitle "Leland Stanford on Railroads. A Plea in Behalf of Corporate Rights—Certain Queries Answered." The response in particular he addressed to the Special Committee on Fares and Freights of the Board of Trade and to opinions expressed on the matter by Judge Jeremiah Sullivan Black.

[167]*Chicago Tribune,* Jan 18, 1881.
[168]LS to NY Chamber of Commerce, Jan 20, 1881, in *Sac Record-Union*, Jan 22, 1881; *SF Chronicle*, Jan 22, 1881; and *NY Tribune*, Jan 23, 1881.

Stanford summarized the gist of the widespread questionnaire's interrogatives as dealing with "the control, to a greater or less extent, of property which stockholders of railroad companies believe to be of right their own."[169]

The president of the Central Pacific Railroad elaborated upon ideas he had often expressed elsewhere, but offered nothing new. Yet the intensity of his arguments and language was such that his ideas now took on a new significance. Rather than simply objecting to regulation, Stanford condemned it as the "direct offspring of robbery and rapine enforced by the hand of might," having "originated in a barbarous age." The regulation of the economy, he said, would lead to the creation of "commissions of espionage" that were contrary to American traditions, ideals, and constitutional principles. The logical conclusion of the Granger cases would be state control, and therefore state ownership, of all property.

As a good businessman, Stanford believed that the first consideration of railroad managers must be the treasury of their companies; this, after all, was expected and demanded by all stockholders. But he disavowed operating at the limit of whatever the traffic would bear; he reminded his readers, however, that even if he *did* regulate rates on this principle, he would simply be doing what everybody else did. This oft-condemned practice in itself was a *good* thing, he argued, because the free market was the best regulator. The principle of gearing rates to a market free of regulation was practiced by all professional men, including merchants, manufacturers, lawyers, doctors, and farmers.

Stanford repeated his claim that the only time the railroad involved itself in politics was when self-protection demanded it. Management and regulation of railroad property, he insisted, should be left entirely in the hands of the railroad owners and managers; the state had no jurisdiction unless it condemned the roads by right of eminent domain and reimbursed the owners for the property thus confiscated.

The committee's first interrogatory, Stanford insisted, begged the whole question by assuming Judge Black's argument that railroads were public highways. This he rejected. Corporations are formed, he contended, throughout all the states of the Union under general incorporation laws and were formed by the "corporators." Thus the property of the corporation was contributed by the stockholders and was owned by them. The state created neither the corporation nor its property.[170]

Since the committee had provided Stanford with a copy of Judge Black's response, he felt at liberty to answer Black's specific points, particularly those pertaining to the Central Pacific Railroad:

> The Judge has fallen into a great error, and one which, I am sure, when he comes to be aware of the facts, he will very much regret.[171] So far from the aid of the Gov-

---

[169]*NY Tribune,* Jan 23, 1881.   [170]*NY Times,* Jan 23, 1881.

[171]This shows how little LS knew Judge Jeremiah Black!

ernment being sufficient to build the Central Pacific Railroad, I can say, because I know whereof I speak, that every dollar derived from the loan of the Government credit went into the construction of the railroad, together with a much larger amount derived from the other resources of the company, and had the company developed and created no more business than existed when the roads were commenced, we would never have heard of such wild arguments as those of Judge Black, because the roads would long since have passed into the hands of their creditors. It is susceptible of easy demonstration that the work of grading the first 150 miles of the Central Pacific Railroad from Sacramento eastward was more than would suffice to grade the road for a single track from the Rocky Mountains to the Hudson River.

These Pacific roads have, in their construction and in their operation, redeemed every promise and every hope that the public entertained.[172]

To the objection that railroads charged what the market would bear, Stanford agreed that this was true and was exactly what they should be doing. He offended some readers by suggesting that what railroads charged was nobody else's business.

In response to one of the committee's questions, as to whether criticism of railroads were provocative or communist, or whether they set capital and labor against each other, he replied that should railroads be left alone and uncrippled, and their control left to themselves, there would never be a reason for such a question. Communism, he declared, did not come from those trying to manage their own property, but from those who wished to control and regulate other people's property. He then said that the regulation and control championed by the committee and by Judge Black was "on a par with principles contended for by the Communists and the agitator [Denis] Kearney."

A later journalist summarized Stanford's position as follows: state regulation of corporations, not "uncontrolled power of large railroad corporations," was responsible for the growing spirit of communism.[173]

Stanford's position had been as one-sided and extreme as Black's, which led to a barrage of criticism from the eastern press. In a lengthy editorial on Stanford's response to Black (and indirectly to the position of the Chamber of Commerce and even the *Times* itself), the editor of the *Times* dubbed him the "Pacific Coast champion of railroad abuses."[174] Stanford, he wrote, attacked the "established principles of law, whether embedded in legislation or judicial decrees" with a view to "overthrowing the whole system of modern jurisprudence."

The Chamber of Commerce and the *Times* had sought support for the principles laid down in the ill-concealed form of interrogatives in its questionnaire, but in Leland Stanford's response, unlike that of Judge Black, they did not get what they wanted.

---

[172]*SF Chronicle*, Jan 2, 1881.   [173]*SBar News-Press*, Jan 22, 1956.
[174]*NY Times*, Jan 25, 1881.

Frank Morrison Pixley

One year later, in the fall of 1882, editor Frank Morrison Pixley of the *Argonaut* gave his old friend Leland Stanford an opportunity to reply in print to a series of anti-railroad charges made by a convention that assembled in San José to investigate the railroad and which subsequently recommended substantial reductions in passenger and traffic rates.[175]

Pixley, known as "exceptional for his governmental service in the period 1851–1890," was more than a newspaperman: he was or had been a forceful muckraker, author, publisher, and entrepreneur. Pixley as a journalist was described as "widely admired and widely felt."[176] It was said of his literary contributions, "No crisper English is current, and none straighter to its mark, than he wielded; and even people who were enraged by his editorials could not forbear to read."[177] One close student of the career of Pixley paid the multi-faceted man his greatest tribute:

> Pixley probably exerted a more commanding influence upon the public mind of California in his time than any other man. In his turn he was a lawyer, miner, journalist, politician and capitalist. His voice was heard afar. He made and unmade men, and was almost as much to be feared by an opponent as Ambrose Bierce.[178]

It was certainly good to have Pixley in your corner.

The Governor and Pixley were indeed very close friends; it is thought that Frank's failing health was the only thing that kept him from being named to Stanford University's first Board of Trustees.[179]

Stanford's Reply to Pixley's "Invitation"

In his lengthy reply to Pixley's "challenge," Stanford delineated in even greater detail his economic philosophy. The first charge he answered was that the Central Pacific had a monopoly on transportation. He repeated his earlier explanation that the railroad was a destroyer of monopolies; besides, water transportation was present to compete with the railroad, thus keeping its rates as low as possible. Not only would water routes keep railroad rates down, but the railroad had actually brought water rates down. Rates through the Isthmus had dropped from one hundred dollars per ton to seventeen dollars per ton as soon as the Southern Pacific system opened. So far as railroad rates being excessive, he reiterated, the rate was only

---

[175]FMP to LS, Aug 14, 1882, in *SF Argonaut*, Aug 19, 1882.

[176]Charles F. Lummis, ed., "A Jason of the Coast [FMP obit.]," *LSSM* 1895 3 (Jun–Nov): 237.

[177]Ibid.

[178]Bailey Millard, *History of the San Francisco Bay Region* (3 vols., Chicago, SF, and NY, 1924), I, 432; Helen Van Cleave Park, ed., and Elinor Burt, asst. ed., "Remembering Frank Morrison Pixley," *MCHSB* 1967 1 (2): 3.

[179]Weber, "Pixley of Pixley," 19.

studied law in New York and Michigan before joining the gold rush to California.[a] Twenty-four-year-old pioneer Pixley left Michigan for California in the fall of 1848.[b] He spent the winter with an uncle in Missouri and continued his westward trip the following spring, by wagon train, riding a mule.[c] He arrived in El Dorado County in September 1849, and afterwards spent two years in Plumas County working the mines on the North Fork of the Yuba River.[d] In 1851 Pixley moved to San Francisco, where he began practicing law as an assistant to his maternal uncle, Judge Roderick N. Morrison.[e] He served as city and county attorney of San Francisco from May 1851 to January 1852.[f] Lorenzo Sawyer, later a federal judge, was employed by Pixley as his assistant in this position. Later, they formed a law practice together.

From 1852 to 1854, besides practicing law, Pixley was one of the publishers and proprietors of the *San Francisco Daily Whig*.[g] He represented San Francisco in the tenth session of the California Assembly in 1859. Frank Pixley held the position of attorney general during Stanford's term as governor and later served as a regent of the University of California.[h]

When men drilling for water in Tulare County hit an artesian belt twenty-five miles long and fifteen miles wide, the underground pressure was great enough to force the water out of the wells without pumping. These drillers then tried to get the Southern Pacific Railroad to build a station there.[i] In 1866 they got Frank Pixley to join them to form the Pixley Townsite Company—five miles south of Tipton—and then named the town after him.

The Tulare County town of Pixley, built fifteen miles south of the town of Tulare, was later described as a very desirable place to live.[j] Pixley not only got the railroad to build a station there, which, with the addition of a warehouse, made Pixley into a grain shipping center, but he built a three-storey hotel on the site, to be used in part as a railroad restaurant.[k] This hotel—named at first the Naoma and changed to the Artesia when its artesian well was developed—also housed one of the town's two saloons.[l] The hotel was gutted by fire on the morning of October 22, 1945.[m] Pixley's two-storey office building, built a block south of the hotel, was named the Argonaut, for his San Francisco newspaper of the same name.[n] The town soon boasted what was described as a "monster artesian well," a brick store building, a two-storey school, large grain warehouses, livery stables, and a blacksmith shop.[o]

[a]William E. Swasey, *The Early Days and Men of California* (Oakland: PPPC, 1891), "Frank M. Pixley," 311.

[b]Phelps, *Contemporary Biography of California's Representative Men,* I, 309.

[c]Ibid.; Carl I. Wheat, "'California's Bantam Cock'—The Journals of Charles F. De Long, 1854–1863," *CHSQ* 1931 10 (1): 64; Katherine Pixley Robson, "Frank Morrison Pixley," *MCHSB* 1967 1 (2): 4–5, was in error about Pixley's age and when he came to Calif.   [d]*SF Argonaut*, Aug 19, 1895.   [e]Ibid.

[f]Robson, "Frank Morrison Pixley," 4.   [g]Swasey, "Frank M. Pixley," 312.

[h]David C. Weber, "Pixley of Pixley: An Artesian Spring in the Valley," *BCCQN* 1997 62 (1): 15; John L. Levinsohn, *Frank Morrison Pixley of the Argonaut* (SF: BCC, 1989). Pixley's chronology is not at all certain and varies from one pub. source to another.   [i]Weber, "Pixley of Pixley," 17.

[j]Angel, comp., *A Memorial and Biographical History of the Counties of Fresno, Tulare, and Kern, California*, 225.

[k]*Terra Bella News*, Mar 19, 1943.   [l]Ibid.

[m]*Visalia Times Delta*, Oct 23, 1945.   [n]*Terra Bella News*, Mar 19, 1943.

[o]Angel, *A Memorial and Biographical History of the Counties of Fresno, Tulare, and Kern, California*, 225.

> ### Jane Stanford's "Relatives"—A Case of Mistaken Identity
>
> The following story merits mention only because it has been quoted and retold so many times:
>
> After Pixley was established it was reputed that some of Jane Stanford's "relatives" (they are not identified) bought a section of railroad land just southwest of Pixley—a tract of land later known as the Schiffman Ranch—where they developed a large artesian well.[a] The water flowed with such pressure that it had to be capped most of the time. The Lathrops built a "tea-room" house and caused a local sensation by having breakfast at ten in the morning, a formal dinner every evening, and poetry reading in the middle of the day. The Lathrop house was eventually moved into Pixley and became the Kangaroo Inn.[b]
>
> The lifestyle of these Lathrops certainly does not fit that of Charles or Ariel Lathrop. The Lathrop house—whoever the Lathrops were—is not to be confused with any house in the town of Lathrop, first a railroad center and now a commercial town just outside Stockton along Interstate 5, which was laid out by Stanford in 1887 and was named for his brother-in-law Charles Lathrop. The only Lathrop whom real estate records show to have owned land in Tulare County was B[enjamin] G[ordon] Lathrop of Redwood City fame.
>
> [a]Cora L. Keagle, "Pixley's History, 1886–1922," in unidentified newspaper account, found in Vertical File, Pixley Branch of the Tulare County Lib., repeated in another unidentified newspaper which credits the *Pixley Enterprise*.
>
> [b] Edwin G. Gudde, *California Place Names: The Origin and Etymology of Current Geographical Names* (Berkeley: UCP, 1969), 174.

about two cents per ton per mile, less than one-seventh the amount allowable by law.

The next charge was that the government had subsidized the transcontinental railroad and therefore had the authority to regulate it. This Stanford denied, not only on the grounds that such regulation was unconstitutional, but that the railroads had not been subsidized by the government. The government had not given money to the railroads; rather, at most it had only *lent* them money in the form of bonds, which had to be—and were—repaid with interest. The only gift was in land that for a long time—some areas until the present!—was worthless. Stanford pointed out that in terms of money saved by having the railroad, even if all the interest on the debts were forfeited, the federal government and the people of California would still come out far ahead.[180]

In a later edition of the *Argonaut*, the editor commented extensively on Stanford's response and outlined in detail the great advances made in California because of the state's various railroad enterprises.[181]

---

[180]LS to FMP, in *SF Argonaut*, Aug 22, 1882. [181]Ibid., Sep 30, 1882.

Sen. Roscoe Conkling of New York wrote an opinion on the right of the California Railroad Commission to regulate rates of the Central and Southern Pacific railroads. His sixteen-page analysis of the constitutional framework of the nation and the state and the powers of the commission was devastating to the commission. He argued that if the commission had the right to regulate fares and rates there would be no limit to how low they could be set: "Of course, the power to reduce rates, if possessed by California, has no limits but her pleasure."[182] The power to set rates was held by Congress alone, and there could not be two sovereigns possessing the same power.

Sen. Roscoe Conkling's Opinion

First—That the State of California has no power to take away from the corporations [Central and Southern Pacific railroads], or from either of them, the rights, franchises, or privileges which California did not give, but which were received wholly from Congress.

Second—That an Act of California in form repealing or attempting to repeal their or either of their charters, would not work a dissolution, or impair the right to continue under the Acts of Congress.

Third—That the right to charge for carrying passengers and freight is a specific grant from Congress inwrought with the rights and interests of the United States, and that the whole subject of rates of fare and freight in respect of legislative control is committed absolutely to Congress, and is put effectively beyond the reach of the State of California.

Fourth—That the two corporations named are not subject to the constitutional and statutory provisions recited in the beginning of this opinion.*

*Roscoe Conkling, *An Opinion as to the Power of the Railroad Commissioners of the State of California to Regulate Fares and Freights on the Central and Southern Pacific Railroads* (SF: HSCC, 1882), 16.

Threats from Within—The Ellen M. Colton Case

Over the years Leland Stanford and his Associates faced scores of legal challenges to their railroad empire, but none more threatening—or painful—than that from an insider.

By an agreement dated August 27, 1879, Huntington persuaded Ellen Colton to settle her deceased husband's interests with the railroad partners. When Stanford was later questioned about this agreement, he explained:

I was in very bad health for most of the time, and unable to give any attention to business from the 1st of January, 1879, until sometime in August of that same year, except

---

[182]Roscoe Conkling, *An Opinion as to the Power of the Railroad Commissioners of the State of California to Regulate Fares and Freights on the Central and Southern Pacific Railroads* (SF: HSCC, 1882), 15.

as far as necessity compelled. Owing to the condition of my health I had but very little part in the negotiations which led to the agreement of August 27, 1879.[183]

Huntington said that Ellen Colton received in settlement $100,000 more than he would have given David Colton had the settlement been made during Colton's lifetime. Stanford, ever the diplomat, said that he would gladly have settled with Mrs. Colton for $100,000 more than she had coming rather than give her any cause of complaint after the settlement was made.[184]

Ellen Colton signed the agreement, but later—deciding she had been robbed—filed a Superior Court suit in San Francisco County on May 24, 1882, to reopen the transaction and set the agreement aside.[185]

Lloyd Tevis cautioned his railroad friends that they could not afford to have litigation with the plaintiff, the widow of their old associate, on grounds that a lawsuit would be prejudicial to themselves as individuals and to all their enterprises.[186]

By stipulation of all parties to the trial, on September 5, 1883, the venue was changed to Santa Rosa, in Sonoma County, where it opened on November 5, 1883, while the Stanfords were in Europe.[187] Ellen Colton alleged that the agreed-to settlement was fraudulent. The case—almost ten thousand pages filling eighteen volumes—dragged on until the last testimony was taken on the eightieth day, July 24, 1884.[188] A verdict was not reached until October 6, 1885, after Stanford had taken his seat in the U.S. Senate. Judge Jackson Temple found in favor of the defendants: "Upon the foregoing facts I find, as a conclusion of law, that plaintiff is not entitled to the relief, or any portion of the relief, prayed for in her amended complaint, and that the defendants are entitled to judgement in this action dismissing said amended complaint, and for their costs."[189]

Charley Crocker was so pleased—relieved?—by the decision that on December 1, 1885, he gave a stag dinner party in San Francisco to celebrate the occasion, an affair described as "one of the most elegant dinner parties that has taken place here for years."[190] The guests of honor at his residence on California Street included a large number of railroad officials and all the attorneys and others who were connected with the famous case. Pixley's *Argonaut* published a complete list of the notable celebrants.[191] Stanford missed the gala affair, having left San Francisco for the East on Nvember 28. He was scheduled to arrive in Washington on December 5.[192]

[183]LS test., *Colton Case Depositions*, II, 5–6, 9.   [184]Ibid., II, 9.

[185]SupC, SoC, *Ellen M. Colton vs. Leland Stanford et als.,* in *Colton Case*, V, 1.

[186]*CSCR*, Vol. 82, Case No. 11983, *Ellen M. Colton, Plaintiff and Appellant, vs. Leland Stanford, et als.*, Defendants and Respondents, and Opinion of the Supreme Court in the Colton Case, Jun 4th, 5th, and 6th, 1889, pp. 410–411.

[187]SupC, SoC, Case N. 7061-5 No. 905, bound in *Colton Case*, V, 1.   [188]*Colton Case*, XVIII, 9689.

[189]In the SupC., SoC, State of Calif. Dept. No 2. *Ellen M. Colton, Plaintiff, vs. Leland Stanford, et als., Defendants. Findings* (SF: HSCC, 1886). This includes a 123-page decision in the *Colton Case*. In *Colton Case Depositions*, II, Doc. 5.

[190]*SF Argonaut*, Dec 5, 1885.   [191]Ibid.

[192]*SF Chronicle*, Nov 29, 1885; *SF Argonaut*, Dec 5, 1885.

Mrs. Colton appealed her case to the California Supreme Court, which in January 1890 sustained Judge Temple's decision by a vote of four to nothing (two judges abstained, one not having heard the case and the other deeming himself unqualified to vote on the matter).[193] The case cost each side approximately $100,000.[194]

The Central Pacific Associates had won the case . . . or so it would seem. In December 1883, during the course of the trial, the plaintiff's attorneys introduced into evidence a volume of correspondence known as the "Colton Letters." These letters were written by Huntington to Colton between October 8, 1874, and October 8, 1878—letters apparently stolen from the Southern Pacific Railroad offices. The letters dealt primarily with the construction of the Southern Pacific through California to Yuma. They described a variety of political matters, particularly Huntington's activities to prevent Tom Scott from getting his own bill through Congress. The damning letters—all 213 of them—were published by the editor of the *San Francisco Chronicle*. He insisted that these letters showed "the full extent of the arrogance, corruption and duplicity of the Central Pacific monopoly, and the fact that for years past the company had been systematically engaged in debauching Senators and Representatives, buying up Legislatures, presenting fraudulent reports, declaring dividends with borrowed money."[195]

In one of the embarrassing letters Huntington wrote to Colton that would later return to haunt him *and* his railroad partners, he confided that the Southern Pacific could not get a certain piece of legislation passed without paying more for it than it was worth.[196]

This Colton case had another side, perhaps brighter for Ellen Colton than she ever realized. She had been relieved of the responsibility of a note for $1 million signed by her husband upon entering the company. Also, she was guaranteed a sizable income under the terms of the agreement. In a long editorial, the editor of the *Argonaut* defended the Central Pacific Associates.[197] Cerinda Evans, Huntington's biographer, catalogs in detail the support received by Mrs. Colton from the Associates, whom she in her own peculiar way calls the "Huntington Group."[198]

Ellen Colton was not as generous with her largess as were her erstwhile partners. Her husband's will had provided for the maintenance of his mother and sister—Abagail [sic] R. and Martha Colton. Ellen Colton refused to follow the provisions of his will, and in 1883 they brought suit against her and lost. In 1888 the case was appealed to the U.S. Supreme Court. On January 27, 1891, the decision of

[193]*CSCR*, No. 1192, Jan 2, 1890. Vol. 82, 351–412. *Ellen M. Colton v. Leland Stanford, et al.* Also in *Colton Case Papers.* See also No 11983 in the Supreme Court of the State of California, *Ellen M. Colton, Plaintiff and Appellant, vs. Leland Stanford, et als*, Defendants and Respondents, and Opinion of the Supreme Court in the Colton Case, Jun 4, 5, and 6, 1889.

[194]Evans, *Huntington*, I, 346–347.

[195]*SF Chronicle*, Dec 23, 1883; the text of most, if not all, the letters may be found in *Colton Case*, IV, 1607–1848.

[196]CPH to David Colton, Nov 9, 1877, in *Colton Case*, IV, 1802–1803.

[197]*SF Argonaut*, Dec 29, 1883.   [198]Evans, *Huntington*, I, 348 ff.

the U.S. Circuit Court was reversed and Colton's mother and sister won the support that David Colton had given them.[199]

It is hardly an exaggeration to say that every California legislature from 1866 on—even those regarded as pro-railroad—had forces determined to regulate freight and passenger fares and to bring down what they regarded as extravagant profits for upper management.

Nor is it an exaggeration to say that Leland Stanford was called in to lead the forces in defense against almost every threat to his railroad empire. He was known for being well informed, honest, logical—and for being a scrapper when he had to be. It is significant that he was invited by one Assembly and Senate Corporation Committee after another to inform the members of those committees about railroad affairs, not just in California, but in the nation as a whole. It is significant, too, that his words were heeded by political foe as well as friend. It was largely Stanford's efforts that saved the Central Pacific and Southern Pacific of California from the attacks during the decades from 1865 to 1890 that might otherwise have brought these railroads into receivership—as was the fate of almost all other transcontinental railroads.

But in the background loomed a specter more threatening, more menacing, and more powerful than the California legislature—reformers and anti-railroad voices at the national level, inside and outside Congress. They were to make themselves heard and felt in the late 1880s.

[199] SF Examiner, Jan 28, 1891.

THE COLTON CASE.

JUDGE TEMPLE'S DECISION IN FULL.

A COMPLETE REVIEW OF THE GREAT CASE AGAINST THE RAILROAD MANGERS.

The Railroad People Acted In Good Faith Towards Plaintiff.

At Colton's Death the Association Was Entirely Ended.

The Judge Finds No Concealment or Intentional Misrepresentation on the Part of Stanford. et al.

MRS. COLTON TRIED TO RETIRE FROM THE BUSINESS WITH AS MUCH AS POSSIBLE.

The Door Opened Very Wide For Admission of Evidence.

A Graphic and Concise Showing of The Character of the Negotiations.

The Unfortunate Year in which the Compromise Was Made.

HOW LAWYER WILSON FIGURES IN THE CASE.

Parties to Contracts Must Look out For Themselves.

He Renders Judgment for the Defendants.*

*SF CSTUJ, Oct 10, 1885.

CHAPTER 14

The CP/SP Associates Help Complete Three Southern Transcontinentals
1878–1883
Rival Transcontinental Lines Were Invading[1]

Early Movements for a Southern Transcontinental Railroad

E arly debates over the construction of a transcontinental railroad focused on whether it would follow a northern or southern route. Railroads planned— and in some places already under construction—across the southern United States in the 1870s, therefore, did not come as a surprise to the Central Pacific/ Southern Pacific Associates. Fearing the disastrous consequences to their own rail empire should such a system ever be built, they had followed closely all attempts to construct a second, southern transcontinental.

Several transcontinental railroad companies were formed after the close of the Civil War to link Missouri, Louisiana, Texas, and other states with California. John Frémont joined other speculators in introducing a bill into Congress on December 11, 1865, to charter a railroad from Missouri and Arkansas to the Pacific Coast.[2] On July 27, 1866, President Andrew Johnson signed into law a bill that created the Atlantic & Pacific Railroad.[3] This line was chartered to run from or near Spring- field, Missouri, and then along the Canadian River to Albuquerque, from there

---

[1]McAfee, *California's Railroad Era*, 181.

[2]*USCG*, 29th Cong., 1st Sess., 17 (Dec 11, 1865). Keith Bryant, Jr., *History of the Atchison, Topeka and Santa Fe Railway* (NY: Mac, 1974), 84, identifies the supporters of the bill.

[3]14 *US Stats* 292–299 (39th Cong, 1st Sess. [Dec 4, 1865–Jul 28, 1866]), Chap. 278, *An Act granting Lands to aid in the Construction of a Railroad and Telegraph Line from the States of Missouri and Arkansas to the Pacific Coast*. App. Jul 27, 1866. The A & PRR, based in St. Louis, is not to be confused with the altogether different A & PRR promoted by Thomas Butler King and Robert John Walker, and chartered in NY to build a transcontinental railroad. Nor should the simi- larity of names permit it to be confused with the 1851 P & A, the precursor of the SF & SJ. See Art. of Assn. *(continued)*

along the thirty-fifth parallel to the Colorado River, "thence by the most practicable and eligible route to the Pacific."[4]

The federal government provided a large subsidy to encourage the building of this transcontinental railroad. It granted a 200-foot right-of-way, a land grant of twenty odd-numbered sections of land per mile on alternate sides of the track in territories and ten sections per mile in states, with a capitalization of $100 million. The line was to be completed by July 4, 1878.[5]

There was an unusual clause in the enabling act that would create unforeseen problems in the future. Section 18 of the law stipulated that the Southern Pacific Railroad of California was "authorized to connect with the said Atlantic & Pacific Railroad formed under this act, at such point, near the boundary line of the State of California, as they shall deem most suitable for a railroad line to San Francisco."[6] This passage teems with ambiguities. The Southern Pacific was *authorized* to meet the Atlantic & Pacific, but such a link-up was not *mandatory*. It could meet the Atlantic & Pacific *near* the state line, not necessarily *at* it. When the two roads were 1,250 miles apart, how much leeway is involved in *near* the state line? Thus, the roads could have met in California, at the Colorado River, in Arizona Territory, or even farther east than that. And in the statement, "as they shall deem most suitable," who are *they*? Southern Pacific owners and directors could make a good case that they themselves were best qualified to select the most suitable railroad line to San Francisco. To complicate matters even more, between the passage of the law in 1866 and the required completion date of 1878, the Central Pacific Associates had taken over the Southern Pacific Railroad.

The Southern Pacific terminated in San Francisco via the San Francisco & San José Railroad. The proposed southern line was to end in San Francisco and thereby offer to that city the advantages of a line also enjoyed by Sacramento, the terminus of the Union Pacific-Central Pacific road.

This new transcontinental as defined in 1866 would definitely pose a threat to the Central Pacific. The Associates feared that if a southern transcontinental railroad were built, it would gain the lion's share of traffic from New York to San Francisco. To forestall this eventuality, the Central Pacific Associates bought the Southern Pacific Railroad and its rails running into San Francisco.

(*continued*) of the P & A Rail Road Co., signed Oct 24, filed Oct 25, 1851. File 144, CSA. See Amended Arts. of Assn. of the P & A, signed Sep 6, filed Sep 14, 1853. File 144, CSA. This early railroad was organized in SF on Aug 21, 1851. For details, see Winther, "The Story of San Jose, 1777–1869," 163–164.

[4] 14 *US Stats* 292–299 (39th Cong., 1st Sess.), Chap. 278, *An Act granting Lands to aid in the Construction of a Railroad and Telegraph Line from the States of Missouri and Arkansas to the Pacific Coast*. App. Jul 27, 1866. Sect. 1, p. 293.

[5] Ibid., Sect. 3, p. 294, and Sect. 8, p. 297.

[6] Ibid., Sect. 18, p. 299.

Early Central Pacific and Southern Pacific Opposition to a Southern Transcontinental

As a railroad tycoon, Stanford was confronted by a host of problems in the two decades following completion of the nation's first transcontinental railroad. By the 1880s he and Huntington and Crocker expanded their railroad empire into a second, southern transcontinental by new construction, consolidation with old roads, and leasing existing railroads. To do all this, of course, they had to find desperately needed money: shortage of funds was a constant problem.

Stanford had primary responsibility for coping with a steadily rising public, journalistic, and political opposition to the Central and Southern Pacific railroads. These roads were being depicted increasingly as octopus-like monsters—though the term itself was not yet applied to them—stretching their greedy arms into every area of California's economic and political life. The Associates' railroads—so all railroad enemies and many reformers thought—charged fraudulently high freight and passenger rates and were responsible for all the social ills of the Golden State.

To guarantee the planned extension of the Southern Pacific, the Associates had to take steps to keep other railroads out of "their territory"—and the definition of this concept grew with time. Besides the threat of invasion posed by the Atlantic & Pacific Railroad of 1866, yet another southern line that threatened the Southern Pacific was created on March 3, 1871, when Congress chartered the Texas Pacific Railroad Company (its name was changed on May 2, 1872, to The Texas & Pacific Railway Company),[7] to build from Marshall, Texas, to "ship's channel" in San Diego Bay. As in the case of the Atlantic & Pacific, five years earlier, this law further authorized the Southern Pacific Railroad to build from a point at or near Tehachapi Pass, by way of Los Angeles, and then to link up with the Texas Pacific at or near the Colorado River, thus providing for still another southern transcontinental railroad.[8]

Thomas Scott, serving simultaneously as president of both the Pennsylvania Railroad and the Texas & Pacific, planned to purchase roads on both ends and fill in the system by new construction; he hoped to acquire the San Diego and Gila road, which had been organized in 1854 and later incorporated into the Memphis, El Paso, & Pacific Railroad.[9] But before construction on the Texas & Pacific got underway,

---

[7]George Werner, Texas railroad historian, to the writer, Sep 28, 2002.

[8]16 US Stats 573–580, 41st Cong., 3rd Sess. (Dec 5, 1870–Mar 3, 1871), Chap. 122, *An Act to incorporate the Texas Pacific Railroad Company, and to aid in the Construction of its Road, and for other Purposes.* App. Mar 3, 1871, by Pres. Ulysses S. Grant (R).

The story of the subsequent conflict is told by Lewis Lesley, "A Southern Transcontinental Railroad into California: Texas and Pacific versus Southern Pacific, 1865 to 1885," *PHR* 1936 5 (1): 52–60; see also Ralph Traxler, Jr., "Collis P. Huntington and the Texas and Pacific Railroad Land Grant," *NMHR* 1959 34 (2): 117–133.

[9]Lesley, "Southern Transcontinental," 52–53; Daggett, *Chapters on the History of the Southern Pacific*, 202 n12.

the Panic of 1873 halted almost all railroad building.[10] When in 1874 its managers asked for federal assistance to build the Texas & Pacific to a point of connection with the Atlantic & Pacific, they encountered fierce opposition from the Central Pacific Associates. After all, the Texas & Pacific law granted their Southern Pacific Railroad the right to build to the Colorado River, there to connect with the Texas & Pacific.[11]

Scott decided to push his Texas & Pacific Railway across the state into San Diego. Meanwhile, the Southern Pacific managers had made plans to build south from San Gorgonio Pass (the pass between San Gorgonio and San Jacinto, containing today the towns of Beaumont and Banning, among others) and then to Yuma; there was even talk of building the Southern Pacific to the Gulf of Mexico and shipping cargo from there to the East Coast.[12] If Scott had built to San Diego through the same pass, the two roads would have run parallel. The Associates decided to fight Scott for control of the Southwest.

As early as January 29, 1875, the San Francisco Chamber of Commerce held a meeting to consider petitioning Congress to allow the Southern Pacific to build beyond the Colorado River until it met the Texas & Pacific. Stanford was invited to the meeting, which was designed to sound out public opinion on the proposal. He praised the idea of allowing an expression of thinking on the part of the city's leading citizens, and he made a strong statement in favor of the proposed extension of the Southern Pacific Railroad. This was the earliest date his interests in a southern transcontinental found public expression.

At the close of the meeting, the trustees of the Chamber unanimously adopted the following resolutions:

> Resolved, That the President of the Chamber is hereby directed to request our Senators and Representatives in Congress to favor the extension and construction by the Southern Pacific Railroad of its line east of the Colorado to a junction with the Texas Pacific and Atlantic and Pacific roads, upon terms equally favorable with such other roads until a junction is made with a constructed road or roads.
>
> Resolved, That a copy of the foregoing preamble and resolutions be sent by telegraph to each of our Senators and Representatives in Congress.[13]

On May 18, 1875, Stanford was interviewed by the *San Francisco Chronicle* on the building of the Southern Pacific. In giving his reasons for wanting to build the road, he said, "Had Tom Scott built his road to the Pacific he would have taken from us our best prospective traffic and carried it east. He would have given San Francisco a blow from which she would never have recovered."[14]

---

[10]*HMD 6*, 43rd Cong., 2nd Sess. (Dec 7, 1874–Mar 3, 1875), "Memorial of the Texas and Pacific Railway Company and the Atlantic and Pacific Railroad Company," Dec 8, 1874. SSN 1653. *Galveston Daily News*, Dec 2, 1883.

[11] 16 *US Stats* 573–579, 41st Cong., 3rd Sess., Chap. 122, *An Act to incorporate the Texas Pacific Railroad Company*.

[12]LS to FMP, Aug 22, 1882, in *SF Argonaut*, Aug 26, 1882.

[13]*SF Chronicle*, Jan 30 and 31, 1875; also reported in the [Salem, Ore.] *Willamette Farmer*, Feb 5, 1875.

[14]*SF Chronicle*, May 19, 1875.

Crocker, in his testimony in the 1887 Pacific Railroad hearings, repeated that the Associates did not at first want to extend the Southern Pacific Railroad and make a transcontinental railroad out of it, but they recognized that if they did not build it, Scott would have, and his competition in California would have ruined the Central Pacific. Echoing what Stanford had said in 1875, Crocker insisted that he and the Associates had fought for this right in order to keep the Texas & Pacific out of California, knowing that if that road crossed the Colorado, "Tom Scott was bound to scalp the Central Pacific."[15]

The southern California press was divided over the contest between the Central Pacific and the Texas & Pacific. The *Los Angeles Republican* favored Scott, while the editorial pages of the *Los Angeles Star* backed Stanford.[16]

Meanwhile, by 1872 the Atlantic & Pacific had been able to build only 361 miles, from Pacific, Missouri, near St. Louis, to Vinita, in Indian Territory.[17] At one point, Atlantic & Pacific managers leased the entire Missouri Pacific system in order to secure its entrance into St. Louis and build up a monopoly of Missouri business. This move proved unfortunate when the over-extended system was almost destroyed by the Panic of 1873; financial problems drove the road into receivership in 1875.[18] The lease of the Missouri Pacific was set aside and work on the main line came to a halt.[19]

Optimism among San Diegans that their city would become a terminus of a transcontinental railroad had at first rested with the Memphis, El Paso & Pacific Railroad Company, of which the ubiquitous John C. Frémont was president.[20] This company had planned to build to San Diego, but in 1870 had gone bankrupt. San Diegans then petitioned the Atlantic & Pacific to survey a line to San Diego, but that road was more interested in building to San Francisco. Railroad dreams of this border village with a population of approximately 2,400 were dashed on June 12, 1873, when the Memphis, El Paso & Pacific Railroad was sold to the Texas & Pacific.[21]

On September 10, 1876, a new line—the St. Louis & San Francisco Railroad, nicknamed the "Frisco"—was created to revive the Atlantic & Pacific.[22] The *Railroad Gazette* of New York quipped that the new railroad was to be called the St. Louis & San Francisco Railway Company, "because, perhaps, it has no terminus in either

---

[15]CC test., Sep 20, 1887, *USPRC*, VII, 3683.   [16]*LA Republican*, quoted in *LA Star*, Sep 20, 1877.

[17]H. Craig Miner, *The St. Louis-San Francisco Transcontinental Railroad, the Thirty-fifth Parallel Project, 1853–1890* (Lawrence: UPK, 1972), 75–77.   [18]Ibid., 91.

[19]Ibid., 93.   [20]McAfee, *California's Railroad Era*, 113.

[21]Population: Dept. of the Int., *Compendium of the Ninth Census (June 1, 1870)*. Francis A. Walker, supt. of census (Wash.: GPO, 1872), 128. Sale: Douglas Campbell, *Closing Argument of Douglas Campbell, Esq. in reply to Gov. John C. Brown, J.A. Davenport, Esq., and Major James Turner, before the Judiciary Committee of the House of Representatives, in regard to the title of the Texas and Pacific Railway Company to the property of the Memphis, El Paso and Pacific Railroad Company. April 24, 1878* (Wash.: TM & C, 1878), 3. This doc. was not pub. in the Serial Set.

[22]Miner, *The St. Louis-San Francisco Transcontinental Railroad*, 94, 96, and 172.

city."[23] This new road was to take over most of the Atlantic & Pacific track, thus preserving the fiction that the road and its huge 1866 land grant still existed as a separate and viable entity.

For the next four years the Frisco built aggressively across Missouri and into southern Kansas.[24] Rumors that either Jay Gould or Huntington was about to seize the line caused Thomas E. Nickerson, president of the Atchison, Topeka & Santa Fé Railroad, to turn the Frisco into an ally. At first the Atchison (later known simply as the Santa Fé) was a local Kansas railroad that afterward developed transcontinental ambitions. In the fall of 1879 Nickerson—president of the Santa Fé from 1874 to 1880 and of the Atlantic & Pacific from 1880 to 1881—entered into negotiations with James D. Fish, president of the Frisco. They agreed that the Atchison, Topeka & Santa Fé, the Frisco, and the Atlantic & Pacific would cooperate to build a transcontinental under the original Atlantic & Pacific charter.[25]

Santa Fé engineer Albert A. Robinson immediately began building the line. Considerable friction developed between the engineers of the Santa Fé and the Frisco as the Atlantic & Pacific was being built. Having stopped at Vinita, the Atlantic & Pacific resumed construction at Isleta, New Mexico Territory, leaving a widening gap between Isleta and Vinita as it pushed rapidly across both New Mexico and Arizona.[26]

In 1879 San Diego land developers Frank and Warren Kimball were rebuffed by Charles Crocker of the Central Pacific *and* by Jay Gould, who then controlled the Union Pacific, in their bid for a railroad into San Diego. In the fall of that year, the Kimballs persuaded the Atchison, Topeka & Santa Fé Railroad to build to San Diego.[27] The Santa Fé wanted to facilitate this project by acquiring the Atlantic & Pacific, which still had a right to its large 1866 land grant. The concurrent plan for the Atlantic & Pacific, as the Pacific link of the Santa Fé, to enter California at Needles, near the 35th parallel, in effect nullified the San Diego agreement. A new plan was created for the California Southern to build from San Diego toward San Bernardino, there to link up with the Atlantic & Pacific. Los Angeles interests, fearful that this proposed transcontinental would by-pass their city, attempted to get Congress to nullify the 1866 land grant, a move that almost succeeded.[28]

---

[23]*Railroad Gazette*, Sep 1, 1876.

[24]Bryant, *History of the Atchison, Topeka and Santa Fe Railway*, 85.

[25]William E. Bain, *Frisco Folks: Stories and Pictures of the great* [sic] *Steam Days of the Frisco Road (St. Louis-San Francisco Railway Company)* (Denver: SageB, 1961), 21–22; Miner, *The St. Louis-San Francisco Transcontinental Railroad*, 121–126.   [26]George Werner to the writer, Sep 28, 2002.

[27]Bryant, *History of the Atchison, Topeka and Santa Fe*, 95–96.

[28]William Greever, *Arid Domain, The Santa Fe Railway and Its Western Land Grant* (Stanford: SUP, 1954), 34–35; Franklin Hoyt, "Railroad Development in Southern California, 1868 to 1900," Ph.D. diss. (USC, 1951), 256 and 295–296; Lewis B. Lesley, "The Struggle of San Diego for a Southern Transcontinental Railroad Connection, 1854–1891," Ph.D. diss. (UCB, 1933), 264.

Death of Mark Hopkins—March 29, 1878

A great deal happened to the Central Pacific Associates in the year and a half following Colton's "We want rest" letter to Huntington. The years 1878 and 1879 were critical for them, with the death of two key men and the near-death of a third.

On March 29, 1878, less than three years after the death of Edwin Crocker, the Central Pacific Associates lost the second of their powerful team of railroad entrepreneurs. For years Mark Hopkins had suffered from sciatica and rheumatism.[29] Charles Crocker said he had been ill for the last four years of his life.[30] When Hopkins' doctor advised a change of climate, he built a log cabin near the summit of the Sierra Nevada and spent some time there, where he remained active—and more often than not hard at work. As he grew older and his bouts with these besetting maladies increased in number and severity, his doctor advised a warmer climate. To try this cure, he and a group of friends boarded a train for Fort Yuma in Arizona Territory. There it was thought that he showed signs of improvement, but on the night of March 29 he died.

Hopkins was known as a man of few words, but every member of the Central Pacific team regarded his counsel as invaluable. At times they all sought his advice; Huntington would hardly make a move without Hopkins' approval. One eulogist, praising Hopkins for the part he played in the early history of the Central Pacific Railroad Company, called him the "keystone of the arch."[31]

Death of David Douty Colton—October 9, 1878

In late August 1878, David Colton was at a San Francisco dinner party given by Charles Crocker in honor of Pennsylvania Judge Jeremiah Sullivan Black, attended by Leland Stanford, Collis Huntington, and "other gentlemen of distinction."[32] Shortly afterward, Colton, who was something of a horseman, suffered what seemed at first to be nothing more than superficial injuries when thrown from a bucking mustang.[33] But his condition worsened.

Correspondence from Fred Crocker to Huntington shows how important Colton had become by then to the eastward expansion of the Southern Pacific system. And we know from a letter Colton sent Huntington that in September he was active in the

---

[29]Phelps, *Contemporary Biography of California's Representative Men*, II, 30.

[30]CC test., Jul 8, 1884, *Colton Case*, XVII, 8874.

[31]*SF Chronicle*, Mar 30, 1878.

[32]*SF Argonaut*, Sep 7, 1878. On Aug 14, Black, AAS, and a star-studded group of celebrities made a tour of Chinatown. *SF Alta California*, Aug 15, 1878. *Sac Bee*, Aug 21, 1878, reports that Black had left the capital city the day before to return to Wash.

[33]*SF Chronicle*, Oct 9, 10, and 11, 1878.

organization of the Southern Pacific Railroad of New Mexico to continue the rail-road from Arizona across New Mexico Territory to a point near El Paso.[34]

Stanford, Charles Crocker, and Lloyd Tevis had boarded a train together for New York on September 11, 1878, Stanford and Tevis to work on a Wells Fargo financial contract involving the Southern Pacific Railroad, and Crocker to make a health-restoring vacation in Europe.[35] Mrs. Colton and daughter, and Charles Crocker were all reported on September 19 as having registered at the Windsor Hotel in New York.[36] It was noted a week or so later that Stanford was also there, but no mention of when he arrived, though probably at the same time.[37]

Crocker boarded the *Germanic* and sailed for Liverpool on September 28, 1878, to join his wife, Mary, his daughter, Hattie, and sons George and William in Europe, where they had gone in June.[38] On October 6, with Stanford and Huntington still in New York, Crocker arrived in Liverpool.[39] On the following day, Edward H. Miller, Jr., reported—or complained—in a letter to Huntington about the effect of Colton's condition on daily operations of their business: "General Colton is sick. Will not be able to do business for a month. There is no one here to manage money interests or negotiate loans if any are required."[40] Colton was expected to survive, but it would be at least three weeks before he could even be consulted about business affairs.[41]

Alban Towne, general superintendant of the Central Pacific Railroad, then sent Huntington a detailed letter about Colton's illness, telling him that Judge [Robert] Robinson and Fred Crocker were on the way to Yuma taking with them Colton's power of attorney so that they could complete critical business negotiations there.[42]

Since Colton's illness had not been considered serious, Towne wrote to Huntington, he had been confined to bed for only four or five days, taking a patent medicine for what was thought to be a minor illness. Towne went on to say that Colton's doctors finally became concerned enough with their patient's worsening condition that they began looking for an explanation of how he might have received what more and more looked to be very serious injuries. This was not done until Sunday, October 6. That was when the accident with the horse was found to have caused the rupture of small blood vessels that had led to the formation of abscesses, from which a flow of black blood caused blood poisoning.[43] On October 9, 1878, David Colton died unex-pectedly from what his doctor described as a ruptured blood vessel in his abdomen.[44]

Since Colton seemed to have been on the road to recovery from minor injuries, his

[34]DDC to CPH, Sep 25, 1878.   [35]DDC to CPH, Sep 11, 1878.
[36]*SF Chronicle*, Sep 20, 1878.   [37]*NY Times*, Sep 27, 1878.
[38]Ibid., Jun 21 and Sep 28, 1878.
[39]Their ship reached Queenstown at noon, Oct 6, and proceeded at once to Liverpool. *NY Times*, Oct 7, 1878.
[40]EHM, Jr., to CPH, Oct 7, 1878.   [41]EHM, Jr., to CPH, Oct 8, 1878.
[42]ANT to CPH, Oct 9, 1878. Judge Robinson was the father of att. Edward I. Robinson of the SPBRR.
[43]ANT to CPH, Oct 9, 1878.   [44]*SF Chronicle*, Oct 10, 1878.

death caused rumors that he must have died from some physical violence. To stifle these rumors, Colton's physician, Army surgeon Lt. Col. Charles C. Keeney, published a detailed statement on his patient's symptoms and condition for the days October 2 through 9.[45] This report concluded with the description of an autopsy performed by Dr. Levi C. Lane, professor of surgery and surgical anatomy at the Medical College of the Pacific, whose own report con-

> OSCAR LEWIS HAS COLTON MURDERED
>
> Rumors that Colton had died from some kind of violence had themselves been put to death . . . until the inventive historical-fiction writer Oscar Lewis happened upon them. He later informed his readers that Colton had died after being *stabbed*, that he was *murdered*, "but details of the mystery—if it was a mystery—never reached the public."*
>
> *Oscar Lewis, *The Big Four*, 302.

cluded: "Not one mark of violence was found to justify the villainous reports which have been current in regard to the matter."[46]

Colton died at 10 P.M. on the very day Towne wrote his letter to Huntington. The following day Fred Crocker—knowing of Colton's death—sent Huntington a report on how he and Judge Robinson had completed the organization of the Southern Pacific Railroad of Arizona.[47]

With the news of Colton's unexpected death, his own family and the Stanfords hurried home to San Francisco.[48] When notified by cable of Colton's death only three days after he had reached England, in what was the shortest European trip Crocker ever made, he cancelled his vacation and made arrangements to return home immediately. On November 7, they boarded the *Britannic* and landed in New York ten days later.[49]

Charley Crocker cried when he called at the Colton house.[50]

It was discovered not long after Colton's death that for some time his handling of the Associates' financial affairs had been "irregular," to say the least. Within less than four years after Colton had joined them, they had become aware of the enormity of some of these irregularities.[51] Crocker wrote to Huntington in December 1878 giving him details of some of Colton's financial manipulations.[52] The following February Crocker told Huntington that they had discovered much "crookedness" in the affairs of the Rocky Mountain Coal & Iron Company, of which Colton had been president. He added that there was even more crookedness in certain Ione coal purchases and other Central Pacific matters; this promised to make an earlier financial scandal the company faced seem like "small potatoes" in comparison.[53]

[45]C[harles] Keeney, M.D., "Case of General Colton, and the Causes of His Death," *PMSJ* 1878 21 (7): 309–316; repr. in *SF Alta California*, Dec 22, 1878. See also *SFCD*, 1877–1878, 481, for bio. info. on Keeney.

[46]Keeney, "Case of General Colton," 316; *SFCD*, 1878–79, 501. [47]CFC to CPH, Oct 10, 1878.

[48]*SF Chronicle*, Oct 11, 1878. [49]*NY Times*, Nov 18, 1878.

[50]*Colton Case*, V, 2485. [51]See Evans, *Huntington*, I, 340ff., for an examination of the DDC affair.

[52]CC to CPH, Dec 2, 1878. [53]CC to CPH, Feb 15, 1879; Evans, *Huntington*, I, 345.

Pacific Improvement Company—October 31, 1878

Following Mark Hopkins' death, his widow refused to participate in any new railroad construction. Because of this, the three remaining Associates superseded—though they did not dissolve—the Western Development Company, and replaced it by a new vehicle of construction they created in October 1878.[54]

It was Stanford's idea. On October 26, he suggested the plan to Huntington and sought his partner's reading on his idea: "Have not organized new company. Am not entirely clear on the subject. What is your opinion?"[55] Three days later, Stanford sent the vice president a telegram recommending the creation of the new construction company, naming Strobridge president and soliciting Huntington's approval.

Not aware of Stanford's correspondence with Huntington, on the same day Fred Crocker wrote Huntington: "Governor Stanford proposes to organize a new construction company for this extension [across Arizona], making Strobridge President and Manager, with a salary of $10,000. I do not know whether he has conferred with you or not."[56]

The idea of calling it the General Improvement Company was dropped in favor of thr name Pacific Improvement Company, whose Articles of Incorporation they signed in San Francisco on October 31, 1878, and filed with the Secretary of State on November 4.[57] Strobridge was, indeed, named president.[58]

Soon thereafter, Charles Crocker could report to Huntington,

> I have just returned from a trip to the front on the Gila, where I found Strobridge in full blast. He is full of energy—as much so as I ever saw him, and I assure you the work under his charge is going forward splendidly & economically. . . . It seemed like old times to meet "Stro," out there, & hear him order things around.[59]

The Pacific Improvement Company performed largely the same services as had the Western Development Company.[60] The new company was owned at first only by Stanford, Huntington, and Crocker, but Mrs. Hopkins had a change of heart and joined them.[61] Huntington later sold his stock to the Hopkins estate, giving the Hopkins interest 50 percent, with the Stanford and Crocker interests remaining owners of 25 percent each.[62]

Unlike its predecessors, the Pacific Improvement Company was not dissolved at the time that the Associates created another construction company. It continued to

---

[54]The corp. hist. of the WDC is difficult to follow. CSS records show that its charter was forfeited on Dec 30, 1906, for failure to pay its license tax. Then new Arts. of Inc. were signed and filed May 19, 1909. File 57371, CSA; Arts. of Inc. signed Feb 11, filed Feb 16, 1911. File 64367, CSA; Arts. of Inc. were again signed Apr 28, filed Jun 17, 1933. File 154404, CSA. All were for fifty-year corps.   [55]LS to CPH, Oct 26, 1878.

[56]CFC to CPH, Oct 29, 1878.

[57]LS test., *USPRC*, V, 2672; CFC telegram to CPH, Nov 2, 1878. Date of signing and filing, and Cert. of Diminution of Capital Stock, Jul 28, 1920. File 12018, CSA.   [58]LS test., *USPRC*, V, 2672.

[59]CC to CPH, Dec 10, 1878.   [60]LS test., *USPRC*, V, 2658–2662.

[61]Frank S. Douty test., *USPCR*, V, 2672.   [62]Daggett, *Chapters on the History of the Southern Pacific*, 134.

own a great deal of real estate and property in California and New York, stocks and bonds in a number of railroad companies, and stock in the Oakland Waterfront Company. It continued to be a valuable financial plum for some investors until it was dissolved in the mid-twentieth century. As late as the summer of 1887 Stanford still owned $1.25 million in Pacific Improvement stock.[63]

SOUTHERN PACIFIC CONSTRUCTION ACROSS ARIZONA TERRITORY— NOVEMBER 19, 1878–OCTOBER 18, 1880

On February 7, 1877, the legislature of Arizona Territory passed a law allowing the Southern Pacific to build across its territory.[64] The railroad had reached Yuma on May 20, 1877, but did not cross the Colorado River until Sunday, September 30, 1877, when 4-4-0 (a designation for the number of wheels: four leading trucks, four drivers, and no trailing trucks) *Engine 31* crossed the river into Arizona—even though not yet authorized by Congress to build outside the state of California.[65] A Southern Pacific annual report verifies the often-disputed date of this event: "Trains commenced running over the Bridge to the Depot in Yuma, carrying the United States mails, passengers, freight, etc., on the thirtieth day of September, 1877."[66] On that day, The Texas & Pacific Railway, which was to join the Southern Pacific at that point, was still 1,200 miles away.[67]

Over the strong objection of Tom Scott, Huntington persuaded a congressional committee that the Southern Pacific could and should keep building eastward until it met the Texas & Pacific.[68]

In 1877 Huntington was the only one of the Associates who wanted to build a southern transcontinental railroad. On October 15, 1877, Colton had written him:

> Crocker, Governor Stanford, and myself had a consultation yesterday (Mr. Hopkins not able to be in his office) and I think we agreed fully. . . . I think I can speak for all your associates on this side that we do not want to build any more roads east of the Colorado River on the 32nd parallel for some time. We want rest. Stop building roads until we can pay our debts. Get strong once again.

[63]LS test., *USPRC*, V, 2662. Edwin Truman Coman, Jr., "Sidelights on the Investment Policies of Stanford, Huntington, Hopkins, and Crocker," *BBHS* 1942 16 (Nov): 85–89, identifies the broad and extensive investments of the PIC. His source of info. was a set of the company's records, including 279 ledgers, journals, and minute books, 42 cases of corres., and 150 drawers of vouchers dealing with subsidiary companies. This coll. is now housed in the SUA.

[64]No. 33, "An Act To secure the construction and operation of certain railroad and telegraph lines, and to provide for other matters relating thereto." App. Feb 7, 1877, by the Leg. Assy. of the Terr. of Ariz.

[65]Frank Love, hist. researcher, Yuma, Ariz., Apr 19, 2002. Photos commemorating this event are on file at the AHS. Evans, *Huntington*, I, 252; Grodinsky, *Transcontinental Railway Strategy*, 64, says early Oct.

[66]George E. Gray's "Chief Engineer's Report," in *AR SPRRC*, for the eighteen months ending Dec 31, 1878, 57. See Clifford [*sic*] Earl Trafzer, *Yuma: A Short History of a Southwestern Crossing* (Yuma: YCHS, 1974), 28.

[67]See map, Miner, *The St. Louis-San Francisco Transcontinental Railroad*, 123; Evans, *Huntington*, I, 252.

[68]"From Trail to Rail—The Story of [*sic*] Beginning of Southern Pacific," Chap. 36, "Completion of 'Sunset Route' from Pacific Coast to Gulf of Mexico: Race with Texas and Pacific East of El Paso," *SPB* 1928 (12): 12.

Then, later in the seventies—"if memory serves me, about 1877," reminisced William Benson Storey, Central Pacific and Southern Pacific surveyor, builder of the San Francisco & San Joaquin Valley Railway and long-time president of the Santa Fé[69]—Charles Crocker became dissatisfied with the construction of the Associates' portion of the second transcontinental, so he got James Strobridge to return and take up his former duties as superintendent of construction. According to Storey, a deal was made with Strobridge that he would not have to live at the site, as he had during the building of the Central Pacific. Strobridge agreed to organize the work and visit the construction site as often as *he* deemed it necessary.[70]

This oft-quoted account of Strobridge's return from retirement is mentioned only because it has been used in so many erroneous accounts of Strobridge's career. Storey's chronology was off a bit, and his time perspective failed him even more. At no time in 1877 had there been any eastward construction for Crocker to become dissatisfied with its lack of progress. In fact, Yuma remained the terminus for about a year and a half. Moreover, Strobridge never went into retirement, so could not have been called out of it.

The Southern Pacific Railroad of Arizona was incorporated September 20, 1878, to build a railroad from Yuma to the eastern boundary of Arizona.[71] Strobridge's contribution to the building of the southern transcontinental railroad obviously came after he assumed charge of construction from Yuma. Fred Crocker wrote Huntington on November 2, 1878, saying that Strobridge had taken charge the day before and "goes to Yuma today." On the same day, Stanford wrote Huntington, "J. H. Strobridge goes to the front tonight to take charge of the work with instructions to push it with the greatest force consistent with economy." A Yuma newspaper reported that Strobridge was on the site in late November and that men and materials were there for the drive eastward.[72]

The Central/Southern Pacific Associates never had a more faithful or more enthusiastic supporter than Frank Pixley's *Argonaut*. With the railroad gearing up for eastward construction from Yuba, on November, 16, 1878, this journal seized on the theme of the benefits to be derived by San Francisco if Tom Scott's plans were frustrated in the Southwest.[73]

A week later the *Argonaut* published another encomium of the Southern Pacific Railroad and a blast at Tom Scott:

---

[69]Bryant, *History of the Atchison, Topeka and Santa Fe Railway*, 175ff. There is a sketch of the railroad career of William Benson Storey in Lawrence Waters, *Steel Trails to Santa Fe* (Lawrence: UKP, 1950), 344–345n, and an account of the purchase and completion of the SJVRR on 344–346.

[70]William Storey's account is in John Galloway, *The First Transcontinental Railroad*, 88.

[71]"From Trail to Rail," Chap. 34, "Southern Pacific Extends Line Over Arizona and New Mexico Into Texas: Stage Coach and Freighting Teams of the Southwest," *SPB* 1928 16 (10): 13. Ed. comment and synopsis, Unmerger Case (*Brief of Defendants*), 37.   [72][Yuma] *Arizona Sentinel*, Oct 12, and Nov 9 and 23, 1878.

[73]*SF Argonaut*, Nov 16, 1878. Pixley's ed. was quoted in full in the previous chap.

The same conflict is now going on southward between Tom Scott and the Southern Pacific corporation [*sic*]. The contest is now for the trade of Southern California, New Mexico, Arizona, the Mexican states of Chihuahua, Sonora, and the great valley of Mexico. It is a splendid prize for which these athletes in the railroad ring are contending. If Stanford and company succeed, all this trade comes to our port, enriches our people, stimulates our industries, and builds up San Francisco to become one of the greatest and richest of the commercial emporiums of the world. If Tom Scott succeeds, he will steal away our trade, leave our port, in comparison with what it ought to be, an embarcadero for hides and tallow.[74]

Ground was broken at Yuma on November 19, 1878, for construction of the Southern Pacific across Arizona.[75]

Strobridge was a cautious man, and never presumed to make critical decisions or to build without specific orders. As an example, and as a testimony to his confidence of the abilities of Crocker and Stanford in making decisions on engineering or geographical matters, he sent the following telegram to San Francisco:

> End of Track, Arizona
> Dec. 4, 1878
>
> To
> Chas Crocker,
> Bates & I have been 30 miles out to-day.[76] He is running a new line commencing one mile from Gila City. He can get a good line from that point, that we can build clear through, one & one-half miles per day. On the old line we cannot build one half-mile per day. I want you or the Governor to come down as soon as possible & determine which line we will take. It must be decided very soon, for if we are to take the old line, there are heavy points that must be covered, now to get them out of the way. Don't send anybody, but come one of you. Answer.
>
> J.H. Strobridge

A copy of this telegram was sent as an enclosure in a letter to Huntington in which Crocker wrote, "[I] shall go down to Yuma tomorrow."[77]

Construction eastward by the Southern Pacific of Arizona began in earnest in 1879, and within a year President Strobridge's Pacific Improvement Company had laid almost three hundred miles of rails.[78]

Only two weeks after the railroad from Yuma had reached Adonde Wells[79] (later named Wellton), thirty-one miles eastward,[80] a very annoyed Charles Crocker

---

[74]Ibid., Nov 23, 1878.

[75]"Trail to Rail," Chap. 34, "Southern Pacific Extends Line Over Arizona and New Mexico Into Texas," *SPB* 1928 16 (10): 13.   [76]Joseph H. Bates was an asst. eng. for the CPRR. *SFCD*, 1878, 121.

[77]CC to CPH, Dec 5, 1878.

[78]William Hood, chief eng. of the SPC after 1885, test., Unmerger Case, II R. 434–435 (*Brief of Defendants*, 37 and 41).

[79]The suggestion of JHS for "Gila" as a name for this station was rejected because the railroad wanted a station at Gila Bend. The name "Adonde" was selected by David Neahr, a Yuma merchant. ANT to CPH, Dec 30, 1878. Neahr was also a stockholder in the SPRR of Ariz. CC to CPH, Feb 7, 1879.

[80]"Trail to Rail," Chap. 34, "Southern Pacific Extends Line Over Arizona and New Mexico Into Texas," *SPB* 1928 34 (10): 13–14.

added his protest to the one Colton had made in the fall of 1877. He, too, complained to Huntington about the mad construction rush. His annoyance and pique are obvious from a letter to his New York Associate: "I assure you Mr. Huntington, that I really think we ought to get out of debt, before we build any more road. We are all of us getting old, and I feel like putting my house in order before I die."[81]

Crocker's frustration most likely resulted less from growing old with too many loose ends than to the recent deaths of Hopkins and Colton, the critical illness of Stanford, and the feeling that he (Crocker) was carrying the entire executive burden west of New York.

Huntington got his way: his Associates settled their differences about building beyond the state line and followed his lead in seeking support for their construction of a second, southern transcontinental—later nicknamed the "Sunset Route," a name used by the Galveston, Harrisburg & San Antonio since the early 1870s.[82] Their line would extend through to New Orleans.[83] They hoped in this way to stop the Atlantic & Pacific and the Texas & Pacific. To do this, they had to control the only two available crossings of the Colorado River—those at Yuma and Needles.[84]

STANFORD'S FIRST SERIOUS ILLNESS—1878–1879

Hard on the heels of the death of Hopkins and Colton, and with railroad construction in Arizona hardly begun, in the winter of 1878–1879 Stanford was laid low by a mysterious malady that caused his friends to despair for his life.

In the middle of December 1878 Stanford was still active in railroad affairs, dealing, specifically, as shown in a conversation he had on December 12 with Fred Crocker, with the fact that Huntington had not been kept informed about the laying of rails east of Yuma. Young Crocker wrote Huntington that same day promising to keep him informed on a daily basis, if possible, on their progress.[85]

The first inkling that something might have been wrong with Stanford was a letter he sent to Huntington penned and signed by Frank Shay, the day following Stanford's conversation with Fred Crocker.[86] The earliest documented report of Stanford's illness is found in a letter from Charles Crocker to Huntington written two weeks later, in which he said, "Governor Stanford is sick at home, but when he comes to the office again, we will talk over what to do with them [steel rails]."[87]

[81]CC to CPH, Jan 22, 1879.   [82]George Werner to the writer, Sep 28, 2002.

[83]Evans, *Huntington*, I, 252–260, summarizes these differences.

[84]Lynn Farrar points out that the Yuma crossing used by the SPRR in 1877 was not the best one: "The T & P [Texas & Pacific Railway] had staked out a better one north and prior to where the SP built and it was not until ca [sic] 1926 that a line change put the alignment on the T & P surveyed line." Letter to the writer, Sep 16, 2002.

[85]CFC to CPH, Dec 12, 1878.   [86]LS [per Frank Shay] to CPH, Dec 13, 1878.

[87]CC to CPH, Dec 26, 1878.

Crocker wrote again a few days later that he had presented an item of business to the Governor, who seemed not to want it done. This seeming lack of interest prompted Crocker to say, "I will see him again."[88]

On January 20, 1879, in still another letter to Huntington, Crocker wrote, optimistically, "Gov. Stanford has been ill for the last two weeks and over. This morning I understand that he is out of bed, and will probably be around again in a week or so."

Crocker's next medical report was penned only two days later: "Gov. Stanford as I wrote you a few days ago, has been quite sick, and at one time was threatened with a more serious illness. He is now up and about the house, & intends as soon as he gets able, to go east with his wife who has also been sick." And on January 24, Crocker's optimism seemed justified: "Stanford is getting better, and is up & about the house now. Expect him to be out in a few days."

Crocker reported again on February 6, 1879, that Stanford was still sick, but not seriously. Crocker mistakenly believed that Stanford had recovered, so his letter to Huntington written on February 10 sounded more like a complaint than a report of the Governor's condition:

> I stopped in at Governor Stanford's this morning, on my way to the office, and found him still in bed.
>
> He has been up and around the house, & out driving, but every time I go there I find him in bed.
>
> I hope it is nothing more serious than appears on the surface the matter with him.

On February 15, 1879, Crocker again wrote to Huntington, "I am waiting for the Governor to get out to see if we can get a settlement of these matters; but he scatters so much, and changes his mind so often, that I wish you would come out here and assist in fixing them up; it needs firmness to deal with this matter."

A week later, when Crocker again reported on Stanford's illness, he had the first concrete suggestion as to its cause—sewer gas poison. Charley was not sure whether the poisoning occurred at home or at the office.[89]

The full explanation surfaced in Crocker's letter of February 25, 1879:

> I am sorry to say that Mr. Stanford is worse again. It has been ascertained that there was a privy vault in the cellar of his house at the ranch, where they have lived most of the time for the past two years, and they have been breathing the poison from that. The result is that it has thoroughly poisoned the whole family, and the Doctors say that it will require at least a year to eradicate this poison from his system.
>
> I saw him yesterday for a few moments, and he looked worse than he has at any time since he has been sick. I saw him again for a few moments this morning. He was in bed, & feeling some better, having had a good nights [sic] sleep.

---

[88]CC to CPH, Dec 31, 1878.   [89]CC to CPH, Feb 22, 1879.

The Doctors think there is no doubt but what he will ultimately recover, but then you know a man in his condition is so liable to colds, & backsets, and one thing & another, that there's no telling what may occur, and in view of that, I assure you I think it is best for us to go slow, very slow.

You know the state of his finances, and in case of his death, his obligations must be paid. I hope for the best and really do not feel alarmed, but at the same time I deem it necessary to be cautious.

On February 27, 1879, Crocker saw one of Stanford's doctors, who confided in him that in his opinion his patient would be disabled for a year.[90]

Stanford worsened, and on March 1, Crocker reported to Huntington that he was not allowed to see Stanford, and that no letters or any other business affairs were permitted. He closed, "I cannot communicate with him in any way."

A week later Crocker could see no prospect of Stanford's being able to work for months.[91] But the worse was still to come. In the middle of March he suggested to Huntington that they reconsider their railroad operations in Arizona in view of the Governor's likely death:

For the first time since Gov. Stanford's illness, I feel somewhat alarmed. I called there this morning but he was asleep, and I did not see him. I saw Mrs. Stanford, and while I have no doubt she greatly exagerates [sic], yet at the same time, the fact is that the Gov'r is constantly getting worse.

He is worse now, than he has been at any time. He has not been able to keep anything on his stomach with the exception of milk, since his first attack, & he is now troubled to keep even that on. The heat of his body is $101\frac{1}{2}$, and I am told that 104 is the highest stage of typhoid fever, and 98 the normal condition. With such a fever raging in his system, and inability to keep anything on his stomach, the strongest man is bound to give way.

For these reasons, I feel alarmed, and it becomes necessary for us to look the thing square in the face. Whether or not, the probable loss of Governor Stanford, should have any effect on our work in Arizona, is a matter for consideration.

You know the large amount of indebtedness he is carrying for himself personally, and of course, in the even of his death, that could not be carried for any length of time.[92]

Crocker went down to the farm and visited Stanford on March 30. His ailing partner was feeble, but was sure that things were going to improve. He was able to eat again, and had almost entirely given up medicines. In fact, Stanford was sure it was the medicines that kept his stomach so upset that he couldn't keep food down.[93]

Stanford wrote to Huntington on April 3, saying he had been back on his feet for five or six days, that he had given up all medicine, and that his greatest trouble at the

[90]CC to CPH, Feb 27, 1879.   [91]CC to CPH, Mar 8, 1879.
[92]CC to CPH, Mar 14, 1879.   [93]CC to CPH, Mar 31, 1879.

time was from rheumatism. Though feeling much better, he said, it would probably take several months of rest before he regained his complete strength.

Crocker's next report on Stanford's health, the day after the Stanford letter, described how the Governor was improving. Though "looking pretty thin," he was, nonetheless, "bright and cheerful."[94]

When Crocker received word from Huntington that he was going to Texas on business, he wrote, twice in one letter, "I wish you would come out here." He alluded at the same time to the fact that Nick Smith was filling in for Stanford in his office, and that—apropos "statements of account between ourselves," Stanford's account was going up very fast and Captain Smith was carrying a large cash tag for him.[95] Stanford's illness obviously had serious repercussions on the building of their expanding railroad system, and on company and personal finances.

But slowly, Stanford's condition began to turn around, as Crocker wrote: "Stanford still remains unwell, though he is slowly improving. He has not been to the city since he went to his farm, so there has been no consultation about business with him, for several months."[96] And then, in a second letter written the same day:

> Governor Stanford has returned from his Ranch, and I called on him this morning. He is looking very much better, but is far from being a well man. His sides, legs and back are all drawn up with rheumatism and he has got to be very careful of himself.

Crocker closed this letter with an uncharacteristically personal note: "I wish you could come out before he goes away. So we could all be together for a few days."

Though he survived the life-threatening crisis, in mid-May Stanford was still too sick to do any business, owing primarily to his rheumatism.[97]

As late as the first week of June 1879, Stanford was still too sick to put in an appearance at his office, and even a slight change in the weather made him worse. Jane Stanford went to the office on June 6 to assure Crocker that her husband would recover completely. She said she thought they should go away for awhile for a change of climate, but her husband was against it.[98]

Pressing business matters that he was conducting single-handedly were getting Crocker down, especially the need to settle the Colton estate. On June 7, 1879, he wrote to Huntington:

> I hope you can come out here very soon as the Colton estate really ought to be settled up, and I have everything now so that it can be quickly done. Governor Stanford has not been in the office since January 5, and there is no immediate prospect of his coming here.

---

[94]CC to CPH, Apr 4, 1879.   [95]CC to CPH, Apr 8, 1879.
[96]CC to CPH, Apr 23, 1879.   [97]CC to CPH, May 17, 1879.
[98]CC to CPH, Jun 6, 1879.

Crocker was sure as late as the middle of June that Stanford would not be fit for business for a long time to come.[99]

Stanford continued to improve, and gradually began to appear in public, but he was not well for a long time, and it is not much of an exaggeration to say that he never recovered fully from this life-threatening illness of the first half of 1879.

RAILROAD CONSTRUCTION IN ARIZONA IS SUSPENDED AND RESUMED—1879

Construction activity was suspended during the torrid summer months of 1879. The terminus of the Southern Pacific Railroad remained in Casa Grande, Arizona, in the exact middle of the Territory, from May 19, 1879, to March 17, 1880, even though construction eastward had continued during this time.[100] There was said to be material for building 150 miles of track, and Strobridge, it was reported, was under orders to complete one and a half miles per day.[101] (It is highly unlikely that railroad officials would have told James Harvey Strobridge how to go about his business under the hot Arizona sun.)

As the Associates continued their relentless efforts to complete their own southern transcontinental railroad, it was reported in January 1880 that Strobridge had taken another large force of railroad builders to Arizona.[102]

The *Argonaut* was delighted to report that after what it scoffed at as "a short interruption," construction had been resumed and was again speeding its way toward New Orleans.[103] "With abundant iron rails, ties, and other material," by February 1880 Strobridge was again "pushing his construction from Casa Grande eastward." Since resumption of work on the line, he had already built sixteen miles, and, barring some unforeseen obstacles to impede the work, the railroad was expected to reach the Gulf of Mexico in record time. Three years had been allotted for the completion of this "second great trans-continental highway," but Stanford and Crocker expected it to be finished in less than two.[104]

Stanford had become exuberant about the prospects of regional and national prosperity the completion of their southern transcontinental foreshadowed. As early as February 7, 1880, while the Southern Pacific was still only halfway across Arizona, he was quoted as envisioning the completion of the Southern Pacific's transcontinental railroad, when there would be nothing standing in the way of

---

[99]CC to CPH, Jun 17, 1879.

[100]"Trail to Rail," Chap. 34, "Southern Pacific Extends Line Over Arizona and New Mexico Into Texas," *SPB* 1928 34 (10): 14; Julius Kruttschnitt, chairman of the Exec. Comm. of the Board of Directors of the SPC, test., Unmerger Case, II R. 724 (*Brief of Defendants*), 39, gave May 15, 1879, as the arrival date at Casa Grande.

[101]*SF Argonaut*, Jan 24, 1880.   [102]Ibid., Jan 10, 1880.

[103]Ibid., Feb 7, 1880.   [104]Ibid.

An Interesting Sidelight on 1880 Railroad Construction

"We have now, in process of building and built, five transcontinental railroads:
  1. The Central Pacific and Union Pacific, accomplished;
  2. The Southern Pacific, building;
  3. The Northern Road, from Lake Superior to Puget Sound, building;
  4. The Canadian Road, building;
  5. The Atchison, Topeka and Kansas [sic], threatened."*

*SF Argonaut, Feb 7, 1880.

bringing immigrants from Liverpool to San Francisco for fifteen dollars per head, with their tools and household goods. Every industrious man would find there a twenty- or forty-acre piece of land just waiting for working men to come from the eastern states or Europe to occupy it.[105]

Once the Associates determined to build their own southern transcontinental to New Orleans, they were relentless in their drive eastward. The Southern Pacific reached Tucson, two-thirds of the way across Arizona, on March 17, 1880, and three days later the first passenger train entered that city.[106]

Pixley's *Argonaut* again caught the spirit of their determination in late August 1880, when the Southern Pacific was building between Benson and San Simon, quickly approaching New Mexico:

> The Southern Pacific Railroad Company is pressing the construction of its line eastward with great energy. It is now nearly a hundred and fifteen miles beyond Tucson. On Tuesday of this week nearly two and one-quarter miles of track were laid. Mr. Charles Crocker goes East week after next with his family, leaving his younger son, William, at Cambridge, and the ladies in New York. Messrs. Huntington and Crocker will visit Texas, and in the same private car with which they leave San Francisco. It is their intention to there await the connection of the Southern Pacific road with the Santa Fe, Atchison & Topeka line, and return to San Francisco by way of the Southern road. The trip is a business one, to make arrangements in the Eastern States for the new transcontinental railroad that we shall then have over the new southern route. This southern route ought to do our city a vast deal of good. It ought to extend our trade jurisdiction to new territory, and bring to our city a large and continually increasing business. It will, if our merchants have the energy and the enterprise to reach out and secure what the railroad company has brought within their grasp. The company has done its duty, but we fear that our merchants will not do theirs. They

---

[105]Ibid.
[106]"Trail to Rail," Chap. 34, "Southern Pacific Extends Line Over Arizona and New Mexico Into Texas," *SPB* 1928 (10): 14.

are slow, and lack daring. They allow the Saint Louis and Chicago people to outwit them. Chicago comes to our very borders, and steals away trade from under the very noses of our merchants. The Southern Road makes an independent route for carrying passengers and merchandise, and, when connected with the Gulf of Mexico, will enable the California railroad people to become entirely independent of the Union Pacific and the Eastern connections between the Missouri River and the Atlantic seaboard. As an immigrant route, it ought to do a large business.[107]

Mussel Slough Showdown—May 11, 1880

Only a few months after the 1879 hiatus in railroad construction in Arizona, the Associates faced one of their most serious challenges and crises at home, as violence erupted over an issue that had plagued the Associates for a number of years.

Settlers had been lured into the San Joaquin Valley by glowing descriptions of the lands available from the railroad at reasonable prices. One of them, written by Jerome Madden, one of the railroad's land agents, read in part as follows: "The vast suppliers of water and magnificent timber in the adjacent Sierra, and the facilities for bringing them to the plains, will be of great value."[108] Wanting to believe in their wildest dreams, settlers poured in and began squatting on railroad lands at random, hoping they could make good their claims when legally challenged to do so.

As the Southern Pacific Railroad of California pressed its inexorable drive up and down the state and into every town of any importance, and after 1878 was driving its rails across the south to complete a transcontinental railroad to New Orleans, there were only occasional acts of resistance worthy of notice.

The Mussel Slough incident in California was one of these. It had serious repercussions for the railroad in all its endeavors, and its beleaguered image was tarnished even more, some thought entirely beyond repair.

Stanford played his role of public relations expert with commendable skill, but when the road pushed into the Mussel Slough area of Tulare County (which was absorbed into King's County in 1893), all that changed.

In the 1870s the Mussel Slough district, now called the Lucerne Valley, was filling up fast with settlers who never bothered to purchase the government lands they squatted on, lands for which the Southern Pacific had tried to secure federal patents for years.[109] Most of these squatters, Stanford's secretary Frank Shay later wrote, were members of William C. Quantrill's guerrilla band in confederate Missouri during the Civil War.[110] The railroad efforts to repossess the land only

---

[107] SF Argonaut, Aug 28, 1880.

[108] Jerome Madden, *The Lands of the Southern Pacific Railroad Company of California* (SF: SPRR Journal, 1877), 12–13.

[109] One of the best accounts of the events leading up to the Mussel Slough tragedy and the battle itself is in Wallace Smith, *Garden of the Sun: A History of the San Joaquin Valley, 1772–1939* (LA: LHP, 1939), 259–290 and 545.

[110] Shay, "A Lifetime in California," 120.

alarmed the squatters, but its managers sought to allay the squatters' fears. They assured them that if the Southern Pacific Railroad Company got possession of this land it would be sold for the usual price of $2.50 per acre, *without* regard to improvements.[111] In 1877 the Southern Pacific finally won clear title to the long sought-after lands.[112]

In response to a rumor that the railroad intended to charge more than $2.50 per acre, a Settlers' Land League was formed at Hanford, on April 12, 1878, composed of several hundred farmers pledging not to pay a higher price.[113] Then, "A quasi-military organization that was coexistent with the League" was formed, having membership that overlapped though was not identical to that of the league.[114] This organization was placed under the command of former Confederate Army major Thomas Jefferson McQuiddy of Tennessee, who was also president of the league.[115] It was said that his troops were organized as a cavalry and, wearing masks, trained at night in the towns of Hanford, Grangeville, and Lemoore (or Lemore), where they patrolled the roads on horseback.[116]

On March 4, 1879, three hundred people, some of them determined to "make trouble" if they did not win their fight with the railroad, met in the farming town of Hanford to protest the eviction decisions. They organized five military companies of sixty men each.[117] The settlers recognized the railroad's legal right to the land, according to the decision of the United States Circuit Court, but felt that they had a moral right to it, based on their interpretation of earlier railroad promises. As one writer defined the issue: "The company fought for its property; the settler, for his home."[118]

The prices the railroad eventually demanded reportedly ranged from eleven to forty dollars per acre, depending upon location *and* improvements the settlers had made.[119] This announcement prompted sporadic violence against the property of the Southern Pacific and its agents.

Finding it impossible for new owners who had bought in the interim the lands from the railroad to take possession of their property from the people who were squatting on the land, Charles Crocker, the president, and Stanford, who was not a

---

[111]Benjamin B. Redding (Pacific Coast Land Bureau, comp.), *California Guide Book, The Lands of the Central Pacific and Southern Pacific Railroad Companies in California, Nevada, and Utah* (SF: PCLB, Jan 1, 1875), 17; Settlers Committee of the Mussel Slough Company, *The Struggle of the Mussel Slough Settlers for their Homes. An Appeal to the People. History of the Land Troubles in Tulare and Fresno Counties. The Grasping Greed of the Railroad Monopoly* (Visalia: DPE, 1880), a 32-p. pam.; James Brown, *The Mussel Slough Tragedy* (Fresno: [n.p.], 1958), and, by the same author, "More Fictional Memorials to Mussel Slough," *PHR* 1957 26 (4): 373–377.

[112]Irving McKee, "Notable Memorials to Mussel Slough," *PHR* 1948 17 (1): 20; see also William McKinney, "The Mussel Slough Episode, a Chapter in the Settlement of the San Joaquin Valley, 1865–1880," MA thesis (UCB, 1948).

[113]Brown, *The Mussel Slough Tragedy*, 41–42; *SF Alta California*, Apr 13, 1878; Evans, *Huntington*, I, 291.

[114]Brown, *The Mussel Slough Tragedy*, 45.   [115]Ibid., 46; Evans, *Huntington*, I, 291.

[116]Smith, *Garden of the Sun*, 265–267.   [117]*Sac Union*, Mar 5, 1879; McKee, "Notable Memorials," 21.

[118]Smith, *Garden of the Sun*, 260.

[119]Angel, *A Memorial and Biographical History of the Counties of Fresno, Tulare, and Kern, California*, 166.

company officer, decided in 1878 to seek ejectment judgments against the squatters.[120]

One night in early November 1878 a masked band burned the ranch house of Perry C. Phillips, a man who had paid the railroad its higher price for his land. Another man, Walter J. Crow, was threatened for the same offense.[121]

In early 1879, twenty-three cases for damages and ejectment were brought against settlers by the Southern Pacific Railroad.[122] On December 15, 1879, in the case of *Southern Pacific v.* [Pierpont] *Orton*, Judge Lorenzo Sawyer decided in favor of the railroad:

> It follows that the title to the lands in question is in the plaintiff, and the defendant has no title, and his possession is wrongful. There must be findings and judgment for the plaintiff, and it is so ordered.[123]

In 1880 the settlers, many of whom were now farmers, tried to negotiate with Charles Crocker. Failing in this, they sent a committee to appeal to Stanford—neither an officer nor a director of the Southern Pacific Railroad, but now listed for the first time as a "General Agent."[124] The settlers appealed to Stanford because of his reputation for fair play and approachability.[125] A conference followed, reportedly marked by "a mutual spirit of concession and compromise," and resulted in an understanding that Stanford would visit the valley and confer with the settlers in an attempt to find an amicable solution to the dispute.[126] On the basis of this agreement, a Stockton journalist reported that some ill-advised friends of Stanford, without his knowledge, circulated a groundless rumor that Crocker was the cause of the Mussel Slough troubles and that Stanford had begged friend Charley to be lenient with the farmers.[127]

Stanford arrived in Hanford on March 11 to see firsthand the land under dispute and hear the farmers' complaints.[128] The settlers were satisfied that Stanford's interest guaranteed that there would be fair play and fair concessions on the part of the railroad.[129] One San Francisco newspaper reporter, who said that Governor Stanford seemed willing to work out a compromise with the settlers, was sure that the Governor would offer liberal concessions in order to make peace.[130] The committee

[120]CC to CPH, Nov 30, 1878, in Evans, *Huntington*, I, 291–292.

[121]*SF Post*, Nov 8, 1878.

[122]Att. J. Jacobs Jr. to U.S. Att. Gen. Charles Devens, May 7, 1879, in Brown, *The Mussel Slough Tragedy*, 134–135.

[123]This case is found in 32 *Federal Reporter*, 457–480, 480 cited.

[124]*AR SPRR*, For the Year Ending Dec 31st, 1880 (SF: HSCC, 1880), all directors, officers, and agents are listed on an unnumbered page facing the title page. Brown, *The Mussel Slough Tragedy*, 56, is wrong in thinking that LS was a SPRR director. CRC, *First Annual Report of the Board of Railroad Commissioners*, 253.

[125]*SF Call*, May 13, 1880.   [126]*Sac Record-Union*, Mar 12, 1880.

[127]*Stockton Mail*, Apr 12, 1890.

[128]McKee, "Notable Memorials to Mussel Slough," 21; Smith, *Garden of the Sun*, 268.

[129]McKee, "Notable Memorials to Mussel Slough," 21.   [130]*SF Call*, Mar 12, 1880.

reported that Stanford had agreed to stay all legal proceedings until the matter had been investigated further.[131]

Hopes for a peaceful settlement with the Settlers' Land League were dashed on April 10, 1880, when Southern Pacific land agent Daniel Parkhurst went to Hanford to handle the sale of railroad lands at the increased prices. The settlers warned him for his own safety to leave town. Because of Parkhurst's activities, the squatters accused Stanford of bad faith.[132] Stanford was squeezed by both sides in the dispute: pressure was applied not only by the squatters, but by other people who had bought and were yet unable to occupy the lands on which the illegal settlers had built.[133]

The railroad finally insisted that a United States marshal deliver eviction notices.[134] Southern Pacific authorities later claimed they did everything with-

JUDGE LORENZO SAWYER

was a transplanted New Yorker who had also practiced law in Wisconsin. He was practicing law in Virginia City, Nevada Territory, until he received a telegram from Governor Stanford offering him the judgeship of the twelfth judicial district, comprising San Mateo County and part of San Francisco. Sawyer accepted the appointment. That fall he was elected to a full six-year term and in January 1864 he took his seat as one of five new justices on the California Supreme Court. After serving the six-year term—the last two as chief justice—Sawyer was defeated in his bid for the regular ten-year term as an associate justice; he was later appointed federal circuit judge for the northern district of California.[a]

Sawyer and Stanford remained friends for life; the justice later served as one of the original trustees of Stanford University.[b]

[a]Johnson, *History of the California Supreme Court, 1850–1900*, I, 96.

[b]*The Leland Stanford Junior University*. Includes Senator Stanford's Plan for its Organization, The Grant Founding and Endowing the University, Description of the Property Embraced in Grant, and Portraits of the Trustees (SF: BC, 1888), 15.

in their power to avoid conflict and had gone out of the way to be fair by not taking possession of disputed lands until the United States Circuit Court had declared the settlers in wrongful possession, and until the time for appeal by the Settlers' Land League to the United States Supreme Court had expired.[135]

Stanford, accused of duplicity and insincerity, insisted that the Settlers' League had violated its agreement with the Southern Pacific Railroad by filing appeals on ejectment cases that had gone against them.[136]

Faced with defeat at every turn, the committee agreed to meet the railroad price halfway, but Stanford, for some unexplained reason, refused. His sudden change in attitude has often been attributed to what one critic called Huntington's unwilling-

---

[131]McKee, "Notable Memorials to Mussel Slough," 21.

[132]*SF Call*, Dec 4, 1880; *Sac Record-Union*, May 11, 1880.

[133]Mills D. Hartt to LS, May 5, 1880, in *Sac Record-Union*, May 13, 1880.

[134]Jerome Madden, SPRR land agent, to Mills D. Hartt, May 8, 1880, in ibid., May 13, 1880.

[135]*Sac Record-Union*, May 13, 1880.

[136]The Settlers Committee, *Struggle of the Mussel Slough Settlers*, 26–29; see also McKee, "Notable Memorials to Mussel Slough," 21.

ness to compromise—to his "inflexible determination."[137] According to this unlikely interpretation, Stanford was inclined toward leniency, but he toughened his stance because of his partner's intransigence. If this were true, Huntington's attitude toward fair land pricing must have changed since the mid-seventies and would have to change again by the early nineties. After similar problems with squatters at the earlier date, Huntington had written to Hopkins:

> It occurs to me that some arrangement might be come to with these squatters as to the amount they shall pay the company when it is decided they are on its lands. If it is possible, get them to agree on something, even less than their value, so as to avoid litigation.[138]

Always the practical man, Huntington added: "Just now we cannot afford to have any more enemies in Congress from the Pacific Coast." Huntington had more problems with squatters after he became president of the Southern Pacific Company. He told his nephew Henry, his first assistant, that the government's lax land policies were more to blame for squatters' trespasses than was the greed or dishonesty of the settlers themselves:

> The settlers do not seem to be to blame in going on and occupying the lands as they did. . . . I hope you will be very careful that the railroad company does not charge them for their improvements, but lets them have the land at the same price that the company would have sold them for before they were occupied.[139]

For whatever reason, a tough line was taken. On May 11, 1880, United States Marshal Alonzo W. Poole and William H. Clark, a railroad agent, armed with a Circuit Court writ ordering the settlers off the land, attempted to dispossess some of them. A gunfight broke out which left eight men dead or wounded: everyone shot eventually died of his wounds.[140] Mills D. Hartt, one of the land purchasers who was considered a tool of the railroad, was one of those killed in the battle.[141]

When the gunfight erupted at Hanford, Stanford was on an eastbound train. He checked into the Windsor Hotel in New York on May 15 and sailed for Europe on May 22.[142] President Crocker of the Southern Pacific Railroad was in San Francisco at the time of the shooting. He wrote to Huntington two days afterward describing the events leading up to the battle and the results of the shootout.[143] Meanwhile, Marshal Poole had returned to San Francisco, Crocker said, and he was having a consultation with him later in the day to decide on the next step to be taken.

---

[137]Brown, *The Mussel Slough Tragedy*, 58; Bean, *California*, 227.   [138]CPH to MH, Apr 10, 1876.
[139]CPH to Henry E. Huntington, Oct 19, 1893.
[140]*SF Call*, May 12 and 13, 1880; *Sac Record-Union*, May 12 and 13, 1880; Thomas Thompson, *Official Historical Site Map of Tulare County, Compiled, Drawn and Published from Personal Examinations and Surveys* (Tulare: THT, 1892); Brown, *The Mussel Slough Tragedy*, 25, 61, and 69; Smith, *Garden of the Sun*, 271.
[141]*SF Call*, May 14, 1880; *Sac Record-Union*, May 14, 1880.   [142]*NY Times*, May 15 and 22, 1880.
[143]CC to CPH, May 13, 1880.

Crocker took a strong, no-compromise position against the farmers. He shared his feelings with Huntington:

> The whole party of the Leaguers, [*sic*] are now in contempt of the U.S. District Court, and also criminals in having obstructed a U.S. Marshal in serving a writ, and all of them are liable to heavy fines and imprisonment in the State Penitentiary for six years, if the Court so decrees.
>
> I propose to see that they are brought up & punished, & unless you say to the contrary, I shall go on prosecuting our rights, and get possession of our property.[144]

Frank Pixley's *San Francisco Argonaut* agreed with the position Crocker had taken. The real issue in the fray, according to an *Argonaut* editorial, was not whether the railroad authorities acted honestly or generously, not whether the settlers had equities, not whether the members of the league did or did not fire the first shot— these were all questions "secondary and unimportant." The real issue was that the members of the Tulare league had "declared war against the United States of America and had inaugurated it by setting at defiance the decree of a United States court—resisting its powers, and by armed violence opposing the service of its mandate by a United States marshal."[145]

Ultimately, of the eleven settlers indicted for obstructing and conspiring to obstruct an officer of the law in execution of his duties, only seven were brought to trial.[146] They were tried in the United States Circuit Court in San Francisco, Judges Ogden Hoffman and Lorenzo Sawyer presiding. Jury selection was completed on November 30, and the verdict rendered on December 23, 1880.[147] Charges against one of the prisoners were dropped two weeks into the trial.[148]

Six defendants were found guilty on the first charge. A new trial was ordered for one of the prisoners, but there is no record of its ever being held.[149] The other five convicted men were sentenced to eight months in prison and a $300 fine plus costs. They were incarcerated in the Santa Clara County jail in San José.[150] The other farmers either moved away or paid the railroad's price.

Following the Mussel Slough incident, the Central Pacific/Southern Pacific Associates continued to lose the public's esteem. Anti-railroad activity became a powerful force in California politics for the next thirty years, and the events at Mussel Slough became the rallying cry of the enemies of the Southern Pacific. Popular, fictionalized versions of the Mussel Slough tragedy were broadcast for generations by authors like Josiah Royce in his *Feud of Oldfield Creek: A Novel of California Life*, and by Frank Norris in *The Octopus*.[151]

---

[144]Ibid. It was business as usual for CC. See letter and telegrams to CPH, May 19 and 20, 1880.

[145]*SF Argonaut*, May 22, 1880.   [146]Brown, *The Mussel Slough Tragedy*, 89.

[147]Smith, *Garden of the Sun*, 279.   [148]Brown, *The Mussel Slough Tragedy*, 93.   [149]Ibid., 95.

[150]For a summary of the trial and of the trial judge's controversial charge to the jury, see *Sac Record-Union*, Jan 22, 1881, and *SF Call*, Dec 2, 1880.

[151]Josiah Royce, *The Feud of Oldfield Creek: A Novel of California Life* (Boston: HMC, 1887), and Norris, *The Octopus*.

The Mussel Slough Prisoners

experienced one of the most bizarre imprisonments on record. They were placed behind bars for eight months at the San José jail, but were given the key to the front door of the jail and allowed to attend church and lodge meetings in town. One prisoner, in ill health, was allowed to live in San José so long as he reported daily to the jail. A recently married settler brought his wife with him and they honeymooned in jail. The other married men were joined by their wives and children and were given three rooms over the jail for keeping house. The one bachelor among them married the jailer's daughter on the day the men were set free![a]

When released, at midnight on September 23, 1881, the convicts were guests of honor at a huge barbecue given by the city and were then escorted to the city limits by the San José municipal band. In Hanford, on October 6, 1881, they were welcomed by a large and enthusiastic demonstration of three thousand people celebrating their homecoming.[b]

The journey home was made by wagon, not railroad!

[a]Smith, *Garden of the Sun*, 285–287.   [b]*SF Chronicle*, Jan 1, 1882.

On Pardoning the Mussel Slough Prisoners

A concurrent resolution introduced in the California State Legislature asking President Rutherford Hayes for presidential clemency was unsuccessful. The senate adopted the resolution by a vote of twenty-four to four.[a] The assembly adopted the measure four days later.[b]

Though Gov. George C. Perkins had exceeded all his predecessors in issuing pardons, since this was a federal, not a California case, the legislature could not appeal to him for clemency. (During his three years in office he granted 84 pardons to state prison inmates, 129 to county jail prisoners, and he issued 50 commutations and made 2 reprieves.[c])

[a]*CSJ*, 24th Sess., 131 and 157–158 (Jan 26 and 29, 1881).
[b]*CAJ*, 24th Sess., 195, 199, and 204 (Feb 2, 1881); *SF Chronicle*, Jan 27, 1881.
[c]Melendy and Gilbert, *The Governors of California*, 197.

Southern Pacific Construction in New Mexico Territory— October 18, 1880–May 19, 1881

Trains were in operation to San Simon, Arizona Territory, eleven miles from the Arizona and New Mexico border, on September 15, 1880, and eastward into Lordsburg, across the line, on October 18, 1880.[152] From there, construction was carried on by the Southern Pacific Railroad Company of New Mexico, incorporated April 14, 1879, to build across the territory to the Rio Grande.[153] From the Arizona-New Mexico boundary to the Texas border at El Paso was only 167.3 miles.[154] During the seven

---

[152]"From Trail to Rail," Chap. 34, "Southern Pacific Extends Line Over Arizona and New Mexico Into Texas," *SPB* 1928 16 (10): 15.   [153]Ed. commentary, Unmerger Case (*Brief of Defendants*), 37.

[154]*Corporate History of the Central Pacific Railway Company as of June 30, 1916*, 32. The *Corporate History of the Southern Pacific Railroad Company as of June 30, 1916*, 109, sets this distance at 167.45. Lynn Farrar thinks the difference of .5 miles is probably due to line changes at the Rio Grande to force the El Paso & Southwestern Railroad Co. (EP & SW) against the Mexican boundary. Letter to the writer, May 4, 2002.

months it took to build between these two points, most of the correspondence of the Associates dwelt on construction matters they would face after they reached Texas.

The need for concerted effort in their construction was reflected in an early 1881 letter from General Superintendent Alban Towne to Huntington about the progress of one of the Associates' competitors. The Atlantic & Pacific Railroad, he reported, building westward from Albuquerque, was "driving the work with all possible dispatch." The road had about 1,700 men grading, 500 or 600 of them Mormons working under John W. Young. And though the Atlantic & Pacific was not yet building west of Prescott, Arizona, he warned that it was expected soon "to break through to the Needles" at the California state line.[155]

Stanford, too, was doing everything he could to push the Southern Pacific eastward. When Towne suggested to him that they extend the Central Pacific track from Willows to Tehama or to Placerville, Stanford told him that rather than extending the existing road, they should "save all the steel to push on towards the Gulf." Towne complained that Crocker felt the same way: "Mr. Crocker is down at the front, although if he were here I would not get much encouragement, if any, from him, as I know how he feels with regard to further extensions."[156]

Stanford was still elated over what reaching New Orleans would mean to the Southern Pacific and to the country as a whole. He wrote Huntington on February 1, 1881, while the railroad was under construction somewhere between Deming, New Mexico (a town in 1880 named by Leland Stanford for the maiden name of Charles Crocker's wife, Mary Deming),[157] and El Paso, Texas: "When our line is completed through to the Gulf of Mexico, we will have the shortest line for all the country west of the Rocky Mountains to tide water, on the Eastern Coast, and the cheapest route, for all that section of country, to Europe."

The need to complete their own transcontinental railroad and to retain control of it affected the contracts the Associates negotiated with other lines and the way they planned to protect their interests in other companies that were a part of their empire, particularly the Pacific Improvement Company and its railroad construction activities.

On a pending contract Huntington had been negotiating with Col. Thomas Wentworth Peirce[158] of the Galveston, Harrisburg & San Antonio Railroad, Stanford wrote a letter to Huntington that would have important ramifications a few weeks later:

---

[155]ANT to CPH, Jan 20, 1881.   [156]ANT to CPH, Jan 21, 1881.   [157]ANT to CPH, Nov 12, 1880.

[158]The following note is from George Werner to the writer, Sep 28, 2002: "Despite what the Southern Pacific shows in its corporate records, Colonel Thomas Wentworth Peirce spelled his name Peirce. No 'i' before 'e' in this instance. When the family immigrated, the name was spelled Pers and I understand that is how still pronounced in Mass. At some point this spelling was changed from Pers to Peirce. The only station named for him in Texas was originally spelled Peirce Junction, but someone who thought they [sic] knew better changed it to Pierce Junction. The station is now well within the corporate limits of Houston." The name is spelled *Pierce* in the 1915 Unmerger Case and in many SPRR records.

I have received yours of the 14th inst. Enclosing copy of contract with Peirce, the general terms of which are satisfactory, but I think that there should have been a division by five and Mrs. Hopkins one of the parties. Perhaps not too late for this arrangement, and I wish that you would give it consideration.[159]

He went on to say that in his opinion, "so far as we are to meet competition, we cannot push the road to completion too soon." And aside from the question of meeting competition, completing their road "at the earliest day practicable" made good business sense, because of the business that would immediately flow over the completed line. He pointed out that from the 1,250,000-ton wheat crop in California in the 1880 harvest, between 6 and 700,000 tons of the grain was still in the state, largely because of lack of transportation for exporting it to the East.

Stanford underscored Towne's report on the construction of the Atlantic & Pacific between Albuquerque and Prescott, and stressed the need for the Southern Pacific to forge ahead. He suggested that they determine just where the greatest need was for construction and that Strobridge be sent there as soon as possible.[160]

Stanford talked with Crocker about how to speed up construction between El Paso and San Antonio, and then wrote Huntington that he thought they could build east from El Paso very rapidly, providing they had the material for the superstructure.[161] He reminded Huntington, "The ties we can have here; but the iron, chairs and spikes of course you must furnish." Stanford suggested that he send some of the needed materials by the Atchison, Topeka & Santa Fé and perhaps another 5,000 to 10,000 tons by the Isthmus route. He also suggested contracting out the construction of the road from San Antonio westward to the canyon of the Rio Grande. "One thing is certain to my mind," he wrote, "that is, the greatest speed possible in construction is the greatest economy, because we will so much sooner have the use of the entire line through to the Gulf, and because of the advantages it will give us with our rivals."

Crocker wrote Huntington telling him of a recent talk he had with Strobridge about construction east from El Paso: "I think we should make our calculations to build between El Paso and S [sic] Antonio within the next eighteen months. We will have to build about 385 miles from El Paso eastward between now and the first of December."[162] Crocker then suggested that if Huntington would arrange to build westward from San Antonio the two crews could meet in the coming winter. He stressed the necessity of expediting the work as rapidly as possible, "for if the Texas & Pacific people get out there much in advance of us they will have established a line of communication, which it will be hard for us to break up."

Writing again the following day, Crocker gave Huntington several arguments in

---

[159]LS to CPH, Jan 24, 1881.   [160]Ibid.

[161]LS to CPH, Jan 26, 1881.   [162]CC to CPH, Jan 26, 1881.

favor of focusing on building eastward. For one, "We can build cheaper from this end with Chinese labor under the supervision of Strobridge, than can be built from the eastern end with white labor." Moreover, building from the west would give the Central Pacific Railroad a good deal of freight business hauling supplies to the construction site. He repeated that he thought that at least 380 to 400 miles should be built from the western end.[163]

The great issue, Crocker said, was how to get steel. Stanford had told him that Huntington had placed an order for 10,000 tons of English steel. Crocker then suggested by way of a question, "Would it not be well to duplicate that order, and have it come as fast as possible?"

Huntington had written to Crocker suggesting that he move Strobridge to San Antonio to take charge of construction there. Strobridge, Crocker, and Stanford were all against this plan. Crocker explained why: "If he goes east, he cannot take his Chinamen with him. They will not go, and he would have to depend on white labor."[164] Crocker continued:

> Everybody agrees that the weather in that cañon is so intensely hot that work cannot be done there during the summer season. I wrote you [see letter of Jan 26] fully on my return from the front, giving Strobridge's and my views in the matter, and Gov. Stanford agrees with me, that we should try by all means to build from this end to the cañon, during this season. Then Strobridge can take hold of that heavy work during the winter season, and early spring, when it is cool.

In January 1880, when the Southern Pacific was only about halfway across Arizona, the Atchison, Topeka & Santa Fé Railroad picked up half-interest in the Atlantic & Pacific from the cash-poor St. Louis & San Francisco in order to further its plans to build to the Pacific Coast.[165] The interest of the Santa Fé in the Atlantic & Pacific posed a threat to both the Gould lines *and* the Southern Pacific. With the Southern Pacific building across Arizona and then New Mexico, and likely to tie up near El Paso with the Texas & Pacific and block once and for all the entry of the Santa Fé into California, Santa Fé officials decided on a terminus of their line near Deming, New Mexico. There on March 8, 1881, they made a connection with the Southern Pacific, thereby becoming a part of the first southern transcontinental railroad.[166]

Even so, ambitious Santa Fé managers still had their eyes on their own complete transcontinental system, as did the Southern Pacific Associates. This is why in the

---

[163]CC to CPH, Jan 27, 1881.   [164]CC to CPH, Feb 2, 1881.

[165]Joseph Nimmo, Jr., chief, Bur. of Stats., Treas. Dept., *Report on the Internal Commerce of the United States,* 1884, 46, in *HED* 7, Part 2, 48th Cong., 2nd Sess. SSN 2295. Miner, *The St. Louis-San Francisco Transcontinental Railroad,* 121; Bryant, *History of the Atchison, Topeka and Santa Fe Railway,* 85.

[166]Edward Chambers, VP of the ATSF, test., Unmerger Case, III R. 939–941 (*Brief of Defendants*), 191; Bryant, *History of the Atchison, Topeka and Santa Fe Railway,* 79.

fall of 1881 Gould and Huntington agreed on a joint purchase of the Frisco line as a means of stopping their common rival—the Atlantic & Pacific—at Needles.[167]

Still hopeful of working out a compromise with the Atlantic & Pacific Railroad in case the arrangement with Gould failed to stop that road, on January 10, 1882, the Southern Pacific Associates bought a controlling interest in the St. Louis & San Francisco Railway, which held half-interest in the Atlantic & Pacific. The Santa Fé owned the other half.[168]

A top-level meeting of all railroads and parties concerned was held in St. Louis on January 27, 1882, at a time when the Southern Pacific was building eastward about one hundred miles beyond Sierra Blanca. The importance of the meeting was described graphically by railroad historian Craig Miner when he wrote that Charles Rogers (Frisco line superintendent intent on protecting the independence of his railroad) must have been dizzied as he attended the January 27 meeting and watched four new directors take their places on the St. Louis & San Francisco Railway Company. They were Huntington, Jay Gould, Russell Sage, and Leland Stanford, who had returned only a month and a half earlier from his second trip to Europe.[169]

Control of the St. Louis & San Francisco and its half-interest in the Atlantic & Pacific with the Santa Fé stopped the Atlantic & Pacific at Needles.[170]

The Atlantic & Pacific was finally allowed to enter California by connecting with a Southern Pacific branch from Mojave; this connection was made on August 3, 1883, with the opening of a pile bridge across the Colorado River to Needles.[171] This arrangement prompted the California Railroad Commissioners to comment, "From and since October 1, 1884, the Atlantic and Pacific Railroad Company, a foreign corporation, . . . has operated the Southern Pacific Railroad, Colorado Division . . . in this State."[172] (The 1884 date was when an agreement to lease the Mojave-Needles line to the Atlantic & Pacific became effective.) But Huntington knew the Atlantic & Pacific was in serious financial trouble; and even though authorized to offer service to San Francisco, the road was operating at a sizable deficit.[173]

After years of fighting, in April 1884 the Southern Pacific agreed to sell its interest in the Atlantic & Pacific to the Santa Fé.[174] Until clear title could be vouchsafed, in August the Southern Pacific agreed to a temporary lease of the Mojave-Needles

[167]Bryant, *History of the Atchison, Topeka and Santa Fe Railway*, 91.

[168]Miner, *The St. Louis-San Francisco Transcontinental Railroad*, 131.

[169]Ibid., 137; SL & SF Railway Co., Minutes of the Board of Directors, Jan 27, 1882. Frisco Archives.

[170]Miner, *The St. Louis-San Francisco Transcontinental Railroad*, 131.

[171]Bryant, *History of the Atchison, Topeka and Santa Fe Railway*, 90. The details of this arrangement are spelled out in *HED* 7, Part 2, 48th Cong., 2 Sess. (Dec 1, 1884–Mar 3, 1885), printed as Nimmo, *Report on the Internal Commerce of the United States*, 1–63. See art. in the *SF Call*, Apr 7, 1883.

[172]CRC, *Fifth Annual Report of the Board of Railroad Commissioners*, 16.

[173]Bryant, *History of the Atchison, Topeka and Santa Fe Railway*, 92.   [174]Ibid.

line to the Atlantic & Pacific—effective on October 1.[175] As part of the package, the Santa Fé was given trackage rights to San Francisco.[176] On December 27, 1911, the sale of the road from Mojave to Needles was finally made to the California, Arizona & Santa Fe Railway Company for $30,000 per mile.[177]

Southern Development Company—January 31, 1881

Texas law prohibited construction in the state by any non-Texas company, so before the Associates could build in Texas, they had to organize a construction company that could work in that state.

The Associates had discussed bringing Thomas Peirce into their organization as a possible way of solving this problem. Stanford warned Huntington that negotiations with Peirce for control of the Galveston, Harrisburg & San Antonio line would require a stock transfer with the Pacific Improvement Company and other companies.

Stanford rejected this transfer of stock. Because of the Pacific Improvement Company's large assets and liabilities, he thought that Peirce should not be taken in; instead, he suggested an alternate plan: the best way to handle the problem would be to create a new organization and make Peirce a stockholder in it.[178]

Three days later he informed Huntington how they [he does not identify the others, but presumably it was Stanford and Crocker] proposed doing this:

> We are today organizing a new Construction Company to be known as the Southern Development Company. . . .

Texas Railroad Law

"Texas law since the mid-1850s required that all railroads operating in Texas must be incorporated in and have their headquarters in the State. These prohibitions were made a part of the State Constitution of 1876. Thus the Southern Pacific companies were all foreign organizations and had no legal right to operate or own track in Texas. The entire railroad east of the center of the Rio Grande was built under the charter of the Galveston, Harrisburg & San Antonio and owned by that company. This includes a section between the center of the river and El Paso. Thus the inclusion of the Texas companies in the Omnibus Lease of 1885 was illegal, and the State forced the Southern Pacific Company to relinquish the lease of the GH & SA and the Texas & New Orleans. These companies continued to be operated by their own forces until 1927 when the T & NO [Texas & New Orleans] leased all the major SP properties in Texas and Louisiana and then merged them in 1934. The T & NO itself continued to be an operating company until 1961 when, with the approval of the Interstate Commerce Commission and legal precedence, the Texas properties were merged into the Southern Pacific. This marked the first time that there was one corporate entity between San Francisco and New Orleans. While the president of the Southern Pacific was the president of the Texas companies, there really was an iron curtain at El Paso dividing the Atlantic and Pacific systems of the Southern Pacific Company."*

*George Werner to the writer, Sep 28, 2002.

---

[175]Nimmo, *Report on the Internal Commerce of the United States*, 45.

[176]Bryant, *History of the Atchison, Topeka and Santa Fe Railway*, 92.

[177]File No. A. 13893, *Corporate History of the Southern Pacific Railroad Company*, 130. Purchase price: Bryant, *History of the Atchison, Topeka and Santa Fe Railway*, 92. [178]LS to CPH, Jan 28, 1881, translation of coded telegram.

The objects declared in the articles of incorporation are as general as those of the Pacific Improvement Company. After the Company is formed and officers elected we will have drawn contracts such as you have sent here for the construction of the road between El Paso and San Antonio, and properly signed by the Company and sent on for the signature of the G. H. and S. A. Ry Co. [Galveston, Harrisburg & San Antonio Railway Company]. One-quarter of the stock, as soon as it can all be issued, will be sent on to be handed to Mr. Pierce [*sic*] or his representative; but I think, as I wrote you before, that this stock ought to be divided into five parts, and Mrs. Hopkins, yourself, Mr. Crocker and myself should each have a fifth interest. When I was over on your side and met Mr. Pierce [*sic*], I remember a conversation that you and I had with him, when it was left optional with us whether we should have a three-quarters interest or a four-fifths interest, and it is possible that Mr. Pierce [*sic*] would now be willing that the interests should be fifths instead of quarters. If so, I recommend that you make the arrangement accordingly.

We shall lose no time in occupying the strategic points East of El Paso.[179]

The articles of incorporation of the Southern Development Company were signed January 31, 1881, and filed with the State of California soon afterward.[180] To do business in Texas (and Louisiana), the company had to have a headquarters in Texas.[181] All of the new company's construction was east of the Rio Grande.[182] It

CPRR, SPRR, AND SPC CONSTRUCTION COMPANIES

1. Charles Crocker & Company
   Dec 24–26, 1862–Oct 28, 1867 (presumed date of dissolution).
2. Contract & Finance Company
   Oct 28, 1867–(dissolved in 1874).
3. Western Development Company
   Dec 15, 1874–Jun 30, 1906 (see note 54).
4. Pacific Improvement Company
   Nov 4, 1878–(dissolved 1966).
5. Southern Development Company
   Jan 31, 1881–(not dissolved, see note in text).*

*Since companies sometimes died a natural death without legal process, and sometimes two companies may have overlapped one another in time, dates of dissolution may be arbitrary or presumptive.

[179]LS to CPH, Jan 31, 1881.

[180]Arts. of Inc. of the SDC, signed Jan 31, endorsed with the clerk of the CCSF, Feb 1, filed Feb 3, 1881. File 12626, CSA.   [181]Lynn Farrar to the writer, Sep 16, 2002.

[182]Daggett is wrong in thinking that the SDC "became responsible for construction east of the Ariz. state [*sic*] line when the Pacific Improvement Company left the field." *Chapters on the History of the Southern Pacific*, 135.

PACIFIC IMPROVEMENT COMPANY

managers decided in 1900 to liquidate the corporation.[a]

San Francisco banker William H. Crocker asked Samuel F. B. Morse—described as a "fifth cousin twice removed" from the famous inventor of the Morse Code—to liquidate the money-losing company.[b] In April 1915, Morse was made general manager of the company for this purpose. A "Certificate of Dissolution of Pacific Improvement Company to wind up and dissolve" was filed on November 1, 1966, and the final Certificate on December 9.[c]

On August 16, 1968, Stanford University received its last check from Pacific Improvement Company funds.[d]

[a]Edward Scott, *A Time for Recollection. A Tribute to Samuel F. B. Morse, Whose Dedicated Purpose for more than Half-a-Century Has Been the Preservation of Del Monte Forest* (Crystal Bay, Tahoe, Nev.: STPC, 1969), [1]. Also, Special Report on the Liquidation of Pacific Improvement Company and of Affiliated Companies, Oct 31, 1923, 3. Pacific Improvement Company Records. SUA.   [b]Inter. with Elmer Lagorio, Oct 24, 2002.
[c]In CSA and SUA.
[d]David S. Jacobson, LSJU sec., to Mrs. Margaret Cordellos, PIC sec., Aug 20, 1968.

was similar in most respects in operation and management to the first three construction companies through which the Associates had operated, but its reasons for being founded were entirely different. It did not in any sense supersede the Pacific Improvement Company.

On June 10, 1881, five months after the incorporation of the Southern Development Company, all construction equipment, including ties, rails, wagons, and horses, were sold by the Pacific Improvement Company to the Southern Development Company for $561,721.28.[183]

Meanwhile, the Texas & Pacific was moving westward from Dallas as rapidly as possible to check the Southern Pacific's incursion into Texas. Construction under the corporate name of Southern Pacific ended at El Paso (actually, in the middle of the Rio Grande) and at that point construction across Texas was carried on by the Associates' Southern Development Company, under the auspices of the Galveston, Harrisburg & San Antonio.[184] Huntington had bought some shares in this company in 1877.[185]

---

[183]SDC, meeting of the board of directors, Jun 10, 1881. The directors listed the assets sold and their prices.

[184]May 19, 1881, date used in *USPRC*, Report of Accountants, Exhibit 35, VIII, 4749. The eastern portion of the GH & SA, from Harrisburg, near Houston, to Richmond had been built between 1851 and 1855 by the Buffalo Bayou, Brazos & Colorado Railroad Company (BBB & CRC) and therefore formed the oldest link in the completed SP transcontinental. "From Trail to Rail," Chap. 36, "Completion of 'Sunset Route' from Pacific Coast to Gulf of Mexico: Race with Texas and Pacific East of El Paso," *SPB* 1928 (12): 12.

[185]"From Trail to Rail," Chap. 36, "Completion of 'Sunset Route' from Pacific Coast to Gulf of Mexico," 12.

Southern Pacific Construction in Texas— May 1881–January 12, 1883

The Southern Pacific had reached El Paso on May 19, 1881, and soon thereafter entered into a major agreement with the Galveston, Harrisburg & San Antonio, which had been in San Antonio since February 5, 1877.[186] With visions of what becoming a part of a transcontinental railroad would do to its profits and image, on July 5, 1881, this road contracted to let the Southern Development Company build its road westward from San Antonio and connect up with the Southern Pacific moving eastward.[187]

In May 1881, Strobridge began laying rails eastward from El Paso "under the auspices of the Galveston, Harrisburg, and San Antonio Railroad."[188] While Strobridge worked on the Texas line of the Southern Pacific a station was briefly named there for him.[189] The town of "Strobridge," pronounced and spelled "Strawbridge" by locals—about halfway between El Paso and San Antonio—was renamed Sanderson in 1882, in honor of Thomas P. Sanderson, construction engineer when the line was being built.[190]

The eastward-driving Southern Pacific (always building under the auspices of the Galveston, Harrisburg & San Antonio) reached Sierra Blanca, Texas, about eighty miles east of El Paso, on November 25, 1881.[191] On the following day Huntington and Jay Gould, who had succeeded Tom Scott as head of the Texas & Pacific, signed an agreement whereby the Texas & Pacific was given trackage rights over Southern Pacific rails from Sierra Blanca to El Paso in exchange for dropping suits against the Southern Pacific for alleged usurpation of its right-of-way to El Paso.[192] The Texas & Pacific and the Southern Pacific made connection at 6 P.M. December 1, 1881.[193] Thus ended the Texas & Pacific's dream of its own railroad to San Diego, though its connection with the Southern Pacific made it part of the second southern transcontinental line.

The Southern Pacific did not stop at Sierra Blanca, but continued to press eastward to meet the Galveston, Harrisburg & San Antonio.[194] Two weeks later it was already fifty miles east of where it was joined to the Texas & Pacific.[195]

California newspapers followed closely the construction of the southern

[186]Ibid.

[187]Minute Book, Boston Board of Directors, G.H. & S.A. (1870–1881), Jul 5, 1881, in James Baughman, *Charles Morgan and the Development of Southern Transportation* (Nashville: VUP, 1968), 223 n33.

[188]Jack Skiles, *Judge Roy Bean Country* (Lubbock: TTUP, 1996), 63.

[189]Lynn Farrar to the writer, Sep 16, 2002.   [190]George Werner to the writer, Sep 28, 2002.

[191]"From Trail to Rail," Chap. 36, "Completion of 'Sunset Route' from Pacific Coast to Gulf of Mexico," 13.

[192]Ibid.

[193]*El Paso Lone Star*, Dec 3, 1881; George Werner to the writer, Sep 28, 2002; ANT to CPH, Dec 2, 1881, reports that the railroads tied up at seven o'clock that evening.   [194]*Galveston Daily News*, Dec 2, 1881.

[195]*El Paso Lone Star*, Dec 17, 1881.

transcontinental. In March 1882 the *Sacramento-Record Union* published a detailed account of the progress being made building across Texas:

> The Southern Pacific Railroad [*sic*] is being built through Texas as rapidly as possible. Two construction gangs, consisting in all of 2,000 men, are at work; one having started from El Paso, and the other working westward from San Antonio. It is thought that these two divisions will meet at the Pecos river [*sic*], which is about 130 miles from San Antonio and 400 miles from El Paso. On the El Paso end of the line over 253 miles of track have been completed, and the work is going on at the rate of about a mile and a half a day. The country is wild and mountainous; deep ravines and gullies abound, and mountain streams run through precipitous canyons. A still worse country for railroad work will be met with in about thirty days, if the present rate of construction is maintained, but the engineers will continue to push steadily forward as fast as possible. English steel rails are used in the construction of this road, and most of the supplies are brought from this city [Sacramento]. A few things are obtained from Los Angeles and the southern country, and some hay and forage for the stock are obtained by the men from the country through which they are passing.[196]

Officials of both the Southern Pacific and the Galveston, Harrisburg & San Antonio were anxious to finish the project as quickly as possible. On April 17, 1882, Crocker, Gray, Hood, and Strobridge of the eastward-moving Southern Pacific crew met with Jim Converse, chief engineer of the eastern road, for an inspection tour of the construction site.[197] Col. Thomas Peirce made a similar inspection on May 22. Both inspections were done with a view to finding a way to hasten the meeting of the two construction crews. Strobridge's crew of five hundred Caucasians and three thousand Chinese laborers reached Sanderson, Texas, in May 1882.[198]

In the spring of 1882 a baseless rumor was spread in San Francisco that Stanford was about to retire from active management of the Central Pacific Railroad. The editor of the *San Francisco Call* made this retirement sound more like a foregone conclusion than just the rumor it was, when he wrote:

> Important changes, which have been pending in the management of the Central Pacific Railroad for some time, were completed yesterday. It is probable that Governor Stanford will retire from the active management of the road, and that hereafter A. N. Towne, who has been appointed General Manager, will be invested with all the power heretofore centred [*sic*] in the Governor. Mr. Towne has long been the Chief Executive officer of the Company, but following the example of a number of the Eastern corporations, the railroad officials have concluded to remove from the shoulders of the President of the Company the open management of its affairs, and have, consequently, reorganized the personnel of the management.[199]

Stanford, of course, did not retire.

---

[196]*Sac Record-Union*, Mar 22, 1882.

[197]*San Antonio Daily Express*, Jun 1, 1882. LS had just returned from Europe the previous month and in Apr was planning a trip to his Vina Ranch.   [198]Skiles, *Judge Roy Bean Country*, 77.

[199]*SF Call*, May 5, 1882.

In the summer of 1882 Crocker and his wife, with daughter Hattie and son William, abandoned the business of railroad building for a much-needed, four-month-long vacation in Europe. They left San Francisco for New York on May 25 or June 2, the record is unclear.[200] They sailed from New York on the *Celtic* on July 5, 1882.[201] After tours of London, Norway, and Russia, they were ready to return home.[202] The Crockers left Liverpool on the *Celtic* on October 31, and sailed into New York on November 10, 1882.[203]

Meanwhile, crews of the Southern Pacific building eastward from El Paso and of the Galveston, Harrisburg & San Antonio driving westward from San Antonio met on January 12, 1883, 227 miles west of San Antonio, or, as a San Francisco newspaper described the site, "in the southwestern part of Texas, about 490 miles from the bridge across the El Paso river, near a tributary of the Rio Grande, called Devil's river."[204] The junction was made exactly two and a half miles west of the old Pecos River bridge. The nearest station was called Painted Cave.[205] It was there that Thomas Peirce "drove a silver spike in the last tie and the 'Sunset Route' became a reality."[206]

The celebrants did not include Stanford, who was very ill in New York and trying to leave the country for a European health tour. Crocker was also in New York.[207]

In anticipation of the opening of the railroad for westward travel, it was announced that the first Southern Pacific train from New Orleans would reach San Antonio on January 31 and leave the next morning for San Francisco.[208] The first through train from Galveston to San Francisco passed through El Paso on February 2, 1883.[209]

The line from California to New Orleans was made up of eight different railroads.[210] And with transshipment at New Orleans for either New York or Europe by ship, it really was a transcontinental line.

OTHER TRANSCONTINENTAL RAILROADS

There were other parallel railroads across the North American continent—the Northern Pacific, the Canadian Pacific Railway, and later the Great Northern. All of them posed some threat to the Central/Southern Pacific Associates' rail system. The Canadian Pacific was especially dangerous to them, since it was subsidized by the British government and, therefore, was free of the restrictions of the American

[200]The *SF Argonaut*, Jun 3, 1882, says "Mr. and Mrs. Charles Crocker and daughter left for the East and Europe last Thursday for several months." The *Argonaut* was pub. on Sat., so the meaning of "last Thursday" is unclear.

[201]*NY Times*, Jul 6, 1882.   [202]*SF Argonaut*, Oct 28, 1882.

[203]*NY Times*, Nov 11, 1882.   [204]*SF Chronicle*, Jan 13, 1883.

[205]"From Trail to Rail," Chap. 36, "Completion of 'Sunset Route' from Pacific Coast to Gulf of Mexico," 13.

[206]Ibid.   [207]*SF Chronicle*, Jan 18, 1873.   [208]*El Paso Lone Star*, Jan 27, 1883.

[209]Ibid., Feb 3, 1883. Ed. commentary, Unmerger Case (*Brief of Defendants*), 38.

[210]The seven companies listed in SPRR records omitted the Louisiana Extension Co., in Texas, that connected the Louisiana Western with the T & NO.

Interstate Commerce Act passed in 1887.[211] This line was willing to join an American railroad pool, but insisted that it be given special consideration because the circuitous route it had to take to deliver goods in San Francisco made it the slowest of the transcontinentals. In 1888 the American roads agreed to its terms and the Canadian line joined the newly-organized pool.[212]

Stanford complained that in one year alone his railroad had lost a million dollars in net earnings because of competition from other transcontinental lines.[213] He was especially bitter about government grants to the Northern Pacific—which completed its transcontinental line into Portland, Oregon, in 1883. This, he insisted, was a violation of the spirit of the government's assistance grant to the Central Pacific and Union Pacific railroads.

Stanford, Huntington, and Crocker argued that government assistance in building the transcontinental railroad had been designed to attract investors, but now those who invested because of this inducement were being injured by competing roads, also assisted by the government. Investors had assumed, with good reason, that the Pacific railroad—which *they* helped finance—would be the only government-aided transcontinental line and that it would get all the cross-country business.[214] Thus, the government had violated the terms of this arrangement when it subsequently aided three other Pacific roads, giving them twice the land grants awarded the Central Pacific. To make matters worse, all the lands that these roads traversed were more valuable than those through which the Central Pacific had to build. Central Pacific president Stanford thought it only fair that these investors be reimbursed by the government for all losses sustained because of other assisted roads.[215]

Stanford was also piqued by the fact that other government-aided roads had hesitated—in fact, had made no move at all—until the Central Pacific had demonstrated the practicability of operating a through road; the Central was a true pioneer road whose success encouraged others to enter the field.[216] That the other roads were now receiving special consideration from the government after their past hesitation to risk anything was particularly galling to him.

ORGANIZATION OF THE SOUTHERN PACIFIC COMPANY
OF KENTUCKY—1884–1885

The arrangement made on January 1, 1880, leasing the Southern Pacific Railroad to the Central Pacific for five years, had given the Associates a fixed profit off their

---

[211] James O'Meara, "The Union or the Dominion?" *OM* 1889 14 (82): 419–420.

[212] For an explanation of the rate wars, see Grodinsky, *Transcontinental Railway Strategy*, 328–330.

[213] LS test., *USPRC*, V, 2475 and 2752. [214] LS inter. with *Cincinnati Inquirer*, Feb 18, 1887.

[215] LS test., *USPRC*, V, 2752–2753. [216] Ibid., V, 2757.

Southern Pacific Railroad holdings.[217] But by 1884 the economic prospects of this road looked so bright that they became dissatisfied with the old arrangement. A key factor in their decision to reorganize their railroad holdings was that Central Pacific stock was selling so well that they no longer held a majority of it.[218] It was estimated that their combined holdings amounted to less than 30 percent.[219] In contrast, the three Associates and the Hopkins estate still owned almost all of the Southern Pacific Railroad stock as late as 1885. Another reason for the reorganization was that the Southern Pacific was at the point of cashing in on the lucrative transcontinental business. Stanford explained to the Pacific Railway Commissioners in 1887 that the Southern Pacific had become so large and its interests so varied that the smaller Central Pacific could no longer control it, thus the relative position of the two railroads had reversed.[220] This and other factors led in 1884 to the creation of the Southern Pacific Company, a holding company, not itself a railroad until much later.

The most authoritative and detailed account of the creation of the Southern Pacific Company is found in Timothy Hopkins' testimony in the 1915 Unmerger Case, which covered in painstaking detail the steps taken between March 17, 1884, and April 1, 1885, for the organization of the Southern Pacific Company, for the termination of leases held by the Central Pacific Railroad, and for the leasing of the Central Pacific and Southern Pacific lines to the new Southern Pacific Company.[221]

One of the best kept "open" railroad secrets of 1884—which was no secret at all to anyone who read the newspapers or followed the happenings in railroad circles—must have been the creation in Kentucky of the Southern Pacific Company. A Kentucky bill to incorporate the new company in that state was signed into law by Gov. J. Proctor Knott on March 17, 1884.[222] The law was simple, requiring only that the new corporation maintain an office in the state and that a clerk or assistant clerk be a resident of Kentucky. The law allowed the company to keep offices at such places outside the state as the board of directors might from time to time require.[223]

---

[217]A copy of this lease is in *HED 60*, 49th Cong., 1st Sess., 2. SSN 2398.

[218]George T. Klink test., in Unmerger Case, II. 613–618. Klink became a clerk in the accountant dept. of the CPRR in 1883 and was appointed auditor of disbursements for the SPC in 1885, a position he held until 1904. Unmerger Case (*Brief of Defendants*), 70. See more on Klink in the *SF Chronicle*, Jan 12, 1905. MH died on Mar 29, 1878.

[219]Daggett, *Chapters on the History of the Southern Pacific*, 147–148.

[220]LS test., *USPRC*, VI, 3616.

[221]TNH test., summarized in Unmerger Case (*Brief of Defendants*), 77ff.

[222]Carol Parris, Law Librarian, Univ. of Ky., to the writer, Jan 30, 2002. Chap. 403, *An Act to incorporate the Southern Pacific Company, Acts of the General Assembly of the Commonwealth of Kentucky, Passed at the Regular Session of the General Assembly, which was begun and held in the City of Frankfort on Monday, the thirty-first Day of December, Eighteen Hundred and eighty-three* (Frankfort: Ky. Yeoman Office, 1884), I, 725–728. A copy of this law is in *HED 60*, 49th Cong., 1st Sess., 6. SSN 2398. The CRC recognizes Mar 17, 1884, as the inc. and official date of the SPC, not early 1885, when the operation of the co. was agreed upon. CRC, *Seventh Annual Report of the Board of Railroad Commissioners*, 322.

[223]Chapter 403, "An Act to incorporate the Southern Pacific Company," 728.

Bibliographical Note on the Unmerger Case

What is generally known as the Unmerger Case was the *United States of America versus Southern Pacific Company, Central Pacific Railroad* [Rail*way* after 1899], *and Union Trust Company of New York*, United States District Court, District of Utah, Case No. 3575 (Equity Case 420), Entry 3, "Combined Bankruptcy, Civil, and Criminal Case Files, 1880–1931," National Archives and Records Administration, Rocky Mountain Region, Denver.

Timothy Hopkins' testimony begins on March 9, 1915, Box 370, Vol. 16, 1300–1390. The essence of Hopkins' testimony is summarized in Unmerger Case (*Brief of Defendant*), 77ff.

This case was filed on February 11, 1914, under the antitrust law of 1890 to compel the separation of the Central Pacific Railroad from the Southern Pacific Company. In the course of the testimony, the history of the Central Pacific Railroad, the Southern Pacific Railroad, and the Southern Pacific Company was discussed in considerable detail. The 1914 Unmerger Case is synopsized in the one-volume *Brief of Defendants*. The charter of the Southern Pacific Company is in Haney, *Congressional History, 1850–1887*, 134–137.

The best brief analyses of the case are found in two pamphlets published in 1922. One was written by Stuart Daggett, "The Southern Pacific Unmerger: Judicial Proceedings for the Separation of the Central Pacific and Southern Pacific Railroad Lines," *University of California Chronicle*, October 22, 1922 24 (4): 465–496; reprinted as a 32-page pamphlet of the same title (Berkeley?: [n.p.], 1922). The second was written by Fred G. Athearn, *The Separation of The Central Pacific and The Southern Pacific Railroads: A Plain Statement of the Facts* (SF: Union Pacific Railroad, 1922).

It was explained that Huntington incorporated this holding company in Kentucky so that California lawsuits could be handled in federal rather than state courts.[224]

Leland Stanford, having returned to New York from Europe less than three months earlier with the body of his dead son, spent the week of August 4, 1884, at the Long Branch Hotel.[225] He was only one of many senior Central Pacific officials making their way quietly to the nation's financial and business capital. The *Argonaut* reported that there would be a sizeable number of Central Pacific officials in New York after those on the way and those still to leave San Francisco reached there. The gathering of Central Pacific Railroad officers in New York in late August gave rise to a spate of speculative newspaper articles.

Obviously a high-level Central Pacific Railroad business meeting was in the making, the nature of which was not released to the press, though what it was all about was in no way concealed from outsiders.[226]

---

[224]George T. Klink test., Unmerger Case, II R. 621–622, in Daggett, *Chapters on the History of the Southern Pacific*, 151 n21.   [225]*SF Argonaut*, Aug 9, 1884.   [226]Ibid., Aug 23, 1884.

Rumor had it at the time that the Stanfords planned to move their permanent residence to New York.[227]

The impressive list of Central Pacific officials already in the East or on the way to the meeting included:

> Leland Stanford, President
> Collis P. Huntington, Vice-President
> Charles Crocker, Second Vice-President
> Timothy Hopkins, Treasurer
> Alban Towne, General Manager
> John Christian Spayd Stubbs, Freight Traffic Manager
> Theodore H. Goodman, General Ticket Agent.[228]

Timothy Hopkins tells of having received a telegram from Stanford, who was already in New York, summoning him from San Francisco to attend a meeting. He left for the East in the latter part of July and found Stanford, Huntington, and Crocker already busy on the matters at hand. There he learned that the purpose of the meeting was to go over railroad affairs in general and to take up the question of the organization of a new company for the purpose of holding and operating the railroad companies owned and controlled by the Central/Southern Pacific Associates, those under the management of the Central Pacific, and those east of El Paso in Texas and Louisiana. This promised to be one of the most far-reaching railroad alignments ever made.[229]

The plan of the new organization and the agenda at the New York conferences are found in the minutes of the meetings kept by William E. Brown, who was appointed secretary.[230] The first matter of business was to find a basis of agreement with Thomas W. Peirce of Boston, a major stockholder in the Galveston, Harrisburg & San Antonio, the Louisiana Western, and the Texas & New Orleans railroads. Apparently Peirce also held 20 percent of the stock in the Associates' Southern Development Company, which had constructed the line in Texas between El Paso and San Antonio; the other 80 percent was held by Huntington, Stanford, Crocker, and the Hopkins estate. As part of the plan they worked out, Peirce was to sell his shares in the Galveston, Harrisburg & San Antonio and of the Texas & New Orleans and be credited for the total amount of these two roads on the books of the Southern Development Company. In addition, Peirce agreed to put in his 28,059 shares of stock in the Galveston, Harrisburg & San Antonio in

[227]Ibid., Oct 18, 1884.
[228]*Illustrated Fraternal Directory including Educational Institutions of the Pacific Coast, giving a Succinct Description of the Aims and Objects of Beneficiary and Fraternal Societies and a Brief Synopsis of the Leading Colleges and Private Seminaries compiled from Official Records and Society Archives* (SF: BC, 1889).
[229]TNH test., Unmerger Case, II R. 655–657 (*Brief of Defendants*), 77–78.
[230]Unmerger Case, V R. 1688 (*Brief of Defendants*), 77.

exchange for 150 shares of the Southern Pacific Company for each 100 shares of the Galveston, Harrisburg & San Antonio stock.[231]

Following the negotiation of this agreement, the Central Pacific officers turned their attention to the organization of the Southern Pacific Company. The minutes of the September 10 meeting described an analysis of all assets and liabilities of the four Associates and estates to determine how they stood financially in undertaking the new railroad alignment. This behind them, at a meeting on the following day the Associates decided on an agenda to discuss the following items:

1. The consolidation of all lines of the Southern Pacific system into one company.
2. The separation of Central Pacific business from Southern Pacific business.
3. The leasing of the Central Pacific system to the new Southern Pacific Company.
4. The general consolidation of all their lines from San Francisco to Newport News (a Huntington proposal).

The main object of the holding company, Hopkins testified, was to take over and operate the entire line from New Orleans to California. When asked why this was necessary, what was wrong with the Central Pacific Railroad Company and its system of leased lines, he answered:

> The Central Pacific leased lines system had become very much smaller than the Southern Pacific [Railroad] Company interests had become; in fact, the Southern Pacific lines, when completed through to New Orleans, were at least twice as long as that of the Central Pacific main lines, and we considered it advisable that as long as the larger interests were concentrated in the Southern Pacific [Railroad] Company, it should be the operating line, and accordingly we discussed and arranged what was considered a fair and equal manner of doing it, and we put that into effect.

At an October 1 meeting the group appointed Leland Stanford a committee of one to formulate a plan for leasing the several roads of the through lines to the Southern Pacific Company.

To help raise money for their ambitious plan, they decided to increase the capital stock of the Southern Pacific Company to $100 million. Hopkins said they had made this decision in the spring of 1884 after the Kentucky legislature had approved their new company. The increase in stock was made at the October 1 meeting, and temporary stock certificates were then issued.

It was decided at the same meeting that the new corporation would have seven directors: C. P. Huntington of New York, Thomas W. Peirce of Boston, and five others to be selected from San Francisco, where the company's general offices would be located.

The group held another meeting on November 5, 1884, at which details of the

---

[231]Peirce (b. Aug 16, 1818) died at age sixty-seven on Oct 2, 1885, not long after these financial arrangements were agreed to. Obit., *Boston Evening Transcript*, May 3, 1885; Mason Hart, in *New Handbook of Texas* (Austin: TSHA, 1996), V, 129–130.

leasing arrangement were worked out and agreed to. Temporarily, the lease payments would be fixed charges, with a guaranteed return of 2 percent on capital
stock per year, and all the earnings of the Central Pacific system over and above that
percentage, until the amount reached 6 percent; any profits above 6 percent would
be paid to the Southern Pacific Company.[232]

Stanford worked hard to create a workable plan of consolidation.[233] Under the
following terms the Southern Pacific Company was deemed fully organized on
February 10, 1885:

1. Beginning February 10, 1885, the Southern Pacific Company became the lessee,
for a term of ninety-nine years, of all the railroad properties of the eight companies (including the often-overlooked Louisiana Western Extension Company)
whose roads made up the Sunset-Gulf route of the Southern Pacific Company.[234]
2. The issuance of the agreed-upon $100 million in capital stock.
3. The Southern Pacific Company would lease the Southern Pacific railroads of California, Arizona, and New Mexico for ninety-nine years, dating from February 10, 1885.
4. On February 17, 1885, the official date of the transaction, the Central Pacific Railroad Company would lease all its properties to the Southern Pacific Company for
ninety-nine years for annual rents of from $1.2 million to $3.6 million, depending
upon its earnings. This lease was to begin on April 1, 1885.[235]

On March 1, 1885, the Southern Pacific Company took over operations of the
Southern Pacific Railroad of California, the Southern Pacific Railroad of Arizona,
and the Southern Pacific of New Mexico. On April 1 it assumed control of the Central Pacific. In addition to those railroads listed above, Stanford later identified the
following lines leased at one time by the Central Pacific and afterward leased by the
Southern Pacific Company:

> Berkeley Branch Railroad Company,
> Northern Railway Company,[236]
> Stockton and Copperopolis Railroad Company,
> San Pablo and Tulare Rail Road Company,
> Amador Branch Railroad Company,
> California Pacific Railroad,
> Southern Pacific Railroad (of California),
> Southern Pacific Railroad (of Arizona),
> Southern Pacific Railroad (of New Mexico),
> The Los Angeles and San Diego Railroad Company, and
> The Los Angeles and Independence Rail Road Company.[237]

[232]TNH test., Unmerger Case, II R. 660–665 (Brief of Defendants), 78–81.   [233]Ibid., 80.
[234]George T. Klink test., Unmerger Case, II R. 666–668 (Brief of Defendants), 81–82.
[235]The lease is in HED 60, 49th Cong., 1st Sess. (Jan 27, 1886), 3–5. SSN, 2398. "Contracts between Southern
Pacific Railroad [sic] and other Companies," 2–5. Exhibit A, Unmerger Case, I R. 13 (Brief of Defendants), 81–82.
[236]Organized by the CPA. Arts. of Inc. of the NRC, signed and filed Jul 19, 1871. File 21, CSA.
[237]LS test., USPRC, V, 2498–2499.

CLAUSES OF THE 1885 LEASE OF CENTRAL PACIFIC PROPERTIES
TO THE SOUTHERN PACIFIC COMPANY

"The said Central Pacific Railroad Company hereby assigns to the said Southern Pacific Company all the leases which it now holds of railroads and other property situated in said State of California and lying and being north of the town of Goshen, in the county of Tulare, with the right to take, hold, operate, maintain, and enjoy said railroads and other property in the same manner as the said Central Pacific Railroad Company holds, operates, enjoys, and maintains the same under the said leases, and with the right to receive the rents, issues, and profits thereof.

"And the said Central Pacific Railroad Company hereby releases the Southern Pacific Railroad Company, a corporation formed and existing under the laws of the United States and of the State of California, and the Southern Pacific Railroad Company, a corporation formed and existing under the laws of the Territory of Arizona, and the Southern Pacific Railroad Company, a corporation formed and existing under the laws of the Territory of New Mexico, and each of them, from all and every obligation under or by virtue of any in every lease made by said three last-mentioned railroad companies, or either of them, to the said Central Pacific Railroad Company, and transfers and surrenders unto the said Southern Pacific Company the possession of all the property in said leases, or any of them, mentioned or described, with the right to receive the rents, issues and profits thereof free from all claim of the said Central Pacific Railroad Company to the same or any part thereof."*

*HED 60, 49th Cong., 1st Sess. (Jan 27, 1886), 3–5.

On February 27, 1885, Leland Stanford issued a circular notice from the Office of the President of the Southern Pacific Company, announcing to all concerned that the new leasing arrangement had been consummated.

Under the terms of this lease, the Central Pacific Railroad Company and the Southern Pacific Railroad—though still retaining their own corporate identities—became operational parts of the system of the new Southern Pacific Company.[238] At a directors' meeting on February 18, 1885, Stanford, still president of the Central Pacific, was named president of the Southern Pacific of Kentucky. Huntington and Crocker were made first and second vice presidents, and Timothy Hopkins—whom Mark Hopkins' widow, Frances Sherwood Hopkins, had officially adopted five years before—was named treasurer. Charles Crocker remained president of the Southern Pacific Railroad of California.

---

[238]*Agreement between the Southern Pacific Company and the Central Pacific Railroad Company, February 17, 1885.* A copy of this lease is in *HED 60*, 49th Cong., 1st Sess., 3–5. SSN 2398.

CIRCULAR NOTICE.
SOUTHERN PACIFIC COMPANY,
Office of the president.
San Francisco, Feb. 27th, 1885.

Arrangements having been effected by the various railway companies interested between San Francisco and New Orleans, comprising the following roads, namely: The Southern Pacific, [sic] of California, Southern Pacific, of Arizona, Southern Pacific, of New Mexico, Galveston, Harrisburg and San Antonio, Louisiana Western, Texas and New Orleans and Morgan's Louisiana and Texas Railway and Steamship Lines, and roads controlled by the said companies, for a unification of their joint administration, and with a view to a more economical working of the properties, it has been decided that on and after March 1st, 1885, these properties will be operated under one general organization, known as the Southern Pacific Company, with headquarters at San Francisco, Cal., divided into two sections; all west of El Paso will be known as the Pacific System and all east thereof as the Atlantic System.

The organization for the administration of the general conduct of the business of the Company will be briefly as follows: Under the direction of the President the General Managers will attend generally to the business of the Company, having the supervision and direction of all the departments of the service of the Company within their respective jurisdictions, the financial and accounting departments excepted, and their orders will be obeyed and respected accordingly.

The Secretary and Controller will have charge of all of the books and accounts, and will, subject to confirmation by the President, nominate and fix the compensation of suitable persons for the heads of the various offices of the accounting department.

The Treasurer will have charge of all revenues of the Company, and will appoint, subject to confirmation by the President, such assistants as may be necessary for the conduct of the business.

The General Traffic Manager, under the direction of the General Manager of the Pacific System, will be charged with handling of all through business of the Company, and that interchanged by, or which may be competitive between, the Pacific and the Atlantic Systems.

OFFICIALS OF THE LINE.

A.N. Towne, General Manager Pacific System, San Francisco, Cal. A.C. Hutchinson, General Manager, Atlantic System, New Orleans, La.

J.C. Stubbs, General Traffic Manager, San Francisco, Cal.

All other officers and agents will be continued on the various roads and divisions as under the previous organization until further notice by the general managers.

LELAND STANFORD, President.*

*Unmerger Case, Pratt Exhibit No. 2, 491–492 (*Brief of Defendants*), 83–84. The purchase of the Morgan Line by Huntington was reported in the *SF Chronicle*, Feb 18, 1883.

THE EXTENT OF THE ASSOCIATES' RAILROAD EMPIRE IN 1885

Between 1881 and 1884 the Associates' railroad empire had grown by leaps and bounds through construction and consolidation. An 1881 editorial sketched the Central Pacific holdings as follows:

> Main line, 833¼ miles; Oregon division, 151½; San Joachin [sic] division, 146½; branches, 35¼; total, 1,216 [sic]; tributary roads, 450½ miles; aggregate, 1,916½.
>
> Besides, there are in progress the Oregon extension, 150 miles; Yosemite Valley extension, 100 miles; total, 250 miles. The company also owns and operates steamer lines on the Sacramento river, 294 miles; on the Colorado river, 365 miles; total, 659 miles of river line. The Southern Pacific system, which is under the same management, now consists of about 1,288 miles completed and 200 in progress, making 1,488 miles. The entire system, therefore, including the mileage now in progress, aggregates 3,404 miles of railway and 659 miles of steamer lines, or 4,063 miles of transportation lines in all.[239]

Before the end of 1884 the Associates owned and controlled more than 5,500 miles of railroad, including all the lines that ran in and out of San Francisco, Sacramento, Stockton, and Los Angeles. The entire broad-gauge system of the state was centralized under one management.

Critics insisted that the management of the system could be, and often was, tyrannical. But had the scattered system been in a dozen different hands, its development might have been sporadic and feeble . . . or a Jay Gould might have stepped in and taken control.

Huntington was not satisfied. He wanted to include some of his own eastern holdings to give him and his partners control of a coast-to-coast line not shared by the Union Pacific and others. But Stanford and Crocker—both more conservative empire builders than Huntington—were against incorporating into their railroad system any roads east of New Orleans.[240] Moreover, by the late seventies Stanford had become involved in extra-railroad activities such as horseracing and winemaking and did not wish to tie up all of his money and time in railroad construction and consolidation.

The Central Pacific Associates owned the new Southern Pacific of Kentucky, so there was no danger on their part of losing money as a result of any curtailment of Central Pacific business to this new transcontinental. Any loss in Central Pacific business would also be a loss in Union Pacific revenue, since that road would handle the eastern portion of transcontinental railroad shipping. As it was, the Central Pacific and the Southern Pacific Railroad Company would not be in competition.

---

[239] *The Railway Age*, Feb 24, 1881, 101.

[240] TNH test., Unmerger Case, II R. 666 (*Brief of Defendants*), 79. The CPH plan to consolidate railroads from SF to Newport News was rejected. See Lavender, *The Great Persuader*, 358.

Stanford himself conceded that these two systems together competed with other railroads, but not with each other.[241] John C. Stubbs, general traffic manager of the Southern Pacific, acknowledged that if the Texas & Pacific had built the southern transcontinental, there would have been no effective check on free competition, thus creating a rivalry that would have hurt the Central Pacific.[242] Control of the Southern Pacific route was all that saved the Central Pacific from extermination, said Stubbs, since competition with the Texas & Pacific would have bankrupted their road.[243] Alban Towne, general manager of the Central Pacific, corroborated Stubbs' assessment. When questioned about what would have happened to the Central Pacific if the Southern Pacific Railroad had been in the hands of competitors, he said that the Central Pacific would have been in the hands of a receiver; it would not have been able to earn sufficient money to pay even its operating expenses and fixed charges. He added that having both railroads under the same management had neutralized the effects of destructive competition.[244]

RAILROADS CONTROLLED AND OPERATED BY THE SOUTHERN PACIFIC COMPANY, JUNE 1885	
	Mileage
Central Pacific R.R.	1,254.24
Northern Ry.	153.63
San Pablo & Tulare R.R.	46.51
Berkeley Branch R.R.	3.84
California Pacific R.R.	115.44
Stockton & Copperopolis R.R.	49.00
Amador Branch R.R.	27.20
Southern Pacific R.R. of California.	552.85
Southern Pacific R.R. of Arizona.	384.25
Southern Pacific R.R. of New Mexico.	167.30
Galves'n, Harrisburg & San Antonio Ry.	936.74
Mexican International, R.R.	171.00
Texas & New Orleans R.R.	105.10
Louisiana Western R.R.	112.00
Morgan's Louisiana & Texas R.R. and Steamship Company.	281.00
Sabine & East Texas R.R.	104.00
Los Angeles & San Diego R.R.	27.60
Los Angeles & Independence R.R.	16.83
Southern Pacific R.R. of Cal. (No. Div.).	202.50
Total Rail Lines	4711.03*

*Unmerger Case, Petitioner's Exhibit No 28, IV R. 1522 (*Brief of Defendants*), 92, excerpted from *Southern Pacific Company Travelers' Official Guide*, Jun 1885, 223.

Charles Crocker also agreed that the Central Pacific needed what the new arrangement offered. He told the Pacific Railway Commissioners in 1887 that the Southern Pacific served as a defense for the Central Pacific, that their sole reason for building the southern line was to protect the Central Pacific. Other than this, he and his partners had no ambition to build the Southern Pacific Railroad.[245]

The Southern Pacific did not hurt the Central Pacific Associates so far as their own personal income was concerned, but it *did* injure the Central Pacific-Union Pacific as a system. Union Pacific president Charles Francis Adams testified in 1887

[241]LS test., *USPRC*, V, 2823–2824.
[243]Ibid., 3389.
[245]CC test., *USPRC*, VII, 3683.
[242]John C. Stubbs test., *USPRC*, VI, 3363.
[244]ANT test., *USPRC*, VI, 3407.

that the earnings of his railroad had been "enormous" until the completion of the Northern Pacific, the Denver and Rio Grande to Ogden, and the Southern Pacific. These lines annually took $4 million worth of business away from his road.[246]

Since the Union Pacific was only one-half of a transcontinental system, one could not expect the Central Pacific Associates to sacrifice their Southern Pacific interests, which they owned outright, for their Central Pacific business; in the latter railroad they owned less than half a company that in itself was only half of a transcontinental network.

As late as 1885 some people believed that Stanford and his partners were on the verge of bankruptcy, owing largely to the fact that the Southern Pacific and Northern Pacific were cutting into their business.[247] Even the Pacific Railway Commissioners, as hostile as they were toward the Associates, conceded that Central Pacific profits had dropped

JOHN C. STUBBS,

general traffic manager of the Central Pacific Railroad, was widely recognized as the greatest traffic man in the country. He began service as a clerk in the freight office of the Central Pacific Railroad Company in Sacramento, soon after the completion of the road. When the general offices of the company were moved to San Francisco in 1873, Stubbs was appointed general freight agent. At that time there were no rules or precedents governing the transportation of overland freight or relating to the construction of freight schedules. It was the duty of Stubbs to make rules, schedules, contracts, etc., and he proved equal to the task. It was not long before he was recognized as the best traffic agent in the country, a reputation which he maintained until he retired from service under pension rules, at which time he was vice president in charge of freight and passenger traffic.*

*Frank Shay, "A Lifetime in California," 222.

considerably after 1883.[248] But Stanford assured the public that there was nothing fundamentally wrong with the soundness of the Central Pacific operation that caused the current decline in prices. He promised that he and his Associates would see to it that their road would not suffer from loss of business taken by the other roads.[249]

In addition to these railroads, the Southern Pacific Company operated Sacramento River steamers, ferry transfer steamers, river steamers and barges, and ocean steamships.

Owing to a business depression and lower rates than customary, the gross earnings in 1885 were less than the year before, but they still exceeded company expectations. Stanford interpreted this as a result of the wisdom of placing several properties under one management company, resulting in greater economy and efficiency and more satisfactory service to the patrons of the railroad.

One of the advantages of the "Sunset Route," which connected with the water

[246]Charles Francis Adams test., *USPRC*, I, 85.
[248]*RUSPRC*, 90.
[247]Ellen M. Colton, in *SF CSTUJ*, Oct 10, 1885.
[249]*Boston Transcript*, May 21, 1883.

Leland Stanford's Summary of the Size and Composition of the Associates' 1885 Railroad Empire, from a Different Perspective

I. The Pacific System (all lines west of El Paso):

A. Central Pacific Railroad and Leased Lines:

	Mileage
Central Pacific Railroad	1,248.60
Berkeley Branch Railroad	3.84
California Pacific Railroad	115.44
Northern Railway	153.63
San Pablo & Tulare Railroad	46.51
Sacramento & Placerville Railroad	5.64

[The distance given here is wrong. CRC, *Ninth Annual Report of the Board of Railroad Commissioners,* 31.]

Stockton & Copperopolis Railroad	49.00
Amador Branch Railroad	27.20
Total	1,649.86

B. Southern Pacific Lines and Leased Properties:

SPRR, California, Northern Division	202.21
SPRR, California, Southern Division	553.36
SPRR, Arizona	383.74
SPRR, New Mexico	171.06
Los Angeles & San Diego Railroad	27.60
LA & Independence Railroad	16.83
Total	1,354.80

II. Atlantic System (all lines east of El Paso):

Galveston, Harrisburg & San Antonio Railway	932.90
Texas & New Orleans Railroad	208.67
Louisiana Western Railroad	112.00
Morgan's Louisiana & Texas Railroad	281.30
Morgan's Louisiana & Texas Steamships	
New York, Texas & Mexican Railway	92.00
Gulf, Western Texas & Pacific Railway	66.00
Total	1,692.87
Grand Total of miles of railroad operated	4,697.53

III. Rolling Stock of the Southern Pacific Company:

Cars	Pacific	Atlantic	Total
Passenger and Officers	261	80	341
Sleeping and Parlor	55	17	72
Excursion	19	—	19
Emigrant Sleeper	96	12	108
Passenger and baggage	2	17	19
Baggage, Mail and Express	109	34	143
Caboose	144	66	210
Box—Freight, Stock, Fruit, etc.	5,010	3,088	8,098
Flat—Freight, Water, Work, etc.	3,340	2,534	5,874
Total	9,036	5,848	14,884
Locomotives (not including dump hand, section, or four-wheeled work cars)	462	204	666*

*Leland Stanford, President, Southern Pacific Company, *Annual Report of the Southern Pacific Company. 1885,* 1–9.

route between New York and New Orleans, was that there was only one transfer required—that from ships to railroad cars at New Orleans. This proved to be one of the company's most popular services to shippers. It carried 70 percent of the Associates' through-freight from New York to San Francisco in 1885.

Stanford pointed out, too, in his 1885 report, that the Southern Pacific Company controlled the shortest transcontinental route. He predicted that with the expected increase in California's population and the construction of additional branch lines and feeders, the business of the company would grow even more.

RAILROAD POOLS AND THE 1887 RATE WAR

From the beginning, the Associates had worked hard to gain control of actual or potential competitors or to negotiate agreements with them to keep prices high enough so that they would not threaten each other. Throughout the 1880s, a series of nationwide railroad pools was organized, lessening the loss of revenue from cutthroat competition, but this means of reducing destructive competition fell apart in 1887.[250] At best, pools did not destroy competition; as John Stubbs later explained to the Pacific Railway commissioners, while pools averted rate wars, they did not eliminate competition, which was always present, though in modified form.[251]

The Transcontinental Traffic Association, one of the country's greatest railroad pools, attempted to prevent competition over the transcontinental lines, but it was dealt a serious blow in January 1886 when the Atchison, Topeka & Santa Fé Railroad withdrew, precipitating one of the greatest rate wars of all time.[252]

In early 1887 the Santa Fé management suggested a new pooling arrangement with the Southern Pacific, keeping 50 percent of the railroad business in southern California and 27 percent of that in the northern part of the state for itself. The Southern Pacific rejected this offer, whereupon the Santa Fé declared all-out war against what it called the monopoly of its rival.[253]

When the first transcontinental railroad opened for business in the spring of 1869, it cost $130 to travel first-class by rail from Chicago to San Francisco. Four years later first-class fare was $118, and by 1885 had dropped to $100.[254] The 1887 rate war caused the bottom to fall out of these high fares. The battle intensified in early March, when on the fourth of the month passenger fares from San Francisco to Boston plummeted to $47, those from San Francisco to New York dropped to

---

[250]LS test., *USPRC*, V, 2573–2574.   [251]John C. Stubbs test., *USPRC*, VI, 3329.

[252]Glenn S. Dumke, *The Boom of the Eighties in Southern California* (San Marino: HL, 1944), 23; see Joseph Netz, "The Great Los Angeles Real Estate Boom of 1887," *APHSSC* 1915 10 (Annual): 54–68, particularly 56.

[253]Dumke, *Boom*, 24.   [254]Ibid.

Southern Pacific Railroad Consolidations, 1888 to 1902

On May 4, 1888, the biggest Southern Pacific Railroad consolidation of all time took place when the following eighteen lines became part of the Southern Pacific Railroad:

1. Southern Pacific Railroad Company,
2. The San Jose & Almaden Railroad Company,
3. The Pajaro & Santa Cruz Railroad Company,
4. The Monterey Railroad Company,
5. The Monterey Extension Railroad Company,
6. The Southern Pacific Branch Railway Company,
7. The San Pablo & Tulare Railroad Company,
8. The San Pablo & Tulare Extension Railroad Company,
9. The San Ramon Valley Railroad Company,
10. The Stockton & Copperopolis Railroad Company,
11. The Stockton & Tulare Railroad Company,
12. The San Joaquin Valley & Yosemite Railroad Company,
13. The Los Angeles & San Diego Railroad Company,
14. The Los Angeles & Independence Railroad Company,
15. The Long Beach, Whittier & Los Angeles County Railroad Company,
16. The Long Beach Railroad Company,
17. The Southern Pacific Railroad Extension Company, and
18. The Ramona & San Bernardino Railroad Company.[a]

On April 13, 1898, the Southern Pacific Railroad entered into a four-party consolidation of the following railroads:

1. The Southern Pacific Railroad Company,
2. The Northern Railway Company,
3. The Northern California Railway Company, and
4. The California Pacific Railroad Company.[b]

On March 7, 1902, the Southern Pacific Railroad Company entered into a consolidation that placed all the Southern Pacific railroads of the Southwest under one corporate structure. They included:

1. The Southern Pacific Railroad Company (of California),
2. The Southern Pacific Railroad Company (of Arizona), and
3. The Southern Pacific Railroad Company (of New Mexico).[c]

The corporate existence of the Southern Pacific Railroad of Arizona and of the Southern Pacific Railroad of New Mexico were terminated on February 10, 1902, by consolidation into the Southern Pacific Railroad of California. The articles of consolidation are missing from the California State Archives.

[a]Arts. of Assn., Inc., Amal., and Consol. of the SPRR and seventeen other railroads, dated May 4, filed May 12, 1888. File 651, CSA.

[b]Arts. of Consol., Amal., and Inc. of the SPRR, the NRC, the NCRC, and the CPRC, signed Apr 13, filed Apr 14, 1898, File 1004, CSA.　　　　[c]*Corporate History of the Southern Pacific Railroad*, 107–108.

$45, and the fare to Chicago fell to $32.[255] The next day these fares were reduced $4, $5, and $7, respectively.[256]

On the morning of March 6, 1887, the two companies decided to fight to the finish over the cost of traveling from Kansas City to Los Angeles. The two giants opened even at $12; when the Santa Fé dropped to $10 and then to $8, both fares were promptly matched by the Southern Pacific. The Southern Pacific then took the initiative and dropped its rates again to $6 and then $4, and in the early afternoon of the same day announced the all time low of $1 for the 1,800-mile trip from the Missouri River to Los Angeles.[257] These rates quickly bounced back again, but never to the highs of the 1870s. For a year the cost of traveling to California remained less than $25.[258]

The social and economic effects of this rate war are incalculable: hundreds of thousands of people decided there would never be a better opportunity of finding their way to the Golden State—*El Dorado*. The Southern Pacific alone carried 120,000 immigrants west in a twelve-month period.[259]

There was very little significant extension of the mileage of the Associates' railroad empire after the new leasing arrangement of the Southern Pacific Company of Kentucky had been worked out. By the late 1880s, in fact, there was almost no new construction anywhere in the Southwest. The remaining Associates, primarily Huntington, would continue to strengthen their positions in the Southern Pacific Company and build new feeder lines from the main lines to the various byways along it. Yet by 1890 growth of the system had nearly halted. The decade from the mid-eighties to the mid-nineties ended an era in the growth of the major California railroads.

CALIFORNIA

LONG KNOWN AS

America's Greatest Winter Resort

...IS THE...

GREATEST SUMMER RESORT

IN THE WORLD

Clear, dry days, cool nights, no sunstroke or tornados. Magnificent beach, island and mountain resorts, including Shasta region, Lake County and the Springs, Lake Tahoe, Yosemite Valley, Kings River Canyon, Big Trees, Kern River Canyon, San Francisco, Santa Cruz and Santa Cruz Mountains, Del Monte, Monterey, Santa Barbara, Santa Monica, Long Beach and Catalina, besides

A THOUSAND MINERAL SPRINGS

Excellent shooting and fishing. Best summer camping-ground in the world. For literature about the resorts and information concerning the journey address or call on any agent

SOUTHERN PACIFIC

99. California is America's greatest winter and summer resort.
Union Pacific Collection.

---

[255]*LA Times*, Mar 5, 1887.
[256]Ibid., Mar 6, 1887.
[257]Dumke, *Boom*, 24–25.
[258]Ibid., 25.
[259]For a vivid description of this rate war and its political and social effects, see Wilson and Taylor, *Southern Pacific*, 86–88; and McAfee, *California's Railroad Era,* 188–199.

100. Emigrant train on the way to California, 1886. *Union Pacific Collection.*

THE SOUTHERN PACIFIC COMPANY IN THE PROMOTION OF THE WEST

Southern Pacific officials believed the success of their railroad and the success of California agriculture went hand-in-hand. As early as 1863 Governor Stanford addressed the State Agricultural Society on the need to remedy the state's slack population growth by fostering easier transportation and perfecting the state's agricultural resources. He introduced his subject by surveying a number of biblical and classical personalities and their remarks on agriculture. He then assured his listeners that all labor in legitimate pursuits was honorable and that the farmers' profession was the oldest and noblest on earth. He praised California's cities and the growth of its agricultural pursuits and then got down to the point: despite California's tremendous growth, as reflected in the 1860 federal census report, it had not grown nearly as much as it should have. He told his audience: "We are in a position to invite immigration from every portion of our country." A number of states, among them Iowa and Wisconsin, had grown proportionally faster. Two things, he said, would encourage a greater growth in California:

1. To spread out before the farming communities of the other States authentic information, in the shape of reliable statistics, as to the productions of our soil, and the noble field that is here offered for the industrious and energetic farmer.

James Harvey Strobridge Retires, But Only from Railroad Construction

In 1883, following the completion of the southern transcontinental, the indomitable railroad builder J. H. Strobridge shifted operations and started a railroad line up the Sacramento River Valley for Oregon. He remained president of the Pacific Improvement Company until sometime in the fall of 1890. Fred Crocker notified Huntington that Strobridge had handed him his resignation when a grading contract was signed without his approval, an action he regarded as a "reflection upon his management."[a] Crocker did not act upon the letter right away, hoping to get Strobridge to change his mind. He wrote to Strobridge on August 13, accepting his letter of retirement, but Strobridge remained with the railroad and with the Pacific Improvement Company until approximately October; the exact date is difficult to pin down.[b] Strobridge finally retired, after spending twenty-six years largely with the Central Pacific/Southern Pacific Associates.

Respect for Strobridge's versatility and talents was shown on April 25, 1892, when he was made a director of the new Bank of Sisson, Crocker & Company—Joseph S. Sisson and Clark W. Crocker.[c]

Strobridge was also president of the Farmers and Merchants Bank in Hayward from 1910 to 1921, at which time it was purchased by the Bank of Italy (later the Bank of America). He was also a director of the First National Bank of Hayward from 1911 to 1921 when it, too, was purchased by the Bank of Italy.[d] National currency issued by the First National Bank of Hayward on March 25, 1915, bears the signature of Strobridge as president of the bank.[e] Strobridge must have been pleased by the knowledge that not one of his wealthier associates had his signature on a piece of United States national currency.

Strobridge died a happy man on his Hayward farm on July 27, 1921—at the age of ninety-four, outliving his wealthier colleagues by decades.[f]

[a]CFC to CPH, Jun 24, 1890.   [b]CFC to JHS, Aug 13, 1890.
[c]SF Argonaut, Jan 2 and Mar 27, 1893, doing business at 322 Pine Street. SFCD, 1893, 209. Author inter. with Robert J. Chandler, Wells Fargo Bank historian, Mar 12, 2003.
[d]James E. Babbitt, archivist, Bank of America, to Edson T. Strobridge, Oct 14, 1977.
[e]Copy in the writer's coll., thanks to the generosity of Ian Ferguson of Redwood City, Calif., nephew of Strobridge's adopted daughter Carrie Ferguson.
[f]SF Chronicle, Jul 28, 1921; "The Strobridge Family," AT 1970 6 (4): 8–12.

2. To provide all who desire to emigrate, a safe, expeditious, and easy means of accomplishing their purpose.[260]

At this point the value of the coming railroad was praised: nobody would reap richer benefits from a transcontinental railroad than those whose livelihood was agriculture. Through the railroads alone the attention of the world would be attracted to California.

Benjamin B. Redding, land agent of the Central Pacific and Southern Pacific railroads until 1882, firmly supported developing California along with the state's railroads. He wrote a number of articles on agricultural topics, including the need for

[260]"Address of Leland Stanford at the Opening of the Tenth Annual Fair of the State Agricultural Society," 49.

irrigation, citrus and olive culture, wheat production, and the effect of California's salubrious climate on agriculture. His bibliography on the subject is impressive.[261]

Since the era of Progressive Republicanism and Democratic New Dealism of the early twentieth century, it has been fashionable to think that anyone having an exorbitant amount of wealth acquired it dishonestly. Terms like *Captains of Industry, Robber Barons, Big Four,* and *Monopolists* were created to collect classes of men under titles that would summarily condemn them. In the late-nineteenth century, railroad owners were the favorite whipping boys of the reformists and progressives, the self-appointed consciences of the nation.

Now, two-thirds of a century after the New Deal, historians are beginning to weigh the facts more carefully. Historian Richard Orsi accepts what he calls "the essential truth" of traditional, derogatory accounts of Southern Pacific managers; he even falls into the trap of accepting the name "Big Four" for the Central/Southern Pacific Associates, a term used by railroad enemies like Oscar Lewis and others to be as damning as *Robber Barons.* But Orsi balances the account somewhat as follows: "The extensive agricultural and land promotional activities of the Southern Pacific and its officials suggest that, contrary to the traditional interpretation, the railroad during the late nineteenth and early twentieth centuries in many ways linked its own interest with the progress of the state."[262] As a result of company policy, the Southern Pacific often used its power to strengthen and diversify the state's economy and further the welfare of her citizens.

By the end of the nineteenth century, the Southern Pacific assumed responsibility for some portion of California's social and intellectual improvement. In 1898 it began publishing *Sunset Magazine* as an in-house means of advertising railroad lands that were for sale. Indeed, it was in large part because of the railroad's existence and its policies that the "Far West emerged from a colonial to a mature and more balanced economy."[263] The 1890 census showed that—largely a result of railroad transportation—California's wheat harvest was worth almost twice that of its gold, and was second only to Minnesota's in the entire country.[264]

One historian of the American West concluded: "Most of the early promotion of the scenic and climatic conditions of the West was in some degree an undertaking of the Western railroads."[265] Railroads brought tourism, tourism brought permanent settlers, and permanent settlers brought skills, talents, and wealth. It is no exaggeration to say that the great railroads made the great state of California.

---

[261]Richard Orsi, "The Octopus Reconsidered: The Southern Pacific and Agricultural Modernization in California, 1865–1915," *CHSQ* 1975 54 (3): 214 n14, for a partial list of Redding's writings.   [262]Ibid., 198.

[263]Earl Pomeroy, *The Pacific Slope: A History of California, Oregon, Washington, Idaho, Utah, and Nevada* (NY: AAK, 1965), 102. See footnotes and their referents in Chap. 5, "A Broader Economic Basis," 83–119, of this work, showing the transformation in Calif.'s economy as a result of the state's many railroads, of which the SPRR was by far the largest.   [264]*Statistical Abstracts*, 1889–1900 (Wash.: GPO, 1900), (wheat) 312–313; ibid., 1892, (gold) 49.

[265]Pomeroy, *The Pacific Slope*, 335; McAfee, *California's Railroad Era*, 181.

CHAPTER 15

COMPETITION ON LAND, RIVERS, AND SEAS

Laissez Faire, But Not Free Enterprise!

Cooperation will add new energy to civilized life, because it will increase the pros-
perity of laboring men, and enlarge in every respect the scope of their lives.... The
introduction of the cooperative principle into the industrial systems of our coun-
try means a general advance in the conditions of all classes.

—Leland Stanford[1]

Unrestricted competition would have been ruinous for both companies [Central
Pacific Railroad and Pacific Mail Steamship Company], so a compromise was
effected. —Cerinda Evans[2]

RHETORIC OF COMPETITION

It was one thing for Leland Stanford and his Associates to argue, as they often did, on the side of a free-wheeling, laissez-faire economic structure in which their railroad empire could operate free of all government constraints; it was quite another to tolerate ruinous competition when there were ways of eliminating it, or at the very least of mitigating its harmful effects. They were not at all bothered by the possibility that unrestricted competition was self-defeating, or that it led inevitably to monopoly: they expected to survive the system. Yet when their own survival seemed threatened, they seemed to deny their competitors the rights reserved to themselves.

To stifle competition, the Associates bought into nonrailroad businesses in order to force down prices they themselves had to pay. True, this was a case of competition lowering prices, but it was not at all a working of the free market, since they entered businesses in which they had no other interest except allowing themselves to be bought off. As a case in point, they bought the Coos Bay Coal Company to avoid paying high prices for coal; the result of this purchase was a drop in their cost

---

[1]An inter. in SF with a representative of the *NY Tribune*, pub. May 4, 1887, in which LS explains a Sen. bill he had intro. Feb 16, 1887; HHB *Stanford*, 159 and 181. [2]Evans, *Huntington*, I, 273.

from eight dollars to four and one-half dollars per ton.[3] In another instance, in 1876, they used their own Western Development funds to build a railroad to the town of Ione, to develop a coal mine they had bought.[4]

THE PACIFIC EXPRESS AND WELLS FARGO EXPRESS DEAL

Even before the completion of the transcontinental railroad, the Central Pacific Associates had been faced with competition from different kinds of businesses. Express companies, for example, which hauled merchandise between customers and railroads, cashed in on a considerable portion of potential railroad profits. Lloyd Tevis later testified that in 1869 he had conceived the idea of organizing an express company to compete with Wells Fargo. He proposed this to Stanford and his Associates and after considerable negotiation they agreed to form their own company—the Pacific Express.[5]

Tevis' testimony was not entirely accurate. The articles of incorporation of the original Pacific Express Company were filed on June 21, 1855, providing for a $100,000 stock investment of two hundred shares at $500 each. It was authorized to run for fifty years.[6]

What the Tevis-Stanford group did was to create new articles of incorporation of the Pacific Express Company, which they signed on July 1, 1869, and filed four days later.[7] The directors of the "new" company were Josiah Stanford, Darius O. Mills, real estate investor Henry D. Bacon, Lloyd Tevis, and Oakland capitalist Lewis Cunningham.[8]

By employing economic leverage, the new Pacific Express Company eventually forced an agreement out of Wells Fargo. The result was that the company stayed out of the express business. It never did any business of its own, and, having attained their goals, the directors allowed their company to be *in effect* consolidated into Wells Fargo. The deal between the two companies led to a complete reorganization of the established firm, wherein Stanford and Crocker became directors of the Wells Fargo Express Company.[9]

There was no formal consolidation of the two companies, but in exchange for one-third of the total Wells Fargo stock, Stanford, Crocker, and Hopkins dissolved the Pacific Express. Before the stock was transferred to the three Central Pacific Associates, it was increased from $10 million to $15 million in total shares, a stock-

---

[3]LS test., *USPRC*, V, 2497.   [4]Ibid., 2692.
[5]Lloyd Tevis test., ibid., VI, 3119.
[6]The CSA no longer has the orig. Arts. of Inc. File 7428, CSA.
[7]Arts. of Inc., PEC, signed Jul 1, filed Jul 5, 1869. File 7432, CSA.
[8]Ibid. Bacon, *SFCD*, 1877–78, 110; Cunningham, *OCD*, 1877–78, 831.
[9]Lloyd Tevis test., *USPRC*, VI, 3114–3115.

watering job that was later condemned as one of the Central Pacific's most calcu-lated swindles.[10] A number of years afterwards, when the *Washington* [D.C.] *Sun* published a detailed history of what it labeled the "frauds and swindles" of the Cen-tral Pacific, it included this deal with Wells Fargo on its list of railroads "gobbled up" by the Associates.[11]

As part of this agreement, Wells Fargo was guaranteed the business of the Cen-tral Pacific for a period of ten years. Each of the three railroad men had to put up one-third of one-half million dollars, working capital to enable the new Wells Fargo organization to do banking. Thus, for a total cash outlay of only half a million, they gained control of $5 million in Wells Fargo stock, a swap that proved extremely rewarding to the railroad Associates. Wells Fargo had no cause for complaint: Pres-ident Tevis later testified that the new arrangement was even *more* beneficial to Wells Fargo; the company had never been a profitable concern until this arrange-ment with the Central Pacific was made.[12]

Later, when questioned about the details of the agreement, Stanford replied that he was unclear as to its terms, but he did recall that Wells Fargo was not given any special consideration; the contract simply guaranteed that no other company would be given special consideration.[13] He was wrong. The agreement reached was based on the recognition by both companies that Wells Fargo and the Pacific Express would be mutually injurious if they were both hauling freight. Despite Stanford's equivocating, it is clear that Wells Fargo *was* accorded a special relation-ship to the Central Pacific. The terms of agreement acknowledged that the pro-jected Pacific Express Company had an "advantageous" contract with the Central Pacific, and under the new arrangement Wells Fargo was to inherit *that* company's contract.[14] As it turned out, as late as 1887 Wells Fargo still had a monopoly on the Central Pacific and Southern Pacific express business.[15]

CALIFORNIA STEAM NAVIGATION COMPANY

Water transportation presented almost as great a threat to the Central Pacific as did rail. San Francisco lay at the mouth of the Sacramento and San Joaquin rivers, along which commercial steamboats had long plied their way inland to and from the port city. Besides this, the coast-to-coast traffic of steamship companies drew heavily from actual or potential railroad business.

The California Steam Navigation Company had been organized on March 1,

[10]This agreement was repr. in ibid., 3120.

[11]Repr. in *SF Bulletin*, Jul 21, 1873.

[12]Lloyd Tevis test., *USPRC*, VI, 3118.

[13]LS test., ibid., V, 2921–2922.

[14]For the contract between the PEC and the CPRR, see ibid., VI, 3121.

[15]Lloyd Tevis test., ibid., 3127.

1854.[16] Its $2.5 million capital stock allowed it to begin operations on the Sacramento and San Joaquin rivers with a large number of steamers. As early as 1856 two daily steamers ran from San Francisco to Sacramento while two others ran in the opposite direction.[17] This steamboat company had been bought by the California Pacific Railroad Company, which had been organized in January 1865 to extend from Vallejo to Sacramento by way of Davisville. The California Pacific in turn was purchased by the Central Pacific Railroad on April 1, 1871. The steamship company was bought by the railroad Associates for $620,000.[18] Huntington later said that he himself did the trading for the company's steamships: he made it clear that they were not bought by the Central Pacific but that he and his partners had bought a majority of the company's stock as an individual purchase.[19]

By the late 1860s the California Steamship Company had gradually won control of most of the inland steamer traffic to San Francisco. In 1869, the year the transcontinental was completed, the steamship company sold its steamers to the Central Pacific, giving the railroad Associates a near-monopoly on transportation from Ogden to San Francisco. Edward H. Miller, Jr., the Central Pacific's secretary and a director of the company, later testified that in 1872 the Associates bought interest in a number of steamships owned by the California Pacific Railroad Company.[20] Their intention was to destroy competition on the Sacramento River, allowing them to keep railroad rates high.[21] From that time on, the Central Pacific controlled all the water and rail routes from the capital city to the coast: no further competition was tolerated.

Further consolidation of their river-bound competition took place in 1878, when Stanford, his three Associates, and David Colton, acting through the Western Development Company, purchased the Colorado River Steam Navigation Company, whose ships started at Yuma, Arizona, and ran up the Colorado River.[22] There was heavy traffic in government supplies along the Colorado for the forts, reservations, and mines that had opened there. Rather than have a competing firm transport the supplies to the place where the railroad began, the Associates bought this steamship company, which gave them control of the business for the entire distance.[23] In an arrangement that proved extremely rewarding to Stanford and his partners, the Central Pacific managed the steamship company and turned all profits over to the Western Development Company—which *they* owned.

---

[16]For a hist. sketch of the steam navigation companies in Calif. and, in particular, the CSNC, see William D. Johnson, "Inland Steam Navigation in California," M.A. thesis (LSJU, 1952); see also Evans, *Huntington*, I, 272–273.

[17]William Ladd Willis, *History of Sacramento County, California* (LA: HRC, 1913), 204.

[18]CPH test., *USPRC*, I, 14–15.   [19]Ibid., 15.

[20]EHM, Jr., test., ibid., V, 3069. EHM, Jr., had been sec. of the CPRR since 1864.

[21]Ibid., 3070.   [22]Frank S. Douty test., ibid., 2698–2699.

[23]Ibid.

Once they had weakened or destroyed most of the competition with their coast-to-coast railroad business, the Associates turned their eyes to the lucrative Pacific Ocean trade. San Francisco's international trade was far more extensive than that of any other West Coast city. Losing the sea-going business of this city was unthinkable to Leland Stanford and Associates.

Pacific Mail Steamship Company

The Pacific Mail Steamship Company was organized in New York in April 1848 and sent its first steamers around South America that same year.[24] The company ran its ships on five lines: (1) between New York and Aspinwall, (2) between Panamá and various Central America ports, (3) between Panamá and various Mexican ports, (4) between Panamá and San Francisco, later extended to Astoria, Oregon, and (5) between San Francisco and Hong Kong and Yokohama.[25] Since 1849 the Pacific Mail had provided sea-going transportation between Panamá and the North Pacific, but it was not until 1867 that the company initiated its trans-oceanic trade when it sent the *Colorado* to the Far East.[26] To make it feasible for the Pacific Mail to operate between the East Coast of the United States and the Orient, Congress awarded the company a subsidy.[27] It was hoped that having steamers on both the East and West coasts and a railroad across Panamá would siphon off traffic between western Europe and the Orient—away from the Suez Canal and Cape of Good Hope routes.

Empire building across the plains and the oceans of the world had more than a profit-motive: there was competition, the desire to create wealth, the challenge to be first, *but* there was also vision, the desire to make the world a smaller place in which transportation networks could bring—to all men—luxury never dreamed of. Walt Whitman, cited earlier, anticipated this in poetry (see next page).

Six months after the Central and Union Pacific railroads were joined at Promontory, Ferdinand de Lesseps oversaw the completion of the Suez Canal, shortening the distance between Europe and the Orient by several thousand miles. This shorter water route threatened to destroy the prospects that goods from the Far East to Europe would cross the American continent.[28] Ocean vessels in many

---

[24]Will Lawson, *Pacific Steamers* (Glasgow: BSFC, 1927), 5; see 15–28 for a brief hist. of the PMSC. See also, John Haskell Kemble, "The Genesis of the Pacific Mail Steamship Company—Part I," Chap. I, "The Pacific Mail Steamship Company" (240–247); Chap. II, "Three Ships" (247–254), *CHSQ* 1934 13 (3): 240–254; ibid. 13 (4): "The Genesis of the Pacific Mail Steamship Company (Concluded)," Chap. III, "Getting Under Way," 386–406.

[25]Evans, *Huntington*, I, 273.

[26]John Haskell Kemble, "The Big Four at Sea, the History of the Occidental and Oriental Steamship Company," *HLQ* 1940 3 (3): 339.   [27]Ibid., 340.

[28]John Haskell Kemble, "The Transpacific Railroads, 1869–1915," *PHR* 1949 18 (3): 334–335.

A SELECTION FROM *PASSAGE TO INDIA*,
by Walt Whitman

Passage to India!
Lo, soul, for thee, of tableaus twain
I see, in one, the Suez canal initiated, open'd,
I see the procession of steamships, the *Empress Eugenie*'s leading the van;
I mark, from on deck, the level sand in the distance;
I pass swiftly the picturesque groups, the workmen gather'd,
The gigantic dredging machines.
I see over my own continent the Pacific Railroad.*

*Whitman, *Passage to India*, 6–7.

instances could transport goods more cheaply than could railroads. If America's railroads were going to protect that portion of their transcontinental freight business that originated in Asia, which was then carried across the country to the East Coast, much of which was then transshipped to Europe, it was thought that they would have to come to terms with steamship companies, and vice versa, or enter into direct competition with steamship companies of their own.

The opening of the transcontinental railroad—just two years after the Pacific Mail had first crossed the Pacific—made it possible to travel from New York to San Francisco in less than a week and shortened the trip from New York to the Far East by two weeks. It was obvious to the managers of the Pacific Mail and the Central Pacific that they posed a threat to each other. The traffic on the Panamá Railroad would certainly decline in importance as a result of the transcontinental railroad. There was a need for cooperation between the Pacific Mail and the Central Pacific to insure profitable travel and transportation of goods from the East Coast and the Orient. Though the situation called for cooperation, there was always the danger that *competition* rather than cooperation would develop.

No secret was made of the fact that the Central and Union Pacific railroads bought off the Pacific Mail, paying the seagoing competitor over $4 million to maintain high rates, effectively protecting their lower shipping rates. Until 1872 the transcontinental railroads and the Pacific Mail worked together so smoothly that it was rumored, erroneously, that the steamship company had been bought out by the Central Pacific.[29] One San Francisco editor was especially suspicious of what he regarded as a conspiracy to destroy competition; he informed his readers that there

[29]*Sac Union*, Dec 6, 1872.

had been an arrangement between Stanford and his Associates and the Pacific Mail for over a year whereby freight rates had been regulated. He hinted at total amalgamation of the two concerns, suggesting that the San Francisco agents of the Pacific Mail had already resigned their present positions. This alarmed journalist warned his readers: if Californians were not careful, they would have no means of traveling or shipping to the outside world except through Stanford's railroad, sailing vessels, or ox teams.[30]

The goodwill and cooperation enjoyed by the Central Pacific and the Pacific Mail were sabotaged in 1873. Rufus Hatch, the new manager of the Pacific Mail, announced that instead of depositing transoceanic and transcontinental freight from Asia at San Francisco, his company was going to take it *directly* to Panamá, with only a brief stop in San Francisco for the purpose of unloading local freight.[31] The rest would be sent across the Isthmus by railroad and then carried to New York by Pacific Mail steamships. By placing the entire route (except for the Panama Railroad stretch) in the hands of a single company, rates would be lower even though the service would take slightly longer.[32] Hatch was sure his scheme would be accepted by shippers, owing to the fact that they would save railroad charges across the continent.[33]

Occidental & Oriental Steamship Company

Pacific Mail's move prompted the Central Pacific Associates to act; otherwise, they argued, their railroad system could have been destroyed. One railroad agent insisted that the railroads could not make a profit if unlimited competition with the Pacific Mail were to continue.[34]

One of the most neglected and consequently least known of Leland Stanford's many careers is that of founder and president of the Occidental & Oriental Steamship Company.[35] His interest in steam navigation began in the late 1860s; it can be traced directly to his desire to keep the Central Pacific as free as possible from crippling competition, or effective competition of any kind.

The Central Pacific owners had not been standing idly by watching the Pacific Mail cut into their profits. While negotiating on an acceptable working agreement with the Pacific Mail Steamship Company, they organized their own sea-going business—the Occidental & Oriental Steamship Company.

The articles of incorporation of the Occidental & Oriental, calling for a duration

---

[30]*SF Bulletin*, Dec 5, 1872.　　　　　　[31]Kemble, "The Big Four at Sea," 340.
[32]John C. Stubbs test., *USPRC*, VI, 3309.　　[33]HHB, *Chronicles of the Builders*, V, 440–441.
[34]John C. Stubbs test., *USPRC*, VI, 3349–3350.
[35]NET, "Leland Stanford, President of the Occidental and Oriental Steamship Company," *AN* 1971 31 (2): 120–129.

of fifty years, were signed in San Francisco on November 25, 1874, and filed in Sacramento three days later.[36] This company began operations with a capital stock of $10 million divided into 100,000 shares at $100 each.[37] The Union and Central Pacific railroad companies divided the stock *almost* evenly—the West Coast partners holding slightly more than half—with Stanford, Huntington, Crocker, Hopkins, Colton, and Tevis each having 9,000 shares.[38] The original directors of the company were Stanford, Crocker, Hopkins, Colton, and Tevis. Though Huntington's eastern responsibilities prevented his serving on the board of directors, he had a "deep interest in the company" and "exerted great influence in its policies;" indeed, he was an active participant in all Occidental & Oriental affairs.[39]

Thus the Occidental & Oriental Steamship Company developed out of the battle with the Pacific Mail. Stanford and his friends organized their company to gain control of a through-route to the Orient and to force the Pacific Mail to resume use of San Francisco as a terminus. Other developments also worked in their favor.

The desired result was achieved when the Pacific Mail was forced to negotiate an agreement with the railroads. So far as the relations between the Pacific Mail and the Central Pacific, the "new" agreement was simply a return to the original system of depositing Pacific Mail freight in San Francisco and then shipping it overland by rail.[40]

Huntington wrote to Mark Hopkins that this deal between the Pacific Mail and the railroad companies was actually the work of Jay Gould—virtual head of the Union Pacific from 1874 to 1878—done to protect his own stock speculation.[41] Gould and Sidney Dillon had tried to get Huntington to put pressure on the Pacific Mail board of directors, but Huntington refused, reasoning that most of the Pacific Mail stock was held by speculators (including Gould). Huntington did not like the fact that Gould was in *actual* control of both the Pacific Mail and the Union Pacific; he pledged himself to continue looking after Central Pacific interests, whatever that might take.[42] A year later Gould urged Huntington to have the Central Pacific join the Union Pacific in purchasing the Pacific Mail outright. A past-due indebtedness of $2 million made the Pacific Mail vulnerable to almost any takeover. Huntington was sure that for $1.5 million they could control the entire steamship line.[43] Huntington was sure, too, that an arrangement could be made to give the Central Pacific eventual control over the Pacific Mail, without buying the company. But he still wanted nothing to do with Gould's deal.[44]

Then, in early 1876, the Panama Railroad terminated its contract with the steam-

[36]Arts. of Inc. of the O & O, signed Nov 25, filed Nov 28, 1874. File 6953, CSA.
[37]Ibid. See also LS test., *USPRC*, V, 2924.
[38]Arts. of Inc. of the O & O; LS test., *USPRC*, V, 2924; *O &O Record* (Minutes of the Board of Directors, 1874–1908), 1–5.   [39]Evans, *Huntington*, I, 279.
[40]Kemble, "The Transpacific Railroads," 334–337; LS test., *USPRC*, V, 2924.
[41]CPH to MH, Mar 4, 1875.   [42]CPH to MH, Apr 19, 1875.
[43]CPH to MH, Apr 6, 1876.   [44]CPH to MH, Apr 9, 1876.

ship company, citing their reasons as irregular Pacific Mail shipments and excessive losses of packages and goods.[45] This move nearly ruined the Pacific Mail.[46]

A new Pacific Mail board of directors—charged with saving the company from bankruptcy and ruin—was later impaneled in the spring of 1876. Railroad men were placed at the helm of the troubled steamship company. There is no evidence, however, that the Central Pacific Associates had any interest in controlling the Pacific Mail, so long as the two companies could cooperate amicably.[47]

At least a majority—and occasionally all—of the rapidly changing five-man membership of the board of directors of the Occidental & Oriental Steamship Company were from the Central Pacific group. And they actually *managed* the line.[48] The Union Pacific members never attended board meetings, but they did take an active part in dividing the traffic among the cooperating companies.[49] Stanford, a director of the company for the rest of his life, was elected president on December 15, 1874.[50] On July 8, 1875, George H. Bradbury, a former president of the Pacific Mail, succeeded him.[51] Bradbury was reelected on July 6, 1876, and July 24, 1877.[52] He resigned on July 3, 1878, and was succeeded as president by David Colton.[53] Following the death of Colton on October 9, 1878, Stanford was again reelected president on October 29, a position he held for the rest of his life.[54]

Mark Hopkins was the company's first treasurer. He resigned on October 21, 1875, and was succeeded by the London and San Francisco Bank, Ltd.[55] In 1878 a Central Pacific subsidiary, the Western Development Company, assumed the duties of treasurer, and a year later was superseded by the Pacific Improvement Company. After the various construction companies began functioning legally as treasurers, the office in effect was left vacant, until 1899, when Frank S. Douty, treasurer of several Central and Southern Pacific subsidiaries, was named to the post as treasurer of the Occidental & Oriental.

Stanford served actively during the first few years of the company's life, when one to five board meetings per year were held. As he grew older he gradually withdrew from the actual management of the company, due to travel abroad and ill health. By the late 1880s and early 1890s the directorship had shifted from the old heavyweights like Huntington, Charles Crocker, Sidney Dillon, and Jay Gould to younger Central Pacific officials.

---

[45]Report of B. Mosely, gen. supt. of the PRR, Mar 21, 1876, cited in Evans, *Huntington*, I, 276.

[46]For the story of the political machinations in NY pertaining to this matter, and the involvement of Jay Gould, Trenor W. Park, and others, see the *Daily Panama Star and Herald*, Jan 25 and 31, 1876. This is the same Trenor Park who bought the LS mine in Sutter Creek in 1872.

[47]Edward R. Gundelfinger, "The Pacific Mail Steamship Company, 1847–1917: Its Relations with the Railroads," B.A. thesis (UCB, 1917), 39.

[48]*O & O Record*, 1.

[49]LS test., *USPRC*, V, 2925.

[50]*O & O Record*, 10.

[51]Ibid., 23.

[52]Ibid., 37 and 47.

[53]Ibid., 52.

[54]Ibid., 54.

[55]Ibid., 26.

101. *Governor Stanford* steamer, Lake Tahoe, 1884. *Stanford University Archives.*

One of the luminaries among these younger men was Charles Crocker's son Charles Frederick "Fred" Crocker. After January 26, 1880, when Republican governor George C. Perkins appointed the twenty-five-year-old Crocker scion as aide-de-camp on the staff of the Commander-in-Chief of the National Guard of California with the rank of lieutenant colonel, Fred Crocker was known as Colonel Crocker.[56] Other successors to the old guard were Timothy Hopkins, Frank S. Douty, and Willard Vincent Huntington, one of Collis Huntington's nephews.[57]

Fred Crocker was elected vice president of the Occidental & Oriental October 29, 1878, and since Stanford was frequently absent from business meetings, he regularly presided over the meetings of the board.[58] In 1875 David D. Stubbs—brother of John C. S. Stubbs—was appointed secretary of the Occidental & Oriental Steamship Company. In 1898 he was appointed to the new position of general manager and held both posts until 1908.

[56]Official Record, CED, Admin. of Governor Perkins. Register of Official Transactions, 1880–1883. CSA, File F3639-10, p. 15; Calif., *Annual Report of the Adjutant-General of the State of California, 1880.* Vol. 3, 1872–1884, Table G, "Roster of Officers of the National Guard of California, July 31st, 1880," 39; *SF Examiner*, Jan 27, 1880. Perkins was the first gov. elected under the new Calif. constitution and was the only gov. ever elected to a three-year term. He served from Jan 8, 1880, to Jan 10, 1883. Melendy and Gilbert, *The Governors of California*, 188–203.

[57]*O & O Record*, 50 and 111.   [58]Ibid., 52, 58, 62, and 111.

THE STEAMER *GOVERNOR STANFORD*

A little-known aspect of Stanford's ties with water travel is that a mail and passenger steamer bore his name. It was reported on October 1, 1872, that George Middlemas and William A. Boole of San Francisco had under construction a steamer for the account of William "Billy" W. Lapham, owner of Lapham's Hotel at South Stateline, Nevada.[a] The owner was James McM[illam] Shafter of San Francisco.[b]

When finished, the steamer was 92 feet long, 16.5 feet wide, and had a draft of 4.5, and a "measurement" of 64.18 tons. It was estimated that the *Stanford* could carry 125 passengers. On December 6, 1872, the $15,000 *Governor Stanford* was slid into Lake Tahoe's Discovery Bay, and four days later made her trial run across the lake to Tahoe City.

The *Stanford* was a disappointment: seven knots was her maximum speed, and within slightly over two years her boiler was replaced with one designed to double her speed.

The owner's mail steamer contract called for the steamer to make tri-weekly cruises from Tahoe City to Hot Springs, Glenbrook, Lapham's Landing, and Rowland's Station.

A contemporary writer described the regular itinerary of the ship as follows: "The *Governor Stanford* makes regular trips around the lake daily, touching at all Post-office and other settlement points. It leaves Tahoe City shortly after the arrival of the stage from Truckee, and returns in time for the evening stage. This gives parties from San Francisco at four o'clock Saturday evening several hours upon the lake and home again Monday morning."[c]

In 1881, the boat was sold and the new owners eventually advertised "$1.00 per person cruises to any Particular Land Place On The Lake." Two years later, the *Stanford*'s steam boiler was condemned by district boiler inspectors. The owners then decided to convert her into a wood-carrying barge.

On December 29, 1883, before the conversion was made, a storm ground the ship to pieces against the pilings of J. M. Short's store at the lumbering settlement.

[a]*Nevada Register*, Oct 1, 1873, quoted by Edward B. Scott, *The Saga of Lake Tahoe, A Complete Documentation of Lake Tahoe's Development over the last One Hundred Years* (Crystal Bay, Nev.: TPC, 1957), 395. Middlemas and Boole were doing business at 403 Spear Street, *SFCD*, 1873, 436.

[b]For the story of the *Stanford*, see Scott, *The Saga of Lake Tahoe*, 394–396. James McM Shafter was later named one of the original trustees of LSJU.   [c]*SF Argonaut*, Aug 28, 1880.

Collis Huntington once suggested to Stanford that the Central Pacific ought to acquire a controlling interest in the Union Pacific. He felt that a single transcontinental line could bargain better with the Pacific Mail, but his suggestion was never followed up.[59] In February 1875 a contract was signed by the managers of the Central Pacific, the Union Pacific, and the Occidental & Oriental in which the officers of the three companies pledged to do everything within their power to recover the trade the railroads had lost to the Pacific Mail's Panamá route. So intent were they at succeeding that they were willing to operate at a loss by carrying ocean trade at railroad rates. According to the terms of their agreement, two-thirds of through-passenger fares would go to the Occidental & Oriental, while the two railroads would divide

[59]CPH to LS, Mar 15, 1875.

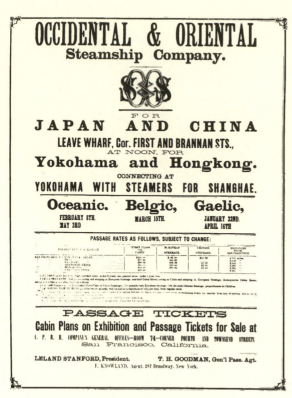

102. Leland Stanford, president of the
Occidental & Oriental Steamship Company.
Stanford University Archives.

the other third equally. Freight fares were to be divided equally between the steamship company and the two railroads. The Occidental & Oriental was authorized to use the wharves of the Central Pacific Railroad Company free of charge.

The financial operations of the Occidental & Oriental leave no doubt that the line was a tool of the Central and Union Pacific railroads. In 1877, when the directors of the Occidental & Oriental needed money, they floated a $150,000 loan from the Western Development Company, owned—of course —by the Central Pacific Associates! The promissory note covering the loan was signed by Stanford, Huntington, Hopkins, and Colton.[60]

The Pacific Mail finally accepted the fact that the Occidental & Oriental was going to be a rival line and not just a paper competitor. The steamship company's managers took immediate steps toward a peaceful settlement of the dispute with the railroads to forestall the eruption of a disastrous rate war— which the railroads were bound to win.

In February 1875 the Pacific Mail sold to Lloyd Tevis—now an agent of the Central Pacific—some San Francisco waterfront property for a price below market value: sixteen lots, a number of wharves, sheds, warehouses, and coal yards. The editor of the *San Francisco Bulletin*, suspicious that the Pacific Mail had sold out to the Central Pacific, thereby ending all competition between them, repeated the story spread by the *Sacramento Union* three years earlier. Their interests, he said, were too similar to allow for opposition between the parties. He concluded: "There will be no Occidental line of steamers, nor any other competing line by the procurement of the Central Pacific combination. The transfer of this magnificent property at about half its actual value don't [*sic*] mean opposition."[61]

[60] *O & O Record*, 50, meeting of Nov 21, 1877.   [61] *SF Bulletin*, Feb 12, 1875.

The two steamship companies agreed in June 1875 that each would open a monthly transoceanic passenger service, alternately leaving San Francisco every fifteen days. Both companies were to work closely with the Central and Union Pacific railroads, and would divide equally the profits for cargo carried by the railroads *and* the Pacific Mail. The railroads, for their part, guaranteed the Pacific Mail six hundred tons of freight each month.[62] These arrangements went into effect before the first Occidental & Oriental steamship ever sailed, and lasted for the lifetime of the new company.

San Francisco wharves were shared by the two steamship companies, but the long-rumored merger never came about.[63] Nevertheless, by threatening to swing southward into the lucrative Panamá trade, the Occidental & Oriental kept the Pacific Mail in line and also gave the railroad men a voice in setting steamship rates between the East and West coasts. The Associates found later that this practice could work both ways: the Northern Pacific later demanded a subsidy from the Occidental & Oriental for agreeing not to compete with *it*![64]

The Pacific Mail's relationship with the three cooperating companies was not always harmonious. Periodic rumors of an impending rate war continued to circulate.[65] The particulars of an expected battle between the two steamship companies were spelled out in detail in a series of editorials in the *San Francisco Bulletin*—by an editor who wrote as though he might have some inside information, though he did not. It was titled "The War between Pacific Mail and the Pacific Railroads."[66]

The railroads canceled their contract with the Pacific Mail in the spring of 1879; they were unwilling to agree to another because of a high subsidy increase demanded by the rival steamship company. The Pacific Mail took the initiative in negotiating with the railroads, but when this effort proved futile, the company lowered its passenger rates. The Union Pacific shrugged this off, pointing out that the sea-going competitor was already carrying its capacity and that it was almost impossible to lease or buy more ships. Because of this, the Pacific Mail could not have hauled more freight and passengers even if the business had been available. There appears to have been considerable bluster here, for it was generally understood that the railroads were preparing to make sizable retaliatory reductions on through-rates.[67]

On March 1, 1880, the Pacific Mail won the still-undeclared war—which had been reduced to little more than a battle of words—by wringing from the railroads a five-year contract granting it a subsidy increase from $60,000 to $110,000 per month.[68] Stanford later speculated that without its railroad subsidy, the Pacific Mail

---

[62] *Sac Record-Union*, Mar 4 and 9, 1875.

[64] Grodinsky, *Railway Strategy*, 262.

[66] Ibid., Jan 31, 1880.

[68] Ibid., Mar 2, 1880.

[63] *SF Bulletin*, Mar 30, 1876.

[65] *SF Bulletin*, Jul 11, 1879.

[67] Ibid.

would have gone bankrupt. When the subsidy ended, with the passage of the Interstate Commerce Act of 1887, the Pacific Mail cut its rates and again became a competitor. Contrary to earlier threats of the outcome had genuine competition been permitted, the company did not go bankrupt.[69] By then Stanford said that the competition of the Pacific Mail was insignificant. The harmful competition was now coming from other railroads.[70]

Collis Huntington and Jay Gould, who had bought large shares of stock in the Union Pacific and remained in control of the railroad from 1874 to 1878, got complete control of the Pacific Mail in March 1880 and brought that company entirely under the control of the Union Pacific/Central Pacific trans-continental railroad system.[71] Still, there was no merger. The two steamship companies—the Pacific Mail and the Occidental & Oriental—continued to operate separately, though the value of goods shipped by the Pacific Mail between San Francisco and New York dropped sharply and steadily from over $70 million in 1869 to just slightly more than $2.3 million in 1884.[72] In 1880 Huntington bought just enough shares in the Pacific Mail to qualify as a member of the board of directors. He gained control of the Pacific Mail Steamship Company on May 31, 1893, when, just before Stanford died, Huntington was named president of the Pacific Mail.[73] (Under his management the company prospered as never before.)

Bradbury, Stanford's short-term successor as president of the Occidental & Oriental, made arrangements in England for the ships the company needed. Eventually, the *Oceanic*, *Belgic*, and *Gaelic* were leased from the Oceanic Steam Navigation Company. One steamship historian was led to the erroneous conclusion that the Occidental & Oriental belonged to the White Star line since most of the Occidental & Oriental's fleet of nine ships was chartered from it.[74] Another scholar mistakenly classed it as a White Star subsidiary.[75] Other White Star steamships leased by the Occidental & Oriental were the *Coptic*, the *Arabic*, and the *Doric*. The British freighter *Evandale* was charted for a single voyage in 1895.[76] Three years later the Occidental & Oriental chartered the British freighter *Venus*, also for a single voyage.[77] The only American steamship sailed by the Occidental & Oriental was the *San Pablo*, chartered in 1884 from the Pacific Improvement Company. Because the owners of this company were directors of the Occidental & Oriental, they actually chartered the ship from themselves.[78] Most of these ships had between one hundred and two hundred first-cabin passenger berths.[79]

[69]LS test., *USPRC*, V, 2929.   [70]Ibid., 2930.   [71]*SF Bulletin*, Mar 15, 1880.

[72]Nimmo, *Report on the Internal Commerce of the United States, 1884*, 55.

[73]Evans, *Huntington*, II, 498. Jay Gould died on Dec 2, 1892.

[74]Lawson, *Pacific Steamers*, 9.   [75]Smith, *Passenger Ships of the World, Past and Present*, 728.

[76]*SF Chronicle*, Oct 20, 1895.   [77]Ibid., Apr 18, 22, and 23, 1898.

[78]*SF Alta California*, Jul 13, 1884.   [79]Ibid., Jun 3, 1875, for a description of the *Oceanic*.

101. Occidental & Oriental Steamship Company's *SS Belgic* in about 1893.
Mariners' Museum, Newport News, Virginia.

These steamers were the most modern and most comfortable built at the time. The *Oceanic* had all the luxuries of a palace: a saloon, library, grand piano, and two fireplaces. Outside staterooms were provided with running water, call bells, and bathing facilities. The ship was launched on August 27, 1870. It weighed in at 3,808 gross tons, having a length of 420 feet (overall length, 432 feet), a width of almost 41 feet, and a depth of just under 23½ feet. It was placed in service in 1871 and made the Liverpool to New York run for four years. Chartered by the Occidental & Oriental from 1875 to 1895, it was in service between San Francisco and Hong Kong. This liner was scrapped in London in 1896.[80]

Initially, the Occidental & Oriental liners sailed from San Francisco in the middle of the month, crossing to Yokohama or Hong Kong and returning by the same route, completing a round trip that took about three months. After 1883 the service was increased to three sailings per month: the one-way trip from Hong Kong to San Francisco was cut to about three weeks. In 1889 the *Oceanic* set the trans-Pacific record when she steamed into San Francisco only thirteen and one-half days out of

[80]Smith, *Passenger Ships of the World*, 191, and *passim*, for info. on several of the other leased ships. Kemble, "The Big Four at Sea," 348.

Yokohama.[81] Three years later Honolulu was added as an occasional port of call and before the turn of the twentieth century became a regular stop on the trans-Pacific trip.[82] Still later, Manila was added.[83]

Until 1896, having been bought off by prominent Japanese steamship companies, the Occidental & Oriental stayed out of the coastwise trade of the Far East. But in that year both the Pacific Mail and the Occidental & Oriental began competing with the Japanese companies in the China-Japan trade.[84] As with American competitors, the Occidental & Oriental and the Japanese-owned Toyo Kisen Kabushiki Kaisha agreed on schedules, rate-setting, and the division of profits, an arrangement similar to that worked out by the Occidental & Oriental and the Pacific Mail.

The cargo trade carried by the Occidental & Oriental was far more profitable than its passenger business; only about thirty to seventy first-class passengers traveled on each ship, most of whom were government representatives, naval officers, merchants, tourists, and missionaries.[85]

The Occidental & Oriental proved to be a profitable enterprise—an unexpected development, as it turned out. When Stanford explained to the Pacific Railway commissioners in 1887 that he and his partners had organized the Occidental & Oriental to force the Pacific Mail to bring its freight to San Francisco, he said that they expected to lose $100,000 per year on their new business venture. But, surprisingly, the Occidental & Oriental had "paid nicely" and had even brought its owners handsome profits.[86] Charles Francis Adams, named president of the Union Pacific to add respectability to that company, said the Occidental & Oriental had been a source of profit to his road as well.[87] Profits were so good that in 1878 the company began paying dividends, the first of forty-six paid between that year and 1900, with an average of about 6 percent. The total dividends paid amounted to forty dollars per hundred-dollar share, but since only three dollars per share had ever been paid in, the 1887 dividends amounted to over 200 percent of money actually invested, averaging about 60 percent for the lifetime returns of the company.[88]

Surplus funds accumulated by the Occidental & Oriental were held by the Central Pacific, until it was discovered that some of this money—$150,000 in one case—had been lent interest-free to the Western Development Company and the Pacific Improvement Company.[89] This was a dubious loan at best, since 50 percent of the money belonged to the Union Pacific. When the managers of the Union

[81]SF Chronicle, Jan 2, 1883, and Aug 1 and Sep 3, 1875; SF Alta California, Nov 12, 1889.

[82]SF Chronicle, Jan 10, 1892, Jan 8, 1893, Feb 22, 1896, Dec 30, 1897, and Dec 31, 1898.

[83]Ibid., Jun 7 and Dec 31, 1902, Dec 31, 1903, and Dec 27, 1905.

[84]O & O Record, 29–33 and 82–88.

[85]Kemble, "Big Four at Sea," 353; O & O passenger lists are in the PMSC coll. at the HL.

[86]LS test., USPRC, V, 2924. [87]Charles Francis Adams test., ibid., I, 83.

[88]O &O Record, 91–97. [89]Colton Case, IV, 1584–1587.

Pacific discovered what was happening, they demanded their share of the profits at once, thus ending for the Central Pacific partners a very convenient source of interest-free, ready cash.[90]

David D. Stubbs, secretary of the Occidental & Oriental, admitted on December 14, 1883, that strict records were not kept of such transactions and that a bookkeeper examining the books of the Occidental & Oriental Steamship Company would not have discovered such loans.[91] Money was "deposited" by the Occidental & Oriental as if the Central Pacific were a bank, and then was withdrawn as needed; no receipts on money so deposited or lent was kept; for a number of years the Occidental & Oriental did not even have a treasurer.[92]

From 1900 on, the Occidental & Oriental's business steadily declined. It went out of business in 1908, having achieved all its original goals. The end was signaled by the election of Rennie P. Schwerin, a vice president and general manager of the Pacific Mail, to the presidency of the Occidental & Oriental. The Pacific Mail added new and improved ships to its line with which the Occidental & Oriental ships could not compete. The *Coptic* and the *Doric*—the last of the Occidental & Oriental ships—were sold by the White Star line to the Pacific Mail in the summer of 1906. The inevitable end of the Occidental & Oriental Steamship Company came on July 23, 1908, when a meeting of the board of directors was called . . . and only the secretary showed up.[93] The company's suspension of operation on November 8, 1908, was its practical end, but not the legal end: for some reason, the company was reincorporated for fifty years on April 30, 1917, and its operations suspended on March 4, 1922.[94]

REALITY OF COMPETITION

Stanford's economic philosophy, especially his ideas on the working of the free market, were expressed time and time again over the years, with one unchanging theme—that competition was the best regulator of the market in railroad and other businesses. If prices or costs got too high, unregulated competition would lower them by attracting competition into the field. But when it came to implementing these notions of laissez-faire capitalism, he and his partners found themselves driven to reducing competition by one means or another.

For a number of years the Associates had destroyed or weakened railroad competition by buying out competing roads and incorporating them into the Central Pacific-Southern Pacific system. No sooner had the transcontinental railroad been completed than the managers of the Central and Union agreed to maintain rates at

[90]Ibid., XV, 7646–7654.   [91]Ibid., IV, 1573.
[92]Ibid., 1577–1578.   [93]O & O Record, 233.
[94]Arts. of Inc. of the O & O, dated Apr 30, filed May 8, 1917. File 84451, CSA.

a given level without competing against one another.[95] Competition could be eliminated from within the system; it could be avoided by private agreement. The
inconsistency of this position never bothered Stanford or his Associates; in fact, he
admitted later that in certain instances in the 1870s the Central Pacific prospered
only because it was able to fix its rates "free of competition;" he also complained
that when competing lines opened up, the incomes of the Central Pacific and its
spur roads fell off.[96] Yet, consistent with his earlier arguments, he must have seen
that this was the result of the natural laws of economics at work and was therefore
good for the economy as a whole.

Instead of allowing this "beneficent" competition, however, Stanford and his
partners set about to eliminate it whenever possible. In the 1887 railroad investigation, one of the Pacific Railroad commissioners' strongest criticisms of the Central
Pacific Associates was that they regularly "destroyed possible competitors," paying
out almost $26 million for rebates, subsidies, and pools. They did this, ironically, to
eliminate the competition that Stanford professed was beneficial to the national
economy.[97]

The Associates wanted a system of laissez faire, but rejected free enterprise; they
did not want government regulation, but neither did they desire free competition.
The philosophy of laissez faire, in their thinking, applied only to government controls. They proved themselves "fittest to survive," in terms of contemporary social
Darwinism, which espoused the survival of the fittest in business. But enemies of
their system, and others like it, regarded pooling arrangements, monopolies, and
other noncompetitive agreements as a conspiracy against the public; yet the public,
the Associates discovered, through its representatives in government, was going to
insist upon its right to protect itself by forcing competition, or by guaranteeing that
competition could exist. This government intervention in the free enterprise system, then, could be regarded as a higher application of the principle of social Darwinism.

---

[95]Peter B. Shelby test., *USPRC*, IV, 2122.   [96]LS test., ibid., V, 2849.
[97]*RUSPRC*, 141–142.

CHAPTER 16

EARLY LIFE OF LELAND, JR., AND THE FIRST EUROPEAN TOUR
1868–1881

In Pursuit of Culture Prescribed for All American Millionaires

Leland's birth eclipsed his father's professional interests. Even the completion of the transcontinental railroad, the major symbol of Stanford's success, was far less important to the proud parents than the birth of their only child.
—Linda J. Long[1]

LELAND JUNIOR IS BORN IN SACRAMENTO—MAY 14, 1868

In their house at Eighth and N streets in Sacramento, a son—their first and only child—was born to forty-four-year-old Leland and thirty-nine-year-old Jane Stanford at two o'clock in the morning on May 14, 1868, following eighteen years of marriage. Harvey Willson Harkness, M.D., was "Physician in Attendance."[2] Jane's sister Anna, her brothers Charlie and Henry, and the mothers of both proud parents were present for the great event.[3] Nothing could have meant more to the Stanfords at that moment; a later writer would see the birth of Leland, Jr., as "almost as much a public event as if an heir had been born to a reigning prince."[4]

---

[1]Linda J. Long, "The Stanfords as Parents," *S & T* 1991 15 (1): 10–13, 12 cited here, a well-balanced and judicious examination of the subject, written by the Public Services Lib. SUA.

[2]LSJ's birth cert., dated SF, Jul 12, 1898, in LSJ papers. SUA.

[3]BB, *Mrs. Stanford*, 14; GTC, *Stanford*, 380, later wrote that young Leland's birth had made such a profound impression on LS that—for the only time in her life—Mrs. Stanford witnessed him on his knees praying, giving thanks for their baby and for the mother's good health. Clark cites no authority for this touching scene.

[4]*Sac Bee*, Jun 6, 1939. LS was a proud new father and undoubtedly played the part, but not in the ridiculous way related by Jane's biographer: "When the baby was only a few weeks old, Mr. Stanford asked Mrs. Stanford to arrange a dinner party for a group of their particular friends. It was a large party, and when they were seated the waiter brought in a large silver platter with a cover and placed it in the center of the table. Mrs. Stanford was very much surprised, for she had planned nothing of the sort, and also had not seen the platter before. Then Mr. Stanford arose and said, 'My friends, I wish now to introduce my son to you.' When the cover of the silver dish was lifted, the baby was discovered lying in it on blossoms. He was carried around the table and shown to each guest. He was smiling, and went through his introduction very nicely." BB, *Mrs. Stanford*, 15. Only BB knew of this anecdote, though it has been quoted often since she concocted it.

104. Leland Stanford, Jr., age seven (1875), wearing a velvet suit. *Stanford University Archives.*

Little Leland DeWitt Stanford—the middle name was for the Governor's unmarried brother DeWitt, who had died six years before in Australia—was treated as though he were much more than an ordinary child. Baby Leland was cherished—almost revered—by his parents, and he quickly became the center of their lives.[5]

On one occasion when Leland was away, presumably on the Central Pacific construction site, Jane took the baby to San Francisco to get Dr. J. D. B. Stillman to inoculate the infant against smallpox. Between the lines of an undated letter sent by Jane from her hotel, one can feel the tender foolishness that comes with parenthood. She writes that the baby was "very fretful, crying" as a result of a vaccination in the arm. "I sent for the Dr. and he ordered a hot bath and a gin sling—which quieted him [the baby, not the doctor!]."

This letter also contains a series of gentle complaints and confessions to her husband:

---

[5]Wenzel, "Finding Facts about the Stanfords," 253.

I see so little of you now days. A letter is more dear than ever. I feel as though I have so much to tell you about your being so good to me doing so much I am so much occupied with baby I am afraid I don't do my duty to you when I do have you with me. But my heart is full of love running over with the feeling I have for you my blessed husband. I am not half good enough. I would like to be perfect that you might think me the best of wives. I shall be glad when we can be together all the time. I feel so lonesome even here in the Hotel. I miss you all the time. With many kisses and a heart full of love, affectionately yours, Jane. Baby sends lots of kisses.[6]

Whenever little Leland appeared with his mother in public, he was bedecked like a little prince. Until the age of six he wore velvet suits, big white collars, and had his hair in long curls. At six, his Uncle Ariel took him to a barber shop "and had his hair cut boy-fashion and bought him a pair of colorful boots with red tops and copper toes." (The next day he gave these boots to his pal Fritz, a neighborhood playmate who had no shoes.[7])

YOUNG LELAND

Unlike so many spoiled sons of the very rich, Leland Stanford, Jr., "made good use of his talents and opportunities and was on the way to becoming a well rounded and exceptionally well-informed young man when his life ended." These are the words of Gunther Nagel, one of Jane Stanford's biographers.[8] Young Leland's letters, written between the ages of eleven and two months short of what would have been his sixteen birthday, reveal a great deal about his thoughts and activities.[9]

Following the completion of their San Francisco mansion in the spring of 1876, the Stanfords traveled east to visit the Centennial Exposition in Philadelphia. Their eight-year-old son showed particular interest in the mechanical exhibitions and handmade articles. His father bought him a woodcarving set, and some time later, if we credit Bertha Berner on this fact, his own works were displayed in the Mechanics Pavilion in San Francisco.[10] The Stanford University Museum's exhibit of the boy's playthings, his collection of archeological and historical objects, and some of his own paintings demonstrate his wide range of talents and interests. In one of his practice account books, there are pictures of ships and buildings drawn by Leland.[11]

Collecting was one of Leland's earliest hobbies, beginning with pinecones at age eight.[12] His rooms in the San Francisco mansion and the Palo Alto Stock Farm home were transformed into miniature museums.

---

[6]JLS to LS, undated letter in JLS papers.   [7]BB, *Mrs. Stanford*, 40.
[8]Gunther Nagel, "Boy in a Gilded Age," *CH* 1978/79 57 (4): 321.
[9]LSJ's corres. is now preserved in the LSJ papers.   [10]BB, *Mrs. Stanford*, 17.
[11]LSJ papers.
[12]Fisher, "Stanford," 28.

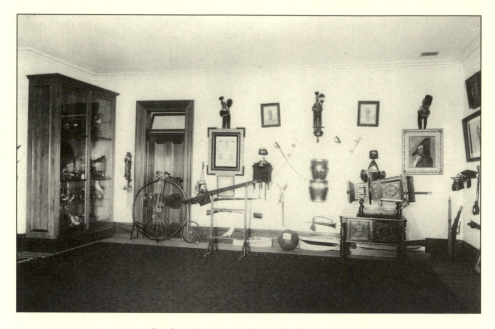

105. Leland, Jr.'s room in the Palo Alto Farm house.
Stanford University Archives.

A CHRISTMAS PARTY

In 1877 nine-year-old Leland was host of the first social event held in the Stanfords' new San Francisco home—a Christmas reception and dance, the largest children's party yet held in the city.[13] His card of invitation read:

> Master Leland Stanford
> requests the pleasure of your company
> at S. West Corner of Cal'a & Powell Sts.
> Friday afternoon; Dec'r 28th
> at two o'clock
> 1877
> R.S.V.P.   Dancing

There were about 150 young guests, plus parents and guardians.[14] Very few regrets were returned. The guest list, published in a society sheet, is a genealogist's dream.[15] Numbered among the guests were Leland's life-long friend Wilson G. (Wilsie) Taylor and Leland Senior's namesake, seven-year-old Leland Stanford

---

[13]*SF Morning Call*, Dec 29, 1877.   [14]Ibid.

[15]"Society, Master Leland D. W. [*sic*] Stanford's Brilliant Reception," in unidentified jour., Dec 29, 1877. SUA.

Stillman, the son of family friend and doctor J. D. B. Stillman.[16] Nathan Ballenberg's Band played near the mansion's entrance to greet the young merrymakers.[17] Dance teacher "Professor" Oliver A. Lunt was master of ceremonies.[18] Mrs. Stanford and Anna Marie Lathrop, Leland's aunt, joined him in receiving guests in the parlor on the left of the main entrance as the guests pulled up under the portico on the east side of the house.[19] "The carriages made a long line outside, and umbrellas, with silks and satins under them, kept coming up the steps."[20] All the "masters" wore kid gloves, considered indispensable at children's parties; the "misses" were dressed not only in silks and satins, but others introduced point lace, and many wore "brilliants" in their ears.[21]

Gaslights were turned on as though the party were an evening affair, which it later became.[22] At four o'clock the young people were marched to the "upper room," where they were served ice cream, cake, candies, and bon bons. When the prize cakes were cut, there was the additional surprise of having a gold ring baked inside two of them![23] The rings were finally won by a young miss and a lad who "carried off the trophies of good luck amidst applause."[24] Santa Claus appeared at the party with an immense bag of presents, something for everyone.

The afternoon party ended at seven o'clock, the last waltz ushering in nightfall.

Not Exactly Another Transcontinental, But . . . It was Leland's Train

At home at the Palo Alto Stock Farm, Leland was able to indulge his mechanical bent by building—or having built—a miniature railroad near the house. After the boy had made his own train by tying a row of chairs together and sliding them about in the house, Stanford decided to bring a railroad engineer down to the farm to build his son a small railroad. This engineer dutifully assembled a wooden railroad on the front lawn, between four hundred and six hundred feet long, depending on which authority we accept, with wires, switches, and all the paraphernalia of a real railroad.[25]

Eleven-year-old Leland had asked a Mr. Benson, foreman of the Central Pacific boiler shop, whether a small boiler could be built for his "stationary" train. The reply was that it could be built, for a cost of fifteen dollars, but *only* with the autho-

[16]NET and ELT, unpub. mss. "Friends of Leland Stanford Jr: Lizzie Hull and Wilsie Taylor," and "The Family of Miss Lizzie Hull."   [17]SF Morning Call, Dec 29, 1877; Nathan Ballenberg, Bio. File. CSL.
[18]SFCD, 1877, 546; SF Blue Book, 1888, lxi, 55.
[19]SF Morning Call, Dec 29, 1877.
[20]"Society, Master Leland D. W. [sic] Stanford's Brilliant Reception."   [21]SF Morning Call, Dec 29, 1877.
[22]Ibid.   [23]Ibid.   [24]Ibid.
[25]SF Examiner, Jun 22, 1893 (200 yards). [HCN], In Memoriam. Leland Stanford Jr., 21 (400 feet).

rization of Engineer John T. Wilson. Leland wrote to Wilson: "If it is possible for you to grant this you would oblige me very much."[26] The boy's father took care of the details and Wilson—who along with his Central Pacific duties held the imposing position of Master of Machinery of the Southern Pacific Railroad Company—built the boiler.[27] Afterward, Leland wrote Wilson a thoughtful thank-you letter:

> Palo Alto Menlo Park
> June 19th 79
>
> Mr. Wilson
>
> Dear Sir
>
> I am very pleased with my car. I did not expect it would be so light and handy as it is. I am now laying the track and hope to have it completed and in running order by the last of the week, and I thank you very much for the pain you have taken to please me.
>
> Respectfully yours
> Leland Stanford Jr.[28]

The following day Leland wrote to a New York friend, Harvey Farrington, Jr., telling him that the next time he visited the Palo Alto farm he could have a ride on the train, which would reach from the house to the stable, when he finished extending it. The single car, he said, would do until he extended the road.[29]

Many glimpses of young Leland's friendships as a boy are seen in the writings and reminiscences of people who knew him in those times. As late as 1941 San Franciscan Maude Pettus wrote of Leland as her "constant and only playmate" when she was a ten-year-old girl living a block and a half down California Street from the Stanfords. Every day after school, she reminisced, she would change into her play clothes and walk up the street "and find the little boy waiting for her at Powell Street, diagonally opposite from the Stanford mansion, where the Stanford stables had been built."

Looking back over the years, she mused:

> I have often wondered since then why we have heard so little of that small boy—of his schooling, his pleasures, his aims; of his traits of character, for certainly because of his natural qualities and the privileges of his birth, he was in the making of someone whose life would be outstanding. I have never seen or heard any description of him, but he stands out very brightly in the memories of my childhood.[30]

---

[26]LSJ to John T. Wilson, [undated, but before Jun 19, 1879], in LSJ papers.

[27]SPRR, *Annual Report of the Southern Pacific Railroad Company, years ending Jun 30, 1876 and 1877* (SF: SPRR, 1877). All officers are listed on an unnumbered page facing the title page.

[28]LSJ to [John T.] Wilson, Jun 19, 1879. These letters were later returned to JLS. NTS to JLS, Dec 23, 1893: "Mr. J. T. Wilson handed me a short time since the enclosed letters written to him by your darling boy in Jun 1879."

[29]LSJ to Harvey Farrington, Jr., Jun 20, 1879.

[30]*Oakland Tribune, Knave*, Nov 16, 1941.

106. Leland, Jr.'s railroad at the Palo Alto farm house. *Stanford University Archives.*

LELAND'S EDUCATION AND TRAINING

At home in San Francisco, in the Palo Alto country home near Menlo Park, on trips across the country, or while traveling abroad, Herbert C. Nash, serving as the Governor's personal secretary, did double duty as young Leland's tutor. Nash's $75-per-month salary, along with the fringe benefits—living and accompanying one of the nation's first families, rubbing shoulders with famous and powerful people, and living in what popular exaggeration called a multi-million-dollar mansion in San Francisco—would have been any secretary-tutor's dream.[31]

Nash was born in Nice, France, of English parents (his father operated a school in Nice) on August 25, 1857.[32] He was educated in various French colleges and served as vice-consul of the United States at Nice from 1877 to 1881. Nash met Stanford in Nice in 1880 and Mrs. Stanford in May 1881 when she was visiting southern France.[33] Stanford, who was in the United States at the time, had recommended Nash to Jane, and she hired the twenty-four-year-old Nash as Leland's tutor.[34]

---

[31]Frank Shay's Payroll Account Book, SUA.
[32]HCN, "Dictation by H.C. Nash on Leland Stanford, 9/14/89," 90. BL. *SF Chronicle,* Jun 8, 1902. HCN and JLS shared the same birthday.   [33]HCN, "Dictation," 90.
[34]Ibid. *SF Chronicle,* Jun 8, 1902.

Nash said that Stanford gave him the general supervision of all branches of Leland's education.[35] He was to teach Leland and hire other tutors for those subjects he was not able to teach.

David Starr Jordan is the sole source for the story that Leland, Jr., was once enrolled in a San Francisco kindergarten taught by his former student, Mary Frazer Macdonald.[36] This school was founded by Sarah B. Cooper and was later endowed by Jane Stanford.

Apparently Leland enrolled in only one formal course of study—along *with* his ever-present tutor—an accounting class at the Heald's Business College in San Francisco. On June 22, 1882, the school wrote his father: "We hereby agree to allow your son Leland Stanford, Jr. and Herbert Nash to attend this College deducting such time as they may be detained by your request and permission and to complete the full term of six months by actual attendance."[37]

Everyone who has remarked on the subject of Leland's education and training has agreed that he was a good student and learned quickly. Mathematics and history were his favorite subjects. Unlike Nash's other students, who were taught by the customary routine of books and regular lessons, the new tutor said that he saw at once that this system would not do for his new charge: "I found that he was accustomed to imbibe information all the time, whenever he could get it—at play, at meals, in walks, and everywhere."[38] Nash said that Leland was quick at learning. He learned his lessons in history, geography, botany, or other sciences as quickly as his tutor could present the lessons. Leland seemed to be a "natural born mathematician" and would take up a problem and master it right away. Moreover, Nash went on, "He was far ahead of any boy of his age I had ever known."[39]

When Nash undertook Leland's tutorship the boy already knew French and German well; he was particularly advanced in German. He was also well advanced in history and geography, "but had not begun the study of the dead languages—perhaps that was the only respect in which he was backward." At this point Nash introduced him to Latin and reported that his young student made very rapid progress in it. Leland's later illness in Paris delayed Nash's intended introduction of Greek into his curriculum.

Leland spent considerable time and money collecting antiques and art objects, but as a rule he was given only small sums at a time by his parents for spending, and was required to keep close accounts and avoid extravagance. On his trips to Europe

[35]HCN, "Dictation," in intro. statement.   [36]DSJ, *Days of a Man*, I, 121–122.

[37][Frank C.] Woodbury, sec., and [Charles S.] Haley to LS, Jun 22, 1882, orig. in Heald Colleges files, SF; inter. with Karen Iversen, Education and External Projects admin., Heald Colleges, SF, Mar 14, 1997. LS must have forgotten about this term at Heald. In 1889 he told an interviewer, "My own son never went to any school except the kindergarten." *Sac Record-Union*, Oct 26, 1889.

[38]HCN, "Dictation," 90.   [39]Ibid., 91.

he kept an account book of every penny he spent, detailing the cost of carriage rides and what might seem trivial expenses, among them string, which he bought for five cents, and a half-dollar loan he had repaid to Nash.[40]

Nash tells us of an incident that occurred in Athens that gives some insight into the character and self-image of young Leland. The two of them had visited several antique shops and Leland had found some ancient glass curios that he wanted to buy, but did not have the six-hundred-dollar purchase price. He spoke to his father about the curios and was given the money needed. Nash was surprised that Leland did not run out immediately and purchase the treasures: nor did he buy them the next day. Finally, Nash asked him, "Don't you want those things?" The surprising answer was: "Yes, I do, but my father gave me this money and I don't want him to think that because I have it, I am going to spend it at once. I want him to think that I have a little self-control, and that money does not go right through my hands."[41]

This incident illustrates another trait of Leland's character—an intense desire to please his father, for whom he had the greatest love and respect. Nash explained:

> He wanted his father to have perfect confidence in him. He had great affection for his mother, as his was a very fond, loving disposition, and his heart went out to his mother. He knew that his father was a great man and in addition to his own estimate, he saw everyone treating his father with deference in his business, and this impressed him still more. He knew that the best model he could take was his father and he therefore tried to do as he thought his father would do under similar circumstances.[42]

Nash furnishes us with the most complete physical description of Leland given anywhere. He described him as a tall boy for his age.[43] He had never been very muscular, but he was always healthy. He had a very good profile—"a large nose, not as large as his father's, but better shaped. He had a very short upper lip, with a low bow in it, and a strong chin. . . . His eyes were very large, with wide space between them, his eye-brows dark, while his hair was of a light brown shade."

William T. Ross, addressed always as "Professor," tutored Leland in reading and elocution.[44] Ross, a Harvard graduate—described as a "cultured gentleman and a scholar having twenty years' experience in the field—was known as San Francisco's most prominent elocutionist and received the patronage of leading families statewide."[45]

Young Stanford's education was described as sensible and practical, with emphasis on the basic skills that would allow him to develop later according to his own interests and inclinations, most likely for engineering.

---

[40]His report is in the LSJ papers.   [41]HCN, "Dictation," 97.   [42]Ibid.
[43]Ibid., 100.   [44]LSJ papers; *SFCD*, 1883, 904.
[45]Harvard ref. in William T. Ross to his sister Mary, undated, in LSJ papers; Ross' description of Leland, Jr., appeared in *Vanity Fair*, Sep 9, 1882, and is quoted in clipping in SUA; Lyle E. Cook, LSJU asst. gen. sec., to Ruth Scibird, SUL, Mar 22, 1951, also quotes the *Vanity Fair* art. SUA.

The boy's technological interest could lead at times to nearly disastrous consequences, as in a case chronicled by Frank Shay. In one of his many enlightening anecdotes about the Stanfords, Shay describes sitting with the Governor and Jane one evening in the library of the San Francisco house when they heard an explosion from the floor above. Shay ran up the stairs while the parents took the elevator. Leland, Jr., had a workroom all his own on the third floor; now clouds of steam were pouring from the open door into the hall. The boy was sitting on the floor holding a handkerchief to his face. In response to Frank's "what happened?" Leland pointed to a wrecked apparatus on the floor and replied, "Boiler exploded." The boy explained that he had tried to build a steam engine; for a boiler he had used a five-gallon kerosene can, filled with water, under which he had placed a lighted alcohol heater. The hastily summoned doctor assured the parents that Leland had sustained no serious injuries, that the burns on his face and hands were superficial. The room, however, didn't fare so well: the windows were blown out, pieces of tin and other metals were imbedded in the walls, and the workroom was in ruins! Shay concluded: "Leland tried out no further inventions until they had been examined and approved by experts."[46]

CHERISHED BIRTHDAY GIFTS

For his father's fifty-sixth birthday, Leland gave him a set of three "pearl" shirt studs. A little later the Governor found out that his eleven-year-old son had expended his entire capital—fifty cents—to make the purchase. For the rest of his life these studs decorated the front of Stanford's shirt. One day while serving in the U.S. Senate, in Washington, Stanford had a photograph taken of himself that showed the studs perfectly. He then had four copies of the photograph made: one for Shay, one for Timothy Hopkins, one for the San Francisco house, and one for the country home.[47]

Two months after Stanford received his gift of shirt studs, Jane gave their son a gold watch and chain for his twelfth birthday. One day when Frank Shay was at the Stanford house talking with Jane, Leland entered. "Leland," said his mother, "show Mr. Shay your new watch." The boy unbuttoned his vest and from an inside pocket produced the watch and chain. When asked why he concealed them inside his vest, Leland replied, "You know that most of the boys are not rich and haven't any watches. I didn't want to hurt their feelings so I put mine in my inside pocket before I went out to play."[48]

---

[46]Frank Shay, "A Lifetime in California," 125A.   [47]Ibid.
[48]Ibid., 125–125A.

LELAND AND JANE STANFORD AS PARENTS

Young Leland was given the best of everything that money could buy, yet there is no evidence that he was spoiled; his father and mother were *parents*, not benefactors. Both parents were from what today would be called hard-working, middle-class families and they instilled in their son the values they both learned as children and modeled as adults.[49] The parents were determined to rear their young son as sensibly as possible.[50] They were happy that very early he showed a predilection towards learning and showed no traces of rebelliousness or indifference. Both parents not only adored their child, but also spent as much time with him as they could.

Leland Senior encouraged his son to play with those "toys" that were "educational," especially ones that would develop a mechanical or artistic talent, including a carpenter's bench, woodcarving tools, a stationary engine, a small locomotive, and telegraph and telephone instruments.

Young Leland loved the out-of-doors and was encouraged to work and play there. He rode his pony and romped with his dogs. On his bicycle he looked like any other young boy pedaling around with his friends, whether at the country home, in San Francisco, or in the East.

Leland made his own friends: his parents did not invade this area of his life. He chose his friends on the basis of similarity of interests, regardless of their social or economic conditions. He could and did bring all his friends home to visit. For some time one of his constant companions was the son of a shoemaker. Leland's parents treated both boys alike.[51]

Nothing reflects better the maturity, loving consideration, and parental affection young Leland showed than when he cared for his ailing mother on his trips abroad. In letters home, the young man tells his father of their tours, his mother's illnesses and treatments, and how he cared for her. On his mother's fifty-fifth birthday, he wrote to his father: "This is Mama's birthday. We tried to make it as cheerful and as pleasant as we could . . . with much love from your loving son."[52]

Not all the praise for young Stanford came from his parents or his mother's biographer and not all the applause for the parents came from family friends or later biographers. An unidentified San Francisco newspaper reporter is quoted as having written in 1877 of the nine-year-old Leland: "The Governor believed in bringing up the boy in the spirit of self-dependence, so that if the father's riches do be-wing themselves, the son will be able to take care of himself."[53]

Leland was bright, scholarly, kind, generous, and exceptionally well rounded in

---

[49]Long, "The Stanfords as Parents," 10–13.
[51]HCN, "Dictation," 100.
[53]Long, "The Stanfords as Parents," 13.
[50]BB, *Mrs. Stanford*, 39.
[52]LSJ to his father, Aug 25, 1883.

his human relationships. He was also outstanding in his academic pursuits, his hobbies, and his preparations for a professional career. Yes, Leland Stanford, Jr., was a good boy, perhaps because Leland and Jane were good parents.

Many of his letters to boyhood friends and relatives make it perfectly clear that—despite his princely lifestyle—Leland was allowed to be a child and a young boy. He enjoyed his boyhood, telling his friend Wilsie Taylor about playing in the snow with his dog, Wellington, while visiting the Sierra Nevada.[54] Later, he wrote Wilsie about his stamp collection, his eight-member bicycle club, and another dog, this one a female named Cootsie: "She is a rowdy for sure, the other day she ate up my pigeons."[55]

THE STANFORDS' FIRST EUROPEAN TOUR—
MAY 22, 1880–DECEMBER 11, 1881[56]

In the spring of 1880 the fifty-six-year-old Governor, fifty-one-year-old Jennie, and their twelve-year-old son left on the first of their European tours in pursuit of the culture prescribed for all American millionaires. For the parents it was also a quest for better health.[57]

The elder Stanford stayed in New York during the winter of 1879, where he suffered a relapse from an earlier illness. One day he became so engrossed in business in his New York office that he neglected to turn the heat on and was oblivious to the temperature drop; when he got ready to go home, he was so stiff he could hardly rise from his chair. That evening he attended a dinner at the home of Secretary of State Hamilton Fish, and on the way home he became seriously ill again. The next day his nervous spasms returned, and for several weeks his friends and family feared for his life.[58]

Stanford checked into New York's fashionable Windsor Hotel on May 15, 1880, to complete preparations for the trip abroad.[59] His choice of the Windsor as a home-away-from-home and as his business headquarters when in New York was later explained by a New York journalist:

> Stanford always made his headquarters at the Windsor Hotel while he was in this city. He began to go there when the house was first opened, about twenty years ago. He usually occupied a suite on the first floor on the Fifth Avenue side, where he could see the walking and driving that were always going on in that thoroughfare.[60]

A week later, on May 22, the family, accompanied by Dr. Harvey Harkness, boarded the Pacific Steam Navigation Company's 2,866-ton *Patagonia* for Liver-

---

[54]LSJ to Wilsie Taylor, Oct 21, 1879. In early letters LSJ sometimes spelled his friend's name "Wilsey" or even "Wiltsy."   [55]LSJ to Wilsie Taylor, Mar 30, 1880.   [56]*SF Argonaut*, Dec 17, 1881.
[57]LS made six European trips, Jane made five (before her husband's death), and LSJ two.
[58]HHB, *Stanford*, 64, later wrote that when the friends of LS saw him off on the trip to Europe, some of them never expected to see him alive again.   [59]*NY Times*, May 15, 1880.
[60]*NY Daily Tribune*, Jun 22, 1893.

pool. This ship, which was built the same year the transcontinental railroad was completed, was the smallest and oldest ship they would ever sail on.[61] They arrived at their destination on June 2.[62]

For a year and a half the Stanford party toured Europe, visiting Ireland, Scotland, England, France, Belgium, the Netherlands, Germany, Switzerland, Austria, and Italy. For eleven months of this time the family was without the Governor.

During the first part of this trip, while still in England, Jane was taken ill and put under the care of Sir William Jenner, a noted London physician.[63] On their departure for France, Dr. Jenner sent a medical report describing Jane's treatment to Dr. Adolf Kussmaul, who practiced in Homburg and about fifty miles away in Strassburg. He was one of the world's leading specialists in a number of fields, among them respiratory ailments.[64] Dr. Kussmaul checked on Mrs. Stanford once a week.[65]

Meanwhile, father and son made a number of excursions together, all dutifully reported in letters to "Mama."

After returning to Paris from a tour of Italy, Stanford delivered an address to a gathering of "Fellow Countrymen" at Fourth of July celebrations at the Hotel Continental. There he discussed American commercial advantages, the need for international cooperation in trading that would benefit all parties, and the hope that standing armies—a blight upon the body politic—would someday be dissolved and their members become producers instead of consumers—but he drew his greatest applause when he said that considering its present state of civilization, man must "rest mainly upon the surer principle of self-interest."[66]

Unexpectedly, Stanford had to interrupt his European trip to return home for undisclosed urgent railroad business. The *Argonaut* reported that he was on his way home from England, where he had gone "for the purpose of furthering his design of promoting direct connection in freight and passenger travel between Liverpool and San Francisco."[67] If this were the case, nothing seems to have come of it.

Stanford was unable to return to Europe to join his family for almost a year. During his long absence, his wife—apparently in improved health—and his son continued their tour. They visited Berlin, the Netherlands, Belgium, France, and Italy again, always hoping that Stanford would soon rejoin them. So it was that the Stanford entourage, often without Leland, Sr., followed the tour typical of American aristocracy, visiting major European capitals and principal resorts and spas.

---

[61] *NY Times*, May 22, 1880; Smith, *Passenger Ships of the World—Past and Present*, 447.

[62] *Times* (of London), Jun 4, 1880.

[63] Arthur W. Hafner, ed., "William Jenner," *Directory of Deceased American Physicians 1804–1929*, I, 798; "Sir William Jenner," *JAMA* 1970 214 (5): 907–908; Kenneth F. Kiple, ed., *The Cambridge World History of Human Disease* (Cambridge: CaUP, [1992], 1993), 18 and 50; Sidney L. Landau, ed.-in-chief, *IDMB* (3 vols., NY: JWS, 1986), II, 1315; Dawson Williams, ed., "Obituary, Sir William Jenner," *BMJ* 1898 2 (Oct–Dec): 249–252.

[64] "Adolf Kussmaul, obituary," *DDAP 1804–1929*, I, 883.   [65] BB, *Mrs. Stanford*, 29.

[66] In GTC papers.   [67] *SF Argonaut*, Jul 17 and 24, 1880.

Early in this first European trip, when Stanford was still with them, the family had visited a number of European health spas and "thermal stations." Mrs. Stanford's letters to her husband from Berlin and Antwerp in November 1880 showed that she was familiar with many German health resorts. In later years, the ailing Stanford spent a great deal of time "taking the cures" in these resorts, especially at Bad Kissingen, about halfway between Nuremberg and Kassel.

As mentioned, part of the reason the Stanfords made the Grand Tour was to broaden their son's education. Such a tour had to be enlightening to the intelligent, alert young man, and his and his mother's letters home attest to the education he was receiving. From Brussels the doting mother wrote her husband that Leland was speaking both German and French and was so fluent in French it seemed he had spoken it all his life.[68]

Their itinerary can be reconstructed from letters and telegrams sent home by Jane and Leland and from Leland's "log book for 1881."[69] This log is the best record of the journey; in it his recorded observations of the cities and people reflected his maturity.[70]

Leland wrote his father from Berlin about going to the cathedral, where Emperor William had ninety opera singers sing High Mass every Sunday morning. The Stanford party missed both the service and the chance to see the emperor, but they did see Crown Prince Frederick.[71] They also caught a glimpse of Prince Frederick Charles of Prussia, the nephew of Emperor William and cousin of Frederick, as he passed them in his carriage. Later, while visiting the Royal Picture Gallery opposite the Imperial Palace, Leland saw from the window crowds of people "bowing and scraping" as the emperor drove up and entered the Palace.[72]

The family then made its way to Paris, where Jane Stanford was again "not very well."

In Nice the Stanfords visited a silk factory and saw weavers at work.[73] The Caesars' Palace at Rome, the Coliseum, and a grand review of troops observed by Leland and his mother prompted another "Dear Papa" letter.[74] Jane and Leland were among two hundred visitors received by Pope Leo XIII. Leland said that the Roman Pontiff had placed his hands on their heads even though they were not Catholics.[75] The following week they visited Pompeii.[76]

---

[68]JLS to LS, Nov 8 and 11, 1880.

[69]Now in LSJ papers. Some of the key guides to their locations and dates are in Jane's letters to LS, dated Nov 14, 1880, from Antwerp; Nov 17, 1880, from Brussels; Mar 16, 1881, from Naples; Mar 28, 1881, from Rome. All in JLS papers.

[70]The account of Frank Pixley in the *Argonaut* is another indispensable source of info. about the Stanfords' travels.

[71]Crown Prince Frederick, the son of the emperor and the father of William II, was Emperor Frederick III for ninety-nine days in 1888.   [72]LSJ to his father, Nov 8, 1880.

[73]LSJ to his father, Dec 19, 1880.   [74]LSJ to his father, Mar 13, 1881.

[75]LSJ to grandma [Jane Lathrop], Mar 14, 1881.   [76]LSJ to his father, Mar 19, 1881.

STANFORD'S SECOND EUROPEAN TRIP—HE REJOINS HIS FAMILY—
JUNE 4–DECEMBER 11, 1881

Stanford was able to rejoin his family in the spring of 1881. He left San Francisco for New York on May 10, on the first leg of his return trip to Europe.[77] He sailed from New York on June 4, again on the *Germanic*.[78] Apparently he had no intention of hurrying home: the *Argonaut* said that it was the Governor's intention to remain away for six months, and possibly even a year.[79] He arrived in London on June 13.[80]

The reunited family spent a great deal of time traveling and shopping during the next few months. At this time Stanford purchased most of his wife's jewelry that became part of her famous collection, and her collection of laces.[81] Besides visits to the tourist centers, the Stanfords were able to accept many invitations from individuals they had met in California. On a number of occasions, European travelers to California who returned to New York to sail for Europe were given complimentary passage on the Occidental & Oriental lines to the Orient. In return for his generosity, Stanford was said to have won a number of invitations to visit Europe again.[82]

While visiting Paris in 1881, each of the three Stanfords had a portrait painted by a famous French artist. From about June 26 until July 13 Stanford sat for his portrait by Meissonier.[83] Mrs. Stanford's portrait was painted by Léon Bonnat, and their son's by Carolus-Duran (Charles Auguste Émile Durand), both in the fall.[84] An adulatory editorial titled:

NEW PORTRAITS,
PORTRAITS OF GOVERNOR STANFORD,
WIFE AND SON,
Painted by Meissonier, Bonnat and Carolus
Duran—Description of the
New Works

bearing a dateline of Paris, November 14, 1881, was reprinted in Sacramento the following month.[85] Bonnat has been quoted as having said that his portrait of Jane Stanford was the most elaborate he had ever undertaken, that all his earlier works had been quite simple by contrast.[86]

Stanford sat for his portrait in the early summer of 1881. Leland, Jr., noted in a letter that his father had returned to Paris on June 14.[87] Two weeks later he wrote that the family was supposed to go to Fontainebleau, but the trip was canceled

---

[77]*SF Argonaut*, May 14, 1881.
[78]*NY Times*, Jun 4, 1881.
[79]*SF Argonaut*, May 28, 1881.
[80]Ibid., Jun 18, 1881.
[81]BB, *Mrs. Stanford*, 29; Fisher, "Stanford," 29.
[82]BB, *Mrs. Stanford*, 24.
[83]See Chap. 11, *supra*.
[84]Osborne, *Museum Builders of the West*, 44. Duran's name appears in various forms and spelling.
[85]Printed in the *Sac Record-Union*, Dec 10, 1881.
[86]*Yankee Reporter*, Nov 5, 1881, as quoted by Osborne, "Stanford Family Portraits by Bonnat, Carolus-Duran, Meissonier, and Other French Artists of the 1880s," 6.
[87]LSJ, "Logbook" [*sic*], Apr 17–Aug 10, 1881, in LSJ papers.

107. Leland Stanford, Jr. *Stanford University Archives.*

because "Papa had to go to Mr. Meissonier and never came home until twelve o'clock."[88] In another two weeks the painting was finished, and our reporter tells us that on July 13 "we drove to Mr. Meissonier in the after noon [*sic*] and saw him put his signature to Papas [*sic*] picture."[89]

We have very little information on what the Stanfords did on the last four months of their tour. The periodic reports of the family's travels published in Pixley's *Argonaut* provide some outline of their itinerary, but it must be remembered that plans that never materialized are often reported in this newspaper as though they had been carried out.

A society gossip section of the *Argonaut* titled "Bella's Letter" contained frequent mention of the Stanford travels.[90] For example, this is the only report we have of the Stanford family's trip to Switzerland in late July for a visit that was to last two months, or of the fact that Stanford was in London on Saturday, August 6.[91] "Bella's

[88]Ibid., Jun 26, 1881.   [89]Ibid., Jul 13, 1881.
[90]Ben C. Truman wrote the arts. in Pixley's paper signed Hebe or Bella. *SF Argonaut*, Mar 13, 1883.
[91]Ibid., Jul 30 and Aug 20, 1881.

108. Louis Meissonier portrait of Stanford,
Paris 1881. *Stanford University Archives.*

Letter" is also the only indication we have that the Stanfords were in Geneva on
August 13 and were planning to sail for home from Liverpool on October 8.[92] They
were later reported as being in Paris on October 5 and planning to leave for home
on the nineteenth.[93]

If the reports of "Bella's Letter" were accurate, the Stanfords must have changed
their plans, for they were still in Paris on November 26, 1881, when Eadweard Muybridge—still a friend at that time—saw them off on the first step of their return
trip home. On December 1 they sailed from Liverpool on the *Britannic* and arrived
in New York at 8 P.M. on December 11, 1881, where they checked into the Hotel
Bristol.[94] They finally reached California on March 13, 1882.[95]

---

[92]Ibid., Aug 13, 1881.   [93]Ibid., Oct 5, 1881.

[94]*Times* (of London), departure, Dec 2, arrival, 13, 1881; *NY Times*, arrival, Dec 12, Windsor Hotel, Dec 13, 1881.
The *SF Argonaut*, Dec 17, 1881, gives the incorrect date of the 12th for their arrival in NY.

[95]*SF Argonaut*, Mar 18, 1882.

CHAPTER 17

UNIVERSITY OF CALIFORNIA REGENT
1882–1883

They Are Regents Between Their Appointments and Resignations[1]

*In reply to your favor of the 21st inst I have the pleasure to inform you that . . .
Gov. Stanford was appointed Regent. September 14, 1882.* ——Albert Hart[2]

*I hereby notify you that Regents of the University have been appointed as follows:
George T. Marye vice Stanford resigned.* ——W. W. Moreland[3]

SOCIAL LIFE OF THE STANFORDS IN 1882

The year 1882 was busy and hectic for the Stanfords, filled with railroad business, lawsuits, an active social life, plans being made for the future, and a serious illness of Stanford.

While still in New York, on December 22, 1881, Stanford was interviewed by Frank Pixley about his ideas on the protective tariff (which had cost the Central Pacific Associates $11 million more than they would have paid had there been no tariff), the possibility of a place for Aaron Sargent in President Chester Arthur's cabinet, and Stanford's attitude in general toward President Arthur.[4] Obviously, a few months out of the country had not diminished Stanford's interest in politics.

Finally at home again, after an absence of over a year and a half for Mrs. Stanford and about seven months for the Governor, the Stanfords immediately resumed their place in California politics and high society. On Wednesday, March 29, 1882, Stanford slipped back into the swing of San Francisco social life by honoring his old friend Aaron Sargent with a spectacular party at the California Street residence. The party was described as a delightful affair that "took place in the large dining-room, which had been artistically decorated for the occasion, and otherwise adorned by objects of *vertu*, lately selected by Mrs. Stanford during her tour abroad." Among the guests were Gov. George Perkins, Charles Crocker, and Lloyd Tevis.[5]

---

[1]Verne A. Stadtman, *The University of California 1868–1968* (NY: MGH, 1970), 524 n25. Ellipses omitted.

[2]A[lbert] Hart, priv. sec. to Gov. George Perkins, to J. H[armon] S. Bonté, sec., UC Board of Regents, Sep 23, 1882.

[3]W[illiam] W[alter] Moreland, priv. sec. to Gov. George Stoneman, to J. H[armon] S. Bonté, sec., UC Board of Regents, Mar 30, 1883.   [4]*SF Argonaut*, Jan 14, 1882.   [5]Ibid., Apr 1, 1882.

Six weeks later, on May 11, Jane Stanford celebrated her own return to California society with a "kettledrum"—characterized as a tea with music and dancing—at the San Francisco house.[6] Mrs. Stanford adorned herself in a robe of royal-purple velvet trimmed with rich lace, and a diamond necklace and pendant brooch. The affair was described as the "most delightful event of the week" in San Francisco, one that attracted a large number of guests, among them Mrs. Adam Grant and her son Joseph, Mrs. Mark Hopkins, Mrs. Alban Towne, Capt. and Mrs. Richard Campbell Hooker, Mrs. Senator William M. Stewart, Capt. and Mrs. Nick Smith, and Mr. and Mrs. Charles Crocker.[7]

The society columns of the *Argonaut* announced shortly afterward that the peripatetic Mrs. Stanford had gone to Palo Alto for the summer, then she took a trip to

TEAS AND KETTLEDRUMS . . .
SOCIETY IS AGITATED.

An important social question is being considered, viz., "What is the difference between a kettledrum and a tea? We know that at a kettledrum there are music and dancing; at a tea there are peanuts and conversation, and the guests bring their own peanuts."*

*SF Argonaut, Feb 7, 1880.

Los Angeles, followed almost immediately by a short visit to Monterey.[8] By June, Stanford was again in New York tending to railroad business and missed many of these festivities.[9] Stanford's whereabouts in the summer and fall of 1882 can be traced through his letters. On June 6 he wrote his wife that he had reached New York safely from California.[10] Two days later he went to Albany to visit his mother-in-law and wrote Jane a letter reporting on his brief trip

and her mother's health. Back home again from the East in mid-summer, he wrote J. D. B. Stillman from San Francisco on July 28 and October 23.[11]

On August 29, the Stanfords gave a party for several close friends, another that was described as the city's "social event of the week."[12] On October 15, Stanford honored the retiring general Irwin McDowell with a dinner; the guests included a number of high-ranking military and naval officers and wives.[13]

San Francisco society's event of events in the fall of 1882 was a visit paid the city by Queen Victoria's daughter, Princess Louise. It is unclear how much the Stanfords participated in San Francisco's regal entertaining of the princess. The royal

[6] Ibid., May 13, 1882; kettledrum, ibid., Jan 31, 1880.

[7] Ibid., May 13, 1882; the Hookers were present at society gatherings in SF throughout the late-nineteenth century. Elizabeth "Bessie" (Stewart) Hooker was the daughter of Sen. William Stewart, see Ruth Hermann, *Gold and Silver Colossus William Morris Stewart and his Southern Bride* (Sparks, Nev.: DPP, 1975), 244; the Hookers were divorced in 1889 in proceedings held in a judge's chambers and "kept very quiet," *SF Call*, Jun 16, 1889.

[8] *SF Argonaut*, May 20 and Jun 10 and 17, 1882.
[9] Ibid., Jun 10, 1882.
[10] LS to JLS, Jun 6, 1882.
[11] LS to JDBS, Jul 28 and Oct 23, 1882.
[12] *SF Argonaut*, Sep 2, 1882.
[13] Ibid.

visitor and her new husband, the Marquis of Lorne, who was governor-general of Canada, arrived at the Palace Hotel in San Francisco on September 13, 1882.[14] Three days later they left on the *H.M.S. Comus* to visit British Columbia. It was reported at the time that the Stanfords were making plans to entertain them upon their return from Canada.[15]

However, the Stanfords left San Francisco on November 9 to lease a house in New York where they would live while young Leland attended Harvard.[16] A report in the *Argonaut* recognized that the closure of the Nob Hill mansion did not "promise much for the festivities which were to have been accorded royalty on their return here."[17]

On Sunday, December 10, the *Comus* redeposited the "vice-regal party" near Goat Island on the ship *General McPherson*, which carried the festive visitors to San Francisco, back to their same suites at the Palace.[18] The next day the princess and her husband visited Menlo Park and were given a tour of the Palo Alto Stock Farm, even though the Stanfords were away. On the following evening, December 12, 1882, they attended the opening concert of Christine Nilsson at the Grand Opera House.[19]

STANFORD AS A REGENT OF THE UNIVERSITY OF CALIFORNIA— SEPTEMBER 14, 1882–FEBRUARY 26, 1883

On September 14, 1882, while the legislature was not in session, Republican governor George C. Perkins appointed Leland Stanford to the Board of Regents of the University of California.[20] Stanford's appointment was announced to the board on October 7, 1882.

On January 17, 1883, the names of three appointees—Nathaniel Greene Curtis, Isaias William Hellman, and Leland Stanford—were presented to the senate for confirmation.[21] By this time, the Democrats were in control of the senate and Perkins had been succeeded by Democratic governor George Stoneman. Rather than vote that day for confirmation, the senate, as was customary, referred all three names to the fourteen-member Senate Judiciary Committee.[22]

---

[14]Ibid., Sep 16, 1882. [15]Ibid.

[16]Ibid., Nov 11, 1882. [17]Altrocchi, *Spectacular San Franciscans*, 221; *SF Argonaut*, Nov 18, 1882.

[18]*SF Argonaut*, Dec 16, 1882. [19]Ibid.

[20]Letter from A[lbert] Hart to J. H[armon] S. Bonté, Sep 23, 1882, announcing the appt. of LS to the UC Board of Regents on Sep 14, 1882. BL. *SF Argonaut*, Sep 16, 1882; *SCD*, 1882, 114.

[21]*CSJ*, 25th Sess., 39–41 (Jan 17, 1883).

[22]The following men made up the Comm.: Chairman Charles W. Cross (D), Clay W. Taylor (D), Dennis Spencer (D), Patrick Reddy (D), Franklin T. Baldwin (D), George A. Johnson (D), Henry Vrooman (R), Kirk Etna Kelley (D), William W. Kellogg (D), Frank J. Sullivan (D), David McClure (R), Reginaldo Francisco Del Valle (D), George H. Perry (R), and George E. Whitney (R), ibid., 32. Party identification and first names are given alphabetically in Driscoll and White, *List of Constitutional Officers*.

It has been alleged that the Judiciary Committee was heavily stacked—10 to 4, or 71 percent—in favor of the Democrats. However, since the Senate in the Twenty-fifth Session of the legislature had 31 Democrats to only 9 Republicans—or 77.5 percent Democrats—the membership of the Judiciary Committee was about as proportionate to the full senate partisan division as it could have been.[23]

That the delay involved in referring the appointees to the Judiciary Committee was a deliberate political partisan move—as has long been suggested—is not borne out by the facts. Appointee Curtis was a Democrat who had served as a member of the lower house of the California legislature in the twelfth session (with Charles Crocker) and as a state senator in the seventeenth, eighteenth, and twenty-second sessions; his name, too, was referred to the Judiciary Committee.[24]

Curtis, however, had a long and unpleasant record with the California State Senate. On December 6, 1880, Governor Perkins had appointed him a regent. His letter of appointment reached the senate on January 6, 1881, and five days later he was rejected by the senate by the narrow margin of 20 to 18.[25] The vote was strictly along party lines. Of the 38 senators voting, 21 were Republicans, 7 were Democrats, and 10 were Workingmen (Denis Kearney's California Workingmen's Party had a large Irish membership and focused on the labor issue as primarily a Chinese issue—its socialist line was largely motto and bluster). In favor of confirmation were 4 Republicans (19 percent), 7 Democrats (100 percent), and 7 Workingmen (70 percent); against confirmation were 17 Republicans (81 percent), 3 Workingmen (30 percent), and no Democrats.[26]

Historian Theodore Hittell traces this rejection of Curtis to his pro-Confederacy stand during the Civil War.[27]

Governor Perkins then nominated Curtis a second time; the senate rejected him for the second time, this time by a vote of 19 to 15.[28] Again the vote divided along party lines. Of the 34 senators voting, 17 were Republicans, 7 were Democrats, and 10 were Workingmen. In favor of confirmation were 1 Republican (6 percent), 7 Democrats (100 percent), and 7 Workingmen (70 percent); opposed were 16 Republicans (94 percent), 3 Workingmen (30 percent), and no Democrats.

Now Curtis was up for confirmation for the third time and was not about to get it, despite his being a Democrat. When Curtis' name (and immediately thereafter Stanford's and Hellman's) was presented to the senate and was referred to the Judi-

[23]*CSJ*, 25th Sess., 139.
[24]CC and Curtis, *CAJ*, 12th Sess., 6 (Jan 7, 1861); Driscoll and White, *List of Constitutional Officers*, 41 and 83; *CSJ*, 25th Sess., 39 (Jan 17, 1883).
[25]*CSJ*, 24th Sess., letter of appt., 18 (Jan 6, 1881); rejection by the Sen. (Jan 11, 1881), 40.
[26]Ibid., 40; Driscoll and White, *List of Constitutional Officers*, 38–63.
[27]Hittell, *History*, IV, 675.
[28]*CSJ*, 24th Sess., 78 (Jan 18, 1881).

ciary Committee, that committee was instructed to decide whether, "under section one thousand four hundred and twenty eight of the Political Code, it was proper for this nomination to be considered by the Senate."[29] Thus, this was the issue: "Does the Senate have to confirm interim appointments?" Section 1428 of the *Political Code* states: "Whenever a vacancy occurs in the Board [of Regency] the Governor must appoint some person to fill it, and the person so appointed holds for the remainder of the term."[30] Nothing is said therein about senate confirmation.

On February 9, the Judiciary Committee presented a majority *and* minority report to the full senate.[31] The issue was delineated clearly:

> Mr. President: By vote of the Senate the following questions were submitted to the Judiciary Committee for its consideration and decision thereon:
> *First*—Upon an appointment by the Governor of a member of the Board of Regents of the University of California, to fill a vacancy for an unexpired term, is it necessary that the name of such appointee should be submitted to the Senate for confirmation?
> *Second*—If submitted, should the Senate take action thereon?
> The committee, having had the question submitted under consideration at several meetings, have arrived at a conclusion, and a majority make the following replies:
> *First*—That it is not necessary that such appointments should be submitted to the Senate for confirmation.
> *Second*—That if submitted, the Senate should take no action thereon.

This majority report was signed by Kirk Etna Kelley (D), Patrick Reddy (D), George E. Whitney (R), George A. Johnson (D), William W. Kellogg (D), David McClure (R), Henry Vrooman (R), George H. Perry (R), and Franklin T. Baldwin (D).

A two-point minority report, taking the opposite position, was then submitted, as follows:

> *First*—That it is necessary that such appointments should be submitted to the Senate for confirmation.
> *Second*—That if submitted, the sSenate should take action thereon.

Senators Dennis Spencer (D), Frank J. Sullivan (D), Reginaldo Francisco Del Valle (D), Clay W. Taylor (D), and Charles W. Cross (D) signed this report.

In yet another clearly partisan vote, those deciding for the majority proposition that the governor did *not* have to have senate approval for interim appointments was 9 out of 14 (64 percent); 5 (36 percent) thought that he did. Of those voting with the majority, the partisan division was almost even: 5 out of 9 (56 percent) were

[29]Ibid., 25th Sess., 39 (Jan 17, 1883).

[30]*The Political Code of the State of California,* annotated by Creed Haymond and John C. Burch, of the California Code Commission (2 vols., Sac: HHCC, 1872), I, 298.   [31]*CSJ,* 25th Sess., 151 (Feb 9, 1883).

Democrats, 4 (44 percent) were Republicans; those voting *for* the minority resolution were *all* Democrats.[32]

Thus it seemed for the time being that Stanford and the others did not need senate confirmation to continue serving as regents. But the drama was not over yet. The matter, it seemed, had to be presented to the full senate, as it was, on February 13, at which time it was postponed until February 20.[33] On that day the matter was an object of political chicanery almost unheard of in California Senate annals. Democrat Kellogg moved to adopt the majority report, which he had helped frame.[34] Fellow Democrat Cross, who favored the minority report, moved instead that the word *majority* in the majority report be changed to *minority*. At once, a vote on the question of switching the words was demanded by Democrats Del Valle and Pierce H. Ryan and Republican Thomas Fraser. As it turned out, the vote to continue requiring senate approval for gubernatorial interim appointments carried by the barest of all possible margins—17 to 16, with 7 not voting.[35]

The partisan division on this vote is obvious and shows that the senate was not going to sacrifice any of its real or assumed prerogatives—particularly when 77.5 percent of them (80 percent after February 23) were Democrats, as was Governor Stoneman—to any Judiciary Committee's legal decision.[36] Every vote in favor of the legislative legerdemain that could convert a minority report into a majority report and vice-versa—by simply reversing two words—was cast by Democrats; all Republicans—with no abstentions or absences—voted to retain the reports as submitted to the Judiciary Committee . . . as did 7 recalcitrant Democrats.

If it had been the intention of the new senate to embarrass either outgoing Republican governor Perkins or any or all of his appointees, it could simply have voted to reject them. This it did not do.

It is significant that the letter announcing Stanford's replacement says that Stanford resigned from the Board of Regents. Moreover, the official list of University of California Regents *also* lists him as a regent who had resigned. The fact is that while confirmation was pending, an appointee was *in fact* a regent, having the right to

<hr>

[32]Ibid.   [33]Ibid., 176 (Feb 13, 1883).   [34]Ibid., 227 (Feb 20, 1883).

[35]The ayes on the question were Leonard Buck (D), William Cronan (D), Charles Cross (D), Reginaldo Francisco Del Valle (D), Warren English (D), Joseph Filcher (D), Charles Foster (D), John Harrigan (D), Martin Kelly (D), Jeremiah Lynch (D), Cabel H. Maddox (D), Charles D. Reynolds (D), Pierce Ryan (D), Dennis Spencer (D), Frank Sullivan (D), Clay W. Taylor (D), and John Wolfskill (D).

Those opposed to renaming and reversing the reports by the stratagem of switching the words *majority* and *minority* were Franklin T. Baldwin (D), August L. Chandler (R), John T. Dougherty (D), Thomas Fraser (R), George A. Johnson (D), Kirk Kelley (D), William W. Kellogg (D), David McClure (R), Thorwald K. Nelson (D), George H. Perry (R), Patrick Reddy (D), Joseph Routier (R), George Steele (R), Henry Vrooman (R), Hyram W. Wallis (R), and George E. Whitney (R), ibid.

[36]There were nine Reps. in the 25th Sess. until Feb 23, 1883, when Martin J. Brooks (D) successfully contested the seat of George Steele (R), thus changing the numbers to thirty-two Dems. (80 percent) and eight Reps. Driscoll and White, *List of Constitutional Officers*, 40.

attend the meetings of the Board of Regents and to vote on issues before that body: Verne A. Stadtman, historian of the University of California, wrote: "Curtis and Stanford were appointed between sessions (biennial) of the legislature and, although their appointments were not confirmed, they had a right to attend all meetings and vote. Thus, historically, they are considered former regents of the university between the dates of their appointments and resignations."[37]

Stanford, then, was a regent from 1882 to 1883, as listed in the biographical sketches of regents—"Appointed to fill the unexpired term of Regent Redding, Sept, 1882–1898; resigned before appointment was confirmed by state senate, March 1883," he was not just an appointee pending approval.[38] In fact, he was in attendance at the meeting when his appointment was announced. At 1:30 on the afternoon of October 7, 1882, a special meeting of the board was called to order at 310 Pine Street in San Francisco.[39] Gov. George C. Perkins was the chairman. The minutes of the meeting began, "The roll was called and the following Regents answered to their names:"

1. George C. Perkins (California governor),
2. Frederick McLean Campbell (state superintendent of schools and later president of the National Educational Association),[40]
3. Pierce Barlow Cornwall (president of California Electric Light Company and president of Bellingham Bay and British Columbia Railroad),[41]
4. John Lyman Beard (farmer and fruit-raiser, later state senator),[42]
5. John Sharpenstein Hager (former state senator, judge, U.S. senator, member of the 1879 State Constitutional Convention),
6. Andrew Hallidie (Clay Street Cablecar Company, known by Stanford from cable-car days),
7. Leland Stanford,
8. Dr. Horatio Stebbins (pastor of the First Unitarian Church of San Francisco, who later officiated at Stanford's funeral),
9. William T. Wallace (former California Supreme Court associate justice, in the California Assembly in 1883),
10. Joseph W. Winans (member of the 1879 State Constitutional Convention), and
11. William T. Reid (president of the University of California).[43]

Secretary J. Harmon Bonté then announced that Leland Stanford had been appointed regent to fill out the unexpired term of Regent Benjamin B. Redding, who had died.

---

[37]Stadtman, *The University of California 1868–1968*, 524 n25.

[38]Verne A. Stadtman, comp. and ed., *The Centennial Record of the University of California* (Berkeley: UCP, 1968), 407 and 426.   [39]Minutes of the Regents of the Univ. of Calif., Oct 7, 1882, IV, 353–365.

[40]*Sac Union*, Mar 29, 1905; *SF Call*, Mar 29, 1905.   [41]*SF Examiner*, Dec 25, 1891.

[42]*SF Call*, Nov 21, 1903; Driscoll and White, *List of Constitutional Officers*, 38.

[43]Minutes of the Regents of the Univ. of Calif., Oct 7, 1882, IV, 353.

The special meeting of the regents had been called to consider three routine but pressing matters: a report on the Committee on Instruction and Visitation, a report of the Finance Committee, and the report on the Committee of Grounds and Buildings. When matters are referred or adopted, the minutes contain no information about how individuals voted, so the name Stanford does not appear in the minutes after notice of his appointment. Examination of all volumes of the Minutes of the Regents from the meeting at which Stanford's appointment was announced— until he resigned—shows that the regents met on November 1, 1882, December 5, 1882, December 28, 1882, and March 6, 1883.[44] Stanford never attended any of these meetings, but not because of indifference on his part. On November 1, he and his family were packing for a long trip to New York; on December 5 and 28 he was in New York and Washington; and by the spring of 1883, he was too ill even to make a planned trip to California, which had to be cancelled.

On February 23, 1883, Stanford asked Governor Stoneman to remove his name from consideration for senate confirmation of his regent's position. This was done three days later—ending Stanford's 166-day tenure as a regent—when Stoneman sent the following message to the Senate: "Having been requested to withdraw the name of Leland Stanford as a regent of the University, I beg leave to withdraw the name of the said Leland Stanford from the list now pending for confirmation before your honorable body."[45] In the same message he withdrew the names of Hellman and Curtis.

On March 6, 1883, Governor Stoneman reappointed Hellman to succeed himself. On March 20, 1883, it was reported that three new regents had been appointed: Isaac [sic] W. Hellman, to succeed himself (Hellman, like Stanford, had resigned his position). George T. Marye to replace Stanford, and Arthur Rodgers to replace Curtis, who had also resigned.[46] Hellman was confirmed by a vote of 37 to 1, proving that his earlier referral to the Senate Judiciary Committee was not to be construed as a rejection of his appointment.[47]

Democrat Curtis was not reappointed by the Democratic governor for confirmation by the Democratic senate—another argument against the three referrals being a partisan ploy.

---

[44]Ibid., Nov 1, 1882 (Minutes, Vol. IV), Dec 5, 1882 (Minutes, Vol. IV), Dec 28, 1882 (Minutes, Vol. V), and Mar 6, 1883 (Minutes, Vol. V).

[45]*CSJ*, 25th Sess., 256 (Feb 26, 1883). The no. 166 is arrived at by counting both the first and last days of his tenure: Sep 14, 1882, and Feb 26, 1883.

[46]Letter of W[illiam] W[alter] Moreland to J. H[armon] S. Bonté, Mar 30, 1883. Announces the resignation of LS from the Board of Regents of the UC. His successor, George T. Marye, was appointed on Mar 12, 1883, BL; Oscar T. Shuck, "William Walter Moreland," *History of the Bench and Bar of California: being biographies of many remarkable men, a store of humorous and pathetic recollections, accounts of important legislation and extraordinary cases, comprehending the judicial history of the state* (LA: CoPH, 1891), 903.   [47]*CSJ*, 25th Sess., 361 (Mar 20, 1883).

There is no doubt that Stanford would have been confirmed, as was Hellman, had he not persisted in his premature resignation. If we look at the composition of the Judiciary Committee outlined above, to win committee recommendation to the full senate would have taken 8 votes. There is little doubt that Stanford had four of the required votes in the Republicans on the committee. Two years later, the twenty-sixth session of the California legislature had 20 Democrats and 20 Republicans in the senate; in the assembly there were 60 Republicans and 20 Democrats.[48] When Assembly Bill 290—the bill authorizing the creation of Stanford University—came before the legislature, the Senate, as we shall see, voted unanimously in favor of it and it was approved in the Assembly by the lopsided vote of 63 to 4. Had Senate Democrats wanted to embarrass Stanford, this would have been the place to vote as a bloc against him rather than for him.

The fact that 8 of the 10 Democrats on that committee were still in the twenty-sixth session (all but Kellogg and Sullivan) and voted *for* the bill that made Stanford's university possible contradicts the theory that senate Democrats in the twenty-fifth session had sent Stanford's name to the Judiciary Committee as a sure way of killing his appointment to the Board of Regents.[49]

Why, exactly, did Stanford resign from the Board of Regents of the University of California? We may never know. All we can do is speculate, and speculation is not history. Over the years, speculation ranged from harmless surmises to the most ridiculous accusations of Stanford's motives for founding a separate educational institution.

One prominent historian—Theodore H. Hittell—questioned and yet repeated the rumor that Stanford felt deeply chagrined over the entire confirmation fiasco. Hittell stated that "according to some accounts, it was partly for that reason that he determined to build and endow a university of his own." Hittell conceded that "there may have been no truth in these rumors," and went on to point out that soon afterwards Stanford began making plans for his own "magnificent institution."[50]

Others—who opposed the creation of Stanford's new university—imagined further and even baser motives in Stanford's founding of this "unnecessary institution." According to one story, he founded the rival school out of spite for not having been confirmed a regent of the state university a few years earlier. In this new undertaking, this story insists, Stanford's motives were selfish, even sinister: "He was just erecting a monument to himself; or he was attempting to injure the State University out of a spirit of revenge."[51] There was no basis in fact in this charge, but it persisted even after Stanford died.

[48]Driscoll and White, *List of Constitutional Officers*, 139.   [49]Ibid., 41–60.
[50]Hittell, *History*, IV, 676.   [51]Elliott, *Stanford University, the First Twenty-five Years*, 77.

As late as June 11, 1894, eight and a half years after the founding of Stanford University, Congressman Thomas J. Geary—a Democrat from Santa Rosa, and a member of the Committee on Interstate and Foreign Commerce and the Committee on Foreign Affairs—appeared for three hours before the House Committee on Pacific Railroads.[52] During this testimony, he seized the opportunity to repeat with his own amplifications the old slander as to why Stanford had founded his university. The committee was examining the ability of the Central Pacific to pay its outstanding debts to the federal government. Geary urged the government to foreclose against the Central Pacific for all indebtedness rather than try to collect piecemeal from the original stockholders' estates—he had in mind specifically the estates of Huntington and Stanford, since the proceeds of the Hopkins and Crocker estates had already been distributed. As Geary developed his reasoning for the legality and desirability of foreclosure, he focused more and more on the character of the Central Pacific Associates—notably Stanford. Geary insisted that "these men who have stolen millions" should not be allowed to go scot-free.[53] Comparing Stanford to a burglar who used his ill-gotten gains to build a church, Geary continued: "We are proud of our university but we have nothing to be proud of in the motives which inspired the building of it."

Geary rejected the admonitions of Republican congressman William Henry Blair, a member of the committee: "Judge not, lest ye be judged." He spoke venomously to the committee: "We all know that it was revenge and meanness, and not philanthropy that actuated the founding of the institution. . . . Is it a good thing to teach every boy who graduates from this university that he must go out into the world to make money, no matter how, by honest or dishonest means!"

U.S. senator George Clement Perkins, Stanford's successor in the Senate, was familiar with the facts and refuted Geary's allegations. He made it clear that no personal pique or rivalry with the University of California entered into the Stanfords' benevolence in founding a new university. Perkins and thirty-two other Republican senators, including many of the political powerhouses of the late-nineteenth and early-twentieth centuries, signed a letter to Jane Stanford on June 23, 1894, in which they declared:

> We who knew Senator Stanford well, and honor his memory for his great and charitable undertaking, assure you that his good name cannot be injured by attributing to him selfish or unworthy motives in devoting his time and fortune for the benefit of the present generation and of generations to come. We hope you will not allow this or any other unpleasant incident to disturb your peace of mind while engaged in con-

[52]Geary's comm. positions—*USCR*, 53rd Cong., 1st Sess., 544 (Aug 21, 1893).
[53]"The Funding Bill Opposed Central Pacific Methods," *SF Examiner*, Jun 11, 1894.

summating the great work to which yourself and your husband devoted your lives and fortunes. We do not think anything has been said that will in the slightest degree impugn Mr. Stanford's reputation, or that anything will be done which will affect your good work.[54]

Yours, respectfully,

William P. Frye	[Maine]
John H. Mitchell	[Oregon]
William A. Peffer	[Kansas][55]
Jacob H. Gallinger	[N.H.]
George L. Shoup	[Idaho]
Thomas C. Power	[Mont.]
Henry Cabot Lodge	[Mass.]
William E. Chandler	[N.H.]
James McMillan	[Mich.]
Joseph M. Carey	[Wyo.]
William B. Allison	[Iowa]
Matthew S. Quay	[Penn.]
Redfield Proctor	[Vermont]
Joseph R. Hawley	[Conn.]
John Sherman	[Ohio]
Henry C. Hansbrough	[North Dakota]
William M. Stewart	[Nev.]
John P. Jones	[Nev.]
George F. Hoar	[Mass.]
Joseph N. Dolph	[Ore.]
Henry M. Teller	[Colo.]
Charles F. Manderson	[Neb.]
Orville H. Platt	[Conn.]
George C. Perkins	[Calif.]
James D. Cameron	[Penn.]
Fred T. Dubois	[Idaho]
Cushman K. Davis	[Minn.]
William D. Washburn	[Minn.]
Nelson W. Aldrich	[R.I.]
Eugene Hale	[Maine]
Nathan F. Dixon	[R.I.]

Some indignation on Stanford's part might have been understandable . . . but not toward the state university; even if Stanford had harbored some resentment toward the legislature for not immediately confirming his appointment as regent, which he

[54]This letter is in the SUA. A few days later, DSJ sent Sen. Hoar a thank-you letter for his support. DSJ to Sen. George F. Hoar, Jun 30, 1894.

[55]Peffer was a lifetime Republican who strayed from the flock in 1890 to be elected to the Sen. as a Populist.

did not, the state university was in no way involved. Stanford would have been an asset as a regent of the University of California—a struggling school that in the school year 1882–1883 had sunk to 215 students from its high of 332 in 1878.[56] The University of California needed Stanford more than he needed it—and it wanted him. Millicent Shinn, eminent California writer and the first woman to receive a Ph.D. degree from the University of California, caught the spirit of the institution's feelings for Stanford when she later wrote:

> The *Overland* chances to know, by the very best of all evidence—that of eye and ear— how eager partisans of Governor Stanford the University people were; how great the disappointment and indignation when they failed to obtain him as regent; how hot the comments of the young men and how grave the regrets of the older men.[57]

The attitude of the California legislature toward the University of California had always been less than cordial.[58] In its rocky twenty-three-year history from 1868 to 1891 the institution had seven presidents. The fact that the state university did not grow has been attributed to the legislature's attitude toward higher education; also, the legislature had practically wrecked the state's secondary school system, the feeder from which the university was to grow.[59]

A later Stanford biographer was sure that Stanford had his name withdrawn for the sole purpose of avoiding a partisan confrontation over matters that should have transcended partisanship.[60] The anti-railroad, anti-Stanford *San Francisco Bulletin* tried to lend credence to this account in a front-page story that stated that Stoneman withdrew Stanford's name under pressure and that the humiliated Stanford vowed vengeance on the people of California for thus rejecting him.[61] The editor did not offer a shred of evidence to substantiate his slanderous statement.

So far as Stanford was concerned, his resignation from the Board of Regents was the end of the matter; there is no evidence—nothing said or done by him—that suggests he harbored any grudge over the incident. The journalistic judgment that for a time he was probably "deeply distressed" and resentful of the criticisms leveled at him because of his railroad associations is presumptive and undocumented.[62] Good relations between Stanford and the University of California were never interrupted, and President Martin Kellogg participated in the opening exercises of Stanford University a few years later.

---

[56]Stadtman, *The University of California 1868–1968*, 93.

[57]*OM*, Jan 1886; "Milicent Washburn Shinn," in Max Binheim, comp. and ed., *Women of the West: A Series of Biographical Sketches of Living Eminent Women in the Eleven Western States of the United States of America* (LA: PP, 1928), 83.

[58]Elliott, *Stanford University, The First Twenty-five Years*, 78.

[59]Ibid.

[60]GTC, *Stanford*, 397.

[61]*SF Bulletin*, Mar 31, 1917.

[62]*SF Examiner*, Jun 21, 1893.

The Stanfords in New York in the Winter of 1882–1883

In early November 1882, the Stanfords went east "by the southern route."[63] In late November they contracted to pay a thousand dollars a month to lease the William Henry Vanderbilt mansion on Fifth Avenue in New York City for the winter of 1882–1883.[64]

This would place him near the heart of national railroad operations and national politics, and would provide young Leland with a place to entertain college friends from Harvard. After staying temporarily at the Windsor Hotel, on Fifth Avenue, the Stanfords and their guest Lizzie Hull moved into the house on November 28, 1882.[65]

The Stanfords had no sooner moved in—some reports suggest that the move was made earlier on the same day—than they attended the evening wedding of Tim Hopkins and May Crittenden on November 28 at St. Thomas' Church.[66] The minister who performed the ceremony was William H. Platt, formerly rector of Grace Cathedral in San Francisco. The attendants looked to be the same as though the wedding had been in San Francisco, including William H. Crocker as a groomsman, Joseph D. Grant as an usher, and maids Mary Miller, Miss Easton, and Hattie Crocker, all from San Francisco or the Peninsula.[67]

The Stanfords would not have missed this celebration for anything. Jane was adorned in a black silk dress trimmed with point lace and wearing diamonds in her hair, a necklace of large brilliants, and a heavy band of diamonds. It was not the first time that Jane Stanford had been excoriated by press and public for her inappropriate display of jewels. The *Argonaut* reported:

> Many ladies thought it a strange place to appear quite so brilliantly bedecked; but, perhaps, envy was quite an element in their criticisms. The lady wore a magnificent necklace of diamonds, while below it, extending from shoulder to shoulder, was a row of splendid gems four inches deep. Her ears, head, arms, and dress were ablaze with jewels.[68]

The newlyweds were given a reception in Mrs. Mark Hopkins' suite at the Windsor, and on December 28 she honored them with another in San Francisco.

The guest list included C. P. Huntington and his niece, the Charles Crockers, Mr. and Mrs. D. O. Mills, Ogden Mills, Mrs. Sibley Severance, the bride's sister from San Francisco, Cyrus W. Field, David Dudley Field, and Lloyd Tevis. (Reports do

---

[63]Stanfords went east last Thurs., *SF Argonaut* Nov 11, 1882, by the "southern route." Ibid., Nov 18, 1882.

[64]*NY Times*, Nov 20, 1882; the *SF Argonaut*, Dec 2, 1882, makes the same report, adding, "so good report has it" [probably that of the *Times*]. BB, *Mrs. Stanford*, 30, wrongly identifies the property as the Lorillard House, and Altrocchi, *Spectacular San Franciscans*, 243, citing BB as her source, makes the same property misidentification.

[65]*SF Argonaut*, Nov 25, 1882; LSJ to [Cousin] Joey [JWS], Nov 9, 1882; LSJ to Wilsie Taylor, Dec 5, 1882. Lizzie's close friend Hattie Crocker was also in NY for the winter of 1882–1883. *SF Argonaut*, Dec 9, 1882.

[66]*NY Daily Tribune*, Nov 29, 1882; *SF Call*, Nov 29, 1882.

[67]*NY Daily Tribune*, Nov 29, 1882; *SF Argonaut*, Dec 2, 1882.   [68]*SF Argonaut*, Dec 9, 1882.

May Crittenden Hopkins

was one of the few people whom Jane Stanford ever addressed by her first name in her letters. May was born in St. Louis on June 6, 1863, the youngest of five children, daughter of Hiram Crittenden and Lydia Sherwood.[a] She was the niece of Frances Sherwood, Mark Hopkins' wife. She was educated in and traveled widely in Europe, and when her mother died in Nice, France, on December 8, 1877, May came to San Francisco to visit her Aunt Frances.[b] It was there that she met the Hopkins' son, Timothy.[c]

[a]TNH, *Kelloggs*, 377.   [b]Ibid., 378.   [c]*SF Call*, Jan 24, 1892.

not mention whether Leland, Jr., or Lizzie Hull were present.)

During their stay in New York the Governor continued to expand his circle of powerful friends. It was there that he met Grover Cleveland, a future president of the United States. In January 1883 Stanford had dinner at ex-governor Alonzo B. Cornell's Fifth Avenue mansion with Cornell, Cleveland (he and Stanford might have discussed old school days at Clinton Liberal Institute), Hamilton Fish, William M. Evarts, Joseph B. Choate, Gen. Winfield S. Hancock, John Jacob Astor, William C. Whitney, and J. Pierpont Morgan.[69]

Frank Pixley's society page of January 6, 1883, carried the message "The Stanfords are quite domesticated in the Vanderbilt mansion, and it is said they are soon to startle the Gothamites with one of their princely receptions."[70]

---

[69]Nevins, *Grover Cleveland*, 128.   [70]*SF Argonaut*, Jan 6, 1883.

CHAPTER 18

THE DEATH OF LELAND, JR., ON HIS SECOND EUROPEAN TOUR
1882–1884
It Seems Unnatural for a Young Person to Die[1]

He was fast growing into the ideal of what a man should be, and to my love for the boy was added my admiration of the coming man. —Nick Smith[2]

"For little Leland, from the Governor's Chinese boys." Card from Chinese gardeners at the Palo Alto home, at Leland, Jr., memorial service at Grace Cathedral.
—Bertha Berner[3]

DID YOUNG LELAND STANFORD CHANGE HIS NAME?

Hubert H. Bancroft is the sole source of the story that at some time in 1882 or early 1883 Leland Junior decided to change his name from Leland DeWitt Stanford to Leland Stanford, Jr. The following is Bancroft's version of this event told in his own words:

He was fourteen years of age, when one evening the family were assembled in the library, at their house in San Francisco, Mr. Stanford engaged in executing some legal documents in which it was necessary that his son's name should be accurately mentioned, and the boy deeply absorbed in a book. While the attorney was reading the papers aloud to Mr. Stanford, preparatory to signing them, as he pronounced the words, Leland DeWitt Stanford, the youth looked up quickly and said: "That is not correct; my name is Leland Stanford junior."

His father explained to him the importance of the change, and as it was necessary that his decision should be final, it was suggested that he should take time in which to think further of it.

"Papa," he said, "I have already thought about it, and I want your name exactly."[4]

---

[1]Denis Kearney to LS, May 7, 1884.
[2]NTS to Mr. and Mrs. Stanford, Oct 26, 1884, quoted in Elliott, *Stanford University, the First Twenty-five Years*, 9–10.
[3]BB, *Mrs. Stanford*, 38.   [4]HHB, *Stanford*, 64–65.

Bancroft tells us nothing of his source for this account, but as with so many of his anecdotes, it must be discounted; *rejected* might be better. For one thing, the chronology of Leland's own use of his name or names does not show any sudden change in name. A few examples will suffice to make the point.

As early as June 19, 1879, he signed a letter to railroad engineer John Wilson with the name "Leland Stanford Jr.," three to four years before Bancroft's reported change of name. A few months later, on October 21, 1879, he signed "Leland Stanford, Jr." to a letter written to his friend Wilsie. On one of his "Dear Papa" letters, written on November 8, 1880, he signed his name "Leland D. Stanford," and on another, written March 13, 1881, he used the same full name. To Uncle Ariel, on July 9, 1883, he signed "Leland Stanford Jr."

If the romantic scene described by Bancroft actually took place—and it is much more likely it was only another example of his fanciful reporting—Leland's impulse was not carried through consistently. For the rest of his life he signed his letters by a variety of names, as inconsistently as anyone might. Many letters were signed just plain "Leland," others "Leland Stanford," without a middle name or initial and without the "Jr." tag. Nowhere is there found any reason to think that he had abandoned the name given him at birth for a later name of his own choosing.

LELAND JUNIOR AND FRIENDS—LIZZIE HULL AND WILSIE TAYLOR

Family friend Florence Eliza Hull, known to everyone as Lizzie or Miss Hull, spent the winter of 1882–1883 with the Stanfords in New York.

From New York that winter, Leland wrote to Wilsie Taylor describing his nightlife in the city, which to the fourteen-year-old boy meant staying up every night until midnight and attending one theater after another.[5]

While Leland was away in New York, Wilsie served as his link with everything he held near and dear at home. In one letter he asked Wilsie to go to the Palo Alto farm and check on his dogs.[6] He instructed Wilsie to take his letter to his Uncle Ariel in Room 69 of the Central Pacific Railroad office at Fourth and Townsend, where he could get round trip tickets for the trip to the stock farm. (Leland also remarked in his letter of having heard of a snowstorm in San Francisco.)

Wilsie did as he was asked. He saw Uncle Charley rather than Uncle Ariel, but he got the tickets.[7] He reported back that Leland's puppies looked splendid and that Uncle Charley had sent another puppy to the farm that the workmen named Shorty, because of his missing tail. However, somebody had stolen Leland's little dog Fannie. Leland's horse, Wilsie assured him, was doing fine. The unexpected

---

[5]LSJ to Wilson G. Taylor, Dec 5, 1882.   [6]LSJ to Wilson G. Taylor, Jan 16, 1883.
[7]Wilson G. Taylor to LSJ, Jan 25, 1883.

109. Miss Lizzie Hull.
Gift of Elspeth Grant Bobbs
(*Lizzie's granddaughter*).

snowstorm—the snow lasted only five hours—alluded to in Leland's letter did a lot of damage on the farm, knocking down trees in front of the house.[8]

Wilsie sent his regards to Leland's mother, his Aunt Anna Maria, Miss Hull, and Mr. Nash, and closed, "Any business you wish me to do for you I will only be to [sic] glad to attend to it for you if you will but state it."

SECOND EUROPEAN TOUR (STANFORD'S THIRD)— MAY 26, 1883–MAY 4, 1884

There was to be one more European tour for the Stanfords before Leland began his studies at Harvard University. Apparently Stanford, with his wife and sister-in-law Anna, had planned to make a trip home to California by April 1, 1883, with the intention of leaving for Europe on May 29.[9] By the middle of April, already two weeks behind this schedule because of a severe attack of rheumatism, Stanford changed his plans to leave for the West Coast within a week.[10] By the first week of

---

[8]The Dec 31, 1882, snowstorm was described as the heaviest in SF "since snow was first invented." *SF Call*, Jan 1, 1883. It was the first snow in SF since Jan 12, 1868.

[9]*SF Argonaut*, Mar 17, 1883. JLS had written to a friend that she was anxious to get home to Calif. because of thirteen consecutive Sundays of rain in NY. *SF Call*, Mar 13, 1883.

[10]*SF Argonaut*, Apr 14, 1883. The *SF Chronicle* did not know the extent of his malady when it reported on Apr 16, 1883, that the arrival of LS in SF that day had been postponed because of the Governor's "slight indisposition."

Miss Lizzie Hull

Lizzie was the daughter of Edward Hull, long-time acquaintance of the Stanfords. For several years Hull was a partner in the Sacramento wholesale grocery firm of Hull and Lohmann and then Lindley, Hull & Lohman. During many of his years in business in Sacramento he lived in San Francisco.[a]

Lizzie's mother, Hattie Hull, had died at thirty-two of heart disease in Clinton Springs, New York, on January 20, 1868, when Lizzie was only five and a half years old.[b] Lizzie became almost an adopted daughter to the Stanfords. Born in 1862, she was young, but not young enough for Leland to address in his letters in any form other than "Miss Hull" . . . though she called him Leland. Lizzie was well-educated and was said to have been a brilliant musician; Bertha Berner said that Jane Stanford often described her as a sunbeam in their home.[c]

[a]For the history of Lizzie's family, the life of Lizzie Hull, and her relationship to the Stanford family, see NET and ELT, "The Family of Miss Lizzie Hull." Unpub. ms. in the author's possession, to be a part of a book on the Hull family.

[b]*Sac Daily Bee*, Jan 27, 1868. The *Bee* reports Clinton Springs; the Albany Rural Cemetery gives the place of death as Clifton. Hattie Hull was buried in the Albany Rural Cemetery. Inter. with Virginia B. Bowers, historian, Albany, NY, Nov 23, 1997, and John W. Buszta, registrar, Albany Rural Cemetery, Dec 3, 1997, and Oct 27, 1999.   [c]BB, *Mrs. Stanford*, 30–31.

May his condition had deteriorated to the point that though not confined to his bed in his New York residence, he was being visited twice a day by his physician.[11] This forced him again to postpone his California trip.[12]

The Governor's health continued to be poor, and on May 25, 1883, he wrote a medical friend—an unidentified doctor—that he was confined to the house most of the time, weak from the same illness that had plagued him four years earlier.[13]

Finally, in a condition of health similar to that he suffered from when they left on their first trip abroad, on May 26, 1883, the family—with Herbert Nash still playing the dual role of secretary and tutor—once again sailed for Europe—again on the *R.M.S. Germanic*.[14] The family had no fixed plans or time for returning, but it was reported that Stanford intended to visit Russia on this tour.[15]

Leland wrote his Aunt Kate—Ariel Lathrop's wife, Katherine P. (née Beardsley)—from the *Germanic* that both parents were ailing and that they hoped to reach London as quickly as possible to see Dr. Sir William Jenner again, as his mother had earlier in 1880.[16] They arrived in Liverpool on June 4 and apparently reached London on the same day.[17]

---

[11]An early report of "brain fever" had been discredited, but LS had experienced spasms that kept him within his house for several weeks. *SF Chronicle*, May 2, 1883.   [12]*SF Argonaut*, May 5, 1883.

[13]LS to unidentified doctor, May 25, 1883.   [14]*NY Tribune*, May 26, 1883.

[15]*SF Argonaut*, Jun 2, 1883.

[16]LSJ to Aunt Kate Lathrop, Jun 2, 1883. Catherine [*sic*] P. Beardsley, in Huntington, *A Genealogical Memoir of the Lo-Lathrop Family*, No. 1800.   [17]HHB, *Stanford*, 72.

Leland wrote a letter to Lizzie Hull from Claridge's Hotel on Brook Street at the corner of Davies in London that is a veritable treasure trove of information and insight.[18] First, he reported that the ship's journey of seven days and seventeen hours (actually, it took nine days) was one of the fastest ever made to date, and then he immediately changed the subject to events and anecdotes of their early stay in London. Leland's interest in mechanics is evident from a casual but telling remark he made about locomotive engines, particularly since his parents had promised to give him his own complete machine shop when they returned home.

The personal flavor of this letter revealed a side of the boy that was almost never seen. One aside showed a bit of Leland's temperament and sense of humor, when he described for Lizzie the single run-in he had with Herbert Nash: "Owing to our natural sweetness of temper we have only had one row since we came. That was over the head of Count Corti the Italian ambassador (the one sent to the Berlin congress) whose room was underneath.[19] I think he thought Bedlam was let loose."

Leland never neglected to show concern for his parents when they were not well or to look after them whenever he could. His father suffered from violent head and back pains and weakness in his legs that at times made walking almost impossible. With both parents ailing, Leland kept up his correspondence home. He reported to Lizzie,

> Mama is ill she has had a very inflamed eye she is in a dark room all the time. The Doctor says it is quite serious and she must keep very quiet and that it comes from weakness and inaction of the heart. It is very painful she sleeps very little.
> Papa is no better, he has been out to ride but it jars him very much.[20]

The boy was thankful for the pleasant weather, saying that in the week and a half since they arrived in London it had been foggy only twice. The days were crowded: one day they went to a fish exhibition, they viewed jewels and a boat, they drove around in a hansom every day, and saw the sights of London from the top of a double-decker bus.

He even commented on the short hair styles the young girls were wearing, and then made the only personal comment about Lizzie found in any of his letters: "But I suppose yours is long enough to be fixed quite nicely now." And, on the subject of the fairer sex, "Yesterday we saw the most beautiful girl Mr. N. or I ever saw she was very handsome and very well dressed N. admits it."

In a mood of unusual jollity, he even found amusing a sign over a shop door, "Nash and Hull." And he teased a bit, "I hope you are enjoying yourself at Chicago getting up at 7 oclock in the morning."[21]

---

[18]LSJ to Miss Hull, Jun 15, 1883, from London.

[19]Count Lodovico Corti (Oct 28, 1823–Apr 9, 1888) represented Italy at the Berlin Congress of 1878, called by the signers of the Treaty of Paris of 1856 to reconsider the terms of the Treaty of San Stefano, which Russia had forced on the Ottoman Empire in early 1878.   [20]LSJ to Miss Hull, Jun 15, 1883, from London.

[21]Ibid.

In England Jane Stanford's condition worsened, but in July Leland wrote home that both parents had greatly improved.[22] Then, while in Paris, his mother suffered a relapse, having fainting spells. Because of Mrs. Stanford's poor health, her doctors had advised a therapeutic sea voyage, but, as Leland explained in a letter written while in Paris to his Aunt Kate, his mother was suffering from periodic inflammation of her eyes, which necessitated her staying in a darkened room. Her ailment was eventually diagnosed as blood poisoning.[23]

The family was often separated as a consequence of health problems. Jane and Leland were in Paris for some time while the Governor traveled alone, partially on business; again, he spent some time in Bad Kissingen in Bavaria and Bad Homburg near Frankfurt a.M.[24] Jane and young Leland spent most of August at the spectacular Hotel Frascati in Le Havre, where it was hoped the sea air would help improve her health.

Meanwhile, Leland kept up his studies. His schedule called for a three-hour study session with Herbert Nash every morning, plus daily German lessons. During the evening Nash read *Oliver Twist* to the small family.[25]

The Stanford travels were followed closely by Frank Pixley's society and gossip columns in the *Argonaut*. In September the Stanfords were at the Hotel Bristol in Paris, and the Governor's health had improved so markedly that he was planning to return home in November.[26] Two weeks later, the Stanfords were reported as "testing, with admirable results, the waters of Kissingen."[27] Actually, as noted, only Stanford went there; Jane and Leland, Jr., went to Le Havre.[28]

After a six-week separation, the family was reunited in Paris. They visited Hamburg in late September, where they were spectators at military maneuvers.[29] Next, they stopped over briefly in Paris again, and in October visited Bordeaux, where they observed winemaking and enjoyed a tour of the wine cellars. Stanford went alone to the Château d'Yquem vineyard, where he watched the vintage in progress.[30]

Friends also traveling in Europe delighted in calling on the Stanfords. When Creed Haymond and his wife returned from a four-month trip abroad they brought news regarding the health of Governor and Mrs. Stanford, which Haymond believed to be improving.[31]

And apparently it was. Stanford had intended to sail for home in November. Despite the fact that his health had been "fully established," so it was reported, he and Mrs. Stanford decided to extend their stay another six months. (This proved to be a

---

[22]LSJ to Aunt Kate, Jul 2, 1883, from London; LSJ to Uncle Ariel, Jul 9, 1883, from London. These letters are quoted exactly as they were dashed off by LSJ. LSJ Coll. SUA.

[23]LSJ to Aunt Kate, Aug 2, 1883, from Paris.

[24]LSJ wrote almost daily from Le Havre to his father during Aug: e.g., Aug 9, 15, 16, 19, 21, 22, 25, 1883; LSJ to Miss Hull, and to his father, both from Paris and both dated Sep 2, 1883.   [25]LSJ to his father, Aug 9 and 15, 1883.

[26]*SF Argonaut*, Sep 1, 1883.   [27]Ibid., Sep 15, 1883.

[28]BB, *Mrs. Stanford*, 31.   [29]Fisher, "Stanford," 31; HHB, *Stanford*, 75.

[30]LSJ to Uncle Ariel, Oct 17, 1883, from Paris.   [31]*SF Argonaut*, Oct 20, 1883.

fatal change in plans.) Stanford was still not up to the pressures of business. The *Argonaut* reported, "Under advice of his physician, he deems it prudent to remain abroad for the rest and quiet from business which he could not have in San Francisco."[32]

In the middle of November, the Stanfords were reportedly in Paris again.[33] There they visited numerous museums before making a trip to the Near East. On the way they went to Marseilles, where they visited a number of art galleries and museums; then they stopped at Lyon to visit silkweavers, after which they spent two weeks in Nice. At Arles, they visited Roman ruins.[34]

The Stanford entourage next traveled to Venice for five days, from which Leland wrote home, "Three evenings in succession we took gondolas and hired a boat-load of singers, and had them follow us down the canals and sing under the Rialto."[35]

From Venice the travelers journeyed to Vienna, where they spent Christmas; they stayed in the Austrian capital for ten days. They went out almost every night, seeing the best opera companies and ballets in Europe.[36] On Christmas Day, Leland wrote to Aunt Kate from Vienna that he would next write to her from Constantinople, where he expected to find many objects for his museum.[37]

The Stanford party spent New Year's Day at Bucharest, and left on the fifth of January for a fateful two-week visit to Constantinople, crossing the half-frozen Danube in an open boat at daybreak.

THE MYTH OF STANFORD AND THE ORIENT EXPRESS

Stanford had an interesting experience during his third European visit that is not often recounted. There are three accounts of this episode—Stanford's, that of Lew Wallace, and one by Herbert Nash—that differ so much that it is difficult to sort out the facts.

Gen. Lew Wallace—American minister to Turkey and later writer of the popular novel *Ben Hur*—wrote Stanford on January 16, 1884, informing him that Sultan Abdülhâmid II had received word of his presence in Scutari and wished to interview the famous American railroad builder.[38] Though there is no suggestion that either Wallace or Stanford had requested an interview with the sultan, Wallace notified his fellow American: "The Sultan will receive you in private audience next Friday [probably January 18]." He then coached Stanford on a very important Turkish custom:

[32]Ibid., Nov 17, 1883.
[33]Ibid., Dec 15, 1883.
[34]LSJ to Uncle Ariel, Dec 25, 1883.
[35]LSJ to Miss Hull, Feb 11, 1884.
[36]Ibid.
[37]LSJ to Aunt Kate, Dec 25, 1883.
[38]The sultan was b. Sep 21 or 22, 1842, became sultan Aug 31, 1876, was deposed on Apr 27 or 28, 1909, and d. Feb 10, 1918 (authorities differ on two of these dates). See Joan Haslip, *The Sultan: The Life of Abdul Hamid II* (NY: HRW, [1958], 1973). Known as the Great Assassin and the Red Sultan, between 1894 and 1896 Sultan Abdülhâmid II ordered the genocide of 300,000 Armenians living in the Turkish Empire.

Allow me to hope you will do so for my sake. Such invitations are always received in this country as orders; and if you leave the city before the audience, you leave me without excuse, and in a tight place. Besides, you should remain and talk *railroad* to the Sultan, a subject in which you will find him greatly interested and a quick student.[39]

The Stanfords spent ten days in Constantinople, and saw "pretty much everything that was worth seeing," said Stanford in a lengthy interview with a *San Francisco Call* reporter.[40] Before discussing his interview with Sultan Abdülhâmid II, Stanford told of Mrs. Stanford's reactions to being a guest at several aristocratic harems. In his words, "I must say that my wife was not favorably impressed with the matrimonial condition of Turkish women." There followed a lengthy and detailed examination of the harem wives and specific comments on what the Turkish institution had done to these women.

He then described their visit to see the crown jewels, escorted by aide-de-camp Pangeria [*sic*] Bey. Passing through parallel lines of more than two dozen Turkish officers "in glittering uniforms," they reached the door of the treasure chambers, where two officials broke the wax seals and unlocked the doors and guided them through the spectacular collection of jewels, whose value, Stanford said, could not even be conjectured. But it was safe to say, he did conjecture, that it was more valuable than the $30 million collection in the Green Vaults at Dresden.

According to Stanford's recollection, his invitation to discuss with the sultan the material developments of Turkey came the day before their scheduled departure. When he explained this to the court official bearing the invitation, this official told him that "the matter could easily be accommodated, by delaying the Austrian mail steamer for a day; and this was done by the steamship company in compliance with request from the court."

The following day he and Lew Wallace with Pangiris Bey were ushered into the sultan's private interview room. There he was seated opposite the forty-two-year old despot, known as the Great Assassin. Stanford described him as "a rather slight man, some 35 years of age, with an intelligent face, that showed a somewhat timid character."

After a few minutes of small talk, the sultan came to his point of interest in Stanford, and questioned him closely as to the advisability of building a railroad from Constantinople to the head of the Persian Gulf. Stanford's "private enterprise" answers must not have made much sense to the absolute despot posing the questions; however, Stanford answered as follows:

1. To induce a private company of capitalists to construct such a railroad its success as a commercial enterprise should be made strongly probable.

---

[39]Lew Wallace to LS, Jan 16, 1884.

[40]The LS inter. with Sultan Abdülhâmid II was reported in the *Sac Record-Union*, Jan 13, 1885, with a note that it was repr. from the *SF Call* of Jan 11. The inter. does not appear in the *Call* of Jan 11.

2. To encourage the capitalists, a grant of public lands expected to increase in value as a result of the railroad construction should be made.

3. Military and police protection should be provided during the time of construction.

4. The company should be exempt from taxation for a number of years.

5. The company should have sole right to build other lines, branches, and feeders, as the development of the country and the interests of the company shall require.

6. The company should have the right to set its own terms for compensation for services performed.

7. The government should have priority in the use of the railroad, but should pay the same rates that private individuals would pay.

Stanford's description of the kind of railroad the sultan ought to build sounded a great deal like the Central Pacific, with several items added that he and his partners could only dream of.

Upon completion of the interview, which Stanford remarked seemed to please the sultan, Stanford was asked to submit his responses in the form of a letter so that the sultan might have them at hand for more careful consideration. The visitors then backed out of the room, "in orthodox fashion," and were treated to a "substantial lunch" with the Grand Vizier and a number of other Turkish officials.

Stanford gave a copy of the letter to the *San Francisco Call* reporter, saying that it followed the interview closely and that the writer would get from the document itself a better idea of the way the interview went than Stanford could give him from memory. There is no record now of what happened to this letter.

Herbert Nash was traveling with the Stanfords at the time of the meeting with the sultan. Though not present at the interview, years after the event and just after Stanford's death he published an account of the interview that seems to be a combination of exaggeration and romantic, creative history reporting.[41] According to Nash, while Stanford was in Constantinople he looked into the possibility of constructing a railroad from that city—to be precise, from Scutari (now known as Üsküdar) on the Asian side of the Bosporus—to the Persian Gulf. The heavy traffic through the Suez Canal had long attracted his attention, because it took much of the traffic that otherwise might have gone to his steamship and railroad companies. The Suez provided a shortcut for Asian goods that before had been sent across the Pacific, across the American continent by railroad and then across the Atlantic. According to Nash's account, Stanford observed that much of the trade consisted of fabrics too valuable to be shipped by sea.

Nash said that when rumors of Stanford's inquiries in Constantinople about the feasibility of building a railroad from Constantinople to the Persian Gulf reached the Yldez Palace, Sultan Abdülhâmid II immediately "ordered" an interview with the American railroad builder. Stanford expressed his regrets that he would be

---

[41] HCN narration is found in an UNC in the LS coll. and was repr. in the *PA Daily*, Sep 4, 1893.

unable to make the interview, since he had booked passage on a steamer sailing for Athens the next morning. Word came back from the palace that he would not miss the steamer: it would not be permitted to sail until he was aboard.

Nash went on to say that the sultan asked Stanford to build the railroad and that Stanford considered the proposal for a week and then decided that because of his age the undertaking would be too difficult. In his communication to the sultan declining the offer, Nash added, Stanford made a number of valuable suggestions in regard to financing and building the road, but he never received a reply.

According to Stanford's own statement of his visit with the sultan, unlike later writers' accounts of this interview, Stanford did not claim that the sultan asked him to build the railroad and that owing to his age and poor health he declined.

However, Stanford's account takes on a new dimension only two months after his newspaper interview was published. Jesse Root Grant, the youngest of Ulysses Grant's four children, wrote to him asking about the feasibility of getting a charter to build this railroad.[42] Stanford answered his question as follows: "[The Sultan] asked me if I would undertake the construction and [I] have no doubt if I had consented he would have given most liberal concessions."[43]

If Stanford had turned down a specific request to build this road, why did he not mention it in the earlier interview? Unfortunately, we do not have a copy of the detailed letter that Stanford sent the Sultan so we could learn more of the facts of the matter.

As it turned out, neither Stanford nor Jesse Grant had anything to do with the building of the Orient Express.

ILLNESS AND DEATH OF LELAND JUNIOR—MARCH 13, 1884

Leland, Jr.'s next letter to Lizzie—the last letter he would ever write—is the most detailed account of the trip to the East, especially the visit to Constantinople:

Naples
February 11, 1884

Dear Miss Hull,

I have seen lots of things since I wrote to you last. We went to Nice after leaving Paris and had a very enjoyable time as the American Fleet was at Villefranche and they gave dances every Thursday. From Nice we determined to go to Constantinople. We stopped at Venice five days and had a delightful time. Three evenings in succession we took gondolas and hired a boat load of singers and went down to the Rialto to hear

---

[42]Grant's letter is not found in the SUA, but the LS response makes its contents clear. Grant's children: Frederick Dent (May 30, 1850–Apr 11, 1912), Ulysses "Buck" Simpson, Jr. (Jul 22, 1852–Sep 26, 1929), Ellen "Nellie" (Grant) Wrenshall (Jul 4, 1855–Feb 3, 1889), and Jesse Root (Feb 6, 1858–Jun 8, 1934). On U. S. Grant, Jr.'s date of death, which is frequently printed incorrectly, see SD Union, Sep 27, 1929.   [43]LS to Jesse Grant, Mar 31, 1885.

them sing. We spent Christmas in Vienna staying there altogether ten days, going to the Opera almost every evening and seeing one of the best Opera companies and Ballets in the world. At Buckarest [sic] we spent New Year's day starting on the fifth of Jan. at five in the morning for Varna reaching the Danube at about six at a place called Giurgeva. (You must know that for 10 days everything has been blocked with snow.) There we took sleighs and drove over the ice to a small island where two open boats were waiting to take the passengers across the river between the floating ice for about a mile where at Roustchouk the train for Varna was waiting. When we arrived at Constantinople we all thought we were in the strangest country we had ever been in before. No two Turks seemed to be dressed alike because their clothes are of so many different colors. We became acquainted with Pangiris Bey one of the Sultan's ade-de-camps [sic] and he took us to the Treasury where we saw diamonds literally by the bushel and one emerald as large as your hand, bowls full of emeralds, rubies and pearls and carpets of gold covered with precious stones as close as they could be put on. After we had seen three rooms out of six filled with just such things we were taken to one of the Sultans private Kiosks and given coffee in cups with gold holders set with diamonds and after this a delicious mixture of preserved rose leaves. We saw two other beautiful palaces but it would take a month to tell you all about them so I will wait till I get home.

At Athens we had a very nice meeting with Mr. and Mrs. Schuyler, Gen. Beale's daughter, and Dr. Schliemann and his wife. I bought a good many antiquities for my Museum and Papa gave me 4000 francs for its support. We saw lots of beautiful and wonderful things in Greece and enjoyed our stay very much. We had a very smooth passage from Corinth to Brindisi and I arrived at Naples without having been sea sick from Varna to here.

Papa is pretty well except for his stiffness and does a great deal in the way of sight-seeing. Mama and myself are not well just for the present because we have been going it too hard. Mr. Nash lost his valise in crossing the Danube and now everything that can't be found happened to be in that, it must have been as large as Noah's ark and contained the treasures of the Indies. We are all sorry to hear that you are sick and hope you will be well soon.

Best wishes from all and love from me.

Leland

The thrill of young Leland's life was the time he spent on the Bosporus, sailing from the Golden Horn (a horn-shaped estuary)—the harbor of Constantinople—to the Black Sea, when he was allowed to steer the steamboat. He spent much of the wintry day with the cold wind blowing steam spray in his face. That evening, back in Constantinople, Leland did not feel well. Jane mentioned this to her husband, who attributed the boy's condition to the excitement of the day.[44] This may have been the first sign of his fatal illness.

Apparently the Stanfords left Turkey on about the twentieth of January.[45] When the weary party reached Athens, the city was in the grips of one of its worst winters on record. Knee-deep in snow, Leland visited several temples. While in Athens, as

---

[44]BB, *Mrs. Stanford*, 32.   [45]See Lew Wallace to LS, Jan 16, 1884, on Stanford's inter. with the sultan on Jan 18.

his letter to Lizzie says, he was privileged to meet the world-renowned archeologist Dr. Heinrich Schliemann. The famous scientist invited the party to his private museum and gave young Leland fetishes and charms he had found in the sixth City of Troy. While in Athens, Stanford contributed five hundred dollars to the purchase of books for the library of the American School of Classical Studies.[46]

Then the Stanfords visited the Acropolis. In the evening, after returning from an expedition to the ruins of the Temple of Eleusis, Jane again noticed signs of fatigue in their son, and the boy himself complained of a sore throat and a headache.[47]

Herbert Nash attributed Leland's illness to the very bad sewerage in Constantinople, in which each house had a cesspool, which emanated smells and vapors through the pipes and into the air breathed in other houses.[48]

From Athens the Stanford party crossed the Isthmus of Corinth, then by steamer they traveled to Brindisi. Next, they took a train to Naples. This is where they were when Leland wrote to Lizzie that during the last leg of this trip he was ill again. The elder Stanford did a lot of sightseeing in Naples, without the company of his ill wife and son.

From the "unhealthy city" of Naples, the party went on to Rome, thinking the climate there would be better. A local doctor diagnosed the illness as a "mild case of typhoid fever." Leland reached what his mother called his "highest point," but the doctor advised a minimum of four weeks' confinement.[49] Though the hopeful mother saw her son on the path to renewed health, Leland's condition grew worse. Jane remained concerned about his health and wanted to get him home as soon as possible. They moved him again, this time to Florence, a city that promised an even better climate for the boy's complete recovery. They arrived there on February 21, but almost immediately Leland broke into a fever. Jane wrote Tim and May Hopkins that her son had been ill in Athens and so ill in Naples that he had been confined to bed for a few days.[50] And now, for three weeks Leland lay in a darkened room suffering fits of delirium, as the distraught parents stood by helplessly. On the thirteenth of March 1884—four days after the Governor's sixtieth birthday—Leland Stanford, Jr., age fifteen years and ten months, died at the Bristol Hotel.

Few people experience the success of the Stanfords—wealth, fame, position—but in the end, they were powerless to save their son. They purchased homes, businesses, culture, but this young life, for which they would have gladly exchanged all their wealth, could not be saved.

Shortly afterward Stanford described the last few hours of their son's life:

My son's death was a terrible blow. He contracted the seeds of typhoid fever at Constantinople and the disease did not really take hold of him until we had reached rome

---

[46]*SF Argonaut*, Mar 15, 1884.

[48]HCN, "Dictation by H.C. Nash on Leland Stanford," 100.

[50]JLS to Tim and May Hopkins, Feb 25, 1884.

[47]BB, *Mrs. Stanford*, 32.

[49]Ibid.

[*sic*]. He was strong and cheerful throughout his illness, and when the fever left him we received the congratulations of the attending physicians upon his improvement. The very next day he seemed to have great difficulty in drinking, and this difficulty gradually increased until death ensued. He died quietly and painlessly.[51]

The simple message sent to San Francisco, "Our darling boy went to heaven this morning at half-past seven o'clock after three weeks sickness from typhoid fever," marked the beginning of a new period in their lives.[52] They fell into the depths of despair, but later emerged with a dedication to humanity that made their earlier philanthropies pale in comparison.

Condolences and Memorials

When news reached California of the death of young Leland Stanford, memorial services were held in a number of churches throughout the state. Scores of poems, written in commemoration of their son, were sent to the parents in an effort to console them.[53] There is a beautiful 249-page bound volume in the Stanford Archives, published anonymously, which contains a lengthy sketch of the life of young Leland, copies of letters he wrote home to various people on his last European trip, and many letters and telegrams sent to his bereaved parents following his death. The modest compiler of this splendid volume was the devoted and faithful Herbert Nash.[54]

Copies of this book were sent to many of the Stanfords' friends, including Wilsie Taylor.[55] The names of the letter writers are too numerous to cite: a list of them reads like a roll call of the leading social, political, and economic figures of the United States and Europe, including Darius O. Mills, Whitelaw Reid, Lorenzo Sawyer, Stephen J. Field, Harriet Beecher Stowe, and—from Constantinople—C. Pangiris Bey.

Stanford's long-time railroad associate Collis Huntington wrote, "Am pained beyond expression by your irreparable loss. Accept my kindest sympathy."[56] A voice from earlier decades, Anna Judah—the widow of Theodore Judah—wrote of her own anguish: "Oh, that fatal fever! I know it all."[57]

One letter—so far out of character, it would seem, coming as it did from a long-time political enemy—was particularly touching. Denis Kearney—founder of the Workingmen's Trade and Labor Union—who made a career of terrifying the inhabitants of Nob Hill, wrote:

[51]UNC, May 5, [1884], in SFS 8:7; *SF Examiner*, May 6, 1884.
[52]LS telegram to Ariel Lathrop, Mar 13, 1884, in SFS 8:12. In a similar telegram addressed to Mrs. MH, on the same date, JLS added: "Please pray for us." JLS papers.   [53]BB, *Mrs. Stanford*, 37; SFS 8:7.
[54][HCN], *In Memoriam. Leland Stanford Jr*. The book entry at the CSL identifies HCN as the writer and ed.
[55]Wilson G. Taylor to "My Dear friends Gov. & Mrs. Stanford," Oct 28, 1884.
[56]CPH to LS, Mar 13, 1884.   [57]Anna Judah to JLS, May 13, 1884.

Dear Governor: I deeply sympathize with you and Mrs. Stanford in the loss of your boy—your only darling boy. When the telegraph announced the sad event, it cast a gloom over the entire community. Everybody said, "What a pity" and I can assure you all felt sorry. Still, Governor, it is as natural to die as it is to live, but it seems unnatural for a young person to die. . . . Tell Mrs. Stanford that I will select the proper and necessary help for her when she arrives home, that is if I am worthy of the order.[58]

The great and mighty of the world were saddened by the Stanfords' misfortune and were anxious to convey their condolences:

Paris 8th April 1884

Dear Mr. Stanford,

At the same time that I learn of your being in Paris, I have been informed of the sad bereavement that has befallen yourself and Mrs. Stanford. Believe me I sympathize most sincerely with you both, and I hope that the impression [text is obscure here] of the same kindly feeling poured in on you as it will be by your numerous friends, may, as much as possible, lighten the effects of the heavy blow.

Proposing very shortly to call [text is obscure] you by the hand I remain very truly yours

Ed[mond] de Rothschild

The grief, of course, was shared more closely and more painfully by intimate friends. On March 17, Nick Smith wrote:

My Dear Afflicted Friends,

How my heart aches for you in your great bereavement no one can know. It daily goes out in sympathy for you in your loss and affliction, for there is no greater loss than yours.

In the prime of youth and the promise of a great and noble manhood, your darling boy, loved by all who knew him, has been taken away—truly "death loves a shining mark."

He had lots of friends and everywhere the sorrow and sympathy is deep and sincere.

He must have been called thus early for some divine purpose, perhaps to make it easier for the loved ones he knew to follow in the path he is traveling, and to invite and welcome those coming to that home in the future where good spirits dwell.

But he has not entirely left us, the spirit of his memory will visit the afflicted heart and with whisperings of comfort and promise sanctify it for the great hereafter.

. . . .

Hoping to see you soon

Your ever devoted friend
N T Smith[59]

---

[58]Denis Kearney to LS, May 7, 1884.   [59]NTS to LS and JLS, Mar 17, 1884.

This letter was followed by another written by Nick to Jane after the bereaved parents returned to New York:

San Francisco
May 7, 1884

My Dear Mrs. Stanford

I am very glad to hear you and Mr. Stanford arrived in New York with your health improved.

Everyday my heart goes out in sympathy for you in your great bereavement, and everywhere in California the sympathy and regard expressed for you both seems to be universal; you have no idea how much this friendly feeling has been manifested, the death of Leland is felt by the whole community.

As Dickens says "of every tear that sorrowing mortals shed on such green graves, some good is born, some gentler nature comes."

You will come back with a sad heart, yet with an anguish sweetened with the memory of your darlings face brighter and happier under the shadow of the waiting angel.

He has gone and what a void for you, but you will never be alone, the thoughts of your noble boy and his angel love with which you are blest, will always keep you company.

Even when you are the most weary and lonely, he will come quietly and whisper in your heart words of love and comfort.

I am glad you will bring him to Palo Alto. He was so fond of the place, the hills and trees will be like familiar friends, the birds will sing to him their morning carols, and flowers will shed fragrance on his tomb.

With my best wishes for you both.

Your Ever Sincere Friend
NT Smith

Later, after Nick received his copy of *In Memoriam*, he wrote a letter of thanks, which was in reality another message of condolence:

My Dear Friends

Please accept my heartfelt thanks for your kind remembrance in sending me a copy of "In Memoriam" of dear Leland.

I will always cherish it as I do everything connected with the memory of the bright noble boy.

He and I were old friends—friends in his infancy and childhood; and the hours of companionship we have passed together, boy and man, developed a confidence and love, which will be ever dear to the cherished memories of my heart.

He was fast growing into the ideal of what a man should be, and to my love for the boy was added my admiration of the coming man.

I have several pictures of him but none as late as the one in the book you sent me, which is excellent; but the best picture is stored in my heart's memory, for there I can see it in all its beauty and feel its influence.

I can hardly realise [sic] he is gone, for often he comes to my mind with a reality, like a sweet surprise and welcome greeting.

How he dwells with you, and lives in memory, the idol of your hearts, I can imagine.

Although you can not [sic] see him in flesh, yet you can see him in that soul and spirit, which belongs to a brighter life, and as such he will always be near you.

Cheer up my dear friends; the hope and longing of a fond heart, is the Aurora of promise, which comes from the morning of the future, and perhaps this is a light given us to follow,—a foretaste and promise of the great hereafter.

It may be when the mystery of life and death is understood we can resignedly and cheerfully say "whatever is is right."

I trust you are both well and hope to see you soon.

Ever your Sincere Friend
NT Smith[60]

Lizzie Hull, writing from Menlo Park, poured out her heart to Jane.[61] She had written on March 15, just two days after Leland's death, but apparently that letter was lost. In the second letter, she describes her own heartache, and wishes that the Stanfords were at home surrounded by those who loved them rather than in Europe among strangers. In her most personal letter ever written to Jane, she said:

> It is a great trial to have you so far away that I cannot come to you. If you were only a little nearer home I would come so gladly. So, hurry home and let your little girl try and comfort you. . . . With love to the Gov. and many kisses for your dear self from

Your little girl,
Lizzie Hull

William T. Ross, Leland's grammar and elocution teacher, wrote to Mrs. Stanford that he thought often of Leland's tender treatment of his pets and of his kindness to all animals.[62] He praised the boy for his great sense of honor in the many games and sports that he so enjoyed, and his "high standard of justice and right, and of his ready acquiescence in what his well-balanced mind conceived to be just and true." He marveled at Leland's noble spirit that seemed to dwell only on what was beautiful and good. In his studies he showed a pronounced preference for the spirit of learning, causing his teacher to wonder "at one so wise and yet so young."

Jane's brother Charles Lathrop wrote:

March 15, 1884

Dear Governor.

I can hardly realize that Leland, Jr has been taken from you and Jennie, and gone to a better world. Our sympathies are with you in this sad bereavement. I hope Jennie and yourself will be able to bear up during this great trial.

Your brother in law
Charley

---

[60]NTS to LS and JLS, Oct 26, 1884, quoted in Elliott, *Stanford University, The First Twenty-five Years*, 9–10.

[61]Lizzie Hull to JLS, Mar 29, 1884.   [62]William T. Ross to JLS, Jan 1, 1885, in LSJ papers.

Ariel Lathrop asked, simply, "How is my sister?"[63]

The eloquence and passion of Thomas Welton, Leland Stanford's youngest and favorite brother, whom he had not seen in a quarter of a century, attempted in vain to lessen the pain his brother and sister-in-law were suffering:

Melbourne March 25/84

Hon Mr & Mrs Leland Stanford

Dear Brother & Sister

Your telegram of the 15 inst reached me the following morning. I at once telegraphed a few words in reply, & now by the first mail to California I write you, though I know not when or where this letter will find you.

If your own loss was not a public calamity I would not by word or deed pain you by reference to it, but apart from yourselves, & our family name & interests, the public at large, whether conscious of it or not, were deeply interested in the preservation of a life that seemed so remarkably promising in disposition & ability to receive from you the enormous power, & its responsibility, that you in the course of nature would one day have placed in his hands—a power that only a good & able man should ever possess. How often have I thought with pride & pleasure of the boy who I so frequently heard of, through Mrs. Livingston & others, was a splendid fellow, & who would undoubtedly have sought to continue, perfect & extend its gigantic enterprises, inaugurated by his father, for the public good—to add laurels to his father's fame—to greatly increase our legitimate pride, & to perpetuate our family name. How often, too, did I think with great pleasure of the splendid commercial avenues you had opened for his entrance [illegible] & continuance. & I was anxious of sharing with you the happiness you experienced in laying a solid foundation to the pursuits you intended to engross his future attention, by varying your investments that your son might be saved the dangerous mental strain that always attends long enumerated thought in one particular direction. And I was also conscious of feeling within myself an increasing ambition to add something to the family tree that in your boy bid so fain to attain great heights & fine propositions, giving a grateful shade to an appreciative people. I know that great wealth is regarded with much suspicion & that the rich are seldom loved by the masses, but knowing the stock from whence your son came I was convinced he would never abuse his power, or forget his duties to our common humanity. Now all is changed, so hopelessly changed. The very laudable ambition that stimulated *me* to exertions has suffered a great shock. & if it so affects me, how inexpressively more so must be the effect on yourselves. [illegible] we shall meet again in the spirit world but that is only a suffice satisfaction, & does not give the public the least compensation for the loss of a valuable earthly existence. I do not like to dwell longer on this heart rending subject, still I would like to make one suggestion, though it be at risk of being considered presumptuous. It is this. If you have amongst your nephews one who has great promise of worth & ability would it not be well to adopt him, even to changing of his Christian name, & to concentrate your power in him, & through him carry out the great schemes that have been your aim of your life. Possibly some such

---

[63]Telegram from Ariel Lathrop to LS, at Florence, Italy, Mar 13, 1884.

plan as I have proposed would lessen your great grief & prolong your usefulness, & stay on this earth. Now dear brother & sister I can only say you have my anguished sympathy, and the loneliness of my own life aids me to see more clearly the now loneliness of yours. May you bear up bravely is the prayer of your affectionate brother

Thomas Welton Stanford

Katie [last name unknown], Jane Stanford's maid for five years, though fearful she may have overstepped social bounds, wrote the following touching letter:

Dear Madame!

Learning of the very sad news about Leland, I hope you will excuse my liberty of writing to you. I can never forget your kindness to me in my troubles.

I could not express in words how badley I feel for you in this saedest of tryals.

I would have willingly given my life iff it could have Saved Lelands. Often I think of wen I Saw Leland last what a wonderful yung Gentlemen he hat growen in every way.

I pray to God to give you Strength in tis grat Sorrow.

hoping this few lins will reach you.

I remain yours
respectfully
Katie

THE STANFORDS' GRIEF—AND IDEAS ABOUT RELIGION

Following the death of their son, both of the grief-stricken parents seemed on the verge of nervous collapse. Life no longer seemed to hold any meaning for them, and it was well said that "the light of their lives went out with their boy."[64] On the first night, Bertha Berner said Stanford's condition sank to the point where his sanity and life seemed to hang in the balance.[65] Fearful that her husband might not survive the shock of Leland's death, Mrs. Stanford summoned all the courage she could to help lighten his burden. He gradually regained some of his strength only to have his wife overpowered by her silent grief and anxiety for him; for a time her life, too, hung in the balance.[66] Berner was not a witness to these events, so Jane Stanford must have given her this account.

Frank Pixley, both a journalist and a family friend, said that the cruel blow of the son's death would have overwhelmed Mrs. Stanford had she not been supported "by a firm and confident reliance upon the Infinite Being."[67] Jane Stanford's belief in immortality gave her strength necessary to bear her grief.

The poor health of both Stanfords kept them from leaving Europe right away. Leland's body lay (with several others) for days in the mortuary room of the Amer-

[64]GTC, *Stanford*, 382.
[65]BB, *Mrs. Stanford*, 33.
[66]Ibid., 35.
[67]Frank Pixley, in the *SF Argonaut*, Jun 2, 1884.

ican Church on the Rue de Berri in Paris.[68] During this time they turned again to Bonnat for portraits of the father and son. The posthumous portrait of the boy was done from a photograph, and that of the father was probably done in the same way.[69] The three life-size Bonnat portraits and the smaller Meissonier are at the Stanford University Museum.

Finally able to leave Europe, the Stanfords boarded the *Germanic* in Liverpool on April 24, 1884, six weeks after their son's death, for the long, painful journey home.[70]

In expectation that they would leave immediately for home, on Apr 6, 1884, the Stanfords' private car had been sent east, attached to an overland train.[71] They arrived in New York on May 4 and checked into the Windsor Hotel.[72]

Visiting with commiserating family members in upstate New York, and, very likely, a reluctance to arrive home in California without the light of their lives, contributed to detaining the Stanfords until the fall. Pressing railroad business kept them busy until November. Stanford and his Associates were then busy organizing the Southern Pacific Company of Kentucky holding company.

While Leland and Jane were in New York, Bertha Berner wrote a half-century later, Leland's body was kept for a while in an unoccupied room at Grace Church that was converted into a temporary mausoleum.[73] Leland's body may have been kept there while provisions were being made for temporary burial, but Berner was obviously wrong in thinking that a church room could be a temporary mausoleum. Stanford himself said on May 5 that Leland's body was to be placed temporarily in a vault in Green-Wood Cemetery in New York.[74] The Green-Wood cemetery has no record of Leland, Jr.'s temporary stay, most likely, says the cemetery archivist, because he was not interred there.[75]

It was at this time that President Grant and his wife Julia introduced the Stanfords to their friends Dr. and Mrs. John P. Newman. Newman was a singular figure whose immediate influence upon the Stanfords was considerable. It was he who sparked Jane's interest in the occult. Newman had preached in the Washington church that the Grants attended while in the White House. In their bereavement the Stanfords welcomed the Newmans' consolation; they invited Newman to accompany them to California to preach at Leland's memorial service in San Francisco.[76]

A funeral car carrying the body home to California was draped in black, with a bier in the center holding the casket.[77] The funeral party left New York on Thursday night, November 20, 1884, and made its way across the continent. Once in Califor-

[68]LS inter. with the *NY Herald*, Mar 22, 1885, pub. in the *Herald* on the following day.
[69]Osborne, "Stanford Family Portraits," 10; Judith Amsbaugh, SUM Docent, to the author, Feb 4, 1998.
[70]*Times* (of London), Apr 24, 1884.   [71]*SF Argonaut*, Apr 12, 1884.
[72]*NY Times*, May 5, 1884.   [73]BB, *Mrs. Stanford*, 35.
[74]LS inter., *NY Herald*, Mar 23, 1885; UNC, dated May 5, in SFS 8:7.
[75]Letter to the author from Theresa La Bianca, arch., Green-Wood Cemetery, Brooklyn, NY, Apr 19, 2001.
[76]BB, *Mrs. Stanford*, 35–36.   [77]Ibid., 36.

nia, the train wound its way to a temporary station erected near the country home on the Palo Alto Stock Farm, where the funeral party arrived just past noon on Thursday, November 27.[78]

LELAND STANFORD JUNIOR'S LAST TRAIN RIDE

"At 12:15 o'clock yesterday a train of four cars and a locomotive slowly drew up in front of one of the entrances of Palo Alto farm, one mile below Menlo Park. The engine was draped in mourning and the bell was constantly tolled. It was a special train which, bound on a sorrowful mission, had left Sacramento at 7 o'clock in the morning and arrived at its destination by way of Livermore, Niles and San Jose. Immediately behind the locomotive and a baggage car was the palace car 'California,' in the rear parlor of which, on a low platform, rested six caskets and cases, one within the other, encircling the mortal remains of the youthful Leland Stanford, Jr., who scarcely more than two years previously had left almost the same spot in the bright exuberance of health, vigor and ambition with parents then joyous in fond anticipations of his future, but now sorrowing and cast down in their overwhelming affliction in its untimely fruition. The chamber was filled with mementoes [sic] of sympathizing friends in the form of floral pieces of many descriptions and designs. A fine portrait of the dead hung between the windows on one side. The outer case was bound in sailcloth, fully corded, with the knots sealed with the consular stamps of the countries through which it had passed since it first left the city by the Arno. A day and night watch had been kept perpetually in the chamber from Thursday night of last week, when the train first started on its overland journey. The palace car 'Stanford' was next in the train. It bore the parents of the deceased, ex-Governor and Mrs. Stanford, together with several of their relations. The fourth car was an ordinary passenger one used for general convenience."*

SF Call, Nov 28, 1884.

BURIAL AND MAUSOLEUM OF LELAND JUNIOR

A simple burial service was held on the same day.[79] The body was then placed in a small mausoleum a short distance from the main house on the farm. The crypt was described in considerable detail in the pages of the *San Francisco Argonaut*:

> The mausoleum is to the south of the main building, a distance of one hundred yards. It is one of stone and brick, laid in the firmest cement, and though severely plain in design, is very massive in its appearance. It is guarded by a heavy outer door of iron, painted dark green, and an inner gate of beautiful wrought brass and iron. The interior floor is of small white slabs of marble, with a beautifully designed border in colored stones. The ceiling is richly frescoed. The designs were made in Florence, and the painting done here by E[rnest Etienne] Narjot. Some of the work has been retouched by Tojetti.[80] Immediately over the sarcophagus, the fresco is that of two life-sized angels, bearing upward in their arms the inanimate form of the dead

[78]*SF Call*, Nov 28, 1884.   [79]Ibid.

[80]This art. does not tell the reader whether it was Domenico Tojetti or one of his two sons. All three were artists.

youth, the resemblance of the face being excellent. In the front part of the picture is that of four infant figures, bearing in their hands a long wreath of flowers, with the word "Rest," in golden letters, in the center. In the middle of the ceiling is a stained glass window, divided into three parts, in each of which is a charming cherub's head. The other spaces in the ceiling are occupied by representations of clouds. The sarcophagus is nearly at the back of the mausoleum. It is eight feet four inches long, four feet wide, and three feet six inches high, and built of pressed bricks, with slabs of the purest white Carrara marble, an inch thick, firmly locked to them with cement. The upper slab weighs over one thousand pounds, and is screwed to the lower part with large silver-plated screws. The inscription is cut in the front slab of the sarcophagus, in plain square letters, and reads as follows:

Born in Mortality
May 14, 1868,
Leland Stanford Jr.
Passed to Immortality
March 13, 1884.

The grounds around the mausoleum have been tastily laid out, and already beautiful creeping plants are beginning to cover its outer walls, and in a few months the whole will be buried in foliage. A new pathway has been opened from the house to the tomb, and it was first used yesterday. The massiveness of the mausoleum and sarcophagus, with the defenses offered by two doors, for which only one key exists, which never leaves the possession of Mrs. Stanford, and the constant presence of a night-watchman, would seem to insure the absolute protection of the remains from any sacrilegious hand; but the architect of the tomb, in order to strengthen even these defences [sic], has pervaded its walls with a series of electric wires, so that in case of the slightest portion of them being attacked an alarm will instantly be given in four important and widely separated localities on the grounds and in the buildings, whose locations are kept secret.[81]

MEMORIAL SERVICES FOR LELAND JUNIOR

The editor of the *San Francisco Evening Post* described the November 27 service, when the remains of Leland were placed in his mausoleum, as "simple and elegant."[82] Placed over the bier and the body was a purple pall, and all about the site were flowers. The funeral procession included the bereaved parents, Leland's Uncle Josiah and Aunt Helen, cousins Josiah and Agnes (Uncle Josiah's son and daughter, now wife of Dr. Edward Robeson Taylor), Uncle Ariel and Aunt Kate Lathrop, Uncle Henry Lathrop, cousins Christine and Leland Stanford Lathrop (Uncle Charles Lathrop's children), and about fifty employees of the farm. The pallbearers were sixteen of the longest-serving employees of the farm.[83]

[81] *SF Argonaut*, Dec 13, 1884.   [82] *SF Evening Post*, Nov 28, 1884; *SF Argonaut*, Dec 13, 1884.
[83] *SF Argonaut*, Dec 13, 1884; the *SF Call*, Nov 28, 1884, lists them by name.

At eleven o'clock on Sunday morning, November 30, 1884, a memorial service was held at Grace Cathedral in the city—at its pre-1906 earthquake location at the southeast corner of California and Stockton.[84] The church was filled to overflowing long before the scheduled hour.[85] Hanging from the frontal arch were three arched bands, where it was written in white flowers on a background of green, the words: "In Memoriam—Leland Stanford Jr."[86] A white cross standing in the center aisle that reached up into the vaulted ceiling was a gift of the Chinese gardeners from the Palo Alto farm. They had written on a card: "For little Leland, from the Governor's Chinese boys."[87]

John P. Newman delivered the memorial address.

THE STANFORDS MEET BERTHA BERNER

This memorial service was the occasion of a meeting of Jane Stanford and her future secretary and companion, Bertha Berner. Bertha and her brother had brought their ailing mother to California for the climate. Reading about the funeral of young Leland to be held at Grace Cathedral, Bertha suggested that they attend the service—they were Episcopalians—and listen to the sermon.[88] Bertha was sure her mother would welcome the service, since Bertha's only sister had died recently. Because of the great crowd, the Berners did not attempt to enter the church, but stayed outside near a side entrance on Stockton Street.

Soon two large carriages came down Stockton and stopped at the side entrance. Bertha recognized the Stanfords from pictures in the newspapers. The Berners were about to leave when a curate came through the side door and said that Mrs. Stanford had seen them and wondered whether they might like to come in. They were seated directly behind the Stanfords.

Bertha was then looking for a job and summoned the courage that afternoon to write to Jane Stanford explaining her circumstances and asking if she might help her with correspondence. Two days later she and her mother were invited to an interview. The only question Leland Stanford asked Bertha was whether she had written the letter herself. She had. Jane Stanford then interviewed Bertha's mother. The following Monday Bertha began working at the Stanfords' San Francisco home.

Twenty-three-year-old Bertha Berner—born on July 12, 1861, in Manitowoc, Wisconsin—now embarked on a career of companionship that would last for two decades, until the death of Jane Stanford in 1905.[89]

[84]This was before Grace Cathedral was rebuilt where it now stands, on the Calif. St. site of CC's former residence, about two blocks west of the LS home. *SFCD*, 1884, 507.   [85]*Sac Record-Union*, Dec 1, 1884.
[86]Ibid.   [87]BB, *Mrs. Stanford*, 38.   [88]Ibid., 37–39.
[89]*SF Chronicle*, Mar 12, 1945.

CHAPTER 19

The Birth of
Leland Stanford Junior University
The Children of California Shall Be our Children[1]

And was not Leland Stanford, Junior's, death one of the great blessings of our country? . . . through him started the great university . . . an institution to build up . . . the youth of our country. —Maggie McClure[2]

Through the means of the great university that bears his name, the world of learning is the richer for young Leland Stanford's short stay on earth.
—Gunther Nagel[3]

The Idea of a University Takes Shape

Following the unexpected and tragic death of Leland, Jr., while visiting Europe in the spring of 1884, the physical and mental ill-health of the distraught Stanfords prevented their leaving for home for several weeks.

We now have no way of knowing for sure, but perhaps it was during this time that the idea for founding an educational institution in their son's memory began to take shape. After their ideas on the subject had matured and actual research into what this would entail had begun, it seems that *everyone* had thought of the university idea before the Stanfords did.

One early claimant to having discussed with Stanford ideas of what the parents of the dead boy might do as a memorial for their son, something that would redound to the benefit of others, was Connecticut-born Augustus Field Beard, then serving as pastor of the American Church in Paris.[4] The following account of

---

[1]BB, *Mrs. Stanford*, 45.

[2]"Maggie," Margaret M. McClure, was one of the reigning belles of Calif. in the late 1850s and early 1860s. Maggie McClure to Boutwell Dunlap, in Dunlap, "Some Facts Concerning Leland Stanford," 210.

[3]Nagel, "Boy in a Gilded Age," 320–331.

[4]Augustus Field Beard was born in 1833 and died in 1934, 101 years and 7 months old. He served as pastor of the American Church in Paris from 1883 to 1886, before being transferred back to NY. He was a graduate of Yale, A.B. 1857, A.M. 1860, and a graduate of the Union Theo. Sem. in 1860. He was awarded an honorary doctor of divinity degree by Syracuse Univ. in 1875. Ordained a Congregationalist minister 1860, and corresponding sec. of the Amer. Missionary Assn. (AMA) after 1886. Author of *A Crusade of Brotherhood: A History of the American Missionary Association*   (continued)

Beard's relationship with the Stanfords was given in a 1928 letter he sent to the president of Stanford University:

When young Leland died, his body was brought to the mortuary chapel connected with the American Church in Rue de Berri of which I was pastor. This brought me into a close relationship for the time with his sorrowing parents. They visited the room where his precious remains were, daily or nearly so, where I met them at their request and where we held devotions together. Both were so sadly stricken that I had for them a deep sympathy which they recognized with much confidence. We spoke of our religious hopes and feelings freely. On one occasion, Senator Stanford sought me with a special purpose. He said, "This bereavement has so entirely changed my thoughts and plans of life that I do not see the way before me. I have been successful in the accumulation of property, and all of my thoughts of the future were associated with my dear son. I was living for him and his future. This is what brought us abroad for his education. Now, I was thinking in the night, since Leland is gone what my wealth could do. I was thinking since I could do no more for my boy I might do something for other people's boys in Leland's name. When I was connected with the building of the railroad, I found that many of those engaged in the engineering work [were] inefficient and inexact and poorly prepared for their work. I was thinking I might start a school or institution for civil and mechanical engineers on my grounds in Palo Alto. I have a beautiful situation there. What would you think of that?" I did not know then that he had been Governor of California, and I replied, "Mr. Stanford, that is fine. Leland would be worthily honored and remembered in that way, but could you not enlarge upon that and make it broadly an educational institution of larger scope with applied science as an annex or department, giving a larger fitness for life and for the work?" He was interested at once, saying, "Do you know of any such situation?" I replied that I did, and said, "For example, there is Cornell University. You must know Andrew D. White." "Certainly I do," he said. I continued, "He is a personal friend of mine; was a Syracuse neighbor for years. He is an educator such as you should see and confer with, and Cornell is the type of an institution you would wish to visit. Be sure and see President White and Cornell when you return. You could, I am sure, do no better than that."

Subsequently, a few days later—perhaps a week or so after—I received a request through Mrs. Stanford to be present at their hotel together with Consul-General Walker, an attendant at the church, to witness the will of Mr. Stanford in behalf of a proposed institution at Palo Alto. Mrs. Stanford said to me, "Think of it; it is four million." This was the beginning. I have been told that upon his return Mr. Stanford did visit Mr. White and Cornell, and at Mr. White's suggestion Harvard also.

Thus it came about growing out of our conversations together that I happened to be the first one with whom he conferred. The idea of an institution—technologi-

(continued) (Boston: TPP, 1909), 317. He was long associated with the AMA, an organization founded in 1846 as an interdenominational missionary soc. devoted to abolitionist principles. The AMA founded more than five hundred schools for freed slaves, and ten predominantly black colleges arose from the organization's efforts. See newspaper art. in *Redlands Daily Facts*, Dec 22, 1934, in LSJ papers. See also "Augustus Field Beard," *Who Was Who Among North American Authors, 1921–1939*, Vol. 1.A–J. (Detroit: GRC, 1976), 119, and "Augustus Field Beard," *Who Was Who in America*, Vol. 1, 1897–1942 (Chicago: MarWW, 1960), 74.

cal—was his own; the kind and character the institution was the enlargement of his thought which he acted upon. I was happy that I could make this suggestion. Before he left Paris he had printed a thousand copies of an Easter discourse of mine which he circulated, and sent me through his secretary a personal check of $2500, which, though personal, was devoted to the interest of the church.

When he was Senator, I met him at Washington, and I now have letters from Mrs. Stanford with an invitation to visit them at Palo Alto which I did not find time to do. I have a fine portrait of Leland, Jr., at sixteen years of age which Mrs. Stanford presented to me. This does not relate to your request, but may be of interest to you as showing my relations to Mr. Stanford at the time. Senator Stanford was at once recognized by me as an exceptional man and Mrs. Stanford as an unusual woman.[5]

According to this lengthy statement, Beard listened to Stanford's ideas about the need for a school to train civil and mechanical engineers, and then suggested to him the idea of a school broader in scope, patterned after Cornell.[6] What influence, if any, Beard had in this matter is unclear, but from his own statement, the seminal idea of founding an educational institution must have taken shape in Stanford's mind before their discussion of the matter.

Beard was the first of many people who claimed to have planted the idea in Stanford's mind or caused him to expand upon his own idea as a result of their suggestions. If there is any truth to Berner's statement on the matter, which had to have come from Leland or Jane Stanford, Beard's influence was next to nothing. Berner later wrote that immediately following the death of Leland, when Stanford was himself under medical care, he "indicated that his mind was already beginning to form plans for the application of his resources to an educational institution."[7] She continued:

I heard this episode mentioned by Mr. Stanford himself on two different occasions, and I repeat it here in order to correct a misunderstanding that the plan for a university was suggested by an American minister who happened to stay at the Hotel Bristol in Florence at the time of Leland's death and who was under the impression that he was called on by Mr. Stanford to tell him what to do now that he had lost his only child. This minister did call on Mr. and Mrs. Stanford just before they left for Paris, but was not asked to give advice.

But Beard's role and his self-importance grew with the years. When he died on December 22, 1934, his obituary left no doubt how by then he saw his influence over Stanford. This write-up stated:

While there [Paris] he conducted the funeral of young Leland Stanford and became

---

[5] Augustus F. Beard to Ray Lyman Wilbur, Dec 31, 1928. This letter cannot be found in the Wilbur papers at SUA; it is quoted at length here as pub. by GTC, *Stanford*, 384–385.

[6] DSJ agreed that Cornell was the model: "The Educational Ideas of Leland Stanford," *SS* 1893 3 (2): 19–22; repr. as *Leland Stanford's Views on Higher Education* (Stanford: SUP, 1901), 8. Tenth Annual Commencement Speech.

[7] BB, *Mrs. Stanford*, 34.

intimately acquainted with the parents. When they asked him to suggest a fitting memorial for their son, he outlined the possibility of a university on the Pacific Coast, and the result was the establishment of Leland Stanford University.[8]

Somehow Stanford's thinking that he might establish some sort of training institution reached the United States almost before he did. Shortly after he arrived in New York, his friend Frank Pixley called on him in his New York quarters to get more information on his thinking about founding a school. Pixley wrote home and had published that the Stanfords intended to establish a school for boys and girls at Menlo Park that would prepare them for the realities of life; it was going to focus on practical learning rather than on higher education.[9] Pixley's own words—and certainly he would not have published anything Stanford did not want him to print— were:

> Governor Stanford is restored to perfect health. I have never seen him looking better than now; he seems to be the very type of physical health and mental vigor. The loss of his son is to him a most severe blow. He speaks of it as affecting and changing, in a great degree, his views and purposes. Upon this promising boy he had centred the ambition of his life. This son had satisfied the loving pride of his parents; he gave promise of a useful and brilliant career; and not till his death did they fully realize how much they had depended upon him. The blow was to the mother a most cruel one—it would have been overwhelming had she not been supported by a firm and confident reliance upon the Infinite Being who, in her belief, doeth all things well, and by the strength of the husband upon whom she leaned in the hour of her deep affliction.
>
> Governor Stanford has plans for the establishment of a school for boys and girls at Menlo, where practical education will be afforded in order to fit pupils for the scramble of life. It will be a practical education rather than one upon the higher plane of learning. The plan is not yet matured, but it is sufficiently developed for Governor Stanford to speak freely of it as an important life-work, to which he shall devote much of his time and fortune. Using his own expression, he desires to administer upon his own estate during his own lifetime for the public good. This school will educate boys and girls in such practical industries as will enable them to go out into the world equipped for useful labor, with such practical knowledge as will be of service to them in the battle for bread. It will not be a charitable institution in the undiscriminating sense. Certain scholarships will be provided for the deserving, certain rewards for the diligent. The whole scheme is a brilliant and useful one, and will build for the Stanfords a monument more enduring than one of brass or marble— one that will serve humanity and be of infinite credit to the generous man who endows it with his wealth.[10]

[8] NY Times, Dec 23, 1934.

[9] SF Argonaut, Jun 21, 1884. One of the most detailed statements of the educational ideas of LS was pub. in the SF Examiner, Oct 20, 1889, inter. and repr. under the heading "General Education," in the Sac Record-Union, Oct 26, 1889.

[10] SF Argonaut, Jun 21, 1884.

The Stanfords Seek Professional Advice on Founding a University

Stanford was entering an entirely new field in the business of creating a university, and there lay many obstacles in his path, not least of all his own lack of a university education and lack of almost any experience in dealing with an institution of higher learning. These obstacles were summarized succinctly and tactfully in 1897 by Stanford registrar Orrin Leslie Elliott after the founding of Stanford University: "Senator Stanford was not himself a college man, nor even what would be technically termed an educated man. In setting about the creation of a university he had to feel his way . . . largely in the dark. It is hardly less than amazing that he should have arrived at the result he did."[11]

The Stanfords were practical enough to seek the best advice from the outstanding leaders in a field about which they knew next to nothing. Immediately upon his return from Europe after young Leland's death in the spring of 1884, Stanford contacted a number of the nation's foremost college administrators—described as "the four most daring and revolutionary of the distinguished university presidents in the nation."[12] He interviewed the presidents of Harvard, Johns Hopkins, Cornell, and the Massachusetts Institute of Technology (MIT): Charles W. Eliot of Harvard, who had revolutionized that institution's curriculum by creating an elective system that made classical instruction a matter of student choice; Daniel Coit Gilman (formerly of the University of California) of Johns Hopkins, America's first all-graduate research university; Francis Amasa Walker, who was shaping MIT into a combination university and training school;[13] and Andrew Dickson White of Cornell, who had combined elements of the first three universities into a distinctive coeducational university. On July 5, 1884, the Stanfords spent the entire day at Cornell with President Andrew D. White.[14]

Eliot of Harvard was later reported as having said that the Stanfords had come to him and asked what his plant was worth. When given the figure of $5 million to $6 million, Mrs. Stanford is said to have gushed, "Oh, Leland, we can do it." This conveys the impression that the Stanfords were so naive that they did not appreciate that a university was more than buildings. Jordan later wrote that in response to a request he made to Eliot for more specific information on this interview, he received a letter in which Eliot wrote: "Mrs. Stanford looked grave; but after an appreciable interval Mr. Stanford said with a smile, 'Well, Jane, we could manage

---

[11]Orrin Elliott, "Stanford University," *CCom* 1897 1 (4): 2.

[12]Pease, "The Man," 17.

[13]Jeannette Nichols, "Francis Amasa Walker," *DAB*, X, Part 1, 342–344.

[14]Elliott, *Stanford University, the First Twenty-five Years*, 15. Elliott has the best treatment of the Stanfords' various calls on univ. presidents.

SAMUEL ELIOT'S DINNER PARTY TALK ON THE "SHABBY STANFORDS"

Harvard president Charles W. Eliot's account of a meeting he had with the Stanfords took on an apocryphal luster with each retelling, especially as embellished by his son, Samuel Eliot.

A number of years afterward, at a dinner party at the home of University of Chicago president Henry Pratt Judson, Eliot described "a shabby little man and a shabby little woman"—undoubtedly all spoken tongue-in-cheek, since both Stanfords were always richly and immaculately dressed—who called on his father for advice on building their projected university.[a] The shabby little man is said to have asked: "How much would it cost to duplicate Harvard?" When told that Harvard had a history, a tradition, that could not be duplicated, the "shabby little man" replied: "I mean the plant, the Plant of Harvard, buildings, equipment and such." The story suffers from paraphrase. In the words of young Eliot, the shabby multimillionaire bumbled out, "Oh, I see . . . well." The preposterous conversation concocted by Samuel Eliot—probably intended as nothing more than humorous table-talk—continued: "My father decided to mention a hastily computed round sum and terminate the quite useless conversation: 'Let's say twenty-five million dollars.' Then the shabby little man turned to his shabby little wife in a sort of ecstasy and exclaimed: 'Jane, we can do it! Jane, we can do it!'"[b]

The *report* of what President Eliot is reported to have said was wrong on all accounts: the amount of money in this story was increased fivefold, the Stanfords were not little—Stanford himself weighed over 240 at the time, and his wife almost 170—and they were far from shabby in their dress, as one could see by reading the society columns of any San Francisco, New York, or Washington newspaper.[c] Mrs. Stanford was known as a tall, distinguished, and well-groomed lady of refinement—she would have been the only "shabby little old lady" in the world with a million dollars' worth of jewelry and the reputation of being one of California's best-dressed matrons. Her husband's personal grooming was always impeccable, though at times a bit out of style. While in the Senate it was said of him that though neat, he was one of the most unassumingly dressed men in the capital.[d] His wealth was not reflected in his clothes; he wore an old-fashioned, though not shabby, low-cut vest, but his suits were of the best Irish linen. Stanford almost always wore a butterfly necktie, having a short-ended bow and fastened to the top shirt button by a rubber band.[e] For a number of years this was the only tie he possessed and parted with it only when it was completely worn out. The portrait by Meissonier has him wearing this tie with a rubber band holding it to the top shirt button.[f]

The ridiculous story of the shabby Stanfords, like so many spurious accounts that poke fun at the wealthy and famous, has been repeated for more than a century. The most recent version gained currency on the Internet, when, under the name Malcolm Forbes, a variation on the above account was broadcast for the edification or amusement of the ignorant, the ingenuous, and the gullible.

[a]Judson's dates in the pres. chair were from 1906 to 1907 as acting pres. and from 1907 to 1923 as president, "Harry Pratt Judson," *NCAB* (NY: JTWC, 1929), XX, 24–25. [b]Altrocchi, *Spectacular San Franciscans*, 243–244. [c]UNC, SFS 25:33. [d]Ibid., 18:12. [e]UNC, SUA. [f]Ibid.

that, couldn't we?' And Mrs. Stanford nodded."[15] (A later retelling of this incident has it that when told that it would take about $5 million to endow the university

---

[15]Charles W. Eliot to DSJ, Jun 26, 1919. The original letter is in the DSJ papers, SUA; a copy is in the Orrin Leslie Elliott papers, SUA. See DSJ, *Days of a Man*, I, 367.

they had in mind, Stanford turned to Jane and remarked simply, "Don't you think we had better make it ten millions, my dear?"[16])

Another college administrator from whom Stanford sought advice was Gen. Francis Amasa Walker, president of the Massachusetts Institute of Technology. Walker spent three weeks at the Palo Alto farm beginning in late August 1885 and a number of weeks again in the fall of 1886, advising on the building program.[17] He recommended construction of thirteen single-storey stone buildings. Walker's concepts were used by the architects George Foster Shepley, Charles Hercules Rutan, and Charles Allerton Coolidge, successors to Henry H. Richardson, who was hired by Stanford. Coolidge asked that his firm be considered for the job, and possibly through the influence of Walker (who was Coolidge's mother's cousin), it was given to his firm.[18]

FOUNDING OF LELAND STANFORD JUNIOR UNIVERSITY— NOVEMBER 11, 1885

Back in California after young Leland's death, the Stanfords took immediate steps toward founding their school, but they ran into one difficulty: Stanford insisted upon retaining control during his lifetime over what was now more and more commonly being referred to as a university, whereas California law had no provisions for the incorporation of such a philanthropic institution. His first move, therefore, was to have a bill prepared for introduction into the state legislature that would provide for the creation of the kind of school he wanted to found. He remarked that had such a law not been passed, his own school's trustees could have put him off the grounds. Stanford explained further that he wanted his ideas carried out, so far as they were practical, and since he was going to invest most of his fortune in this school, he would naturally like to humor his own whims.[19] He would not be satisfied making gifts to institutions over which he would have no influence or upon which he could not impress his own ideas. Stanford said that he had seen a number of large estates intended for public use devoured by attorneys and reduced to next to nothing by litigation following the death of the testators; seeing the possibility that this might happen to their estate, he and his wife had resolved to make the gift during their lifetimes and oversee its administration.[20]

Creed Haymond, one of Stanford's attorneys, quickly drew up the appropriate document. San Francisco Republican William B. May presented it to the assembly

---

[16]"Address of [Sen. John W.] Daniel of Virginia," *Memorial Addresses on the Life and Character of Leland Stanford,* 53.

[17]James P. Munroe, *A Life of Francis Amasa Walker* (NY: HHC, 1923), 307; *SJ Mercury,* Sep 18, 1886; *SF Call,* Sep 18, 1886.

[18]Shepley, Rutan, & Coolidge Company letter to DSJ, Jan 29, 1913, in GTC, *Stanford,* 402–403; see Paul V. Turner and Marcia E. Vetrocq, *The Founders and the Architects, the Design of Stanford University* (Stanford: SDA, 1976), passim.

[19]*Wash. Post,* Dec 19, 1886.   [20]*NY Herald,* Mar 23, 1885.

on January 26, 1885, as Assembly Bill 290.[21] On February 17 the assembly—in a house that numbered sixty Democrats and twenty Republicans—passed the bill by a vote of 63 to 4. All four dissenters were Democrats.[22]

On March 5, 1885, the California Senate passed the bill 31 to 0.[23] The passage of this measure came as a birthday gift for the Governor; Governor Stoneman signed it into law on March 9, 1885, Stanford's sixty-first birthday.[24]

Among the key provisions of the twelve-section law, written by Haymond to reflect what Stanford wanted, were the following:

> The person making such grant may therein designate:
> 1. The nature, object, and purpose of the institution.
> 2. The right to name the institution founded.
> 3. The powers and duties of the trustees.
> 4. The manner by which trustees were to be named.
> 5. Rules and regulations for the management of property conveyed.
> 6. The place, time of building, and character of buildings to be erected.[25]

Section 5 of the law permitted Jane Stanford to retain absolute control over the management and affairs of the university if her husband died. She would then hold the power until she voluntarily surrendered her sole trusteeship to the Board of Trustees:

> The person making such grant, by a provision herein, may elect, in relation to the property conveyed, and in relation to the erection, maintenance, and management of such institution or institutions, to perform, during his life, all the duties, and exercise all the powers which, by the terms of the grant, are enjoined upon and vested in the Trustee or Trustees therein named. If the person making such grant, and making the election aforesaid, be a married person, such person may further provide that if the wife of such person survive him, then such wife, during her life, may, in relation to the property conveyed, and in relation to the erection, maintenance, and management of such institution or institutions, perform all the duties and exercise all the powers which, by the terms of the grant, are enjoined upon and vested in the Trustee or Trustees therein named, and in all such cases the powers and duties conferred and imposed by such grant upon the Trustee or Trustees therein named, shall be exercised and performed by the person making such grant, or by his wife during his or her life, as the case may be; *provided*, however, that upon the death of such person, or his surviving wife, as the case may be, such powers and duties shall devolve upon and shall be exercised by the Trustees named in the grant, and their successors.[26]

---

[21]*CAJ*, 26th Sess., 102 (Jan 26, 1885).

[22]Ibid., 318 (Feb 17, 1885). The record says nothing about the missing thirteen members.

[23]Ibid., 586; *CSJ*, 26th Sess., 510 (Feb 17, 1885).

[24]*Calif Stats*, 26th Sess., 49–53, Chap. 47, *An Act to advance learning, the arts and sciences, and to promote the public welfare, by providing for the conveyance, holding, and protection of property, and the creation of trusts for the founding, endowment, erection, and maintenance within this State of universities, colleges, schools, seminaries of learning, mechanical institutes, museums, and galleries of art*. App. Mar 9, 1885, by Gov. George Stoneman (D).   [25]Ibid., 50.   [26]Ibid., 51.

FOUNDER OR FOUNDERS?

When Mrs. Stanford tried to make a change that she considered a defect in one of the provisions in the founding grant, she discovered, as Orrin Leslie Elliott, the first historian of the university, wrote in *Stanford University, the First Twenty-five Years*: "Technically and in law Mrs. Stanford had not been a 'cofounder' of the University, and the power of mending provisions of the Founding Grant could not be reserved to a surviving wife (or anyone else) who was not at the same time a 'co-founder.' These defects were met, as far as it was possible, by the broad provision of the constitutional amendment which 'permitted, approved and confirmed' the provisions of the Founding Grant, the provisions made by Mrs. Stanford, and the 'gifts, grants, bequests, and devises supplementary thereto.'"*

*Elliott, *Stanford University, the First Twenty-five Years*, 325.

SIGNING OF THE FOUNDING GRANT OF
LELAND STANFORD JUNIOR UNIVERSITY—NOVEMBER 11, 1885

Five men—all close friends of Stanford—witnessed the signing by Leland and Jane Stanford of the original grant on November 11, 1885, the birthday of Leland Stanford Junior University.[27] They were Stephen T. Gage, Edward H. Miller, Jr., Nicholas T. Smith, Creed Haymond, and Herbert C. Nash.[28]

The enabling act had provided for twenty-four trustees, each of whom was appointed by Stanford from among his business associates and personal friends.[29] The first meeting of the board was convened in the founders' San Francisco home on November 14, 1885; there, without pomp or ceremony, the trustees were received in the library and had the deed of grant read to them.

The founding grant defined the functions of the trustees and the purposes of the university. The twenty-four-man board was empowered to appoint and remove presidents, fix the salaries of university employees, control the institution and its properties, and use the interest, but not the principal, of these properties.[30] The

[27]The date of the creation of LSJU in 1885 is frequently confused with the date when it opened its doors to students in 1891. This error is broadcast (with almost no complaint) over the doors of the new alumni building, completed in 2001, and on tee shirts, ties, and jackets sold by the thousands at the former Stanford Bookstore, now owned by the Chicago-based Follett Higher Education Group that in 2000 purchased the bookstore from LSJU.

[28]Thomas G. Crothers, "In the matter of the Petition of Leland Stanford, Jr. University and of Timothy Hopkins, Horace Davis, et al." In the SupC of SCC, State of Calif. No. 14912, Dept. 2. Doc. is now in the RCLL "Golden" Coll.

[29]William Ashburner, Isaac S. Belcher, John Boggs, John Q. Brown, CFC, Horace Davis, Matthew P. Deady, Henry L. Dodge, Stephen J. Field, Charles Goodall, George E. Gray, Dr. Harvey Willson Harkness, TNH, Thomas Bard McFarland, John F. Miller, Lorenzo Sawyer, Irving M. Scott, James McM Shafter, Nathan W. Spaulding, Francis E. Spencer, JS, William M. Stewart, Alfred L. Tubbs, and Henry Vrooman. In *The Leland Stanford Junior University* (SF: ALBC, 1888), passim. Includes "Senator Stanford's Plan for its Organization, The Grant Founding and Endowing the University, Description of the Property Embraced in Grant, and Portraits of the Trustees."

[30]The Deed of Grant is repr. in a number of places, including ibid.

purposes of the university were to promote the "public welfare by exercising an influence in behalf of humanity and civilization, to teach the blessings of liberty, and to inculcate love and reverence for the principles of government." The grantors reserved to themselves "absolute dominion over the rents, issues and profits of the real property granted," as though the grant had not been made. To guarantee a curriculum that was practical, not one purely theoretical or speculative, they insisted that instruction be given in the arts, sciences, mechanics, and all branches of agriculture, in order to qualify students for "personal success and direct usefulness in life." Sectarian education was prohibited, but the trustees were to see that the immortality of the soul was taught, as well as the existence of an all-wise and beneficent Creator.

In the presence of one hundred people the Stanfords turned over to the trustees three large tracts of land as an initial endowment, lands located in four counties.[31] The common names for the properties were the Vina ranch, the largest, partly in Butte County and the rest in Tehama; the Gridley farm, in Butte County, planted mostly in wheat; and the Palo Alto Stock Farm, in Santa Clara and San Mateo counties. They were broken down by acreage as follows:

Butte County[32]
Gridley Farm	17,640.00
Other	297.98
Durham tract	318.00
Subtotal	18,255.98
Fractional Sections	3,066.20
Fractional Sections	480.00
Butte County Total	21,802.18

Tehama County[33]
Fractional Sections	16,111.16
Fractional Sections	493.06
Fractional Sections	7,472.53
Fractional Sections	3,200.00
Fractional Sections	8,086.91
Fractional Sections	640.00
Fractional Sections	1,540.00
Grayson Rancho	1,269.00
(Excepting railroad right of way)	
Tehama County Total	38,812.66

[31]See "Stanford's Munificence," in *Sac Record-Union*, Oct 31, 1885, for a description of these properties.

[32]BuC lands are described in SupC of SCC, State of Calif. No. 14912, Dept. 2, 14–18. Rec. on Dec 19, 1885, in BCR, Book Y of Deeds, 762ff.

[33]TC lands are described in SupC of SCC, State of Calif. No. 14912, Dept. 2, 16–19. Rec. on Dec 1, 1885, in TCR, Book W of Deeds, 136ff.

Tehama and Butte counties[34]
Gerke Ranch	10,933.18
(except railroad right of way and the town of Vina)	
Tehama and Butte Total	10,933.18

(The Vina Farm was the total of the last two parcels under Butte County, all of Tehama County, and the total of Butte and Tehama together. This totaled 53,292.04 acres. The discrepancy between this and the official record of 53,291.22 is easily explained by the fact that all acreage was described as "more or less.")

Santa Clara County[35]
Palo Alto Stock Farm	4,437.12
Santa Clara County Total	4,437.12

San Mateo County[36]
Palo Alto Stock Farm	2,526.63
Other	26.14
Other	2.26
San Mateo County Total	2,555.03

Total of all four counties:	78,540.17[37]

With one gift totaling 78,540.17 acres of land, it is little wonder that the Governor was once described—albeit with considerable exaggeration—as the largest landowner in California.[38]

The total value of Stanford's gifts of land to the university is difficult to determine. The *Sacramento Record-Union* estimated it conservatively at $5 million and expected the value to increase to $20 million by the end of the century.[39] This, of course, was sheer guesswork. President Jordan said that Stanford himself had estimated his entire fortune at $30 million.[40] Even Stanford's estimate would have been based upon assigning values to lands that were next to impossible to appraise. Moreover, he did not give all his lands or all his stocks to the university.

For years afterward people would speculate on just how much the original Stanford University grant amounted to. A detailed examination was undertaken by Stanford's old friend Pixley. Admitting at the outset that "few people have any definite idea of the actual sum of money represented by the property," he went on to

[34]The lands in TC and BuC are described in SupC of SCC, State of Calif. No. 14912, Dept. 2, 20.

[35]SCC lands are described in ibid., 20–25. Rec. in SCCR on Jan 8, 1886, Book 83 of Deeds, 23ff.

[36]SMC lands are described in SupC of SCC, State of Calif. No. 14912, Dept. 2, 25–30. Rec. on Feb 18, 1886, in SMCR, Book 40 of Deeds, 1–38.

[37]Ibid., Petition, Thomas G. Crothers, att. for Petitioners. Lists all lands given by the Stanfords to LSJU on Nov 11, 1885. See also, Thomas G. Crothers, "In the matter of the Petition of Leland Stanford, Jr. University and of Timothy Hopkins, Horace Davis, et al." This doc. is now in the RCLL, "Golden" Coll. See also LSJU, *The Founding Grant With Amendments, Legislation, and Court Decrees Published by the University 1971* ([Stanford: SU, 1971]).

[38]"Biographical Sketch," *Memorial Addresses on the Life and Character of Leland Stanford*, 15.

[39]*Sac Record-Union*, Nov 16, 1885.   [40]Jordan, *Days of a Man*, I, 367.

list the acreage of the various Stanford lands, the number of acres in grapes and the
annual quantity of wine produced by the Stanford vineyards. The writer concluded
that if all the land in the Palo Alto property, the Gridley ranch, and the Vina tract
were planted in vines, "it would represent the enormous sum of $200,000,000 and
an annual income of over $11,000,000 a year."[41]

No university in America had anything like such an endowment. "According to
the college registers," wrote Pixley in the *Argonaut*, the leading universities were
endowed as follows:

Columbia	$13,000,000
Harvard	11,000,000
Yale	10,000,000
University of California	7,000,000
Johns Hopkins	3,000,000[42]

The land endowment given by Leland Stanford could not be added to the list,
Pixley said, because no one could make an accurate calculation of its true value.

In the colorful language of the day, just after the death of Stanford, the *Argonaut*
published an assessment of Stanford University and predicted in glowing terms the
bright future it would enjoy. A more recent attempt to assess the value of the Stanford grant has been no more successful that Pixley's. But the conclusion that Stanford's grant was worth somewhere around $20 million is the number often used
today.

Stanford always objected to conventional wisdom, rote learning, or traditional
organization that stifled individual initiative. These attitudes inspired him to create
the kind of institution he originally planned to build. Freedom of individual development was to mark all curricular organization. Degree requirements and traditional sequences of courses were to take secondary place to practical, useful,
individual development. Proper education necessitated absolute freedom of investigation on the part of teachers and students; thus Stanford endorsed "die Luft der
Freiheit weht"—Jordan's phrase—as a proposed motto for the university.[43]

Stanford apparently preferred a sentiment expressed by Jordan himself in his
address at the opening ceremonies of the university: "A generous education should
be the birthright of every man and woman in America."[44] Stanford commented as
follows on Jordan's remark: "This strikes me as a great truth, and of such importance that I would like it to be used as one of the mottoes of the University."[45]

Stanford was convinced that a need existed for the kind of school he intended to

---

[41]*SF Argonaut*, Jul 3, 1893.   [42]Ibid.
[43]DSJ, "The Educational Ideas of Leland Stanford," 20.
[44]*Exercises of the Opening Day, October 1, 1891*. Pub. by LSJU as *Circular No. 5*.
[45]LS to DSJ, Jan 1, 1892.

THE UNIVERSITY OF THE WORLD

"It may be said, without fearing contradiction, that its resources are far in excess of those of any other educational establishment in the world, and that it will never need to deny itself anything, from a library to an observatory or a laboratory, on the ground of expense. It is quite possible that when the properties which are devoted to its support yield their full income, it will find it possible to abolish all fees for tuition and to reduce the charge for board below that which a pupil would cost at home.

"The mind loses itself in the contemplation of the services which such an institution may render to knowledge and civilization. It can afford to enlist a staff of professors embracing the ablest men in each branch in every country in the world. Whenever a man of genius or learning rises above his fellows, the Leland Stanford University can secure him. Even at the same salary, men of eminence would desert places of seclusion to mingle in a society composed of the leaders of human thought in every department of learning. Such a resort might become the intellectual capital of the world, swarming with the uncrowned monarchs of mankind. And what graduates it might turn out! Under such tuition as the Leland Stanford could command, young men with anything in them would be sure to have it developed, and a race of students would be turned out every year who would set the car of progress traveling at a rate unknown to history.

"It is money that tells. In all the great universities of the world, the complaint has ever been that this or that which was eminently desirable could not be done for want of money. Discoveries have not been made, nor problems wrought out to a solution for the want of money. Harvard, which takes the lead among our institutions of higher education, is constantly blocked in its work by the want of money. If Agassiz had had as large an income as he desired to control, there would have been no unsolved problems in ichthyology. If the Lick Observatory had a larger appropriation, it would have done something with its great equatorial. If Yale had the library it should contain, its graduates would not need to go to Europe to prosecute their researches. If Oxford and Cambridge were more munificently endowed, the absurd old fellowships would have been abandoned long ago. Now comes an institution whose work need never be arrested by pecuniary obstacles. It ought to, and under proper management it surely will, some day make itself the university of the world."*

*SF Argonaut, Jul 3, 1893.

build. He insisted that if his university were to be similar to others in the country, he would have given his money to one of *them*; his school, instead, was to be "on a different plan."[46] Stanford felt that existing institutions of higher learning allowed and indeed created a wide separation between the theoretical and the practical, and this he intended to correct. Furthermore, desire and willingness to work and learn were more important to him than were money, family, or social position. As a man who had worked hard and had made a success of himself, Stanford had great faith in the Horatio Alger path of success: success comes to those who work hard, save their money, invest wisely, and spend carefully. One of the major differences between his

[46]*NY Evangelist*, Feb 10, 1891.

Die Luft der Freiheit Weht is Not the Motto of the University

At the time of the trial of Martin Luther, Ulrich von Hutten is reported to have asked in a speech: "*Wisset Ihr nicht, daß die Luft der Freiheit weht?*" ("Don't you know that the air of freedom is blowing?")[a] It turns out that this phrase first appeared in Latin, not German. In the 1859 edition of the works of von Hutten, one finds the words "*videtis illam spirare libertatis auram, homines taedio praesentium innovare hunc rerum statum cupere*" ("You see that breath of liberty blowing, men weary of present things seeking to innovate this new state of affairs.")[b] In David Friederick Strauss' 1858 biography of von Hutten, the writer gives the following German translation of von Hutten's Latin phrase: "*Sehet Ihr nicht, daß die Luft der Freiheit weht, daß die Menschen, des Gegenwärtigen überdrüßig, einen neuen Zustand herbeizuführen suchen?*"[c] ("Do you not see that the breath of freedom is wafting, that the people disgusted with the present situation are seeking to create a new state of affairs?") There are two things to bear in mind here: (1) This is not a translation in any technical sense of the word, particularly since it changes a statement into a question, and (2) von Hutten is talking not about political or intellectual freedom, but rather freedom of conscience or religion.

Stanford University president Gerhard Casper, in a paper delivered to the Stanford Historical Society in which he traces the origins and history of the dubious motto, argues that since *Luft* means "air" rather than "wind"—he would use the literal meaning of the Latin *aura*—a better translation of the English from the German from the Latin would be, "[Don't you] Recognize [see] that the wind of freedom blows [is blowing]."[d] Casper's exacting and incisive examination of the von Hutten text and Jordan's handling and use of it leaves Jordan's history of the motto even *more* questionable. What Jordan was *really* talking about was *Lehrfreiheit* and *Lernfreiheit* (freedom of teaching and freedom of study)—noble concepts that may have caused Jordan and Jane Stanford some uneasiness.[e]

In Jordan's own short publication on the motto, he took the Strauss formulation and omitted the words "don't you see that"—therefore, it seems safe to conclude that the motto is Jordan's, *not* von Hutten's.[f]

An interesting sidelight in support of the Latin origin of the "Stanford motto" is one of Jordan's brief contributions to the literature, prefaced by the words: "German propaganda made it necessary for the University to issue recently a statement explaining that the University has no German motto on its seal." His reasoning in reaching this conclusion was that the "motto" had never been officially adopted and did not appear on the university seal. He made his statement to clarify that just as von Hutten had taken a stand at the beginning of the sixteenth century for freedom in Germany—against what is now called Prussianism—so "on the temporary seal adopted by the professors for their convenience, we put these German words, the words of a German pioneer who was one of the first to fight against the type of officialism that rules in Germany today."[g]

and other universities was that Stanford's would be less expensive; its seven dollars per month (an early guess at the cost of room and board) was geared to help students who could not afford the twenty-five dollars charged at Berkeley.[47]

Students at this school were to be inculcated in the necessity of living sober lives. Stanford estimated that 25 percent of the nation's productive capacity was lost in

---

[47]UNC, SFS 25:15.

Jordan had actually proposed an altogether different motto to Stanford. On March 9, 1894, at the university's first Founders' Day celebration, Jordan recalled that the first time he met Stanford, as they were speaking of the days just after his son had died, Stanford had told him that in the depths of his sorrow, the thought had come to him: "The children of California shall be my children." Sometime afterward Jordan asked Stanford if they could use these words as a motto. The Governor's answer to this proposal was that if at some time in the future the state of California should like to use it, that would be satisfactory, but for the present, he did not wish Jordan to use it.[h]

The controversy over the Stanford University seal was clarified and at the same time intensified when Peter Allen showed that there were, indeed, four Stanford seals:

1. That of the Board of Trustees, with *Semper Virens*—"ever green" or "ever growing"—from the scientific name of the redwood tree (*Sequoia sempervirens*) which appears in the center of the university seal.

2. That of the president's seal, with the words DIE LUFT DER FREIHEIT WEHT encircling the redwood symbol.

3. That of the registrar's seal, with the redwood alone.

4. The Stanford University Press seal, containing a redwood tree with a plain in the background and a fourteen-tree orchard (in some impressions the orchard looks like a flock of sheep), with range after range of mountains stretching into the distant background. This seal has no inscription. Thus, only the president's seal contains the familiar Latin phrase cast in poor German and even worse English.[i]

[a]DSJ, *Ulrich von Hutten* (Knight of the Order of Poets) (Boston: AUA, 1910); (Yonkers-on-Hudson, NY: WB, 1922), 33ff. *Blow* is a bit strong for *weht*; *waft* is probably better.

[b]Eduard Bocking, ed. [*The Works of Ulrich von Hutten*] (7 vols., Leipzig: BGT, 1859–1862), II, 34.

[c]David Friedrich Strauss, *Ulrich von Hutten* (2 vols. pub. as 1, Leipzig: FAB, 1858), II, 176.

[d]Gerhard Casper, "Die Luft der Freiheit weht—on and off," *S & T* 1995 19 (4): 13–23.

[e]Troubled as he and JLS may have been on occasion over professorial misuse of academic position for purposes of political propaganda (as in the Edward A. Ross case).

[f]DSJ, "The Foundation Ideals," *SAM* 1917 18 (Mar): 224–225. Founders' Day Address, Mar 1917. The hist. of the creation of the motto is ably told by Bayard Quincy Morgan, "How Stanford Selected that 'Winds of Freedom' Slogan," *SIR* 1937 39 (9): 22–23; see also Gunther Nagel, "The Legacy of Ulrich von Hutten," *SR* 1962 63 (6): 12–15.

[g]DSJ, "The Wind of Freedom," *SR* 1918 19 (5): 297.

[h]"The First Founders' Day," *SR* 1952 53 (6): 15.

[i]Peter C. Allen, "Quad-Angles . . . with the editor," *SR* 1947 48 (5): 14.

buying, selling, and consuming hard liquors.[48] In keeping with his belief that students were to be kept from the evils of alcohol, the founding deed prohibited forever any kind of "saloon" on campus. In 1888, when Stanford gave his approval for a railway station at Palo Alto, he did so with one reservation: whiskey must never be sold there, near his school.[49]

The cardinal aim of the university was to cultivate individual potential in order to advance humanity. Stanford rejected the idea that there was only a fixed amount of wealth in the world, that only a few could be wealthy, and that the rest were con-

[48]UNC, LS papers.   [49]LS to TNH, Jan 8, 1888.

signed to poverty: "I believe that the comforts and even the elegances of life are the natural heritage of every provident, intelligent man. The earth is inexhaustible in supplies for the gratification of every reasonable want of man."[50] His university would develop the skills needed to help men help themselves; in other words, it would create Horatio Algers.[51] If some of his educational pronouncements had the ring of a farm-boy philosophy, they were sentiments that successful men all over the country could echo and applaud.[52]

Frank Shay, Stanford's private secretary and general factotum, later wrote that Stanford often discussed with him his ideas about founding a great educational institution. According to Shay, Stanford's institution was to consist of a number of schools, beginning with kindergarten and progressing up to what one might call a super high school.[53] Stanford planned a series of workshops for the training of skilled mechanics. Provision was to be made for educating farmers in every branch of agriculture: horticulture, stock raising, and poultry husbandry among them. His general scheme, however, promised to be too difficult to handle satisfactorily, so the Governor allowed himself to be persuaded by Jordan that a "real university, as was afterwards founded, would be better in every way and would be of more benefit to students and to the commonwealth."[54] (Jordan neglected to note the fact that Stanford's plan for a grammar school and technical institute had been abandoned long before he came on the scene, which was only six months before the university opened its doors to students.)

In an 1889 interview with a San Francisco reporter, long before he had ever met Jordan, Stanford was quoted as having used these very words in describing his ideas for the university: "There is in contemplation a complete system of education, from the kindergarten to a post-graduate course."[55] Years later, after David Starr Jordan had become the chancellor of Stanford University, he explained *his* concept of Stanford's philosophy of education. Stanford, he said, believed that no educational system could be complete in which admission to the university was a privilege limited to the chosen few. Stanford believed rather in an unbroken ladder from the kindergarten to the university, "a ladder each should be free to climb, as far as his ability or energy should permit."[56]

Jordan related that Stanford told him on more than one occasion how his short experience on the University of California Board of Regents had taught him a few things about how *not* to manage a university. On one occasion, Jordan said Stanford

---

[50]Inter. in *Sac Record-Union*, Nov 13, 1888.   [51]*Sac Record-Union*, Nov 16, 1885.

[52]Edith Mirrielees, *Stanford, the Story of a University* (NY: GPPS, 1959), 23.

[53]Shay, "A Lifetime in California," 126.   [54]Ibid.

[55]*SF Bulletin*, Jul 22, 1889; repr. in *NY Times*, Aug 5, 1889.

[56]DSJ, "The Foundation Ideals of Stanford University," *LSJUP*, Trustees' Series No. 27 1915, p. 15. Founders' Day Address, Mar 9, 1915.

had told him, when President William T. Reid had asked for an assistant professor of Latin, who would have cost them $1,500 per year, the board sat for an *entire* day haggling over the matter because one of the regents favored a local man he knew who would take the position for $1,000. Having witnessed this, Stanford was determined to put his money into a school where that kind of negotiation and haggling would not be possible.[57] Jordan later repeated the same story to President Martin Kellogg of the University of California.[58] However, this episode did not take place at the only meeting of the Board of Regents attended by the Governor. We must wonder, then, what Jordan's source was.

As the Stanfords discussed the creation of a university as a memorial to their son, the subject of coeducation came up. It was Leland, not Jane, who wanted Stanford university to be coeducational. Girls would be taught how to be better mothers: those in whose hands rested the education of the young must themselves be properly educated.[59] In his 1889 interview with the *Bulletin*, Stanford made his position clear: "Girls will be admitted on equal terms with boys, and they will be entitled to all the privileges of the school, and will be permitted to pursue any course desired."[60] On this issue Stanford met with considerable opposition from his wife.[61]

Jane Stanford objected to a coeducational school. The Governor was surprised to learn that his wife had never considered having girls attend their university. Berner writes that in Mrs. Stanford's mind the institution was to be a memorial to their son, and was therefore for boys only. After considerable discussion, "Mr. Stanford begged Mrs. Stanford to consider the matter; but she had her heart set on the matter."[62] Stanford finally won the argument by reminding her that they had taken the children of California to be their children, and that girls as well as boys were children; with this, she reluctantly gave in, but asked that a limit be placed on the number of female students.[63] Berner said that Mr. Stanford considered this a wise move, but just how wise he thought it to be is seen in the fact that no limit was imposed on the number of women as long as *he* oversaw the university.[64]

Whatever Jane's personal views, the founding grant stated clearly to the trustees at their first meeting, on November 14, 1885, that among the duties of the trustees

---

[57]DSJ to Prof. John C. Branner, Nov 1, 1904, in DSJ, Outgoing Letterbook, XXIV, 497, DSJ papers. SUA.

[58]DSJ to Martin Kellogg, Jun 18, 1894. DSJ papers. SUA.   [59]*NY Times*, May 28, 1888.

[60]*SF Bulletin*, Jul 22, 1889; repr. in *NY Times*, Aug 5, 1889.

[61]There is no telling how Jane's biographer Gunther Nagel got the facts of this disagreement backwards. According to *his* account, "Probably only a few of her intimate friends knew that it was she who suggested to Senator Stanford that women students be allowed in the University." Gunther Nagel, *Jane Stanford: Her Life and Letters* (Stanford: SAA, 1975), 3. This work deals more with JLS corres. than with her life story. Nagel fails to identify a single intimate friend who had this knowledge.   [62]BB, *Mrs. Stanford*, 45.   [63]Ibid.

[64]However, it must be recognized that JLS would not allow any delay in the admission of women in 1891, thus they built the women's dormitory, Roble Hall, out of concrete rather than of sandstone blocks as used on Encina. Elliott, *Stanford University, the First Twenty-five Years*, 177.

was "To afford equal facilities and give equal advantages of association and co-opera-
tion."[65] The next idea expressed by the founders in the Articles of Endowment was:

> We deem it of the first importance that the education of both sexes shall be equally
> full and complete, varied only as nature dictates. The rights of one sex, political and
> otherwise, are the same as those of the other sex, and this equality of rights ought to
> be fully recognized.[66]

Stanford on several occasions reiterated his ideas on this subject. In a newspaper
interview four years later, he said: "I deem it especially important that the education of the female should be equal to that of the male, and I am inclined to think that
if the education of either is neglected, it had better be that of the man than the
woman, because if the mother is well educated she insensibly imparts it to the
child."[67] But the "elastic clause" containing the words "varied only as nature dictates" was an open door for many changes later—among them Jane Stanford's later
limitation on the number of women students—a thing the Governor would *not*
have permitted.

Stanford's views necessarily evolved as the institution took shape. Initially he
believed that women must have the same educational opportunities as men for the
simple reason that for the first seven years of life—the character-building time—
women had the most to do with their children's training, education, and development of values. Here, as in so many places, his ideals were not matched later by
reality, not because of lack of vision on *his* part, but because of later actions by his
widow (discussed further in the section on Stanford University in the Epilogue).

In the last letter he wrote to Jordan, Stanford elucidated the change in his educational philosophy, which he spelled out clearly.[68] In addition to the reason for educating women, he added a commercial consideration: if vocations were thrown open to
women there would be a 25 percent increase in the nation's production, which
would go a long way toward providing comfort and elegance for every American.

Stanford explained in this letter the ways in which some of his ideas were taking
shape. He foresaw the need for training in medicine, law, and political science. The
text in government classes should be the Declaration of Independence, which was a
far more philosophical document than was the Constitution. If men followed the
principles of the Declaration, Stanford was sure there would be an end to warfare.
Chemists, he said, would find a way to produce food in such quantity that no one on
earth should go hungry. Waxing pious, as was seldom his habit, the Governor
stressed the need for an awareness of man's dependence on his Creator.

---

[65]Sect. IV, Art. 16 of the Founding Grant, *The Leland Stanford Junior University,* 25.
[66]Ibid., 45.   [67]*SF Examiner,* Oct 20, 1889.
[68]LS to DSJ, Apr 3, 1893; also, see Pease, "The Man," 16—18.

Proper education must develop the mind, he said, having noticed himself that literature greatly expanded the mind and that technically educated people did not necessarily make the best businessmen. He advocated an education that would cultivate the imagination; a man, after all, could never construct anything he could not first imagine.

Stanford believed that purely technical education limited the imagination, and that everything is opened through imagination and original investigation. Former Stanford professor of history and later university trustee Otis Arnold Pease, speaking at the sesquicentennial celebration of Leland Stanford's birth and the 1974 Founders' Day address, summarized the Stanfords' thinking very succinctly: "Foremost then, in the Stanfords' thoughts about a new institution, was the conviction that the nation's young men and women needed an education that united theory with practice, abstraction with experiment, original investigation with useful application."[69]

REACTIONS TO THE FOUNDING OF STANFORD UNIVERSITY

There was an immediate, worldwide outpouring of praise for Stanford's plan; editors strained for adulatory adjectives with which to describe his magnanimous bequest.[70]

One called it the "most magnificent educational endowment of the world."[71] Another said that the entire plan sprang from the "most unselfish and noblest inspiration."[72] Never was an act performed "with more singleness of purpose and with less ostentation."[73] This gift, "unique in the history of civilization," had no other end than the improvement of humanity.[74] One ecstatic writer called it an act of unparalleled grandeur; never in the whole history of civilization had there been a gift "more princely than this."[75] The Stanford benefaction was unmatched by that of any private citizen in the "whole civilized world." It was California's greatest citizen who created America's greatest university.[76] Another adulated: "The greatest work I should imagine that any single man has ever undertaken for the benefit of others."[77] It was suggested that a monument to Stanford be erected in Santa Clara County to commemorate his creation of "the greatest and most richly endowed

---

[69]Pease, "The Man," 16–18. Pease was then a prof. of hist. at UWa, where he moved in the summer of 1966. In 1967 he was made chairman of that dept. Inter. with Otis Pease, Jul 11, 2001.

[70]*SF Commercial Record*, May 9, 1889.

[71]*Sac Record-Union*, Nov 16, 1885. The issue of Nov 19 quoted seven editorials on "The Stanford Endowment," several of which are noted below.   [72]*Vallejo Chronicle*, quoted in ibid., Nov 19, 1885.

[73]*Sac Record-Union*, Nov 16, 1885.   [74]*SS* 1893 3 (Sep 13), 19.

[75]*Chico Chronicle* and *Marysville Appeal*, quoted in *Sac Record-Union*, Nov 19, 1885.

[76]*West Oakland Star*, Oct 26, 1889, quoted in *Sac Record-Union*, Nov 19, 1885.

[77]Alexander G. Yorke to LS, Sep 19, 1889.

educational institution in the world."[78] Unitarian minister Horace Stebbins praised the projected university in a sermon as the "epitome of the universe."[79]

Not everyone agreed with Stanford's plan to found a school. The lopsided vote in favor of the education bill that created Stanford University and the response to Stanford's grant concealed the fact that there was considerable opposition to it. David Starr Jordan later spread the story of how, while still in Aix-les-Bains, Stanford had met an acquaintance who believed that the Stanford fortune could be put to better use than the creation of another school, arguing that there was already an excess of education in the world, which in itself was a prevalent cause of discontent.[80] Stanford is said to have contradicted him, insisting that there could no more be too much education than too much health or intelligence, and challenged him to produce one man who had too much education. True, there was unwise or unfit learning, but not an excess of education.

Others were sure that there was no need for another university in the San Francisco Bay area, that the state school at Berkeley could handle all the students available and more. One New York editor remarked snidely that there was as much need for a new university in California as for "an asylum for decayed sea-captains in Switzerland."[81]

Still others argued that the grant was merely "restitution" for the Governor's having taken so much from the government and the public.[82] According to this line of reasoning, "Stanford" and "Central Pacific" had been synonymous during the heat of the anti-monopoly agitation in California. Yet, regardless of his inner motives that can never be known for sure, or whatever personal or psychological drives his detractors could conjure up, the grant did work a profound change in the popular feeling toward the Governor. From then on his former detractors would distinguish him even more clearly from his Associates.

Other critics said that Stanford's grant was prompted by partisan considerations, that he was using this "philanthropy" as a means of winning a seat in the United States Senate. It was said later that during a lull in university construction, when the Stanfords were touring abroad, Mrs. Stanford received newspaper clippings from the United States alleging that construction had been halted because Stanford had already won election to the Senate.[83] This charge was not only entirely baseless, but was anachronistic. If Stanford had wanted a Senate seat—and there is no evidence that he had given it any thought as early as 1884—and if the position were for sale, he certainly could have bought one for less than the $20 or 30 million

[78]*SJ Mercury*, Sep 10 and 11, 1889.

[79]Horatio Stebbins, "The Great Gift," preached Sun., Nov 22, 1885, in the First Unitarian Church of SF. Repr. in *Sac Record-Union*, Nov 28, 1885.   [80]DSJ, "The Educational Ideas of Leland Stanford," 20.

[81]Unidentified ed., quoted in Treat, "Golden Key," 60.

[82]*SF Examiner*, Jun 22, 1893.   [83]Treat, "Golden Key," 60.

the university is said to have cost him. Moreover, the university grant was made in November 1885, and construction had gotten underway in 1887, both events after Stanford had already been elected to the Senate in January 1885.

BUILDING AND STAFFING THE UNIVERSITY

Stanford had conceptualized the university broadly:

> Its nature, that of a University with such seminaries of learning as shall make it of the highest grade, including mechanical institutes, museums, galleries of art, laboratories and conservatories, together with all things necessary for the study of agriculture in all its branches, and for mechanical training, and the studies and exercises directed to the cultivation and enlargement of the mind.[84]

The object of the university was to prepare students for personal success and direct usefulness in life.

The Board of Trustees was empowered to appoint the president of the university and to remove him at will without cause.[85] Since the president was to be responsible for all courses of study and for the good conduct and capacity of the professors and teachers, he was to prescribe and enforce the course of all university studies and the mode and manner of teaching. He was given the power to prescribe the duties of professors and teachers and—the idea of tenure never having occurred to the founders—to remove them at will, again, without cause.

If these presidential powers bring a smile of tolerance to the lips of moderns, their tolerance must be strained by the decree of the founders that even though the university was to have no sectarian instruction, it would see to it that the university teach "the immortality of the soul, the existence of an all-wise and benevolent Creator, and that obedience to His laws is the highest duty of man."[86] To clarify by elaboration:

> While the articles of endowment prohibit sectarianism, they direct that there shall be taught that there is an all-wise, benevolent God and that the soul is immortal. It seems to us that the welfare of man on earth depends on the belief in immortality, and that the advantages of every good act and the disadvantages of every evil one, follow man from this life into the next, thereby attaching to him as certainly as individuality is maintained.[87]

With the adjournment of Congress in March 1887, Senator Stanford and his wife returned to California to oversee the beginning of physical construction of the university. He was anxious to get on with the building program to see the fruits of his

---

[84]Art. I of the Founding Grant, in *The Leland Stanford Junior University*, 21; see also NET, "Four Universities: Founders' Visions and Today's Reality: Stanford University," *AQ* 1998 11 (2): 70–73.

[85]Founding Grant, Art. IV, Sect. 9.   [86]Ibid., Art. IV, Sect. 14.

[87]Founding Grant, 44–45.

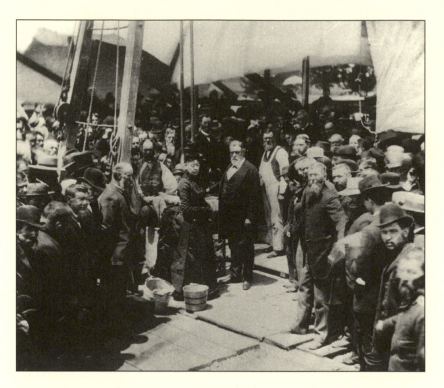

110. Laying the cornerstone at Stanford University, May 14, 1887,
Leland Junior's nineteenth birthday. *Stanford University Archives.*

labor.[88] On May 14, which would have been Leland, Jr.'s nineteenth birthday, the cornerstone of the university was laid, on a site chosen by Stanford and his occasional houseguest, the famous architect Frederick Law Olmsted. Olmstead was not present at the ceremony, but architect Charles A. Coolidge was. Senator Stanford performed the ceremony of mortaring the stone in place.[89] The formality was described by the *Argonaut* as "an important event for the world if the beneficent intentions of the donors are wisely carried out."[90] It was hoped that the school would open its doors a year from that date, but this proved impossible. Openings were subsequently announced for May 14, 1889, and the fall of 1890, but when this last date rolled around, the doors were still closed.

[88]*SF Call*, Apr 16, 1887.

[89]On Olmsted as houseguest, Elizabeth Stevenson, *Park Maker: Frederick Law Olmsted* (NY: MacPC, 1977), 382. For accounts of the laying of the cornerstone, see BB, *Mrs. Stanford*, 48; *SF Alta California*, May 14, 1887; *RC Times and Gazette*, May 14, 1887; *SF Daily Examiner*, May 14, 1887. The Goodrich Quarry, in Almaden Valley, south of SJ, provided the sandstone blocks for LSJU and numerous other SF Bay Area structures between 1875 and 1905.

[90]The *SF Argonaut* of May 14, 1887, carried a long ed. on the event.

111. Early construction scene at Stanford University. *Stanford University Archives.*

Endowments aside, Stanford's decision to manage the building of the university as a personal project soon caused practical difficulties. Lack of ready building funds caused no end of trouble. Whenever Stanford attempted to get some of his money out of the railroad, Huntington would tell him it had all been lent and that there was no cash available. As a result, most of the money the Governor put into construction at this time came from income from the Pacific Improvement Company.[91]

Building a university meant putting together a plant, finding the right man for the presidency, and assembling a faculty. Choosing the president proved by far the most difficult challenge facing Stanford. He offered the position of president to General Walker in 1884, at several times his present salary. Fearful of the effects of a totally new environment upon his family, and desirous of furthering his work at the Massachussetts Institute of Technology, the general declined.[92]

Such unexpected setbacks made Stanford comprehend the scope of the task before him. The talents he wanted were common enough, he thought, but getting them all in one man was another matter. "The scholars," he was said to have remarked, "are plentiful enough, but the executive ability is scarce."[93] He considered business acumen more important than scholarship, and speculated that if he could not combine the two qualifications, he would get a businessman for the job, or possibly hold the presidency *himself* until he could get a suitable man.[94]

[91]Fisher, "Stanford," 41.   [92]*Sac Record-Union*, Nov 13, 1888; Munroe, *A Life of Francis Amasa Walker*, 309.

[93]*SF Examiner*, Apr 17, 1889.   [94]Ibid.

THE STANFORDS AND DAVID STARR JORDAN

It seemed that the university might still be without a president on opening day in the fall of 1891. According to the testimony of President White of Cornell (1867–1885), at the second meeting he had with the Stanfords at Cornell, Leland Stanford had urged him to accept the position, but he had declined.[95] When asked whether there was anyone he would recommend for the position, White advised him to speak with David Starr Jordan, one of his former students, who was now president of Indiana University.[96]

Jordan was away from the campus addressing a meeting at the University of Illinois when he was handed a telegram from Andrew White: "Decline no offer from California till you hear from me."[97] Upon his return to Bloomington on March 22, 1891, Jordan found the Stanfords waiting to see him.

Jordan was immediately drawn to Stanford—"he revealed an unusually attractive personality"—but, more important than this, the educational philosophies of the two men coincided very closely; both, for example, wanted students trained for "usefulness in life." After a short consultation with his wife, Jesse, that same day, Jordan accepted "with some enthusiasm" Stanford's offer of the presidency, despite what he saw as two apparent risks: (1) California was the most individualistic of all the states and still rife with discordant elements [some things never change], and (2) the new institution was to be "personally conducted," its sole trustee a businessman who was active in politics. But the possibilities were so challenging that he could not decline.[98] Several days later Jordan recounted the event as follows: "I never met Senator Stanford until last Sunday, and the proposition involving the presidency of the University was made within ten minutes after I first saw him."[99]

Jordan became interested in the Universalist-Unitarian tradition at an early age. At about the time of their marriage, his parents had left the Baptist church because of its adherence to the tenet of eternal damnation.[100] Jordan was exposed to the Methodist revivals of western New York, but he was, in his own words, "never moved" by the hysterics created by those evangelists who painted such vivid descriptions of hell that "violent nervous disturbances" were observed in the congregation.[101] As a boy Jordan did go forward at a Congregational church revival seeking "salvation," but the experience made no lasting difference in his life.[102]

---

[95] White's memory may have failed him here. He writes that it was after their second conversation at Cornell that the offer of the pres. of LSJU was made. However, White resigned the pres. of Cornell in 1885, and it was not until Mar 1891 that the events surrounding DSJ took place. However, he continued to live in Ithaca, and presumably had an office on campus.

[96] Andrew White, *Autobiography of Andrew Dickson White* (2 vols., NY: CHC, 1922), II, 447.

[97] DSJ, *Days of a Man*, I, 354.
[98] Ibid., 354–356.
[99] Inter. with DSJ, *Indianapolis Journal*, Mar 29, 1891.
[100] DSJ, *Days of a Man*, I, 46.
[101] Ibid., 49.
[102] Ibid.

Jordan's father had a fair-sized library that, in the opinion of the son, possessed too many books dealing with religious controversy to satisfy young David, who at an early age had already become "established" in liberal views.[103] The parents joined the Universalist Church and David remained thereafter thankful for having been "brought up under strong religious influences untouched by conventional ortho-doxy."[104] He early acquired a dislike for theological discussions, believing they had nothing to do with the conduct of life.[105]

Jordan later explained the connection between his middle name and that of Thomas Starr King:

> That passion of mine [his early interest in astronomy] persists curiously in the middle name I have ever since borne, and which I myself chose for two reasons. The one sprang from my love of astronomy; the other had to do with my mother's great admi-ration for the writings of Thomas Starr King and for her profound respect for his personality.[106]

Jordan seems to have forgotten this other explanation of how he had taken the name "Starr" all on his own. In a 1921 response to a query about his name, he wrote, "I was named for Thomas Starr King, a man for whom my mother had a great admira-tion."[107]

Jordan continued his association with Universalists and Unitarians throughout his life. While president of Stanford University he and his wife were members of the Universalist-Unitarian Church of Palo Alto.[108]

His own university education began when eighteen-year-old Jordan entered Cornell University in March 1869, as what he described as a "belated freshman."[109] Three and a half years later, in 1872, as a result of his having taken advanced work in botany, Cornell conferred upon him the degree of master of science, the highest degree according to his own account that he ever earned.[110]

Upon graduation, twenty-one-year-old Jordan accepted a professorship in nat-ural science at Lombard University in Galesburg, Illinois, an institution under the direction of the Universalist Church of Galesburg.[111] After one year he resigned, under pressure.[112] Following this, he spent a year at Louis Agassiz' summer school of science in Penikese, Buzzard's Bay, Massachusetts.[113]

In 1873 Jordan became the principal of the Appleton Collegiate Institute in Apple-ton, Wisconsin, which closed the following year.[114] In 1874 he became a high school teacher of science in Indianapolis. In the following year he was appointed a professor

---

[103]Ibid., 29.   [104]Ibid., 46.   [105]Ibid., 46–47.
[106]Ibid., 21.   [107]DSJ to Mr. S.A. Freeman, Feb 10, 1921, in DSJ papers. SUA.
[108]"Directory [of Members]," Unitarian Church of PA, 1919; author inter. with and letter from Kristina Smith, sec., Universalist-Unitarian Church of PA, Jun 28, 2000.   [109]DSJ, *Days of a Man*, I, 96.
[110]Ibid.   [111]Ibid., 101.   [112]Ibid., 106.
[113]Ibid., 107–112.   [114]Ibid., 120–123.

112. David Starr Jordan,
first president of Stanford University.
Stanford University Archives.

of natural history at Northwestern Christian University—the "burdensome" original name that was later changed to Butler University and then Butler College, named for its founder, Ovid Butler, a member of the Christian Church. Jordan remained there as Dean of Science for four years.[115]

In 1875 Indiana Medical College, where he had been able, in his own words, to "spend some time" while teaching high school, surprised Jordan by conferring upon him an unexpected and gratuitous M.D. degree, which even he admitted he had "scarcely earned."[116] This was in fact an honorary degree, so it was not even "scarcely" earned.[117] In 1877, Butler honored him with an honorary Ph.D.[118] (Neither Jordan's own, massive autobiography nor the longest study ever made of his life and career ever mentions this.[119]) In 1886, Cornell too surprised him with an honorary LL.D. He at first declined this honor, saying he believing that degrees should represent work actually done, but then accepted it under pressure from President White.[120]

In 1879 Jordan became head of the Natural Sciences Department at Indiana University, and on January 1, 1885, was promoted to the presidency.[121]

It is to Leland Stanford's credit that he recognized in Jordan the man he needed to head up the new university. Stanford had consulted a number of prominent administrators of the nation's top universities; however, none of their schools was the exact prototype for Stanford University. His employee and confidant Henry Root, claiming firsthand knowledge in the matter, said that Girard College in

---

[115]Ibid., 140.   [116]Ibid., 146.

[117]On Indiana Medical College, author inter. with Kristen Sanders, asst. arch., IU, Feb 21, 2003.

[118]On Butler Ph.D., inter. with Sally Childs-Helton, arch., Butler Univ., Feb 19, 2003; Sally Childs-Helton to the writer, Feb 20, 2003.

[119]The longest study made on the life of DSJ never addressed this problem. Luther William Spoehr, "Progress' Pilgrim: David Starr Jordan and the Circle of Reform, 1891–1931," Ph.D. diss. (LSJU, 1975).

[120]DSJ, *Days of a Man*, I, 97–98. Cornell as a matter of policy did not award honorary degrees, but the practice was changed in the case of White and DSJ. Immediately thereafter, the orig. policy was readopted.

[121]DSJ, *Days of a Man*, I, 289.

Philadelphia was the model Stanford had in mind.[122] Stanford later said that Cooper Institute in New York was his prototype; it, like his projected institution, stressed the advancement of art, mechanics, and business. At one point Stanford planned for two prep schools, one for girls and one for boys, with a "central collegiate university" between them. Twelve-year-old children would be admitted to these schools for their preparatory work, and would be promoted to the university when they were advanced enough to begin studying for a particular vocation.[123]

As it turned out, Stanford University was organized, built, and then developed quite independently of any fixed model or pattern; its growth reflected the pragmatism and changing ideas of its founders as well as those of its first president.

It is interesting to reflect that before Stanford began examining various universities, he must have considered Harvard the best. It was there that Leland, Jr., was to study.

The Honorary Degrees of David Starr Jordan

At the time of publishing his autobiography, *The Days of a Man*, Jordan wrote: "I still believe that every academic degree should represent work actually done in or under the direction of the institution granting it. At the outset, therefore, I adopted at Stanford University the Cornell rule that no honorary degrees or degrees for studies carried on *in absentia* should be awarded. This regulation has saved us much pressure from various quarters. It seems to me to give the university a certain dignity as existing for purposes of instruction, not for conferring honors on outside persons."*

As he penned these words, he must have reflected that in his own case, except for his Master of Science degree from Cornell, he never earned any other degree. Despite widespread use at Stanford of the tag letters Ph.D. following Jordan's name, this degree did not "represent work actually done."

Honorary M.D., Indiana Medical College, 1875.
Honorary Ph.D., Butler University, 1877.
Honorary LL.D., Cornell University, 1886.

*DSJ, *The Days of a Man*, I, 98 n1.

The Stanfords and Spiritualism

Despite incontrovertible evidence that the Stanfords had sought and followed professional advice in the founding of Leland Stanford Junior University, once it was done, spiritualists, mystics, and soothsayers of every ilk scented an opportunity to publicize their wares by taking credit for establishing the school.

It is true, of course, that both Leland and Jane Stanford saw something bordering on the supernatural in their account of the origins of the plan to build a monument to the memory of their son. In Article 2 of the University Founding Grant, for example, the Stanfords wrote:

---

[122]Root, *Root*, 30. Inter. with Kristina Smith, sec., Universalist-Unitarian Church of PA, Jun 28, 2000.
[123]*SF Chronicle*, Jan 23, 1885.

Since the idea of establishing an institution of this kind for the benefit of mankind came directly and largely from our son and only child, Leland, . . . the institution hereby founded shall bear his name, and shall be known as "The Leland Stanford Junior University."[124]

Stanford attributed the origin of his inspiration for a monument to his son to a dream he had on the night Leland Junior died. Thus, according to this account, in a sense Leland Junior was credited with the expression "live for humanity," which the father remembered from his dream.

There is no doubt that the notion to create a university materialized slowly. The assertion made by Maggie McClure and others that the idea for this memorial came to the Stanfords immediately after their son's death, apart from any suggestion by others, does not hold up to careful scrutiny. McClure says that Jane Stanford often attributed their inspiration to thoughts of the boy, and she quoted Mrs. Stanford as saying that in dreams their son helped her; every new thought and plan seemed to come from him.[125] This last statement does seem to place Jane Stanford on the fringes of another world.

Stanford's widely broadcast and, unfortunately, also widely believed "vision" after his son's death, in which the boy urged him to do something for humanity, lent credibility to the theory held by the credulous that Stanford University was established as a result of spiritualistic communication from a world beyond the grave.[126]

Perhaps the step from faith in immortality to the belief that the departed soul can be contacted by the living is a short one: at any rate, in November 1886 Stanford admitted to his attorney, Samuel M. Wilson, and to Timothy Hopkins that just after Leland's death, when they were the most emotionally unstable and vulnerable, he and Mrs. Stanford had attended séances in Paris in hopes of contacting their dead son, "but were soon convinced of the utter futility of attempting through such means to obtain communication with the departed."[127]

In an interview with the *New York Herald*, in response to a letter from someone in San Francisco published by that paper, Stanford expressed his annoyance with reports of his having any interest in spiritualism and repudiated the false reports spread in the press that he and his wife had a "monomania" or devotion to spiritualism.[128] The Stanfords were *not* spiritualist, he stated, and went on to ridicule allegations that any so-called "monomania" or "devotion to spiritualism" had anything to do with their decision to dedicate their fortune to beneficent purposes. Charges of spiritualistic influences persisted, however, despite all disavowals.

---

[124]*The Leland Stanford Junior University*, 21–23.

[125]Maggie McClure to Boutwell Dunlap, Apr 30, 1923, in Dunlap, "Some Facts Concerning Leland Stanford and His Contemporaries in Placer County," 208–210.

[126]A recent summary of JLS and her dabbling in the supernatural is found in Theresa Johnston, "Mrs. Stanford and the Netherworld," *SM* May/Jun 2000, 68–73.   [127]GTC, *Stanford*, 399.

[128]*NY Herald*, Mar 23, 1885.

Once Stanford University had been founded, based on objective, even scientific principles resulting from advice from leading educational specialists, spurious claims by so-called "mystics" and "spiritualists" of how they had influenced the founding of the school by their supernatural powers and insights began to surface regularly.

Anyone examining the founding of Stanford University will find himself wading through countless nonsensical rehearsals of how the Stanfords were influenced by visions, fortunetellers, séances, and other supernatural drivel.

One prime example is the preposterous claim of one Frederick L. Anderson that his father, Galusha Anderson—Baptist preacher and former president of the old University of Chicago, which closed its doors in insolvency in 1885—spent much time in the Stanford home, and while there planted in his host's mind the "seed thought which later grew into Leland Stanford, Jr., University."[129] More than an exaggeration or even the accretion of faulty memory, this is downright fabrication.

It is true that at times Mrs. Stanford showed that she had a faint hope that spiritualism was not all quackery. One woman requested and apparently received from her a photo of Leland, from which she made a posthumous "physiognomical delineation" of his character.[130] Later, a Madame Diss de Bar said that Leland Stanford once offered her a sizable sum of money for a "spirit portrait," though he denied having any knowledge of her at all.[131]

Even Jane Stanford's memory seems to have been affected by these stories. In 1900 she wrote her attorney the following fanciful death-bed account of her dying son's charge to his father:

> In accordance with his expressed wish to his father only a few hours before he passed away from this life, which was to this effect—"Live for humanity's sake; live to feed the hungry, clothe the naked." His father concluded that the best way to do this, was to educate the sons and daughters of the very poor, who otherwise would not be educated, and thus to furnish the means whereby they might be enabled to feed and clothe themselves.[132]

One recognizes in this unlikely narration a jumbling of New Testament maxims, widespread editorial commentary, and Jane's own equally jumbled educational "ideals."

Leland Stanford was not ashamed to say that a dream of his dead son had set him on the path to creating a memorial to him, but what later became the boy's charge to him assumed a different form with each retelling. In one version, he was much more specific: "Father, do not spend your life in a vain sorrow. Do something for humanity. Build a university for the education of poor young men."[133] Still another

---

[129]Frederick Lincoln Anderson, *Galusha Anderson: Preacher and Educator, 1832–1918* (Wenham, Mass.: ERA, 1933), 19–20.   [130]Mary D. Stanton to LS, Dec 28, 1888.
[131]*SF Bulletin*, Apr 4, 1888.   [132]JLS to Mountford Wilson, Jun 9, 1900.
[133]UNC, in LS papers. Young Leland failed to mention poor young women.

account by newspaper correspondent George Alfred Townsend—who said he was told this by the Stanfords when he visited them at their Palo Alto home in 1887— has the son rebuking his distraught father: "Papa, do not say that. You have a great deal to live for; live for humanity."[134]

Several fanciful accounts purport to describe the events of the night of Leland's death. Bancroft probably interviewed Stanford for his *Founders of the Commonwealth* series, and perhaps it was confidences exchanged there that led to his writing that the exhausted Stanford had a singular dream—some call it a vision—of his dead son. His aching heart, fevered brain, and fitful and disordered sleep had brought on the vision. While Stanford was lamenting in this dream his lack of reason for living, young Leland appeared to him as real as if in the flesh, and comforted him: "Father, be not cast down; all is well; you have much to live for; you can do so much more and better for your fellow men than I."[135]

Bancroft wrote that Stanford had been contemplating a substantial gift to some kind of public institution.[136] In agreement with this, Sen. George Graham Vest of Missouri would say later that Stanford had been undecided as to whether to give his money to a hospital or to a school, but was inclined toward the latter, believing that the safety of the country rested ultimately upon an educated people.[137] Both these statements may have been based on later hindsight, "predicting" that Stanford would do what by then they knew he had already done.

In 1889 a six-column article on prominent men who believed in spiritualism appeared in a New York paper. Stanford was listed among them, though the writer conceded that the California senator denied any spiritualist connections and had no faith in mediums. The identification was based on certain of Stanford's alleged beliefs that smacked of spiritualism. Given the writer's flimsy evidence, however, anyone believing in the supernatural could have been classed as a spiritualist.[138]

In the fall of 1891 rumors were again circulated that Stanford University had been founded through the agency and under the influences of spiritualism. Maud Lord Drake, a spiritualist medium, said she had been the link between the two worlds. Many years later, Jordan said that Stanford, wishing to put an end to such speculation once and for all, asked him in 1892 to draw up a formal memorandum disavowing any faith in spiritualism and disavowing that spiritualistic influences had anything to do with his founding of Stanford University. Jordan's account of the 1892 episode reads as follows:

---

[134]*Cincinnati Enquirer*, Oct 21, 1887, and *NY Commercial Advertiser*, Jun 27, 1893. Still other forms appear elsewhere, as in J. H. Seals, "Leland Stanford's Dream," in LS papers.   [135]HHB, *Stanford*, 83.

[136]Ibid., 89.

[137]Address of George G. Vest, Sen. from Mo., *Memorial Addresses on the Life and Character of Leland Stanford*, 65.

[138]*NY Press*, Feb 17, 1889.

Mr. Stanford made his will, looking to the endowment of the university, in Paris, April 24, 1884. Mrs. Stanford made her will also, and copies were sent to America. Mrs. Maud Lord Drake was unknown to them until they met her at a *séance* with the Grants [Ulysses and Julia] in October, 1884. At about that time Mrs. Drake was detected in fraud. No spiritualistic influence affected the decision [to found the university]. Mrs. Drake had no more to do with it than a babe unborn.[139]

This entire account may have been a concoction. There is no evidence that Stanford rewrote his will in Paris—where he had neither the legal assistance nor the documentation at hand for such an undertaking. Nor has the 1892 statement surfaced.

Jordan did not deny that the Stanfords attended séances in Washington with the Grants, visits prompted by curiosity as well as hope. As he wrote, "Mr. and Mrs. Stanford were for some time deeply interested in certain phases of spiritualism which seemed perhaps to give the basis for a demonstrable belief in immortality, a faith in which they found great consolation." But, he concluded, "they never received through mediums any evidence they regarded as convincing."[140]

Methodist minister John P. Newman also tried to influence the Stanfords by preying on Mrs. Stanford's interest in contacting her son. It appears that Newman wanted the presidency of Stanford University. Stanford rejected all of Newman's hints about making the university a religious school, but Mrs. Stanford *was* interested in Newman's views—an interest she apparently never got over.[141] Newman and his wife took it upon themselves to arrange a series of séances in the Stanfords' San Francisco home. Stanford was invited to join the circle, but he refused. The Newmans eventually claimed a contact, but Mrs. Stanford was unconvinced, saying the voice she heard was not Leland's. Still, she found it difficult to break away from the Newman circle. When her husband reasoned with her and advised her against further attendance, she finally agreed to give it up. The unsuccessful Newmans returned home to New York, but, it was said, Mrs. Stanford's "preoccupation with the subject lasted for years."[142] As her secretary said, Mrs. Stanford's whole subject of conversation was young Leland. Her grief was always in her mind, so much so that the San Francisco house itself seemed grief stricken.[143]

Patronizing spiritualistic mediums was not a socially acceptable practice among members of Stanford's social and economic class. The friends and relatives trying to protect their public image protested against the couple's interest in séances. Still,

---

[139]DSJ, *Days of a Man*, I, 365–366; DSJ to HCN, Jul 27, 1901; a copy of this statement was signed by DSJ on Apr 27, 1917, and placed in the SUA. When DSJ read an art. in the *Chronicle* repeating the absurd claim of Mrs. Drake, since deceased, he sent a copy of this statement to the *Chronicle* ed., who pub. it in the Jul 10, 1925, ed. of the paper. Mrs. Drake died on Sep 26, 1924, of injuries received when her home in Boulder Creek, Calif., was destroyed by fire. A *SF Examiner* obit. (pub. on Sep 29, 1924) identified her as the former Comtesse Eugene [*sic*] de Coriche.

[140]DSJ, *Days of a Man*, I, 366n.   [141]BB, *Mrs. Stanford*, 42.

[142]Ibid., 43–44.   [143]Ibid., 39 and 41.

Mrs. Stanford's ongoing interest could not be denied. Archibald Jennings Treat, for one, a Central Pacific Railroad employee after 1879 and later a San Francisco attorney, who labeled the rumor that Mrs. Stanford was a spiritualist "alley gossip" and assured his readers that she was not a medium—as was sometimes alleged—nor did she hire them. To the undeniable report that she tried to commune with her dead son, all Treat said was: "If that be true, then it is a beautiful thought."[144]

Following Mrs. Stanford's death in 1905, the spiritualism issue was revived. One journalist alleged that the Stanfords retired at eight o'clock each evening and extinguished all the lights in their San Francisco mansion or Palo Alto farm residence (wherever they happened to be), "so that the father and mother could commune with the spirit of the departed lad." "This nightly occurrence was an admitted fact," he added, but he offered no evidence of any kind to substantiate his fantastic statement nor did he identify the people by whom the fact was admitted.[145]

Leroy, Illinois, spiritualist Simeon H. West later revived the story that the inspiration for the university came from the dead boy through spiritualist means. That the Stanfords were faithful spiritualists, he said in 1906, had been known in California for a number of years. West went on to assert that a Mrs. John J. Whitney of San Francisco was the Stanfords' private medium of sixteen years.[146] (Of course since Stanford died in 1893, his relations with Mr. Whitney would have started in 1877, seven years before young Leland died.) West asserted that newspapers later attributed the founding of the university to a dream because it sounded "much milder to orthodox ears than to say spirits." Stanford, like most men in influential positions, West wrote, did not "proclaim his spiritualism from the housetops," since to have done so would have forfeited his influence with people.[147] Therefore, the Stanfords did not "mingle with the common herd of spiritualists" but employed their own private medium to hold family séances in their home. West assured his readers that his information came firsthand from "the spirit world," though he offered no explanation as to what this meant. The report of these occurrences was as reliable as that which told that President Lincoln held private séances in the White House: it was Lincoln—a regular visitor at West's séances—who had told him so![148]

Jane Stanford's early interest with spiritualism became for a time something of an obsession. Even Bertha Berner, who almost always downplayed criticism of Jane, wrote as follows about some of her employer's experiences:

---

[144]Treat, "Golden Key," 93. Treat began his railroad career as an office boy and telegrapher. He worked his way up to become Stephen T. Gage's sec. During the construction of LSJU, Treat took photographs of the work in progress and sent them to LS to keep him informed. Treat Papers, SUA.

[145]*Chicago Examiner*, Mar 2, 1905.

[146]There is an ed. on Mrs. John J. Whitney in the *SF News-Letter*, Jun 30, 1894, 41.

[147]Simeon H. West to *Bloomington* [Ill.] *Pantograph*, Jun 19, 1906, pub. Jun 22.

[148]Ibid., Jun 25, 1906.

The hope for a spirit manifestation, however, had been given to Mrs. Stanford, and she determined to investigate the subject. She prayed so earnestly for light, which meant to behold Leland, that it was pitiful. She often attended demonstrations; we witnessed about all of the examples offered, but they were never satisfying to her. Mr. Stanford reasoned with her and advised her against further attendance, and she heeded his objection for a long time. Her preoccupation with the subject lasted for years. At one time Dr. Jordan, knowing of Mrs. Stanford's interest in the subject, visited Dr. Hermann, the magician, an expert in sleight-of-hand performances, and was shown how the slate writing was done as well as many other so-called spirit manifestations. When the subject was next mentioned Dr. Jordan explained what he had learned of the matter. After this Mrs. Stanford did not attend seances as before but still read almost exclusively on these subjects.[149]

Stanford's brother Thomas Welton, in Australia, was a confirmed spiritualist and on his death he willed money to his brother's university for carrying on psychic research.[150] But in extant letters exchanged by the two brothers there is not so much as an allusion to Leland Stanford's having ever had any faith in spiritualism. After Stanford's death, Jane corresponded with Thomas Welton and her interest in spiritualism was renewed briefly by these letters; she even made a trip to Australia where she hoped to see "an honest demonstration."[151] She was disappointed.

The University Opens

On October 1, 1891, six years after the institution was organized, opening ceremonies were held at Leland Stanford Junior University.[152] For three days trains brought visitors to Menlo Park, Mayfield, and Redwood City, and a special train of six cars was dispatched to carry those who overflowed the regular runs. One journalist estimated that five thousand people crowded into the quadrangle, including many of the state's most distinguished citizens, for opening ceremonies.[153] A stage decorated with palms, pampas grass, and grapevines, weighted down with fresh grapes, was erected at the north end of the quad beneath a huge arch. American flags made up the background and in the center was a full-length oil portrait of Leland Stanford Junior. Among the distinguished guests seated on the platform were faculty members from the University of California, two United States senators, and a number of Stanford's intimate railroad associates. Collis Huntington was conspicuous by his absence.

---

[149]BB, *Mrs. Stanford*, 43–44.   [150]See TWS papers, SUA.
[151]TWS to JLS, Sep 14, 1904. Interest of JLS in spiritualism reportedly carried her to the fringes of Swedenborgianism, *Milw. Journal*, May 23, 1895. Emanuel Swedenborg was a Swedish mystic who claimed in 1747 that "heaven was opened to him" and that spirits and angels revealed supernatural knowledge to him.
[152]Exercises of the Opening Day, Oct 1, 1891. Pub. by LSJU as Circular No. 5.
[153]*Sac Record-Union*, Oct 2, 1891.

113. San Francisco *Wasp* cartoon.
"THE DOORS THROWN OPEN."
"Senator Stanford—It is all for you, my boy,
and for the coming generations. My ambition
is now satisfied. I have less desire to be President than to be founder of an institution that
will make Presidents!"

This *Wasp* caption was almost prophetic,
considering that Herbert Hoover graduated
with Stanford University's Pioneer Class—
the first full four-year class—in May 1895.
Author's Collection.

On opening day there were 559 matriculated students, compared to 520 at the
University of California.[154] Living facilities for students are described first-hand by
university historian Orrin Leslie Elliott, as are student social life, sports, and other
aspects of a student's daily life.[155]

Following the singing of a hymn, Stanford delivered the first address; it was brief
and to the point, without containing anything new in the way of ideas or charges to
the faculty, trustees, and students. President Martin Kellogg of the University of
California also spoke briefly, followed by David Starr Jordan. Trustee Dr. Horatio
Stebbins offered a prayer, and Judge Lorenzo Sawyer, president of the Board of
Trustees, delivered a short, scholarly address, in which he praised the founders for
their generosity and wisdom, and charged the trustees to carry out their intentions; if they developed the university according to the purposes of the founders, he
predicted, its power for good would go on "from age to age, to the end of time."[156]

[154]Elliott, *Stanford University, the First Twenty-five Years*, 94.   [155]Ibid., 175–176.
[156]*Sac Record-Union*, Oct 2, 1891.

EARLY OPERATION AND MANAGEMENT OF THE UNIVERSITY

Stanford kept his hand on active management of the university, but basically did what he said he would do—hire a president who would run the place. He advised Jordan of the desirability of offering a good dining program for the students for less than three dollars per week.[157] He also made decisions on some trivial financial matters, as when he directed that students away from school for more than a week during holidays be credited with the amount of their board during their absence.[158] He chose the names for the men's and women's dormitories.[159]

Stanford followed closely the completion of the initial building program. He advised on the scope and cost and the kind of library needed, and when it came to constructing additional buildings, he traveled back to California from Washington to advise Jordan about them.[160] He even advised on details such as the heating of the gymnasium.[161]

Even if Stanford had wished, and there is no indication that he did, he could not have retired entirely from the operation of the university. His name was too well known across the country, and, to many people, he was probably considered much more accessible than an academic man like Jordan. His philanthropic record suggested that he might be a soft touch. As a result, there are stacks of letters on file written to Stanford by parents hoping to get their children admitted to the university through his personal intervention.[162] Just as many wrote recommending others. In certain cases he did intervene, as when he asked Jordan's special care for a potential student who had served for a number of years as Stanford's page in the Senate.[163]

For years prior to the opening of the university, Stanford had been inundated by job requests.[164] Once President Jordan was hired, Stanford nearly always referred this kind of correspondence to him.[165] The practice, however, was flexible, and on occasion he went beyond merely advising Jordan on faculty matters.[166] In one case Stanford responded directly: "I am leaving the selection of Professors to President Jordan, but when I see him I will confer with him in regard to your case."[167]

Stanford sought and respected Jordan's advice. Once when a professor resigned whom Stanford wanted to keep, he offered to make him a vice president, subject to Jordan's approval.[168] For the commencement speaker in the spring of 1893, Stanford chose U.S. senator George Franklin Edmunds of Vermont, provided that Jor-

[157]LS to DSJ, Aug 30, 1892.

[159]LS telegram to DSJ, May 9 and 16, 1891.

[161]LS telegram to DSJ, Feb 18, 1892.

[163]LS to DSJ, May 29, 1891 [date is blurred, possibly 1892 or 1893].

[164]See Morales, Stanford University, Chap. 4, "Gathering the Faculty," for a detailed study of how the faculty was assembled.

[166]LS telegram to DSJ, Apr 13, 1891.

[168]LS to DSJ, Apr 3, 1893.

[158]HCN to unidentified corres., Dec 13, 1891.

[160]LS telegram to DSJ, May 26, 1891.

[162]LS papers.

[165]HCN to M. St. Myrick, May 25, 1891; HCN to A.L. Ware, Nov 28, 1891.

[167]LS to Prof. Alexander Hogg, Apr 20, 1891.

dan had not already made other arrangements.[169] At other times he was less solicitous, as when he telegraphed his president not to hire a certain professor, adding that he would explain later: "Do not engage Nissen for professor of gymnastics. I will write you."[170] Occasionally Mrs. Stanford also recommended someone to Jordan for a position on the staff, but this was rare.[171]

At times Jordan sought Stanford's support to make certain appointments to the faculty.[172] There is no record of such requests ever being denied.[173] But, in cases where Stanford had no special concern or extraordinary knowledge about applicants, he refused to advise, telling Jordan to exercise his own judgment.[174] In one notable exception, Stanford invited a distinguished speaker, his friend ex-President Benjamin Harrison—known to his friends as "Little Ben," since he stood only five feet six inches tall—to deliver a series of lectures at the university, and Jordan first read of the appointment in the newspapers.[175]

Following his leaving the White House, Harrison was to deliver lectures in the fall of 1893 on international law.[176] In a letter to Stanford, written less than four months before the California senator's death, Harrison accepted Stanford's speaking invitation.[177] Harrison was to concentrate on certain aspects of international law, especially that relating to the solution of problems by arbitration. He arrived at the university in the spring of 1894, a year after Stanford's death, and delivered one lecture per week, a modification of Stanford's original intention, to be sure.[178]

Stanford also helped to govern the extra-curricular activities of his faculty members. On one occasion he objected that Jordan let a professor travel to Pasadena at university expense to lecture there. Stanford suggested the need for a rule governing such matters: "When our Professors lecture for other institutions it seems to me that their expenses should be paid by the people for whom they lecture, especially if they have to go as far as Pasadena."[179]

Management of the physical plant of the new university was in the hands of Ariel Lathrop, Stanford's brother-in-law and business manager. This selection of managers was unfortunate, since Lathrop, who also managed the stock farm, did not approve of the university.[180] Whether he thought Stanford could have done better

---

[169]LS telegram to DSJ, Mar 10, 1893.   [170]LS telegram to DSJ, May 30, 1891.

[171]JLS to DSJ, Oct 15, 1891.   [172]LS to DSJ, Sep 28, 1892.

[173]LS to DSJ, Aug 24, 1892.   [174]LS telegram to DSJ, Feb 17, 1892.

[175]LS to DSJ, Mar 10, 1893. See SFS 21:2 and LS papers for considerable info. on the part of LS in the hiring of teachers.   [176]Ibid.

[177]Benjamin Harrison to LS, Mar 2, 1893. On his acceptance, see JLS to DSJ, Mar 2, 1893.

[178]SF Examiner, Mar 7, 1894. Harrison's wife died on Oct 25, 1892, and on Apr 6, 1896, he married his former wife's widowed niece and sec., Mary (Scott) [Lord] Dimmick. NY Times, Oct 25, 1892, and Apr 6 and 7, 1896. In early 1894, JLS was embarrassed in having to deny that, contrary to an anonymous dispatch she had received from Indianapolis, she was not engaged to be married to Harrison. NY Times, Feb 7, 1894.

[179]LS to DSJ, Feb 17, 1892.   [180]GTC, Stanford, 414.

with his money or whether he was concerned lest the Stanford heirs be left penni-less is uncertain, but he appeared decidedly negative about the whole business.

Young Ray Lyman Wilbur, a future president of the university but in the fall of 1892 only a freshman student, remembered an increase to twenty-eight dollars a month that Lathrop made in Encina Hall students' room and board. The boys' atti-tude toward Ariel Lathrop resulted in the first Stanford yell Wilbur heard:

> A-R-I-E-L
> Go to Hell—
> LATHROP!

The boys were anxiously awaiting the return of the Stanfords from one of their foreign trips, Wilbur said, thinking their return would mean a lowering of expenses.[181] They were right. Stanford no sooner reached home in October 1892 that he wrote Lathrop ordering that the rate be cut to five dollars per week. This, he said, was enough for poor students to pay, since it was predominantly these stu-dents whom he intended to help.[182]

As Lathrop stood more and more in the way of smooth operation, he was unwill-ing to accept such rebukes. It is no surprise that at about this time he resigned and returned to Albany.[183] Those who insist that there was no falling out between Lath-rop and Stanford have to answer the question: "Why was it that when Ariel Lathrop died, his sizeable estate provided for a number of eastern charities, and $500,000 to his brother Charles but not a single penny went to Stanford University."[184]

An important source of ill feelings between the two brothers-in-law may in fact have predated the opening of the university. In February 1890, Ariel Lathrop was a director of the Southern Pacific Company. When the battle between Stanford and Huntington was shaping up, Huntington demanded the ouster of Stanford's old friend Stephen Gage from the directorate. Huntington regarded Gage as nothing but a politician and capable of getting the railroad involved in unnecessary political entanglements. Stanford pointed to Gage's long years of service to the railroad, and refused to dump him. In a compromise move that ultimately strengthened the Huntington-Searles interests at the expense of the Stanford-Crocker position, Stanford agreed to replace Ariel by Thomas H. Hubbard, an attorney for the Searles group. Perhaps Ariel resented the fact that Stanford stood up for Gage yet was will-ing to sacrifice him.[185]

Mrs. Stanford's younger brother Charles replaced Ariel on the university's

---

[181]Edgar Robinson, and Paul Carroll Edwards, eds., *The Memoirs of Ray Lyman Wilbur, 1875–1949* (Stanford: SUP, 1960), 39–41.   [182]LS to Ariel Lathrop, May 30, 1892.

[183]*SF Examiner*, Jun 22, 1893.

[184]*SS*, Dec 7, 1892; *SA* 1908 10 (3): 103, and 1914 15 (9): 405–406; and *SF Call*, Mar 5, 1909, and Jul 8, 1913.

[185]*SF Examiner*, Apr 13, 1890.

Board of Trustees. Charles was thought by some to be harder to work with than Ariel. Complaints against him reportedly streamed into Stanford's office from workers at all levels, but Charles was kept on, undoubtedly because of the deep affection between him and his sister. The younger Lathrop, known for years as the university president's "hair shirt," saw the university completed and later became its treasurer and business manager, a position that reported to the Board of Trustees, not to the university president.[186]

In the estimation of Andrew D. White, the Romanesque style buildings of the inner quad in their "simplicity, beauty, and fitness, far surpassed any other which had at that time been erected for university purposes in the United States."[187] White regarded the Palo Alto school and Jefferson's University of Virginia as the only exceptions to the general rule that American universities were a hodgepodge of incongruous architectural styles.

Often a sick man, Stanford must have been in a poor state of health to miss the first commencement at his beloved university, which took place on June 15, 1892.[188] Too ill to travel home from Europe, he missed the pleasure of watching twenty-nine students receive their bachelor's degrees and another nine their master's.[189] Leland Stanford returned in October 1892 from what would be his last European tour.

Even though not intimates, Stanford and Jordan nonetheless had become friends over the past two years. While away and ailing, Stanford managed to keep in touch with the president. He wrote Jordan about university matters and discussed at length their shared educational philosophies. In one letter, as an example, he expressed satisfaction with Jordan's belief that physics should be taught by experimentation rather than merely by lectures and recitation.[190] Such exchanges had been common. These two men complemented one another very effectively; their personalities were different, but not abrasive. Stanford would write long, respectful letters to Jordan, expounding on educational, religious, and philosophic ideas, and on how best to put them into practice. He hoped that together they could make Stanford University an example of original methods of instruction.

The men's close relationship was underscored at Stanford University's second commencement exercises, on May 31, 1893. When a *San Francisco Call* reporter asked Jordan about a rumor that his relationship with the university was about to be severed, Jordan knotted his brow and answered:

It is a fake. You know the source of the rumor? Then you will not be surprised to hear that there is absolutely no foundation for it. Several weeks ago my appointment was

---

[186]Morales, *Stanford University*, 28. [187]White, *Autobiography*, II, 448.

[188]*SF Call*, Jun 16, 1892. *The Leland Stanford Junior University First Annual Register 1891–1892* (PA: LSJU, 1892), 5; Elliott, *Stanford University, the First Twenty-five Years*, 206; DSJ, *Days of a Man*, I, 428.

[189]*NY Tribune*, Jun 19, 1892. [190]LS to DSJ, Aug 24, 1892.

reconfirmed, and the relations between myself and Governor Stanford are perfectly harmonious.[191]

Just after lunch with Jordan and several university trustees, Stanford was asked about the rumor. His response was even more emphatic than Jordan's. "I have never replied to any newspaper criticism in my life," said the senator emphatically, "but as this rumor might hurt Dr. Jordan here I would like to say that the more I see of him and his work the more I appreciate him, and that I have never entertained for an instant any idea of severing our relations." Turning to Jordan, Stanford asked, "How is that, doctor?"[192]

Jordan answered, "That is so, Governor. I believe we are as one in respect to the university."[193]

As Stanford grew older and his health worsened, he talked more and more about immortality; even in his later letters to Jordan he showed a growing interest in religion. Musing on classical and contemporary world civilizations, he decided that the Greeks and Romans were highly educated, but lacked what he called "true human civilization." He was firmly convinced that a civilization could not long endure "without a belief in the immortality of the soul, and in the beneficence and justice of the laws of the Creator."[194]

All this had bearing on the university. The founder told his president that the university's aim was to "fit men to realize the possibilities of humanity." Their graduates, in a sense, were to be missionaries to spread correct ideas of what constituted a true civilization. The true foundation of humanitarianism was neither intellectual nor moral development alone, but the Golden Rule. This was to be the guide in the development of the "religious element in man."

As Stanford's plans had matured and as the university became truly an institution of higher learning, plans for a comprehensive school system from kindergarten through college had been entirely abandoned. Leland Stanford Junior University looked more and more like other American universities. Ultimately, its curriculum would differ widely from what Stanford had in mind when he founded it, now encompassing a traditional undergraduate and graduate curriculum. And rather than being simply a trade school, today it is regarded as one of the best universities in the world.

Stanford's monument is complete: the Leland Stanford Junior University is his monument.

---

[191] *SF Call*, Jun 1, 1893.
[193] Ibid.

[192] Ibid.
[194] LS to DSJ, Feb 17, 1892.

CHAPTER 20

First Term as a U.S. Senator
March 4, 1885–March 3, 1891
Senator in Fact as Well as in Name

For a whole month there had been a cyclone of public opinion formulated in Stanford's favor, among Democrats as well as Republicans.
—Nevada State Journal[1]

Stanford will be the peer of any man in the Senate. . . . He is recognized as the greatest man among the Central Pacific Railroad associates. He is naturally a man of sound judgment, possessing a thorough acquaintance with public measures . . . the attributes of his nature rank with those of the best and greatest men of history.
—Arizona Mining Record[2]

California Senate Race in 1885

Aaron A. Sargent was a faithful supporter of the Central Pacific Railroad; he served the railroad well in its early, faltering years—from 1861 to 1863—while he was a California congressman. Indeed, he and Theodore Judah were co-authors of the first Pacific railroad bill and Sargent worked to help push the railroad act of 1862 through Congress. He later fought hard but unsuccessfully for the Goat Island grant. Though Sargent had served the railroad cause well, he was no railroad lackey. He had run unsuccessfully for the U.S. Senate in 1867, but in 1868 and 1870 he had again been elected to the U.S. House of Representatives where he served in the Forty-first and Forty-second Congresses. He was not a candidate for reelection in 1872, having again become a candidate for the U.S. Senate. This time he won and served from March 4, 1873, to March 3, 1879, after which he returned to San Francisco and practiced law for three years. In 1882 President Chester Arthur appointed him minister to Germany, a post he filled until resigning in April 1884; he turned down another offer to serve as minister to Russia and returned again to California to practice law.

---

[1] *Nev. State Journal*, Jan 24, 1885.   [2] *Ariz. Mining Record*, UNC, in SFS 11:17.

In 1885 Sargent was the leading contender for Democrat James T. Farley's Senate seat and he had every reason to expect the support of his friend Leland Stanford. The California legislature elected in 1884 seemed favorably disposed toward Sargent and he expected to be elected without significant opposition. Stanford, whose health was not good, was busy as president of the Central Pacific Railroad and Southern Pacific Company.

When Sargent had made his earlier bid for the Senate, his tireless service to the railroad caused a number of people to oppose him as being a "railroad candidate."[3] Now many of his political enemies began resurfacing. In early 1885 it looked like he might lose the nomination, so Sargent wrote a letter to Stanford—labeled "personal and confidential"—asking him to put pressure on a number of influential Republicans to stop their opposition.[4] Sargent was sure he had a safe majority at the time, but there was widespread concern within the party that his many political liabilities left him no chance of victory; in addition, the San Francisco Chronicle labeled him the railroad candidate and opposed him. As requested, the Southern Pacific Associates met and agreed to support Sargent.[5]

Stanford invited close associate Henry Vrooman, a confirmed enemy of Sargent, to the Palo Alto farm for a conference. He urged Vrooman to set aside his personal animosities and support the former senator. They argued for two hours, but Vrooman still refused. This scene was repeated a few days later, whereupon Vrooman peremptorily refused either to vote for or assist in the election of his old enemy. He stated, furthermore, that he and his friends were determined to elect *Stanford* senator, in spite of all Stanford was trying to do for Sargent.[6] Though repeatedly urged to do so, Stanford refused to place himself in the running; he called on Vrooman at least a dozen times, repeating his insistence that he and his associates relent and support Sargent.[7] Every associate and friend with whom Stanford discussed the senatorial contest was asked to support Sargent.

Stanford's reluctance to involve himself in the senatorial contest was evident; Frank Pixley complained on January 3, 1885, that not only was Stanford not a candidate, but that he would not even allow friends to seek support for his potential candidacy. Pixley was convinced, however, that if the Republican members of the legislature could not readily agree on another man and would tender Stanford "the unsolicited compliment" of a nomination, he would not feel at liberty to turn it down.[8] Was Stanford inviting a draft, or was this just Pixley's wishful thinking? There is no way of answering this. If Stanford were really seeking a call to the office,

---

[3]AAS to LS, Nov 11, 1884; *Stockton Independent*, Jul 18, 1873.   [4]AAS to LS, Nov 11, 1884, and Jan 11, 1885.
[5]Skinner, *History of California*, IV, 454–455.
[6]Henry Vrooman, "Honorable Leland Stanford," in HHB coll. BL.
[7]Ibid.   [8]*SF Argonaut*, Jan 3, 1885.

his tracks are too well covered to reconstruct what occurred behind the scenes; nothing has been found in the contemporary sources to suggest any other explanation than that Stanford *did* support Sargent and was not seeking the senatorial seat for himself.

The idea of Stanford's candidacy was not suddenly sprung upon the people of California. As early as December 1884 several California editors had endorsed him for the position, though his friend and powerful rival, George Hearst, hoped to win the Democratic nomination. When rumors of a possible Stanford candidacy leaked to the press in early 1885, there was a widespread reaction almost universally in his favor.[9] Even the anti-railroad editor of the *San Francisco Chronicle* endorsed Stanford, possibly because he saw the handwriting on the wall—that otherwise Sargent was going to win the nomination over his protests. Though the newspaper *may* have compromised on Stanford as less undesirable than Sargent, its support for Stanford appeared genuine.[10]

Another San Francisco journalist reported that since the "first gathering of the clans," a poetic allusion to the precaucus Republican negotiations, Stanford's name had been prominently mentioned as a candidate.[11]

Stanford's Journalistic Boom for the Senate

Sargent enjoyed a journalistic boom of his own in late November 1884 when the *San Francisco Call* published the comments of a dozen and a half California newspaper endorsements of his candidacy under the title "SARGENT FOR SENATOR, Eulogistic Indorsements [*sic*] of the Interior Press."[12]

But Stanford supporters were not to be outdone. Shortly afterward, the earliest and strongest statements from the California press in favor of Stanford's candidacy for United States senator were published on the pages of the January 12, 1885, *Sacramento Bee*. The writer stated that it was settled beyond a doubt that Stanford would accept the nomination if it were offered to him spontaneously. This news sparked a panic among other candidates, every one of them knowing that with Stanford in the race his own candidacy was doomed. The *Bee* writer said that whatever hope others entertained were "based on an insecure foundation," and he predicted that if a ballot were taken at once all other hopefuls would be "hopelessly in the minority."

The word *spontaneously* appeared to guide Stanford's actions. Stanford never sought the nomination. As the *Bee* editor described the situation:

No one, as far as known, has ever charged him with being a candidate—in the sense

[9] *SF CSTUJ*, Dec 20, 1884.
[10] *Sac Bee*, Jan 16, 1885.
[11] *SF Alta California*, Jan 13, 1885.
[12] *SF Call*, Nov 30, 1884.

in which politicians construe the word. He is not button-holing, connubiating, wire-pulling and importuning, as others are. The most that has ever been hoped for or claimed by those favoring Stanford is that he would accept the position if the Republican caucus would honor him, themselves and the State by tendering it to him. And he has not yet said he would not. Whilst he declines to enter a hurley-burley, go-as-you-please contest for the Senatorship, he inspires the belief and hope that he would accept the position. Stanford is still available for Senator, and is the man, of all others, who should be chosen.[13]

In an article with the title "THE STANFORD BOOM" blazoned across the page, the editor of the *Bee* summarized journalistic thinking about Stanford in newspapers in Nevada, Utah, and, among the Democratic and Republican press in California.[14]

This journalist cited two out-of-state papers, first, the *Virginia City Chronicle*, for praising Stanford as one of the noblest and ablest men in California, a man who would enter the Senate with "no masters to serve." And the *Salt Lake City Tribune* said that Stanford, a poor man at the time, was elected governor of California on the basis of his ability and integrity.

Several in-state Democratic papers endorsed Stanford's candidacy, among them the *Stockton Mail, Colusa Sun, Woodland Democrat, Fresno Expositor, San Francisco Examiner, San Francisco Alta California, Red Bluff Sentinel, Merced Express, Los Angeles Herald, Lakeport Bee-Democrat,* and several others not listed.

The *Los Angeles Times*, the leading Republican organ of southern California, reprinted with its blessing the following Sacramento endorsement of Stanford as a senatorial candidate:

> The current report of Stanford's possible entry into the contest for United States Senator has grown into a full grown possibility. There is very strong feeling here in favor of Stanford. Prominent men discuss his intellectual and pecuniary influence over the State and his landed interests common to the farming classes, and generally think he will deal fairly as between people and railroad. I would judge from rumor and hearsay that all Perkins' and Estes' support will go to Stanford if he is proposed, and a large portion of Sargent's followers, owing to the general feeling against Sargent.

The *Lodi Valley Review* wrote:

> There is no doubt that Leland Stanford would make a good Senator. He made a good Governor. The Central Pacific Railroad was brought to completion by his energy and ability. . . . The great administrative ability of Leland Stanford would advance the power of the State far in excess of its mere voting power.

Under the banner "KIND WORDS FROM AN OPPONENT," the *Placer Herald* remarked:

---

[13]*Sac Bee*, Jan 13, 1885.   [14]Ibid.

The name of Governor Leland Stanford, in connection with the United States Senatorship, is received with great favor by politicians in general, and a portion of Republican press is highly complementary to that distinguished gentleman.

The *San Franciscan* of a late date said:

It has doubtless surprised both the *Stockton Mail* and the *San Francisco Examiner* with what favor Governor Stanford's name has been received by the interior press. Even Democratic newspapers, which up to the last election made a specialty of gnashing their teeth at the railroads, are quite warm in their approval. Governor Stanford, we presume, has no desire to go to the Senate, but it certainly must be gratifying to him to see how well he stands with the press of the State, which is a tolerably good reflector of public sentiment. The cordiality shown him personally is, besides, an indication of popular feeling toward the transportation companies with which he is conspicuously connected.

On January 16, 1885, just four days before the Republicans in the state legislature chose their candidate for the seat in the U.S. Senate, the editor of the *Bee* added to his push for Stanford with the following endorsement:

The demand for the election of Stanford to the United States Senate seems to be universal throughout California. Even the most pronounced of the anti-railroad papers concede his great ability and high character as a citizen. There is no man in the State who better represents its many varied interests. The State would be honored should he be her representative at Washington, where he would take a leading position in the councils of the nation.

The trust which friends and enemies felt for Stanford is no better exemplified than in the following lengthy and adulatory statement that a man opposed to the railroad interests of Stanford handed the editor of the *Bee* to publish:

I'm not so prejudiced but that I can do a man justice. Leland Stanford is, in my eyes, an intellectual Olympus when compared with those who have been named for the Senatorship. He is a remarkable man, and his integrity is as unimpeachable as his energy is indefatigable. I recognize in him one who is greater even than the railroad. When I say that, I mean that I believe he could rise far above his own personal interests to do that which would benefit the State at large. I have always had the highest respect for him personally, while antagonistic to the public and political acts of the corporation. I believe that Stanford will make a model Senator, if he should be chosen, and I am not so certain but that the best way out of our railroad difficulties would be to send him to the Senate. It would bring the railroad and the people closer together, and the latter could certainly obtain more justice from Stanford himself than they have so far been able to obtain from their Representatives and Legislators. If I had a vote in this present Legislature, I would cast it for Stanford, and be proud to do so.[15]

---

[15]Ibid., Jan 17, 1885.

When rumors of a possible switch in candidates reached Huntington, he found it incredible, and promptly dispatched a telegram in code to Stanford: "It is reported here that you are in the field against Sargent. I cannot believe it, please telegraph me at once."[16] The next day Sargent wrote Stanford from Sacramento, again pleading with him to call off his friends—especially Creed Haymond, a Southern Pacific attorney and long-time Stanford business associate—who were busy pulling Sargent votes from a number of legislators and pledging them to Stanford. The disgruntled Sargent said that the whole affair was inconsistent with a letter he had received from Stanford just a day earlier promising his support: "I appreciate the friendship these men have for you, & that their zeal for you is the cause of their acts. But they should not trifle with your honor, or force you into opposition to me, which they are now doing."[17] Yes, Sargent was disgruntled—and he had good reason to be—as reflected in the way he addressed his old friend in the two letters written on January 13, 1885, very formally as "Hon. Leland Stanford," whereas in his November 11, 1884, letter he had addressed him as "My dear Governor."

The California legislature elected on November 4, 1884, consisted of an evenly divided senate, twenty Republicans and twenty Democrats; the assembly, however, was heavily Republican, outnumbering the Democrats sixty to twenty.[18] This made the election of a Republican senator a foregone conclusion, unless a candidate was nominated who was not acceptable to a powerful group within his party. A number of Republican hopefuls—Morris M. Estee (former assemblyman and perennial candidate for public office), George C. Perkins (the first California governor under the new state constitution and later a U.S. senator), and Aaron A. Sargent—immediately entered the contest. Estee, the *Chronicle*'s favorite, was expected to lead the Republican party into an anti-monopoly position if he won; his candidacy was largely a matter of revenge for having been beaten earlier in the race for governor, allegedly by the railroad.[19] Perkins, thinking he had very little chance himself, joined in the scheme to elect Estee. Yet the whole cabal, according to Sargent's appraisal of the situation, favored Stanford's candidacy over his own: if Stanford won, it would be obvious that he had won because of railroad funds; the party would then be disgusted by the railroad and would become anti-monopoly.[20]

The legislature was Republican, but it was *also* anti-railroad, and *not* just for public consumption. The railroad men in the legislature were almost solidly for Sargent, but the opposition to him was considerable and growing. There was Vrooman's determined opposition, and he was now a state senator from Alameda County; there was the genuine conviction—even among some of Sargent's supporters—that he

[16]CPH telegram to LS, Jan 12, 1885.   [17]AAS to LS, Jan 13, 1885.
[18]*SF Chronicle*, Nov 5–7, 1884. Until 1913, U.S. senators were elected by state party caucuses, not by popular vote.
[19]AAS to LS, Jan 13, 1885; AAS to LS, Jan 11, 1885.   [20]Ibid.

could not defeat a strong Democratic contender, regardless of the Republican majority in the legislature.

There was an equally genuine *popular* movement for Stanford. Californians who were against having the Central Pacific in politics had long made it a policy to distinguish between Stanford and his railroad. His friends rightly believed it would be easy to persuade the people of California—and their legislators—that Leland Stanford should be rewarded with a seat in the Senate.

Stanford is Nominated for the U.S. Senate—January 20, 1885

The Republicans in the legislature caucused on Tuesday evening, January 20, 1885, to choose their candidate. Sargent was still confident of a majority of twenty votes, if Creed Haymond and Stephen T. Gage, another railroad man who was backing Stanford, would speak in his behalf; he believed he had a slight majority without the active support of Haymond and Gage, if they would just remain neutral, or at least silent; in short, the only way he could be beaten was by Stanford supporters.[21] The eighty Republicans in the legislature showed themselves hopelessly divided on the first ballot: Sargent led the tally with twenty-six, followed by Perkins who got twenty-two, then came Estee with nineteen, and two minor candidates captured six votes. Stanford, the "non-candidate," received seven votes.

On the second ballot, Vrooman, true to his promise—or threat—entered Stanford's name. Perkins' vote immediately fell to one, and Sargent's and Estee's supporters to sixteen each; Stanford's name—like magic—drew forty-seven votes, more than enough for the nomination. Estee and Sargent supporters were understandably infuriated by this unexpected turn of events and refused to make the vote unanimous. One disgruntled assemblyman muttered, "This is the worst blow that has ever been struck at the Republican party in this State," and a state senator echoed these sentiments, saying, "The Republican party has gone to hell."[22]

Soon after Huntington's plaintive telegram reached Stanford, who was no longer able to evade the issue, the Governor announced his decision to run for the U.S. Senate. He cited the importunity of powerful political friends urging that only *his* (Stanford's) candidacy could insure harmony within the party. Moreover, they impressed upon him that this was a popular call that he could not very well refuse.[23]

Some of Stanford's friends believed that the Senate would be a kind of therapy for him; he needed to get away from the Palo Alto farm with its ubiquitous reminders of happier days—before the death of young Leland. When the position

[21]Ibid., Jan 13, 1885.   [22]*Butte Record*, Jan 24, 1885.
[23]HHB, *History*, VII, 431–432.

was offered him, he reportedly left the decision entirely to his wife, suggesting to her that life in Washington might prove a welcome diversion.[24]

Stanford did not seek the Republican nomination, but he accepted it without hesitation when it was offered. Politicians often claim this sort of detachment, all the time lobbying and manipulating economic and political strings behind a curtain of pious indifference. But Stanford was different: he sought to avoid being nominated and actively supported the candidacy of Sargent. This could not be said about his friends, who were legion, and determined. Vrooman later said that Stanford's loyalty to Sargent and his own lack of political ambition were unique: he was nominated *against* his consent and *over* his protest.[25]

Jerome Hart, associate editor of the *Argonaut*, later attributed the entire Stanford boom to Frank Pixley, another of Sargent's confirmed foes.[26] In 1859 Sargent had run for attorney general on Stanford's unsuccessful ticket, whereas Pixley had won this position in 1861 when Stanford was victorious.[27] According to Hart, the enmity between Pixley and Sargent could be traced to the failure of the one and the success of the other. Pixley confided to Hart in early 1885, under pledge of secrecy, that he was going to prevail upon Stanford to run for the Senate. Hart doubted that Stanford would betray his "most loyal henchman," but events, Hart said, were to prove him wrong; the appeal to Stanford's vanity was irresistible, and he gave in to Pixley.[28] Hart said it was then left to Vrooman and William H. Mills, land agent for the Southern Pacific Company, to persuade Stanford that Sargent would surely lose while he, Stanford, could easily win. Thus, the moving forces behind Stanford's election were Henry Vrooman, Stephen Gage, Creed Haymond, and William Mills. Gage's brother Norris Gage later said that it was Stephen who used the argument that the change in environment in Washington might be good for Mrs. Stanford; he was sure that it was his brother who finally persuaded Stanford to accept the nomination.[29]

This explanation is possible, but it is unlikely that this was the only persuasive factor. If Stanford had wanted a more salubrious social climate he could have afforded it without the added burdens of Senate duties and the very insalubrious natural climate of Washington, D.C. And if there were something morally treacherous or dishonest—depending upon one's point of view—in his supplanting Sargent, such an argument would not have mitigated the injustice and would not have persuaded him to do it. It seems obvious that Stanford was convinced that the voice of his friends and the voice of the California legislature were indeed the voice of the people. Perhaps the tight first ballot convinced him that Sargent could not have

---

[24]BB, *Mrs. Stanford*, 55.   [25]Vrooman, "Honorable Leland Stanford."

[26]Jerome Hart, *In Our Second Century, from an Editor's Note-Book* (SF: PiP, 1931), 127.

[27]For an indication of FMP's long-time hatred of AAS, see *SF Argonaut*, Jul 12, 1879.

[28]Hart, *In Our Second Century*, 127.   [29]Norris L. Gage to Edgar E. Robinson, May 23, 1917.

beaten the Democratic candidate even if he had managed to win over the strong opposition in the Republican caucus.

Another reason for Pixley's dislike of Sargent that is overlooked by political pundits seeking reasons for editorial dislike for Sargent in early 1885 can be traced to an event that occurred in 1877. It was reported on July 26 of that year that Sargent had filed a libel suit against Pixley in the Twelfth District Court charging that in the *Argonaut* of July 14, 1877, Pixley had accused him of causing the loss of $1.5 million to the laboring classes of San Francisco by using his influence to retain George M. Pinney in the Pay-Inspector's Office while he was using Navy Department Certificates of indebtedness to raise money from various local savings banks.[30]

Sargent had filed a similar libel suit against Charles and Michael H. de Young of the *Chronicle* charging that in their issue of May 15, 1877, they had published libelous statements about him.[31]

As his reason for accepting the nomination, Stanford himself fell back on the argument that Sargent could not beat the Democratic candidate. A year later, he told a *Sacramento Record-Union* reporter that the candidate he favored (Sargent) fell short of the votes needed in the California Senate to elect him.[32]

Stanford's long-time friend Judge William W. Morrow subscribed to this interpretation.[33] He had been chairman of the Republican state central committee of California, delegate to the Republican nominating convention in Chicago in 1884, and this political powerhouse would be congressman from California from 1885 to 1891, and United States district judge from 1891 to 1897. When asked many years later whether Stanford had double-crossed Sargent, Morrow emphatically denied the charge, saying, "Stanford became a candidate only after he was convinced that Sargent could not be elected."[34]

Pioneer journalist Frank A. Leach, California assemblyman in the Twenty-third and Twenty-fourth Legislatures, referred to Stanford's nomination as a "daring, defiant, skillful, and expeditious piece of political work" that never had its equal in California.[35] A Sargent supporter himself, he did not recognize any opposition to Sargent except the "railroad cabal" that foisted Stanford upon a reluctant legislature and equally reluctant state. The facts do not bear out Leach's interpretation. Indeed, if there were little likelihood that Sargent could win, Stanford was entirely justified in replacing him; the purpose of political parties is to win elections, and Stanford *could* do that.

---

[30]*SF Alta*, Jul 26, 1877.

[31]Ibid. Under a heading of "RANK RASCALITY," the *SF Chronicle* discussed "Senator Sargent's Protection of the Whiskey Swindlers." *SF Chronicle*, May 15, 1877. [32]*Sac Record-Union*, Feb 13, 1886.

[33]"William W. Morrow," *BDAC 1774–1961* (Wash.: GPO, 1961), 1363.

[34]GTC, inter. of William W. Morrow, Oct 28, 1927, in "Record" book (Spring 1907), 1.

[35]Leach, *Recollections of a Newspaperman*, 264; obit., *SF Chronicle*, Jun 20, 1929.

Stanford's old friend Marcus Boruck, editor of the *California Spirit of the Times*, wrote Stanford on February 25, 1885—*after* his senatorial election—explaining that the position of Vrooman and others was based on one simple fact: Sargent was a turncoat who denounced the railroad as a monopoly and "often in Sargent's room . . . the railroad was roundly abused by Sargent and his henchmen."[36] This was reported to Vrooman at a meeting in Judge Samuel C. Denson's office by Assemblyman Charles F. McGlashan of Nevada City.[37] Thus Boruck "confirmed" the rumor that Sargent had been planning to double-cross the railroad: while supposedly a loyal railroad supporter, he was also posing as an anti-monopoly candidate.

Stanford must have known better—or at least suspected otherwise—when he got reports of Sargent's duplicity. He had never before had cause to doubt Sargent's loyalty to the railroad interests of the Associates.[38] Even in 1885, more than a decade after his oft-cited speech to the workingmen at the Sacramento railroad paint shop (delivered on March 10, 1873), Stanford's own words about the role of Sargent in the passage of the Pacific railroad bill must have still rung in his ears:

> He [Sargent] was the most active man in Congress, in the passage of the Pacific Railroad Bill. He did more for it probably than any other man in Washington. [Applause.] He deserves more credit for its passage than any other man in the United States that *ever* was in Congress.[39]

This alleged betrayal by Sargent does not seem probable. It is more likely that Boruck's report was designed to make Stanford's own position more palatable to Stanford himself, to remove any moral doubts about supplanting Sargent. How better could this be done than to convince himself that he had supplanted a traitor?

Stanford and Sargent had been close friends, and they trusted each other. Sargent never recovered from the apparent treachery of Stanford. He died on August 14, 1887, when Stanford was serving in only his second year in the Senate.

STANFORD'S ELECTION TO THE U.S. SENATE—JANUARY 28, 1885

Stanford's election to the Senate was a foregone conclusion. On January 28, 79 of the state's 120 legislators (119 voted)—66 percent—made his election final; it was the greatest vote received by a senatorial candidate in twenty years.[40] Democrat George Hearst—who had served one term in the state legislature as an assem-

[36]Marcus D. Boruck to LS, Feb 2, 1885.

[37]Ibid. Denson had been judge of the Sixth District Court from Jan 3, 1876, until Dec 31, 1879, when, following the adoption of the new state constitution, this court ceased to exist. Willis, *History of Sacramento County*, 223; Woolridge, *History of the Sacramento Valley California*, I, 275.

[38]It must not be forgotten that on Mar 4, 1872, MH wrote a letter to CPH complaining about the attempt of AAS to modify the 1866 railroad act, generally considered a "Company Act," in the words of MH. The amendment proposed by AAS is a story in itself, but MH described its terms as a "hard blow" to the CPRR.

[39]"Leland Stanford," *CMB* 1874 5 (4): xv.   [40]*Sac Record-Union*, Jan 29, 1885.

blyman from San Francisco in 1865 (sixteenth session)—ran second, drawing only 37 votes, less than half of what Stanford polled.[41]

Henry Vrooman deserved most of the credit for Stanford's victory. An Oakland editor praised him as a maker of United States senators, and predicted that Stanford's "spontaneous" nomination would restore faith in the material interests of the Pacific Coast—interests that had been demoralized by, of all things, communist ideas. This enraptured journalist wrote that if an honest man were the "noblest work of God," then California was going to be represented in the Senate by "one of the noblest works of the Creator." Stanford's victory, he exulted, was a defeat for the "corrupt and venal politicians" who wished to sell the Senate seat to the highest bidder.[42]

It was ironic that the man who could have outbid all others was able to win nomination singularly free from the corrupting influences of money. Stanford's nomination was recognized as the result of a friendly conspiracy on the part of his friends, and simultaneously accepted as an expression of public confidence in the man himself. It was further evidence that the people did not oppose railroad men, as such, but were still able and willing to discriminate among them. Stanford was praised as one of the few men who had no political ambitions; he would make an excellent senator because he would transcend partisanship.[43]

REACTIONS TO STANFORD'S ELECTION

With remarkably few dissenters, most of California's newspaper editors as well as those of other states were happy with Stanford's nomination and election.[44] The editor of the *Los Angeles Times* was unenthusiastic but accepted it as the best possible nomination, given the four candidates, saying that it was preferable that the head of the railroad be a senator who had not purchased the position than to have one of the railroad's attorneys buy the candidate's way in with railroad money.[45] In this way the interests of the people would be protected by the "high character, known integrity, and distinguished ability" of Stanford. Most people, he said, trusted Stanford to do the right thing as senator. He was a man who could not be bought with gold, of which he already had a surfeit—he was too wealthy to be corrupted. This writer mused that Stanford must have derived considerable satisfaction in being so popular with the same people who persistently and bitterly attacked the corporation he headed.

---

[41]*CSJ*, 26th Sess., 150–151, and 169–170 (Jan 28, 1885); Assemblyman, Driscoll and White, *Constitutional Officers*, 96.
[42]*Oakland Tribune*, Jan 21, 1885.   [43]Ibid., Jan 22, 1885.
[44]SFS 11 and 12:39–109, contain hundreds of clippings from scores of newspapers in Calif. and the rest of the country, almost all endorsing LS and praising the leg. that elected him.
[45]*LA Times*, Jan 21, 1885.

One California newspaper editor predicted that the great "railroad king" would exert a more beneficial influence in the Senate for the state of California than could any other candidate.[46] Another rejoiced in the defeat of Sargent, who was, he wrote, "simply a politician of the narrowest and bitterest stripe."[47] This journalist saw the impending election of Stanford as a foreshadowing of the destruction of the Republican party, since Stanford would not be partisan enough for his compatriots. A Nevada County journalist traced the nomination of Stanford entirely to his popularity among the people of the state; neither money nor manipulation was needed or used to elect the people's candidate.[48] For a whole month, he said, there had been a "cyclone" of public opinion formulated in Stanford's favor, among Democrats as well as Republicans. This coincides with Stanford's later claim that many Democrats had pressed the Republicans to have him run.[49]

Bipartisan praise for Stanford's probable election was voiced in many big city papers. One editor who was a long-standing Stanford supporter was confident that Stanford's nomination met with the hearty approval of every honest man in the state. This "honest, patriotic, industrious, and unselfish gentleman" was not a seeker after office, and the senatorship was literally forced upon him.[50] Another said that the legislature had simply obeyed a public sentiment which was so emphatic that no one dared resist it; he predicted the dawn of a new and more prosperous era in the state as a result of Stanford's election; it was proof that the "calm, reasoning intelligence" of the people would guide the political affairs of the state in the future.[51]

Boruck viewed the nomination as an honor "unsought, unbought, unsolicited."[52] The noted noncandidate, he wrote, was admired, respected, and esteemed for his "honorable impulses, ability and intelligence, for his clear intellect and magnificent brainpower." Certain that Stanford was just a little lower than the angels—and not much lower, at that—Boruck continued: "He is a man who, in all the great essentials which constitute manhood in its highest type, stands pre-eminent among men. His name is a glory to the state, and his life the brightest page in her history. Hail! All Hail! Leland Stanford, Senator."

If the widespread acceptance of Stanford's nomination by the people of California was any reflection on the wisdom of the move, the Republicans had made the best choice possible. As a popular candidate rather than a machine politician, his selection seemed to some a return to the tradition of the founding fathers.[53] And since he was a railroad man, and the state's first ranking railroader at that, his ready acceptance testified eloquently to the fact that people respected his personal

---

[46]*San Joaquin Valley Argus*, Jan 24, 1885.   [47]*Butte Record*, Jan 24, 1885.

[48]*Nev. State Journal*, Jan 24, 1885.

[49]Inter. with corres. of the *Cincinnati Enquirer*, repr. in *SF CSTFJ*, n.d., clipping in LS papers.

[50]*SF Argus*, Jan 24, 1885.   [51]*SF News-Letter*, Jan 24, 1885.

[52]*SF CSTUJ*, Jan 24, 1885.   [53]Ibid.

integrity and felt confident that the public good would hold first priority in his actions for the coming six years; his character alone was a sure guarantee that California could trust him always to act in the public interest.

Not everyone was easily reconciled to having a railroad senator; not that they had any personal animus toward Stanford the man, but some still regarded his election as a "political outrage," an assertion that *the people* must not be allowed to rule.[54] Others, more cynical, could not believe that he had not purchased the Senate seat, as so many were doing in his day; one wit observed that Stanford's horseflesh was more creditable to him than his rank as a statesman, "though he paid as high for one as for the other."[55]

Stanford entered upon his new office with trepidation. Shortly after his election he reminded the California Republican League that this was his first experience with legislative office, and that he felt much better suited to an administrative position. Republican though he was, he was going to Washington with little partisan feeling; his main concern, he promised, was to advance the interests of California.[56]

A year later, on May 8, 1886, C. P. Huntington wrote to Steve Gage, whose official title then was Assistant to the President of the Southern Pacific Company, thanking him for some California newspapers he had sent and asking Gage to keep him informed on political affairs in the Golden State. He took this opportunity to comment on Stanford's election to the Senate and to give Gage his ideas on who the *next* senator should be.

In a statement that seems entirely devoid of truth, he wrote:

> The election of Gov. Stanford, of course, was not expected. When the Governor was here sometime before his election the thought of his election never came into my mind; but I could say nothing against it, because he would naturally have been my first choice, as he is not only a clean pure man but able, only his election placed me in a somewhat equivocal position with the other party, which I very much regret.[57]

Huntington went on to say that to elect Sargent in the next election—in 1887 as Stanford's colleague, not in 1891 as Stanford's opponent—would serve the best interests of the state:

> I would like very much personally to see him elected, not only because I like the man, but because he would ably represent the state and I feel that in this way justice will be done to him as well as to myself and others who had promised him our support to the best of our ability.

This never happened, for reasons shown below surrounding the death of Republican senator John F. Miller.

[54]UNC, 1885, SFS 12:43.   [55]Ibid., 22:1.
[56]Speech before Calif. Rep. League, Feb 11, 1885, repr. in UNC, SFS 12:23.
[57]CPH to Stephen T. Gage, May 8, 1886.

STANFORD AS A U.S. SENATOR

Following Stanford's election to the upper house and before he assumed his senatorial duties, he did some extensive sightseeing in Mexico. Sometime late in January 1885, he and Alban Towne traveled to Mexico City together.[58] A month later the *Argonaut* reported: "Senator-elect and Mrs. Leland Stanford, Secretary E. H. Miller, Jr., General Manager A. N. Towne, General Traffic Manager J. C. Stubbs, and Assistant Superintendent George Crocker, of the Central Pacific Railroad, arrived in New Orleans on Thursday, February 26."[59] It was Mardi Gras time for the Stanfords and friends.

After three days in New Orleans, the Stanfords headed for Washington, arriving there on the second of March.[60]

FORTY-NINTH CONGRESS, SPECIAL SESSION OF THE SENATE— MARCH 4–APRIL 2, 1885

Though the opening of the Forty-ninth Congress would not normally take place until December 7, 1885, Stanford's Senate career began on March 4, for a special Senate session that had been called.[61] When Leland Stanford took the oath of office as a United States senator that day, he believed that he was answering a popular call. Although he was the wealthiest man in that august body, and the seventh-richest in the United States—after John D. Rockefeller, William W. Astor, Jay Gould, Cornelius Vanderbilt, William Vanderbilt, and Collis Huntington—he had neither bought nor bargained his way into office. Therefore, he was free of all political encumbrances.[62]

But unconscionable political enemies struck wherever they thought they could hurt or call into question Stanford's mental capacity to sit in the U.S. Senate. A letter to the *New York Herald* from someone in California spread the malicious rumor that the death of Stanford's son had "unsettled" the new senator's mind. The *Herald* published the letter, but rejected the ideas express in it for the nonsense they were. The *Herald* answered the attack as follows:

> No one who sees him, or speaks with him or with Mrs. Stanford, will have a doubt that both of them bear a very grievous blow with fortitude and self-possession, and than neither of them is so engrossed by a great grief as to justify the ill natured and injurious reports which have been circulated about them.[63]

---

[58]*SF Argonaut*, Jan 24, 1885.   [59]Ibid., Feb 28, 1885.

[60]Ibid., Mar 7, 1885.

[61]*USCR*, 49th Cong., 1st Sess., 177 (Mar 4, 1885).

[62]*NY World*, UNC, SFS 25:55; cited in Wilson and Taylor, *Southern Pacific*, 105.

[63]*NY Herald*, Mar 23, 1885.

A ROMANTIC DESCRIPTION OF STANFORD'S OATH OF OFFICE

Congressman Joseph Wheeler of Alabama later wrote the following picturesque portrayal of the event when Stanford took the oath of office in the United States Senate: "On March 4, 1885, the most distinguished and noted men of our land were assembled in the Hall of the United States Senate. All eyes were turned toward the desk of the Vice-President as a handsome form ascended the steps, raised his hand, and took the Senator's oath of office. A well-poised head, an expression indicating firmness of character and intellectual power, showed the superior type of this calm, dignified man. It was the monarch of the great West—LELAND STANFORD, of California."

Wheeler went on to explain his meaning: Stanford was the "monarch of material development."*

*Memorial Addresses on the Life and Character of Leland Stanford, 101.

On March 30, 1885, the Stanfords took out a four-year lease with a two-year option—to begin November 1, 1885—on a Washington mansion known as the Brady House. It was at 1701 K Street, opposite Farragut Square, and was one of only three houses on K between Connecticut Avenue and Seventeenth Street.[64] This house, with the furniture included, cost them five thousand dollars per year.[65]

FORTY-NINTH CONGRESS, FIRST SESSION—
DECEMBER 7, 1885–AUGUST 5, 1886

In the fall of 1885, with Senate duties in the first session of the Forty-ninth Congress about to begin, the Stanfords, at home in California, packed up and returned to Washington, reaching the capital city on December 5, 1885.[66] They lived temporarily in the Reverdy Johnson annex to the Arlington House until their residence on Farragut Square was ready for occupancy.[67] Because she was still in mourning for her son, it was expected that Mrs. Stanford would not go into society that winter.[68] Moreover, her sixty-six-year-old brother-in-law, Charles Stanford, had died at his summer residence in Schenectady, New York, on August 24.[69]

---

[64]Russell J. Wilson to a Col. Levi Maish, Jun 8, 1895, in LS papers; UNC, Wash. DC, paper dated Dec 3, 18(??), in SFS 18:47.   [65]SF Argonaut, Dec 26, 1885.   [66]Ibid., Nov 28 and Dec 5, 1885.

[67]Ibid., Dec 19, 1885. On May 19, 1929, John Clagett Proctor pub. a hist. of the Arlington House in the Wash. Sunday Star. The Arlington had been built in 1869 on the site of the home of Francis Scott Key. In 1919 the hotel was demolished to be replaced by a federal building, the headquarters of the Veterans Bureau. The hotel faced Vermont Ave. near the corner of I St. This art. contains several pictures of the famous structure along with photos of other historic buildings in the area. The same author pub. another art. on these and other buildings in the Wash. Star, Oct 9, 1938.

[68]SF Argonaut, Nov 28 and Dec 26, 1885.

[69]Sac Daily Bee, Aug 25, 1885; CS had been honored in the "Self-Made Men of Our Times" sect. of the SF Alta California on Jul 18, 1869, where it was written of him: "No man in the United States, by pure force of character and intelligence, has done more in business and public life to give himself a distinctive and honorable reputation than the subject of our present notice (Hon. Charles Stanford, of Schenectady, New York)" [Chicago] RA 1885 10 (Sep 3): 568.

114. The Stanfords' residence in Washington, D.C.
The Brady House at 1701 K Street, between Connecticut Avenue
and Seventeenth Street. *Stanford University Archives.*

The mourning never stopped for the Stanfords. They undoubtedly found some solace and perhaps even comfort, too, in the full-length portrait of Leland, Jr., that graced the wall of the senator's library in their Washington home-away-from-home.[70]

Having only one month's experience in office, during the special session in the spring of 1885, the junior senator from California—junior to Republican Maj. Gen. John Franklin Miller—quickly assumed his official duties and was soon described by one journalist as the busiest man in the Senate.[71] Jane wrote with pride that her husband "was devoted to the Senate Chamber [and] is always in his seat at the opening and rarely leaves till the Senate adjourns. He seems to adapt himself to the extra cares with the same calm poise as he ever has in the past to new duties."[72] But Stanford soon found these duties irksome; he missed the easygoing and efficient life he had lived in California. After only a month in office he began complaining that his constituents were working him to death, that they had made him an errand boy, a

[70]*Sac Record-Union*, Feb 13, 1886.   [71]UNC, SFS 10:4.
[72]JLS to May Hopkins, Jan 29, 1886.

packhorse.[73] He had one hundred letters a day to answer, and the writers all expected him to respond personally.[74] Accustomed as Stanford was to direct response whenever he as chief executive of the Central Pacific Railroad spoke, the deliberative processes of the Senate, it was said, were especially annoying to him.[75]

Stanford's first address in the Senate was a brief speech on February 9, 1886, about the need for a new post office in San Francisco.[76]

When Republican senator John F. Miller died on March 8, 1886, Governor Stoneman appointed Democrat George Hearst in his place. On Friday, April 9, 1886, Senator Stanford presented George Hearst's credentials to the upper house and introduced the new senator from California.[77]

On April 12, 1886, Stanford presented a petition by Col. Jonathan Drake Stevenson to be "compensated for certain services rendered the Government during the Mexican war." Stevenson's petition was referred to the committee on claims.[78] The next day, Stanford introduced Senate Bill 2127 requesting relief for Col. Stevenson, who during the Mexican War had been commander of the Seventh (later renamed the First) Regiment of New York Volunteers.[79] This bill was read twice and referred to the Senate Committee on Claims. Apparently the bill was not approved or died in committee, because on June 1, 1886, Stanford introduced a second bill (SB 2579) for Stevenson's relief.[80] It, too, was referred to the Senate Committee on Claims. (Ninety-four-year-old Stevenson died in San Francisco on February 14, 1894.[81])

Two weeks after Stanford's first petition for Stevenson's relief, on April 26, 1886, and again on May 10, he spoke at length against the Interstate Commerce Bill.[82] In what was for Stanford a powerful presentation, he told his Senate colleagues that he recognized the Interstate Commerce Bill for what it *was,* rather than what its title *purported* it to be: it was a bill not to regulate *all* commerce, but just the carriers—that is, railroads. Its authors had failed to define commerce, which included trading, bartering, and interchange of commodities; as it stood, Stanford suggested, it ought to be renamed "a bill to regulate carriers." He conceded that Congress had the right to regulate interstate commerce, but he maintained strongly that the bill's selective definition of commerce—to cover railroads that crossed state lines—would convert "nonphysical lines" into barriers, or "frontiers between the states." He appealed to his states' rights colleagues to oppose the bill on the ground that the rights of states were being infringed upon.

[73]UNC, SFS 10:1–2.
[74]Ibid., 10:4.
[75]Ibid., 25.
[76]USCR, 49th Cong., 1st Sess., 1237 (Feb 9, 1886).
[77]Ibid., 3302 (Apr 9, 1886).
[78]Ibid., 3375 (Apr 12, 1886).
[79]Ibid., 3420 (Apr 13, 1886).
[80]Ibid., 5095 (Jun 1, 1886).
[81]SF Call, Feb 15, 1894. Stevenson was born on Jan 1, 1800. SJ Pioneer, Mar 15, 1894.
[82]USCR, 49th Cong., 1st Sess., 3827 (Apr 26, 1886), and 4316–4318 (May 10, 1886).

Stanford attacked a major argument used in the bill's defense, namely, that a government has a *right* to regulate that which it creates. He insisted that this argument did not apply in this case, since the states, not Congress, had incorporated the railroads. But by far his greatest objection was that this bill violated constitutional guarantees against having one's property confiscated without due process of law. Rate control was a form of confiscation, since it deprived railroads of anticipated profit, and anticipated profit *was* property.

Senator Stanford objected further that the proposed law destroyed competition. As it was, some railroads were making long hauls, often at a loss, at a lower rate than short hauls, in order to steal traffic from other roads. But, he added, if the federal government made them adhere to these long-haul rates, and then cut the short rates to a proportion of the long rates, as it intended to do, the roads would go bankrupt.

Kentucky senator James B. Beck, a Democrat who most persistently questioned Stanford during the Californian's speech, discredited himself and embarrassed supporters of the bill with his lack of accurate information:

> Mr. Beck. Virginia City is 700 miles [from the Pacific Coast], and Reno three or four hundred.
> Mr. Stanford. Virginia City is only 30 or 40 miles from Reno.
> Mr. Beck. Then I have it wrong.[83]

This was the last time Senator Beck interrupted Stanford to set him right! It also demonstrated to his colleagues that Stanford was no mere Western millionaire who could be badgered or treated with impunity. Senators learned to respect him for the profound knowledge underlying his spoken word.

On April 28, 1886, Stanford introduced another bill providing for the relief of a California veteran, George Percy Ihrie, a former aide-de-camp of Gen. Ulysses S. Grant.[84]

Senator Stanford gave notice on May 12 that on May 27 he would deliver a eulogy on his senatorial colleague from California, Sen. John Franklin Miller, who had died on March 8.[85] Also on May 12, Stanford presented a memorial of California woolgrowers remonstrating against the placing of wool on the "free list." This memorial was referred to the Senate Committee on Finance.[86]

On May 14, 1886, Stanford introduced Senate Bill 2428 to grant "certain seal rocks to the City and County of San Francisco in trust for the people of the United States."[87] This proposal was referred to the Senate Committee on Public Lands.

On May 26, 1886, Stanford introduced Senate Bill 2541 to authorize "the estab-

[83]Ibid., 4317.
[84]Ibid., SB 2277, 3917(Apr 28, 1886).
[85]Ibid., 4395 (May 12, 1886).
[86]Ibid.
[87]Ibid., SB 2428, 4494 (May 14, 1886).

lishment of export tobacco manufactories, and for drawback upon imported articles used in manufacturing exported tobacco."[88] This bill was referred to the Senate Committee on Finance.

The next day, May 27, 1886, Stanford delivered a eulogy on the life and military career of Gen. John Franklin Miller.[89]

Several eastern papers broadcast the rumor in the summer of 1886 that Stanford was tired of public life and was planning to resign his Senate seat.[90] The only thing that kept him from resigning, speculated a number of Californians, was the knowledge that Governor Stoneman would appoint a Democrat to succeed him. They predicted, however, that if California elected a Republican governor in 1886, thus eliminating this prospect, Stanford would almost certainly resign.[91] That summer of 1886 Frank Shay was responsible for the content of political editorials of the *Oakland Times*, and the journal emphatically denied the rumors of resignation: "How such stories originate it is hard to determine, but there is no truth whatever in the foregoing statement. Stanford is in the best of health, and has had no attack of apoplexy and says the whole story is a lie from beginning to end."[92]

FORTY-NINTH CONGRESS, SECOND SESSION— DECEMBER 6, 1886–MARCH 3, 1887

As Stanford reflected on his experiences as a young man in business and his observations of miners at work, he became more and more convinced of the need for greater cooperation among individuals and classes. This became his panacea for all social ills, especially the conflicts between capital and labor that were making the headlines with increasing regularity. He tried in various ways to encourage individuals who wished to form cooperative associations, and introduced a bill (SB 3022) on December 20, 1886, that was designed to help them create such associations.[93] The bill was limited to the District of Columbia, but laws in the District allowed anyone to form corporations there, regardless of home state; besides, Stanford hoped some states would use this bill as an example for their own legislation.[94]

On January 10, 1887, Senator Stanford delivered another speech against the Interstate Commerce Bill.[95] The ideas he expressed in this and the earlier speech were not new: he had used them time and time again when he had resisted state regulation of railroads earlier, and now as he spoke both inside and outside the Senate against public control of private business. Control, after all, was the essence of

[88] Ibid., 4941 (May 26, 1886).
[90] *Oakland Morning Times*, Jul 11, 1886.
[92] *Oakland Morning Times*, Jul 11, 1886.
[94] *Cincinnati Enquirer*, Feb 18, 1887.

[89] Ibid., 4992–4993 (May 27, 1886).
[91] UNC, SFS, X, 1, 2, and 4.
[93] *USCR*, 49th Cong., 2nd Sess., 272 (Dec 20, 1886).
[95] *USCR*, 49th Cong., 2nd Sess., 490–492 (Jan 10, 1887).

ownership; government control would destroy the income-producing quality of private property.[96]

Stanford again pointed out that cutthroat competition with water travel was evidence that the railroads did not have a monopoly: "If it is a monopoly it is only a beneficent one, helping and facilitating travel and commerce."[97] He complained that the Interstate Commerce Bill was a guarantee that water transport would be cheaper than rail, thereby making it impossible for railroads to compete. He omitted all reference to pools and gentlemen's agreements made to avoid competition whenever possible, and failed to acknowledge that most waterways were either owned or controlled by railroad interests, and that, in effect, competition from water carriers had *already* been destroyed. In his Senate speech Stanford made the Interstate Commerce Bill sound disastrous to all railroads, but when interviewed after it was signed into law, he said that the recently enacted law would not hurt roads east of Chicago. These roads would benefit from the law because they already had pooling agreements that were more stringent than the terms of the law, yet he insisted that West Coast railroads would be hurt by having their rates forced below water rates.[98]

San Francisco newspapers, particularly the *Argonaut*, which carried the entire text of Stanford's speech, praised both his stand and his speech on the issue of the Interstate Commerce Bill:

> Senator Stanford, on the 10th day of January, addressed the Senate of the United States in opposition to the adoption of the commerce report of the Interstate Commerce Bill, in reply to Senators [James B.] Beck [Democrat] of Kentucky and [Shelby M.] Cullom [Republican] of Illinois. This is really the first and most ambitious attempt of our Senator since his membership of the Senate. It is a dignified, logical, and, in our judgment, unanswerable statement of his side of the question. In it we recognize an entire absence at oratorical effort, and its methods and modesty of statement more nearly resemble the manner of debate in the English Parliament than in the Congress of the United States.[99]

Stanford may have overwhelmed his audience with his knowledge of the facts in the case, and he may have propounded unanswerable arguments, but he misjudged the mood of the nation. More was at stake than ambitious politicians seeking votes; there *was* going to be regulation of railroads, regardless of constitutional niceties, because—as signaled by the reversal of the Granger cases—state regulation had failed. Regulation was being demanded by an increasing number of responsible voices. Since the U.S. Supreme Court had said in effect that the states could not regulate commerce that crossed state lines, the only agency left was the federal government.

The Interstate Commerce Act, as signed into law on February 4, 1887, was weak

---

[96]Ibid., 491.   [97]Ibid.
[98]*Cincinnati Enquirer*, Feb 18, 1887.   [99]*SF Argonaut*, Jan 15, 1887.

and largely ineffective, but it was a beginning for those who wished to regulate commerce on a national level.[100] Once such a law was on the books and had withstood a court test, the old walls against regulation were doomed to collapse; once accepted, it would be much easier to strengthen such legislation to make it effective.

Stanford's Ideas on Cooperative Associations

On February 16, 1887, Stanford addressed the Senate on his ideas about cooperative associations.[101] He argued that civilization itself ultimately rested upon principles of cooperation. The cooperative associations that he was espousing would allow workers to share the fruits of their industry. Not only would the material goals alone justify such legislation, but cooperation involved another dimension: it would create a more intelligent people.[102] The purpose of cooperation, as he saw it, was to allow those with little capital to unite in economic ventures that they could not afford individually. The anticipated objection that this bill was asking for an already guaranteed right was true, Stanford conceded, but before a group could incorporate for any specific purpose under existing laws, it had to show financial solvency. His bill provided for the association of individuals—he left all this vague and undefined—with or without capital.

In early May of 1887, the *New York Tribune* published Stanford's lengthy explanation of his ideas and of his bill.[103] There he reiterated his earlier assertion that it would help people realize that there was no fundamental conflict between labor and capital. He explained in greater detail how their interests were the same; each needed the other, and both were working for the same ends. Capital was the product of labor, so there could no more be antagonism between them than between cause and effect. By helping people realize that capital was but labor organized, that corporations were extended partnerships, and that all laborers with intelligence could organize cooperative societies and work for themselves, Stanford hoped to prove that their disparity was more imagined than real.

The employer was—temporarily at any rate—not only a necessity in the economic system, he was a benefactor. Yet as labor became more educated, to the point that it could employ itself, the employer would no longer be necessary. Stanford thus justified the present profit system: the initiative of the employer had made profit possible and had put labor to work, and such initiative must be rewarded. Labor could organize and put itself to work, but was unwilling, or was, from lack of knowledge, unable to do this. But perfect cooperation, which was inevitable,

---

[100]*USCR*, 49th Cong., 2nd Sess., 1435 (Feb 4, 1887).   [101]Ibid., 1804–1805 (Feb 16, 1887).

[102]LS was neither espousing nor was he interested in the Rochdale-type distributive cooperative. See J. Murray Luck, "Cooperation—An Aspect of the Social Philosophy of Leland Stanford," *Co-op News*, Apr 13, 27, and May 11, 1950.

[103]*NY Tribune*, May 4, 1887.

would gradually eliminate the employer class. In other words, while labor was *indispensable,* capital was only *useful.*[104]

Stanford believed in what was then being called the "Gospel of Wealth." He agreed with the Carnegies and the Rockefellers that the wealthy were only trustees of their wealth, but he parted company with them on one point—he insisted that their usefulness—and his—as a class would someday end:

> What I believe is the time has come when the laboring men can perform for themselves the office of becoming their own employers; that the employer class is less indispensable in the modern organization of industries because the laboring men themselves possess sufficient intelligence to organize into co-operative relation and enjoy the entire benefits of their own labor.[105]

This was not intended as an endorsement of a primitive communism or share-the-wealth scheme. Any man who demanded of another a portion of his property was claiming a portion of his manhood, a share in his productive capacities, Stanford said. He favored a distribution of wealth, but only as a result of labor. Distribution of wealth would come from a more equal distribution of the productive capacity of men, and this would result from cooperation. Stanford's plan would produce not a *forced* distribution of wealth but a *natural* distribution that would not destroy individual initiative and personal rewards resulting from diligent work and self development.

When Stanford later wrote to David Starr Jordan that cooperation was one of the most important things that could be taught in the university, he reasoned that education tended to distribute wealth more evenly.[106] Economic equality would introduce social equality, so that no industrious man would feel himself the social inferior of any other man.[107]

In this theorizing Stanford seemed at times to betray his own class. His ideas, however, had no tinge of European radicalism, no socialism, no call for revolution. He simply recognized that overall prosperity depended upon an enlightened working class, a class that would possess the wherewithal to buy and enjoy the products that it was paid to produce.

Once again Pixley's *Argonaut* carried the full text of Stanford's speech on cooperative associations, along with commentary and commendation:

---

[104] *SF Argonaut,* Jun 11, 1887.   [105] *NY Tribune,* May 4, 1887.

[106] LS to DSJ, printed in the *SF Examiner,* Jun 22, 1893. According to the *Examiner,* this was the last *signed* letter of LS, dictated to his private secretary [HCN], just a few days before LS died. I have not been able to locate this letter in the LS corres. files. In any case, the *Examiner's* claim is wrong: the last letter signed by LS was addressed to Frank Shay and was sent by Shay to LSJU Pres. Ray Wilbur Lyman, with an enclosed cover letter, dated Jan 24, 1925: "I enclose the last letter written by Senator Leland Stanford shortly before he died. It occurs to me that you might wish to place it in the museum with other relics." LS letter to Shay was dated Jun 19, 1893, and it was signed. Shay's letter and a copy of the LS letter are in the GTC papers, SUA.   [107] LS, "The Future of Our State," in UNC, LS papers.

We print . . . Governor Stanford's speech in the Senate of the United States in support of a bill introduced by him to aid wage-workers by a legalized scheme of cooperation. This scheme for the association and organization of individual workers who have not the aid of capital to enable them to carry out the larger industrial operations, has been for many years a favorite idea of the Senator, suggested, doubtless, and strengthened by his personal experiences in carrying to successful completion the great enterprise of a trans-continental road. At the time this road was projected by himself and his associates, it was regarded as a gigantic enterprise, one that would have embarrassed the strongest government to assume, and which there was no available personal fortune in this country strong enough to undertake. Yet by the association of five gentlemen of moderate fortunes, aided to a limited extent by the loan of government credit—which has been to the last dollar of obligation promptly and honorably met—and by the donation of public lands that were comparatively worthless at the time of their concession and made valuable by the enterprise they were given to aid, the great work was entered upon and pressed to a speedy completion. It was at the time one of the greatest undertakings that had been conceived, and its successful completion is an illustration of what may be accomplished by brains and organization without the use of great capital. This calm, deliberative, and well-reasoned argument in favor of labor organization is characteristic of Governor Stanford, and proves that, in the enjoyment of his great wealth, he has not lost sympathy with the working-class of which he was and still continues to be one.

We do not know whether the Senator is a candidate for the Presidential nomination, and if he is, we do not know whether such a speech as the one delivered by him is as well calculated to meet popular countenance as the more ingenious and artful attempts of shallow partisans to commend themselves to popular favor by pandering to popular prejudice.[108]

Stanford's bill passed the appropriate committee, but never appeared on the Senate calendar again.

Sen. George Hearst, whose short-term tenure in the Senate lasted from March 23 until the end of the session on August 4, 1886, was replaced by Republican Abram P. Williams, who had been elected to fill out Sen. John F. Miller's term. Williams served from August 4, 1886, until the end of the congressional session he had been elected to fill out, which ended on March 3, 1887.

The indefatigable George Hearst was undaunted by his loss to Stanford in the 1885 senatorial contest, and his brief four-month tenure as an appointee to the upper house whetted his appetite for another try. He was successful in his 1887 bid for election to the Senate and again it was Leland Stanford who for the second time within a year presented the credentials of his old friend and political adversary to the upper house, on March 3, 1887, the last day of the session. Hearst then served in the Senate until his death on February 28, 1891.

[108] *SF Argonaut*, Feb 19, 1887.

FIFTIETH CONGRESS, FIRST SESSION—
DECEMBER 5, 1887–OCTOBER 20, 1888

The Stanfords spent most of the summer of 1887 at home on the farm, traveling about the state, or entertaining in San Francisco. On November 22 they left for Washington to attend the opening of the first session of the Fiftieth Congress on December 5.[109]

Memories of the Civil War had kept sectionalism alive in Congress, and they resulted in widespread "waving of the bloody shirt" at election time, when bills of a sectional nature appeared, or when appointments were made. An event occurred in 1888 that proved Stanford disinclined to carry on this sectionalism and showed that he was willing to forsake his party on an important vote when personal convictions thus directed him. On December 6, 1887, President Grover Cleveland sent the name of fellow Democrat Lucius Quintus Cincinnatus Lamar (or L. Q. C., as he was known) to the Senate for confirmation to a seat on the United States Supreme Court.[110] Lamar had been a member of the Thirty-fifth, Thirty-sixth, Forty-third, and Forty-fourth Congresses and U.S. senator from Mississippi from March 4, 1877, until March 6, 1885, when he became Secretary of the Interior. Unfortunately for Lamar, he had also been an outstanding Confederate officer and political office-holder.

The Senate Judiciary Committee conceded that Lamar was fully qualified for the office, but insisted that his former Confederate connections rendered him unfit for it: the official reasons given for rejecting him were his advanced age (he was sixty-two at the time of his appointment) and that he had not practiced law long enough to be qualified for a seat on the high bench.[111] The Lamar hearing was held in secret "executive session" from 1 until 4:30 on the afternoon of January 16, 1888.[112] For this reason the record of the proceedings did not appear officially in any documents, not even in the *Congressional Record*. It was expected to be a close vote, and party whips worked overtime getting their members in line. The *Congressional Record* reported only that the appointment had been confirmed—nothing more was said about it.[113] But newspapers all over the country printed the story immediately.[114]

Lamar was approved thirty-two to twenty-eight, with only two Republicans supporting him: Stanford was one of them; the other was William M. Stewart of Nevada.[115] The independent-thinking Stanford was praised for this action. The editor of a San Francisco paper, for example, was sure that Stanford's stand "argued a

---

[109]*USCR*, 49th Cong., 2nd Sess., 2591 (Nov 26, 1887).

[110]Wirt Armistead Cate, *Lucius Q. C. Lamar, Secession and Reunion* (ChH: UNCP, 1935), 458.

[111]Ibid., 482–483.   [112]*USCR*, 50th Cong., 1st Sess., 475 (Jan 16, 1888).   [113]Ibid.

[114]See Edward Mayes, *Lucius Q. C. Lamar: His Life, Times, and Speeches* (Nashville: PHMECS, 1896), 525ff, for a synopsis of ed. reactions to Lamar's approval.

[115]Cate, *Lamar*, 485; Mayes, *Lamar*, 525ff; Nevins, *Grover Cleveland*, 339; Vest eulogy, *Memorial Addresses on the Life and Character of Leland Stanford*, 66.

great amount of moral force" for a man (Stanford) in whom there was "nothing of the politician."[116]

The *San Francisco Argus* published a cartoon titled "THE FUNERAL OF THE BLOODY SHIRT," depicting Blind Justice hovering over a casket in which "The Bloody Shirt" is being buried, with Stewart and Stanford standing next to the grave, shovels in hand![117]

Democratic senator George Graham Vest of Missouri, himself a former member of the Confederate House of Representatives and Senate, later disclosed what Stanford had confided to him about his support of the Lamar appointment:

> When the nomination of Lamar was sent to the Senate for associate justice of the Supreme Court of the United States a determined effort was made to defeat it. Party lines were attempted to be drawn and sectional feeling was attempted to be aroused. Governor STANFORD, in a conversation with me, gave his reasons for favoring that confirmation. He said: "No man sympathized more sincerely than myself with the cause of the Union or deprecated more the course of the South. I would have given fortune and life to have defeated that cause. But the war has terminated, and what this country needs now is absolute and profound peace. Lamar was a representative Southern man and adhered to the convictions of his boyhood and manhood. I respect such a man. There can never be pacification in this country until these war memories are obliterated by the action of the Executive and of Congress."[118]

STANFORD'S PRESIDENTIAL "BOOM" OF 1888

Leland Stanford, president of the United States! This was considered the pinnacle of success for any United States senator, and was the dream of many. Indeed, it was not beyond the pale of possibility for Stanford—at least to hear his friends and ardent supporters tell the story. Stanford's presidential booms are the most surprisingly neglected aspects of his whole career. This is not because there was any chance that he might have become president, but just because they *happened*. A number of people for more than six years thought it either a distinct likelihood or at least a remote possibility, and so they catapulted him to a position in politics that was expected to bring him at the very least a cabinet position.

Even before his election to the Senate was confirmed, it was rumored that Stanford would capture the Republican presidential nomination in 1888.[119] With the party conspicuously lacking in new talent, and with Democrat Grover Cleveland taking office in the spring of 1885, it was not surprising that rumor made every popular Republican a candidate. Stanford denied emphatically that he *was* a candidate,

---

[116]*SF City Argus*, n.d., SFS 16:3 and 19:4.   [117]Ibid., Jan 29, 1888.

[118]Vest eulogy, *Memorial Addresses on the Life and Character of Leland Stanford*, 66.   [119]*SF News-Letter*, Jan 24, 1885.

but conceded what everyone already knew: that few men in the country would reject the nomination if it were offered.[120]

A number of California editors endorsed Stanford's candidacy. One pointed to his "breadth of intellect of early American statesmen" and his thorough knowledge of business as prime qualifications for the office.[121] After all, political administrators needed to know business in order to run the government, and Stanford was a proven master at this. As early as the spring of 1886 the *Sacramento Record-Union*, one of the most influential California newspapers, had also endorsed Stanford's candidacy.[122] Several San Francisco journalists regarded Stanford as the strongest man in the Republican party in 1886, and backed him for the presidency, predicting that his nomination would please all classes and all parties in the state.[123] About the same time an unidentified Nevada politician asserted that Stanford probably had a better chance of winning in 1888 than any one else in the party, including the perennially hopeful and one-time candidate James G. Blaine—congressman, U.S. senator, and secretary of state under three presidents (two at this time, and later under Harrison)—who was still hungering for the nation's highest office.[124] If Stanford were nominated, the Nevada supporter predicted he could easily beat the unpopular President Cleveland.[125]

Two years after his Senate career was launched, Stanford's name as a possible presidential candidate was heard more and more insistently in the East. An editor in Washington predicted that his nomination would command the respect of all Americans, something that could not be said of many Republican prospects.[126] In the mind of one midwestern journalist, Stanford was in fact being groomed as the party's 1888 candidate.[127] And barely a year before the next presidential election, he was billed in California as the next president, given that he alone could carry New York, his home state, where he was "universally admired."[128] What could be more natural than his "manifest destiny?" Leland Stanford: railroad magnate, governor of California, United States senator, and *finally*, president of the United States![129]

An *Argonaut* editorial reported on how Stanford felt about the Republican nomination and how he would refuse to stoop to the usual political tactics to capture it:

> Governor Stanford has been again suggested in connection with the Presidential nomination by the Republicans. He takes the same position to-day that he has occupied from the beginning. He is not, and has not been, and will not become a Presidential candidate, as candidacy is worked by such active politicians as Blaine, Sherman, and others, who plan campaigns and send pledged friends to the National

[120]UNC, n.d., 1885, in SFS 10:10. This scrapbook contains scores of clippings on LS pres. prospects for 1888.

[121]*Yolo Mail*, n.d., SFS 10:10.   [122]*Sac Record-Union*, Mar 31, 1886.

[123]E.g., *SF Argonaut*, n.d., 1886, SFS "C."

[124]NET, *James Gillespie Blaine and the Presidency: A Documentary Study and Source Book* (NY: PLP, 1989), *passim.*

[125]Nev. man in UNC, Jan 1886, SFS 10:12.   [126]*Wash. National Republican*, Jun 22, 1887.

[127]*Jerseyville* [Ill.] *Republican-Examiner*, Feb 25, 1887.   [128]*SF Post*, Nov 11, 1887.

[129]*California Farmer*, Dec 1887, in SUA.

THE NEW YORK HERALD.

NO. 18,862.   NEW YORK, FRIDAY, APRIL 13, 1888.   TRIPLE SHEET   PRICE T:

115. Senator Stanford's boom for the presidency. *New York Herald.*

SENATOR STANFORD'S BOOM.

A CALIFORNIAN SAYS HE WOULD RECEIVE THE VOTE OF THE ENTIRE PACIFIC COAST.

[BY TELEGRAPH TO THE HERALD.]

WASHINGTON, April 12, 1888.—Mr. Walter Van Dyke, formerly United States District Attorney for California, is here on business connected with the National Soldiers' Home. He was asked to-night what he thought of the candidacy of Senator Stanford for the republican nomination for the Presidency. Mr. Van Dyke said:—

"Governor Stanford will receive the support of the California delegation, and no doubt of the whole Pacific coast if he should be a candidate, as I understand since arriving here he will be. The objection raised against him is his connection with railroads. This objection, if tenable, would shut out from political preferment some of our greatest republican statesmen, for they can be mentioned by the score as either officers or stockholders in some of the great railroads. And it may be noted to the credit of Governor Stanford and his associates that although they have been engaged in constructing and operating railroads for near a quarter of a century, and much of that time on a grand scale, they never have had a strike on their hands and many of their employés have been with them from the beginning."

Senator Stanford was California's war Governor and was one of the best Governors that State has had, and is now making her a faithful, able and conservative Senator. If nominated he would receive a larger majority on the Pacific coast than has been polled by any candidate since war times.

Convention. Governor Stanford will not decline the nomination in a letter; he will make no political speeches in the Senate for political effect; he will pay no money for a literary bureau; he will send no partisan friends out to manipulate delegates to the convention; he will set up no journal to advocate his claims; but if he should be nominated by the National Republican Convention as its candidate for the exalted office of chief magistrate and executive of the nation, he will esteem the honor too great to be declined. This was the position taken by him in California, when in the earlier days he led the Republican forlorn hope for State treasurer, and later when he led the Republicans to their first victory as governor, and when he was chosen senator of the United States. The position does him honor, and his candidacy would honor the Republican national party.[130]

Two of Stanford's most persistent boosters were Robert E. Culbreth, editor of the *San Francisco City Argus*, and Culbreth's political cartoonist, Theodore C. Boyd.[131] In Culbreth's editorial pages and with some of the cleverest political cartoons of the day—rivaling those of Thomas Nast, political cartoonist of *Harper's Weekly*—the *Argus* promoted Stanford for the White House. The California senator was a "fitting

---

[130]*SF Argonaut*, Apr 11, 1888.

[131]Theodore Boyd had long been a woodcut artist and political cartoonist in SF. *SFCD*, 1888, 249.

successor" to Lincoln; he was the strongest and most available candidate for the office; also, he had never been involved in party quarrels or dissensions, and therefore had no enemies to stab him in the back.[132] He was not only more likely to carry New York than any of the prominently mentioned candidates, he was also very popular in the South. If William T. Sherman, Roscoe Conkling, or Walter Gresham did not capture the nomination, Stanford would. Of these possibilities, only Stanford could carry any southern states, and no one could *possibly* doubt his ability to carry the whole Pacific Coast.[133]

Early in 1888 the editor of the *Argus* was sure that all the leading journals wanted Stanford, especially since Blaine had by then withdrawn. One of this editor's political cartoons showed Blaine leading Stanford to the presidential chair and bidding him sit there. Blaine's "withdrawal" was obviously taken too much at face value.[134] Other journalists wanted Stanford nominated, but did not see Blaine "giving" him the White House; rather, they saw a political battle shaping up between the California senator and the former secretary of state. In their view, the nomination depended on the results of this contest.[135] Another editor, more sophisticated in the workings of party machinery, insisted that Stanford was incapable of winning the machine support necessary to capture the nomination; he was "too much a man of the people for the party 'sachems' to accept."[136]

Walter Van Dyke, former United States district attorney for California, when asked by the *New York Herald* what Stanford's chances were for the presidency, answered, "Governor Stanford will receive the support of the California delegation, and no doubt of the whole Pacific Coast, if he should be a candidate. The only objection raised against him is his connection with the railroad."[137] Van Dyke went on to comment on an aspect of Stanford's labor relations that has almost never been touched upon:

> It may be noted as to the credit of Stanford and his associates that, although they have been engaged in the construction and opening of railroads for a quarter of a century, and much of that time on a grand scale, they have never had a strike on their hands and many of their employees have been with them from the beginning.[138]

Stanford did not win the nomination in 1888, nor did he try to. His name was not up as a candidate and he did not get any votes. It is not very likely that Californians were "disappointed and chagrined" that the delegates at the Chicago convention passed him by, as was asserted by one of his friends.[139] Gen. Benjamin Harrison

[132]*SF City Argus*, Apr 28, 1888; SFS 19:4.

[134]Ibid., n.d., in SFS 16:6, and *Argus,* Sep 4, 1886.

[136]UNC, SFS 2:151.

[137]*NY Herald*, Apr 12, 1888; repr. in the *SF Daily Argus*, Apr 14, 1888.

[139]*SF Argonaut*, Aug 13, 1888; *Sac Record-Union*, Jul 5, 1888.

[133]Ibid., n.d., in SFS 19:10.

[135]*Marysville Appeal*, n.d., in SFS 10:4.

[138]Ibid.

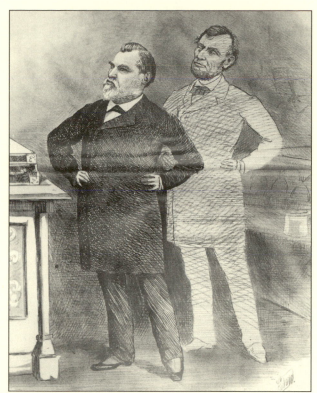

116. Stanford a "Fitting Successor
to Lincoln." *San Francisco City Argus.*

117. Stanford's "presidential boom."
A San Francisco journalist depicts
"Kingmaker" James G. Blaine offering
Stanford the presidential chair.
San Francisco City Argus.

118. Cartoon of the "Presidential Derby." *San Francisco City Argus.*

received fifteen of the Golden State's sixteen electoral votes when he won the nomination on the eighth ballot.[140] (James G. Blaine received one.)

Senator Stanford and his wife, meanwhile, had turned to things within their reach, such as lavish banquets and foreign travel. Stanford was in Europe from spring through fall of 1888, and did not take part in the election. In October, just after returning home, he regarded the tariff as the most important single issue in the presidential race; the free trade policy favored by the Democrats, to his way of thinking, would be ruinous to the industrialists as well as the workingmen. And Cleveland's administration, he insisted, had been a failure ever since the president had come out in support of the gold standard.[141] Cleveland favored tariff protection, while making a distinction between a protective tariff, which he supported, and a revenue tariff, which he opposed on the ground that the latter levied an inequitable tax on the people. Riding the political current of his day, and playing on the country's anti-British sentiment, Stanford summed up the whole campaign and defined all the issues in one terse sentence: "Every Englishman is for Cleveland."[142]

Perhaps it was Stanford's appreciation for the talent of political figures in either party and his ability to work with them that attracted Cleveland to him. On the evening of January 12, 1889, the Stanfords "gave a dinner of eighteen covers" at their Washington home.[143] The guest list included more Democrats than Republicans, several of them members of Cleveland's cabinet.

Despite basic partisan and philosophical differences between Stanford and

---

[140]Rep. Party, *Official Proceedings of the Republican National Convention held at Chicago, June 3, 4, 5, and 6, 1884* (Minneapolis: CWJ, 1903), 199; NET, *James Gillespie Blaine and the Presidency*, 300–301.

[141]LS inter., printed in the *SF Chronicle*, Nov 11, 1888, and *Sac Record-Union*, Nov 11, 1888.

[142]*Sac Record-Union*, Oct 20, 1888; NET, *James Gillespie Blaine and the Presidency*, 78.   [143]*NY Times*, Jan 12, 1889.

LELAND STANFORD'S JANUARY 12, 1889,
DINNER PARTY GUEST LIST:

Secretary of the Navy William Collins Whitney (D) and wife.
Postmaster General Donald M. Dickinson (D) and wife.
Secretary of State Thomas Francis Bayard (D).
U.S. Supreme Court Justice Stephen J. Field (D) and wife.
U.S. Supreme Court Justice L. Q. C. Lamar (D).
Nebraska Senator Charles Frederick Manderson (R) and wife.
Michigan Senator Thomas Witherell Palmer (R) and wife.
Mrs. J. Thompson Swann and Mrs. Condit Smith (unidentified).*

*NY Times, Jan 12, 1889.

Cleveland, the president showed the greatest respect for the California senator's judgment. He frequently consulted Stanford on matters of policy and, particularly, West Coast appointments to office. On January 19, 1889, in a letter addressed "My dear Senator," the president asked, "Will you please come and see me this morning, or if this is not convenient, as soon as you can?"[144]

A few months later the *Alta California* reported the workings of federal patronage in California as follows: "Senator Stanford has gone to Monterey and Congressman [William] Vandever did not arrive yesterday, consequently the expected meeting of the Congressional delegation to apportion out the Federal offices did not come off."[145] Both Vandever and Stanford were Republicans, while the president of the United States, who would be making the appointments, was Grover Cleveland.

A later editorial in a Cincinnati paper, following the death of Stanford, paid him a retrospective tribute regarding his relations with President Cleveland:

> Senator Stanford was always a welcome guest at Mr. Cleveland's board. President Cleveland held the highest opinion of the California Senator's business shrewdness, and he has had absolute confidence in the advice given him by Mr. Stanford. It is safe to say that Senator Stanford decided the fate of more Presidential appointments on the Pacific Slope during Mr. Cleveland's first administration than did all the Pacific Slope Democrats combined. The last visit he ever made to the White House was last April, when he drove up to the Executive Mansion to ask Mr. Cleveland for the promotion of a young army officer in whom he was interested. The request was promptly granted.[146]

Stanford's friendship with President Benjamin Harrison followed a similar course. His faithfulness to the party and its candidate, and his unflagging popularity merited a cabinet position; it was rumored that Harrison would reward him with one. But the call never came.[147] Stanford did, however, exercise a great deal of

---

[144]Grover Cleveland to LS, Jan 19, 1889, in LS papers.
[146]*Cincinnati Tribune*, Jun 22, 1893.

[145]*SF Alta California*, Jul 27, 1889.
[147]*NY Herald*, Oct 27, 1888.

influence on the Harrison administration so far as West Coast patronage was concerned. He was characterized as the supreme arbiter in the distribution of federal appointments and favors in California.[148]

FIFTIETH CONGRESS, SECOND SESSION— DECEMBER 3, 1888–MARCH 3, 1889

In October 1888 the Stanford party returned home to California from Europe. They returned to Washington on November 28 for the opening of the short session of the Fiftieth Congress, which ended on March 3, 1889. The session opened on December 3; there is no explanation of why Stanford did not attend until the seventeenth of the month, when a note appeared in the *Congressional Record* stating, "Leland Stanford, a Senator from the State of California, appeared in his seat to-day."[149]

Two days later, on December 18, Stanford was appointed one of three Senate conferees on a House of Representatives amendment to Senate Bill 1931, dealing with the purchase of sites for new federal buildings in San Francisco.[150]

On January 11, 1889, Stanford introduced a joint resolution (SR 128) to appoint a manager for the national home for disabled soldiers: it was referred to the Committee on Military Affairs.[151] A few days later, on the sixteenth, he presented to the Senate a petition of the Board of Trade of San Luis Obispo, California, for an appropriation for the construction of a breakwater in that town's port: it was referred to the Committee on Commerce.[152] A week later, on January 22, he presented an amendment to a tariff bill on "wine-spirits."[153] On February 11, he introduced two bills: Senate Bill 3954, which provided for the relief of two petitioners and which was referred to the Committee on Claims, and Senate Bill 3955, which provided for the establishment of a light and fog signal to mark the entrance to the harbor at San Pedro, California, referred to the Committee on Commerce. Stanford also proposed an amendment to an Army appropriations bill and another to a civil appropriations bill (both were ordered to be printed).[154] A few days later he offered an amendment to another civil appropriations bill: it was ordered to be printed and then with accompanying papers was referred to the Committee on Appropriations.[155]

On February 19 Stanford presented another amendment to an Army appropriations bill, which, like the first, was referred to the Committee on Military Affairs.[156] Senator Stanford concluded his activities in the Second Session of the Fiftieth Congress by presenting to the upper house a concurrent resolution of the California state legislature calling for federal legislation to exclude Chinese immigrants from entering the country.[157]

[148]UNC, SFS 25:6.

[150]Ibid., 339 (Dec 18, 1888).

[153]Ibid., 1096 (Jan 22, 1889).

[156]Ibid., 2047 (Feb 19, 1889).

[149]*USCR*, 50th Cong., 2nd Sess., 271 (Dec 17, 1888).

[151]Ibid., 652 (Jan 11, 1889).

[154]Ibid., 1742 (Feb 11, 1889).

[157]Ibid., 2081 (Feb 20, 1889).

[152]Ibid., 831 (Jan 16, 1889).

[155]Ibid., 1919 (Feb 15, 1889).

FIFTY-FIRST CONGRESS, SPECIAL SESSION OF THE SENATE—
MARCH 4–APRIL 2, 1889
FIFTY-FIRST CONGRESS, FIRST SESSION—
DECEMBER 2, 1889–OCTOBER 1, 1890

Stanford did not attend the special session of the Fifty-first Congress. On November 28, 1889, the Stanfords again returned to Washington, just in time for the convening of the first session of the Fifty-first Congress on December 2. They had just experienced one of the happiest periods of their lives since young Leland's death, and were entering—though they had no way of knowing it—one of the most difficult: failing health and unprecedented railroad problems lay ahead.[158] Despite ill health and pressing railroad business, Stanford tried his best to be present at most Senate roll calls.

A matter of special interest to Senator Stanford had come up with the introduction of the controversial Blair education bill. Years before, Congressman Gilbert C. Walker of Georgia had introduced House Resolution 748, which called for applying the proceeds of all public land sales to education. On July 29, 1876, Congressman Henry William Blair of New Hampshire spoke in favor of this measure.[159] Similar bills introduced by Blair passed the Senate on three occasions only to be killed in the House of Representatives. The present bill frightened states' rights enthusiasts by providing federal aid to schools where such aid was deemed needed by the bill's authors; an initial grant of $77 million was to be apportioned among the states in proportion to their illiteracy rates.

On May 25, 1888, Henry Blair—now U.S. *senator*—of New Hampshire proposed a constitutional amendment (SR 86) requiring states to maintain free, non-sectarian schools for all children.[160] Later Blair introduced Senate Bill 185, to incorporate his earlier resolution into law. Stanford spoke in favor of the measure on February 25, 1890.[161] He rejected without consideration the argument that the bill was unconstitutional, maintaining that the important consideration was whether there existed a *need* for it. Believing that the national government could have no more important object than the improvement of the intelligence of the nation's citizens, and inasmuch as a number of states could not afford to meet the educational demands imposed upon them, he concluded that the bill was not only constitutional, but necessary. Reminiscent of the founding grant of Stanford University, and reflecting a growing interest in religion, Stanford argued that literacy and intelligence were needed to foster the morality and religious beliefs that were in harmony with a "sublime, all-wise, always beneficent Creator." Education, he believed, was the solution to all problems, religious, political, or industrial; this bill would cer-

---

[158] *Sac Record-Union*, Sep 17, 1889.

[159] *USCR*, 44th Cong., 1st Sess., App., 235–245 (Jul 29, 1876).

[160] *USCR*, 50th Cong., 1st Sess., 4615 (May 25, 1888).

[161] Ibid., 51st Cong., 1st Sess., 1687 (Feb 25, 1890).

tainly render humanity morally stronger, wiser, and happier. Earlier, Stanford had attributed the nation's poverty to the sale and use of liquor, lack of manual labor, and ignorance of how to save money. The Blair bill would help eliminate poverty by giving to the people an education, a sense of values, and the ability to work.[162]

At home in California, Pixley's *Argonaut*, as might be expected, supported Stanford's position on the Blair bill, as reflected in the following editorial excerpt:

> The bill under consideration has for its object the lessening of ignorance in all parts of the country in proportion to the illiteracy of all parts. It seems to me to proceed upon the right principle and in recognition of the importance of education to insure the prosperity of the country and the happiness of its citizens.[163]

The *San Francisco Chronicle,* on the other hand, opposed Stanford's stand on the education bill and offered such illogical, almost bizarre, reasoning that Stanford's stand seemed brilliant by contrast.[164] First, the *Chronicle* editor rejected Stanford's argument that education contributed to man's ability to control the various forces of nature and thereby helped him provide for his needs; chance and circumstance, the *Chronicle* writer insisted, and not education, controlled these forces. This editor rejected as nonsense Senator Stanford's idea that the wealth of one man in no way implied or necessitated the poverty of another: wealth, after all, the journalist wrote, was fixed in amount. If the proponents of the Blair bill had to contend with no more substantial arguments than this, their bill would not have been defeated— as it was—by southern states' rights opponents.

Stanford's legislative interests were limited in number and scope, but he was very interested in national finances. He was sure that an increase in the amount of circulating currency was all that was needed to solve the nation's economic problems. In this he agreed with the Populists and Farmers' Alliance men, but their agreement ended there. Stanford surprised his fellow millionaires by concluding that the nation's economic system should not only be more flexible, but ought to give every man the credit he needed, based upon his industry, character, and ability to repay.[165] It was the farmer, Stanford believed, who had the indestructible security that could best furnish the government with the means of supplying the needed money that would give the nation's economic system flexibility. On March 10, 1890, he submitted a resolution—not a bill—to the Senate requesting that the Committee on Finance inquire into the possibility of making loans directly to farmers, with their real estate as security:

> Whereas there is a stringency in money and much consequent distress, the ener-

[162]*Sac Record-Union*, Feb 22, 1888.

[163]*SF Argonaut*, Mar 17, 1890, on LS Sen. speech on Tue., Feb 25, 1890, on SB 185, a proposal "to aid in the establishment and temporary support of common schools," in *USCR*, 51st Cong., 1st Sess., 1687 (Feb 25, 1890).

[164]*SF Argonaut*, Apr 14, 1890; *SF Chronicle*, Mar 31, 1890.   [165]*NY Evangelist*, Feb 19, 1891.

gies of the country being depressed, large portions of the farming communities heavily burdened and struggling for relief; and

Whereas the United Sates Government is alone authorized to make money which shall be a legal tender, whether it be by stamp upon paper, silver, or gold; and

Whereas the value of the three commodities when used as money depends entirely upon the stamp of the Government making it legal tender; and

Whereas it has been found that the money advanced by the Government upon its own bonds to the holders thereof has furnished the best and most acceptable currency, through which to-day in our country most of the exchanges are made; and

Whereas the present stringency is largely due to the retirement of Government bonds which have been so largely the basis of our circulating medium; and

Whereas it is of great consequence to national and individual interests that credit should be established, where merited, as far as is safe and practicable; and

Whereas the Government can do this abundantly, without risk to itself, upon much of the property of the country, as it is now doing upon its own bonds, on which it is paying interest: [sic] and

Whereas loans upon a property basis would furnish all the money needed without cost to the Government, and a fair interest paid by the borrower would give to the Government for the use of its credits in bills a large income: Therefore,

Be it resolved, That the Committee on Finance be instructed to inquire what relief may be furnished by the United States Government, and particularly whether loans may not be made by the Government upon mortgages deposited with it upon real estate, independent of improvements, at such rate and to such an amount only as will make the security to the Government perfect, the Government to receive some small rate of interest, from 1 to 2 per cent., ample compensation for the use of its credit, and to prevent the undue applications for loans beyond the needs of the country. And the Government, as further restraint and provision against an overissue (if such a thing be possible upon perfect security, where the interest is very slight), shall provide to call in a percentage of its loans, from time to time, upon reasonable notice, as it may deem necessary, at its own discretion, for the welfare of the nation.[166]

The committee sidetracked the loan resolution for two months without action. Stanford was not one to be ignored, and he pressed the matter on the floor of the Senate. On May 23 he introduced his Land Loan Bill (SB 3889), a bill which directed the Secretary of the Treasury to print $100 million worth of paper money secured by land at no more than 50 percent of the land value.[167] This, he said, was far safer than the present policy of lending 90 percent on government bonds and would also allow those without liquid capital to "energize" their assets.

Stanford was asked to explain the difference between his bill and the sub-treasury scheme advocated by the Farmers' Alliance. The Alliance plan, he argued, called for temporary loans secured by the products of the farmers' lands, loans that

---

[166]USCR, 51st Cong., 1st Sess., 2068 (Mar 10, 1890).

[167]Ibid., 5169–5170 (May 23, 1890); a letter to the SF Argonaut on Apr 14, 1890, pointed to a similar, but far more generous and more revolutionary bill before Parliament allowing Irish farmers to purchase their farms with 100 percent of the price being lent by the British govt.

had to be repaid as soon as a crop was harvested; his scheme, however, provided for long-term loans at 2 percent interest secured by the *land itself*.[168] Some of his critics were unable to see the difference! The *San Francisco Argonaut* carried several lengthy editorials explaining the terms and intentions of Stanford's government loan plan.[169] On June 11, 1890, the Senate Committee on Finance indefinitely postponed his land loan measure.[170] The ailing Stanford had just reached France on his fifth trip abroad when this action was taken.

FIFTY-FIRST CONGRESS, SECOND SESSION—
DECEMBER 1, 1890–MARCH 2, 1891

The issue of legal tender was again on everybody's mind, so on December 5, 1890, Stanford revived the land loan matter, calling up his Senate Bill 4528 (admittedly, it was substantially the same as his Senate Bill 3889) for debate.[171] In the second session of the Fifty-first Congress the senior senator from California devoted even more time to pushing for his bill. After discussing the matter at some length in the Senate on December 19, he concluded, simply: legal tender is created by the imprint of the United States government regardless of material used.[172] Moreover, since the federal government reserved to itself the right to make money, it had the "correlative duty to furnish an ample supply."[173] Stanford's bill was referred to the Committee on Finance.

In a six-page report issued on February 17, 1891, this committee rejected Stanford's bill—"reported adversely," to use the technical language of Senate Report 2267—which, of course, was tantamount to a rejection by the entire Senate. In the language of the committee, "Some of the minor objections to the bill might perhaps be removed by amendment, but the objections to its substance, constitutionality, and to the principle involved, are ineradicable."[174]

The Lamar appointment of 1888 had shown Stanford's political independence, when he voted for a fully qualified Confederate officer to sit on the nation's highest court. This independence was demonstrated again in early 1891 when an elections bill (introduced in the lower house on June 19, 1890), sometimes called the Force bill or Lodge bill, came before the Senate. It was named for Henry Cabot Lodge, its author in the House of Representatives, where it passed on July 2. This proposal dealt with one of the most heated political issues of the time: to provide federal

[168]LS inter. with *Cincinnati Enquirer*, repr. in pam. form, in LS papers.
[169]*SF Argonaut*, Sep 15, 1890, Jan 5 and 19, 1891, and Feb 2, 1891.
[170]*USCR*, 51st Cong., 1st Sess., 5922 (Jun 11, 1890).
[171]Ibid., 2nd Sess., 112 (Dec 5, 1890); 667–668 (Dec 19, 1890).
[172]Ibid., 2nd Sess., 667–668 (Dec 19, 1890); *National Review*, Mar 22, 1890; *SF Argonaut*, Apr 7, 1890.
[173]*USCR*, 51st Cong., 2nd Sess., 667 (Dec 19, 1890).   [174]*SR 2267*, 51st Cong., 2nd Sess., 6 (Feb 17, 1891).

protection for Negroes when they were voting. Stanford opposed the bill, and in so doing aligned himself against the overwhelming majority of his fellow Republicans. He conceded that the present election system had a number of "evils" in it, but the Force bill, in his estimation, was a greater evil than that which it hoped to correct. By regulating the voting procedures of the states, Stanford argued, it endangered the principle of self-government. What was worse, by encouraging or possibly requiring that local and national elections be held at the same time, the measure would allow regulation of local and national elections.[175]

Senate Republicans were determined to pass this measure and even tried to press the cloture system into service, but eight western Republicans joined the Democrats in sidetracking the bill. Stanford was one of the eight, and even though he was absent when the crucial vote was taken, he was paired against it.[176] As it turned out, Stanford's absence did not affect the outcome of the cloture vote: it simply reduced the majority against the bill from two to one.[177] Sen. William Stewart in his *Reminiscences* gives a graphic account of a hasty trip he made to New York to get Stanford to pair himself against the bill.[178]

Stanford had gone to New York on Sunday, January 25, 1891, to inspect a number of his horses that were to be sold. The next morning, on his way to the American Institute Building at Sixty-third Street and Third Avenue where the sale was to take place, he was involved in an accident that could have cost him his life.[179] Accompanied by John McCarthy, his private secretary, the coupé in which they were riding was struck by a speeding horse car with such force that both vehicles were overturned and Stanford was ejected onto the stone pavement. He received several bruises and a gash on his forehead. At first it was thought that the injured senator had suffered a broken arm or shoulder and broken ribs, possibly even a skull fracture, but the dazed man soon regained complete consciousness. Several passengers in the badly damaged horse car that hit him were shaken up and the frightened driver left the scene in haste. Stanford's wound was "plastered up" by a surgeon, and despite protestations from the doctor and McCarthy he insisted on continuing to the American Institute Building. This incident caused him to miss the 4:30 train to Washington. The next morning they returned to the capital, where he was a guest of President Harrison in the evening.

In the waning days of Stanford's first term as senator, on February 28, 1891, at ten minutes after nine in the evening, Sen. George Hearst died in his home in Washing-

---

[175] *NY Evangelist*, Feb 19, 1891.

[176] If two sen. were on opposite sides on a matter to be voted on, it was a common practice to "pair," meaning that neither had to attend the sess. and vote. If one sen. of a pair were present, he would abstain on the bill in which he was paired.

[177] *NY Herald*, Jan 27, 1891.

[178] William M. Stewart, *Reminiscences of Senator William M. Stewart of Nevada* (NY: NPC, 1908), 305–307.

[179] "Senator Stanford's Escape from Death," *NY Herald*, Jan 27, 1891.

ton of a long illness described as "alimentary."[180] He had made a trip to New York in December 1890 to place himself more closely under the care of his physician, Dr. Charles Ward. With the gravity of his illness confirmed, he returned to Washington to die in the company of his wife, Phoebe, and his son, William Randolph, who had come east to be with his father during his last days.[181]

Shortly after midnight in the United States Senate, Stanford arose to announce that his colleague had died. Despite its involvement in a tumultuous, all-night session, the Senate adjourned out of respect.[182]

Hearst's body lay in state at his Washington home at 1400 North Hampshire Avenue until March 5, when a memorial service was held there.[183] Afterward, the casket was place on a funeral train of six Pullman sleepers and day coaches. The train carried besides the immediate family members eight United States senators and nine representatives. The fourth car in the procession was *Car Stanford.* Pixley's paper reported almost daily on the cross-country trek of the funeral procession: "Senator and Mrs. Stanford are on their way West [sic] on the funeral train of the late Senator Hearst."[184] As expected, the *Examiner,* owned by Hearst's only son, William Randolph Hearst, provided the most complete coverage.

At home in California, the state legislature adjourned. More than half its members went to San Francisco for the funeral. Hearst lay in state in Grace Episcopal Church from March 12, when his train arrived in San Francisco, until Sunday, March 15, when funeral services were held.[185] Hearst was buried at the Mountain View Cemetery in Oakland; once his mausoleum was prepared, his remains were moved to Cypress Lawn in Colma, on the San Francisco Peninsula.[186]

In his Senate eulogy of George Hearst, on March 25, 1892, Stanford praised his departed colleague as a man of calm and keen judgment, a man who had the faculty of making and retaining strong friendships. Hearst was a man of industry, perseverance, good judgment and truth. "Such were the qualities which enabled my friend and colleague to bring to a successful close the great battle of life."[187]

---

[180]*SF Examiner*, Mar 1, 1891.

[181]Mr. and Mrs. Fremont Older, *George Hearst, California Pioneer* (LA: Westernlore, 1966), 226.

[182]*SF Examiner*, Mar 1, 1891. It is interesting to note that tucked away among the various eulogistic notices in the *Examiner* of Hearst's death is the "Prattle," a column written by Ambrose Bierce, a man who, five years before Hearst's death, had written one of his infamous "malogies," *SF Wasp*, Aug 21, 1886:

Ex-Senator Hearst	The righteous, God hath said, shall rise the first:
The friend of Stoneman and of	O peaceful be thy long, long sleep,
Haggin here	George Hearst.
Rests from the labors of his high career.	

Either William Randolph Hearst was a forgiving employer, or he was not a reader of the *Wasp.*

[183]*Wash. Star*, Feb 5, 1891; *SF Examiner*, Mar 5, 1891.

[184]*SF Argonaut*, Mar 9, 1891.   [185]*SF Examiner*, Mar 13–16, 1891.

[186]LS eulogy of George Hearst, Mar 25, 1892, in *USCR*, 52nd Cong., 1st Sess., 2560–2561 (Mar 25, 1892), Vol. V. SSN 3068.   [187]Ibid., 2561.

CHAPTER 21

STANFORD AND THE U.S. PACIFIC RAILWAY COMMISSION OF 1887

The Pacific Railway Commission is Not a Judicial Body[1]

We feel that where we have complied with all of the requirements of the law, where we have annually reported to the United States Secretary of the Treasury, as required under the act of 1862, where we have submitted the affairs of the company to the investigation of all the officials charged with the investigation of the same, and where we have complied with every requirement of the law, oppressively as it has sometimes borne upon the company, and where the properly-authorized officers of the Government have accepted and received the reports of the company, fully showing the condition of its affairs as required by law, up to the 31st of December, 1886, it is hardly in keeping with the solemn compact made between the company and Congress, under the act of July, 1862, that no addition to, alteration in, or amendment to that act should be made without having due regard for the rights of the company, on the 3rd of March, 1887, to pass the act of Congress authorizing the present investigation, under which we are called upon to go over now and investigate transactions reported to the Government over a quarter of a century ago, and long since settled and closed.

—U.S. senator Leland Stanford[2]

PRESIDENT GROVER CLEVELAND APPOINTS A PACIFIC RAILWAY COMMISSION, APRIL 15, 1887

There was no little concern inside and outside of Congress that the railroads receiving government loans for initial construction never intended—nor would ever be able—to repay these debts. Various attempts were made to require that a percentage of net profits be set aside in a sinking fund to repay the debts. Later government-assisted railroads must have rued the day in 1862 that

---

[1] Stated in the first of 12 "Opinions of Mr. Justice [Stephen] Field, and Judges [Lorenzo] Sawyer and [George M.] Sabin, delivered in the U.S. Circuit Court at San Francisco, August 29, 1887," *USPRC*, VII, 4215.

[2] "Answer of Leland Stanford. In the Circuit Court of the United States for the Northern District of California. In the Matter of the United States Pacific Railway Commission." *USPRC*, VII, 4173; see Evans, *Huntington*, II, 432, for an examination of the events surrounding this test.

Aaron Sargent first mentioned the possible use of a sinking fund to guarantee repayment of any debts owed to the government.[3]

On May 7, 1878, Congress passed the Thurman Act, an *ex post facto* measure that modified the original railroad act of 1862 by requiring that federally-assisted railroads deposit 25 percent of their net earnings into a sinking fund to be established by the United States Treasury. These funds were to be used to liquidate railroad obligations to the federal government when their debts came due.[4] The railroads argued, quite rightly, that this law legalized a way to secure repayment of the debts even *before* they were due and thus deprive the affected railroads of capital needed for operating expenses and expansion.

Congress later decided to investigate the federally-assisted railroads in response to complaints about excessive railroad profits, squandering of money from the public treasury, and lawsuits—some spurious, others not—against the railroads. A federal bill was passed by Congress and signed into law by President Cleveland on March 3, 1887. Its title, which called for making an investigation of the books, accounts, and methods of railroads that had received aid from the United States, "and for other purposes," bespoke its cumbersome mission.[5]

On April 15, 1887, President Cleveland appointed a three-man Pacific Railway Commission—independent of Congress—to investigate all western railroads receiving federal land grants and loans. The appointment of this commission launched one of the most grueling railroad investigations ever conducted. The principal hearings were held in San Francisco (at the Palace Hotel and in the offices of the Central Pacific Railroad), New York, Boston, and Omaha, while others were held in various towns off the beaten path.[6] Every major figure in the building or management of the Central Pacific, the Union Pacific, and the Southern Pacific railroads was eventually subjected to an almost inquisitional probing into not only his business accounts but also his personal affairs.

The various railroad investigations by the California legislature were a nuisance, but had not threatened the Southern Pacific partners. The congressional investigation of 1887 was another matter.

Cleveland's investigative commission was stacked with reform-minded Democrats in the persons of Chairman Robert Emory Pattison of Pennsylvania and Elbert

---

[3]*USCG*, 37th Cong., 2nd Sess., 602 (Jan 31, 1862).

[4]20 *US Stats* 56–61, 45th Cong., 2nd Sess. (Dec 3, 1877–Jun 20, 1878), Chap. 96, *An Act to alter and amend the act entitled "An act to aid in the construction of a railroad and telegraph line from the Missouri River to the Pacific Ocean, and to secure to the Government the use of the same for postal, military and other purposes"*, [sic] *approved July first, eighteen hundred and sixty-two, and also to alter and amend the act of Congress approved July second, eighteen hundred and sixty-four, in amendment of said first-named act.* App. May 7, 1878. The law was named for Ohio senator Allen Granberry Thurman (D).

[5]*RUSPRC*, 3; 24 *US Stats* 488–492, 49th Cong., 2nd Sess. (Dec 6, 1886–Mar 3, 1887), Chap. 345, *An act authorizing an investigation of the books, accounts, and methods of railroads which have received aid from the United States, and for other purposes.* App. Mar 3, 1887.   [6]*RUSPRC*, 4.

Ellery Anderson of New York, and David T. Littler, a reform-minded Republican from Illinois.

Robert Pattison had been the Democratic governor of Pennsylvania from 1883 to 1887. His administration was committed to economy and reform—and to strong executive action in holding railroads and canal companies in strict conformity to the letter of the law.[7] Politically and philosophically, Pattison was a natural for Cleveland's choice to serve as chairman of the Pacific Railway Commission.

Anderson had a long record as an attorney committed to political reform, serving at one time as president of the Reform Club. He conducted proceedings against Jay Gould and the Texas Railway Company and was successful in recovering $2 million interest on income bonds.[8] He was active in the prosecution and overthrow of the William Tweed Ring. Anderson was a strong advocate of tariff reform and was opposed to the coinage of silver. He turned down several offers of a seat on the Supreme Court.[9]

Ohio-born Littler was an Illinois lawyer and state senator.[10] In 1866 President Andrew Johnson appointed him Collector of Internal Revenue for the Eighth District. He later resigned this position to become a partner in a prestigious Springfield, Illinois, law firm in partnership with Henry S. Greene. In 1882 and 1886 Littler was elevated to the lower house of the state legislature and in 1886 and 1894 was elected to the state's upper house. In both houses of the legislature he took a prominent part in legislation dealing with questions of revenue.

The commissioners were given fifty-eight specific subjects for their guidance: twenty-three were charges that the railroad companies had failed in their duties to the government; nineteen related to the monetary values of the companies, holdings of stock, salaries, and payments made to influence legislation; six contained specific instructions to the commissioners; and ten were related to allegations by the railroad companies that the government had not treated them fairly.[11]

Two hundred and fifty-two people in all, including attorneys accompanying witnesses, were called upon to testify or be heard, including state and territorial governors, city mayors, state legislators, newspaper editors, hotel proprietors, bankers, miners, brokers, merchants, and railroad owners and managers.[12] The witnesses were subjected to unrelenting interrogation by the committee. The entire set of reports and testimonies filled 5,600 pages and was published in ten volumes (with the commissioners' reports) as *Senate Executive Document 51* of the First Session of the Fiftieth Congress.

---

[7]John Frederick, "Robert Emory Pattison," *DAB*, VII, Part 2, 313–314.   [8]*NY Times*, Feb 25, 1903.

[9]Ibid. The "Boss" William Marcy Tweed Ring consisted of henchmen Peter Sweeny, Richard B. Connolly, and A. Oakey Hall. They dominated the Democratic party in New York City during the 1860s, through their Tammany Hall connections. Tweed died in prison. Alvin F. Harlow, "William Marcy Tweed," *DAB* X, Part I, 79–82.

[10]Newton Bateman and Paul Selby, eds., "Littler, David T.," *HEI*, I, 341.   [11]*RUSPRC*, 106–129.

[12]They are listed in the Alphabetical Index to the *USPRC*, IX, 5399–5401.

Afterward, on March 17 and 20, and April 7, 1888, Creed Haymond, the general solicitor of the Central Pacific Railroad, testified before a select committee of the U.S. Senate, in which he summarized the results of the 1887 investigation as it pertained to the Central Pacific. His arguments were later published in book form.[13]

The commission's unwieldy task was made even more challenging by the fact that its members found it difficult to understand the railroad structure that it was called upon to investigate. The similarity of the names Southern Pacific Railroad [of California] and Southern Pacific Company [of Kentucky] has been a source of confusion from 1885 to the present day. In the Senate on February 3, 1887, while the bill to investigate railroads receiving government assistance was yet under discussion, the relationship between the Central Pacific and the Southern Pacific came up. Stanford interrupted the proceedings to say, quite bluntly and yet quite rightly, "Misstatements are made everywhere. The Senator from New Jersey [John Rhoderic McPherson (D)] talks of that about which evidently he knows nothing."[14] In answer to a request by Nebraska senator Charles Henry Van Wyck (R) for an explanation of this confusing nomenclature—a question still raised by students of railroad history and not understood by many writers on the subject—Stanford attempted in vain to clarify the relationship between the Southern Pacific Railroad and the Southern Pacific Company:

> Mr. VAN WYCK. "I should like to ask the Senator for information, what was the name of the corporation which built from San Francisco south?"
> Mr. STANFORD. "The Southern Pacific."
> Mr. VAN WYCK. "The Southern Pacific of what?"
> Mr. STANFORD. "Of California."
> Mr. VAN WYCK. "The Southern Pacific Railroad of California?"
> Mr. STANFORD. "Yes."
> Mr. VAN WYCK. "Then why is it that in this bill, in which it is spoken of as the assignee of the Central Pacific, it is called the Southern Pacific?"
> Mr. STANFORD. "For the reason that there was a consolidation. The Southern Pacific Company of Kentucky purchased the stock of all these various railroads, fourteen of them, and it is made up of those various companies. It is a through line; and for convenience, as there was no local law by which we could consolidate them, they obtained a charter from Kentucky to make a through line, with one set of officers and expenses. It is better and it harms nobody. It is a through line under one management, instead of being under fourteen different managers."
> Mr. VAN WYCK. "If the Senator will allow me, I wish to ask a further question. When the Central Pacific first leased to some other company, what was the designation of the company to which it was first leased?"

[13]Creed Haymond, *The Central Pacific Railroad Co. Its Relations to the Government. It Has Performed Every Obligation* (SF: HSCC, 1888).

[14]*USCR*, 49th Cong., 2nd Sess., 2636 (Mar 3, 1887). LS did not address the difference between a purchase and exchange. There was no way the SP could have bought all fourteen of these companies.

Mr. STANFORD. "The Southern Pacific."
Mr. VAN WYCK. "The Southern Pacific Railroad Company?"
Mr. STANFORD. "The Southern Pacific Company."[15]

And so it went.

EARLY INVESTIGATION OF THE MISSING BOOKS OF THE CONTRACT & FINANCE COMPANY

The location of the Contract & Finance Company books had been raised as early as September 2, 1880, in a case before the Supreme Court of New York in which Huntington, Stanford, and Crocker were defendants.[16] Stanford and Crocker were deposed in San Francisco. When asked if he knew who had possession of the company's records, Stanford answered that he did not know.[17]

The question put to Charles Crocker was more specific: "Are there not records extant within your knowledge of that corporation that will show whether or not the stock of these plaintiffs passed through their hands?" Crocker answered: "I don't know anything about the records; I have not seen any of them for a number of years."[18]

So far nothing had been said to suggest that the records were missing or perhaps no longer existed.

It was another matter, however, in the spring of 1883 when *Colton Case* depositions were being taken. There the possibility that the Contract & Finance books had been hidden or perhaps destroyed was discussed at length.[19] During the Stanford deposition, the deposing counsel suggested—without any explanation of his innuendo—that the books had been sent to a warehouse in London or somewhere else in England to prevent their being seen or examined by anyone other than Stanford, Huntington, Crocker, or Hopkins, or someone authorized by them.[20]

In early 1883 the California Railroad Commissioners, during an inquiry into Central Pacific freights and fares, stumbled upon and subsequently investigated the fact of the lost books of Charles Crocker & Company and those of the Contract & Finance Company.[21] Even before hearing testimony on this subject, they described the Contract & Finance Company as "a twin organization with the Credit Mobilier."[22]

---

[15] *USCR*, 49th Cong., 2nd Sess., 2636 (Mar 3, 1887).

[16] Supreme Court, of the State of New York, City and County of New York. *David Stewart, vs. Collis P. Huntington, Leland Stanford, Charles Crocker, &c. Lloyd Aspinwall, and o[the]rs, Ex'rs, &c., vs. The Same. William Paton, vs. The Same. Elizabeth S. Paton, Ex'r'x, &c., vs. The Same. John T. Agnew, et al., Sur'g Part'rs, &c., vs. The Same* (NY: CSH, 1982), 42–43. Bound in Vol. 7, Pam. 1, of CPRR Pams.   [17] Ibid., 43.   [18] Ibid., 80–81.

[19] The records of this case are a major source for anyone probing the story of the C & FC books.

[20] LS dep., *Colton Case Depositions*, II, 35–36.

[21] CRC, *Fourth Annual Report of the Board of Railroad Commissioners*, Year Ending Dec 31, 1883, 118–221.

[22] Ibid., 118.

On March 19, they subpoenaed William E. Brown, secretary of the Contract & Finance Company from 1868 to 1872, to testify. Brown denied having been asked by anyone to take the missing books to Europe, and added that, in fact, knowing he was to be questioned by the commission, he had spent two or three days looking for the books. He explained that when he went to Europe in 1873 on his own private business he personally boxed the books up because they were full, thinking his successor would not need ready access to them. Brown thought that Samuel Hopkins, Mark Hopkins' nephew, probably had charge of the removal of the books. Sam Hopkins, unfortunately, had died at sea "about six or seven years ago," Brown said.[23]

Testimony by Charles Crocker shed no light on what happened to the missing books, as reflected in the following exchange on the Charles Crocker & Company books of either company:

Question—Do you know what the Central Pacific line cost per mile from Sacramento—I mean the average per mile from Sacramento to the State line, while under your supervision?

Answer—I could not tell you now, sir; I don't remember. It cost a very large amount though.

Q. Have you any figures by which you could give us that information—any books?

A. No, sir; I have not.

Q. Were there not books kept?

A. Well, yes; I kept books—my accounts.

Q. Any of them in existence?

A. I do not believe there are. I have not seen them for ten years.

Q. Do you know what has become of them?

A. No, sir.

Q. And you cannot give us any information as to what became of them?

A. I closed them up and I think they were put in boxes at Sacramento, and where they are now, I could not tell you.

Q. Do you know if they are in—

Witness (interrupting)—They are closed up. I owed nobody and nobody owed me, and I did not consider them of any value.

Q. Well, then, is there any way, in your judgment, by which the original cost to you of the Central Pacific Railroad from Sacramento and within this State could be ascertained?

A. I cannot, only to ascertain it in a general way.

Q. But there are no books in existence to your knowledge, now, by which these figures could be given, are there?

A. No; none.

Q. And you have no knowledge of what has become of the books?

A. No.

Q. They were rather voluminous, were they not—a good many books?

---

[23]Brown's test. was pub. in the *SF Call*, Mar 20, 1883.

A. Well, no; not very. I kept them in a very simple manner. I kept an account of what coin I received and what I paid out; that is about all. And about all I had left when I got through was the stock. The money was all spent that I received on the contract.[24]

It is not difficult to understand why the commissioners' report on this aspect of their investigation reflected their frustration:

> Mr. Crocker's books are lost, and he does not remember the cost. The Contract and Finance Company's books are likewise lost. Under these circumstances it is impossible to determine from documentary evidence what the actual cost of the Central Pacific Railroad was to the Contract and Finance Company. It is equally impossible to ascertain the fact from living witnesses, as they do not remember. By actual cost, I do not mean the money nominally expended upon it by the Central Pacific Railroad Company, for Mr. Towne gives us the figures to a cent, $138,553,459.29.
>
> What I do mean is what it really cost the Contract and Finance Company, for that was its true cost to the railroad company. During the whole of my examination of Mr. Crocker, answers to questions upon this subject (actual cost) were constantly evaded, and finally objections to them were sustained.[25]

On March 26, 1883, the hearings were adjourned until Monday, April 2, and the presence of Charles Crocker was requested to testify on April 3, 1883.[26] On that day he was in Arizona, so his testimony was postponed until he returned.[27]

A week later, on the afternoon of April 9, Crocker was examined. After a brief discussion of Central Pacific construction costs, when asked "Were there ever any efforts to sell out?" the following bantering exchange ensued:

> CROCKER: No, not exactly. There was an effort to get other capital interested; that was why the Contract and Finance Company came to be formed. There was nobody then fool enough to buy us out. I would many times willingly have sold out for a clean shirt. Commissioner WILLIAM WINTER FOOTE: You would not sell out for a clean shirt now?
> CROCKER: Well no. I have several clean shirts at present.[28]

Crocker was questioned again on April 12, but the commissioners never mentioned the missing Contract & Finance Company books.[29]

The unexplained and questionable disappearance of the financial books of the Contract & Finance Company added to the suspicion of wrongdoing by the Central Pacific Associates.[30]

Governor Low later told H. H. Bancroft that the real story of the Contract & Finance Company could never be told. The reason, he said, was because of what he

---

[24]CRC, *Fourth Annual Report of the Board of Railroad Commissioners*, 118–119.   [25]Ibid., 120.
[26]*SF Call*, Mar 27, 1883.   [27]Ibid., Apr 3, 1883.   [28]Ibid., Apr 10, 1883.
[29]Ibid., Apr 13, 1883.
[30]Lavender, *The Great Persuader*, 292–293, sets the no. of vols. at fifteen. He says that the CPA burned the books in the basement of the railroad office building in the summer of 1873. Unfortunately, he did not doc. the source of his info. in either case so that readers could share his knowledge.

termed "inside workings." No one on the outside could get to the inside, and those on the inside who knew the truth would never tell.[31]

Thus there was nothing new about the fact that the Crocker Company books and those of the Contract & Finance Company were missing in the summer of 1887 when the Pacific Railway Commissioners attacked the matter. They had been handed a target to train their investigative guns on well in advance of the testimony given them.

For years after the completion of the transcontinental, the cost of financing new construction and maintaining and operating the system continued to be a problem. Substantial profits from the road itself were only slowly realized. The *real* money came from the Associates' various construction companies, the first of which was the Crocker organization. But the profits from this firm were insignificant compared to the fortunes realized under its successor, the Contract & Finance Company. This company built over 550 miles of road, for which it received in excess of $47 million, half in gold and half in stock, amounting to $86,000 per mile.[32]

Somehow, probably in the summer of 1873, the financial records of the Contract & Finance Company disappeared—lost, some said; destroyed, undoubtedly to cover up excessive profits made in building the transcontinental railroad, argued the enemies of the Associates.

In the various investigations of the missing books, one explanation surfaced time and time again, that the books had been packaged for the railroad's move from Sacramento to San Francisco and were never seen again. Daniel Yost, Stanford's private secretary, testified on August 1, 1887, that the last time he saw the books, Mark Hopkins was packing them for the company's move from Sacramento to San Francisco.[33]

In Charles Crocker's testimony, given in New York on September 20, he, too, speculated that Mark Hopkins may have destroyed the books, thinking that they were not worth keeping.[34] Hopkins, of course, had now been dead for years and could not deny or explain the actions attributed to him.

STANFORD'S TESTIMONY BEFORE THE
U.S. PACIFIC RAILWAY COMMISSIONERS

The most embarrassing episode of Sen. Leland Stanford's life was undoubtedly his experience before the Pacific Railway Commissioners.[35] He was sworn in and

---

[31]HHB inter. of Frederick Low, in Low papers. Low was wrong in thinking that no accounting of the cost of building the CPRR could be made without the missing books of the C & FC. Between 1966 and 1967 Lynn Farrar and his seventeen-man SPRR research team, along with almost unlimited institutional help from others, did just that. Lynn Farrar to the writer, Jul 27, 2002.   [32]EHM, Jr., test., *USPRC*, V, 3061–3063.

[33]DZY test., *USPRC*, V, 2712–2713.   [34]CC test., *USPRC*, VII, 3664–3665.

[35]LS test., Jul 28 (*USPRC*, V, 2460–2519), Jul 29 (V, 2519–2671), Aug 2 (V, 2729–2747, 2750–2768), Aug 3 (V, 2768–2837), Aug 5 (V, 2917–2951, 2958), Aug 10 (VI, 3160–3200), and Aug 31 (VI, 3607–3620).

gave his first testimony at the Palace Hotel in San Francisco on July 28, 1887. On this first day of testimony Stanford answered forty of the fifty-eight questions to be asked by the commissioners. These questions dealt with a variety of matters, including surveys, routes, the Railroad Acts of 1862 and 1864, construction, consolidations, financing, earnings, assets, litigation, taxes paid by the Central Pacific, and a host of related topics. Though it was a grueling day, there was no particular conflict between the commissioners and the witness, though the commissioners were not satisfied that Stanford had given a direct answer to their question of how much money had been paid to influence legislation.[36]

Stanford's second day of testimony was July 29. The major subject discussed related to the financing of the construction and expansion of the Central Pacific. The commissioners spent a great deal of time scrutinizing the creation, ownership, and profits of the various construction companies that built the Central Pacific. Stanford and his Associates were all owners of the Crocker Construction Company. The commissioners doubted that he was entirely truthful in testifying that he did not profit from the proceeds of that company.[37] He said that Charles Crocker turned over to the Contract & Finance Company all railroad stock received for his construction costs. This stock of the Crocker company had a par value at one time of $14 million, though the market value was far less; in fact, Crocker later testified that he gave the stock to the Contract & Finance Company because it was *worthless*.[38]

Commissioner Anderson put a direct question to Stanford about the location of the missing Contract & Finance Company books:

Q. In regard to the books of the Contract and Finance Company, when did you last see them?
A. I have no distinct recollection as to the time when I last saw them. I suppose that the time when I last saw them was the time that I was last in the office of that company.
Q. In whose custody were they then?
A. I think that Mr. Brown was still there.
Q. Mr. Brown has stated that he passed them over to Mr. John Miller. Do you know Mr. John Miller?
A. Yes, sir; he succeeded Mr. Brown. I have no recollection at all of the books, but as I frequently passed the door of his office going to my own, which was directly opposite, I have no doubt that I have seen the books hundreds of times lying on his desk, but I never examined them, and any recollection that I have as to the last time that I saw them would simply be as having seen them lying on the desk.[39]

The impatient Anderson snapped:

The contract and books of the Contract and Finance Company have never been accessible, and that no satisfactory explanation of their disappearance has ever been

[36]LS test., *USPRC*, V, 2495; his entire day's test. is found in V, 2460–2519.   [37]Ibid., V, 2636 and 2648–2649.
[38]CC test., *USPRC*, VII, 3651 and 3661.   [39]LS test., *USPRC*, V, 2640.

given, has led this Commission to take a great deal of interest in the matter, and to move it to do what it can to solve the mystery. Therefore, on behalf of the Commission, I would invite you to give any explanation that you can as to the whereabouts of the books, and also to produce John Miller, who appears to be the last person in whose custody the books were.[40]

In the course of Stanford's testimony on August 2, 1887, his third day of grilling, a serious problem did arise. The investigating panel requested permission to see the railroad's written records, and then Commissioner Anderson added, "As commissioners, we would be bound to make public, through our report to the President, all that we concluded to be evidence bearing on the issue."[41] Stanford seemed willing to accept this, but he first wanted to consult with legal counsel about the matter.[42]

Stanford was represented by counsel at the hearings, and as the investigation proceeded, one of his attorneys, Alfred Andrew Cohen, frequently interjected objections and advised his client not to answer specific questions he thought were personal or did not pertain to the investigation.[43] In the matter at hand, Cohen did not object to showing the commissioners the records they wanted to see, as one would show documents to a judge; but he did object to making everything public that the commissioners were allowed to see.[44]

Creed Haymond, another of Stanford's attorneys, suggested a solution should a disagreement arise as to which documents were relevant: "Suppose that these books were submitted to you gentlemen, and you should select certain things which we might think ought not to be published. That question could be left to the circuit court by a friendly proceeding, and could be speedily passed on."[45]

Stanford accepted this *modus operandi*.

But Commissioner Anderson took a hard line and left no doubt as to what he considered his powers to be. The ensuing exchange defined the differences between the two sides in the matter:

> ANDERSON: If I ruled, or if the Commission ruled, that a certain account was relevant, it would be considered as belonging to the world from that moment.[46]
> HAYMOND: Yes; providing your ruling could be sustained by the court.
> ANDERSON: The court would not have time to interfere, because as soon as it would be decided relevant [by the Commission], it would be in evidence.
> COHEN: I would suggest, although I think it is hardly necessary to make such a suggestion to a lawyer of your great experience, Mr. Chairman, that you are asking more here than a court would ask, or that the court to which you would apply would ask. That is, the production of books and papers by wholesale.
> LITTLER: We have found it utterly impossible to be governed by the rules of evidence

---

[40]*USPRC*, V, 2641.   [41]LS test., ibid., V, 2742.   [42]Ibid., V, 2743.
[43]It is interesting to note that Cohen was back in the good graces of LS and the other CPAs after an earlier falling-out.
[44]LS test., *USPRC*, V, 2744.   [45]Ibid., 2745.   [46]Ibid.

in conducting this examination. We take all sorts of statements—hearsay and everything else.
STANFORD: I think that the hearsay evidence has reached you first.

The lines of battle were drawn.

Right or wrong, the railway commissioners did not have a case that would stand
up in court. Following this heated exchange between Stanford's attorneys and the
commissioners, Commissioner Littler's admission that he and his colleagues were
unable to be governed by the rules of evidence proved legally to be a fatal, self-
inflicted blow by the commissioners. What attorney would have carried such an
admission into court in a serious attempt to win his case?

On August 3, 1887, Stanford's fourth day of testimony, things did not go any
more smoothly. Following pressure by Anderson for Stanford to answer a question
the way the commissioner wanted it answered rather than the way Stanford tried to
answer it, the following exchange ensued:

> STANFORD: If you will allow me to say it, it seems to me that your commission,
> instead of being disinterested and trying to investigate between the railroad com-
> pany and the Government, is all on the side of the Government. It seems to me more
> like a prosecution against this company than an investigation, and perhaps I might
> add, inquisition.
> ANDERSON: We will not stop to discuss that. I shall have to pursue my own method.[47]

In the afternoon session, Anderson grilled Stanford on why he and his Associates
had gone to Kentucky for a charter for the Southern Pacific Company. Stanford
answered, flippantly (or was it candidly?), "To get a charter that was favorable—
that would allow us to lease all the roads in the country."[48]

There was no way that the Southern Pacific Company could have bought all of
the companies it controlled or owned, and Stanford explained the difference
between an outright purchase and an exchange using bonds.

Anderson asked him: "What security have you for the performance of such
obligations as the Southern Pacific of Kentucky may enter into it to guarantee
bonds or payments of rentals, if it should cease to be advantageous to it—how
could you enforce any such obligation against the Southern Pacific of Kentucky?"
Stanford answered:

> I will tell you. I think when we formed that company there were twelve different
> companies forming a through line to New Orleans, and we had to keep up those dif-
> ferent organizations.
> They all had different interests, and it was very inconvenient and somewhat expen-
> sive; so we formed this company in Kentucky for the purpose, practically, of making it
> one company controlling all these roads. The roads are under the same ownership in

[47]Ibid., 2793.   [48]Ibid., 2809.

119. Cartoon portraying the intentions of the 1887 Railway Commission investigation. *San Francisco City Argus.*

120. Cartoon picturing the Central Pacific Associates' tug of war with Robert E. Pattison, chairman of the 1887 Railway Commission, David T. Littler, and E. Ellery Anderson, members of the commission. *San Francisco City Argus.*

reality. We formed this Kentucky company and owned it, so we took the lines of these roads and we valued them. Then we took the stock, for instance, of the Southern Pacific Company and appraised that at so much, and exchanged that for so much stock of the Southern Pacific of Kentucky. So that the Southern Pacific of Kentucky practically owns the Southern Pacific. So through Arizona, and so through New Mexico and all the lines through to New Orleans and those branch lines in Texas—I think some eight or ten hundred miles altogether there—they are owned really by the Southern Pacific. The Southern Pacific really owns all these roads, excepting just enough stock to keep up the organization of these different companies, so that it is the value of those roads and whatever they have got as assets that makes the Southern Pacific Company.[49]

In the August 5 interrogation, when the commissioners asked specifically about the use of money earned by the Dutch Flat wagon road, Stanford became extremely irritated: he resented the insinuation that he and his Associates had robbed the Pacific railroad by appropriating its money to themselves.[50] In one of his sharpest statements to the commission, he snapped:

> I have been called all sorts of names by demagogues on the stump and by hostile newspapers, and by enemies of the road, and they have never injured me. At one time I was charged with having a connection with bunko sharps and three-card monte men and gamblers, who were robbing passengers on the railroad. I do not suppose that anybody believed that, but still the charge was made. While I wish to treat the Commission with all courtesy, I do not feel like answering questions suggested by that class of complaints and that class of individuals.[51]

On August 10, the commissioners carefully scrutinized the finances and fortunes of all the witnesses called. One of their persistent questions involved the use of railroad funds for political influence. Stanford explained that his company employed many agents, but insisted that they were commissioned to work against legislation harmful to the company; they did very little in the way of promoting "affirmative legislation" beneficial to the company.[52] *He* handled matters of this nature in the California legislature.

When Stanford was asked if one particular large sum of money had been used to influence legislation, his counsel, Alfred Cohen, would not allow him to answer, on the ground that the question was designed not to get information, but as "seeking to pander to a public scandal," which was in no way related to the affairs of the committee.[53]

Stanford told the commissioners that there had hardly been a session of the California legislature from 1863 or 1864 that had not proposed legislation hostile to the railroad. It was because of this, he insisted, that a number of attorneys regularly

---

[49]Ibid. [50]Ibid., 2928. [51]Ibid., 2929.
[52]Ibid., VI, 3162. [53]Ibid., VI, 3164.

represented the railroad as legitimate lobbyists before legislative committees in Sacramento. He continued: "I must say that I have had many an argument before committees, and had many a talk, too, with the individual members of the legislature on behalf of the company, and I have tried to use all the influence I could in various ways."[54] But he insisted that he had never used any illegitimate influence. When a commissioner asked Stanford to name some lawyers who had attended the legislature with him, he again refused—"under counsel."[55]

The commissioners asked the Governor directly whether he had ever corrupted any state legislator or congressmen by buying votes, to which he replied: "I never corrupted a member of the legislature in my life, and I do not know that any of my agents ever did." He stated, further, that he had never made a trip to Washington to exercise political influence there; in fact, he had refused to pay a ten thousand dollar bribe that would have secured the votes needed to get Goat Island when the railroad wanted it as its West Coast terminus.

Chairman Pattison repeated the question about corrupting legislators, and the annoyed Stanford blurted out: "I certainly never corrupted an official in my life, nor attempted to." When the persistent chairman posed the question yet another time, Stanford accused him of ungentlemanly behavior: "It is your right and your duty to be a gentleman in asking your questions."[56] The commissioners then asked whether Western Development Company funds had ever been used to influence legislation. Stanford answered that he had no knowledge of such a thing.[57]

The investigators then directed their attention to what they called *unaccounted* money, used allegedly to purchase legislative support. Stanford refused to discuss the matter, but was badgered by the committee into denying that such a thing had happened. The committee then leveled a barrage of questions at him, each naming a specific individual allegedly influenced by railroad money.[58] Again, a series of refusals to answer followed.

When Thomas I. Bergin, another of Stanford's attorneys, said, "We decline to answer for the reasons already stated," Commissioner Anderson insisted that Stanford himself refuse to answer the question, because "We want to present the matter to the court, and therefore desire to have it in proper form."[59] Stanford, not intimidated by the hostile commissioners, responded: "I adopt Mr. Bergin's remarks."[60]

This could have led to a constitutional crisis, involving, as it did, the authority of a presidential commission regarding a federal law. From then on, Stanford refused to answer *any* incriminating questions, but the commissioners would not back off;

[54]Ibid., VI, 3168—3169; see also DZY test., ibid., V, 2720.   [55]LS test., ibid., VI, 3169.
[56]Ibid., 3172.   [57]Ibid., 3170—3172 and 3180.
[58]Ibid., 3185—3187.   [59]Ibid., 3185.
[60]Ibid. Bergin was an att. in the SF firm of McAllister & Co. *SFCD*, 1887, 223.

believing his answers were needed for the proper conduct of the investigations, they petitioned the California Circuit Court to compel him to answer.[61] It was widely feared that a court decision in his favor would annul the Interstate Commerce Act, passed earlier that year.[62]

The arguments were heard by the Circuit Court of the United States, San Francisco, Justices Stephen Field, Lorenzo Sawyer, George M. Sabin, and Ogden Hoffman presiding.[63]

On August 16, when subpoenaed to testify before this court, Stanford stated:

> The Commission insists upon answers to questions insistence upon which can have no possible effect upon any of the just relations between this company [Central Pacific Railroad] and the Government, and can only tend to cast doubt and suspicion upon parties whose names may be mentioned in the course of such investigation. As the subjects to which these questions are propounded are of an exclusive private character and in no ways affecting the interests of the Government, neither the company nor its officers feel called upon to answer them.
>
> . . . .
>
> Questions have been propounded, and a line of examination pursued, manifestly prompted by disaffected and hostile parties, whose aim was more the pursuit of personal enmity of a private character than the interests of the public at large or the ends of justice. To answer any of the objectionable questions propounded necessarily gives rise to the implication that all persons whose names may be mentioned in the questions to which answers are declined are guilty of the acts, commission of which is implied in the bare asking of the question.
>
> In my testimony given to the Commissioners I have said in substance, and now repeat, that I have never corrupted or attempted to corrupt any member of the legislature, or any member of Congress, or any public official, nor have I authorized any agent to do so.[64]

The court decided in Stanford's favor and dismissed the petition, with only Judge Hoffman dissenting. The majority opinion, delivered on August 29, 1887, read as follows:

1. The Pacific Railway Commission is not a judicial body and possesses no judicial powers . . . and can determine no rights of the Government or of the corporations whose affairs it is appointed to investigate.
2. Congress can not [sic] compel the production of private books and papers of citizens for its inspection, except in the course of judicial proceedings.
3. The courts are open to the United States as to private parties to secure protection for their legal rights and interests, by regular proceedings.

---

[61]*Proceedings in the Circuit Court of the United States for the Northern District of California. In the matter of the Application of the United States Pacific Railway Commission to compel Leland Stanford to answer certain interrogatories and to him propounded by said Commission.* Bound in *USPRC*, VII, 4164–4250.   [62]*Stockton Mail*, Sep 16, 1887.

[63]Justices Field and Sawyer were serving as trustees of LSJU at the time of this hearing. Sabin was a U.S. district judge of Nev. *USPRC*, VII, 4250.

[64]*Proceedings in the Circuit Court . . . in the matter of . . . Leland Stanford, USPRC*, VII, 4174.

4. Congress can not empower a commission to investigate the private affairs, books, and papers of the officers and employés of corporations indebted to the Government as to their relations to other companies with which such corporations have had dealings, except so far as such officers and employés are willing to submit the same for inspection; and the investigation of the Pacific Railway Commission into the affairs of officers and employés of the Pacific Railway Companies under the act of March 3, 1887, is limited to that extent.

5. The United States have no interest in expenditures of the Central Pacific Railroad Company under vouchers which have not been charged against the Government in the accounts between them; and the Pacific Railway Commission under the act of Congress of March 3, 1887, no power to investigate such expenditures against the will of the company and its officers.

6. The judicial power of the United States is limited to "cases" and "controversies" enumerated in Article III, Section 1, of the Constitution as modified by the eleventh amendment, and to petitions on habeas corpus and cannot be extended by Congress; and by such "cases" and "controversies" are meant the claims of litigants brought for determination by regular judicial proceedings established by law or custom. [In other words, neither the federal government nor Congress could make the courts instruments in conducting legislative investigations.]

7. The judicial department is independent of the legislative, in the Federal Government, and Congress cannot make the courts its instruments in conducting mere legislative investigations.

8. The power of United States courts to authorize the taking of depositions on letters rogatory from courts of foreign jurisdictions exists by international comity; but no comity of any kind can be invoked by a mere investigating committee appointed by Congress.

9. The Central Pacific Railroad Company is a State corporation not subject to Federal control, any further than a natural person similarly situated would be. Per Sawyer, J.

10. The Central Pacific Railroad Company is absolute owner of the lands and bonds granted to it by the Government, having complied with the Act making the grant, subject to the lien of the Government to secure its advances, in the same way and to the same extent as a natural person in like situation. Per Sawyer, J.

11. The relation of creditor exists between the United States and the Central Pacific Railroad Company, under the act granting aid to the latter, with like force and effect as if both were natural persons, the relation being private and having nothing to do with the power of the Government as sovereign. Per Sawyer, J.

12. The United States, as creditor, cannot institute a compulsory investigation into the private affairs of the Central Pacific Railroad Company, or require it to exhibit its books and papers for inspection in any other way, or to any greater extent, than would be lawful in the case of private creditors and debtors. Per Sawyer, J.

13. The United States, as Creditor, have the same remedy as a private creditor, and no other, to compel payment of any moneys due it from the Central Pacific Railroad Company, as their debtor, or to prevent the latter from wasting its assets before the debt matures, and that remedy, if any, must be by regular judicial proceedings in due course of law; and Congress has no power to institute a roving legislative

121. Uncle Sam defends the Central Pacific against Railroad Commissioners
Robert E. Pattison, David T. Littler, and E. Ellery Anderson. *Author's Collection.*

inquisition into the affairs of the company to ascertain what it has done or is doing
with its money. Per Sawyer, J.[65]

A chastened commission questioned Stanford for the last time on August 31. In
this session there was no sarcasm, no innuendoes, no ill-concealed charges of
malfeasance, or any other hostile action or attitude manifested that had been common in earlier sessions.[66]

CONCLUSIONS OF THE PACIFIC RAILWAY COMMISSIONERS

In their December 1, 1887, report to President Cleveland the commissioners
protested that the San Francisco Circuit Court decision made it impossible to conduct *any* investigation except with information that would be given willingly, thus
precluding intelligent legislation based upon congressional fact-finding missions.[67]

But the hostile commissioners had met their match—got their "comeuppance,"

---

[65]Ibid., the "Opinion of the Court" is in *USPRC*, VII, 4215–4239 and 4250; the decision is cited on 4215–4216.
[66]LS test., *USPRC*, VI, 3607–3620.   [67]*RUSPRC*, 85.

as Huntington biographer Cerinda Evans described the result of the court case—and the decision stood.[68]

Evans argued that one principle at play when the court decided that the commissioners could not compel witnesses to open their books and expose to the world other businesses they might be engaged in was that citizens could not be prohibited from engaging in other lawful business just because of their connection with the Central Pacific Railroad Company. American citizens were entitled to the same protection from inquisitorial investigation as any other citizen engaged in business: that the congressional committee could not destroy the checks and balances of the United States Constitution by usurping the powers of another branch of the government.[69]

If challenged—which it was not—the court's decision also could have resulted in a major constitutional crisis.

The 1887 Pacific Railway Commissioners were convinced that the construction of the road cost far less than the amount paid to the companies working on it. They decided that the cost of construction of the Central Pacific Railroad from Sacramento to Promontory—a total distance the commission set at 737.5 miles—could not have cost more than $36 million.[70]

The commissioners stated in their report that even Stanford had conceded that the balance of the stock distributed by the Contract & Finance Company in the amount of $54 million, less $3 million in company debt, was a net profit. This would have amounted to a profit of $15 million. The commissioners cited testimony by Stanford and William E. Brown to substantiate this conclusion.[71] However, the page of Stanford testimony cited never even mentioned the value of bonds received; moreover, the Stanford statement expressly denied most of what the commissioners averred that he admitted. On the page following the one cited, Stanford said that the railroad received $50 million in government securities, less its indebtedness.[72]

Still less did the Brown testimony substantiate the commissioners' conclusion. In fact, Brown said the indebtedness may had been $4 million rather than $3 million, and he went on to testify that the stock received had absolutely no borrowing value on the market.[73]

Despite their claim that they had no documentary evidence on which to base costs, expenses, and payments to Charles Crocker & Company and to the Contract & Finance Company, the commissioners' *Report* cited the pages-long reconstruction of these statistics by "expert accountant" Richard F. Stevens.[74]

Stanford, Huntington, Hopkins, and the Crocker brothers were equal co-own-

---

[68]Evans, *Huntington*, II, 441.   [69]Ibid., 442.   [70]*RUSPRC*, 74–75.
[71]Ibid., 75.   [72]LS test., *USPRC*, V, 2969–2970.
[73]William E. Brown test., *USPRC*, V, 2979.
[74]*USPRC* citation, *RUSPRC*, 75; Richard F. Stevens' test., *USPRC*, VI, 3501–3536.

ers of the Contract & Finance Company, and from it each (or their estates) received approximately $13 million in Central Pacific stock when the company was dissolved.[75]

Following their investigation, the Pacific Railway Commissioners criticized the Central Pacific business arrangements and charged the Associates with violating a rule of equity in dealing with themselves; it was also unethical, they argued, to be, in fact, both parties to what was passed off as a series of legitimate contracts.[76]

The commissioners took a strong stand on the matter of the missing books, stopping just short of charging criminal actions on the part of the owners and caretakers of these books:

> Putting all these facts together—the existence of a strong motive on the part of Stanford, Huntington, Hopkins and Crocker to suppress the books; the impossibility of accounting for their disappearance, except in pursuance of the act or direction of one of these four persons; the evidence of Yost that he saw Hopkins engaged in packing the books in boxes; the evidence of John Miller of their sudden disappearance, and the statement of Mr. Crocker connecting their disappearance with Mark Hopkins—it is impossible to avoid the conclusion that the suppression of these books has been intentional and willful.[77]

There was never any hard evidence offered or even suggested to implicate Stanford in the corruption of public officials, but the Pacific Railway Commissioners were sure that guilt was strongly implied by his evasiveness, by his refusal to answer certain questions they posed. With the available testimony and what sketchy evidence they could amass, the commissioners concluded that the Central Pacific railroad spent over $2.25 million to influence legislation, money it listed under "general expenses."[78] Of the $5 million earlier alleged as taken by the Associates, the commissioners reported: "There is no room for doubt that a large portion of this money was used for the purpose of influencing legislation and of preventing the passage of measures deemed to be hostile to the interests of the company, and for the purpose of influencing elections."[79] They said it was impossible to read Huntington's correspondence and his testimony without concluding that he had expended large sums of money in Congress to defeat the passage of railroad bills. According to the commission, the fact that the Associates had attempted to conceal some of their financial transactions was in itself evidence of irregularity: their objectives must have been illegitimate.

The commissioners were sure that Stanford and his Associates were guilty of bribery, which was patently illegal. Why, then, did they take no steps to prove their suspicions? Attempting to influence legislation, of course, was perfectly legal,

[75]LS test., *USPRC*, V, 2648–2656 and 2669–2670.

[76]Gerrit Lansing, *Relations Between the Central Pacific Railroad Company and the U.S. Government. Summary of Facts* (SF: HSCC, 1889), 76 and 82.   [77]*RUSPRC*, 74.   [78]Ibid., 144.   [79]Ibid., 84.

though the commissioners failed to distinguish between trying to influence law-makers, which for some reason they thought illegal, and lobbying, which then as now was considered a legitimate and sometimes expensive practice, but perfectly acceptable in ethics and law.

The commissioners decided that the Associates had made excessive profits from their railroad interests, but they never cited or tried to establish a rule or guideline for determining what was or was not excessive.

They said Crocker, for example, had been paid almost twice what it cost to build some sections of the railroad; even though he claimed that he had no partners in his company, a railroad official admitted that it was composed of Charles Crocker, Stanford, Huntington, Hopkins, and Edward H. Miller.[80] Whether a formal partnership existed between the Associates or not, there was "an explicit understanding that they should share equally" in profits from construction, repairs, branch lines, leases, express business, and the sale of materials and coal.[81]

The investigating commission decided that on construction contracts alone the Associates had made over $100 million in stocks and in excess of $5 million in bonds; furthermore, they had cleared $12 million in gold and $52 million in stock on the government-aided construction of the Central and Western Pacific railroads. Besides this, they had spent, or allowed their agents to spend, almost $5 million without requiring any sufficient vouchers disclosing the purpose to which it was applied. The investigators concluded: "On the face of the books the barren fact appears that Leland Stanford and C. P. Huntington have taken from the assets of this company, over which they had absolute control, the sum aforesaid of $4,818,355.67."[82]

The railroad commissioners argued that a detailed study of the finances of the whole Central Pacific network showed that this railroad and its subsidiaries cost $58 million to build, but since it had received $120 million in bonds, stocks, and cash, there was $62 million excess. They were certain that most of this was clear profit, paid entirely to Stanford, Huntington, Hopkins, and Crocker—"voted to themselves by their own votes." As if this were not enough, similar profits were taken from leased roads.[83] The flaw in the commissioners' reasoning was their failure to distinguish between real money and inflated stock values.

The commissioners attacked the Central Pacific Associates for awarding contracts beneficial to themselves. They condemned universally the practice of giving contracts to companies in which the directors had a personal interest.[84]

They went on to trace the Central Pacific's weak financial condition to the fact that contracts with Crocker & Company, the Contract & Finance Company, the

---

[80]Richard F. Stevens test., *USPRC*, VI, 3501–3512; DWS test. and CC test., ibid., V, 2865 and VII, 3641.

[81]Carman and Mueller, "Contract and Finance Company," 338.			[82]*RUSPRC*, 84, 138–139.

[83]Ibid., 81–82.					[84]Ibid., 82–83.

Western Development Company, and the Pacific Improvement Company had drained the Central Pacific of its resources. They concluded that "certain individuals" had issued to themselves enormous quantities of stock and bonds of this company, had paid themselves dividends on the stock, and had made the interest charge on the bonds exceedingly heavy. The railroad company's financial straits, they found, were caused by these factors alone.[85]

The commissioners conceded that Stanford and his partners had received little money from government lands and railroad bonds during the first few years of the railroad's operation, but insisted that they had made sizable profits later, not only from their ownership of the construction companies, but from their railroads. Up to 1870 they showed profits of almost $2.5 million; from 1870 to 1873 over $6.5 million; and more than $52.5 million between 1874 and 1884. This was *net*, not gross income—it was profits, money left after operating expenses, taxes, and interest on loans had been paid. Between 1874 and 1884 over $34 million was distributed to stockholders in dividends, and since Stanford, Huntington, Hopkins, and Crocker were virtually the only stockholders during most of this time, they received nearly the entire amount of dividends declared during these years. The investigating body concluded: "The distribution of this vast sum of money to these four persons, whose stock represented substantially no contribution whatever to the actual value of the railroad, was most improvident, and was in plain disregard of the obligations incurred by the company to the United States."[86]

According to the commissioners, as of December 31, 1886, the Central Pacific had piled up a total public and government liability of almost $172 million.[87] Until this time there had been no effort made to retire the large government loans (in fact, there was no payback provision that required prepayment before maturity). This led the commissioners to charge that the Central Pacific, as well as other bond-aided companies, had defrauded the government of its advances and the shippers of a large proportion of their cash.[88] In a searing condemnation of the financial and political operations of the government-assisted companies, the commissioners stated:

> The aided companies combined with others to tax the communities which they served, and they forced the consuming classes in all sections of the country to contribute to the payment of interest and dividend upon the fictitious capital which they had created. They increased the cost of living. They laid proprietary claim to the traffic of large sections of the country. They squandered millions of their money to "protect" their territorial claims, while expending other millions in encroachments upon the territory claimed by other companies. They constituted themselves the arbiters of trade. They attempted to dictate the channels that trade should follow and fixed rates of transportation that were extortionate. They charged all that the traffic would

[85]*USPRC*, V, 2630.   [86]*RUSPRC*, 87–88.   [87]Ibid., 147.
[88]See Carman and Mueller, "Contract and Finance Company," 340 n69, for payment of these notes.

bear, and appropriated a share of the profits of every industry by charging the greater part of the difference between the actual cost of production and the price of the article in the market. They discriminated between individuals, between localities, and between articles. They favored particular individuals and companies. They destroyed possible competitors, and they built up particular localities to the injury of other localities, until matters had reached such a pass, that no man dared engage in any business in which transportation largely entered without first soliciting and obtaining the permission of a railroad manager. They departed from their legitimate sphere as common carriers and engaged in mining articles for transportation over their own lines. They exerted a terrorism over merchants and over communities, thus interfering with the lawful pursuits of the people. They participated in election contests. By secret cuts and violent and rapid fluctuations in rates they menaced business, paralyzed capital, and retarded investment and development.[89]

But there was another side to the story, and the railroad had countless supporters in its battle with the railway commissioners. San Francisco journalist Marcus Boruck, for one, summed up the Pacific Railway Commissions' campaign against the railroad in a lengthy editorial that resounded across the state. He accused the commission of having entered the city of San Francisco with a hand raised against everyone in the employment of the railroad. Worse yet, he wrote, the commissioners had reached their decision long before reaching California. The commission individually and collectively occupied a singular position, he wrote: "It is the Judge, the Jury, the 'persecutor,' the Counsel, all combined, and arrayed against the railroad."[90]

Frank Pixley's *Argonaut*, in an extensive analysis of the investigation that pointed to the prosperity the transcontinental railroad had brought to individual states and to the country as a whole, concluded the Railway Commission's investigation was entirely unnecessary.[91]

This journal interpreted the entire railroad investigation as motivated by nothing but political concerns: the Railway Commission was "appointed under a recent law of a Democratic Congress, to enable a Democratic President to make Democratic politics out of all railroads that had received aid from the general government."[92] The minority and majority reports of the commission were unfair, but, "Pattison's minority report is simply scandalous. It is the production of a malignant and biased mind that lacks ability to hurt where it has the disposition to destroy."[93] Moreover, the railroad Associates had complied with every term of their contract with the federal government, and, in cases where there was disagreement submitted to courts for determination, they had "in all cases performed whatever requirement" was demanded by the courts.[94]

[89]*RUSPRC*, 141.   [90]*SF CSTUJ*, Aug 6, 1887.   [91]*SF Argonaut*, Aug 27, 1887.
[92]Ibid., Jan 7, 1888.   [93]Ibid.   [94]Ibid.

Again, the Pixley journal attacked the motives and character of the commissioners:

> These gentlemen . . . were governed by none other than the meaner motives that prompt men to hunt for something wrong . . . to propitiate the masses of the more ignorant voters by pandering to their jealousies and inciting their resentments against property-owners and successful business men.[95]

The Central Pacific Associates' Account of Railroad Finances and Assets

Congressional and state investigating committees could uncover vast fortunes the Associates had amassed, but they turned a deaf ear to the other side of the question. In early 1870 Huntington complained that earnings from the Central Pacific barely paid interest on their accounts and that there was hardly enough left to cover maintenance and routine improvements.[96]

Huntington later testified that the Central Pacific had always been short of money. When he tried to get funds for building it, the richest men in New York, Boston, and San Francisco refused to invest in the venture. Huntington said that the words of Commodore [Cornelius Kingsland] Garrison expressed the way they all responded to his entreaties: "Huntington, the risk is too great, and the profits, if any, are too remote. We cannot take the risk."[97] Huntington said he contacted financiers and bankers in California, among them D. O. Mills, Eugene Kelly, and John Parrott, and they all turned him away, "some saying the risks were too great, and others that we were crazy."[98]

In corroboration, San Francisco attorney and investor Alfred A. Cohen told the 1887 Railway Commission that when the road was first completed, he would not have taken its stock as a *gift* if he had to be responsible for its debts.[99]

In his March 10, 1873, "Paint Shop" speech, Stanford had pointed out that the completion of the Central Pacific Railroad *seven* years ahead of schedule was saving the federal treasury a minimum of $7 million per year, but its cost of construction was 50 percent higher than it would have been if the road had not been completed until 1876.[100] He showed, too, that at current discounts the amount of money received from the federal government—when reduced to gold coin—would not

---

[95]Ibid.   [96]CPH to LS, Jan 4, 1870.

[97]SR 778, Vol. 4, Part 2, 54th Cong., 1st Sess., 38 (Feb 20, 1896). SSN 3365. Garrison had been mayor of SF from Oct 3, 1853–Oct 1, 1854. He returned to NY in 1859 and became a shipbuilder, businessman, and philanthropist. He died on May 1, 1885, in NYC.

[98]Ibid. Kelly was the NY rep. of Donohoe, Ralston & Co. *SFCD*, 1863–64, 208; Parrott was a SF banker, Parrott & Co. *SFCD*, 1863–64, 286.   [99]Alfred A. Cohen test., *USPRC*, V, 2394.

[100]*Sac Record*, Mar 11, 1873; LS test., *USPRC*, V, 2465.

have carried the road over the mountains, let alone build it to Ogden. Besides that, the government had received far more in securities for its loans than it required, since the Central Pacific had put up its entire railroad system as collateral rather than just the original transcontinental line.

Because of forced discounts, the company realized only sixty cents on the dollar in gold on the government bonds; therefore only about $16 million was received from government bonds for the building of the entire Central Pacific line.[101] The Pacific Railway Commissioners, who listed the values at par, rejected the railroad's suggestion that the government loan be reduced to the gold or salable value. They expressed some doubt that government bonds had been discounted, and argued that even if they had been, the government debt to the public for these bonds had to be repaid at par.[102] Stanford insisted that in calculating the railroad's debt they ought to take into account the fact that the railroad was paying interest on $20 million it never received.[103]

In 1895 the thirty-year government securities put up to build the Central Pacific would be due. Detractors argued that before the eighties the road had not done anything toward repaying this debt—indeed, it was not required that any payment be made until the due date—which led critics to believe, or at least pretend to believe and to argue, that the railroad had no intention of ever repaying it.

Stanford had told Huntington that it was clear that instead of the Southern Pacific owing the government, the government actually owed to the railroad all the money it had saved the national treasury. "I think we ought to take that position," he confided, "and decline to make any offer of future payment."[104] Huntington had said this years earlier and Stanford was now simply agreeing with him. Huntington had pointed out in 1876 that before the completion of the transcontinental railroad the United States government had paid between seven and eighteen million dollars per year to move mail, troops, munitions, and supplies westward. It was obvious that the railroad saved the country far more than the interest on the railroad bonds and would still come out ahead if the interest were never paid.[105]

PRESIDENT CLEVELAND'S REPORT TO CONGRESS

President Cleveland said in his accompanying message on January 17, 1888, when he submitted the reports of the 1887 Pacific railway investigation to Congress, "No one, I think, expects that these railroad companies will be able to pay their immense

[101]*Sac Record*, Sep 13, 1873.   [102]*RUSPRC*, 91.
[103]LS test., *USPRC*, V, 2526.   [104]LS telegram to CPH, Sep 23, 1887.
[105]"Letter from C.P. Huntington, vice-president of the Central Pacific Railroad Company, to Hon. George F. Edmunds, United States Senate, in Relation to a Bill to create a sinking-fund for the liquidation of the Government bonds advanced to the Central and Western Pacific Railroad Companies," in *SMD 85*, 44th Cong., 1st Sess., 1–4 (Apr 3, 1876).

indebtedness to the Government at its maturity."[106] He said that—even considering the public importance of the Pacific railroads—there had been a "reckless and unguarded appropriation of the public funds and the public domain."[107] The minority report of the Pacific Railway Commission recommended that the charters of the roads be forfeited and that a receiver be appointed to work out a system whereby the government would be repaid. Despite what the railway commissioners, former President Cleveland, or any other skeptics had said, on the first of February 1899 the federal government and the Southern Pacific Railroad resolved the whole problem of the debt owed the government: settlement was made for over $58 million in principal and interest at face value of the bonds.[108]

Stanford and his Associates were embarrassed by the Pacific Railway Commissioners, but they survived with their railroad empire intact and in fairly good shape. Pixley viewed the commission cynically as a "smelling" committee prompted more by per-diem pay and increased recognition than by a desire to root out genuine ills in the economic system.[109]

But for another twenty years California politics would continue to focus upon the "octopus" spawned by enemies of the Southern Pacific. Of the original Central Pacific giants, Judge Crocker had died in 1875, Hopkins in 1878, and Charley Crocker in 1888, leaving only Stanford and Huntington. Stanford had always branched out to pursue other interests, at times even abandoning any really active participation in the counsels of their railroad, having gradually given up to Huntington the primacy that Huntington had always wanted and which at times he exercised behind the scenes. After Stanford's entrance into politics in the mid-eighties and the great battle between the two old partners in 1890 saw Huntington step into the presidency of the Southern Pacific Company, another era in Stanford's life closed. Yet much of the story of his varied career during the two decades following the completion of the transcontinental in 1869 remains to be told . . . in another context.

---

[106]*RUSPRC*, Part. 1, iv.   [107]Ibid., iii.

[108]*HED* 238, 55th Cong., 3rd Sess., 1–9 (Feb 15, 1899). SSN 3812.

[109]*SF Argonaut*, Aug 20, 1887.

122. Col. Charles Frederick Crocker.
Stanford University Archives.

123. Timothy Nolan Hopkins.
Stanford University Archives.

CHAPTER 22

SOUTHERN PACIFIC
COMPANY PRESIDENCY

Huntington's Love of Power and His Desire for Vengeance[1]

I think that Leland Stanford would always tell the truth, to the best of his knowledge and belief. —Collis P. Huntington, 1896[2]

I am rather proud of the enemies I have made. All I ask is that they do not praise me, for then my friends would say: "What has Huntington been doing now, that such fellows would praise him?" —Collis P. Huntington[3]

MORE ON STANFORD'S ELECTION TO THE U.S. SENATE

Appearances in the nation's upper house by California's peripatetic Senator Stanford in February and March of 1890 were made at the same time he was waging another form of political battle—that with C. P. Huntington in New York and San Francisco over the future management of the Southern Pacific Company. To understand Stanford's contest for reelection to the Senate in 1890 and early 1891 it is important that the railroad battles be dealt with first: they affected his campaign strategy and, indeed, could have influenced the outcome of the 1890 election of the California legislature and thereby Stanford's reelection to the U.S. Senate by the state legislature.

Much ink has been spilled over how Stanford's first Senate election, in 1885, had destroyed all remaining cordiality between him and partner C. P. Huntington. Huntington was sure that both he and Aaron Sargent had been double-crossed by their politically ambitious associate. After all, he and Stanford had promised to back their faithful legislator-politician-railroad attorney Sargent. Later events have shown that the importance Huntington allegedly placed on Stanford's selection

---

[1]Evans, *Huntington*, I, 268. These are Evans' words, taken out of context by selective quoting; she did not endorse their sentiment.

[2]CPH test., "Government Debt of the Pacific Railroads," *SR 778*, 54th Cong., 1st Sess., 179 (printed May 1, 1896). SSN 3365.   [3]Quoted without doc. in Kraus, *High Road to Promontory*, 295.

rather than Sargent's has been greatly exaggerated, as evidenced by remarks made by Huntington himself.

In 1886 Huntington wrote to Stephen Gage that he, Stanford, and Crocker had held a conference on whom to support for the Senate in 1887, when the California legislature would be electing another senator.[4] Huntington did not identify the man on whom they had agreed, but this letter contained some remarks not expressed when Stanford was elected a year earlier. Huntington had said then that Stanford's election was not expected when the two had met just before the election; in fact, Stanford's election had never entered his (Huntington's) mind. This is not surprising, since it had not entered *anybody's* mind. But, Huntington went on, he could not say anything negative about Stanford's election, because—if it had been a subject of discussion—Stanford in fact would have been his first choice! His colleague was a "clean" and "able" man; Huntington's only regret was that Stanford's sudden acceptance of the nomination placed him in an "equivocable" position with Sargent.

As for the 1887 election, Huntington had once again endorsed Sargent. He did this based on Sargent's being the best man to look after the overall interests of the state. He would like to see Sargent elected, he stated, not only because he liked him personally and thought he would ably represent the state, but to repay him for the loss of a promised seat in 1885: "I feel that in this way justice will be done to him as well as to myself and others who had promised him our support to the best of our ability."[5]

Late 1884 and 1885 was a busy time for Stanford. In January 1885 he was elected to the U.S. Senate; less than three weeks following this, he was named president of the newly-formed holding company, the Southern Pacific Company of Kentucky. In November of 1885 he founded his university, which he personally managed for a number of years before it opened in 1891. Few men even in *good* health—regardless of stamina, drive, or good intentions—could have done justice to more than *one* of these positions, let alone all three.

Collis Huntington, for one, was sure that the interests of the Associates' railroad empire were suffering from Stanford's neglect. Over the years the relationship between the two men had grown more and more strained, not just over the railroad, but also political matters, particularly involving the Sargent affair.

Huntington expressed this major objection: that as a senator and university manager, Stanford no longer paid sufficient interest to his railroad duties. Stanford himself realized this and tried to resign from the railroad presidency in 1889, but all of his Associates—except Huntington—prevailed upon him to stay on a while longer.[6] Meanwhile, Stanford continued absenting himself from company business

---

[4]CPH to Stephen Gage, May 8, 1886.   [5]Ibid.   [6]*SF Examiner*, Apr 12, 1890.

for long periods of time, as he already had for two or three years. Huntington objected to this, and during the last year complained more often.[7]

Wineries, horses, stables, foreign travels, and railroad business had usurped much of Stanford's time even before he took on all the added responsibilities of the Senate. He had served for twenty-nine years as president of the Central Pacific, in fact as well as name; he was neither a figurehead nor just a titular head (this road had always been known to its enemies as Stanford's road or Stanford and Company— never Huntington and Company).[8] But Stanford *was* hardly more than titular head of the Southern Pacific Company; thus Huntington reasoned that if Stanford was not going to use his favored Senate position among Californians for the benefit of the railroad, he should be replaced by the man who was functioning as president . . . Huntington himself.

In late 1889 and early 1890 it seemed that open warfare between the two would break out. Frequent visits of Southern Pacific Company officials to New York caused considerable gossip about what might be going on within the upper echelon of the company.

When questioned about the meaning of the frequent trips to New York by major railroad officials, one company spokesman in California answered:

> It means that in reality the headquarters of the Southern Pacific Company is in New York. The officials all go to New York to consult Huntington, who is running things now more than he ever did before. Of course we still have the general offices of the company in this city, which must always be the case. . . . But here is where only the details are carried on; the general policy is formulated in New York, and it is the Mecca where the officials are now going to get their instructions.
>
> This has been brought about for several reasons. Stanford is almost wholly taken away from the railroad on account of his university project and his political duties. This being the case, and with Chas. Crocker dead Huntington is the only one left to direct affairs from day to day.[9]

Tim Hopkins spent several weeks in New York in the fall of 1889, and Col. Fred Crocker made two trips there within one year, possibly to act as a mediator between Stanford and Huntington. He returned to San Francisco under the impression that matters had been smoothed out, but he was wrong.[10] Finally, when open war between Stanford and Collis Huntington seemed imminent, Crocker and Hopkins met again in New York where they negotiated and signed a veritable peace treaty. The agreement—in the handwriting of Herbert Nash—was signed or initialed by all involved parties on February 28, 1890.

This agreement, which put Huntington at the head of the Southern Pacific Com-

---

[7] Ibid.   [8] *SF Bulletin*, Jul 13, 1872.
[9] UNC, in LS papers.   [10] *SF Chronicle*, Apr 11, 1890.

Huntington-Stanford Peace Treaty*

First:

The following to be and constitute the Board of Directors of the Southern Pacific Company for the ensuing year: Leland Stanford, C.P. Huntington, Chas. F. Crocker, J.C. Stubbs, W.E. Brown, A.N. Towne, Thos. E. Stillman, S.T. Gage, E.H. Miller Jr., W.V. Huntington, Thomas H. Hubbard.

Second:

That C.P. Huntington be elected President for the ensuing year.

Third:

That an executive Committee be appointed by the Board to consist of the following Directors. Leland Stanford, C.P. Huntington, Chas. F. Crocker and Thomas H. Hubbard, with Leland Stanford Chairman thereof.

Fourth:

That the papers in possession of C.P. Huntington in reference to the Sargent matters be either destroyed or delivered sealed to the undersigned to be disposed of as they shall see fit [this titillating point was not elaborated upon].

Fifth:

That all the parties owning or representing interests in the property of the Pacific Improvement Company shall in good faith refrain from hostile or injurious expressions concerning each other and shall in good faith co-operate for the election of Leland Stanford as Senator in the next term of the U.S. Senate.

Dated, Feby. 28. 1890.

C.P.H. Initials   Signed T.E. Stillman
L.S.   Thomas H. Hubbard
                               C.F. Crocker

*A copy of this agreement, in HCN's handwriting, was later found among JLS papers; it is *now* in a bound vol. of LS corres. in LS papers.

pany, was certainly *not* the firing or humiliation of Leland Stanford as has been depicted. Not only was Stanford not well at the time, but also he was preoccupied with other matters. And although for some time he had been on the verge of stepping down from the presidency of the Southern Pacific Company, he was *not* thrown out or cast aside with no power. Huntington was elected president only for the ensuing year, not necessarily forever. Of the eleven-man board of directors, seven were in the Stanford camp (Stanford, Crocker, Stubbs, Brown, Towne, Gage, and Miller). The members of the Executive Committee were divided evenly in their loyalties, with Stanford as chairman. And had the agreement been kept by all parties endorsing it, Stanford would have come out ahead on two accounts: he

would rid himself of any further embarrassment over the Sargent affair, and in gar-
nering the undivided support of his Associates in the upcoming election.

On his way back to California, on April 3, 1890—just before the Southern
Pacific Company's annual meeting in San Francisco—Stanford told a reporter in
Wadsworth, Nevada, that he had notified his Associates to expect his resignation
from the Southern Pacific presidency: "If I have my way I'll turn over the Presidency to another man at the directors' meeting next week."[11] The choice of a new
president, he said, depended largely upon the preferences of the Searles and Huntington interests, but he expected a smooth transition, that the directors would
make "a harmonious choice."

The subtitle of the *Sacramento Bee* article on Stanford, "HE IS NOT IN GOOD
HEALTH," dwelt upon the senator's failing health and an upcoming trip to Europe
advised by his New York physicians.

Stanford reached home on Friday, April 5, 1890, and granted a *Chronicle* reporter
an interview in his Nob Hill mansion the next day.[12] In the course of his conversation
he repeated his intention to free himself of some of his railroad responsibilities:

> I shall tender my resignation as president of the Southern Pacific Company at the
> annual session of the board of directors to-morrow or next day: It will, I suppose, be
> accepted by my associates, and, unless he declines, my successor will be C. P. Hunt-
> ington. My only motive in resigning is to relieve myself of the active duties con-
> nected with the office. While I am without any organic disease, I am troubled at times
> with a sort of nervous derangement, and am, consequently, desirous of greater lib-
> erty of action.

Stanford, then, gave ill health as one of his reasons, but said nothing of the prior
agreement that had already been ratified. Perhaps he was trying to soften any loss of
his own prestige in stepping down. This was not a hasty move on Stanford's part, he
assured the press: he had been considering it for years, wanting more time to devote
to the university and to his senatorial duties.[13] When questioned about a possible
successor, he verified rumors that Huntington would succeed him, tacitly conceding
that all the details for the impending changes had been worked out in advance.[14]

Several factors pointed to the fact that it was time for Stanford to step aside as
president of the Southern Pacific Company:

1. His already ill health was further declining.
2. His devotion to building the university drained the time and strength needed in
   the management of the railroad empire.
3. The Southern Pacific Company had become more and more a New York-run
   enterprise.

---

[11] *Sac Bee*, Apr 5, 1890; *SF Chronicle*, Apr 5, 1890.   [12] *SF Chronicle*, Apr 7, 1890.
[13] *SF Call*, Apr 8, 1890.   [14] *SF Chronicle*, Apr 8 and 9, 1890.

4. The management of the Hopkins-Searles interests in the Southern Pacific Company were being managed by Judge Thomas E. Stillman of New York.
5. With the death of Hopkins and Crocker and the loss of Stanford as a full-time participant, only Huntington was left to run the company.

Stanford recognized all this, which is why he volunteered to step aside. The problem lay not with how the transition was made, but in the accusations afterward leveled by Huntington that slandered Stanford's use of the railroad power he had long enjoyed.

Huntington Replaces Stanford as President of the Southern Pacific Company

The 1887 ordeal with the Pacific Railway Commissioners was probably the most embarrassing event in Stanford's life; the circumstances surrounding his surrendering of the presidency of the Southern Pacific Company to Huntington in 1890 proved to be the most humiliating—not so much that he was replaced by Huntington, but *how* the transfer of power was handled. The annual meeting of Southern Pacific stockholders was held in the San Francisco offices of the railroad on April 9, 1890.

Huntington read his inaugural message from a prepared manuscript, thanking the officers for electing him president, as though it had been spontaneous, and pledging his continuing loyalty to the company. With studied malice he directed the following statement at Stanford and the 1885 senatorial election: "In no case will I use this great corporation to advance my personal ambition at the expense of its owners, or put my hands into the treasury to defeat the people's choice, and thereby put myself in positions that should be filled by others."[15]

Huntington's remarks both during and following the meeting in which he was catapulted into the presidency of the Southern Pacific Company—a position he always thought he deserved—created a sensation in the press. Shortly after Huntington made his address, an *Examiner* reporter interviewed him at his Fourth and Townsend office, where Huntington elaborated on his objections to politics in the railroad office. He said that the company had entered too often and too deeply into politics. Without the slightest embarrassment about his own New York and Washington political activities, he said, "This building [the Fourth and Townsend headquarters] has been overrun with politics, and it is time to call a halt."[16]

Huntington continued:

From this time on we are going to follow one business. We are railroad men and

---

[15]*SF Examiner*, Apr 10, 1890.   [16]Ibid.

intend to conduct a legitimate railroad business. To do that successfully politics must be let alone. The two don't go well together. If a man wants to make a business of politics, all well and good; if he wants to manage a railroad, all well and good; but he can't do both at the same time.

I have seen the ante-rooms down here in this building full of men trying to learn or get something out of politics. Why should they come here? This is no place for them. But then they were not to blame. The tip went forth that political work was being done at Fourth and Townsend streets, and they merely followed the tip. Well, there won't be any more tips sent out of these railroad offices. Politics have worked enough demoralization in our company already, and they have gone out of the door never to return. I'm not down on politics, mind you. In a free country like ours men should take an interest in politics, and it is laudable for them to have political ambitions, but it is wrong to mix it with business.

But Huntington was not yet finished. When the reporter asked him about his prickly relations with Stanford, he answered:

Now, I do not wish the public to have that impression. I have nothing personal against him. He has many good points that I like, and it was never my intention to say anything that would give him offense. We get along in business all right, and our personal relations are kept up the same as usual.

But, don't you think that it is a queer sight to see politicians continually hanging around a railroad office? It is to me, and if I have to stay around here for 365 days in a year I'll see that there is no more of it. Things have got to such a state that if a man wants to be a constable he thinks he has first got to come down to Fourth and Townsend streets to get permission. Hereafter people who come to Fourth and Townsend streets must have railroad business to transact. The Southern Pacific Company is out of politics, and will attend to its business like any other private company or individual should do.

Even though the changes made at this fateful meeting had been agreed to in Huntington's New York office, when the time came for the changeover, the unexpected criticism and savage attack from Huntington—Stanford's partner of three decades—left Stanford, according to one account, reeling and seething.[17] This is an exaggeration, but even though the change had been agreed to several weeks earlier, nothing prepared anyone present for Huntington's brutal remarks.

Bertha Berner later wrote that when Stanford returned to the country home

---

[17]The word *ouster*, used by the *LA Times*, Jul 24, 1897, was not CFC's word, as it is represented as being. I have rejected as spurious hearsay and have therefore ignored this long piece of what may be nothing more than journalistic fiction. It purports to tell of an intimate conversation in San Francisco's Pacific-Union Club in which CFC cast aside all discretion and told the "true story" of the annual railroad meeting to an unidentified confidant. According to this report, CFC recounts a fantastic encounter in the railroad offices, minutes before the annual company meeting, in which LS and CPH "closed in death grip" and in which LS told CPH that all of the Associates distrusted him. The story appears out of character for CFC, and smacks of fabrication throughout. It was pub. only after the death of CFC, allowing no opportunity for refutation, modification, or correction. For what it is worth, serious students may wish to examine this item.

COLLIS P. HUNTINGTON IS ARRESTED!

Apparently running a railroad by strict business principles would not have permitted giving passes to one's attorney for free passage over "all lines of the Southern Pacific Railroad."[a] But for this very offense, which was considered a violation of the Interstate Commerce Act, in 1895 Huntington was arrested on a San Francisco warrant sent to New York with a demand for his rendition to the Golden State to stand trial.

His case came before Judge Brown of the United States District Court in New York. Brown threw the case out, arguing that the indictment was "fatally defective in not averring that any use was ever made of the pass, or that any transportation was ever furnished under it." The law, in other words, forbade free transportation, but not free passes that may not have been used.[b]

Huntington offered the following as the real reason for the case against him:

"I think the root of the whole matter lies in the fact that when I became president of the Southern Pacific railway [sic] I discharged twenty-three men in San Francisco who were so far as I could see merely political agents and go-betweens for politicians. They did no work for the railway so I cut them off. Perhaps they are hungry now and have got to make a strike somewhere."[c]

[a]*Milw. Sentinel*, Jan 14 and 17, Feb 16, and Mar 24, 1895, and *SF Chronicle*, Apr 23, 1895.   [b]*SF Chronicle*, May 8, 1895.   [c]*Milw. Sentinel*, Apr 23, 1895.

that night he looked ten years older than when he left for the offices in the morning. It was then that he told his wife he was no longer the president of the Southern Pacific Company and that Huntington had succeeded him.[18]

Berner is the only source of an interesting personal note to the deteriorating relationship between Stanford and Huntington. Following the death of his first wife, she said, Huntington married again and then acquired his own home on Nob Hill. One day Huntington said to Stanford, "I wish you would ask Mrs. Stanford to call on Mrs. Huntington." In reply came the icy response: "I do not regulate Mrs. Stanford's social activities."[19] If this unlikely scene actually took place, Huntington certainly would never have forgotten it.

On April 11, responding to a reporter's importunities for him to comment on the charges Huntington had made against him, Stanford said,

I never in my life used a penny of the company's money for my individual benefit; not one cent for any one of my personal purposes. On the subject of the last Senatorial election I can say, as I have always said, that I was never a candidate for the United States Senate. Representations were made to me that it was for the best interests of the party that I should accept the nomination. I withheld my consent. I positively refused to be a candidate. I consented to nothing that would in any way make me a candidate. Finally representations were put to me that the party and its leading men wanted me to take the nomination and called upon me to accept it to benefit the party. I then replied, "Well, if that is the case, I suppose I must accept."[20]

Huntington's statement that he, unlike Stanford, had kept the railroad out of politics was as far from the truth as it could possibly be; it was common knowledge

---

[18]BB, *Mrs. Stanford*, 85. After five years in the household, even BB should have known the difference between the SPRR and the SPC. She is also wrong in implying that this move took LS by surprise.

[19]Ibid., 86; *SF Argonaut*, Apr 21, 1890; *Chicago Examiner*, Mar 2, 1905.   [20]*SF Examiner*, Apr 12, 1890.

that he had been politically involved throughout his whole railroad career. For years he had lobbied in Washington, and afterward had employed attorneys as his agents in Congress. In terms of the railroad empire, he as well as everyone else realized the importance of a few key, strategically placed lobbyists.

In 1882 George E. Whitney, a candidate for state senator, found out that the railroad was against him and confronted Stanford and Huntington in their offices. Stanford expressed his hope that Whitney would be elected, but Huntington said he was not interested in politics. Whitney, who shared the widely accepted estimation of Huntington's political activities, retorted: "While you say you are not in politics, I think you are."[21] Stanford's friend Archibald Treat agreed; he charged that the "ruthless" Huntington was "steeped from his feet to his eyebrows in politics."[22]

REACTIONS TO HUNTINGTON'S BECOMING PRESIDENT OF THE SOUTHERN PACIFIC COMPANY

Huntington's wish came true: his enemies did *not* praise him. A survey of the California press reveals only one editor who accepted Huntington's statement that he was above politics.[23] Most California journalists recognized that it would be difficult to persuade California that Stanford, *not* Huntington, was responsible for railroad politics, especially after Huntington's letters had been aired at the Colton trial, letters that were "fragrant of a political fund."[24]

The editor of the *San Francisco Examiner* wrote a number of pro-Stanford articles. He asserted that even the bitterest anti-railroad critics would prefer Stanford to Huntington as the head of the Southern Pacific Company: Stanford was more humane, more responsive to public opinion, and more interested in the prosperity of California.[25] Unlike Stanford, who was a Californian with California ideas, Huntington had become a New Yorker, and a bitterly anti-California, pro-Chinese New Yorker at that. This editor had earlier said that Huntington was not "loved greatly" or "respected overmuch" in California. However, his stronger statement—that money was "Huntington's only god"—echoed the low opinion most Californians had of Huntington. This was reflected by scores of letters from total strangers that poured in supporting Stanford in the controversy with Huntington.[26]

Shortly after Stanford's resignation, Henry Vinson Morehouse, an attorney and president of the Bank of San José, wrote the following testimonial of his support for

[21]Treat, "Golden Key," 43.   [22]Ibid., 44 and 46.

[23]*Colusa Morning Gazette*, May 1890, in SFS 1:106. HHB later agreed, but only after falling out with LS. According to HHB, CPH had needed a Calif. resident as head of the SPC, but now, to save the corp. from politics, he was exercising his option of placing himself at the head of the road. *Builders of the Commonwealth*, V, 98–101. One has but to consult the Kentucky law to see that there is nothing in it requiring that the company head be a Calif. resident.

[24]*Eureka Times*, Apr 19, 1890.   [25]*SF Examiner*, Apr 10, 1890.

[26]Ibid., Jan 7, 1889; *SF Argonaut*, Apr 21, 1890; in LS papers.

Stanford: "I write you simply to say that I want to be placed on your list of friends, as one who thinks that you are one of the greatest men of this age and the greatest philanthropist this world has ever known."[27] In a similar vein, John W. Wilcox, the manager of a San Francisco wharf, wrote Creed Haymond, "If Mr. Huntington expects to ride to popular favor on the fall of the best man in the state, he will find that he has made a great mistake."[28]

Some of the most excoriating newspaper cartoons appearing in San Francisco, indeed, in the entire state, were published in the pages of the *San Francisco City Argus*. In one, captioned "Conspiracy Against Senator Stanford," Huntington was depicted with Michael Harry (Mike) De Young—who "had his eye on the [U.S.] Senate," and Stephen M. White, another Senate hopeful, throwing snakes into a caldron filled with deadly witches' brew into which Stanford was to be thrown.[29] Huntington was labeled the embodiment of "Jealousy." A poem in the upper left corner of the full-page cartoon titled "The Witches' Anthem," based on the witches' chant from *Macbeth*, read as follows:

> Round about the caldron go
> Mike, White, Huntington and Co.,
> Throwing in their venom dark;
> What's the object? Listen! Mark!
> Mike for social recognition
> Would sink to fathomless perdition;
> Stanford kicked him like a poodle,
> And he couldn't get his boodle.
> White's abnormal vanity
> Leads one to doubt his sanity;
> As for Judas Huntington,
> Spite and malice rolled in one
> Only half express it. Fie, oh!
> Fie! You precious, precious trio![30]

The editor of the *Chronicle* also championed the Stanford cause, identifying Huntington with Brutus and Stanford with Caesar, attributing Huntington's attack on Stanford to the senator's plan for lending government money at low interest. Huntington, Hubbard, and Stillman were allegedly disgusted by Stanford's money-lending plan, believing it would injure their company.[31] In a similar vein, the editor of the *Sacramento Bee*, also one of Stanford's staunchest defenders, condemned what he called Huntington's "intentional public insult" to Stanford and called the latter's retirement "a blow to the people," a "great public calamity."[32]

From the railroad Associates' inner circle came the story that Huntington and

[27]Henry Vinson Morehouse to LS, Apr 12, 1890.   [28]John W. Wilcox to Creed Haymond, Apr 15, 1890.
[29]SF City Argus, Dec 14, 1892.   [30]Ibid., Jul 5, 1890.
[31]SF Chronicle, Apr 10, 1890.   [32]Sac Bee, Apr 10, 1890.

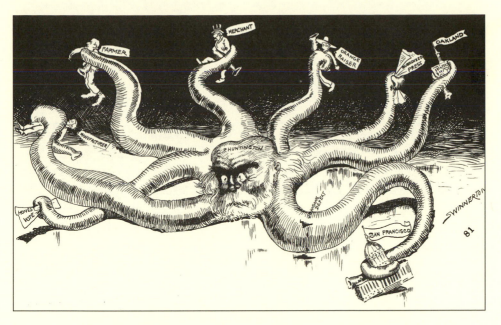

124. Collis P. Huntington depicted as an octopus. *Bancroft Library.*

Stillman had, indeed, gone after Stanford in an attempt to force him into retirement.[33] Allegedly Stanford's neglect of railroad affairs and his political ambition were the basis for their discontent; however, this source confided, it was Senator Stanford's scheme to lend government money at low interest that finally precipitated a declaration of war between himself and Huntington.[34]

Creed Haymond, who subsequently resigned as head of the railroad's legal department, realized that there was no place in the company for him under the new regime. He told the *Chronicle* that Huntington's statements about Stanford's election to the Senate were most unfortunate and resulted from his not knowing the full details.[35] Sargent's election, he said, was impossible because of circumstances unrelated to railroad matters and of which Huntington never dreamed; Huntington never made an effort to learn the facts.[36] Haymond, too, insisted that Stanford had not wanted the senatorship, but that in accepting it he had wronged no one, especially Huntington. If Stanford had not taken Sargent's place, Haymond reiterated, someone else would have. Then he added, cryptically: "The reason why Sargent was not elected Senator is known probably to only three men in all the world. Yes, one of them is Creed Haymond."[37]

[33] *SF Chronicle*, Apr 10, 1890.   [34] *SF Argonaut*, Aug 18, 1890.   [35] *SF Chronicle*, Apr 11, 1890.
[36] *SF Examiner*, Apr 12, 1890.   [37] *SF Chronicle*, Apr 11, 1890.

On April 12, 1890, Haymond decided it was time for Huntington to know the whole truth about the Sargent fiasco. He spent two hours closeted with the new Southern Pacific Company president and explained why Stephen Gage, Henry Vrooman, and himself, Creed Haymond, had so disliked Sargent and why they had bent all their energies to his defeat. Some of their grudges had been kept alive for more than a quarter of a century.[38]

Huntington listened, but he was not convinced. Stanford had benefited from their campaign against Sargent, and he "could have ordered them to keep their hands off." Because Stanford ended up with a seat in the Senate, he was sure that Stanford had "sympathized with them in their political crusade against Sargent."

Huntington did not find it easy to be wrong or to admit that he was wrong. Likening himself to Julius Caesar, he explained his position on Stanford with these ringing words:

> They [Gage, Vrooman, and Haymond] were the first to stab Caesar, and for Stanford to gain the fruit of their work I know of no other expression better suited to express my opinion of the latter than to say, "Et tu, Brute."

The editor of the *Argonaut* argued that Huntington's insane attack on Stanford would redound to Stanford's favor.[39] The Huntington speech was in bad taste, not at all consistent with the friendly relations that had so long existed between the two partners. The editor said it had come like a thunderbolt out of a cloudless sky. But whatever may have been Mr. Huntington's intention, no one could have been more stunned by the recoil than he himself. If Governor Stanford wanted to be reelected to the United States Senate [which he did], after Huntington's inept and ill-timed attack, no other Republican would have had a chance. Indeed, no other name afterwards was even mentioned in the party. If before that time Governor Stanford had had enemies, the *Argonaut* continued, after Huntington's *faux pas* Stanford had only friends. And if the Governor's connection with railroad legislation, litigation, or personal controversies over fares and freights had embittered anyone in business circles, these offenses were all excused by an adulatory public or attributed to his more "wicked partners."

The *Argonaut* said that by almost universal consent—thanks to Huntington—the charities, personal character, and generous acts of the Governor and his wife were publicized to the world. In a word, "Mr. Huntington's very unkind, and, as we deem it, ungenerous and undeserved, assault threw the mantle of oblivion over all the vulnerable acts of Governor Stanford and threw calcium-light upon a thousand unremembered and generous acts."[40]

---

[38] *SF Examiner*, Apr 13, 1890.   [39] *SF Argonaut*, Aug 18, 1890
[40] Ibid.

Huntington's Nominal "Dear Governor" Apology

Stanford was so appalled by Huntington's insinuations that railroad money had bought his Senate seat that he immediately sent a letter to the board of directors demanding an investigation into the charges. In the event of an investigation, it was expected that Stanford would have been vindicated. But no matter *who* won, the railroad would be the loser.[41] Railroad securities, it was said, would have "tumbled like a house of cards stricken by a tornado."[42]

Fred Crocker again tried hard to patch up the quarrel—before it came before the directors for official consideration.[43] He, Stillman, and Hubbard—acting together—persuaded Stanford to withdraw the letter to the board of directors.[44] The argument that finally won him over was this: that he had no right to force the other railroad owners to choose between him and Huntington because of their personal feud.[45] But Stanford was said to have demanded of Huntington either a retraction of his charges or complete vindication by the board.[46] In a very *limited* sense, he got the retraction.

Huntington was prevailed upon to make peace with Stanford before the railroad's position on the market was damaged. On April 15, 1890, he obligingly addressed a letter of apology to Stanford—wrung from him by railroad Associates. In his "Dear Governor" letter he made it clear that their mutual friends had insisted upon his writing, and then expressed his regrets that his inaugural statement had been construed as an attack upon his partner.

Huntington's letter, written privately to Stanford, was not so much an apology as a repetition of his earlier charges, but Stanford accepted it as an apology, simply because he wanted and needed one so badly. It saved face, but not *much* face. Stanford announced that he did not wish to be interviewed by the press on the contents of the letter; even though it was not the complete vindication he wanted, he knew he had gotten more from Huntington than he had expected. He soon made the letter public, and allowed it to be printed in most of the San Francisco newspapers.

The two men remained in their offices at Fourth and Townsend all day long while the press was outside busily speculating about a rumored truce.[47] Meanwhile, railroad officials continued to assure the public—and themselves—that the quarrel would have no adverse effects on the company's bonds or credit. On the sixteenth of April 1890 an *entente cordiale* was restored.[48] The two men greeted each other amidst smiles and awkward pleasantries, and then the whole group of railroad Associates in the office went to lunch together. It was reportedly "not a hungry

[41] *SF Examiner*, Apr 13, 1890.

[43] *SF Examiner*, Apr 12, 1890.

[45] Ibid.; *SF Chronicle*, Apr 15, 1890.

[47] *SF Examiner*, Apr 16, 1890.

[42] *Stockton Mail*, Apr 12, 1890.

[44] Ibid., Apr 15, 1890.

[46] *SF Chronicle*, Apr 16, 1890.

[48] Ibid., Apr 17, 1890.

Huntington's "Dear Governor" Apology Letter*

Dear Governor:

So many items mentioning your name and mine have lately appeared in the daily papers that some of our friends think it would be well for me to write you a letter. Hence, this communication; although I do not apprehend any danger that you and I will be put in a hostile attitude in our business—or, for that matter, personal—relations; but the intervention of others who do not altogether understand our difference may tend to separate our friends. Our views when at variance have been freely expressed and it is needless to allude to them further than to say that we have each of us agreed to disagree.

The remarks that I recently made at the Southern Pacific Board meeting were intended only as a reasonable expression of my view upon these subjects. My words and especially the phrase which relates to campaign uses of company's funds, or, as I expressed it, "putting hands into the treasury of the company to defeat the people's choice" have been construed in some quarters as a personal attack on you. Allow me to say that I greatly regret this impression since I did not intend to make such attack or to charge that you had used the company's money to advance your personal interests or in any improper manner, & I am satisfied that you have not done so. Allow me also to express the wish that our relations may continue as friendly hereafter as they have been heretofore.

Yours very truly,
C P Huntington

*CPH to LS, Apr 15, 1890.

gathering," but a sociable one, and afterward they all returned to Stanford's office for the remainder of the afternoon; this was the longest Stanford and Huntington had been together for five years. Thus an armistice—though not a peace—had been reached, as demonstrated by the way Huntington continued to jab at Stanford afterward.[49]

When the shakeup in the Southern Pacific management failed to improve business relations among the Associates, Stanford and Fred Crocker insisted on new ground rules for conducting business. They dispatched a letter to the Huntington-Searles group demanding that in the future they get along; as there was one dissenting voice among the four, there were to be no new enterprises started. "Success without harmony is possible," they wrote, "but hardly probable."[50]

Following Huntington's taking over the presidency of the Southern Pacific Company (Stanford remained president of the Central Pacific for life) the Stanfords returned to Washington on Senate business and then sailed for Europe on May 28. Countless friends and associates kept the Governor informed about political and

---

[49] *SF Argonaut*, May 19, Jun 2, and Aug 4, 1890.
[50] LS and CFC to CPH, Thomas E. Stillman, and Thomas H. Hubbard, Apr 22, 1892.

railroad news while he was away. Steve Gage wrote to Stanford in Kissingen that the most popularly discussed topic in California was Huntington's denial of his charges against him (Stanford)—"over his own signature"—and his frequent reiterations of the charges he had made against Stanford.[51]

Stanford believed that Huntington had been less offended in 1885 than was thought by most people. He wrote to Steve Gage soon after resigning the presidency of the Southern Pacific Company to ask for a number of adulatory letters written to him by Huntington in 1886; they were to be turned over to Ariel Lathrop for safekeeping.[52]

Long before the anti-Stanford diatribes, there was no more certain way of earning the criticism of political and social reformers than by association with Collis Potter Huntington. Guilt by association was inevitable. A case in

JOSEPH H. MOORE ON COLLIS P. HUNTINGTON

"If a persistent intermeddler without proper warrant in Government affairs, an unscrupulous dealer in threats and promises amongst public men, a constant menace to sworn servants of the people in their offices of trust, a tempter of the corrupt and a terror to the timid who are delegated to power, a remorseless enemy to wholesome legislation, a constant friend to conspirators against the common welfare for private gain—if such a compound of dangerous and insolent qualities merged in one personality, active, vigilant, unblushing, be a Lobbyist—then Collis P. Huntington is a Lobbyist at the doors of Congress, in its corridors and in its councils, at Washington.

"He is the spirit incarnate of Monopoly in its most aggressive form. Among the intrenched [sic] powers which have sapped the vitality and are a menace to the existence of our form of republican government, he is strong with their strength, dangerous with their power, perilous with the insolence of their courtesies, the blandishment of their open or covert threats."*

*Joseph H. Moore, *An Open Letter. A Protest and a Petition. From a Citizen of California to the United States Congress* (SF: JHBC, [1876]), 1–2.

point: In 1876 Joseph H. Moore had written a widely-circulated open letter to Congress holding up to public scrutiny the "villainies" of Huntington as reflected in his own letters, which Moore cited and quoted at length. It is only after more than a dozen pages of this sort of condemnation of Huntington that the writer turned to the wrongs of California and, lumping the Associates together, concluded that defrauding the government of millions of dollars was first in the hearts and minds of Leland Stanford and his Associates.[53]

SUMMARY

Obviously *something* had happened between 1886 and 1890 to destroy the cordial relations between Stanford and Huntington, and one does not have to look far to find it.

Huntington's first "grumblings" about his Central Pacific Associates had been

---

[51]Stephen Gage to LS, Jul 2, 1890.   [52]LS to Stephen Gage, Apr 29, 1890.

[53]Joseph H. Moore, *An Open Letter. A Protest and a Petition. From a Citizen of California to the United States Congress* (SF: JHBC, [1876]), 13.

heard years earlier, when they began building their mansions on Nob Hill. But this had long since been forgotten, particularly since Huntington himself now owned one of those Nob Hill castles.[54] He was especially rankled by Stanford's putting his fortune into a university. Often when Californians called on Huntington in New York, he would tell them that Stanford was a fool, throwing away his money on horses and on building a school, which he reportedly called "Stanford's circus."[55] Huntington thought that any spare money Stanford had to throw around could best be plowed back into their railroad empire.

Later, Stanford's friend James Bassett, the writer of the famous "Dear Pard" letters, said that Stanford came to regard Huntington as a shady character whom he would not trust any farther than he could throw Trinity Church up the side of Mt. Shasta. Huntington's response was that Stanford was a "blanked old fool."[56]

JAMES MADISON BASSETT

was for many years one of the most conspicuous characters on the Pacific Coast. A Hoosier from Marion County, Indiana, as a boy he learned the printer's trade, and, after 1850—the year he arrived in California—he worked on or owned an interest in several West Coast newspapers.[a] In the 1870s he worked for Stanford as a railroad purchasing agent and the two became fast friends. As a close friend of the top man, he learned a great deal about the inner operations of the railroad empire and, in particular, about Huntington's role. Bassett used business secrets acquired while Stanford was alive in his later fight with Huntington—after the latter dispensed with his services following the death of Stanford.[b] Bassett, who detested Collis Huntington, is best known for his "Dear Pard Letters." A series of epistles designed to discredit Huntington, they were later serialized for the public to read.[c]

[a]*SF Chronicle*, Apr 25, 1903.   [b]Ibid.
[c]In the *SF Daily Report*, Nov 7, 1892, and weekly thereafter.

Some of Stanford's friends conceded that there was further widening of the breach between the old partners because their wives did not get along.[57] As mentioned, Mrs. Stanford had allegedly snubbed the new Mrs. Huntington by refusing to call on her. It was later reported that Mrs. Huntington's desire to spite and humble Mrs. Stanford resulted in Huntington's attempt to purchase opposition to Stanford in his senatorial race. Other contemporaries, however, played this down. They attributed Huntington's attack on Stanford to his long-seething jealousy of his famous and respected colleague.[58] Stanford had been governor of California, was now a U.S. senator, and he was being suggested for the presidency of the United States. Meanwhile Huntington, in the opinion of one writer, remained a friendless, money-worshipping, glorified village trader—unknown and unnoticed (compared to the fame enjoyed by Stanford)—and was regarded almost universally as "tricky, hypocritical, and insincere."[59]

[54]CPH to MH, Mar 23, 1877; *SF Argonaut*, Apr 21, 1890.   [55]Treat, "Golden Key," 45.
[56]J[ames] M. Bassett to CPH, Jun 25, 1894, in *SF Daily Report*, Jul 21, 1894.
[57]*Stockton Mail*, Apr 12, 1890; *SF Examiner*, Jun 21, 1893.   [58]*Stockton Mail*, Apr 12, 1890.
[59]*SF Argonaut*, Apr 21, 1890.

In trying to find a reason for why Huntington decided to declare war on Stanford at this time and not earlier, Bancroft wrote mistakenly that the Southern Pacific Company had needed a California resident as president, but now, to save the corporation from politics, Huntington was exercising his option of placing himself at the head of the company.[60] This explanation has no basis in fact at all. First, the articles of incorporation of the Southern Pacific Company did not stipulate that its head had to be a California resident.[61] Moreover, Huntington had no "option" to place at its head whomever he wished.

Stanford's surrender of the presidency of the Southern Pacific Company has also been misinterpreted as a total ouster from railroad affairs, but this was not the case. When he announced his intention to resign, he made it clear that his interests in railroad affairs were as great as ever and that he would continue to take an active part in them.[62] After Stanford stepped down from the presidency of the Southern Pacific Company, the executive committee put him in another powerful position, as head of the committee. This position relieved him of the duties of the presidency while still allowing him to supervise many of the affairs of the corporation. Several people surmised, inaccurately as it proved, that as chairman of the newly created executive committee he would still be at the head of the great railway system.[63] It was one editor's wishful thinking when he predicted that Stanford's voice would be as strong as ever in the company.[64]

Stanford remained an active railroad man until his death.[65] He was president of the Central Pacific Railroad from inception until his death; after he died, the position of president was listed as "vacancy."[66] Under the Southern Pacific Company associated lines, he was president of the South Pacific Coast Railway in 1892.[67] He was also president of the California & Oregon Railroad and the California Pacific until he died.

Stanford's friends asserted that his resignation from the presidency of the Southern Pacific Company was entirely his own decision, that his poor health also made it impossible for him to perform his senatorial duties and made him less active in university affairs. These assertions may have been an attempt to protect him from the stigma of outright defeat.[68] Stanford himself explained that his principal interest in

[60]HHB, *Builders of the Commonwealth*, V, 98–101. Also see n23 above.

[61]Chap. 403, "An Act to incorporate the Southern Pacific Company," Acts of the General Assembly of the Commonwealth of Kentucky, Passed at the Regular Session of the General Assembly, which was begun and held in the City of Frankfort on Monday, the thirty-first Day of December, Eighteen Hundred and eighty-three, I, 725–728.

[62]*SF Alta California*, Apr 8, 1890.   [63]Ibid., Apr 10, 1890; HHB, *History of California*, VII, 632.

[64]*Sac Record-Union*, Apr 10, 1890.   [65]Ibid.

[66]Ibid., 134. In addition to his many railroad involvements, LS was also pres. of the A & P Telegraph Co., doing business at 639 Market St. *SFCD*, 1873–1874, 575.

[67]Henry V. Poor, and Henry W. Poor, *Poor's Directory of Railway Officials and Manual of American Street Railways* (NY: ABNC, 1892), 133.   [68]*SF Examiner*, Apr 7, 1890.

railroads had been construction, and now that the Southern Pacific system was completed, he wished to leave its management to others.[69] If this were so, why did he remain president of the Central Pacific?

Though Stanford's position in the company was undoubtedly weakened, it was not to the extent suggested by the following newspaper report: that he had "as little to say about the exercise of the powers he had so long wielded as the boy which [sic] ran the elevator that took him downstairs after the meeting."[70] Stanford did not surrender his positions with other railroads; as stated, he continued as president of the Central Pacific, with Huntington remaining, as he always had, as first vice president.[71] He also retained his position as president of the "Amador, Berkeley, Sacramento & Placerville, San Pablo & Tulare, Stockton & Copperopolis, Vaca Valley & Clear Lake, and South Coast branch lines," which were, of course, part of the Southern Pacific Company system.[72]

Oscar Lewis was right in this, if in nothing else he wrote about them—that the Central Pacific/Southern Pacific Associates held the center of the stage in California for more than a third of a century and there was hardly an issue of a California newspaper or magazine that did not carry some reference to their activities.[73]

Stanford and Huntington were such different personalities that perhaps conflict was inevitable. The remarkable thing is not that their relationship fell apart, but that they had even worked together so effectively for so long. It is also remarkable that their railroad empire suffered so little from these internecine battles. They both recognized the consequences of all-out warfare and were willing to swallow some pride and continue working together. Therefore, the railroad battle in some respects brought out the best in both their characters—or was it the *worst*?

[69]*SF Alta California*, Apr 8, 1890.

[71]*SF Alta California*, Apr 10, 1890.

[73]Lewis, *The Big Four*, vi.

[70]*LA Times*, Jul 24, 1897.

[72]*SF Examiner*, Apr 7, 1890.

CHAPTER 23

THE ELECTION OF 1890
AND STANFORD'S SECOND TERM
IN THE U.S. SENATE
1890–1893

It Was Simply Stanford[1]

Mr. Stanford was not very conspicuous in the debates in the Senate, though he took an active part in the work of the body and was an influential member of a number of leading committees. His name will forever be associated with the Land-Loan bill, which he originated and presented to the Senate. His addresses on this measure have been quoted in works on political economy in every language of civilization.[2]

Whatever the Government agrees to Receive in payment of the public dues is money, no matter what its form may be; [sic] Treasure notes, drafts, etc. Such bills or paper, issued under the authority of the United States, are money.
                                        —paraphrase of Henry Clay remarks in the U.S. Senate
                                              in 1837, quoted by Senator Stanford[3]

THE CALIFORNIA STATE ELECTION—NOVEMBER 4, 1890

Huntington immediately violated the terms of the February 28, 1890, agreement in which he was to support Stanford's bid for reelection to the Senate. In fact, he probably never intended to carry out this term of their peace pact. Huntington's duplicity was the occasion for a lengthy *Argonaut* editorial that placed the political activities of the two antagonists in proper perspective. Because the Pixley paper examined so many aspects of the railroad warfare and cited so many specific instances of Huntington's oft-denied political activities, I quote at length:

---

[1] *Wash. Post*, Nov 10, 1890.   [2] *Memorial Addresses on the Life and Character of Leland Stanford*, 16.
[3] *USCG*, 25th Cong., 1st Sess., 33 (Sep 25, 1837); *USCR*, 52nd Cong., 1st Sess., 469 (Jan 21, 1892).

We learn from *Themis*, a weekly journal published at Sacramento, that a correspondence has taken place between Grove L. Johnson, formerly a senator from Sacramento, and President Huntington, of the Southern Pacific Company, in reference to the duty of employees in the company's shops to abstain from interference in politics. Mr. Huntington is intent upon preventing the mechanics and working-men in the company's employ from using their influence to assist Governor Stanford to be returned to the United States Senate. We wish Mr. Huntington would abstain from intermeddling in the affairs of the Republican party, and leave Governor Stanford and the Republicans of California to determine the election of a United States Senator in accordance with party usages. While we are unreservedly in favor of the election of Governor Stanford to a second senatorial term, we do not remember to have taken issue with the newly elected president of the company for any honest effort he has made to withdraw the railroad company from endeavoring to control and direct the politics of the State. We have not approved of the employment of any politicians—[George C.] Gorham, [William R.] Carr, [William] Stow, [Aaron] Sargent, [William] Higgins, or anybody else—to manage party affairs or to control party conventions. To the extent that the railroad company has been compelled to fight upon the defensive in order to protect itself from spoliation, we have sympathized with it. We have seen it unjustly assailed on every side and compelled to stand upon the defensive in the halls of Congress, in the lobbies of State legislatures, and in the boards of supervisors in every county through which it has passed. Sometimes we have thought the company right and sometimes we have thought it wrong. But we have always deprecated the necessity of employing professional politicians to stand between it and harm. We have been of the opinion that if the company had depended upon the public and its representatives, and had made no political organization in its defense, it would have saved money, trouble, and unending annoyance. So when Mr. Huntington asserted the position that the company should not act in its corporate capacity politically, we were glad of it. We never have believed that Governor Stanford expended any money to secure his election to the Senate of the United States and he was never as active to elect himself as was Mr. Huntington to elect Mr. Sargent. We have been informed that money has been used in Washington to secure political results, but we have been informed and have believed that Mr. Huntington was the active disbursing agent and that more money had been expended in Washington than in California, Oregon, and Nevada. We have understood that Mr. Huntington took a very active part in the campaign against William A. Piper, and that he caused money to be expended to prevent his re-election to Congress. We thought we had gained this information from Mr. Huntington's correspondence with Mr. D. D. Colton, and if we are correctly informed, Mr. Huntington has for many years played an important part in the management of the political affairs of all the railroads before all the legislators, judges, and assessing officials in which they have been concerned. We are quite sure that Governor Stanford is entirely willing to submit his claims to the legislature of California for re-election if Mr. Huntington will keep his hands entirely free from intermeddling. Nor do we think that it is possible for Governor Stanford to be beaten in this contest, whether Mr. Huntington expends money or refrains from using it, nor whether Mr. Grove L. Johnson does or does not favor the return of Governor Stanford to the United States Senate. We think the people of Sacramento will elect members of the senate and the legislature favoring his return. Sacramento is a Republican city and county; in it Governor Stanford has spent his active life; there is his home; his neighbors know him, and will, in our judgment, favor his re-election to the Senate of the United States. We would be entirely willing to trust his re-election to the working-classes of California, because with working-men he has had no quarrel. Employing more mechanical, skilled, and common laborers than any other individual on the Pacific Coast, he has paid his men better wages than any other corporation. There has never been a strike against any company or any concern over which the governor has presided or whose interests he has managed. Wherever and whenever there has been any misunderstanding, every laborer knew he could appeal to Governor Stanford with confidence that justice and equity would be measured out to him in kindness and generosity with common sense. On one occasion, some years ago, Mr. Colton undertook to pay off the men in silver, then at a discount. Upon a statement of the case to the president of the corporation, Governor Stanford at once corrected the mistake and paid the men in gold coin. Governor Stanford has always held with his working-men the kindest of relations, has paid them the highest of wages to the extent of his influence, and contended to keep the wages of labor well sustained. We do not doubt that Governor Stanford is the choice of this State for any office to which he may aspire; that office is the one he now holds, and is the only one he has sought since in the years 1862–3 he filled the gubernatorial chair. He has filled his senatorial position with honesty, ability, and dignity; he has made no ostentatious display of his wealth; he has performed his official duties with industry, and has in all respects made a good senator. He ought to be returned, and if the decision is left to the intelligent property-owners, mechanics, laboring-men, farmers, and toilers, he will undoubtedly be chosen. All the opposition that Governor Stanford will receive will be from other than the working-men of California. The men who will support him will be the fathers who have children to educate, and every stone and arch and column that is piled at Palo Alto, in building the Leland Stanford Jr. University, will counterbalance in weight and influence more than all the Grove L. Johnsons and Collis P. Huntingtons, all the coin and *Chronicles*, all the piece-clubs [*sic*] and demagogic politicians that money will buy or bribery influence at the polls in November or in the legislative halls at Sacramento.[4]

The California election of 1890 was a bitterly contested event. The election of a Republican governor and legislature was by no means a foregone conclusion; there were conflicting elements at work in both parties that made the outcome of the election difficult to call. Particularly, Huntington seemed to be at war with Leland Stanford and that made it impossible to forecast the result of the senatorial election. Huntington's role of spoiler was so extreme that according to the *Argonaut* he actually supported the Democratic candidate.[5] Pixley conceded that since Huntington was so "willing to pour out his money freely in aid of a Democratic opponent" it was very hard to determine what would be the outcome of the election. Of course if

---

[4]*SF Argonaut*, Jul 14, 1890.   [5]Ibid., Jul 28, 1890.

Huntington really intended to keep himself and his business associates out of politics, and do nothing against Stanford, the Governor would have been returned to the Senate with no opposition from within the Republican party.

In other words, if Huntington stayed out of politics—as he always claimed he had—the contest would have been between Stanford and Stephen M. White, the Democratic opponent. In this case, there was little doubt that the people of California would elect a legislature that would return Stanford to the Senate.

Although Huntington worked hard behind the scenes—and not too far behind them at that—to defeat his business partner, he must have been disappointed with his singular lack of success. As the Huntington conspiracy grew, so did the defense of Stanford by Pixley's influential *Argonaut* and a number of other California journalists. Pixley's editorial columns did not mince words in showing the editor's profound contempt for Huntington:

> The net result, however, of all Mr. Huntington's efforts to organize a conspiracy for the political overthrow of Governor Stanford must be to him as surprising as it is disappointing. In any State of the Union a senator, no matter how irreproachable his character and distinguished his services has about him elements of opposition in his own party, bred of rival ambitions, disapproval of his acts, chagrin at not getting appointed to office, the spirit of faction, or what not. Doubtless all these elements exist in California with reference to Senator Stanford. It would be very strange, indeed, if they did not. But Mr. Huntington has sought in vain to fuse and use them. He turned to the business community and meanly slandered his partner, the late president of the Southern Pacific, as a business man, and there was no response—at least not of the kind that was desired. The business community—the merchants, the bankers, and manufacturers, men of substance generally—do not, as a rule, interest themselves greatly in politics, but Mr. Huntington has found them to be steadfast, if quiet, partisans in this case. Some of them may not agree at all with the senator's views on finance or other matters, but they all have confidence in the excellence of his intentions. They are for Governor Stanford because they have met and known him in their business life. Mr. Huntington has discovered a like disheartening condition of things at the other end of the financial and social scale. The mechanics and laborers, who are much keener politicians than the business men, know all about what the Senator has done in Washington, and approve his course there as being in their interest. They have recognized the mind and heart behind the distinctive measure proposed by him as the same that, in his conduct of a great property, have never failed to be fair and sympathetic toward themselves. They know Governor Stanford, and feel toward him only gratitude, liking, and esteem. If the presidency of the railroad company depended upon the votes of the employees, and an election were to take place to-morrow, how many votes would be cast against Stanford? Mr. Huntington can derive from this unique popularity of his partner the reason why he has not been able to rally even the disgruntled small politicians of the Republican party against him. Politicians' heads have an antipathy for stone walls. In the Democratic

party—which Mr. Huntington made happy with hope when he began his open warfare on Senator Stanford—matters have not progressed in a flattering way. The cry raised for young Mr. White, of Los Angeles, sounded quite cheerful and vigorous for a time, but it has died down. The widely spread report that Mr. Huntington was behind Mr. White's candidacy, which report has not been authoritatively denied, has apparently had the reverse of the intended effect. It has deprived an otherwise legitimate candidature of respectability. The *Examiner*'s nominee, the Hon. Tom Clunie, has evoked considerably less Democratic enthusiasm than Mr. White. We have heard no Democrat, other than these two, mentioned as a possible candidate in opposition to Stanford. It is our present judgment that there will be no serious attempt to elect a Democratic senator, Collis P. Huntington's aid and comfort notwithstanding. The common sense of California favors the return of Governor Stanford for a second term, since it is his wish to serve his State further. There is not enough partisanship going in these days and latitudes to make it a matter of much concern to the ordinary citizen whether he is represented in Washington by a Republican or a Democrat. It is our practice, in fact, to keep a senator of each party there, an arrangement which bears good practical fruit in the way of appropriations, which we all want. Why should Mr. Huntington suppose himself to be able to come into a State to whose people and interests he has become a stranger, not to say an enemy, and induce it to exchange Senator Stanford for Senator White? We desire the latter gentleman and all his friends to understand that we mean no disrespect either to his character or abilities when we say that it is the prevailing belief that it would be folly to retire Governor Stanford to make room for him. Mr. White is a young man of notable qualities. He is one of the very few natives of the State who has achieved something like distinction. As a lawyer, a large practice testifies to his possession of brains and legal knowledge. In the State legislature, his career was marked at once by conspicuous integrity and a great deal of shrewdness. But something more than cleverness and youthful energy are required in a senator. As for the Hon. Tom Clunie, that young gentleman is doing very well where he is, and, we suspect, has had too much intelligence to take his nomination by the *Examiner* seriously. He is industriously rearing a pyramid of appropriations, cementing the same, of course, with the immortal principles of Jefferson and Jackson, and doubtless hopes to step, a few years hence, from the golden summit of his structure into the Senate chamber. Given the Democratic party of the State were on either of these two young men—which it is not and can not be brought to be—it could not, though reinforced with all Huntington's hate, influence, and money, come within miles of success. Governor Stanford would divide with any candidate the votes of the men of intelligence and substance in the Democratic party. They know that it is not alone in the Senate chamber that a senator accomplishes his work. Social position, weight of personal character, the prestige of mighty personal achievement in the field of industrial enterprise, the gravity of ripe years—all these are Governor Stanford's, and all tell in Washington in the State's interest. Therefore the State, waiving party lines, will crown his first term with the approval of another. The *Argonaut* extends its sincere commiseration to Collis P. Huntington. By wanton public assault, by private insult and secret plotting, he has endeavored to break down one whose business partner and personal associate he had been for the better part of a life-time, and who had upon him claims for respect and consideration which any man of loyalty and breadth of nature could not have ignored. Huntington could and did ignore them, and that is why we commiserate him. But we have no pity for the kind of suffering that must be his in finding that it needed only his attempt to wound the man, whose moral and intellectual superiority embittered him, to bring to that man's support and defense the clean citizenship of his State, whether in political sympathy with him or not. He asked California the question: "Do you want Leland Stanford for senator?" And California has already answered: "Yes, but whether we do nor not, we do not want Collis P. Huntington for senator or anything else. It is the snake that has been hurt by its own venomous bite."[6]

It appears that Huntington did not continue his assault upon Stanford for long. He probably saw that Stanford was going to be reelected despite his campaign against him and was politically astute enough to realize that Stanford as a U.S. senator *and* as an enemy could do him a great deal of harm.[7] Huntington, of course, had always insisted that his actions were neither personal, vindictive, nor political, and that he had no interest in doing anything more than keeping the railroad from interfering or meddling in politics. In other words, the effect of Huntington's assault was not what he expected, since it appears that it *helped* rather than hurt Stanford. It drew out expressions of good feeling from men of all parties; if there had been a popular election for senator, it was almost certain that Governor Stanford would have won overwhelmingly.

In his anti-Stanford campaign Huntington committed one serious *faux pas*, almost humorous in its likely result. On June 12, 1890, he responded to a letter from Grove Lawrence Johnson—Sacramento Republican politician and father of later California governor Hiram Johnson—informing him that many employees of the Southern Pacific Company were spending a great proportion of their time in political efforts.[8] Huntington took this opportunity to blast Stanford. He expressed regret that the company had been used "too long, and by those who knew better, as an instrument to advance the personal interests of individuals." As the new president, he promised to do everything within his power to see that this practice was not repeated.

This letter was mild compared to what was to come.

A copy of this letter fell into the hands of the editor of the *Kern County Californian* and he published it on June 28. From his New York office, Huntington penned a letter to this editor in which he approved what that journalist had written about "the rottenness of the politics of the State [California] as conducted by Leland Stanford, through which he used the Southern Pacific Company very much to its own disadvantage in order to accomplish his own selfish purposes."[9]

[6]Ibid., Aug 4, 1890.   [7]Ibid., Aug 18, 1890.

[8]CPH to Grove L. Johnson, Jun 12, 1890, pub. in the *Sac Bee* on Jun 21.

[9]CPH to ed. of the *Kern County Californian*, Aug 8, 1890, pub. in ed. of Aug 23.

Huntington charged that Stanford had advanced his own political interests by reducing fares and freight below the real cost of transporting passengers and merchandise. After offering the following gratuitous dissimulation,

> I sincerely hope that the *Kern County Californian* and all other journals in the State will do what they can to bring political morality on to a much higher level than it has occupied heretofore,

Huntington concluded:

> You will readily see that not only the interests of the people but of the stockholders have been sacrificed for the personal aggrandizement of one man.

The editor of the *San Francisco Argonaut* reported this correspondence and then explained the obvious:

> If there is anything that Governor Stanford can do to reconcile the people of California to his political advancement, it would be the one thing that Mr. Huntington complains of. The average country representative is not anxious to retire Governor Stanford from his political career, or drive him from his position in the United States Senate, if the result is to enable the newly elected president of the Southern Pacific roads to advance fares and freights upon their lines.[10]

A question uppermost in the minds of many California politicos was what line of action Huntington would take in his proposed visit to California in September of 1890. It was rumored that Huntington would discontinue his anti-Stanford campaign entirely, and for reasons not expected by anyone. The controversy apparently had become the subject of discussion in the highest political circles in Washington; it was reported that President Harrison, Secretary of State Blaine, and "very many of the leading senators" had notified Huntington that it would be wise for him to refrain from active hostilities, lest it should help defeat the Republican party in California, and, more to the point for his *own* interests, they warned, lest it be injurious to railroad measures now before Congress.[11]

The *New York Sun* reported that officials of the Southern Pacific Company were hoping that Huntington would not visit San Francisco for the rest of the year: "influences have been at work to induce him to stay till after the November election, in order that there may not be open hostility between him and the friends of Governor Stanford."[12]

The actions by Huntington had given hope to many Democrats: Stephen White, for example, who seemed almost assured of the Democratic nomination for governor in 1890, abandoned those efforts when it seemed that the U.S. Senate seat might be had. He had even given up a lucrative position with the Southern Pacific

---

[10]*SF Argonaut*, Sep 8, 1890.   [11]Ibid., Aug 18, 1890.
[12]*NY Sun*, Aug 6, 1890.

Company—all in hopes of defeating Stanford in the senate race, a hope that could only be realized with the continuing assistance of an unexpected supporter—Collis P. Huntington.[13]

As mentioned, Huntington not only violated the February 1890 agreement to *support* Stanford for reelection, but went out of his way to *oppose* him. The following August, for example, he spoke of the "rottenness of the politics of the state as conducted by Leland Stanford."[14] Much of the California press had by then written Huntington off as a hopeless, incorrigible hypocrite, but much more was to come.[15] In September he wrote that he was not going to make any organized effort to defeat Stanford, but he left no doubt where he stood: "My preference is naturally for Republicans. But I would much rather have a good clean Democrat than a Dirty Republican."[16] Remarks like these prompted rumors of another impending clash between the two railroad giants.[17]

The Republican gubernatorial nomination of Col. Henry H. Markham of Los Angeles, after a long and bitter contest, was viewed by many as a triumph over machine politics, political bosses, and federal officials meddling in California politics. It was also seen as a victory over San Francisco's political dominance in the state, and over partisan and dictatorial newspaper journalists. Stanford's campaign manager, William Stow, took no part in the gubernatorial contest and was not even present in the city of Sacramento while the Republican convention was in session. The editorial writer of the *Argonaut* exulted: "Fortunate is it for the railroad that not a man in authority, or in supposed alliance with it, or in the fight for Senator Stanford, attended or took part in the proceedings of the gubernatorial nomination. No one belonging to the railroad, or friendly to Governor Stanford."

Indeed, all of Stanford's closest railroad friends and associates kept their distance: Stephen Gage took his family on a visit to Yosemite; Creed Haymond did not

---

[13]*SF Argonaut*, Aug 18, 1890; on Oct 6, 1890, just before the election, the *Argonaut* repr. a story attributed to the *Journal of Finance*, pub. in NY: "It is reported that when Senator Stanford returns from Europe he will oust C.P. Huntington from the presidency of the Southern Pacific Railroad and put Colonel Charles F. Crocker in his place. This being repeated to Mr. Huntington, he laughed in derision, and said: 'I can't waste my time paying attention to such remarks. I have been in business a good many years, and I have attained some success by attending to my own affairs and not minding what other people say they are going to do. Stanford is all the time giving vent to remarks of this character, but nothing comes of them, and I never heed their utterance. Mr. Crocker is a nice young man, an exceedingly nice young man, quite clever and quite rich. He is ambitious, but he must not expect to be president of the Southern Pacific for some time to come. Oh, no, not yet,' and Mr. Huntington smiled cheerfully." The ed. of the *Argonaut* went on to deny the veracity of this story: "It is probable that Governor Stanford has never made any threat against Mr. Huntington, and it is improbable that Mr. Huntington has made any sarcastic remarks against Colonel Crocker, for it must be apparent that Mr. Huntington would not willingly wish to make of Colonel Crocker an enemy, because, in the ordinary course of human events, he will continue in the administration of the Southern Pacific Railroad affairs for many years after Mr. Huntington shall have been translated to happier realms."
[14]CPH to ed. of the *Kern County Californian*, Aug 8, 1890, in issue of Aug 23, repr. in *SF Examiner*, Aug 26, 1890.
[15]*SF Examiner*, Aug 28, 1890; *Stockton Mail*, Sep 13, 1890.   [16]*SF Examiner*, Sep 18, 1890.
[17]Ibid. *Stockton Mail*, Sep 9, 10, and 13, 1890.

leave San Francisco; Fred Crocker was too busy arranging for the contemplated celebration of the "Native Sons of the Golden West" on the anniversary of the admission of the state into the Union; and Stanford was in Kissengen, Germany, and not even in telegraphic touch with the men who were most interested in his fight.[18]

Stephen White carried on a campaign directed more against Stanford in particular than against the Republican party in general. To dissuade Democrats from voting for Stanford, he declared that anyone who voted the Republican legislative ticket would endorse the election of Governor Stanford, who was "being pushed forward by the corrupt use of money."[19]

White tried, unsuccessfully, to make Stanford out to be a machine politician who sought reelection by manipulating that machine. In a portion of a five-column self-endorsement, White wrote:

> I start out with the assumption that if the next legislature is not Democratic, Leland Stanford will be reelected. That I am right about this, I have no doubt. Everything is set that way. No other name will be presented to the caucus. All other members of the Republican party are disqualified. There is a large number of prominent and able members of that organization in California who would grace the senatorial office, and who would like to occupy it, and who would make the attempt to win the honor if a square deal was in order. But they are not permitted to compete for the prize. The managers of the present Republican candidate are instructed to pay without limit; to bar out all competition. How do the Republicans to whom I am alluding—and I am glad to say that I know several of them personally—like this, and how does the rank and file of the party enjoy the pleasing spectacle? Not only does Mr. Stanford claim that he holds an iron-clad mortgage upon the party, but he goes further, and, through his ministers, declares that the lien has been foreclosed, and that the time of redemption has passed. Candidly, what remedy does the present situation afford? Is there any way out of it other than the election of a Democratic legislature?
>
> Everyone is aware that no Republican will be permitted to run for the legislature unless his case has been thoroughly diagnosed, his political pulse felt. Moreover, his professions of fealty "to the powers that be" must be unequivocal, and, strange to say, his morals are inquired into, but only for the purpose of finding out whether he will "stay bought"; for be it remembered that the policy of these senatorial managers begets slippery men. I know that there are powerful journalistic influences opposed to the "programme." I think that the leading independent Republican journals of the State do not approve of the perpetuation of the present dynasty; but, in their advocacy of the election of a Republican legislature, they are, without intending it, doubtless aiding in fastening upon the people the very bossism and political dishonesty which they so much deplore.
>
> The enterprising and progressive proprietor of the *Chronicle* [Republican Michael H. de Young], who is ten times more competent to be our United States Senator than

---

[18] *SF Argonaut*, Aug 18, 1890.   [19] Ibid., Sep 22, 1890.

the present Republican incumbent, and whose services clearly entitle him to the distinction—should his party be victorious—is naturally restive under the burden. Is it logical or right in any Republican to assist in the consummation of that which he believes to be a crime, merely because, if he acts otherwise, a Democrat will be elected?

Pause a moment, and hear the senatorial managers. In speaking of this campaign, they declare that expense cuts no figure. They say "we must have satisfactory legislative candidates, even if we salary them. We must have weak Democratic opponents, even if we have to pay them to be knocked down. We must exert ourselves to pull out strong candidates who are against us. We must buy the people to approve the purchase of our seat. We must hire the corrupt to chant our praises. We must threaten the cowardly that they may not tell the truth about us. We must prostitute the Republican organization which we falsely pretend to admire to consummate our scheme. We must appeal to party pride, that we may overcome individual self-respect, and when we succeed, we will laugh at the honest voter. We have cheated him for years, we will cheat him again. His bigotry will be strong enough to hold him to vote the ticket which we have prepared."

Let me ask whether the foregoing is not a true presentation of the actual inwardness of this contest? Is it not the unvarnished truth? The entire question may be thus presented: Do the voters of California approve of the buying of a senatorship? All who so approve will signify their assent by voting the Republican legislature ticket. All opposed, [sic] will support the Democratic ticket. The proposition is now in process of submission. The solution will be reached in November.

This modest effusion was signed by Stephen M. White and dated "Los Angeles, September 6, 1890."[20]

Pixley's editorial pages were not about to let White's innuendoes, charges of corruption, mistaken ideas, and lies go unchallenged:

If it is true that no other name than that of Leland Stanford is presented to the Republican caucus for nomination as senator, might not Mr. White concede that the other younger and ambitious men had renounced their candidacy out of respect to Governor Stanford's superior years and superior service in the ranks of their party?

White's column, the *Argonaut* charged, reeked of "libelous malevolence." Moreover,

if the Democratic party must have a leader, none is more worthy than Mr. White, of Los Angeles. Vituperative and malevolent demagogy we had not anticipated; slanderous, personal vilification against an abler, an older, and a better political opponent, in whose employ he had been and whose service he has but recently left, we could not have expected.[21]

The results of the 1890 election would show that the people of the state and their legislators agreed with the *Argonaut*'s interpretation of the character and motives of Governor Stanford. In a ringing endorsement of the man, the Pixley journal

---

[20]Ibid.   [21]Ibid.

insisted that the voters of California were faced in most cases with nothing other than the qualifications, experience, integrity, and general character of the candidates. Stanford had a track record inside and outside government for the voters to examine. The kind of senator he would be if reelected could be judged by his *past* service in the upper house. And his present absence from his seat in the Senate occurred because he was abroad seeking to improve his health; his pursuit also was for information that would be beneficial to his state and his country. Stanford had been visiting Germany, England, and other European states, the *Argonaut* said, to discover the best way to direct the course of the university he had founded by visiting their institutions of higher education.[22]

White's campaign of smear continued—a "disgraceful and bitter campaign" of "unkind, unjust, and scandalous" charges against Stanford.[23] At a meeting in Metropolitan Hall in San Francisco on the night of October 3, White attacked Stanford with charges of criminal acts in his election to the Senate six years earlier and in his bid for reelection now. The next morning the *Chronicle* carried a report of the meeting under the title:

STANFORD PILLORIED
Stephen M. White Acts as Torturer
A Vehement Denunciation of His Methods.[24]

White proclaimed at the meeting: "I know that there exists to-day in this city a sort of bureau where men hired by Stanford and acting as his agents are supplied with blank checks signed by him with which they buy men to run for the legislature, pledging them to return Stanford to the Senate." The speaker, warming to his own rhetoric, continued, saying there could be no doubt about the facts: men from his own county had told him how they had been sent for by the bureau, and how a certain amount of money had been offered them as campaign expenses, even more to aid them in living in Sacramento, if elected, during the sessions of the legislature, and still more for their reputations. One cannot help wondering on which bank these checks were drawn and why Stanford enemies never produced one—cancelled or otherwise—as evidence of these absurd charges.

White declared in conclusion that the open manner in which Stanford had bought his seat in the U.S. Senate six years earlier was the most infamous crime that ever disgraced the political annals of the state of California.

In response to White's praise of de Young—himself a Republican hopeful for a Senate seat—Ambrose Bierce made a contribution to the campaign literature that was probably the only thing he wrote that won Stanford's whole-hearted approval:

[22]Ibid., Sep 29, 1890.   [23]Ibid., Oct 20, 1890.
[24]*SF Chronicle*, Oct 4, 1890.

What! You a senator? You, Mike De Young?
Still reeking of the gutter whence you sprung?
Sir, if all senators were such as you—
Their hands so slender and so crimson, too,
So black their hearts, so lily-white their livers—
The toga's touch would give a man the shivers.[25]

STANFORD CAMPAIGNS FOR REELECTION TO THE U.S. SENATE

The Stanfords had left for Europe on May 28, 1890, but by the middle of October they were back home in San Francisco to campaign for reelection.[26] Steve Gage, as mentioned, had kept Stanford apprised of how things were going in California, while Edward Curtis, a lawyer-turned-journalist who worked for the Central Pacific and Southern Pacific Company, and Jerome A. Fillmore, general superintendent of the Southern Pacific, kept him abreast of railroad affairs.[27] In one letter Gage told Stanford that California had never before thought and commented so much about a man as it had the vacationing senator.[28] On the recent Huntington charges, Gage had this to say:

> The attack made upon you by Mr. H., his subsequent denial of his charges over his own signature, and his frequent re-itterations [sic] since of the original attack have been, and is, a topic more generally discussed than any I have ever known concerning men in California. But one opinion prevails concerning it; you have lost nothing in the respect and esteem of the people of the Coast. Your enemy will do all that he can to encompass your defeat. But I have no confidence in the success of the methods employed by him, and at this moment I have no fear of the ultimate result.[29]

Gage then quoted Nathan Weston Spaulding, assistant U.S. treasurer for San Francisco, a mutual friend who regularly came into contact with lumbermen—"most of whom are Republicans"—that among this group there was universal support for Stanford in the Huntington matter.[30] Gage went on to say that following a Huntington meeting with two powerful Republican senators, his (Huntington's) attitude on California politics changed—or at least his overt actions were redirected. Among these Republicans were James G. Blaine of Maine,[31] William M.

[25]Richard O'Connor, *Ambrose Bierce, A Biography* (Boston: LBC, 1967), 140.

[26]JLS to May Hopkins, Jul 4, 1890.

[27]Stephen Gage to LS, Jul 2, 1890; Curtis, *SF Call*, Feb 15, 1893; Fillmore, *SF Call*, Feb 28, 1902.

[28]Stephen Gage to LS, Jul 2, 1890.   [29]Ibid.

[30]Ibid. *SF Argonaut*, Mar 17, 1883, and *SF Call*, Jan 1, 1892. Spaulding was the inventor of removable teeth for large circular saws. Hittell, *Commerce and Industries of the Pacific Coast*, 424–425.

[31]James G. Blaine and family and the Stanfords had become personal friends as well as political allies, as evidenced by the fact that the Stanfords were invited to the wedding of Blaine's daughter, Margaret Isabella Blaine, to Walter Damrosch, on Sat., May 17, 1890. Wedding invitation in JLS papers.

Stewart and John P. Jones of Nevada, and John J. Ingalls of Kansas. Huntington told William H. Mills that he realized a Republican victory in the Senate was essential and that he would rather have Stanford out of the way in Washington than back in California as a defeated candidate![32]

Despite Gage's assurances, Stanford's campaign had not been progressing satisfactorily during the senator's absence. The newspapers had blown his feud with Huntington out of proportion and were telling the voters how even *Huntington* had conceded that Stanford's Senate seat had been purchased with railroad funds. Stephen White realized that if the Republicans captured the legislature no name other than Stanford's would be presented to the Republican caucus. Because of this, White barnstormed in favor of electing senators by convention rather than caucus—thus approximating a direct popular vote for United States senators, a measure that would not be ushered in until the Seventeenth Amendment to the U.S. Constitution was adopted in 1913.[33] As if these problems were not enough, a nationwide recession during Harrison's administration reflected on Republicans everywhere. Stanford was also saddled with the unpopular McKinley tariff, which was blamed for the high cost of living and which *he* had supported.

Fortunately, William Stow, who was managing Stanford's reelection campaign, recognized that there were obstacles in their path and that Stanford's reelection was not going to be automatic. For this reason he called the senator back from his European tour two weeks early.[34] The Stanfords cut their trip short and left England on October 1; they were in New York a week later and at home in San Francisco on the fifteenth of the month.[35]

Stow's role in all this is interesting in light of Frank Shay's later explanation of how the political affairs of the Central Pacific Railroad were managed: Shay said that when Judge Silas Sanderson was head of the railroad's legal department, political matters were not handled by that department; Huntington looked after political affairs in the East, and in the West Stanford appointed two "special agents" to look after them.[36] These were William Stow, a San Francisco attorney, and Stephen Gage. Gage handled things in Nevada, which required very little time, and then assisted Stow, the California "special agent."[37] Stow and Gage had both served in the California Assembly back in the early days, Stow as a Whig in the fifth and sixth sessions in 1854 and 1855 (he was Speaker of the Assembly in 1855, the year Nick Smith was in the assembly), and Gage in the seventh session, in 1856.

---

[32]Stephen Gage to LS, Jul 2, 1890. Mills was formerly the manager of the *Sac Record-Union* and afterwards long-time manager of the CPRR Land Office.   [33]*SF Wave*, Sep 13, 1890.

[34]*Wash. Post*, Nov 12, 1890.

[35]*Times* (of London), Oct 3, 1890; *NY Times*, Oct 9, 1890; *SF Argonaut*, Oct 20, 1890.

[36]Shay, "A Lifetime in California," 224.   [37]Ibid.

Meanwhile, there were several forces at work that could have cost Stanford votes in 1890. Anti-Stanford diatribes, such as that penned by Fred M. Campbell of Oakland, in which he detailed four pages of reasons why his (Campbell's) fellow Republicans should not vote for Stanford, probably had no effect on the members of the legislature, who still elected senators in those days.[38] But Stanford's health and consequent absences from the upper house certainly cast doubt on his being returned automatically to the U.S. Senate. Then there were the political machinations within the California legislature itself.

Once on the campaign trail, the Stanfords were welcomed by tumultuous crowds everywhere they went—in Sacramento, Stockton, Auburn, and Colfax.[39] In the state capital a public reception following a torchlight procession from the train was given in their honor.[40] It was characterized as a spontaneous, nonpolitical affair, but the presence of several Republican organizations gave away the event's real purpose. On the following day, October 15, this scene was repeated at Stockton, where it was reported that multitudes of all political hues turned out to see this "great, good, and wise man," this "true servant of the people," this "benefactor of his race."[41] In honor of the Stanfords' generosity toward education, the public schools were closed at 11:30 to give children an opportunity to see their benefactors.[42]

Stanford delivered a nonpartisan address to the crowd assembled in the huge pavilion and praised people of both parties for their patriotism and their consensus on most political principles; the parties differed on a few issues, most important of which was the tariff. He explained briefly that his protectionism was intended to induce people to engage in all classes of industry. At the close of the senator's speech the crowd burst forth with three hearty cheers, and the Stanfords boarded their train to move on, eventually touring all the way to San Diego.[43]

In an interview with a Washington reporter, Creed Haymond explained Stanford's popular reception during the campaign as follows:

> The candidacy of Senator Stanford for re-election lent intense interest to the campaign. With Mrs. Stanford and Tom Fitch he started in at San Francisco and canvassed the State from Chico to San Diego. It was like an old Roman triumph to some conquering general. The grandest ovations that ever the slope gave were tendered them. When Gen. Grant, who was very popular with our people, came to San Francisco the reception given him was on a big scale, but it didn't begin to equal the demonstration gotten up for Stanford, and all over the State it was the same way.[44]

---

[38]Fred M. Campbell, "Senator Stanford! To My Fellow Republicans of California." Oakland: Fred M. Campbell, Oct 16, 1890. Four-page broadside that inveighs against the reelection of LS to the U.S. Sen.

[39]*FLIN*, Nov 8, 1890. [40]*Sac Bee*, Oct 14 and 15, 1890.

[41]*Stockton Mail*, Oct 16, 1890. [42]Ibid., Oct 15, 1890.

[43]Ibid.

[44]*Wash. Post*, Nov 15, 1890.

It was an easy matter for Californians to choose between Stanford and his opposition; at the polls there was no doubt about the voters' choice. The immediate issue, of course, was control of the legislature. If the Republicans won this, Stanford was in. On election day the people not only voted in a Republican legislature—the Democrats captured only 20 percent of the seats—but, for the first time in nine years, chose a Republican governor. The heavy Republican victory was even more remarkable since the nation as a whole had gone the other way. When asked what made this lopsided victory possible, one California politician answered: "It was simply Stanford."[45]

Farmers of both parties had supported Stanford because of his land-loan bill; city workers and anti-Chinese labor groups supported him because of his stand on immigration. The Chinese immigration problem had hurt Stanford personally, culminating in his firing Chinese workers on a number of his farms in order to satisfy the public. His ideas on this sensitive issue had been solicited time and time again, especially after Huntington had come out against any kind of immigration restriction whatsoever.[46] Stanford preferred his own race, but he justified exclusion on other than racist grounds. Magnanimously, he conceded that the Chinese were a disturbing element in American society because the *laws* kept them from becoming citizens. On the ground that they were "sojourners," and not colonists, the senator felt that present restrictive legislation was sufficient.[47] He rejected the argument that their presence reduced the demand for white labor; now that the mines, the principal attraction for Chinese labor, had almost been depleted, they presented even less of a threat than ever.[48]

So far Stanford had said little that would win the support of the racists in the state and much that would offend them. Yet his support of restrictive legislation, his belief that the Chinese were racially inferior to Caucasians, and his opposition to all forms of integration bespoke a position that was at least *palatable* to most voters. He also made it clear that the amalgamation of Negroes and Caucasians was also out of the question.[49]

Stanford was praised for an exceptionally clean campaign. When circumstances might have justified mud-slinging in retaliation, "in no instance did he condescend to reply to the attacks that were made upon him," wrote the *Argonaut* editor.[50] If Stanford was confident that he had the respect and would receive the support of the people of California, his confidence was justified by the result of the election.

---

[45]Ibid., Nov 10, 1890.
[46]*SF Examiner,* Jan 7, 1889.
[47]Ibid., Jan 6, 1889.
[48]Ibid., Jan 8, 1889; *SF Call,* Apr 6, 1890.
[49]*SF Call,* Apr 6, 1890.
[50]*SF Argonaut,* Nov 17, 1890.

STANFORD'S REELECTION TO THE SENATE—JANUARY 14, 1891

White was right: the "solution" was reached in November, though it was not at all what he had hoped for or expected. On November 4, 1890, the sun shone on Republicans in California, while in the eastern states the party "met a most disastrous Waterloo."[51] But, matters concerning currency, revenue, and race wars were not the questions prominent on the Pacific Coast. According to the *Argonaut*, "They were deliberately retired into the background, and Governor Stanford was dragged prominently to the front, and around him and upon him seemed to centre the party fight."[52] The people of the state almost without distinction of party greeted and welcomed him everywhere. The result was *his* triumph and that of the entire state and its municipalities in favor of Republicans.

On January 14, 1891, the California legislature reelected Stanford by a vote of eighty-six to thirty, despite the fact that his fragile health continued to make it impossible for him to perform his duties with the energy they required. The vote demonstrated the legislature's satisfaction with Stanford as a senator *and* its affection for him.[53] His reelection was endorsed all over the country as a well-merited honor, as a tribute to the man who, more than any other in the state, deserved to be treated well by the people. Hardly anyone—aside from hardcore anti-railroad voices—suggested that money had been used to win his support in the legislature. Still, there can be no doubt that his continuing generosity toward the university and other philanthropies had much to do with his popularity and therefore his reelection.[54]

FIFTY-SECOND CONGRESS, FIRST SESSION— DECEMBER 7, 1891–AUGUST 5, 1892

On December 17, 1891, Stanford was appointed to Senate Committees on Education and Labor, Fisheries, and Naval Affairs.[55] Five days later he took the oath of office.[56] On that same day, December 22, 1891, Stanford introduced several bills. He reintroduced his bill (SB 1213) on cooperative associations, which was postponed ("went over without prejudice," to use the terminology of the Senate); it came up for discussion on April 9, 1892, when he was critically ill and absent from the Senate; thus this bill died once and for all.[57]

Also on December 22 he reintroduced Senate Bill 1204, his land loan bill, designed "to provide the Government with means sufficient to supply the national

---

[51]Ibid.   [52]Ibid.
[53]*SF Alta California*, Jan 14, 1891.
[54]*Wash. Post*, Jan 1, 1891; *Wash. National View*, Feb 7, 1891; *Phil. Record*, Jan 15, 1891; UNC, SFS 2:5.
[55]*USCR*, 52nd Cong., 1st Sess., 73 (Dec 17, 1891).   [56]Ibid., 88 (Dec 22, 1891).
[57]Ibid., 92 (Dec 22, 1891), 3412 (Apr 19, 1892).

It was simply Stanford.

"Senator Stanford returned from Europe, just four weeks ago today. He returned two weeks earlier than he intended on urgent telegrams that his presence was needed to save the State to his party. Well, he came and took hold of things with both hands. In ten hours after he was in the State the change could be noticed. The betting men, who had been putting up rather stiff odds in favor of the Democratic candidate, Pond, began hedging, and for the last two weeks there was not a dollar bet. It was all one way, and the people saw it.

"Stanford personally visited every place of importance in the State and talked to the people, not as political stumpers do, but he simply talked to them. Mrs. Stanford was with him and so was Tom Fitch, the old time Nevada orator. This was the entire outfit. The crowds this trio drew were never equaled in the history of California. The enthusiasm they created cannot be described. They kept going until 12 o'clock on the night before the election, starting out in the mountains and winding up in San Diego, which borders on Mexico. The vote shows that they carried everything with them, and not only elected the governor and the entire State ticket, but also an entire Republican delegation, and turned what was a Democratic into a Republican legislature by a four-fifth majority. This, in the face of the balance of the country going the other way, is a remarkable achievement. The farmers, Republican and Democratic, and all the granger and labor organizations, supported Stanford on account of his land loan mortgage bill. Stanford was not only stronger than his party, but he got the vote of the three parties that had tickets in the field.

"The people were determined that he should be returned to the Senate, and, to make it sure, elected a legislature 80 per cent Republican, while nearly half of the Democrats elected are also pledged to vote for him as Senator. The whole thing is so clear that nearly every man elected to an office in the State, which has gone Republican by over 10,000, has written or will write him thanking him for putting them through. Another thing about it is that Stanford never said or insinuated a mean thing or an unpleasant thing about any man or party during his tour, and never made what could be called a strict partisan speech during the whole time."*

*Wash. Post, Nov 10, 1890.

want of a sound circulating medium."[58] Stanford asked that the bill be allowed to lie on the table until he called it up for future consideration.

Stanford did this on January 21, 1892.[59] This was the same bill (at that time SB 4528) presented by Stanford earlier that had been reacted to adversely by the Committee of Finance on February 17, 1891.[60] This time he fought for it more strongly inside as well as outside of Congress. He began by accusing the committee—which had twice killed his bills—of not having considered the economic principles underlying them. Rather, it had relied on superficial comparisons of his system and those that had failed in other countries . . . because of insufficient security.[61]

---

[58]Ibid., 92 (Dec 22, 1891).

[60]SR 2267, 51st Cong., 2nd Sess., 1–6 (Feb 17, 1891).

[59]Ibid., 468–471 (Jan 21, 1892).

[61]USCR, 52nd Cong., 1st Sess., 468 (Jan 21, 1892).

The major difference between Stanford and the members of the finance commit-tee was that they believed that paper currency would inevitably depreciate, whereas he was convinced that paper money was just as substantial as coined money.[62] But his scheme sounded too much like the Populists' "potato bank" plan for traditional specie advocates to accept; it was a plan that in itself was designed to favor one par-ticular class of people—the farmers. Stanford emphatically denied this. He insisted that his only goal was to increase the nation's circulating currency, a goal accepted by a considerable portion of the Democratic party and perennial third parties, though it was very unpopular in his own. He stressed that farmers as a class would benefit from his measure, but not at the expense of other groups or the economy as a whole. If the farmers of his state *alone* could "energize" one-half the value of their lands at a nominal rate of interest, a large amount of money would be placed in circulation—money that would develop the industries of the country as a whole.

Stanford had been told that a legal-tender dollar was not worth as much as a specie dollar, so on February 29, 1892, he introduced Senate Bill 2397, a bill designed to determine the value of legal-tender currency. The Senate voted to table his mea-sure.[63]

This bill was followed almost immediately—on March 4, 1892—by another Stanford bill (SB 2468), calling for the coining of silver bullion.[64]

On March 30, 1892, Stanford delivered his last Senate speech. He opened his remarks by reviewing his bill (SB 2397), which defined the dollar as having as a stan-dard a content of 25.8 grains of gold, whether "the stamp of the Government making the dollar be on gold, silver, paper, or any other material."[65] He then added that to understand the bill on the value of the legal-tender dollar, one must consider its ideas together with those contained in his bills 1204 (the land-loan measure) and 2468 (the silver-bullion bill). He read that portion of his silver-bullion bill, which directed that all legal tender, made so by the stamp of the government, be accepted at par for all debts public and private.[66] To avoid the rush of speculators buying silver that had followed the passage of the Sherman Silver Purchase Act, Stanford's bill did *not* provide that the government had to exchange one kind of currency for another: all would be accepted at par. At the end of this speech, which was one of Stanford's best, he concluded that since the government did not by law allow any political agency to create money, it owed it to the people to create an adequate supply.[67]

In the *San Francisco Argonaut* Frank Pixley gave all of Stanford's money bills his editorial endorsement, but a number of midwestern editors saw the land-loan

[62]Ibid., 469 (Jan 21, 1892); LS to *Stockton Mail*, Feb 18, 1892.

[63]*USCR*, 52nd Cong., 1st Sess., 1535 (Feb 29, 1892).   [64]Ibid., 1713 (Mar 4, 1892).

[65]Ibid., 2684 (Mar 30, 1892).   [66]Ibid., 2686.

[67]Ibid., 2684.

measure as nothing more than a crazy fiat (creation of money by government decree) scheme.[68] They described its author as "a success as a railroad operator but a dreadful failure as a statesman."[69] Some people thought the plan for increasing the currency proposed by this "most sagacious financier in the Senate" was a practical solution to the nation's financial problems; others believed it constituted an outright rejection of American capitalism, and showed that he was "fully impregnated with socialistic ideas."[70] Others felt that Stanford's plan demonstrated his "broad statesmanship" and lack of self-interest, while others suspected that his own interests would profit more than they should, since railroads might qualify for low-interest, long-term loans secured by government land grants.[71] A San Francisco editor objected that in case of widespread default on loans and foreclosure by the federal government, the tax burden of the entire state would fall upon those landowners whose property was *not* in default.[72]

Unfortunately the California senator failed to recognize the strength of the widespread aversion to fiat currency. He reiterated his theme that legal money was entirely the creation of the law. He actually preferred paper money to specie, pointing out that gold was hardly ever seen east of the Rockies and all the silver available, even if minted, would have been but a "drop in the bucket" of currency needed.[73] Paper money based upon unimpeachable security was what the country needed. When a "gold bug" senator objected even to the use of silver, which he called a "debased" coin, Stanford met him on the practical level; drawing from his pocket a silver dollar, he challenged his colleague: "You say that this dollar piece is only worth eighty-five cents, do you? Well, sir, I will give you ninety-nine and a half cents each for a hundred thousand of them."[74] The gold enthusiast was silenced.

Another incident further confirmed the senator's position: when he tried to pay for his lunch in the nation's capital with a gold coin, it was twice refused. Returning to the Senate, he told the story to some gold supporters and wanted an explanation. When told that the gold coin was not legal tender, he replied: "That's it exactly. It's the stamp that makes money and not the materials of which the money is composed."[75] This kind of argument silenced the opposition, but it converted no one to the senator's cause.[76]

---

[68]On this, see George Macesich, *Political Economy of Money: emerging fiat monetary regime* (London: Praeger, 1999), passim.   [69]*SF Argonaut*, Mar 23, 1891; *Chicago Tribune*, Jan 20, 1891.

[70]*Petaluma Argus*, Mar 15, 1890; UNC, SFS 1:10.

[71]UNC, SFS 10:3. The first vol. of the SFS contains scores of eds. on this issue; *USCR*, 52nd Cong., 1st Sess., 470 (Jan 21, 1892).   [72]*SF Chronicle*, Dec 30, 1890.

[73]*Wash. Post*, Apr 27, 1893.   [74]*St. Louis Journal of Agriculture*, quoted in UNC, SFS 10:7.

[75]*Phoenix Herald*, n.d., 1891, in SFS 2:45.

[76]To get his theories on money in print for distribution, an inter. was arranged with LS at the PASF. It was pub. anonymously as a 42-p. pam. titled *The Great Question, An Interview with Senator Stanford on Money*. In LS papers.

STANFORD'S PRESIDENTIAL "BOOM" OF 1891–1892

If Stanford's bruited candidacy for the presidency in 1888 seems incredible, his second presidential boom, as the Populist candidate in 1892, must appear one of the all-time political absurdities. It is true that this movement never got off the ground, but that it could even have been launched—or conceived of, for that matter—is significant. For some Farmers' Alliance men to give serious consideration to having the wealthiest man in the Senate as the candidate for a party whose motto was "down with the money power" was indeed incredible. Yet it happened. Stanford's money bill was too much for some of them to resist. Stanford's name was mentioned as a Populist candidate, and so the Populist convention that year in fact cast one vote for Stanford.[77] It is clear that Stanford's financial plans alone prompted this interest. But a similarity of views on one financial measure could not—by any stretch of the imagination—induce Stanford to support the radical doctrines of the Populists. Some of these doctrines he would have condemned as un-American or communistic: direct election of senators, government ownership of railroads and utilities, and a graduated income tax, to name a few.[78] In the summer of 1891 he stated explicitly that he was not a candidate for the presidency.[79]

But some of Stanford's enthusiastic supporters would not take no for an answer. They did not always make it clear for *which* party's nomination they were endorsing him, however. The election of 1888 was hardly over when his boosters began touting him as the presidential candidate in four years. His nomination in 1892, an Idaho journalist wrote, "would brand the American people as being the greatest discriminators of human excellence on earth."[80] The *Stockton Mail* wanted him as the People's Party candidate and insisted that if one went over the country with a "moral garden rake" he would not find a man better qualified for the position.[81] The editors of the *Argonaut* and the *San Francisco Argus* also favored Stanford as the Farmer's Alliance candidate; with him running on the People's (Populist) Party ticket, which they expected the Alliance men to support—the party would sweep the country from Maine to Texas.[82] He was undoubtedly the "coming man," and one enthusiastic journalist listed a number of Stanford supporters: thirteen prominent governors, senators, other high-ranking public officials, and a number of outstanding businessmen who supported Stanford for the presidency.[83] An editor in Pennsylvania gave Stanford one of the strongest endorsements for president ever to appear in print.[84]

[77]George Harmon Knoles, *The Presidential Campaign and Election of 1892*. LSJU Pubs., University Series. *History, Economics, and Political Science*, Vol. V, No. 1. (Stanford: SUP, 1942), 106 and 108.

[78]*Wash. National View*, Jan 1891, SFS 2:6.   [79]LS to Col. Joseph K. Rickey, Jul 1, 1891, in *SF Examiner*, Jul 22, 1891.

[80]*Idaho Citizen*, Oct 25, 1889.   [81]*Stockton Mail*, Nov 3, 1891.

[82]*SF Argonaut*, Mar 16, 1891, and *SF City Argus*, in Vol. 2 of SFS. This vol. contains scores of newspaper clippings nationwide endorsing LS as the Alliance candidate.

[83]*SF City Argus*, various issues, 1891, in SFS 2:89 and 131, 17:76–77, and 19:10.

[84]*Lewisburg* [Penn.] *News*, Jul 26, 1890.

125. Leland Stanford is "Popular with all Classes for the Presidency."
San Francisco City Argus.

126. The Presidential Circus. *Author's Collection.*

127. The Pacific Coast's favorite for the presidency. *Author's Collection.*

Rumors were heard from Alliance people all over the country that Stanford was to be their presidential nominee. The *New York Sun* described a Farmers' Alliance movement "in Washington and throughout the country looking to the nomination of Senator Leland Stanford for President."[85] The *Grand Rapids Press* wrote that Stanford "at this hour appears to be approaching the White House with triumphal millions of workingmen from farm and factory."[86]

An Alliance meeting in Florida discussed Stanford's candidacy. In spite of his own indifference, Stanford clubs—organized groups of supporters—began springing up all over the West; California people, it was said, were all behind him, as were many from the Mississippi Valley, silver people from the West, and farmers from the Pacific Northwest.[87] If the Alliance men endorsed him, they believed, they could elect him president!

Unlike 1888, when Stanford's candidacy as a Republican might have been feasible, in the 1891 boom there developed considerable opposition; most people recognized the ridiculousness of the whole affair. The influential *New York Times* shrugged off the Alliance plan as a luxury that an active mind and a deep purse could afford. This was patently untrue; there is no evidence that Stanford himself had anything to

---

[85]Quoted in the *SF Argonaut*, Mar 16, 1891.   [86]Ibid.
[87]UNC, Dec 1890, in LS papers.

do with the candidacy boom.[88] Most out-of-state people knew very little about Stanford other than that he was a millionaire. This in itself, however, rendered him dishonest or crazed with ambition. One journalist suggested that if the Alliance men wanted a "bloated monopolist" they should go *all* the way and get Jay Gould.[89] Another judged Stanford entirely on his railroad connections and depicted him as the "embodiment of greed," having pockets that bulged with money belonging to the government.[90] It was ironic that this kind of criticism should come after a number of his railroad connections had been weakened and after he had given the bulk of his fortune to Stanford University.

Another critic, claiming more knowledge of Stanford's political dealings than did his most astute critics in California, called Stanford a hypocrite for befriending farmers just to get their votes.[91] But the criticism of the Stanford boom that made the most sense was heard the least often—that it was based upon too narrow a political affinity with the Alliance doctrines. The San José [California] Grange opposed him and his financial schemes, as did a number of farmers from the Northwest.[92]

128. The people's choice in 1892.
San Francisco City Argus, *February 13, 1892.*

In 1892, owing to the number of powerful Republican favorites in the field, it seemed a good time to bring out a dark horse such as Leland Stanford.[93] When interviewed about his candidacy in March 1892, Stanford told a reporter, "I am not lying awake nights thinking about a Presidential nomination."[94]

In fact, Stanford paid little attention to this talk of his presidential candidacy. He at least recognized it for what it was—a form of tribute by his friends and admirers

---

[88] *NY Times,* Dec 10, 1891.   [89] *Omaha Bee,* Jan 25, 1891.

[90] *Atlanta Journal,* Jan 23, 1891.

[91] *Omaha Herald,* Jan 18, 1891; *Albany Evening Journal,* Jan 25, 1887.

[92] SJ Grange meeting, May 17, 1890, reported in UNC, SFS 1:38; *Northwest Pacific Farmer,* n.d., 1890, in SFS 1:49.

[93] Knoles, *Presidential Campaign and Election of 1892,* 40–41.

[94] *NY Herald,* Mar 6, 1892.

and the daydream of a handful of Alliance men who wanted a winning candidate at any cost.

The ailing senator sat out the 1892 presidential campaign, unable even to contribute much to Harrison's cause. He no longer believed that the tariff was the paramount issue, as in 1888. The nation was compelled to have a revenue tariff, so for all practical purposes the protective tariff men won. Politically, Stanford said, the only question was whether the Democrats or Republicans would control the government.

FIFTY-SECOND CONGRESS, SECOND SESSION— DECEMBER 5, 1892–MARCH 3, 1893

FIFTY-THIRD CONGRESS, SPECIAL SESSION OF THE SENATE— MARCH 4–APRIL 15, 1893

Ill health continued to plague Senator Stanford, and he was unable to leave San Francisco for Washington until February 7, 1893.[95] Mrs. Stanford, in a letter to Tim and May Hopkins, noted that he attended the Senate on March 1, when the *Congressional Record* found it noteworthy to report, "Leland Stanford, a Senator from the State of California appeared in his seat today."[96] His last appearance in the Senate was five days later, on March 6.[97] Thus his active Senate career ended just a little more than three months before his death, which was announced by his political colleague and adversary Stephen M. White in the Senate on August 7, 1893.[98]

EVALUATION OF LELAND STANFORD AS A U.S. SENATOR

One man seldom exhibits the qualities found in Stanford—for *any* undertaking. He had political experience—far more than many of the senators serving with him—and though not a brilliant man, his intellectual development was as great as that of most of his colleagues; and certainly no one would have denied that he was one of the foremost business managers in the upper house. In short, he had the material out of which statesmen are made: education, experience, political astuteness, a good business sense, integrity, and the respect and trust of his constituents and colleagues.

Stanford performed creditably as a senator, considering the condition of his health for the eight years he served, but it must be said that he was neither an outstanding legislator nor a great orator, and he authored no great legislation. Stanford

---

[95]*SF Argonaut*, Feb 13, 1893.   [96]JLS to DSJ, Mar 2, 1893; *USCR*, 52nd Cong., 2nd Sess., 2314 (Mar 1, 1893).
[97]*USCR*, 53rd Cong., Spec. Sess., 4 (Mar 6, 1893).   [98]Ibid., 53rd Cong., 1st Sess., 16 (Aug 7, 1893).

loved to give speeches, as he had often done during his business and political careers. Yet owing in part to his frequent and lengthy absences, due mostly to ill health and extended European tours in search of health, he addressed the Senate during his eight years there fewer than two dozen times.

It is impossible to determine with any degree of accuracy Stanford's attendance record in the Senate. For one thing, roll calls are reported only sporadically. Often a senator would come into chambers late, after a morning roll call had listed him as absent, though he was actually present and took part in Senate business that day. Nor is the voting record a sure mark of presence or absence. Almost the only sure indication or presence other than answering to a roll call was casting a ballot. If a senator abstained, the record simply reports "not voting." And if a man were paired with someone else he

LELAND STANFORD

was sworn in as a United States senator from California on March 4, 1885, and took his seat in the Forty-ninth Congress on the same day.

First Term

Forty-ninth Congress:
    Special Session, March 4–April 2, 1885.
    First Session, December 7, 1885–August 5, 1886.
    Second Session, December 6, 1886–March 3, 1887.
Fiftieth Congress:
    First Session, December 5, 1887,–October 20, 1888.
    Second Session, December 3, 1888–March 3, 1889.
Fifty-first Congress:
    Special Session, March 4–April 2, 1889.
    First Session, December 2, 1889–October 1, 1890.
    Second Session, December 1, 1890–March 2, 1891.

Second Term

Fifty-second Congress:
    First Session, December 7, 1891–August 5, 1892.
    Second Session, December 5, 1892–March 3, 1893.
Fifty-third Congress:
    Special Session, March 4–April 15, 1893.

Stanford served in the Senate until his death on the night of June 20/21, 1893.

would abstain even though occupying his seat at the time the vote was taken. Thus voting meant "present," but not voting did not mean "absent." A perusal of the *Congressional Record* for every day of the years Stanford served in the Senate shows the impossibility of tracking down his or any other senator's attendance record.

We do know the dates of Stanford's foreign travels, and he was away (absent) for extended periods of time. Occasionally, records of his movements show him to have been elsewhere when the Senate was in session, but these incidents are totally inadequate to determine what his attendance record was.

No aspect of Stanford's Senate career received more widespread publicity than his money bills; they were discussed from one end of the country to the other. Reactions ranged from the warmest praise and talk of electing him president to questions about his sanity.

Stanford served on a number of committees, among them Manufactures, Civil Service, Education and Labor, Fisheries, Naval Affairs, Public Buildings and

Grounds, and Epidemic Diseases.[99] Until his health kept him from attending, he spent a respectable amount of time on the floor of the Senate: he was, indeed, a senator in fact as well as name, but if the Governor had looked to his Senate career for securing his place in posterity few people today would ever have heard of him.

During his Senate tenure, Stanford created and then helped manage Stanford University; he continued to contribute to his philanthropies; and he presented bills and voted on measures that won him the commendation of both parties in his state. He became a sort of political senior citizen; one hesitates to say senior statesman. Most Californians were more than satisfied with Stanford's Senate career, and this, after all, is what *really* counted. Several of his votes showed that he was not an obsequious partisan, and his occasional stand against bills favorable to railroads showed that he was unwilling to favor legislation that was not good for the nation as a whole, regardless of his own—or his Associates'—economic interests. When a railroad attorney reproached him for voting against a certain railroad bill, he replied, good-naturedly: "Oh, I forgot all about the fact that I was interested in railroads; I'll do better next time."[100] But he did not.

Perhaps no higher compliment could be paid Stanford as a public official than that of Sen. William M. Stewart of Nevada: "Every suggestion he made, every speech he delivered, and every bill he introduced had for its object the good of all the people."[101] Nothing more could be expected of any public servant.

---

[99]Ibid., 49th Cong., Spec. Sess., 37 (Mar 13, 1885); 1st Sess., 3098 (Dec 18, 1885).

[100]Related by John B. McCarthy, Sen. sec. of LS, in Military Order of the Loyal Legion of the United States, Circular 38, Nov 29, 1904; see "Senator Stanford, Generous Deeds Told About by His Private Secretary," by the Wash. corres. of the *Troy Times*, repr. in *SF Call*, Jul 3, 1893.

[101]*Memorial Addresses on the Life and Character of Leland Stanford*, 61.

CHAPTER 24

SOCIAL LIFE AND TRAVELS
DURING THE SENATE YEARS
1885–1893

The Stanfords Entertained in a Regal Manner[1]

Mrs. Stanford's calling list never numbered less than one thousand names in Washington.
— Bertha Berner[2]

[Governor Stanford] is now absent from his seat in the Senate in pursuit not of pleasure but of health in a foreign country. He is in pursuit of information . . . , visiting Germany, England, and other European states with a view to the study of their institutions of learning, for the purpose which will best carry out his generous views in reference to the Leland Stanford Jr. University.
— San Francisco Argonaut[3]

THE STANFORDS' SOCIAL LIFE IN CALIFORNIA BETWEEN THE SPECIAL SESSION AND THE FIRST SESSION OF THE FORTY-NINTH CONGRESS—APRIL 2–DECEMBER 7, 1885

The 1885 special session of Congress ended after only a month, on April 2, 1885, and two nights later the Stanfords stayed at the Windsor House in New York.[4] Two weeks afterward they were home in California.[5]

In his later years, as the Governor gradually withdrew from railroad affairs, the Palo Alto home became his haven; upon returning from European travels or senatorial duties in Washington, he would hurry down to the farm and spend as much time there as business would allow.[6]

While living in Washington the Stanfords continued to maintain their primary residence in California, though once in the Senate it was difficult to separate their social life from their political life.

---

[1]BB, *Mrs. Leland Stanford*, 82. [2]Ibid. [3]*SF Argonaut*, Sep 29, 1890.
[4]Ibid., May 2, 1885. [5]Ibid., May 16, 1885. [6]*SF Examiner*, Jun 22, 1893.

On September 15, 1885, the Stanfords entertained a number of political and business associates in their beautiful Sacramento home.[7] This was the first time that guests had been invited to the Sacramento mansion since President Hayes and his party visited five years earlier.[8] The guest list included Gen. Francis Amasa Walker, president of the Massachusetts Institute of Technology; Congressman William Walter Phelps of New Jersey; Steve Gage of the Central Pacific Railroad; San Francisco socialite Maj. Jared Lawrence Rathbone,[9] and Edward Curtis, another San Francisco social figure, who in 1880 had published a sketch of the life of Stanford.[10]

As a public official Stanford's outings were usually social and political, as in the fall of 1885 when he visited the small country town of what was then called Salinas City, guest of Jesse Carr, president of the State Agricultural Society.[11] Stanford never lost his love for small country towns and small town people.

The "Senator Stanfords," as Leland and Jane were dubbed at the time, also enjoyed the luxurious Hotel del Monte at Monterey, the favorite watering hole of the elite of San Francisco society. In October 1885 they were among the most honored guests there, along with their friends Timothy and May Hopkins, Maj. Jared Rathbone, and others.[12] But nothing seemed to please Stanford more in his social relations than a spectacular luncheon or dinner at the San Francisco house, as on November 14, 1885, when he entertained a party of thirty gentlemen at lunch, including twenty-four newly appointed trustees of Stanford University on the occasion of the board's first meeting.[13]

SOCIAL LIFE IN CALIFORNIA BETWEEN THE FIRST AND SECOND SESSIONS OF THE FIRTY-NINTH CONGRESS— AUGUST 5–DECEMBER 6, 1886

Following the long session of the Forty-ninth Congress the Stanfords immediately took up their position in California society. They arrived in Sacramento on their way home on Sunday, August 15, 1886, and gave an elegant dinner party the next day at their residence on California Street in San Francisco in honor of Gen. and Mrs. John Alexander Logan, a stalwart Republican Senate colleague from Illinois, and Republican governor Russell Alexander Alger from Michigan and his daughter. These celebrities were joined by friends of the Stanfords and all were entertained at the Palo Alto farm on the following Thursday.[14]

---

[7]*Sac Bee*, Sep 16, 1885; *SF Argonaut*, Sep 19, 1885.   [8]Ibid.

[9]Rathbone was a staunch D, later appointed by Pres. Cleveland to be U.S. consul to Paris, *SF Argonaut,* May 21, 1887; *SF City Argus*, undated Christmas No., 1892; SFOSB, 1894–1895, 92, 146, 329, 346, and 358; and obit., *SF Examiner*, May 3, 1907.   [10]Curtis, *Two California Sketches: William Watt and Leland Stanford*.

[11]*SF Argonaut*, Oct 17, 1885.   [12]Ibid.

[13]Ibid., Nov 21, 1885. This was in conjunction with the founding of LSJU, but the *Argonaut* says nothing about the occasion.   [14]Ibid., Aug 21, 1886.

In September Jane Stanford suffered from one of her many "mild attacks" of malaria and spent a week on the farm recuperating.[15] On Tuesday, September 14, she was well enough to give what was described as an "elegant and elaborate" dinner at the Palo Alto Farm for ex-Sen. and Mrs. James Arkell of New York, along with their daughters Larette and Bestelle, Charles Graham of *Harper's Weekly*, Henry James Ten Eyck of the *Albany Journal*, William J. Arkell of *The Judge*, Congressman George West of Saratoga, New York, James H. Manning of the *Albany Argus*, Ariel Lathrop, Frederick Law Olmstead, Edward Curtis, and many others. The following evening the Stanfords opened their picture gallery at the San Francisco mansion for the entertainment of the Arkell party.[16]

The Stanfords also attended many charity balls, among them an event given for the benefit of the Silver Kindergartens and the Children's Hospital on September 23, 1886. Among the great crowd of high society people who turned out for this event were Mr. and Mrs. Charles Crocker, Mr. and Mrs. Collis Huntington, Miss Lizzie Hull, and Mr. Joseph D. Grant.[17] The Stanfords, Crockers, and Huntingtons each gave checks of five hundred dollars: the proceeds exceeded the manager's greatest expectations.

THE WEDDING OF LIZZIE HULL AND JOSEPH GRANT— NOVEMBER 4, 1886

As the children of the Stanford's friends reached marriageable age, Sen. and Mrs. Leland Stanford were regular guests at weddings among the city's social elite, such as that celebrated on Tuesday, October 5, 1886, at the First Congregational Church on Post Street, when Jennie Whittier, daughter of Mr. W. Frank Whittier of the firm Whittier, Fuller & Co., and Henry E. Botlin, a member of the firm of Botlin, Dallemand & Company, were married.[18]

But no social event of 1886 could have meant as much to the Stanfords as the uniting in marriage of two families long numbered among their closest friends, when Lizzie Hull and Joseph Grant were married, on November 4.[19] With Leland, Jr., now gone, Lizzie must have seemed even more like a daughter to them than she had before. And young Grant, as will be seen later, was a very close friend, owing to the Stanfords' relationship to his father.

The Stanfords received one of the 1,500 engraved invitations:

---

[15]Ibid., Sep 4, 1886.   [16]Ibid., Sep 18, 1886.

[17]Ibid., Sep 25, 1886. Silver Kindergartens is a reference to the SF Silver St. Kindergarten School, the first free school of its kind founded west of the Rocky Mountains. It was founded in 1878. *SF Alta California*, Aug 8, 1881. A new Silver St. Kindergarten Soc. was established in 1882 with Hattie Crocker as pres. *SF Call*, Apr 9, 1882.

[18]*SF Argonaut*, Oct 9, 1886.

[19]Ibid., Nov 6, 1886.

Mr. Edward Hull
requests the honor of your presence
at the marriage ceremony
of his daughter,
Lizzie,
and
Mr. Joseph Donohoe Grant,
on Thursday morning, November the fourth,
Eighteen hundred and eighty-six,
at half-past eleven o'clock,
Trinity Church

The bride was the daughter of Edward Hull and the groom the son of Adam Grant, both business tycoons—Hull in Sacramento and Grant in San Francisco.[20] Prosperity had brought them all to San Francisco, where Adam Grant was now a partner in the firm of Murphy, Grant & Co. and Edward Hull was semiretired, though in 1888 he was still in business with his son Edward V. Hull in St. Louis and listed there as a San Francisco resident.[21]

Twenty-eight-year-old Joseph Grant was born on March 28, 1858, in San Francisco and received his education at the University of California and Harvard.[22] He was the only son of Adam and Emma Grant. The twenty-four-year-old bride was born in Sacramento on August 10, 1862, one of three children.[23]

The society and gossip columns of the San Francisco press had been silent on the engagement of this pair and on their upcoming wedding until almost the day it took place, despite the fact, as the *San Francisco Call* reported, that it had "been looked forward to by society for some time."[24]

One San Francisco editor described the wedding as the most outstanding social event of the week.[25] Another wrote:

> The wedding excited more general interest than has occurred in several months. The contracting couple being well known and both general favorites in the social circles in which they move. The bride is a brunette of pronounced height who has only been in society for a short time. It will be remembered that she made her debut in society at a reception given by Senator and Mrs. Leland Stanford just before they left for

---

[20]LS at 56–58 K St., and Hull at 184 J, both in Sac, and Adam Grant in SF, first at Jansen & Co. at the corner of Jackson and Sansome, then at Eugene Kelly & Co., along with Daniel T. Murphy, Thomas Breeze, and John Deane, and, finally, as a partner in Murphy, Grant & Co., at the NE corner of Bush and Sansome.

[21]Edward V. Hull, pres., National Hardwood Co., res., St. Louis; Edward Hull, vice pres., res. SF, *SLCD* (St. Louis: GDC, 1888), 622. Lizzie's other brother, Thomas H. B. Hull, unknown in the Lizzie literature until we are told that he lived in Phil. at the time of their father's death (from father's will, *SF Call*, Nov 1, 1893).

[22]Joseph Donohoe Grant, *Redwoods and Reminiscences. "The World went very well then." A Chronicle of Traffics and Excursions, of Work and Play, of Ups and Downs, During More Than Half a Century Happily Spent in California and Elsewhere* (SF: SRL & MT, 1973), ix. *SF Argonaut*, Nov 6, 1886. Grant did not graduate from UC. Robert Sibley, ed., *The Golden Book of California* (Berkeley: CAA, 1937), 426.   [23]According to SF's Trinity Church burial records; *SF Chronicle*, Aug 11, 1889.

[24]*SF Call*, Nov 9, 1886.   [25]*SF Examiner*, Nov 11, 1886.

THE LIZZIE HULL AND JOSEPH DONOHOE GRANT
wedding reception guest list reads like a roll call of the political, financial, and business and rail-
road luminaries, among them Fred and Jennie Crocker,[a] George and Phoebe Hearst, Mr. and
Mrs. Joseph D. Redding, Gen. and Mrs. William Henry Linnow Barnes,[b] Mr. and Mrs. John Par-
rott, Jr., Baron and Baroness [John Henry] von Schroeder, Mr. and Mrs. Alban Towne, Mr. and
Mrs. William T. Coleman, Judge and Mrs. [John H.] Hunt, Jr., Mr. and Mrs. Russell J. Wilson,
Mr. and Mrs. Joseph A. Donohoe, Mr. and Mrs. Louis Sloss, Mr. and Mrs. Alfred Tubbs, Mrs.
James Otis, Ellen Colton, Florence Atherton, Edgar Mills, James L. Flood, Col. George Gray,
Judge and Mrs. Lorenzo Sawyer, Ward McAllister—and Sen. and Mrs. Leland Stanford.[c]

[a]Jennie Crocker, who was just two years older than Lizzie, died in childbirth less than four months later, on
Feb 25, 1887, *SF Chronicle*, Feb 28, 1887; *SF Call*, Feb 28, 1887, lists the pallbearers. LS was in Washington serving in the Senate at the time of her death.

[b]Rocq, *California Local History*, 527, has "Linnow;" Altrocchi, *Spectacular San Franciscans*, 377, has "Living-
stone."

[c]*SF Chronicle*, Nov 9, 1886; the von Schroeders were long-time residents of SF and major property holders.
Baroness von Schroeder was Mary Ellen Donahue, daughter of Peter and Anna Downey Donahue. Peter Donahue was one of the originators of the idea of illuminating SF streets with the use of gas. On the von Schroeders,
see *SF Call*, Nov 29, 1883; *SF Examiner*, Dec 11, 1925; *SF Chronicle*, Nov 11, 1927; (Mrs.) Yda Addis Storke, *A Memorial and Biographical History of Santa Barbara, San Luis Obispo and Ventura, California* (Chicago: LPC, 1891), 479–480;
CDI. On Judge Hunt, see *SFCD*, 1886, 637.

their European tour. She is the daughter of Edward Hull, a capitalist of San Francisco.
The groom is the son of Adam Grant who has been identified with the commercial
interests of this coast for over a quarter of a century.[26]

The *Chronicle* editor continued his flowery description of the festivities, as follows:

The bridal gifts occupied one of the largest rooms of the house on the second floor, and
in point of value, variety, and elegance, and good taste, have never been excelled in this
city, the value reaching far above $30,000. . . . The gift of Mr. Grant to the bride was a
pendant of 9 diamonds. . . . Among Mrs. Grant's gifts were some rare and valuable
pearls, while Mr. Hull's gift to his daughter was a check for $10,000. A set of diamond
earrings valued at $5,000 was a gift from Joseph Donohoe [the groom's uncle].[27]

After the wedding the newlyweds boarded a train for a three-month visit in the
East on the first leg of an extended honeymoon trip throughout Europe. It was
reported the following August that they had returned to New York and rejoiced in
the "possession of a son."[28] Baby Douglas Grant was born on August 7, 1887, in Irv-
ington-on-Hudson, New York.[29] By the end of October the three Grants were at
home in San Francisco, where they took up residence in the Adam and Emma Grant
family home at 1112 Bush Street.[30]

---

[26]*SF Chronicle*, Nov 9, 1886.   [27]Ibid.   [28]*SF Argonaut*, Aug 20, 1887.
[29]Inter. with Doreen Herburger at the Mountain View Cemetery, Oakland, Calif., May 5, 1998, on Douglass
Grant burial records; *SF Chronicle*, Mar 19, 1966.   [30]*SF Argonaut*, Oct 22, 1887.

THE STANFORDS AT HOME IN CALIFORNIA BETWEEN
THE SECOND SESSION OF THE FORTY-NINTH CONGRESS AND
THE FIRST SESSION OF THE FIFTIETH CONGRESS—
MARCH 3–DECEMBER 5, 1887

The Stanfords spent a few days in New York City following the close of the Forty-ninth Congress and arrived home in California on Monday, March 21, 1887, in time to help minister to Jane's convalescent sister, Anna Maria, who had been suffering from a prolonged illness.[31]

Jane Stanford gave a spectacular lunch party at the California Street residence on Friday of that week in honor of Mrs. Sen. William Mahone and daughter Otelia, who had been her guests since they arrived in San Francisco. Fourteen of Jane's society friends—described as "mature and young"—were invited. Jane provided her guests with a splendid repast in the dining room:

> The artistically decorated table, in the midst of the beautiful surroundings, was laid with covers for seventeen, and attracted the most favorable comment. An épergne of gold was the center piece, and in it was a collection of white peach, almond, and wild plum blossoms, and at either side, in smaller épergnes, were meadow oats, tulips, white lilacs, and adiantum, tastefully arranged. Delicate blossoms of varied colors were seen in the solid silver vases near by, and there were sprays of ferns and dainty pansies distributed here and there with charming effect.[32]

After the luncheon, another hour was spent inspecting the paintings, statuary, and other treasures in the art gallery.

Among those enjoying this luncheon were Mrs. Alfred L. Tubbs, Mrs. Henry L. Dodge, Mrs. James Carolan, Mrs. Richard Porter Ashe, Mrs. William Ashburner, Mrs. James F. Houghton, Mrs. Frank M. Pixley, and the Misses Otelia Mahone, Gertie Stanford, Jennie Flood, Eva Carolan, Nettie Tubbs, Millie Ashe, Bettie Ashe, and Minnie Houghton.[33]

The society columns were full of charity functions attended by Jane Stanford, such as one in aid of the Pioneer Kindergarten held at Platt's Hall in San Francisco on Monday evening, April 25.[34] But nothing pleased Jane as much as her own soirées at the San Francisco mansion, such as the elegant dinner party she gave on April 12, 1887, in honor of Hattie Crocker and her fiancé, Charles Beatty Alexander of New York. Their parents and other family members attended, as did several close family friends, among them Charles and Mary Crocker, Anna Lathrop, and Herbert Nash.[35]

The following night the proud father of the bride gave a stag party at the Pacific Club. Everyone who was anyone in their professional circle was there, including

[31]Ibid., Mar 12 and 26, 1887.
[32]Ibid., Apr 9, 1887.
[33]Ibid.
[34]Ibid., Apr 16, 1887.
[35]Ibid.

the groom, the groom's father, Henry Martyn Alexander, as well as Leland Stanford, Samuel M. Wilson, Russell J. Wilson, Lorenzo Sawyer, Hall McAllister, Creed Haymond, and Lloyd Tevis, to name but a few.[36]

The wedding of Miss Harriet Valentine Crocker—known to her friends as "Hattie"—and Mr. Charles B. Alexander took place on Tuesday, April 26, 1887, at San Francisco's Grace Church. Pixley's paper said that no San Francisco social event in years had attracted as much attention as this wedding. It was talked about for weeks and the most elaborate preparations were made for its celebration.[37]

The wedding gifts were extravagant. Charles Crocker presented the newlyweds with a house and lot at No. 4 West Fifty-eighth Street in New York City, valued at $400,000. Sen. and Mrs. Leland Stanford—almost an uncle and aunt to Hattie— gave the bride a magnificent set of jewelry, said to have cost $50,000.[38] Among the other presents were a gold jewel-case, enameled in blue and hand-painted, and three massive pieces of silver beautifully ornamented with a decorative grapevine—gifts of Mrs. Mark Hopkins.[39]

Another major wedding, reflecting the constant involvement of the Stanfords in San Francisco society, was that of Jennie Filkins and William B. Tubbs on May 11, 1887, at St. Luke's Church on Van Ness Avenue. The bride was the daughter of Mrs. Emily L. Filkins (widow of Judge Charles E. Filkins) of Marysville;[40] the groom was the son of Mr. and Mrs. Alfred L. Tubbs. Alfred Tubbs was the proprietor of a rope and cordage works in South San Francisco and long-time resident of San Francisco. About five hundred invitations were issued to friends on the Pacific Coast and in the East. The wedding guests included the Stanfords, the Charles G. and Robert C. Hookers, and the Adam Grants.[41]

Stanford, Fred Crocker—whose wife Jennie had died barely three months earlier—and Alban Towne spent several days in May in Los Angeles on railroad business.[42] The summer of 1887 was, as always, a time of business, local travel, and

---

[36]Ibid.   [37]Ibid., Apr 30, 1887.

[38]Ibid. The bracelet alone contained a ruby, topaz, emerald, purple sapphire, an Indian topaz, a spinel ruby, jardoon, hidenite from Virginia, purple sapphire, blue spinel, and jacinth. The necklace contained the same stones as the bracelet, except that there was a yellow sapphire in the center, five purple sapphires, four rubies, and one rose topaz. There was a set of earrings made of a jardoon and set in diamonds; superb ruby and a turmaline were also contained in this precious casket. Each stone was numbered, and a small book, delicately bound in white parchment, described the jewels and where they were found.

[39]Ibid. The *Argonaut* account continues: "The bride was born in Sacramento, and most of her life has been passed in this State, except when she went to Geneva in 1870 for educational advantages, and four other visits subsequently to Europe, and one of which was extended to a tour of the world. She is greatly endeared to all who know her, and has the esteem of many others who respect her for her goodness of heart, her charm of manner, and her manifold charitable deeds. The groom is the son of Mr. H. M. Alexander of New York City, and is a member of the law firm Alexander & Green. He is recognized as one of the most able barristers in the Eastern metropolis, and is well liked by all of his associates."

[40]Mary Robertson, lib. tech., John Q. Packard Lib. of YC, to author, May 7, 1998; *Yuba County Cemetery Book*, 1894–1895, 22; *Marysville Appeal*, Jan 18, 1901.   [41]*SF Argonaut*, May 14, 1887.

[42]Ibid., May 28, 1887.

spectacular parties. On August 3, 1887, the Stanfords demonstrated how generous they could be by turning over the San Francisco mansion to Dr. and Mrs. John P. Newman, who were in town from Washington, D.C., and wanted to receive a number of their friends. The spacious parlors on the first floor were brilliantly illuminated and thrown open for the reception of the guests. The beautiful frescoes and other magnificent works of art that adorned the hall and salons created an incredible atmosphere.[43]

The Newmans and the Stanfords joined in greeting the guests as they arrived. They were entertained by professional musicians and singers. Following this, a light meal was served at half past nine, and at eleven the party wound down as appreciative guests made their way home.[44]

A few weeks later, on September 1, 1887, Judge Lorenzo Sawyer gave an elaborate dinner party at his 734 Sutter Street residence in honor of U.S. Supreme Court Associate Justice Stephen Field.[45] (Back in 1880, Field had been mentioned as a possible candidate for the presidency, and Leland Stanford was quoted as having said that Field would have been the strongest candidate the Democrats could run to win the California vote.[46]) The Sawyer party was described as one of "much enjoyment to the guests," among whom were many of Sawyer's long-time friends, including Leland Stanford and Judge Ogden Hoffman.[47]

On September 6, 1887, a large dinner party was given in honor of Justice Field at the home of Attorney Samuel M. Wilson at 711 Pine Street—the house the Stanfords had rented while theirs was under construction.[48] Among the crowd of political and business dignitaries were Wilson, Field, Russell J. Wilson, Judge Sawyer, Judge George M. Sabin, Hall McAllister, Creed Haymond, John R. Jarboe, Col. Joseph P. Hoge, Judge Selden S. Wright, William Matthews, Col. John P. Irish, Sen. William Stewart, Judge Lewis D. McKisick, Senator Stanford, George E. Whitney, Robert V. Hayne, and Judge John Garber.

A combination business-politics trip to Oregon and Washington Territory was made by the Stanfords in late September; they were joined by Fred Crocker and Alban Towne and a few other business associates and personal friends.[49] The Stanfords afterward continued on to a fair in Stockton.[50]

One of the memorable social events of 1887 was an elaborate banquet in honor of the Stanfords given by the trustees of Stanford University at San Francisco's Palace Hotel on October 25. First, a formal reception was held in the second-floor parlors; at seven o'clock everyone adjourned to the children's dining room at the floor's west end. In the center was a "bounteously provided table set with elegant ware and deco-

[43]Ibid., Aug 6, 1887.

[45]Ibid., Sep 3, 1887; *SFCD*, 1890, 1162.

[47]*SF Argonaut*, Sep 3, 1887.

[49]*SF Argonaut*, Sep 24, 1887.

[44]Ibid.

[46]*SF Chronicle*, May 17, 1880.

[48]Ibid., Sep 10, 1887; *SFCD*, 1890, 1378.

[50]Ibid., Oct 1, 1887.

rated with trophies of the culinary art, masses of bright flowers, and luscious fruit interwoven with scarfs [*sic*] of fanciful colors."[51] The five chandeliers were embellished with begonias and ferns, and the mantel was adorned with chrysanthemums and silk draperies. Each lady and gentleman received either a corsage or a boutonnière. Several hours were devoted to table talk, after which a complimentary address was read and presented to Mrs. Stanford by the trustees and their wives.

JAPANESE PLENIPOTENTIARY JUSANUMI R. KUKI was honored by a large feast given by Leland Stanford. The illuminati of both California and national politics and business were present, among them Gov. Robert W. Waterman, Adm. George Eugene Belknap, Gen. Oliver Otis Howard, Charles Crocker, John W. Mackay, James C. Flood, Sen. James G. Fair, Sen. William Stewart, Sen. John Jones, Senator George Hearst, Charles N. Felton, William W. Morrow, San Francisco Mayor Edward B. Pond, Judge Lorenzo Sawyer, Judge Thomas McFarland, Gov. Frederick Low, Samuel M. Wilson, Creed Haymond, and William T. Coleman.*

**SF Argonaut, Nov 12, 1887.*

One of the most elaborate affairs to take place at the Stanford mansion was a dinner party which Senator Stanford gave on Tuesday evening, November 3, 1887, in honor of Jusanumi R. Kuki, the Japanese minister plenipotentiary. Twenty-eight guests assembled in the elegantly appointed dining room at half past six.[52] The broad table was set with a wealth of gold and silver service, combined with exquisitely cut glassware, rare Sèvres china, and beautiful floral arrangements. This spectacular decoration, characteristic of the empire of the Mikado, honored the minister and several officers of the Japanese man-of-war *Tsukuba* who were present. From the array of blossoms arose a massive épergne of gold and silver, ornamented with artistically molded figures. Each one of these held small bamboo staffs, which bore the national colors of America and Japan.

Following the three-hour dinner there was general conversation in the drawing rooms for another hour.

SENATOR STANFORD'S POOR HEALTH: HIS FOURTH (JANE'S THIRD) EUROPEAN TOUR—MAY 29 TO OCTOBER 19, 1888

Despite the illnesses that plagued Stanford in the winter and spring of 1888 while they were in Washington, in January he and his wife took the time to give a party for their long-time friend Julia Grant, President Grant's widow, who was visiting from New York.[53] Several United States government officials and military and naval officers were present. Shortly afterward, on February 29, the Stanfords left Washing-

---

[51]Ibid., Oct 29, 1887.   [52]Ibid., Nov 12, 1887.
[53]Ibid., Jan 28, 1888. Two years later it was said of Julia Grant that she seemed to have found the elixir of youth. Although age sixty-six in 1890, she was as agile as a woman of thirty and still enjoyed perfect health, ibid., Jul 7, 1890.

ton for the more salubrious winter climate of Florida.[54] But this did nothing, for in early May Jane suffered from another bout with "malarial fever."[55]

From 1888 on, the senator's health declined steadily. In May of that year, Leland and Jane were both advised to take another cure at Bad Kissingen. Subsequently, it was reported: "Senator and Mrs. Leland Stanford have left New York for Liverpool, en route to the Carlsbad Springs in Bohemia, where Mrs. Stanford, who is in ill-health, will test the efficacy of the medicinal waters."[56] The Stanfords sailed on the Guion Line's 6,392-ton *Alaska*—the largest ship to date they had sailed on—on May 29, in the middle of the long (first) session of the Fiftieth Congress.[57] The *Alaska* was built to carry half cargo and half passengers, but Berner writes that all of the passenger accommodations were reserved for the Stanford party.[58] Bertha Berner's description of the *Alaska* as a "slow steamer" is misleading, since this ship had won the Atlantic Blue Ribbon in April 1882 for crossing the Atlantic in a record seven days, six hours, and forty-three minutes at an average speed of 16.10 knots.[59]

This trip began just a few months after the Stanfords laid the cornerstone for the university; they followed the progress of its construction throughout the trip. This European tour is the best-documented of their five trips together owing to the copious correspondence sent and received about the building of the university.

The *Alaska* failed to make the usual stop at Queenstown owing to heavy fog and steamed into Liverpool at noon on June 6, 1888, their eighth day out.[60] When the Stanfords arrived in London, U.S. Marine captain Otway C. Berryman, the European agent of the Southern Pacific and the Pacific Improvement Company and Stanford's long-time friend, met their steamer with a private tug and helped the Stanford entourage move quickly through customs and into the private railroad car of Baron Edmond Rothschild, another Stanford friend, who had been made peer of the realm in 1885.[61] The Stanfords checked into the centrally-located Bristol Hotel, today's Holiday Inn Mayfair.[62] For longer stays they used Claridge's, about half a mile away.[63]

[54]Ibid., Mar 3, 1888.   [55]Ibid., May 2, 1888.   [56]Ibid., May 30, 1888.

[57]Ibid., reported that the Stanfords had left NY for Liverpool, but did not give the exact date of departure; BB, *Mrs. Stanford*, 62, later said that they had sailed on the *Alaska*, and the *NY Times* of May 29, 1888, reports the sailing of the *Alaska* on that date. On the *Alaska*, see Smith, *Passenger Ships of the World*, 3. On their date of return, the *Argonaut* of Oct 22, 1888, reported that Sen. and Mrs. LS had arrived in NY, but did not specify the date of their arrival.

[58]BB, *Mrs. Stanford*, 62–81.   [59]Ibid., 62; Smith, *Passenger Ships of the World*, 3.

[60]*Times* (of London), Jun 7, 1888. BB is wrong in describing this as a ten-day trip, *Mrs. Stanford*, 62.

[61]On Oct 9, 1879, Miss Zalie Watson, daughter of the late Com. Watson, married Marine Lt. Otway Berryman, *SF Argonaut*, Oct 18, 1879; see also the issue of Aug 30, 1879; JLS later described Berryman as the agent and insurance broker of the India Office [presumably of the SPC]. She sent TNH Berryman's home add., 27 Leadenhall St., London E.C., tel. no. 4306. JLS to May Hopkins, Oct 5, 1892. BB, *Mrs. Stanford*, 63–64; *Register of the Commissioned and Warrant Officers of the Navy of the United States, and the Marine Corps, to Jan 1, 1893* (Wash.: GPO, 1893), 122.

[62]David Melrose, gen. manager, Holiday Inn, Garden Court, London, to the author, Jun 19, 2000, gives add. as Garden Court. In a letter to Tim and May Hopkins, on Jun 10, 1892, JLS gives the name as Bristol at Burlington Gardens.

[63]BB, *Mrs. Stanford*, 64.

While in London, Stanford took care of business involving the Southern Pacific Company and the Pacific Improvement Company, attended to some shipments of wine from Vina, and shopped with his wife for art treasures. He purchased a copy of an expensive Bartolomé Esteban Murillo painting and a number of items for the university, especially the museum, among them two old watches to add to the collection begun by Leland Junior.[64]

The purpose of the trip had been the thermal cure, but Stanford's health had improved so he did not go directly to Bad Kissingen; instead, the party made an extended tour of the continent. Neither Leland nor Jane was seriously ill at the time so they enjoyed some of the most tranquil and pleasant moments of their lives since young Leland's death. They were honored everywhere they went.

Following a brief stay in Paris, they moved on to the Grand Hotel in Metz, on the border of France and Germany. There two German officers invited the Stanford party on a personally conducted tour of the fortifications and on the way out, the party was given a military escort. The officers had been told in advance of the Stanfords' impending visit, and were thus able to make arrangements to guarantee them a comfortable stay.[65] The only chronology of this part of the trip we have is Berner's, which contains many errors, so one *must* check her against other sources. She has the Stanfords inconvenienced at Metz because of the arrival of news of the death of Kaiser William I, who in fact had died on March 9, even before the Stanfords had left home.[66] If we assume that she confused the death of Wilhelm I with that of his successor, Kaiser Frederick III, which occurred on June 15, then the Stanfords most likely arrived in Metz from Paris on June 15.[67]

Metz proved to be a virtual military camp. The Stanfords toured the city briefly, but were happy to leave its depressing martial atmosphere. The next morning they moved on to Frankfurt-am-Main. They enjoyed a leisurely drive around the city and then admired the beautiful scenery on the journey from Frankfurt to Bad Kissingen—about a hundred miles—where they arrived the next afternoon.[68]

Once ensconced at Kissingen, the party enjoyed a Sunday afternoon listening to music in the Kurpark, directly opposite their hotel. Since it was a Sunday, it must have been June 17, 1888. Later, the Stanfords were invited to visit the home and garden of Prince Bismarck, a man said to have been very much admired by Stanford.[69]

After an extended stay of six weeks at the springs, Stanford was 20 pounds lighter—though still pressing about 240—but weak; doctors recommended the

---

[64]Ibid., 62–63.   [65]Ibid., 64–65.

[66]Ibid., 65; Smith, *The Century Encyclopedia of Names*, 1063.

[67]Smith, *The Century Encyclopedia of Names*, 410; BB, *Mrs. Stanford*, 64–65.

[68]BB, *Mrs. Stanford*, 66–67. Here BB remarks that on the way from Frankfurt and shortly before arriving in Bad Kissingen, they passed through Augsburg. This is entirely impossible, since Augsburg is about 150 miles south of the line of travel from Frankfurt to Kissengen.   [69]Ibid., 67–68.

"aftercure" at St. Moritz. They took a train to Nuremberg, about a hundred miles southeast of Kissingen. There the Stanfords bought four tile stoves to be placed in the country house in California.[70] (This was the only order the Stanfords ever placed in Europe that was not filled: the stoves never arrived in California.)

After three days in Nuremberg, the Stanford party traveled to Munich. The city was decorated for an International Art Exhibition commemorating (belatedly by two years) the centennial of the birth of King Ludwig I of Bavaria (August 25, 1786–February 29, 1868).[71] According to Bertha Berner's account, the Stanford apartment was located on Maximilian Strasse, opposite the royal residence, where from their balcony they could see from time to time many of the crowned heads of Europe and the men who would someday wear crowns of royalty.[72]

The high point of the festivities celebrating Ludwig's centennial took place on July 29, 30, and 31, 1888.[73] During the last week of festivities, while enjoying the colorful sights of a parade of artists and floats, the Stanfords witnessed a stampede of elephants that occurred on July 31. The elephants were not part of the plan for the festivities, but at the last minute the Circus Hagenbeck, under director Carl Hagenbeck, an internationally known and respected animal trainer and handler, joined the procession with his elephants.[74] Hagenbeck described his elephants as being as peaceful as sheep when they first joined the procession. A steam-driven locomotive outfitted as a "dragon" moved aside to allow the elephants to pass. When it started prematurely, spraying the animals with steam, they panicked and ran amok, as did members of the crowd, which terrified the animals even more. The resulting catastrophe caused scores of injuries and at least two deaths.[75] Later accounts revised this to as high as four.

One of the best, most balanced descriptions of the stampede, removed a century from the errors, passions, and hysteria of contemporary newspaper accounts, was published in 1986 by Munich attorney Otto Gritschneder.[76] An eye-witness report of the calamity was written in 1935 by Bertha Berner, who described the artists' exhibition and the parade in some detail, but, unlike others, her narration includes the following account of how [she thought] the Stanfords witnessed it:

---

[70]Ibid., 71–72.

[71]The festivities had been postponed owing to the fact that just a few weeks before they would have been celebrated in 1886, King Ludwig II had been found dead in the Starnberger See. Two years later a splendid celebration was planned to make up for the earlier plans that had been abandoned. The explanation for the delay is given in Otto Gritschneder, *Weitere Randbemerkungen* (München: OG, 1986), Chap 5, "1888: Elefanten in der Ludwigstraße Festzug zum 100. Geburtstag Ludwigs I," 44–58. See also, *Die Centenar—Feier der Geburt des König Ludwigs I. Von Bayern. Program der Festlichkeiten während der Tage vom 29–31. Juli 1888 in München. Nach Mittheilungen der Festausschüsse im Auftrage des Central-Comité's herausgegeben von Preßausschusse*. From the collection of Wolfgang Hasselmann, with an intro. by Richard Bauer. Repr., Munich: SV, 1986. Also, Ludwig Hollweck, *In München vor hundert Jahren* (München: MV, 1988).

[72]BB, *Mrs. Stanford*, 72.   [73]Gritschneder, "Elefanten in der Ludwigstraße," 45.   [74]Ibid., 46–47.

[75]Ibid., 52–56 for the police report; see also the complete records in the Munich City Archives, cited in the *Münchner Fremdenblatt*, Aug 2, 1888.   [76]Gritschneder, "Elefanten in der Ludwigstraße," 44–58.

At the top of the avenue, before the royal residence opposite our rooms, a turn was made, and when the elephants came opposite the fiery dragon they took fright and stampeded. It was horrible. They dashed into the crowd and threw their riders, two of whom were killed. They trampled three people to death. Pandemonium ruled. At once the high stepladders resting against the lantern posts were knocked down. In front of our windows were two of these lantern posts. On top of our posts, that is, on the two stepladders that reached their tops, sat grandmothers, holding babies, large lunch baskets, and huge colored umbrellas; the other members of the family were draped about the stepladders. These ladders were now knocked over, and the family fell on the people below. The father, in a desire to avenge this injury to his family, began to fight, grabbed the large umbrella, and began to slash about, hitting innocent, unsuspecting people and precipitating a terrible fight. The elephants tore about among the crowd. The royal personages opposite were down in the streets lending aid. Mattresses were lowered from the front windows for the injured.

Our floor was a mezzanine, with low windows. On seeing the terrible catastrophe about to occur, Mr. Stanford leaned away out to warn the people. He leaned so far out that Mrs. Stanford and I caught him by the coat to hold him, but his coat was very loose after the cure and we fell back with the coat in our hands, the Governor still leaning out in his shirtsleeves shouting to the people. I now caught him by the vest and Mrs. Stanford by the belt and we held him.[77]

Writers of Munich history and newspaper journalists have never forgotten this event. In fact, it has grown with the telling. A London newspaper set the number of seriously injured at twenty, with the number of slight injuries much higher.[78] The *official* number of injured people was set at forty-two, but forty-four were counted by another witness.[79] A century later, a 1988 newspaper article reviewing the famous stampede reported that the eight elephants injured *thousands* of people.[80]

As fate would have it, the owner of the elephants, Georges Actingstoll, was an American.[81]

The day after the stampede, if we accept Berner's account, the Stanford party left Munich, apparently on August 1. They went by train as far as Chur, near the Swiss border, where carriages and an experienced mountaineer were waiting for them. Apparently they stayed in Chur that night, for the next night (August 2), they stayed in a small hotel in Albenau, near the Albula Pass, now the site of a golf course.[82]

Berner then relates that they left the *next* day (August 3) and passed through a snowstorm, which is common enough in that area, on the way to St. Moritz, which they reach on *July* 4. Berner's chronology is definitely wrong here. If they arrived in

[77]BB, *Mrs. Stanford*, 74.

[78]*NY Times*, Aug 1, 1888; *London Daily News*, quoted in the *NY Times*, Aug 17, 1888; *NY Herald*, Aug 15, 1888; *Times* (of London), Aug 1, 1888.

[79]*Münchner Fremdenblatt*, Aug 2, 1888; *Münchner Neueste Nachrichten*, Aug 2 and Sep 1, 1888.

[80][Munich] *Süddeutsche Zeitung*, Jul 30/31, 1988.   [81]Gritschneder, "Elefanten in der Ludwigstraße," 56.

[82]Inter. with Helmut Kuen, owner and manager of La Staila Hotel, Silvaplana, Dec 15, 1999.

Bad Kissingen in the middle of June, and then spent six weeks there before traveling on to Nuremberg for three days and then to Munich and back to Switzerland, it is impossible that they could have been in St. Moritz on July 4. Add to this the fact that the elephant stampede occurred on Tuesday, July 31, 1888, making it impossible for them to have arrived in St. Moritz on July 4 *after* leaving the stampede behind in Munich.[83]

Jane's single surviving letter home during this trip provides a better chronological record. Wherever they were on August 16, it was *there* that they would have received news of the death of Charles Crocker, and it turned out that on August 17, Jane wrote to May Hopkins from the Grand Hotel des Bains (Kurhaus) in St. Moritz acknowledging receipt of the news of Crocker's death.[84] (A picture of this hotel, which burned to the ground in 1944, is in Peter Böckli's *Bis zum Tod der Gräfin*; on its site now stands the St. Moritz Post Office.[85])

Bertha Berner relates that Mrs. Stanford was not happy in St. Moritz. The "Kur Arzt" was unsympathetic, and besides burdening Stanford with his diagnosis of the senator's many ailments, he added to Jane's concern with her own state of health. Tiring of the doctor's unwelcome advice and the behavior of her two servants— the valet complained of having a tapeworm and the maid was sure she was about to be struck with apoplexy—Mrs. Stanford "took the bull by the horns." She "muffled the Governor in furs" and gave the order that they were leaving.[86]

Hôtel-Kursaal de la Maloja (Later Known as the Maloja Palace Hotel) and Encina Hall

As the Stanford party made its way to the next major stopping place—Bellagio, on Lake Como—the Stanford coach would have taken the flat road from St. Moritz southwestward toward Lake Como on its seventy-one-mile journey. On the way they would have skirted on their left four lakes one after another—Lake Sankt Moritz (Sankt Moritzer See), Lake Champfèr (Champfèrer See), Lake Silvaplana (Silverplaner See) and Lake Sils (Silser See or Séi, also known locally as Lake Maloja).[87]

After a pleasant drive of less than eleven miles, at the end of Lake Sils Stanford was delighted when he caught sight of the Hôtel-Kursaal de la Maloja (later known

---

[83]Imtraud Stockinger, Leiterin der Monacensia Bibliothek, Munich, to the author, Nov 16, 1999.

[84]They had been expecting this unpleasant news since they last visited him in NY. JLS to May Hopkins, Aug 17, 1888. CC had never fully recovered from injuries sustained from being thrown from his carriage two years earlier in NY. He died at the Hotel del Monte on Aug 14, 1888.

[85]Peter Böckli, *Bis zum Tod der Gräfin: Das Drama um den Hotelpalast des Grafen de Renesse in Maloja* (Zürich: NZZ 1998), 19–20; inter. with Helmut Kuen, Dec 15, 1999.   [86]BB, *Mrs. Stanford*, 75.

[87]Many people in the Engadine speak Romansch. For this reason, in that region one often sees the Romansch names of these four lakes: Lei da San Murezzan, Lei da Champfèr, Lei da Silvaplauna, and Lei da Segl.

as the Maloja Palace). He told Jane that the architecture of this building was exactly
what he had in mind for the boys' dorm at Stanford.

Below is Bertha Berner's firsthand account of the scene:

> As we were nearing the lake, in the midst of a glorious landscape, Mr. Stanford
> said: "I may see the boys' hall built after all." Then he remarked: "I do believe down
> there by the lake I see a hotel very much on the order of the building I have pictured
> in my mind as a suitable one for the boys' dormitory. We must examine it closely."
>
> On reaching the hotel Mr. Stanford asked for the director, explaining his reason
> for wishing to look over the building, and we made a very thorough tour of inspec-
> tion. Mr. Stanford was most favorably impressed and dictated a letter to the architect
> at home, enclosing a pencil drawing of the plan of the building, on the margin of
> which he wrote many suggestions.[88]

Berner purchased two colored picture postcards of the hotel and later had them
framed and presented to the men of Encina Hall.[89] Over the years, the postcards
and the identity of the Encina prototype were lost to the Stanford community.

Thus it was the Hôtel-Kursaal de la Maloja/Maloja Palace that Stanford gazed
upon in approaching Maloja that inspired the design of Encina Hall.[90] Berner had
described the hotel—without naming it—as "relatively new."[91] In fact, it had
opened just four years before, on July 1, 1884.[92]

Encina Hall, the building inspired by the Maloja structure, was a massive stone
building that housed more than three hundred people, including male students and
unmarried male instructors, and, toward the end of its career as a dormitory, even
female students. It was completed in the summer of 1891.[93] Encina was closed as a

---

[88]BB, *Mrs. Stanford*, 76. Mr. J. F. Walther-Denz was the director from 1885 to 1900, Böckli, *Bis zum Tod der Gräfin*, 197.

[89]*Encina* is Span. for "evergreen oak." It is translated from the Latin *Quercus agrifolia* as "live oak," and is generally known as the Calif. or coast live oak, to distinguish it from the *Quercus virginianna*, "live oak or southern live oak," which grows from Virginia to Florida and Mexico. Liberty Hyde Bailey and Ethel Zoe Bailey, comps., *Hortus Third, A Concise Dictionary of Plants Cultivated in the United States and Canada* (NY: MacPC, 1976,c1934), 513–514; Elbert L. Little, *The Audubon Society Field Guide to North American Trees. Western Region* (2 vols., NY: AAK, 1980), 391–393, Plate 175.

[90]Helmut Kuen to the author, Jan 28, 1999. For the hist. of the name "Maloja," see Victor Attinger, ed., *Dictionnaire Historique & Biographique de la Suisse* (Neuchtel: ADHBS, 1928), IV, 647. The name Silvaplana is traced to the Silva family, found in the area as early as the twelfth cent., and to a plain located on the border of Lake Silvaplana. Attinger, ed., *Dictionnaire Historique & Biographique de la Suisse*, 1932, VI, 490–491.   [91]BB, *Mrs. Stanford*, 76.

[92]Böckli, *Bis zum Tod der Gräfin*, 11; the orig. name of the hotel was *Société anonyme de l'Hôtel Kursaal de la Maloja*, 151. The foreword to this book (p. 7) opens with a line that describes perfectly the experience of LS as he gazed upon the hotel for the first time: "Auf der Fahrt von St. Moritz ins Bergell stösst der Blick in einer Kurve vor Maloja auf ein übergrosses, quer in der Talsohle stehendes Gebäude—das Maloja Palace." (On the trip from St. Moritz within the little mountain, in a bend in the road before Maloja, one catches a glimpse of a huge building across the bottom of the valley—the Maloja Palace.) This book contains several pictures of the hotel. Author inter. with Peter Böckli, the writer, Feb 9, 1999; author inter. with Helmut Kuen, Feb 9, 1999.

[93]Completion, DSJ, *Days of a Man*, I, 384–385; men instructors, Elliott, *Stanford University, the First Twenty-five Years*, 175. A dorm. for women had been planned as a duplicate of Encina. By Apr 1891 the basement had been excavated and cut stone was ready for the masons, but the building could not be completed for at least another year. JLS decided that if women had to be admitted at all, they ought to be admitted at the same time as men, so work on the build- *(continued)*

BERTHA BERNER

made several errors in her telling of the above-men-
tioned events. Perhaps she was writing from memory
rather than notes. According to *her* account, as the Stanford entourage descended to Lake Silvaplana from St.
Moritz, and reached milder weather, Stanford's health
showed a decided improvement. This is either an exaggeration or a lapse in memory, since Silvaplana is only
three miles southwest of St. Moritz, the difference in
altitude a scant twenty-three feet.[a] She also confused
the lakes Silvaplana and Sils and the villages of Silvaplana and Maloja. Moreover, Stanford did not look
"down there by the lake," to see the hotel, for the road is
perfectly level.[b]

[a]Inter. with Peter Hansen, summer manager, Hotel Maloja
Palace, Feb 19, 1999. The altitude at St. Moritz, which lies on the
west shore of Lake Saint Moritz, is 5,978 feet (1,822 meters); that
at Silvaplana is 5,955 feet (1,815 meters). From lake to lake, one
actually climbs 96 feet to reach Lake Silvaplana, since the altitude
at Lake St. Moritz is 5,869 (1,789 meters). Berner also errs in
referring to Lake *Silver* Plana. *Mrs. Stanford*, 76.

[b]Writers who have accepted Berner's account uncritically have
now repeated her mistakes for more than a century, e.g., DSJ,
Days of a Man, I, 373; Elliott, *Stanford University*, 37; Paul V. Turner
and Marcia E. Vetrocq, *The Founders and the Architects, the Design of
Stanford University* (Stanford: SDA, 1976), 45; Allen, *Stanford, 25;*
Stanford Publications Service, *Stanford. A man, a woman, and a University* (Stanford: PSEH, 1962), 43.

men's dormitory on January 3, 1956,
and from September 1956 until the
spring of 1957 served as a women's
dorm, until one hundred women students who had been housed there for six
months moved into their new residence
at Florence Moore Hall.[94] After extensive remodeling, Encina was converted
into an administrative office building in
1959.[95] The Maloja Palace closed its
doors to hotel guests in 1934 and it, too,
has served as an administrative building.
Now, owned by a Belgian company, it
serves as a Roman Catholic boys' summer "colony."[96]

Having satisfied himself with his
sketches of what would soon become
the new men's dormitory at the university, Stanford and his party had
lunch and then hurried on their way.
From Maloja to Lake Como there is
about a 1,600-meter drop in altitude,
almost a mile. This descent may have
brought the improvement in Stanford's
health Berner had mentioned. At Lake
Como they caught a boat to Bellagio, where apartments had been reserved for them
at the Hotel Grand Bretagne.[97] At Lake Como on August 25 Jane Stanford celebrated
her sixtieth birthday. Leaving the town of Bellagio with great reluctance, but many
fond memories, the peripatetic couple and retinue next traveled to Milan and afterward spent ten days at Pallanza on Lake Maggiore.

In addition to Bertha Berner's narrative, there were numerous newspaper
reports of the Stanfords' activities in Europe. For example, a news note published
in the *Argonaut* (also chronologically inaccurate) reported, "Among the Californians who passed July and August at St. Moritz, in the Alps, were Senator and Mrs.
Leland Stanford."[98]

(*continued*) -ing was suspended, and in May a concrete structure about a third the size of Encina was begun. Construction was rushed and the building was ready by opening day, ibid., 177. Thus in 1956 the women got their Encina.

[94]*SQ,* 1955, 80, and 1957, 283; *SDM,* Sep 21 and 24, 1956, Jan 10, 1958.

[95] "Encina Hall History and Description," Univ. Architect and Planning Off., 7.

[96]Inter. with Peter Böckli, author of *Bis zum Tod der Gräfin*, Mar 5, 1999.

[97]BB, *Mrs Stanford*, 78.   [98]*SF Argonaut*, Sep 3, 1888.

129. L'Hôtel Kursaal de la Maloja, Switzerland, 1888, later known as
the Maloja Palace (Stanford's model for Encina Hall).
Peter Böckli, Bis zum Tod der Gräfin.

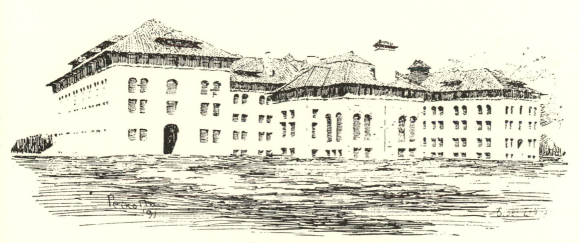

MEN'S DORMITORY

130. Encina Hall. *Overland Monthly, 1891.*

Home Again in California

The Stanfords had planned to return home sometime in October 1888.[99] Their trip from Liverpool to New York and then home was reported in San Francisco in early October.[100] On October 10 the Stanford party steamed out of Liverpool on the White Star Line's *Britannic*, the same ship that had carried them home in December of 1881.[101] Nine days later, on October 19, they arrived in New York.[102] They checked into their apartment at the Windsor Hotel that same day.[103] On the evening of October 21, Senator Stanford hosted a business meeting in his hotel quarters.[104] The Stanfords left for California a few days later.[105]

Once home in California, on Wednesday, November 21, 1888, the Stanfords "threw open their California Street mansion to their many friends." It was intended as an informal reception, to which merely a general invitation had been extended, and the informality made it all the more pleasant.[106]

In December of 1888 Stanford joined other Republicans in celebrating their recent victory at the polls with a "sumptuous banquet" at the Palace Hotel in San Francisco.[107] More than 250 Republicans gathered there to honor Stanford and the rest of the California congressional delegation.

The festivities consisted of "a feast perfect in all its details of tasteful ornamentation, delightful music, inspiring oratory, and delicious viands." The guests included Stanford, Judge Morris M. Estee, Michael H. de Young, owner of the *Chronicle* and later a Republican challenger for the Senate, Gen. William Henry Dimond, former Governor Perkins, and Gov. Robert Whitney Waterman. Stanford delivered a speech in response to a toast to him as "President-elect," playfully tying it to his "presidential boom" of 1888.[108]

The Stanfords at Home Between the Fiftieth and Fifty-first Congresses—March 3–December 2, 1889

On March 3, 1889, the day the Fiftieth Congress adjourned, the Stanfords left Washington to hurry home for the wedding of Anna Lathrop and David Hewes and for a long-planned six-week trip to Alaska with their old friends Justice and Mrs. Stephen J. Field.[109]

Stanford had proposed that an Alaska railway be built linking Alaska and the continent of Asia at the Bering Straits.[110] His recommendation was discussed in Europe

---

[99]Ibid., Aug 20, 1888.

[101]*Times* (of London), Oct 11, 1888; *NY Times*, Oct 17, 1888.

[103]Ibid., Oct 19, 1888.

[105]*SF Argonaut*, Oct 29, 1888.

[107]Ibid., Dec 3, 1888.

[109]Ibid., Apr 8, 1889.

[100]Ibid., Oct 1, 1888.

[102]*NY Times*, Oct 20, 1888.

[104]Ibid., Oct 22, 1888.

[106]Ibid., Oct 10, 1888.

[108]Ibid.

[110]*SF Alta California*, Aug 12, 1889.

and was found by many to be quite feasible. It was certainly thought more feasible than was the laying of the Atlantic cable when Cyrus W. Field (Stephen Field's brother) suggested *that* engineering marvel. The editor of the *Alta* foresaw the day when there would be a schedule of trains running from San Francisco to St. Petersburg, with the trainmaster calling out: "Passengers for Suisun, Sacramento, Shasta, Portland, Puget Sound, Sitka, Omsk, Tomsk, Nijnii-Novogorod, Moscow and St. Petersburg, this way."[111]

The spring and summer of 1889 was a time of mixed sorrow and happiness for the Stanfords. Shortly after arriving home, forty-four-year-old Henry Vrooman, their long-time friend and trustee of Stanford University, died suddenly of a heart attack while driving his daughter from school to their Oakland home.[112] Vrooman, described as a self-made man, had been district attorney of Alameda County and a California state senator from the Seventeenth District. In 1887 he was the unanimous choice of Republicans in the state legislature for United States senator, but was defeated by George Hearst. The Stanfords and the university would sorely miss this trusted friend.[113]

Wedding of Anna Maria Lathrop and David Hewes— June 11, 1889

The marriage of Anna Lathrop to David Hewes—of gold spike fame—was probably the happiest social event for the Stanfords in the year 1889. Anna Maria— the second of Jane's sisters bearing that name—was four years younger than Jane. She first came to California in 1861 and stayed until Leland and Jane had moved [or were preparing to move] to San Francisco, probably in 1873. She then returned to New York to care for their invalid mother.[114] Anna Maria returned to California again in 1882 and lived for many years in her own residence at 2101 Van Ness Avenue, at the corner of Van Ness and Pacific.[115] She had never married and had long been prominently identified with charity work in the city.

Following the death of his wife, on January 3, 1887, Hewes continued for a time living on his Tustin ranch before moving back to San Francisco.[116] In 1888 he built a new gallery for his art collection at the new Oakland house on Madison Street.[117] A prominent feature of both of Hewes' Oakland residences was his valuable gallery of statues and paintings, which was always open to his friends.[118]

Thus it was that Hewes' new Oakland residence came to house his gallery, the

[111]Ibid.
[112]Ibid., Apr 9, 1889.
[113]We do not know where LS was on Apr 10, the day of Vrooman's funeral, but he was not mentioned among those attending the memorial service, *Oakland Tribune*, Apr 11, 1889.
[114]Friis, *David Hewes*, 57.
[115]*SF Argonaut*, Jun 17, 1889.
[116]Hewes, "Hewes, An Autobiography," 260.
[117]Ibid.
[118]Ibid.

David Hewes

was born in Lynnfield, Massachusetts, on May 16, 1822, the son of Col. Joel and Ruthe (Topley) Hewes.[a] His father died when David was five years old, and his mother remarried three years later. By the time he was ten, his stepfather, Oliver Swain, decided that the young man was old enough to earn his keep.[b]

Young Hewes managed to make it to Yale University, and in 1849 he requested and received a leave of absence from his studies, and on December 11, 1849, boarded the *Crescent City* in New York, bound for California.[c] When his steamer broke down off the coast of Florida, he was transferred to a lumber schooner for Panamá, and arrived in San Francisco on the *Unicorn*.[d]

In August 1870 Hewes took a trip to Venice to see a noted physician for treatment of a "serious cutaneous trouble," a type of epithelioma [tumor] on his face.[e] He did not return to California until February of 1872.[f]

While on a trip to the East, on June 30, 1875, in Saratoga Springs, New York, Hewes married Matilda (French), the widow of Franklin C. Gray. Mrs. Gray had a daughter.[g] The newlyweds traveled to England on their honeymoon, and returned to Oakland in the fall of 1877 where they lived until June of 1881.[h]

Owing to the rare illness he had contracted, and perhaps to even more serious ailments his wife suffered, Hewes and wife traveled for two and a-half years in Europe in search of a climate that would serve as a balm for her problem.[i] While in Europe he purchased a number of souvenirs for long-time friends Jane Stanford and Anna Maria Lathrop.[j]

Upon their return to Oakland in the fall of 1877, David and Matilda rented a house at 1218 Oak Street, built in 1876 by Will W. Camron for his new bride.[k]

Josiah Stanford bought the Camron house on September 28, 1882, forcing David Hewes to seek a new domicile. Josiah and family maintained a second residence there while living on the Warm Springs Ranch.[l] Josiah's widow and daughter continued to live there after he died.[m] Today the

result of several years of collecting.[119] This fact changed his very life, for one day the fifty-six-year-old Anna Maria Lathrop visited Hewes' Oakland home to view some works of art in the gallery. They renewed their friendship from Sacramento days, and soon were engaged to be married.[120]

At noon on Tuesday June 11, 1889, David Hewes and Anna Maria Lathrop were married in the drawing room of the Stanford house in San Francisco, where, in the presence of about twenty-five relatives and intimate friends, the Governor gave the bride away to his colleague of thirty years.[121] Hewes' wedding gifts to his bride were a brooch and earrings of sapphires and diamonds and his valuable art collection.[122] Brother Charles gave her sapphire and diamond bracelets, and sister Jane,

---

[119]*SF Argonaut*, Jun 17, 1889. [120]Hewes, "Hewes, An Autobiography," 260–261.

[121]Putnam, *Lieutenant Joshua Hewes*, 195 and 513–516; *SF Chronicle*, Jun 12, 1889; *SF Argonaut*, Jun 17, 1889.

[122]*SF Argonaut*, Jun 17, 1889.

completely restored Camron-Stanford House, as it is now known, stands on the shores of Lake Merritt, the only surviving California home of any of Leland Stanford's brothers.[n]

Giving up the Oakland home, after living in it for a little over three years, Hewes purchased a lot at 1155 Madison Street and built a new home, only a block from his former home and just across the street from where the Oakland Public Library now stands.[o]

David and Matilda Hewes passed a great deal of their lives together on the three-hundred-acre ranch he had bought near the southern California town of Tustin, a spread he called "Anapauma," Spanish for "place of rest," he tells us.[p]

After leaving Oakland they returned to the Tustin Ranch, where they found "at their very door at home" what they had long sought elsewhere, even abroad.[q] There, Matilda's health improved and she passed her remaining years, from June 1881 until the day of her death.

[a]Hewes, "Hewes, An Autobiography," 191; Friis, *David Hewes*, 11.

[b]Hewes, "Hewes, An Autobiography," 225.   [c]Ibid., 233.   [d]Ibid.

[e]Ibid., 253.   [f]Ibid.   [g]Putnam, *Lieutenant Joshua Hewes*, 191.

[h]Hewes, "Hewes, An Autobiography," 256.   [i]Putnam, *Lieutenant Joshua Hewes*, 192.

[j]Hewes, "Hewes, An Autobiography," 260.

[k]UNC in the Oakland Hist. Room of the Oakland Pub. Lib.; *OCD*, 1878–1879, 254; 1879–1880, 262; and 1880–1881, 268.

[l]*OCD*, 1883–1884, 335; 1888–1889, 699. The spelling varies between "Camron" and "Cameron."

[m]*OCD*, 1892, 472.

[n]For the hist. of the Camron-Stanford House, see Wayne A. Mathes, and Frances Hayden Rhodes, "The Camron-Stanford House in Oakland, California," *Antiques* 1984 125 (2): 880–885, and various sketches and newspaper clippings in the Camron-Stanford file in the Oakland Hist. Room. See also Carolyn Sheaff, "Camron-Stanford House, Chain of Title," "Resident Families at 1218 Oak Street, Oakland, California," 4-p. ms. in SUA.

[o]*OCD*, 1881–1882, 257.

[p]Putnam, *Lieutenant Joshua Hewes*, 195–196. I have not been able to confirm the English meaning of this name.

[q]Ibid., 192.

who missed the wedding because she was too ill to make the trip from Palo Alto, gave her a coiffure in the form of a peacock's feather of sapphires and diamonds.[123]

After the wedding, the couple left for the Hotel Vendome in San José, where they stayed until Thursday. Then they journeyed northward to the Palo Alto farm where they had breakfast with Leland and the still-ailing Jane.[124]

An additional wedding gift from the Stanfords was a free trip across the country in their private railroad car—their "mansion on wheels."[125] A week later the newlyweds were in Albany, New York, planning to leave for Europe on June 26, where they would spend a full year traveling and sightseeing.[126] In the following year, they were invited for a week to be guests of Leland and Jane at the Bristol Hotel in London.[127]

[123]Ibid.   [124]Ibid.

[125]Friis, *David Hewes*, 58.   [126]*SF Argonaut*, Jun 24, 1889.

[127]Hewes, "Hewes, An Autobiography," 261.

JUSTICE STEPHEN JOHNSON FIELD

Justice and Mrs. Stephen Johnson Field had arrived in San Francisco in mid-June 1889 for their planned July trip to Alaska.[128] However, owing to Jane Stanford's ill health and Justice Field's assignment to federal judicial duty in southern California, this trip never came off.

The Field entourage did a little sightseeing, spending several days in Yosemite, and left San Francisco on Monday, July 1, on what was expected to be a ten-day trip.[129] Upon their return they were to spend some time at the Hotel del Monte and leave on the 26th for Alaska with the Stanfords.[130] As late as the second week in August, Alaskans were still looking forward to the Fields' visit.[131]

We know from telegrams sent by her husband that Jane Stanford went to the northern California town of Sisson (now Mt. Shasta) in August, where she spent a month at Bailey's Hotel, nursing her health.[132] She was there on August 5 and stayed until at least September 4, 1889.[133] As for Stanford's own health, on July 17, his assistant and friend Steve Gage told a newspaper reporter that his boss was in better health than at any time within the past five years.[134]

Stanford told his wife in this same set of telegrams that he would be in San José on August 7 and would then go on to the Hotel del Monte.[135]

It is not clear when Field was assigned to judicial court sitting with Judge Erskine M. Ross (Ross, too, had been a California Supreme Court justice) in the Circuit Court for the Southern District of California. There he upheld the decision by Ross in passing a severe sentence on ex-Los Angeles Chief of Police Thomas J. Cuddy for attempting to bribe a United States Circuit Court juror.[136]

On his way from Los Angeles to San Francisco, Field had a harrowing experience that undoubtedly caused him to wish he had gone to Alaska. Former Chief Justice of California David S. Terry, who had threatened Field because of a decision unfavorable to Terry's client (now wife), had boarded the train at Fresno that was carrying Field and his wife to the railroad wye at Lathrop—a town built by Leland Stanford and named for Jane Stanford's brother Charles.[137]

---

[128]*SF Argonaut*, Jun 24, 1889.   [129]*SF Alta California*, Jul 3, 1889; *Portland Oregonian*, Jul 3, 1889.

[130]*SF Alta California*, Jul 14, 1889; *SF Argonaut*, Jul 22, 1889.   [131]*Sitka Alaskan*, Aug 3, 1889.

[132]Misspelled Sissou and Sissous in the LS telegrams. A town in Siskiyou County named Strawberry Valley was from 1886 to 1922 named Sisson, for an early settler, Justin Hinckley Sisson (Apr 22, 1826–Nov 18,1893); it was renamed Mount Shasta in 1922. Gudde, *California Place Names*, 328; *Sac Union*, Nov 21, 1893; William Poole, "Shasta," *Via* 1998 (Jul/Aug): 40–45.

[133]LS telegrams to JLS, Aug 6, 7, 24, 25, and 27, and Sep 3, 1889.

[134]*SF Alta California*, Jul 18, 1889.   [135]LS telegrams to JLS, Aug 6 and 7, 1889.

[136]*SF Alta California*, Aug 13, 1889.

[137]Stockton Savings and Loan Assn., "Manteca Memories, Photographic Recollections of the Manteca Area" (Stockton: unpub. pam., n.d.), 10. In the César Chavez Central Lib., Stockton, Calif. This doc. identifies Charles Lathrop erroneously as the husband of the sister of LS.

Terry's political and legal career had been marred by personal acts of violence. In 1856 he had been imprisoned for wounding Vigilance Committee member Sterling Hopkins in the neck with a bowie knife; on September 13, 1859, he had killed Sen. David Broderick in a duel. In 1886 Terry, practicing law in Stockton, had married his client Sarah Althea Hill, the plaintiff in the William Sharon divorce case. Hill claimed that she was the legal wife of former U.S. senator William Sharon under a "contract marriage" and, therefore, was entitled to a share of his fortune. Judgment *for* Hill had been reversed by the California Supreme Court and Terry and Hill had appealed the decision.[138] When Justice Field, acting as Circuit Justice of the Ninth Judicial Circuit, which included California, Oregon, and Nevada, announced his decision and that of Judges Lorenzo Sawyer and George M. Sabin on September 3, 1888, upholding the state Supreme Court finding, a violent scene was precipitated in the San Francisco United States Circuit Court by the new Mrs. Terry, which resulted in the imprisonment of both her and her husband for contempt of court. The *San Francisco Call* later published the following description of the incident:

> Just before the court was opened, Mrs. Terry entered the room in a most attractive costume, and took a seat by her husband and counsel. There was no unnecessary delay when the judges entered and took their seats at eleven o'clock. Mr. Terry placed himself in a most favorable position to hear the reading of the decision, and was perfectly cool and unmoved. Mrs. Terry, on the contrary, was evidently laboring under high-pressure mental excitement. The Chief-Justice [*sic*] had not proceeded very far with the reading when Mrs. Terry, her eyes flashing and her voice quivering with the excitement under which she was laboring, sprang to her feet and exclaimed:
>
> "Judge Field, how much have you been paid for that decision?" For a moment, the most profound silence pervaded the room. Then Justice Field, in a perfectly cool manner, but a shade paler than usual, said, in a quiet manner:
>
> "Take your seat, madam. I will overlook your outbreak this time, but do not let it occur again. Sit down."
>
> "I will not sit down. You have been bought, and I know it," almost screamed the infuriated woman.
>
> The justice then said to Marshal Franks: "Marshal, put that lady out of the court."
>
> This order was the signal for the most intense excitement, and the room was immediately in an uproar. As Marshal Franks advanced to obey the order of the court, Ex-Judge Terry jumped to his feet and warned him not to lay a hand on his wife. Franks pushed Terry to one side, and at the same moment received a most terrible blow in the mouth from the fist of the infuriated man. His teeth were broken, and, the blood flowed freely. Deputy Farish rushed in to assist his chief, and together they bore the maddened husband from the room, while Deputy Taggart performed the same office for the woman.
>
> It was not done, however, without a terrible struggle, Terry and his wife fighting like demons, and disputing every inch of ground. When they reached the hall, Terry

---

[138]Horace H. Hagar, "David Smith Terry," *DAB*, IX, Part 2, 379–380. This work makes use of a number of sources on the life of Terry.

drew a bowie-knife, and would soon have made bad work for the marshal and his deputy had not several others rushed in to their aid, who finally threw him on his back and disarmed him.

Meanwhile, Mrs. Terry had also been forced from the room and taken into the marshal's office, from which place she sent for her reticule, which had been left with a friend. Before giving it to her, it was opened, and a British bull-dog pistol was taken from it. The Terrys had evidently meant business when they went into court that day.

After quiet had been restored, Justice Field continued the reading of the decision, and at its conclusion the court retired for consultation. The result is well known. Terry was sentenced to the Alameda County Jail for six months and Sarah Althea for one month for contempt of court. Terry appealed, but the appeal was denied, and they both served full time.[139]

While serving his sentence in the Alameda County jail, Terry told a friend: "When I get out of here I will horsewhip Judge Field. He will not dare return to California, but the world is not large enough to hide him from me."[140] He went on to boast that he intended to kill Judge Field and Judge Sawyer.[141] Because of this and other, similar threats to Field, the attorney general of the United States assigned David Neagle to travel with Field as a bodyguard.

When Terry—described as a man of "rash judgment and violent impulses"[142]— and wife boarded the San Francisco-bound train at Fresno on August 14, 1889, they had no idea that Field was a fellow passenger. The train reached Lathrop at 7:20 A.M. and Field and Neagle left the train to get breakfast at the hotel.[143] Terry and his wife spotted Field as they entered the dining room. Mrs. Terry returned to the railroad car to get a handbag, leaving Terry seated alone a short distance from Field. Suddenly, the enraged Terry, who was sixty-six at the time, walked over to Field's table and slapped the justice in the face. Neagle ordered him to stop, but Terry doubled his fist and threatened to strike Field again. The bodyguard drew a pistol and shot Terry dead on the spot. Almost immediately Mrs. Terry appeared in the doorway with a traveling bag containing a pistol. She was disarmed.

News of the incident was telephoned to San Francisco and was published there within thirty minutes of the killing.[144]

The train continued on its way to San Francisco, but was stopped at Tracy, where Deputy Marshal Neagle was arrested for murder, handcuffed, and driven back to Lathrop. *In Re Neagle* became a celebrated case in U.S. federal-state relations. Because Neagle was a federal officer acting in the line of duty when he killed Terry, the federal government wished to protect him for prosecution under California law. But, no federal law specifically authorized the appointment of a bodyguard with the

---

[139]*SF Call*, Aug 15, 1889; repr. in the *SF Argonaut*, Aug 19, 1889. The original fracas was reported in the *SF Call* of Sep 4, 1888.

[140]*SF Alta California*, Aug 15, 1889.

[141]*SF Call*, Aug 15, 1889.

[142]Hagan, "David Smith Terry," 380.

[143]*SF Alta California*, Aug 15, 1889.

[144]Ibid.

Supreme Court Justice Stephen Johnson Field,

as Gordon Bakken, one student of his career wrote: "participated in many of the great civil rights cases of the era including the *Test Oath Cases*. In the *Slaughter House Cases* Field fleshed out a constitutional right to pursue any lawful calling based on the Fourteenth Amendment's privileges and immunities clause. His *Munn v. Illinois* dissent established his philosophy of liberty, property, and the limits of government regulation that would resonate in American constitutional law for generations. In *Ah Kow v. Nunan*, the nationally famous Chinese Queue Case, he struck down a San Francisco ordinance requiring the cutting of the queue of Chinese prisoners. Again, he found the substantive due process guarantees of the Fourteenth Amendment and the Bill of Rights to require his ruling against legislation that was 'unworthy of a brave and manly people.' Later, and again involving San Francisco, Field would amplify his position that regulation could be a taking of corporate property without due process of law in *Spring Valley Water Works v. Schottler* (1884)."[a] Following a summary of Field's influence on the Supreme Court and on American jurisprudence, Bakken concluded, "Field indeed left a clear mark."[b] The justice's most recent biographer left an even a stronger testimonial: "He left a legacy that only a handful of other public figures of his day could match."[c]

In April 1897 Field tendered his resignation from the Supreme Court, effective December 1. This allowed him to exceed John Marshall's tenure by two months. President William McKinley wrote to Field, "Entering upon your great office in May, 1863, you will, on the 1st of next December, have served upon this bench for a period of thirty-four years and seven months, a term longer than that of any other member of the court since its creation."[d]

Frank Pixley's *Argonaut* had nothing but unstinting praise for Field's public service when he resigned from the state's high court in January 1863: "The resignation by Judge Field of the office of the Chief Justice of the Supreme Court of California, to take effect on the 20th instant, has been announced. He retires from office without a stain upon his ermine. He retires as poor as when he entered—owing nothing and owning little, except the title to the respect of good men, which malignant mendacity cannot wrest from a public officer who has deserved, by a long and useful career, the grateful appreciation of his fellow-citizens."[e]

[a]Gordon Morris Bakken, "Looking Back: the Court and California Law in 1897," *CSCHSY* 1996–1997 3 (ann.): 121–139. "Postscript: The Retirement of Stephen Field," *CSCHSY* 1996–1997 3 (ann.): 139.   [b]Ibid.
[c]Paul Kens, *Justice Stephen Field: Shaping Liberty from the Gold Rush to the Gilded Age* (Lawrence: UKP, 1996), 285.
[d]See *SF Call*, Aug 5, 1897, and *SF Chronicle*, Oct 13, 1897. The McKinley letter was repr. in the *Call*, Oct 15, 1897, and in the *Chronicle*, Oct 15, 1897.   [e]*SF Argonaut*, Jan 17, 1880

duties Neagle was called upon to perform. The U.S. Supreme Court finally settled the matter by deciding on April 14, 1890, that Neagle's position and action were "fairly and properly inferable" under the U.S. Constitution.[145]

The words of the *Argonaut* editor were prophetic when he had written almost a

[145]USSCR, Vol. 135, p. 1–99. Cases Adjudged in the Supreme Court at Oct Term, 1889. Docket title *Thomas Cunningham, Sheriff of the County of San Joaquin, California, Appellant, v. David Neagle, Petitioner*. The case was argued on Mar 4 and 5, 1890, and was decided Apr 14, 1890. Justice Field did not sit at the hearing of this case and took no part in the decision (p. 99). For application of the decision in *In Re Neagle*, see *USSCR*, Vol. 144, pp. 263–310. Cases Adjudged in the Supreme Court at Oct Term, 1891. Docket title *Logan v. United States*. (Argued Jan 26 and 27, 1892; decided Apr 4, 1892).

year before: "Ex-Judge Terry has brought suit against the United States marshal, threatens Judge Field, and for the absurd comedies enacted we are promised tragedies in the future."[146]

At the time of Terry's death there were five indictments hanging over his head and three against his wife. U.S. District judge Matthew Paul Deady had been instructed by Judge Sawyer to put both defendants on trial.[147]

Indeed, the Stanford-Field trip to Alaska did not come off as planned in August of 1889!

The Death of Lizzie Hull Grant—August 8, 1889

Two months after celebrating the marriage of Jane's sister Anna Maria Lathrop Hewes, the Stanfords "took part" in the heart-wrenching burial of their dear Lizzie Hull, who for years had been like a daughter to them. Jane Stanford was *in absentia* since she was visiting a health resort in Sisson, where she stayed until her husband picked her up in early September.

There was no hint that Lizzie had inherited her mother's heart disease (Hattie Hull died at thirty-two of heart disease on January 20, 1868, when Lizzie was only five years old)[148] until the notices of her death on August 8, 1889, appeared in the local papers.[149] The first notice stated simply:

> Mrs. Grant, wife of Joseph D. Grant of the San Francisco firm of Murphy, Grant & Co., died suddenly at San Mateo last Thursday from heart disease, a complaint with which she had been suffering for some time. Mrs. Grant, formerly Miss Lizzie Hull, was a daughter of Edward Hull, a San Francisco capitalist. She was twenty-seven years of age and leaves a child.[150]

Lizzie died two days before her twenty-seventh birthday.[151]

For the few short years she had been in the public eye, Lizzie had developed a wide range of friendships. The editor of the *Morning Call* did not exaggerate when he wrote of Lizzie, "Society has lost one of its favorites. The world has been deprived of a grand and noble woman, one who moved on the high plain of a true wife and mother."

Friends were invited to attend the funeral service at Trinity Church, Sunday, August 11, 1889. The interment at Laurel Hill Cemetery was private.[153] Therefore, no list was published of those attending, so we have no documentary record that

[146]*SF Argonaut*, Sep 10, 1888.   [147]*SF Alta California*, Aug 15, 1889.

[148]*Sac Daily Bee*, Jan 27, 1868.

[149]This same malady would claim the life of Lizzie's forty-three-year-old brother Edward V. Hull in St. Malo, France, on Sep 26, 1903, in *SF Chronicle*, Oct 2, 1903.   [150]*SMC Times and Gazette*, Aug 10, 1889.

[151]*SF Chronicle*, Aug 11, 1889.   [152]*SF Call*, Aug 10, 1889.

[153]*SF Chronicle*, Aug 11, 1889; *SF Examiner*, Aug 12, 1889.

Leland Stanford was present; but his relationship to the Hulls and the Grants leaves no doubt that he was, since he was in San Francisco at the time of her death. The pallbearers were Edward Whiting Hopkins, Henry T. Scott, Joseph D. Redding, Fred Crocker, Arthur Page, James A. Ford, Daniel T. Murphy, Richard H. Pease, Jr., Edgar Mills, Jr., and Charles S. Baldwin, all close friends of Lizzie and Joseph.[154]

The Trinity Episcopal Church records state that Lizzie Grant was buried in a vault.[155] Today Lizzie rests in the beautiful Mountain View Cemetery in Oakland, overlooking the cities of Oakland and in the distance San Francisco, the San Francisco Bay, and, on a clear day, the wide Pacific. Next to her rests her father, Edward Hull, her parents-in-law, Adam and Emma Grant, her husband, Joseph, and second wife, and Lizzie's seventy-eight-year-old son, Douglas, who died on March 17, 1966, having outlived his mother by more than three-quarters of a century.[156]

The Summer and Fall of 1889

The Stanfords spent much of the summer and early fall of 1889 either at the Palo Alto Stock Farm, the Hotel del Monte in Monterey, or touring the state.

The senator was still a railroad man and spent a great deal of time at his office in San Francisco. It became a place both for intense business dealings and light-hearted social gatherings with old friends. In one of the many "bull" sessions (no pun intended) Leland and friends had in the railroad office, in the summer of 1889, when some "gentlemen" in Leland's office were discussing the senator's early life, Josiah delighted the circle of chums by telling a story of how the Stanford brothers hauled manure away from the boyhood farm in New York.[157] According to Josiah's narration,

> We had the New England habit of wearing a frock which covered our garments and came down to our knees, to protect our clothing, and our pants were tucked inside our boots so as to save them from getting soiled. . . . Leland used to dislike hauling the slaughter house manure because it was so slushy. We would haul it when it was so wet that there would be water on the top of it; we generally left a horrible smell all along the road.

Despite being busy, with politics and business, the Stanfords always found time for social and recreational outings. In early August of 1889 they spent a few days at the Hotel del Monte in Monterey.[158] Then the senator spent a few busy weeks in San

[154] *SF Examiner*, Aug 12, 1889.

[155] Jessie Boudinot Flenner, *Vital Statistics from Records in Trinity Episcopal Church of San Francisco, California* ([SF]: DAR, [1936]). This work contains baptism, marriage, and burial records of the Trinity Epis. Church from 1849 to Jul 1, 1906, but has many errors, including the date of Lizzie's burial.

[156] At the time of writing, the author is in regular contact with Douglas' daughter—Lizzie's granddaughter—Mrs. Elspeth Nora (Grant) Bobbs, who lives half the year in Carmel and the other half in Santa Fé. She and Lizzie share the same birthday, Aug 10.   [157] JM/JS inter., Jul 18, 1889, 4.

[158] *SF Argonaut*, Aug 5, 1889.

Francisco and Palo Alto—often on official Senate duties—while his wife passed the month in Sisson.

On July 23 Stanford had a meeting with a number of Republicans to discuss the need for harmony in the ranks of Oakland Republicans. He said he would recognize no factions and that he would act fairly toward all in the matter of federal patronage.[159] Federal patronage was a subject that came up often in local California politics. Stanford and members of the congressional delegation met often to apportion federal offices in California. Among the offices already filled were those of United States District Attorney, Naval Officer, and Collector of Internal Revenue. The positions of San Francisco Postmaster and United States Marshal, however, were still to be decided.[160]

When Stanford and Republican congressman John Jefferson De Haven of Eureka recommended the appointment of Louis T. Kinsey of Eureka as Indian Agent at Round Table, Mendocino County, Kinsey's appointment was considered a certainty.[161]

On August 20, Stanford entertained a number of friends from San Francisco, New York, and Washington at the Palo Alto farm.[162] On the 26th of August he met with the Senate Committee on Reclamation of Arid Lands, at the office of the State Board of Trade in San Francisco.[163] On the following day, the committee members visited Palo Alto, where they inspected the work on the university, and then enjoyed a splendid repast before continuing on business to San José.[164]

In September the reunited Stanfords spent a week in Sacramento.[165]

Everywhere the Stanfords went people turned out to see them. At Red Bluff in early October they were given a brilliant reception at the Pavilion where the whole depot was decorated with flags and bunting in their honor.[166] The next day they attended a reception held in their honor in Chico; there they were given a military escort to Gen. John Bidwell's ranch, where a large public reception was held.[167] Two brass bands played and a thousand schoolchildren showered their carriage with flowers.

During this trip they were "entertained and feasted" in a number of towns in the northern part of the state.[168]

In late October, having arrived back home again in San Francisco on the seventh of the month, the Stanfords mixed the social, political, and business aspects of their busy lives by royally entertaining the United States Senate Committee on Subsidized Railroads, together with the members of their families and a few friends.[169]

[159]SF Alta California, Jul 24, 1889.
[160]Ibid., Jul 27, 1889.
[161]Ibid., Aug 5, 1889.
[162]Ibid., Aug 25, 1889.
[163]Ibid., Aug 27, 1889.
[164]Ibid., Aug 28, 1889.
[165]SF Argonaut, Aug 26 and Sep 23, 1889.
[166]Sac Bee, Oct 5, 1889.
[167]Ibid.
[168]Ibid., Oct 7 and 14, 1889.
[169]Ibid., Oct 14, 1889.

This was no ordinary dinner party, as the editorial writer of the *San Francisco Argonaut* told his readers:

> The dining-room looked exceptionally attractive that evening, as the elaborate frescoing, the richly finished furnishings, and the novel table decoration combined most harmoniously, and they were accentuated by the elegance of the toilets worn by the ladies and the wealth of flashing jewels which adorned them. The table was embellished primarily with a rustic arch, eight feet long, stretched over the centre and reaching up to the chandelier. It was covered with grape-vines in the tints of both summer and autumn, and laden with luscious clusters of Tokay, Black Hamburg, and Muscat grapes. Below on the damask was a bed of soft moss, having as a centre-piece a large curly cabbage, half opened to display its delicate green heart. Around it were little cup-shaped receptacles formed of bark and of leaves of the curly cabbage, and they contained strawberries, raspberries, melons, and many varieties of fruit. At either end of the arch were silver épergnes, set with fancifully colored bon-bons, and at the ends of the table were silver jardinières holding pink, white, yellow, and terra-cotta-colored chrysanthemums. At each cover was a favor in the form of a satin scroll, bearing a piece of Chinese paper, hand-painted and tied on with parti-colored silk threads. The names were printed in Japanesque script. Throughout all of the apartments were some vases and jars filled with the season's blossoms in all their beautiful colors. The menu was perfect in every particular, and in its enjoyment several hours were most delightfully passed, followed by music and conversation in the drawing-rooms.[170]

SENATE COMMITTEE ON SUBSIDIZED RAILROADS

reception guests of Senator and Mrs. Stanford included Sen. and Mrs. William P. Frye of Maine, Mr. and Mrs. Frederick H. Briggs of the *San Francisco Examiner*, Mr. Woodbury Pulsifer, Sen. Henry L. Dawes and daughter from Massachusetts, Sen. and Mrs. Cushman Kellogg Davis of Minnesota, fellow California senator George Hearst, Sen. David Turpie from Indianapolis, Sen. John Tyler Morgan of Alabama, Sen. Orville Platt of Connecticut, Judge and Mrs. Charles H. Thurston of Marysville,[a] Sen. and Mrs. John P. Jones of Nevada, Mr. and Mrs. Alban Towne, Judge and Mrs. William Morrow, Judge and Mrs. Joseph McKenna, Judge and Mrs. Thomas Jefferson Clunie, Mr. and Mrs. Timothy Phelps, Gen. and Mrs. Nelson A. Miles, Gen. and Mrs. William Dimond, Mr. and Mrs. John H. Jewett (long-time Republican Party workhorse and Marysville bank president whose wife served as president of the Women's Auxiliary of the Society of California Pioneers),[b] Judge Charles N. Felton, and the never-forgotten tutor of the Stanfords' son, Mr. Herbert C. Nash, who must have been overwhelmed, surrounded by such splendor, wealth, and power.[c]

[a]Marysville City Council Minutes, 1884. Mar 17, 1884, on microfilm in the John Q. Packard Lib. of YC.

[b]Jewett came to Calif. in 1849 and worked as a miner. He became pres. of the Marysville Vigilance Committee, the second mayor of Marysville, and an elector for Rutherford B. Hayes, *SF Call*, Jan 17, 1892; Mrs. Jewett, neé May Burtis, *SF Chronicle*, Nov 30, 1902.   [c]*SF Argonaut*, Oct 28, 1889.

---

[170]Ibid.

THE DEATH OF MARY (DEMING) CROCKER—OCTOBER 27, 1889

"Seldom has there been seen in San Francisco so great an exhibition of universal sorrow for the dead and sympathy for the living as was shown at Mrs. Crocker's funeral on Tuesday afternoon," wrote the editor of the *Argonaut* on the death of Charles Crocker's widow, Mary, on October 27, 1889, a little more than a year after her husband's death.[171] The First Congregational Church in the city was far too small to hold the thousands who had come to pay their last respects to "the noble woman whose true sympathy and wide generosity had lightened many another's burden."[172]

The altar was surrounded by beautiful floral emblems from family, friends, and the hundreds to whom Mrs. Crocker had endeared herself. Her brother Theodore and two of his four daughters were at the funeral.[173] Present among the pall bearers were Senator Stanford, Judge Lorenzo Sawyer, Alban Towne, William E. Brown of the Southern Pacific Company, Judge Samuel M. Wilson, former governor George Perkins, Adam Grant, Col. Creed Haymond, Irving M. Scott, William T. Coleman, and Gen. William H. L. Barnes. The funeral sermon was delivered by California pioneer, minister, and family friend Dr. Joseph A. Benton.[174]

At the conclusion of the public ceremonies, the cortège carried Mary's casket to Laura Hill Cemetery, to be placed in Nicholas Luning's vault where the remains of her late husband lay, awaiting the completion of their mausoleum in Mountain View Cemetery in Oakland, which was to be their final resting place.[175]

With three of the five major builders of the Central Pacific Railroad dead—Mark Hopkins and the two Crockers, and now the wife of one of them—Mary Crocker's death must have served as a grim reminder of the mortality of even the rich and powerful.

THE CROCKERS' SILVER WEDDING ANNIVERSARY

On November 27, 1877, as Charles and Mary Crocker were celebrating their silver wedding anniversary (There is no explanation why it was celebrated on the twenty-seventh rather than the twenty-fifth, the actual date of their marriage), Joseph Augustine Benton read a poem to the large assembly of guests. Crocker looked at Benton and said, "Well, you married us twenty-five years ago, and we have clung together this far. Try it again, and see if you can join us for another twenty-five years."[a]

It is a mystery why Crocker made this statement. It was not Benton who had united them in marriage in Mishawaka, Indiana, but Pastor Norman Kellogg of the First Presbyterian Church (see Crocker marriage in Chapter 5 above). In fact, on November 25, 1852, Joseph Benton was in Sacramento officiating at two other weddings.[b]

[a]*SF Call*, Nov 27 and 28, 1877. Citation from Nov 28.
[b]Joseph Augustine Benton, "Record of Preaching," Book 1, under date of Nov 25, 1852, in PSR Archives.

---

[171]*SF Argonaut*, Nov 11, 1889.   [172]Ibid.
[173]*SF Examiner*, Nov 6, 1889. Sketch of the life of Theodore Deming and family in Lyman L. Palmer, *History of Napa and Lake Counties, California* . . . (SF: SBC, c. 1881), 230–231.
[174]Ibid., *SF Argonaut*, Nov 11, 1889.   [175]*SF Argonaut*, Nov 11, 1889.

The following month, on November 21, 1889, the Stanfords were guests of Mrs. Gen. Nelson Appleton Miles who gave a matinée reception at Fort Mason.[176] Her reception included the Stanfords, the Pixleys, the Townes, and Brig. Gen. and Mrs. Alexander James Perry among the four hundred guests.

Leland Stanford's Fifth (Jane's Fourth) European Tour— May 28–October 8, 1890

Even though Stanford was busy with his Senate duties and with trying to resolve railroad problems following his replacement by Huntington as president of the Southern Pacific Company, the ailing California senator decided to return to Europe for another thermal cure. It was April 1890, well before the long session of the Fifty-first Congress closed. Since he was suffering intensely, several prominent New York physicians advised Stanford to visit a number of German bathing resorts to arrest certain unidentified "incipient organic troubles."[177] Early in the month, he and Jane returned briefly to California before leaving for Europe.[178] In Sacramento they were given one of the most "spontaneous and heartfelt manifestations of respect and esteem" ever tendered anyone in the state: ten thousand people turned out to see them, including one thousand school children.[179] Both Leland and Jane were visibly touched by this outpouring of affection.

The *Argonaut* speculated that the Stanfords would probably spend the summer months in Kissingen or Carlsbad and return to California in the fall.[180] The Stanfords left San Francisco on April 25, 1890, and traveled directly to Washington.[181] Stanford was hardly settled after his cross-country trip when word came that his seventy-three-year-old brother, Josiah, had died on May 14.[182] The saddened senator returned briefly to the Senate chambers where on May 23 he introduced his Land Loan Bill (SB 3889) providing for loans to farmers secured by their farm lands.[183]

On May 28, 1890, the Stanfords sailed for Liverpool on the White Star Line's one-year-old, 9,686-ton *Teutonic*.[184] This ship was 50 percent larger than the *Alaska*, the biggest ship they had sailed on before this trip.[185] It was also the fastest: on one trans-Atlantic trip the *Teutonic* won the coveted Blue Ribbon, beating all previous

---

[176]Ibid., Nov 18, 1889.   [177]*SF Examiner*, Apr 5, 1890.

[178]*SF Argonaut*, Apr 14, 1890.

[179]*SF Examiner*, Apr 5, 1890. The best doc. of their fourth European trip is found in the corres. between JLS and May Hopkins, in JLS papers. See also, *Sac Bee*, Apr 5, 1890.   [180]*SF Argonaut*, Apr 14, 1890.

[181]Ibid., Apr 28, 1890.

[182]Josiah's funeral was held at Hamilton Hall, Oakland, with Charles W. Wendte, pastor of the Oak Unitarian Church, officiating. He was buried in Oakland at the Mountain View Cemetery. SCP Marshal's Records, Jul 8, 1888–1894, 94.   [183]*Cong. Rec.*, 51st Cong., 1st Sess., 5169–5170 (May 30, 1890).

[184]*NY Times*, May 29, 1890.   [185]Smith, *Passenger Ships of the World*, 258.

records by steaming from Queenstown to Sandy Hook, a peninsula extending north toward New York Bay, in five days, sixteen hours, and thirty-one minutes, averaging 20.43 knots.[186] The Stanfords arrived in Liverpool at 12:05 P.M. on June 4, seven days out, the shortest of their trans-Atlantic trips to date.[187]

The best documentation of this trip to Europe is found in the correspondence between Jane Stanford and May (Mrs. Timothy) Hopkins. On July 4, Jane wrote to May that they had a pleasant trip across the ocean.[188] On their arrival at the depot in London, they were met by David and Anna Hewes.[189] They stayed in London for three days visiting with Anna, and then went to Paris for two days and from there to Bad Kissingen, where they arrived on June 12; they had been there for three weeks and a day when she wrote to May detailing their itinerary.[190]

In Paris, Herbert Nash took leave of the Stanford party—which included Jane's brother Henry—to visit his parents in Nice.[191]

Stanford was not the only former California governor taking the cure at Bad Kissengen. Ailing Frederick Low—Jane refers to him as Gov. Low—and his family were staying at the hotel next door to the Stanfords, and the two governors and wives met daily in the park. (Apparently Low was on the mend: his daughter Flora told Jane that her mother had said to her, "When your father can get off his jokes and stories at seven o'clock in the morning, you may know your father is himself again.")[192]

The *Argonaut* reported, mistakenly, that the Stanfords had left Germany for a tour of Norway and Sweden.[193] In May, Jane had written to May Hopkins that the trip was to include a tour of Sweden, Norway, Denmark, and Russia, but they had suffered so much from rain and cold that they were reconsidering their northern jaunt.[194] Nothing was ever again said about this proposed tour, so we have no way of knowing whether this part of their "pleasure trip" ever came off, but there is no evidence that it did.

On August 18, 1890, the *Argonaut* published a letter to the editor dated July 29, 1890, from an unnamed correspondent who described a visit he had just enjoyed with Stanford in Germany: "I found him at the Kaiserhoff Hotel, in Berlin, as well or better than he has been for the past ten years. I might say, truthfully, better than ten years ago." Referring to Stanford's Senate bill for low-interest loans to farmers, the writer went on, "He is to-day ready for the fight and a greater champion of the poor man than ever, and they should know it."[195]

The *Argonaut* report continued, "The writer of this note is a resident of San Francisco and has known Governor Stanford for nearly twenty years. The writer is personally known to the editor of the *Argonaut*. His information is reliable."

[186]Ibid.

[188]JLS to May Hopkins, Jul 4, 1890.

[191]Ibid.

[194]JLS to May Hopkins, May 19, 1890.

[187]*Times* (of London) Jun 5, 1890; *NY Times*, Jun 5, 1890.

[189]Ibid.

[192]Ibid.

[195]*SF Argonaut*, Aug 18, 1890.

[190]Ibid.

[193]*SF Argonaut*, Jul 21, 1890.

In mid-August the Stanford party visited Putbus, Germany.[196] In late September the Stanfords were again in England, preparing for their planned departure from Liverpool to New York on October 6, 1890.[197] They left far in advance of the scheduled date, steaming from Liverpool on October 1, again taking the *Teutonic*. Another seven days' journey brought them to New York, on the morning of October 8.[198] On Wednesday, October 15, 1890, they were once again home in California.[199]

SOCIAL LIFE IN CALIFORNIA— OCTOBER 15–NOVEMBER 25, 1890

Jane Stanford, always the gracious hostess, never tired of entertaining her lady friends at luncheons. Shortly after returning from Europe, at one o'clock on the afternoon of Saturday, November 8, 1890, she gave "one of the most elegant affairs of recent date" at the California Street house for thirty of the leading ladies of San Francisco and Peninsula society.[200] After lunch the guests enjoyed an hour in the art gallery and drawing-rooms.

Mrs. Stanford also entertained thirty ladies the following Thursday afternoon. The guest list was as sparkling as the first, with few duplicates.[201]

A week later, on Thursday, November 20, Jane Stanford gave her third luncheon party since returning from Europe.[202] Again, the guest list was a San Francisco *Who's Who*, with the wives of more railroad friends there than at the first two parties.

The *Argonaut* reported that the Stanfords would leave Tuesday, November 25, for Washington, to remain there until March.[203] To bid farewell to friends for the season, the couple held a reception: "To-day [Saturday, November 22] Governor and Mrs. Stanford will receive their friends, ladies and gentlemen, from two until five o'clock in the afternoon, at their city residence on California Street, corner of Powell Street."[204] As scheduled, the Stanfords left town on November 25.[205]

THE DEATH OF WILSON "WILSIE" GRISSIM TAYLOR— DECEMBER 28, 1890

Leland, Jr., and his dearest childhood friends, Lizzie Hull and Wilsie Taylor, died within a period of just over six years. Wilsie had never been well. Bertha Berner

---

[196]Ibid., Sep 1, 1890.
[197]Ibid., Sep 29, 1890.
[198]*NY Times*, Oct 9, 1890; *SF Argonaut*, Oct 13, 1890.
[199]*SF Argonaut*, Oct 20, 1890.
[200]Ibid., Nov 17, 1890.
[201]Ibid.
[202]Ibid., Nov 24, 1890.
[203]Ibid.
[204]Ibid. There is considerable confusion about *Argonaut* pub. dates. The paper was always pub. on Saturdays, but to satisfy complaints from eastern dealers, the management began following an eastern newspaper policy of dating the paper ahead. This practice was explained in the issue of May 2, 1888.
[205]Ibid., Dec 1, 1890.

once mentioned that he was "crippled," without furnishing any details, and in his heart-wrenching letters to the Stanfords after his friend young Leland died, Wilsie mentioned that he was "afflicted, sick, with no future—no object to live for." Yet, again, no mention of his malady.[206]

Wilsie had often spoken to his friend Leland about wanting to become an artist. His letter to Leland of October 16, 1883—having been written on San Francisco Art Association stationery—suggests that the budding artist had realized one of his professional ambitions and become a student at the association.[207] He later also realized another long-time ambition—to study art in Europe.

During the Stanfords' 1883–1884 trip to Europe, Wilsie wrote to Leland, "I am still at the Art School. I am getting along well. I am going to Germany in November to study. I am going to stay in Munich two years and then go to Paris for three years and then come back and try to kill the people with the bad pictures and *don't you forget it*."[208] Three years before his tragic death, the *Argonaut* reported, "Mrs. Emma F. Taylor left on Thursday for New York, where she goes to join her son, Mr. Wilson G. Taylor, who has been absent some time studying art. They will visit the principal cities East before returning."[209]

The Stanfords did not forget their son's friend after young Leland's death. As mentioned, they sent Wilsie a copy of the beautiful volume *In Memoriam*, dedicated to Leland, Jr. In Wilsie's thank you letter, one can begin to glean something about his health—or illness.

San Francisco
Tuesday Oct. 28th 1884

My Dear friends Gov & Mrs. Stanford

I have just received the beautiful book in Memoriam of our dear Leland. It is a most beautiful tribute to his memory—I was so happy to think you remembered me—I shall cherish it, and keep it by me the longest day of my life.

I have been very ill myself—and still confined to my bed with Diphtheria the doctor has pronounced me out of danger, and says with care I will recover. I hope soon to see you both home once more, and that you may be entirely recovered—I am with love sincerely, your friend

Wilson G. Taylor

---

[206]BB, *Mrs. Stanford*, 40; Wilson Taylor to Gov. and Mrs. Stanford, May 14, 1884.
[207]The SF Art Assn. was founded in 1872. In 1884–1885 it was located at 430 Pine St. (*SFCD*, 1884–1885, 955), where it was on May 14, 1884, when Wilsie wrote to the Stanfords; the stationery he used carried an assn. letterhead.
[208]Wilson G. Taylor to "My Dear Leland," n.d.
[209]*SF Argonaut*, Sep 3, 1887; *SF Examiner*, Dec 29, 1890, has Emma J., as does the *SFCD*, 1877–78, 834; Probate records for the estate of Col. John G. Taylor, Wilsie's father, have his mother listed as Emma C. Taylor, executrix. KC, Calif. Case #65. Will, dated Nov 4, 1876, probated Jan 21, 1877.

A terse newspaper obituary on December 29, 1890, announced the end of Wilsie and his dreams:

WILSON GRISSIM TAYLOR

Wilson Grissim Taylor, the artist who has been in Europe for two years, died yesterday in this city. He was 25 years of age and the son of Mrs. Emma J. Taylor. He was a native of California.[210]

Another San Francisco journalist described Wilsie's death as follows:

WILSON G. TAYLOR
Death of a Prominent Young San Francisco Artist

Wilson G. Taylor, the young San Francisco artist, died in this city yesterday morning after a lingering and painful illness.

The young man was the only son of Mrs. Emma J. Taylor and the late Colonel John G. Taylor, nephew of Chief Justice of the Supreme Court Solomon P. Chase.[211]

Young Taylor was one of the most promising artists of this city, but for a few years past he has been suffering from hip disease and lately from Bright's Disease of the kidneys.

Two years ago he left for Europe to pursue his studies in painting, and while there the latter disease was developed to an alarming extent. Eminent physicians were consulted and his case pronounced hopeless. With a determination to die at home surrounded by his family, he started for California on his last sad journey. He arrived here three weeks ago, since which time he has gradually been sinking until death relieved him of his sufferings at an early hour yesterday morning. He was a particular favorite with the artists. A large number of warm personal friends will regret his early demise. He was only twenty-five years of age.

The funeral will take place from the mortuary chapel of Trinity Church to-morrow afternoon at two o'clock.[212]

Wilsie was buried at Laurel Hill Cemetery in San Francisco on December 30, 1890.[213] He was reinterred at the Masonic Cemetery in San Francisco on August 28, 1891.[214] Three of Wilsie's paintings, all tentatively dated about 1880, hang alternately in the Stanford Room of the University Museum. They are *Boat at Sea*, *Mountain Brook*, and *River Scene*.[215]

---

[210]*SF Call*, Dec 29, 1890. Wilsie's father had died at his farm in Bakersfield of what was diagnosed as "quick consumption." Taylor was born in Mo. and had come to Calif. in 1849. He amassed a considerable fortune in his adopted state, and under Pres. Lincoln he was appointed to the SF Customs House. He was thirty-nine at the time of his death on Nov 19, 1876, when his son was eleven years old. *SF Alta California*, Nov 23, 1876; *Bakersfield Southern Californian*, Nov 30, 1876; Wilsie's age, Charles Wells Hayes, *A New Parish Register* (NY: EPD, 1887), Trinity Church, SF, 218–219.

[211]There is, of course, no such office as Chief Justice of the Supreme Court under the U.S. Const. Chase was the Chief Justice of the U.S.   [212]*SF Examiner*, Dec 29, 1890.

[213]Hayes, *A New Parish Register*, Trinity Church, SF, 218–219; *Vital Statistics from Records in Trinity Episcopal Church of San Francisco, California*, 315.

[214]Laurel Hill records, now held by Cypress Lawn Memorial Cemetery, Colma, Calif. Inter. with Marilyn Calvey, Tour and Seminar Dir., Jun 4, 1998.   [215]Inter. with Charlotte Flanagan, Curatorial Asst., LSJM, Jan 17, 2001.

Stanfords' Social Life While in Washington—1885–1893

A new lease for five years and six months on their Washington home, negotiated November 1, 1891, gave the Stanfords an option to purchase the property for $75,000.[216] Stanford was, after all, the richest man in the Senate, and this large white stone house was one of the most beautiful and most fashionable in the capital. Nearby in Washington he kept a stable with a fine stock of twenty horses, though not all were kept within the city.[217]

The senator generally rode to the Capitol in a comfortable carriage, but often he preferred to walk for the exercise. One morning a Washington hackman "accosted the Senator" as he walked along the street and Stanford climbed aboard the old "nightliner" cab and rode to his office.[218] From then until he left Washington, the rusty old hack was his shadow. It always stood on Lafayette Square opposite the Blaine House. When Stanford walked down the street in the morning, the hackman was watching for him. When the senator tired of walking, he called him and climbed aboard. As he left his offices in the afternoon, he found the hack always waiting for him.

The Stanfords' first year in Washington had been spent in mourning for their son; it was not until the second year that they entered Washington society. When they did, it was with much fanfare.[219] When they drove by, people took notice—it was said that they had the "handsomest equipage at the Capital."[220]

On February 9, 1886, Senator and Mrs. Stanford treated the California congressional delegation and other Washington dignitaries to a spectacular dinner, a feast, nay, more than that, an *event*, not soon to be forgotten. The journalist who covered the affair searched for superlatives to describe the evening's décor, foods, wines, and guests:

> The dinner was splendid and beautiful in its appointments. Ten courses were served. California wines were served throughout, save one change to French champagne. California red wine was substituted for Burgundy and white wine went with the oysters. The clusters of fresh fruits, oranges, bananas and apples that brightened the table here and there came in from California, late yesterday afternoon. It was literally a California banquet—a typical banquet from the Golden State. Even the vegetables grew upon the hillsides that slant toward the Pacific ocean. The courses were arranged by Madame Demoret, of this city, but the dishes were prepared by the Senator's caterer. The tea and coffee service of solid gold was from the California mines on massive golden trays; the forks and spoons were of hammered silver, of rich designs; the china was hand-painted Dresden, Vienna and Paris ware, and each

[216]*NY Herald*, Mar 6, 1892.
[217]A detailed description of the home and its furnishings is in UNC, SFS, "C," 36.
[218]George Granthem Bain, in *LA Times*, Jun 25, 1893.   [219]GTC, *Stanford*, 450.
[220]*Wash. Critic*, n.d., in UNC, SFS, "C."

plate was distinct in itself, containing some historic portrait or scene, or some old design. The "Raid on the Sabine Women" adorned the plate of Senator [William M.] Evarts, and the face of Mary, Queen of Scots, looked up at Senator [Joseph N.] Dolph when he reversed his plate. The table was spread in the finest of white damask, relieved in the center by a large basket of roses, flanked on each side by a [sic] oval plaque of Jacqueminots. The company was received in the long oriental parlors, where bright and beautifully blended colors presented an almost enchanting picture.[221]

Jane Stanford's lavish receptions and parties, not to mention her philanthropies, made her one of the most popular ladies in Washington.[222] Mrs. Stanford's calling list in Washington grew to a thousand. And her dinners were regarded as among the grandest the city had ever seen.[223] After reelection to the Senate, the Stanfords increased their dining room capacity far beyond the original eighteen it had seated.

In January 1891 the Stanfords held a gala party for President and Mrs. Benjamin Harrison. Among the guests at this famous affair were Vice President Levi Morton, Chief Justice of the United States Melville W. Fuller, and a number of senators and generals.[224]

A few days later, when the Stanfords were guests at a White House reception, Jane Stanford "literally blazed with diamonds." Her jewels had long been a topic of conversation in social circles and a target of criticism for some journalists. One disgruntled newspaper editor snapped that one month's interest on her jewels would have carpeted the stone floor on which the ladies stood catching cold.[225] Her diamond collection alone was valued at $1 million. In addition, she had a spectacular collection of emeralds, pearls, and rubies. Her accessories surpassed the richest ever seen before in Washington; a single diamond necklace was valued at $600,000.[226] Grover Cleveland's disgruntled biographer wrote, "Mrs. Stanford wore diamonds, as the press put it, 'like a coat of mail,' and at one reception wore $250,000 in gems on her ample throat and bosom."[227] The following estimate of the value of her collection was made in 1882, "She is reputed to have the finest diamonds in that city [New York], except Mrs. John Jacob Astor's."[228]

She must have continued adding to her collection. Entire editorials—with typical journalistic excess—were dedicated to her priceless collection—which included the jewels of the former Queen Isabella of Spain—and to her ostentatious wearing of them. A later estimate of Jane Stanford's collection reported that she owned more diamonds than any royal family in Europe, except the British and Russian.[229] In an attempt to defend any ostentatious use of her jewelry, in 1886 the editor of the *San*

[221] *Sac Record-Union*, Feb 10, 1886.
[223] UNC, SFS 18:7–9.
[225] *Fremont News*, Jan 23, 1891.
[227] Nevins, *Grover Cleveland*, 314.
[229] UNC, SFS 25:19 and 22.
[222] *Wash. News*, Jan 29, 1887.
[224] *Wash. Post*, Jan 16, 1891.
[226] UNC, SFS 10:1 and 53.
[228] *SF Argonaut*, Sep 16, 1882.

Francisco City Argus had written, "Mrs. Leland Stanford has a million in diamonds and seldom wears any. She owns four complete sets bought from Queen Isabella of Spain."[230] One wonders just what inconspicuous use of her jewels made this defense necessary!

All this reminds one of a letter Huntington penned to Colton years earlier on the subject of Jane Stanford's jewels—rather on her wearing of jewels. It had to do with the railroad's negative press coverage by Loring Pickering and George Kenyan Fitch, joint owners and publishers of the *San Francisco Bulletin* and *San Francisco Call*, both of whom "demonstrated a vigorous dislike for any kind of monopoly or display of ostentatious wealth."[231]

Huntington wrote:

> I am satisfied that much of Pickering's bitterness comes from his wife's dislike of Mrs. Stanford. Mrs. S[tanford] has certainly managed to get the ill will of most of the women of Cal[ifornia] that she has come in contact with and much of it is on account of toating [sic] her *Kar* of 30 tons weight around from tea party to tea party.[232]

Unfortunately for later Stanford-Huntington relations, Colton did not follow Huntington's advice to "burn this letter when you have read it."

At their banquets the Stanfords entertained not only presidents, former presidents, senators, congressmen, and Supreme Court justices, but scientists, artists, pageboys, and their own employees. Hardly a day passed that some notable figure did not call at the Stanford home. On at least one occasion they played host to the entire congressional delegation from the Pacific Coast.[233]

Two of Stanford's closest friends in the capital were Democrat Stephen J. Field, who must have given Stanford *some* influence with the Cleveland administration, and Republican congressman Joseph McKenna, later appointed an associate justice of the Supreme Court to succeed Field when he retired in 1897.[234]

Judge William Morrow said later that he often visited the Stanford home in Washington because of the good company to be found there and because he frequently consulted Stanford.[235] Other Stanford friends included John Carlisle, congressman, then senator, and afterward Cleveland's secretary of the treasury, Sen. Justin S. Morrill of Vermont, Sen. William P. Frye of Maine, and the indomitable James G. Blaine, also of Maine.[236]

---

[230] *SF City Argus*, Feb 13, 1886.

[231] Salvador A. Ramírez, ed., *The Octopus Speaks: The Colton Letters* (Carlsbad: TTD, 1982), 131 n13.

[232] CPH to David Colton, Oct 15, 1874.

[233] Fisher, "Stanford," 2–3.

[234] *BDAC*, 1304.

[235] GTC inter. of Morrow, Oct 28, 1927, in "Record" book (Spring 1907), 17.

[236] Fisher, "Stanford," 34. Blaine was born in Penn.

A Note on Stanford Philanthropies

The diversity of Stanford's business interests was matched only by his civic and philanthropic concerns. In 1882 he was listed as the honorary president of the "Carnival Association," which included the Ladies' Protection and Relief Society, the French Benevolent Society, the Old Ladies' Home, the San Francisco Female Hospital, the Pacific Dispensary Hospital, and the Little Sisters' Infant Shelter.[237] And when the Ladies' Silk Culture Society of California was incorporated in 1885, it listed Leland Stanford as a member, without specifying whether honorary or active.[238]

As the Stanfords took their place among the social elite of the nation's capital, their philanthropies grew. They received from twenty-five to forty "begging letters" per day; within one week requests for money came from as far away as Egypt, Ireland, and India.[239] Wherever they went, they assisted needy causes. Jane Stanford gave the Presbyterian church in Menlo Park a new organ; she sponsored five kindergartens in San Francisco, giving them a combined endowment of $100,000.[240] She appointed Fred Crocker, Timothy Hopkins, Joseph Grant, Russell Wilson, and her brother Henry Lathrop as trustees to administer this fund.[241] By 1889 she was sponsoring fifteen different kindergartens.[242] A letter to Jane in 1890 by the president of the Golden Gate Kindergarten Association said that Jane's efforts and gifts had "trained" more than three thousand children in her kindergartens since the death of Leland, Jr.[243] In commemoration of the work of Fr. Junípero Serra, she erected a statue in his honor in Monterey. After attending a church there, she donated $200 for a badly needed carpet.[244] On a short trip to Portland, Oregon, she gave over $500 to an orphans' home.[245] Mrs. Stanford's philanthropies in the East were not as extensive as in the West, but they were considerable. On one occasion Jane Stanford gave $150,000 to a home for old women in Albany, New York.[246] In January 1889 Stanford received a letter of thanks from Maine senator William P. Frye for a gift of $7,000 to Bates College in Maine.[247] Frye praised the Stanfords for their "generous hearts" in doing with their wealth the "greatest possible good to the world." These philanthropies are representative, but do not scratch the surface of the causes to which they contributed during their senatorial tenure. Frank Shay said that the total of Stanford's benefactions "was a large one—written in seven figures."[248]

---

[237]*CRec* 1882 2 (Oct 27), 4.   [238]Evelyn Craig Pattiani, "Silk in Piedmont," *CHSQ* 1952 31 (4): 337.
[239]UNC, SFS "C."
[240]*SF Argonaut*, Dec 1, 1890; UNC, SFS 18:1–4; 25:16; *SF Bulletin*, May 14, 1886; *Portland* [Maine] *Argus*, Jul 1891, in SFS 2:111.   [241]*SF Argonaut*, Dec 1, 1890.
[242]Nash, "Dictation by H.C. Nash on Leland Stanford," 99.
[243]Sarah B. Cooper, pres., Golden Gate Kindergarten Assn., to JLS, Jun 10, 1892.
[244]*Monterey Monitor*, Jul 1891, in UNC, SFS 2:110.   [245]*Portland* [Oregon] *Sunday Mercury*, Sep 24, 1887.
[246]*Sac Record-Union*, May 17, 1886.   [247]William P. Frye to LS, Jan 17, 1889.
[248]Shay, "A Lifetime in California," 110.

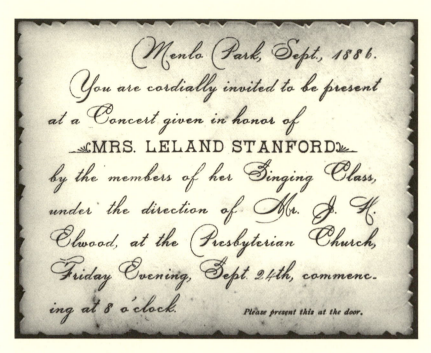

Menlo Park, Sept., 1886.

You are cordially invited to be present at a Concert given in honor of

MRS. LELAND STANFORD

by the members of her Singing Class, under the direction of Mr. J. H. Elwood, at the Presbyterian Church, Friday Evening, Sept. 24th, commencing at 8 o'clock.

Please present this at the door.

131. Concert given in honor of Mrs. Leland Stanford,
Menlo Park Presbyterian Church, September 24, 1886.
Elmo Hayden Collection.

STANFORD FREE KINDERGARTEN.

132. Stanford Free Kindergarten, Mayfield, April 28, 1887.
Stanford University Archives.

133. Stanford Kindergarten, Menlo Park, November 21, 1898.
Elmo Hayden Collection.

The California senator and his wife continued to entertain regally and often, despite official duties and poor health. They once gave a feast for all of Washington's Western Union messenger boys.[249] Every Christmas the Senate pages were invited to a party and given $5 with which to buy a gift.[250] In one year alone the California millionaire was said to have spent over $100,000 for entertaining.[251] With his fortune it is no wonder that Stanford could give his entire Senate salary of $7,000 to his private secretary—or so it was reported—to supplement the secretary's regular salary of $2,500.[252]

[249]BB, *Mrs. Stanford*, 82.
[250]Test. of Carl Loeffler, a Sen. page when LS was a sen., at LSJU Founders' Day celebration, in Wash., Mar 9, 1936, in LS papers.   [251]*Pittsburgh* [Penn.] *Times*, Dec 21, 1887.
[252]Ibid.

Visit of President and Mrs. Benjamin Harrison—
April 14–May 16, 1891
(In California April 25–May 4, 1891)[253]

Returning to California at the close of the short session of the Fifty-first Congress, Jane Stanford was welcomed home with a delightful luncheon-party given by May Hopkins at her Menlo Park estate. Guests included Anna Hewes, Mrs. Henry L. Dodge, Mrs. George Loomis, Mrs. Theodore Payne, Mrs. Alma Park, Mrs. William Kohl, and various "Misses."[254]

Parties such as this were almost a commonplace among the social elite of San Francisco, but the visit by the president of the United States and the first lady was a spectacular affair to be remembered. The Stanfords and the Benjamin Harrisons shared more than political affinity; they had become close friends. In 1891, when the first family traveled to California and took an extended tour of the West Coast, rumor had it that Stanford footed the entire bill.[255] Harrison's presidential train reached Oakland on Saturday, April 25, and the party spent that night at the Palace Hotel in San Francisco.[256] After a restful Sunday in San Francisco, First Lady Caroline Lavinia (Scott) Harrison and other San Francisco ladies were entertained in the evening by Jane Stanford.[257] Two days later, on April 28, 1891, the Stanfords gave one of the city's most magnificent balls in honor of the president and his wife.

After dinner there was a reception to which about five hundred guests were invited, and hundreds turned out to meet the president and First Lady in the Stanford's Nob Hill home, reported to be ablaze with lights into the early hours of the morning.[258]

President and Mrs. Harrison returned to the Palace Hotel at half-past

Stanford's San Francisco Dinner Guest List Honoring President and Mrs. Benjamin Harrison

included Gov. and Mrs. Henry H. Markham, Adm. and Mrs. Andrew E. K. Benham, Judge and Mrs. William Morrow, Mr. and Mrs. Russell Harrison, Mr. and Mrs. Henry L. Dodge, Mr. and Mrs. Morris Estee, Col. and Mrs. John P. Jackson, Mr. and Mrs. George Boyd, Mrs. McKee, Mrs. David Hewes, Mrs. Timothy Hopkins, Mrs. Moses Hopkins, Mrs. Dimmick, Mrs. Gov. Frederick Low, Mrs. Adefia M. Easton, Miss Gwin, Miss Minnie Houghton, Postmaster-General John Wanamaker, Secretary of Agriculture Jeremiah McLain Rusk, Sen. Charles N. Felton, Mayor George Sanderson, Gen. Thomas Howard Ruger, Col. Fred Crocker, Irving Scott, and Lloyd Tevis.*

*SF Argonaut, May 4, 1891; on Benham, see United States Naval Academy, *Register of Alumni: Graduates and former Naval Cadets and Midshipmen* (USNA Alumni Assn., 1972), 3.

---

[253]"Tour of the President, to the Pacific Coast, April 14th to May 16th, 1891." The complete itinerary of Pres. Benjamin Harrison's trip to the Pac. Coast, with tables and maps. In LS Papers.

[254]*SF Argonaut*, Apr 27, 1891.   [255]A number of newspaper eds. repeated this rumor, in UNC, SFS II.

[256]*NY Tribune*, Apr 27, 1891.   [257]*NY Press*, Apr 27, 1891.

[258]*SF Examiner*, Apr 29, 1891; *SF Argonaut*, May 4, 1891.

134. Senator Stanford,
President Benjamin Harrison,
and Postmaster General
John Wanamaker at the
Palo Alto farm house, 1891.
Author's Collection.

eleven, pleased with the delightful way in which they had been entertained. On the following day the presidential party was entertained at luncheon at the Palo Alto farm, where Senator Felton and Governor and Mrs. Markham were again Stanford's guests.[259]

Harrison enjoyed the farm immensely: he toured the university, still under construction, visited the world famous champion trotting-horse stables, and had lunch at the Stanford home.[260] The presidential party traveled to Monterey on Wednesday, April 29, and then went on to visit other parts of the state. Fred Crocker and Mr. and Mrs. William H. Crocker accompanied the presidential party.[261]

The Harrisons were pleased, indeed, with their California visit, described as "a series of public ovations that were without precedent on this side of the continent."[262]

[259]*NY Herald*, Apr 29 and 30, 1891.   [260]*SF Chronicle*, Apr 30, 1891.

[261]*SF Argonaut*, May 4, 1891.   [262]Ibid.

STANFORD'S SIXTH AND LAST (JANE'S FIFTH) EUROPEAN TRIP— JUNE 1–OCTOBER 12, 1892

On Tuesday, April 5, 1892, Senator Stanford, again in the middle of the Senate's long session, returned briefly to California.[263] The trip home lasted less than a month and he was back in Washington on the 28th of April.[264] (Jane had remained at home nursing her seriously ill sister, Anna, and did not leave San Francisco until May 23, when she departed in a private car.[265])

Stanford wrote to Thomas Welton in Australia that he was suffering attacks of the "grippe," which affected his legs and his hearing. The loss of hearing, he said, gave him the most trouble. He added that he and Jennie were leaving on the night of May 30 for New York, where they would sail for another trip to Europe.[266]

About a week earlier, Tim and May Hopkins had left San Francisco for New York to join the Stanfords on their European tour.[267] The Stanfords' friendship with Tim and May had grown so close over the years that Tim seemed almost to fill the role of their lost son.

On June 1, 1892, the four travelers—the Stanfords and the Hopkinses—left New York together on the Inman Line's 10,699-ton steamer *City of Paris* for England, on what would be the Stanfords' final European trip together.[268] Tim Hopkins later said that they sat in adjoining deck chairs and talked chiefly about development of the university.[269]

The party arrived in Liverpool on June 8 and the next day they were in London.[270]

As mentioned earlier, on this tour Stanford's health was worse than it had ever been before.[271] In a letter from Aix-les-Bains, after the two couples had parted, Jane wrote to May lamenting that her husband's health had not improved after a dreary week on the continent; she despaired of his life.[272] On July 4 the Stanfords were still in Aix-les-Bains, but when a physician prescribed a change of air, they made an excursion to Switzerland for the "reaction" part of the cure and then returned to Aix-les-Bains for a second cure.[273] In the middle of July Jane Stanford wrote with considerable relief that her husband was feeling much better.[274] In mid-August they were at Lake Thun, in Switzerland.[275]

---

[263]Ibid., Apr 11, 1892.   [264]Ibid., May 2, 1892.

[265]Ibid., May 30, 1892.

[266]LS to TWS, May 30, 1892; JLS to May and TNH, Mar 10, 1892, from Wash. mentions Jun 1 as the date of departure on their trip to Europe.   [267]*SF Argonaut*, May 23, 1892.

[268]Ibid., Jun 6, 1892; TNH papers, SUA.

[269]TNH to Ray Lyman Wilbur, pres. of LSJU, Apr 21, 1925.

[270]*Times* (of London), Jun 10, 1892; *SF Argonaut*, Jun 13, 1892. THN papers.

[271]See univ. chaplain, *supra*, first LSJU commencement.

[272]JLS to TNH and May Hopkins, Jun 22, 1892; JLS to Mrs. DSJ, Jun 16, 1892.

[273]*SF Argonaut*, Jul 4, 1892.   [274]JLS to Dr. and Mrs. DSJ, Jul 13, 1892.

[275]*SF Argonaut*, Aug 15, 1892.

Timothy Nolan and Mary (May) Crittenden Hopkins

Timothy Nolan Hopkins was the son of Patrick and Catherine (Fallon) Nolan. Born on March 2, 1859, in Hallowell (near Augusta), Maine, he was only nine years older than Leland, Jr.—still young enough to be treated as a son by the Stanfords. Adopted and then rejected by Mary Frances (Sherwood) Hopkins, his foster mother, Tim had found a second adoptive family in the Stanfords.[a]

On November 8, 1887, Frances Hopkins married Edward F. Searles, a wealthy Massachusetts architect, a man twenty-three years younger than she.[b] Within a year she disinherited her adopted son. Following her death on July 25, 1891, it was confirmed in her will that she had left Tim and May without a cent. And Searles was unwilling to divide the estate.[c] As expected, Tim contested the will. On April 10, 1893, Superior Court judge James V. Coffey signed an order distributing all the California portion of the contested will to Hopkins, an amount estimated at $1 million. It was reported that this judgment provided him with a total inheritance, after several compromises with the new Mrs. Searles, of about $2.8 million.[d]

Thus the ailing Stanford lived to see his young friend vindicated.

Timothy Hopkins described himself as a protégé of Leland Stanford.[e]

In 1887 Jane Stanford became godmother to the Hopkinses' daughter Lydia, born at Sherwood Hall in Menlo Park on March 27, 1887.[f] Lydia, who was educated at an "eastern finishing school," enjoyed her debut into society on December 1, 1906, almost two years after the death of her godmother.[g]

[a]JLS papers. On Jul 9, 1879, sixteen months after the death of MH, Mary Frances Hopkins legally adopted twenty-year-old TNH, "before Judge Selden S. Wright of Old County Court." *The World* (not identified by city), Aug 1, 1891; *PA Times*, Jan 9, 1936. Archibald Treat wrote on Aug 18, 1937, that TNH's mother, who lived in Sacramento, refused to allow the Hopkinses to adopt her son, but that after MH died, realizing the opportunity membership in such a family would be to her son, she relented and allowed the adoption to proceed. Treat, "The Stanfords and their Golden Key," 36–37. For an excellent bio. sketch of TNH, see *SF Argonaut*, Aug 3, 1891.
[b]*SF Call*, Nov 9, 1887; Searles' obit., *SF Examiner*, Aug 7, 1920; *SF Chronicle*, Aug 9, 1920.
[c]*SF Examiner*, Aug 13, 1891.   [d]*SF Chronicle*, Apr 11, 1893.
[e]GTC inter. with TNH, Oct 28, 1927, in TNH, "Record" book (Spring 1907), 21–22. In TNH papers, SUA.
[f]Charmayne Kreuz, *A Tradition of New Horizons: The Story of Menlo Park* (Menlo Park: The City of Menlo Park, 1974), 23; Lydia was born after three baby boys were stillborn. Helen H. Kincaid, *Kellogg Research, Incorporated Presents The Hopkins Hoax* (Williamston, NC: KRI, 1973), 54.
[g]*SF Chronicle*, Dec 1, 1906.

The Stanfords spent part of the fall in England and on October 4 stopped over at the North Western Hotel in Liverpool before sailing for home the next day—their first trans-Atlantic crossing on the White Star Line's 9,861-ton *Majestic*, not the longest ship in the world, but at 566 feet the longest ship they had ever traveled on.[276] They arrived in New York on Wednesday, October 12 and a week later were once again home in California.[277]

[276]JLS to May Hopkins, Oct 4, 1892; *Times* (of London), Oct 7, 1892; *SF Argonaut*, Sep 26, 1892.
[277]*SF Argonaut*, Oct 17 and 24, 1892; LS to DSJ, Sep 28, 1892; JLS to TNH and May Hopkins, Oct 30, 1892.

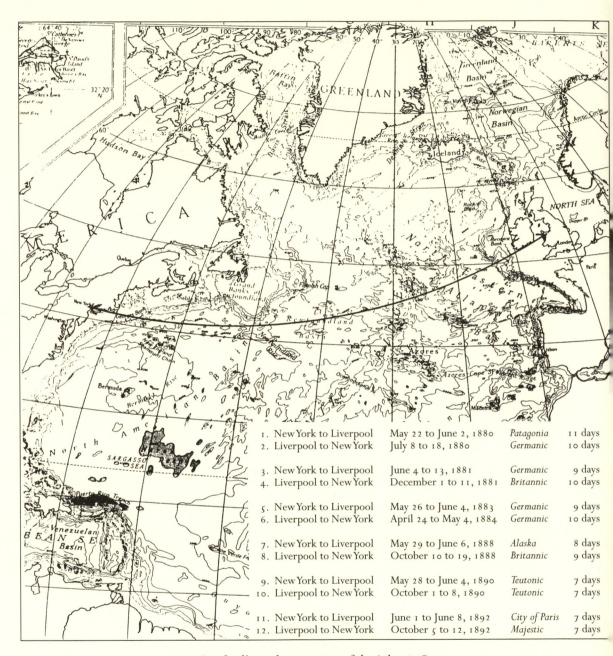

1. New York to Liverpool	May 22 to June 2, 1880	*Patagonia*	11 days
2. Liverpool to New York	July 8 to 18, 1880	*Germanic*	10 days
3. New York to Liverpool	June 4 to 13, 1881	*Germanic*	9 days
4. Liverpool to New York	December 1 to 11, 1881	*Britannic*	10 days
5. New York to Liverpool	May 26 to June 4, 1883	*Germanic*	9 days
6. Liverpool to New York	April 24 to May 4, 1884	*Germanic*	10 days
7. New York to Liverpool	May 29 to June 6, 1888	*Alaska*	8 days
8. Liverpool to New York	October 10 to 19, 1888	*Britannic*	9 days
9. New York to Liverpool	May 28 to June 4, 1890	*Teutonic*	7 days
10. Liverpool to New York	October 1 to 8, 1890	*Teutonic*	7 days
11. New York to Liverpool	June 1 to June 8, 1892	*City of Paris*	7 days
12. Liverpool to New York	October 5 to 12, 1892	*Majestic*	7 days

135. Stanford's twelve crossings of the Atlantic Ocean.
Author's Collection.

The Death of Anna Maria Lathrop Hewes—August 3, 1892

David and Anna Hewes' only published address after they returned from their extended honeymoon in Europe was Anna's San Francisco home at 2101 Van Ness Avenue, where her brother Charles G. Lathrop and his daughter Jennie lived with them.[278] Charles' motherless daughter was described by Hewes as the "light and joy" of their home.[279]

David and Anna Maria Hewes were part of high society in San Francisco and were known for their elaborate dinner parties.[280] While the Stanfords were abroad in 1892, Anna became ill and was placed under the constant vigil of a Mrs. Robertson who lived at 722½ Twentieth Street.[281] The Stanfords arrived at the Grand Hôtel de l'Europe in Aix-les-Bains, about forty miles south of Geneva, on June 14.[282] Two days later, Jane wrote to Mrs. David Starr Jordan, "Never in all my travels from home have I ever felt so joyless, so very depressed. My thoughts travel back to my very sick sister who does not appear to advance since my departure. I fear it depressed her and she cannot rebound."[283]

Writing to May and Tim Hopkins on July 6 from Aix-les-Bains, Jane said she and her husband were leaving for Switzerland the next Wednesday morning [July 13].[284] They had been in Aix-les-Bains for four weeks and the doctor wanted them to return about August 20 for another four weeks. Then the writer added, almost prophetically: "My sister is no better and failing I fear, from the cables I get. I fear I may never see her again in this life."

On their way to Bern, the Stanfords stopped over at the Hôtel Beau Rivage in Geneva.[285] On July 19, in the Swiss capital, Jane received an expected but unwelcome letter from Mrs. Robertson describing Anna's deteriorating condition: "She had a very serious chill last Thursday morning [the 14th] from which she has never rallied enough to make up loss [sic] ground. To me she appears to be gradually sinking every day. She has not taken any solid food for five days."[286]

Anna Hewes died on August 3, 1892, in San Francisco two months short of her sixtieth birthday, only three years after her marriage to David Hewes.[287] Her sister, Jane, had been too ill to attend her wedding in 1889, and was now in Europe at the time of her death.

---

[278]Hewes, "Hewes, An Autobiography," 263; *San Francisco Directory for the Year Commencing May 1, 1891*, 692 and 833. Today this site is occupied by a multistoreyed res.-com.-off. building with a donut shop on the corner.

[279]Hewes, "Hewes, An Autobiography," 263.

[280]On Feb 23, 1891, e.g., *SF Argonaut*, Mar 2, 1891.

[281]*SFCD*, 1896, 1330.

[282]JLS to TNH and May Hopkins, Jun 22, 1892.

[283]JLS to Mrs. DSJ, Jun 16, 1892.

[284]JLS to May and TNH, Jul 6, 1892.

[285]JLS to TNH, Jul 18, 1892.

[286]Mrs. Robertson to JLS, Jul 19, 1892.

[287]*SF Chronicle*, Aug 4, 1892; *Memorial Address on the Life and Character of Mrs. David Hewes, with The Funeral Services Held at the Residence of Her Sister, Mrs. Leland Stanford, San Francisco., Cal., Aug 6, 1892*, gives the date of her death as Aug 3. This 42-p. brochure contains much on the Lathrop family; Friis, *Hewes*, 58, gives Aug 2, 1892, as the date of her death, as does Hewes himself in his "Autobiography," 263.

Following Anna's death, Jane received an unexpected though welcome letter of condolence from a "Mrs. [Catherine] McNeill." She answered the letter upon her return home, and appended to it the note, "From my old housekeeper who lived with me fourteen years at Sacramento home."[288]

JANE STANFORD TO DAVID STARR JORDAN ON JENNIE LATHROP

Kind friend

Since you bade me good bye and left for California, I have thought seriously of our conversation concerning my four years and a half experiences, with its sorrows its cares, its burdens, its sad disappointments almost greater than poor weak human nature could bear, but as the load increased in weight I clung more and more closely to my loving Heavenly Father and have never lost my faith in His promises.

So very many unexpected and new phases in turn are nature have been brought to my attention, and in a way have added to my sorrows. Some hearts have hardened towards me who should have been sympathetic and tender because of my dear husband's loving remembrance of them and these revelations of character have led me into a train of thought that impels me to write this letter to you that you may fully understand the relation that exists betwixt my niece Jennie L. Lathrop and myself.

She is the daughter of my brother Charles G. Lathrop, her mother passed from earth life when she was about four months old, and while she was ill she expressed the wish that I would care for her little daughter if she did not recover from her illness. To comfort her distressed heart I told her I would do the best I could for her child.

When I told my dear husband the request that had been made by Jennie's Mother, he was most decided in his objections to my assuming such a responsibility, first because of my poor health, and because of the great cares I had already to bear, and because of some misunderstanding that might follow were I to assume the care. Some might think it was adoption, which we both felt could never be, and we both felt that our hearts best love had been given, never to be replaced, by any other love for any, but our own dear son.

After duly considering the case I persuaded my sister Anna M Lathrop who was then unmarried to take the responsibility and go live with my brother Charles the Father of the child. She immediately assumed the care and was a loving devoted aunt to Jennie until she was called to her higher better life. Jennie was then seven years old. As my dear sister's life here drew near its close, she requested me to do what I could for "her little girl," the second time. My husband and I discussed the consequence if I took charge of her, and that I must be guarded and careful to let the world and the dear child herself know that I had never adopted her—all this I have been faithful in following—I have clothed her educated her and done the best I knew by her—she has been with me about six years. Another wish expressed by my dear Sister in reference to Jennie L. Lathrop was that she be sent to a convent and kept under the influence of the Sisters until Jennie arrived at the age of eighteen years. My sister made this child her heir, willing to her, her property which amounted to nearly fifty thousand dollars, with the expressed wish that she should not receive any interest until she arrive at the age of eighteen. My husband gave by will to her as well as to all the children of my brothers, except to those who have come since his departure from life here, the sum of one hundred thousand dollars.*

*JLS to DSJ, Nov 11, 1894. [Original punctuation retained.]

---

[288]Mrs. [Catherine] O'Neill to JLS, Oct 28, 1892.

It had been rumored without foundation in fact as early as 1885 that the Stanfords had adopted young Jennie Lathrop, and after the death of Anna the rumor persisted that Jennie had finally became a member of Leland and Jane's family.[289] Even the authority of David Hewes can be used to prove this point, when he wrote, "After the death of Mrs. Hewes [Anna Maria] her niece became a member of her aunt Stanford's family, and by her [Aunt Jane] was educated at the convent in San Jose.[290]

Such was not the case, however, as Jane Stanford made unmistakably clear in a lengthy letter she addressed to David Starr Jordan on November 11, 1894.

Hewes and his brother-in-law Charles Lathrop took the body of Anna to New York, where she was buried next to her parents at the Albany Rural Cemetery.[291] David Hewes provided that every year on the anniversary of her death Anna's grave would be decorated with a mat of flowers.[292]

GUESTS AT THE PALO ALTO FARM

Guests entertained at the Palo Alto farm included the common people as well as the famous; anyone was welcome to call on the affable senator. On May 19, 1893, a committee from the Palo Alto Improvement Club dropped by unannounced to discuss some local problems with Stanford. Though a semi-invalid at the time, he welcomed them. They discussed a number of problems with which Stanford promised to help them. Then the guests, realizing how fragile his health was, tried to excuse themselves. But he insisted that they stay, and they spent the rest of the afternoon discussing anything they wished. The members of the committee were favorably impressed by their host's hospitality and homespun earnestness.[293]

At the San Francisco railroad headquarters at Fourth and Townsend there was a fairly large waiting room, with a desk, two dozen chairs, and a messenger boy.[294] The chairs were usually occupied by people who wanted favors or had something to sell. Newspapermen, businessmen, and would-be politicians did not like the waiting room so they chatted with each other as they stood around in Frank Shay's office nearby, waiting until the Governor would see them. The most persistent callers, Frank Shay said, were women who were reluctant to tell him in advance what they wanted or why they wanted to see Stanford. About 75 percent of them went away with their stories untold; the rest were "firmly eased out."[295]

There were many frequent visitors to the Governor's office from members of

[289]*SF Argonaut*, Aug 29, 1885: "Mrs. Leland Stanford has adopted her niece, Miss Lathrop of Albany, New York, who will hereafter live with her."   [290]Hewes, "Hewes, An Autobiography," 263.

[291]Friis, *Hewes*, 58; Putnam, *Lieutenant Joshua Hewes*, 195.

[292]He did the same for the grave of his first wife, Putnam, *Lieutenant Joshua Hewes*, 263.

[293]Reported in "A Tribute from Citizens of Palo Alto," in LS papers.

[294]Shay, "A Lifetime in California," 111.   [295]Ibid., 112.

the city's journalistic community. (His friends persisted in using this title even after he became a senator.) They included:

STANFORD'S FREQUENT EDITORIAL VISITORS

Frank Pixley of the *San Francisco Argonaut*
Marcus Boruck of the *Spirit of the Times*
John Parker Hale Wentworth of the *Resources of California*
Henry George, the single-tax apostle of the *Post*
John H. Gilmour of the *Call*
Arthur McEwen, a "free-lance satirist and master of vitriolic English"
Fred MacCrellish, owner of the *Alta California*
Fremont Older of the *Bulletin* (later *Call-Bulletin*)
Frank Gassaway, writer, poet, manager of the *Examiner*'s Sunday edition
Edward W. Townsend of the *Examiner*
Fred Marriott, owner of the weekly *Newsletter*
Ned Hamilton of the *Examiner*
John P. de Young of the *Chronicle*
Thomas E. Flynn of the *Wasp*
Ambrose Bierce.[296]

Frank Shay wrote that though these gentlemen called upon the Governor to discuss politics and business affairs, or to get a story, not one of them ever asked for money or favors.

This testifies to their respect for the Governor.

---

[296]Ibid., 112A.

CHAPTER 25

The End of the Line

We Have Known for Months that the End Was Near[1]
March 9, 1824–June 20/21, 1893

Those who view Leland Stanford primarily as one of the Big Four with Mark Hop-kins, Charles Crocker, and Collis P. Huntington, who parlayed others' money into personal fortunes in constructing the Central Pacific and other railroads, show an invidious bias coloring all judgments. —Robert H. Alway, M.D.[2]

RETIREMENT AND FAILING HEALTH

Senator Stanford lived at the Palo Alto farm in a state of semiretirement from the fall of 1892 until his death the following spring. Though ill and confined to his home most of the time, he retained an interest in public affairs, and occasionally invited the entire California Congressional delegation to his country home.[3] The Governor made a brief trip to Washington in February 1893 and put in an appearance in the Senate on March 1.[4] From there he went to New York. Jane Stanford wrote to May and Tim Hopkins that she was "grateful and so deeply thankful" that her husband was "here with us in this life and on this holy day [Good Friday]."[5] He was better than he had been in a long time, though still unable to walk with his old vigor.

As Stanford in his "retirement" took a less and less active part in Southern Pacific counsels, he covered his own interests by making sure that Nick Smith continued not only as the system's treasurer, but after April 5, 1893, as a member of the board of directors.[6] Stanford remained chairman of the executive committee of the Southern Pacific Company and president of the Central Pacific, still one of the Southern Pacific's leased lines, until his death.[7]

---

[1]CPH to *NY Times*, Jun 22, 1893.

[2]Alway, "A History of Stanford Vineyards and Wineries," 5–7. The occasion of this talk was the One Hundred Eighteenth Quarterly Dinner of the SMFW at the LSJU Faculty Club, Jun 1, 1977. The derogatory term "Big Four" was not current during the lives of many of the men insulted by its innuendoes.

[3]*Memorial Addresses on the Life and Character of Leland Stanford*, 82.

[4]JLS to DSJ, Mar 2, 1893.   [5]JLS to May Hopkins, Mar 31, 1893.

[6]*Annual Report of the Southern Pacific Company, Its Proprietary Companies, and Leased Lines, for the Year Ending Dec 31, 1892*, 2.   [7]Ibid., 89 and 97.

136. Southern Pacific Company board of directors.
Southern Pacific Company Annual Report, 1893.

The Stanfords were expected home in May; it was even rumored that they would visit Mexico on their way to California.[8] They did not go to Mexico, but Stanford wanted to attend the Columbian Exposition in Chicago on the way home. Jane was definitely opposed even to a side trip to Chicago. Her reason: "Mr. Stanford would have to go around in a chair and I do not like to subject him to this disagreeable position."[9] But apparently in better health, the Governor had his way, and in April they stopped off for a week in Chicago.[10] They arrived home on May 1.[11] This would be Stanford's last trip east, and it was rumored that he was about to resign his senatorship, a step thought by some long overdue.[12]

In a lengthy editorial on the second Stanford University commencement, which took place on May 31, 1893, the editor of the *San Francisco Call* described the festivities and remarked that Stanford was slated to participate in the program, but "did not feel up to the exaction."[13] Stanford writer Peter Allen goes one step further, writing that Stanford was so weak at the commencement that he had to be steadied by a man on each side as he walked to the platform.[14]

Stanford's doctors attributed his poor health to hardships endured in younger days on the rugged surveying expeditions he made with Theodore Judah and with the way he and his engineers slept on flat cars wrapped in buffalo robes, often find-

[8] *SF Argonaut*, Apr 3 and 10, 1893.
[9] JLS to May Hopkins, Mar 31, 1893.
[10] JLS to TNH and May Hopkins, Jun 12, 1893. JLS wrote that LS was much better, that he was out with his horses and driving around MP. See *SF Argonaut*, May 1, 1893.
[11] *SF Argonaut*, May 4 and 8, 1893.
[12] *SF Chronicle*, Jun 21, 1893.
[13] *SF Call*, Jun 1, 1893.
[14] Peter C. Allen, *Stanford: From the Foothills to the Bay* (PA: SAA & SHS, 1980), 32.

ing themselves covered with snow in the morning. Nick Smith said that Stanford, who was then strong as an ox, had handled *all* the heavy loads that had to be moved out of the water's reach during the flood season.[15]

Every promise of any improvement in her husband's condition, no matter how slight, made Jane extremely happy. Just a week before he died, she wrote a letter to Tim and May Hopkins whose rambling and punctuation lapses bespeak her haste and excitement:

> I have good news to tell you about Mr. Stanford if my heart had not been lightened of its burden somewhat I could not have desired to write you, for I could not have spoken cheer of one so dear—but a change has commenced for the better and I am not deceiving myself for all our friends see it. Mr. Stanford began the "Salisbury Cure" the last week in April under the direction of the doctor while in New York, and under his direction still continues it. It is a meat diet exclusively—and drinking two quarts of hot water daily, a first one hour and a half before each meal—he has been reduced from 240 to 219. Dr. wants him to get down to 200. he sleeps better, breathes freer—has a wonderful appetite, is so cheerful and hopeful and is a thorough believer in the treatment the results have made us both confident in the future. He will be well—he has to continue it perhaps a year but it is not now a hardship as it was the first four weeks—he still has to be aided in walking but the Dr. assures us he will walk when the muscles grow strong.
>
> JLS[16]

During these doubtful times Nick Smith was solicitous of the Governor's worsening health and wrote a letter to Jane expressing how happy he was when it appeared that his old friend was feeling better.[17]

LELAND STANFORD AND NICK SMITH

Tuesday, June 20, 1893, began no differently from any other day for the Governor. His daily activities were fairly routine: he arose at 7:30, ate a leisurely breakfast, and rode down to the paddocks to watch the horses work out. Bertha Berner tells us that after lunch he and Jane went for a ride in their low-wheeled cabriolet to visit Nick and Mary Smith in nearby San Carlos, eight miles away. Nick's house stood at the northwest corner of Cypress (now San Carlos) and Laurel streets, a site presently occupied by the Eureka Bank.[18] The Stanford and Smith homes were, coincidentally, about the same distance from County Road (today partly El Camino Real and partly Old County Road) and also about the same distance from the Palo Alto and San Carlos train depots. The two must have ridden together many times to their San Francisco offices.

---

[15] BB, *Mrs. Stanford*, 14.   [16] JLS to TNH and May Hopkins, Jun 12, 1893.
[17] NTS to JLS, Mar 7, 1892.
[18] NET and ELT, "Captain Nicholas T. Smith, from Schodack to San Carlos," *LP* 1998 31 (2): 3–28.

137. Last photograph of Leland Stanford.
Author's Collection.

Stanford and Smith reminisced about experiences they shared as partners in their stores in Cold Springs and Michigan City back in the fifties. They had lived on the food they stocked, and they slept on the counter. They used buffalo robes for blankets and their rolled-up boots as pillows. In the rainy season the American River overflowed its banks near their store in Cold Springs, so the two partners worked out a precautionary plan against being inundated in their sleep: they took turns dangling their arms over the counter in order to be awakened by the feel of water if it rose that high. Once, when it was Nick's turn for water guard, the water level climbed up his arm but did not awaken him. They awoke to find themselves lying in water. On this last afternoon the two friends spent together, the old Governor teased Nick about the oft-told story.[19]

Nick loved to talk about the "old days." Tim Hopkins later told of an incident when he and some others, among them Nick Smith, were camping in the Santa Cruz Mountains and they got Nick to talking about an incident when he and Stanford were running a store in the "Bluffs." They asked Nick if it were true, as they had heard, that he and Leland mixed sand with the sugar. Smith denied they had ever done that, but said they had at times mixed water and whiskey to make vinegar.[20] One winter there was a scarcity of vinegar, used by the miners to flavor their beans, but they had plenty of whiskey on hand. By diluting it properly it satisfied the demand for vinegar. They must have been the happiest miners in the camp!

If Leland Stanford ever had what one would call a "pal," it was Nick Smith. Nick and Leland were both members of the prestigious Pacific-Union Club in San Francisco.[21] The club's headquarters was destroyed in the earthquake and fire of 1906,

---

[19]BB, *Mrs. Stanford*, 8.

[20]GTC inter. with TNH, Oct 28, 1927, in "Record" book (Spring 1907), 24.

[21]For NTS, see SMC Probate File #1153; *San Mateo City and County Directory 1905–1906* (SF: SBC, 1905); for LS, see *San Francisco Blue Book* (SF: ALBC, 1890), 157; *Our Society Blue Book*, 1894–1895, 157.

but in the following year—the year of Nick's death—the club bought the remains of the Flood mansion at 1000 California Street, where it reopened in 1910 and still operates there.[22]

The 1852 partnership of Smith and Stanford resulted in the friendship of Smith and Stanford—a friendship that had endured for more than forty years when death separated them. Stanford, who had been ill for years and believed in the inevitability of his own death, once told his wife that if the burden on her became too hard to bear, because of his failing strength, there were two old friends she could turn to. One of them was Capt. Nicholas T. Smith.[23] The second remains unnamed—for Bertha Berner, who named Nick as one, never identified the second. She did say that by the time of Stanford's death the unnamed man had come under Huntington's influence and could no longer be trusted.

138. Capt. Nicholas T. Smith.
Author's Collection.

Frank Shay was not the close, life-long friend that Nick Smith was, but as a result of twenty years' close association with Stanford—as an employee of the Central Pacific legal department, as his personal secretary, and as his attorney in later years—he got to know Stanford as few others did. The following anecdote chronicled by Shay illustrates the uncommonly generous side of the Governor's character:

> In all of the twenty years I never saw the Governor lose his temper, although occasionally provoked. He never said an unkind word even about his enemies. On many occasions he went far out of his way to befriend and actively help those who had attacked him and his associates. As an instance I will mention the case of a man who had been prominent in politics and who blamed "the railroad" for his failure to secure nomination and election to high office, and in his stump speeches his denunciations were scathing. He often stated, however, that he had no complaint to make against Governor Stanford and Charles Crocker, personally or as individuals—that it was

---

[22]"The Pacific-Union Club," a 2-p. synopsis of the hist. of the club and of the Flood mansion, sent to the writer by the Pacific-Union Club.   [23]BB, *Mrs. Stanford*, 86 and 134.

"the railroad" that was to blame for most of the ills prevalent in California. Like all of the other anti-railroad orators, however, no particulars were mentioned or proved facts referred to. General denunciation was the rule.

One morning the Governor said that there was a rumor that Mr. ———— was in serious difficulty growing out of the fact that he had invested thirty thousand dollars, a fund of which he was trustee, in a scheme that had failed. He directed me to call upon the gentleman, at his office, and ascertain the facts. At the same time he handed to me a check signed, but with the amount and payee blank. "Write in whatever amount is necessary to square his account and make it payable to him or to bearer, as he may desire," was the final injunction of the Governor.

I shall not attempt to describe the scene that occurred when Mr. ———— realized that his political enemy had come to his rescue. The amount of the check was $35,000.[24]

THE DEATH OF THE GOVERNOR

At home on the evening of the 20th of June 1893, after visiting the Smiths, Stanford had dinner and then did some reading on economic problems facing the nation. Before retiring, he was given his daily massage, to help his circulation: his poor health kept him from exercising on his own.[25] He had suffered from stiffness for quite some time, and his increasing weight was just too much for his limbs to support. For six weeks before his death, Stanford was subjected to the rigorous diet of hashed meat and hot water mentioned in Jane's June 12 letter to Tim and May Hopkins. Just a week earlier he had been almost unable to move without assistance, and

LELAND STANFORD'S EXACT DATE OF DEATH is uncertain; since he died about midnight we have no way of telling whether it was June 20 or 21, 1893. The biographical sketch published in the Senate *Memorial Addresses* gives the date as June 20; the inscription on the marble slab on Stanford's tomb also bears the date June 20.* Most other sources give the now accepted date of June 21.

Memorial Addresses on the Life and Character of Leland Stanford, 5 and 26.

his hearing had been so impaired that it was difficult at times to carry on a conversation with him, though his mind was still alert. On this sad night he had difficulty sleeping, and at 1:25 in the morning of June 21, his valet, Edward Larguy, or Larguy and Mrs Stanford together—the reports vary—entered his room and found the Governor dead.[26] According to a more detailed—or embellished account, we can't tell which—his valet, hearing a gasp coming from Stanford's bedroom, went

[24]Shay, "A Lifetime in California," 110.   [25]*SF Examiner,* Jun 22, 1893.
[26]Whether found by his wife, his valet, or both together will forever remain uncertain. *SF Examiner,* Jun 21 and 22, 1893; *NY Times,* Jun 22, 1893.

first to arouse Mrs. Stanford and then to Herbert Nash's room and the three of them together found the lifeless body of the sixty-nine-year-old Governor.[27]

Stanford's doctor, Joshua H. Stallard, a graduate of the Royal College of Physicians in London and long-time San Francisco physician—now semiretired in Menlo Park—attributed his patient's death to the overexertion of his weak heart from trying to get out of bed, adding that eating such a heavy dinner possibly aggravated his disorder.[28] Several accounts of Stanford's propensity to overeat appeared in print after his death; friends were reported to have said that for two years they had expected him to die at any time because of it. And not just overeating, but he had a clear preference for what were described as "coarse foods"—corned beef and cabbage being his favorites—tastes he had acquired while growing up and working in rural New York state and during his pioneer days in California.[29]

Dr. James Henry Salisbury, Stanford's New York physician, had recently written to Jane Stanford that her husband was suffering from two disorders—fibremia and locomotor ataxia.[30] He had described the first, he told her, in a book he had written, which he had inscribed to her husband.[31] Fibremia, Dr. Salisbury explained, rendered Stanford liable to dizzy spells, which could culminate in sudden paralytic attacks. The second disorder, locomotor ataxia, was the inability to coordinate the muscles in the execution of voluntary movement.[32] Stanford had suffered symptoms of this disease for years.

In a follow-up letter that Dr. Salisbury wrote to Jane Stanford in late May, he underscored the necessity of adhering strictly to the diet and medicinal regimen he had prescribed. The only thing her husband could lose by this diet, Salisbury wrote, was forty pounds of fat—useless material he would be carrying around in his tired, weak state. Salisbury said that his regimen could prolong her husband's life to age ninety or more![33]

---

[27]*NY Voice*, Jun 29, 1893.

[28]*SF Examiner*, Jun 22, 1893; *SFCD*, 1876–1877, 759; Arthur W. Hafner, ed., *Directory of Deceased American Physicians 1804–1929; a Genealogical Guide to over 149,000 Medical Practitioners providing brief Biographical Sketches drawn from the American Medical Association's Deceased Physician Masterfile* (2 vols., Chicago: AMA, 1993), II, 1470; *Official Register of Physicians and Surgeons in the State of California, Jan 31, 1891* (5th ed., SF: BEMSSC, 1891), 104; *Official Register of Physicians and Surgeons in the State of California, Jan 1, 1893* (6th ed., SF: BEMSSC, 189); John Irving Cleese, *Tales of Old Menlo* (MP: MPHA, 1994), 39.

[29]Ed. written on Jun 25, 1893, by a Wash. corres. of the *LA Times* and pub. in the *Times*, Jul 5, 1893.

[30]Dr. J[ames] H[enry] Salisbury to Mrs. [Leland] Stanford, undated letter [Apr 21, 1893], from dated prescription sent the same day the letter was mailed.

[31]James Henry Salisbury, *Microscopic Examinations of Blood; and Vegetations found in Variola, Vaccina, and Typhoid Fever* (NY: MBC, 1868). Dr. Salisbury was a widely recognized specialist. There are two pages of entries of his pub. works in the *National Union Catalogue—Pre-1956*. See also "Salisbury, James Henry," *NCAB*, VIII, 469–470. (This book is now in the Lane Medical School Library at the Stanford University Medical Center.)

[32]Thomas Lathrop Stedman, *SMDic* (25th ed., Baltimore and London: W & W, 1990), 147, 580, and 892.

[33]Dr. J[ames] H[enry] Salisbury to Mrs. [Leland] Stanford, May 23, 1893.

Upon finding her companion of almost forty-three years lifeless, Jane immediately dispatched a carriage to San Carlos to bring Nick to the farm. He got there at daybreak, the first of Stanford's friends to arrive at the scene.[34]

At 4:24 that morning a special train carrying Jane's brother Charles Lathrop left San Francisco, arriving in Palo Alto at 5:36. A carriage awaited him at the station and he was driven to the Stanford home, about a mile away. As word of his death spread all morning, telegraph messages of condolence reached Jane at home, and incoming trains were filled with friends and railroad officials. Five high officials of the Southern Pacific soon arrived: Alban Towne, general superintendent and manager; Jerome A. Fillmore, general superintendent and manager of the Pacific Coast Division; Henry E. Huntington, nephew of Collis Huntington, who held several high offices in Huntington's eastern railroad empire and in the Southern Pacific (it was he who later founded the Huntington Library); Gerrit L. Lansing, auditor and controller; and Rennie P. Schwerin, manager of Southern Pacific Purchase and Supplies Department.[35]

A statement made by Collis Huntington the following day summarized the thinking of many of Stanford's railroad associates:

> We have known for months that the end was near, but were rather shocked at the suddenness of the sad news. The first intelligence we received was through the papers, and later on this morning private telegrams affirmed the sad tidings. I do not anticipate that the death of the Senator will have any direct effect in the conduct of our affairs, for since his retirement he has taken very little interest in the corporation's business. He was too ill or too engrossed with political affairs, and gladly let those at the helm assume the responsibility. In fact, I think that his retirement came as a relief. I know nothing of the Senator's will, and I am at sea regarding the disposition he has made of his railroad affairs. It matters not how he has disposed of the stock, for the controlling interest will remain where it is at present.[36]

A similar prognosis of Stanford's impending death was noted by the editor of the *Cincinnati Tribune*: "Senator Stanford was last in Washington in April. He was very feeble and seemingly on the verge of dissolution. He called on President Cleveland and at that time a congressman who saw him at the White House sorrowfully predicted that the end was not far off."[37]

Pending funeral arrangements, Stanford's body lay in his upstairs bedroom where he had died. Only a few intimate friends were admitted.[38] Jane, with her brother and niece, Agnes Taylor, Josiah's daughter, kept a constant vigil at his bedside. Later in the day the body, in a black cloth-covered casket, was moved to the

[34][SJ] *Pioneer*, Jul 15, 1893.
[35]Edward F. O'Day, *Varied Types* (SF: TTP, 1915), "Rennie P. Schwerin," 253–258.
[36]*NY Times*, Jun 22, 1893.   [37]*Cincinnati Tribune*, Jun 22 (?), 1893, in SFS "D."
[38]The best account of the funeral was pub. in the *SF Chronicle*, Jun 25, 1893; see also *Memorial Addresses on the Life and Character of Leland Stanford*, 19–26.

center of the library for viewing.[39] Emotions ran high. Fred Crocker was on the verge of tears as he said, "He was the best friend I ever had."[40] According to Jane Stanford, this feeling was reciprocated. In 1895 she wrote to forty-year-old Fred Crocker—she generally called him "Col. Fred"[41]—that her husband had considered him his best associate and his closest friend.[42]

Nick Smith remained indoors most of the day, seeing to it that the funeral arrangements were carried out as planned.

Thirty-five-year-old Herbert Nash—who had been at the side of the Governor as his private secretary constantly since the death of Leland, Jr.—assumed the burden of personally supervising matters and looking after the visitors. Most of the time Jane remained in seclusion, seeing only a few of her closest friends.

STANFORD'S FUNERAL

Shortly before noon on June 24, the day of burial, 150 employees of the farm and stables came to the house to view the man everyone considered a friend. Especially notable among them was Charles Corcoran—"Old Charley"—as he was known. Stanford and Charley had wielded picks together in the early days in Michigan City. "Old Charley" was later given a good job at the breeding stables and was told by Stanford that "he need do no work beyond drawing his salary."[43] Charley was persuaded against his will to look at the face of his old friend—the sight sent the seventy-six-year-old man into convulsive sobbing and he had to be led away.

A few minutes before 1 P.M. a black hearse was drawn up to the door of the house; the casket was carried to the hearse by eight long-time employees of the Palo Alto farm.[44]

The first carriage leaving the house carried Jane Stanford and her brother Charles. Until then she had maintained her composure, but now she broke into hysterical sobs and had to be supported by Charles. Their carriage was followed immediately by others bearing relatives and friends, among them Mrs. Charles Lathrop, Dr. and Mrs. Taylor, Mr. and Mrs. Jerome Bonaparte Stanford, and David Hewes. There were twelve carriages. The procession—led by farm and stable employees, then the hearse and pallbearers on foot, and last of all the carriages—passed from the house, down the old County Road, and into the university campus.

---

[39]SF Chronicle, Jun 25, 1893.   [40]Ibid.

[41]JLS to May Hopkins, Aug 5, 1897.

[42]JLS to CFC, Jul 2, 1895. CFC had written JLS about an offensive letter CPH had sent to an assoc., in which he had used insulting language discussing LS and CC. CFC wrote, "Whenever I think of the expressions in C.P.H.'s letter to Mr. Bonn, it is difficult to keep down my indignation, and to determine whether to reply to his insults to and reflections on Gov. Stanford and my father." CFC to JLS, Jan 19, 1894.   [43]SF Chronicle, Jun 25, 1893.

[44]The eight were Henry B. Shackelford, George Woods, Peter Mullen, W. J. McDonald, John Ewett, O. L Mayer, O. T. Gallagher, and Frank Irwin. Ibid.

RESERVED SEATS HAD BEEN PROVIDED FOR THE PALLBEARERS,
including the Congressional delegation, state and city officials, and the employees of Stanford's numerous corporations. This group included Sen. Stephen Mallory White of Los Angeles and Sen. Charles Norton Felton of Menlo Park; Congressmen James George Maguire of San Francisco, Eugene Francis Loud of San Francisco, Samuel Greeley Hilborn of Oakland, and Anthony Caminetti of Jackson; Acting-Gov. John B. Reddick; and the sergeants-at-arms of both houses of the state legislature.[a]

Gov. and Mrs. Henry H. Markham telegraphed their condolences from Chicago on June 21.[b]

There was a strong movement in California to get Acting-Gov. John B. Reddick in the absence of Governor Markham to appoint a senator to fill the vacancy caused by Stanford's death. Judge John F. Davis of Calaveras, Reddick's closest personal friend, assured the public that Reddick would never take such an action.[c] There was even talk of Reddick's naming Markham to the seat so that *he* could be elevated to governor.[d]

George C. Perkins was appointed to the position on Jun 26, 1893, by Governor Markham and was subsequently elected to the position in 1897 and reelected in 1903 and 1909.

[a]*SF Chronicle*, Jun 25, 1893.   [b]*LA Times*, Jun 22, 1893.
[c]*SF Examiner*, Jun 26, 1893.   [d]*SF Call*, Jun 22, 1893.

STANFORD'S HONORARY PALLBEARERS
included many of his closest friends, along with political, business, and railroad associates, among them:

Stephen T. Gage.
Capt. Nicholas Smith.
Col. Fred Crocker.
Wilfred Weed Montague, San Francisco postmaster.
Judge Frank E. Spencer of San José.[a]
Henry L. Dodge.
Judge Joseph McKenna of the U.S. Circuit Court.
Charles Henry Cummings of Sacramento.
Lloyd Tevis.
William W. Stow.
Judge Thomas Bard McFarland.[b]
Former U.S. senator Charles Norton Felton.

Frank McCoppin, former mayor of San Francisco.
Samuel F. Leib.
Alban Towne.
David Starr Jordan.
Alfred L. Tubbs of the Tubbs Cordage Company.
Dr. Charles W. Breyfogle, a San José banker.
Bernard Ulmer Steinman, Stanford protégé and two-time mayor of Sacramento.
William E. Brown, former private secretary to Stanford who held various positions with the railroads and construction companies.
Gen. John F. Houghton.[c]

[a]*Daily Palo Alto*, Apr 25, 1898.
[b]McFarland was one of only fifteen men of the 1878 state Constitutional Convention who voted against the new constitution.   [c]*Oakdale* [California] *Grapevine*, Jun 1893, in UNC, SFS D, 21.

Pallbearers were selected according to Stanford's own directions from among those with the longest railroad service. They included several who had served the railroad from the beginning of construction in 1863, among them several locomotive engineers.[45]

There, on Saturday, June 24, funeral services were held in the open air in the Inner Quad. Sixteen hundred chairs had been arranged for those who might attend, but an estimated five thousand people crowded into the quad.[46]

Following the funeral oration the procession took an hour to pass by the casket.

The simple burial service was performed by William Ford Nicholas, bishop of the Episcopal Diocese of California. Rector Robert C. Foute of Grace Church in San Francisco read the Scriptures, and long-time friend Horatio Stebbins, pastor of First Unitarian Church, delivered the eulogy. Stebbins' charge to the pallbearers was: "Bearers—men of iron hands and iron hearts!—gentle down your strength a little as you bear this body forth—'tis a man ye bear—and lay it softly in its last, strong resting place.

> Such honors Ilium to her hero paid;
> And peaceful slept the mighty Hector's shade."[47]

Following the funeral, as the body was carried into the tomb, Mrs. Stanford broke down again; she was driven home even before the heavy doors were closed.

The casket was placed in the granite Stanford family mausoleum, a half-mile away in the arboretum.[48] (The Stanfords had originally selected this site for a new country home, but with the death of Leland, Jr., these plans were abandoned and all their efforts went into building the university.[49])

Absent from the funeral were Collis Huntington, Ariel Lathrop, and Tim and May Hopkins. The Hopkinses had just returned from Egypt and were at the Plaza Hotel in New York at the time of the death of the man they called their dearest

---

[45]*LA Times*, Jun 22, 1893. The eight engineers were William Scott, Cornelius Collins, and Barney Kelly of Division 110 of the Brotherhood of Locomotive Engineers at Sac; George Cornwall and Walter Lacey of Division 161 in SF; and Samuel C. Clark, James E. Saulpaugh, and James G. Ressegine of Division 283 in Oakland. In Brotherhood of Locomotive Engineers, Leland Stanford Division, No. 238. Ten-p. letter—"Eulogy of Leland Stanford." Addressed only to unidentified "Messrs Editors," 1893. Signed Brotherhood of Locomotive Engineers. LS papers, SUA; see also G.W. Burbank, asst. grand chief eng., Brotherhood of Locomotive Engs., to Con M. Buckley, Nov 1, 1949; *Memorial Addresses on the Life and Character of Leland Stanford,* 21; *SF Chronicle*, Jun 25, 1893. The names and initials of these engs. vary slightly from one source to another. The *LA Times,* Jun 26, 1893, adds John Ewett, Patrick Mullen, and Al Mayer.

[46]*SF Chronicle,* Jun 25, 1893, "Who Were There," lists many of the notables in attendance.

[47]*Memorial Addresses on the Life and Character of Leland Stanford,* 25. It is to the diligence of ref. lib. Eric Heath of Green Library, LSJU, that I owe the observation that Stebbins' quotation from the last two lines of Homer's *Iliad* is from the translation by Alexander Pope, who changed the Greek *Ilium* to the Latin *Ilion. The Iliad and the Odyssey* ("Albion Edition," London: FWC, 1894), 452.

[48]Rosamond Clarke Bacon, "Remarks at the Founders' Day Ceremonies at the Stanford Mausoleum," Mar 9, 1977, a hist. sketch of the building of the Stanford family mausoleum on the LSJU Campus.

[49]Allen, *Stanford: From the Foothills to the Bay*, 19.

139. Floral display at the funeral of Leland Stanford at the Stanford family mausoleum, Stanford University, June 24, 1893. *Stanford University Archives.*

friend.[50] Notified earlier by Jane that the Governor was much better than he had been in a long time, they delayed their trip homeward from the East and did not arrive in San Francisco until July 8.[51] They remembered their dear friend by sending an immense tier of St. Charles lilies, ivy leaves, smilax, and maidenhair ferns.[52]

SENATE EULOGIES

The U.S. Senate set aside September 16, 1893, to pay tribute to its deceased colleague from California; the House of Representatives did the same on February 12, 1894. Stanford was lauded by eight senators and nine congressmen from both parties and all sections of the country.

Sen. Joseph Norton Dolph of Portland, Oregon, said that Stanford's advantages were not superior to thousands of other boys, but by his own ambition, moral character, good judgment, enterprise, energy, and industry, he had made a success of

---

[50]TNH Papers. The *SF Argonaut* of May 15, 1893, reported, "Mr. and Mrs. Timothy Hopkins have finished their tour of Egypt, and are at the Hotel de Londres in Paris." The Hopkinses left Liverpool on the *Majestic* on May 30, and reached NY on Jun 4, in "Timothy Hopkins Chronological Record Book, Jun 15, 1889, to Apr 28, 1928, 43," in TNH papers, SUA.   [51]JLS to May and Tim Hopkins, Jun 12, 1893; TNH papers.

[52]*SF Chronicle*, Jun 25, 1893.

himself.[53] He was as a father to his employees, a genial companion to all, a man simple in manners, generous in hospitality, and unostentatious in his dress and habits.[54] Sen. John Warwick Daniel of Virginia said of Stanford, "The world is better that he lived in it."[55]

Nevada senator William M. Stewart called Stanford the "best of the American type."[56] The millionaire-senator, it was said, was never obtrusive or self-assertive; and even after his great labors had destroyed his physical health, "his judgment was unimpaired."[57]

Missouri senator George G. Vest called Stanford a Christian in the highest and best sense of the term. Stanford, he said, believed in the religion of humanity, and trusted implicitly his welfare here and hereafter to the Sermon on the Mount.[58] Stanford, Vest went on, was a man who proved himself great by throwing off the prejudices of education and geographical section.[59]

THE STANFORD FAMILY MAUSOLEUM was a granite and marble structure completed in 1889. It measured 25 by 40 feet and was built with 8-foot deep foundations, with the superstructure of the best Barre, Vermont, granite. The roof was built of three huge slabs, each 26 feet long. The interior was lined with 8-inch-thick Italian marble from Carrara, secured by bronze anchors.[a] Ernest Etienne Narjot, the pioneer painter of the Pacific Coast, reached the zenith of his fame when he was chosen to decorate the mausoleum.[b]

[a]Allen, *Stanford: From the Foothills to the Bay*, 19.
[b]Louise Narjot Howard, *California's Pioneer Artist, Ernest Narjot: A Brief Resume of the Career of a Versatile Genius* (SF: AD, 1936).

Congressman Samuel G. Hilborn of Oakland, California, told the House of Representatives that he had never heard Leland Stanford speak ill of any human being—"his charity seemed to cover everybody."[60] Hilborn described Stanford's career as one of the most remarkable in history—"romance in real life."[61] Congressman Joseph C. Sibley of Franklin, Pennsylvania, who had visited the Stanfords at their Palo Alto home, said in praise of Stanford, "I never met this man for an hour that I did not have on parting a higher appreciation of his wisdom, a greater respect for his opinions, a warmer admiration for his virtues, greater love for his nobility of character, and a truer sympathy with his aspirations."[62]

Sibley continued, in heartfelt poetry:

> Here reposes royalty in its long, last sleep. Truly, if there be any attributes of kingship which rule the realm of virtues, this man was most of all a king. He was born to conquer and to rule. His conquests cost no tears, made no slaves, marred no lands. He conquered the obstacles of nature, leveled mountains, filled valleys, annihilated distances, overcame time, watered deserts, and made them bloom. . . . He conquered poverty and lack of opportunity for thousands living and thousands yet unborn. He saw in the form of every friendless boy a son. . . .

---

[53]*Memorial Addresses on the Life and Character of Leland Stanford*, 32.   [54]Ibid., 55.
[55]Ibid., 57.   [56]Ibid., 59.   [57]Ibid., 61.
[58]Ibid., 64.   [59]Ibid., 66.   [60]Ibid., 82.
[61]Ibid., 81.   [62]Ibid., 87.

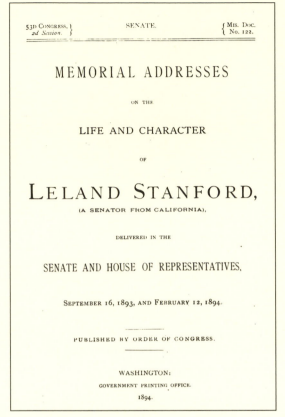

53D CONGRESS, }   SENATE.   { MIS. DOC.
2d Session. }   { No. 122.

MEMORIAL ADDRESSES

ON THE

LIFE AND CHARACTER

OF

LELAND STANFORD,

(A SENATOR FROM CALIFORNIA),

DELIVERED IN THE

SENATE AND HOUSE OF REPRESENTATIVES,

SEPTEMBER 16, 1893, AND FEBRUARY 12, 1894.

PUBLISHED BY ORDER OF CONGRESS.

WASHINGTON:
GOVERNMENT PRINTING OFFICE.
1894.

140. Stanford memorial addresses in the Senate.
Senate Miscellaneous Document.

Near his tomb stands a nobler monument than yet has been erected to earth's heroes. . . . You say he is dead, and I say he has just begun to live.[63]

New Hampshire congressman Henry W. Blair told his fellows in the House of Representatives that Senator Stanford was a *colossus* among men—the wisest and truest friend of the laboring man. He added: "No more impressive personality had ever walked the halls of Congress."[64] South Dakotan John A. Pickler praised this "remarkable character of the nineteenth century in American history" as incomparable: "It would be very difficult to find a parallel in the life of any prominent American contemporary with him."[65]

CALIFORNIA ACCOLADES

When word reached the *Argonaut* of the death of Stanford, the editor, whose policy was not to report deaths, wrote simply, "The untimely hand of death has removed one of the builders of the commonwealth."[66]

Californians in all walks of life offered Stanford their highest praises. Even his old associate C. P. Huntington managed a kind word, as, with trembling voice, he said that he had never known "a more agreeable or more pleasant man."[67]

Groups of California Chinese paid almost unparalleled homage to the Governor: the Chinese Six Companies (associations of Chinese laboring immigrants) honored the memory of the late Leland Stanford as they did that of few white men. They expressed their reverence for the dead senator by placing the yellow flag of China together with the emblem of their particular company at half-staff over the company's headquarters. Not since the death of President Garfield had the flags of

[63]Ibid., 92–93.   [64]Ibid., 97.   [65]Ibid., 106.
[66]*SF Argonaut*, Jun 26, 1893.   [67]*SF Examiner*, Jun 22, 1893.

the Six Companies been thus lowered: "these are the only two occasions upon which the Chinese have shown such marked respect upon the death of a Caucasian."[68]

Bertha Berner later added a personal note about how Stanford treated his employees and how he was regarded by those who worked for him. It was Stanford's custom in Washington to take a nap in his library after dinner, and on awakening would ask, "Is Bertha about?" Then he would dictate to her for about an hour and then ask her to write it out when convenient. She said, "It was always ready for him the next morning. One loved to do things for him, he was so considerate."[69]

Stanford's long-time friend and associate Henry Vrooman had written the following testimonial regarding the character of Leland Stanford:

> During all the years of my intimate relations with the Governor, I have never seen anything in his transactions; I have never heard a word drop from his lips; I have never witnessed a single emotion of his heart that indicated that he was jealous of anybody—and I have been with him in very stormy times and when other people's acts were being reviewed and criticized. But the Governor would say: "Well, boys, let us change the subject—he may have made a mistake, but he is all right—let us be charitable." And that applies to fifteen thousand men on the rolls of the Company from top to bottom. I have never heard him say an unkind word of, or concerning anybody connected with him or in his or the Company's employ in any way or manner.[70]

Stanford admirers were sure that he was California's greatest citizen: "In him California has lost her most noted citizen."[71] As early as 1883 the editor of the *San Francisco Post* remarked that Stanford was considered the foremost and greatest citizen of California.[72] One admirer described Stanford as "Decidedly the most prominent citizen in the state."[73] Another saw him as "California's most illustrious citizen."[74] He was not only the most powerful, but also the most popular man on the Pacific Coast. Upon hearing of Stanford's death, Gov. Henry H. Markham said, "He was one of the grandest men I ever knew."[75]

The story of Stanford was the story of California, and his death, proclaimed the Brotherhood of Locomotive Engineers, was a "public calamity."[76] This organization was sure that every effort of his life had been for the glory of the state of California and for the good of his fellow man.[77] This "greatest man that California ever produced" did more for his adopted state than any other ten men combined. In agriculture, no one else had done a hundredth as much for the Golden State, and his

[68] *Yreka Union*, Jun 29, 1893.

[69] GTC inter. with BB, Dec 12, 1927, in "Record" book (Spring 1907), 43.

[70] Henry Vrooman, "Honorable Leland Stanford," ms. in HHB papers, BL.

[71] *SF Examiner*, Jun 22, 1893.　　　　　　　　　　　　[72] *SF Post*, Nov 28, 1884.

[73] *SF Wave*, Jun 24, 1893.　　　　　　　　　　　　　[74] *Santa Cruz Sentinel*, Jun 21, 1893.

[75] *Cincinnati Tribune*, Jun 22, 1893.

[76] Brotherhood of Locomotive Engs., "Eulogy of Leland Stanford," 6.　　　[77] Ibid.

business probity was unimpeachable.[78] Put only slightly differently, journalist William Alexander Selkirk wrote: "No one person has done a tenth or an hundredth part as much to promote and advance in this state the improvement of live stock and the development of agricultural production."[79]

Paeans of praise for Stanford had appeared in print even before he died. To many, Stanford's character had assumed a grandeur that elicited universal admiration. Marcus Boruck, for one, was sure that Stanford's praises had to be sung rather than spoken: "His name is a glory to the State, and his life the brightest page in her history. Hail! All Hail! Leland Stanford."[80] Following Stanford's death, those who attempted biographical sketches, editorials, or eulogies constantly consulted their thesauri for superlatives. There was no limit to the excessive praise they poured forth. His benefactions made him a "philanthropist-philosopher." His eulogists proclaimed that he was at the same time taciturn, deeply versed in the knowledge of "human nature," and respected for his "magnificent brain power." He was preeminently a thought-producing man. Stanford became the "Sage of Palo Alto."[81] Susan B. Anthony referred to Stanford as Jane's "sainted husband."[82] And the editor of the *San Francisco Examiner* reported (erroneously) that the University of Tennessee had honored Stanford for his contributions to higher education by conferring upon him an honorary LL.D. degree about the time Stanford University opened in the fall of 1891.[83]

Praises were sung to Stanford as a "spiritual giant," as evidenced by the lofty aspirations of his inner life and his nobility of soul. He was one of the noblest works of the Creator—a man of undoubted integrity, spotless private character, far-reaching benevolence, calm judgment, and masterly administrative abilities. His wealth, influence, and popularity all arose from his character and integrity. He was active when other men were idle, generous when others were greedy, lofty when others were base; he seemed always inspired by the noblest and kindliest impulses. To top it all, no man ever lived with more character and goodness in his heart than Leland Stanford.[84]

One New York journalist wrote that Stanford was above all a simple man—despite his wealth.[85] If this "big man with a big heart" had a coat of arms, it, too, would have been the picture of simplicity. As the Governor had once said: "If you make a coat of arms for me, I want a young man driving a pair of oxen hitched to a stoneboat, enthroned on it. That's the way I got my start in life."[86]

[78]UNC in LS papers.
[79]*Petaluma Daily Imprint*, Jun 21, 1893.
[80]*SF CSTUJ*, Jan 24, 1885.
[81]Treat, "The Stanfords and their Golden Key," 32.
[82]Susan B. Anthony to JLS, Jan 29, 1894.
[83]*SF Examiner*, Jun 21, 1893. A detailed perusal of the archives and other records of the Univ. of Tenn. by the univ. arch. and other lib. staff members turned up nothing to substantiate this. Author inter. with univ. arch. Aaron Purcell, Sep 14, 2001.
[84]UNC in LS papers. Another journalist exuded: "Leland Stanford is not only a blessing to the State in which he resides but to the World. He deserves well of his Country." [?] *Daily Journal*, Dec 2, 1876, in SFS B, 58.
[85]UNC [NY] Jun 1893, "Press Notices of Leland Stanford," 92, SUA.
[86]Ibid.

141. Leland Stanford is California's best friend.
San Francisco City Argus.

The California Commandery of the Military Order of the Loyal Legion of the United States remembered Stanford officially as follows:

> In Memoriam
> Leland Stanford
> A Companion of the third Class died at Palo Alto, Cal.
> Wednesday, June 21, 1893[87]

In a special circular the Commandary published honoring their Companion, Stanford was described as:

> A gentleman who, in civil life during the Rebellion, was specially distinguished for conspicuous and consistent loyalty to the National Government, and was active and eminent in maintaining the supremacy of the same.[88]

---

[87]William R. Smedberg, bvt. lt. col., U.S. Army [Recorder]. Military Order of the Loyal Legion of the United States. *In Memoriam Leland Stanford. A Companion of the third Class died at Palo Alto, Cal. Wednesday, Jun 21, 1893.* Headquarters Commandery of the State of California (SF: Calif. Com., 1904). Circular No. 20, Series 1893, Whole No. 335. Jul 3, 1893, SUA. [88]Ibid.

As she faced a multitude of decisions, Jane Stanford also found Nick Smith to be
the loyal friend Leland had known him to be. After the death of Stanford, Nick handled the disposal of a number of horses Jane wanted to sell; he sold 680 horses at
Vina and the Palo Alto Stock Farm, reserving 320 horses in addition to the Thor-
oughbreds and work horses.[89] He was a friend and confidant who offered good
advice, but even more, when Jane could not make ends meet, Nick placed *his* means
at her disposal.[90]

Shortly after Stanford's death, Jane gave Nick her late husband's favorite cuff
links. In spite of their long intimacy, he penned the formal letter of thanks proper
for the time:

> My Dear Mrs. Stanford,
>
> I have just received from you the favorite and beautiful set of pearl sleeve buttons
> of your dear husband and my dearest friend Mr. Stanford.
> I cannot tell you how much I appreciate this sacred souvenir, as my heart is too
> full, but while life lasts the dearest memories will be associated with him and our
> long friendship.
> . . . I must try and see you before you leave for Washington.
> Yours, ever, faithful and devoted friend.
>
> N T Smith[91]

Nick also sent Jane a tender letter of Christmas greetings and consolation just
before Christmas of 1893. Enclosing a letter sent him by Leland Junior in 1879, Nick
wrote:

> The season reminds me that Christmas is near and how lonely you will be, while your
> dear husband and darling boy are where they can only speak to you through the lan-
> guage which loved Spirits whisper to the hearts of those left behind. May your
> Christmas be happy in the thought that they are waiting for you in a better world.[92]

STANFORD'S ATTITUDES TOWARD RELIGION AND CHURCHES

The basic attitudes toward religion and churches expressed by Stanford in his
early years remained almost unchanged throughout his long life. As mentioned earlier, there was no rigid religious discipline in the Stanford house, and no denominational religion imposed upon the Stanford boys, though the father was a
Presbyterian. Leland mentioned once that he was well satisfied with his education
at Cazenovia; the only fault he found was that it was a bit too strict in its religious
observances. And though he did not accept evangelical Christianity as preached by

[89]NTS to JLS, Jul 27, 1893.
[90]BB, *Mrs. Stanford*, 134.
[91]NTS to JLS, Sep 23, 1893.
[92]NTS to JLS, Dec 23, 1893.

the itinerant evangelists he occasionally came in contact with, he was not in any sense irreligious.

Stanford was not a deeply religious man; he believed in a deity and in an after-life, and attended church occasionally, but religion never occupied a place as central to his life as it had to Jane's. Unlike his wife, whose letters and conversations reeked of religiosity and illusion to divine guidance and salvation, Stanford's expressions of religious faith were moderate. The record suggests that he was touched only twice by events that brought him close to a personal religious experience: they were the birth and death of his son.

Stanford was a Christian in the conventional sense of the word. His speeches and conversations are interspersed with occasional allusions to "God," divine guidance, salvation, and so forth, but no more so than were those of other public men of his day and ours. Stanford's mature religious faith was reflected in a number of public statements during his political career, as in his Thanksgiving Day Proclamation of 1862, when as governor of California he reminded his fellow citizens that they had much to be thankful for, and enjoined them to go to their places of worship and engage in acts of devotion that God might continue favoring them with his bless-ings.[93] When his father died, Stanford wrote to his mother that he was happy that his father had gone to a better world, where there was rest for the weary.[94]

The Governor's relationship to various churches reflects a universalism that would defy any attempt to identify him with strict denominationalism. The Stan-fords were married in a Baptist church in Albany, New York, and in Sacramento they sometimes attended a Baptist church.[95] Bertha Berner later wrote that when at home in Palo Alto, the Stanfords and their household generally attended Menlo Park Presbyterian Church.[96] Jane Stanford once gave this church a new organ and supported the church's kindergarten program, but there is no record in the session minutes—despite the fact that Stanford pews were set aside for them—that either of the Stanfords was ever a member of that church.[97]

When a brouhaha arose in 1889 over a mistaken report of Jane's conversion to Catholicism, a reporter asked Stanford whether his wife were a Methodist, Stan-ford replied, "No, but she is as much a Methodist as anything else. We go sometimes to that church."[98] In another journalistic uproar about the rumor that Jane Stanford had become a Roman Catholic, one writer remarked that she had always been regarded as one of the strongest pillars of the Methodist denomination.[99] It was

---

[93]Thanksgiving Day Proclamation, Nov 1, 1862, in CER, Vol. 1058, 364; *Sac Union*, Nov 24, 1862.

[94]LS to his mother, May 23, 1862, and Dec 24, 1865.   [95]*Oakland Morning Times*, Apr 18, 1891.

[96]BB, *Mrs. Stanford*, 49.

[97]Inter. with William Russ, church hist., MP Pres. Church, Jun 28, 2000; *SF Argonaut*, Dec 1, 1890; UNC, SFS 18:1–4; 25:16; *SF Bulletin*, May 14, 1886; *Portland* [Maine] *Argus*, Jul 1891, in UNC, SFS 2:111.

[98]*SF Examiner*, Nov 28, 1889.   [99]*SF Chronicle*, Nov 27, 1890.

well known that the Stanfords and the Grants attended John Newman's Methodist Church in Washington, though it was patently untrue, as one reporter would have it, that they and the Grants "belonged" to that church.[100] By the time this church flap arose, the Stanfords and Newmans had been personal friends for many years.

After Stanford died, a Methodist Episcopal pastor in Washington claimed that the California senator was a member of *his* congregation.[101]

Nor is there any record showing that Stanford was ever a member of an Episcopal church, even though when questioned in 1890 he had remarked that he and his wife were Episcopalians.[102] In 1886, Stanford was a vestryman, a "junior warden," in Trinity Episcopal Church in Menlo Park.[103] The memorial service for Leland, Jr., was conducted in San Francisco's Grace Church, itself Episcopalian, though the Stanfords were never members of that church.

While serving as governor of California, Leland Stanford became acquainted with and worked closely with Unitarian minister Thomas Starr King, particularly in the cause of Unionism, though it is patently inaccurate to refer to Stanford—as did one King biographer—as "Starr King's personal friend and parishioner."[104] The first is an exaggeration; the second an error. King toured the state soliciting funds for the United States Sanitary Commission, an organization that cared for wounded soldiers. He was eminently successful: one-quarter of all funds raised in the nation came from California.[105] In response to King's appeals, Stanford accepted the chairmanship of a committee to canvass Sacramento City and County raising money for this patriotic fund.[106]

One student of Stanford's Sacramento activities has him an active member of St. Paul's Episcopal Church, where he was said to have served as a vestryman.[107] Church records, however, show no evidence that he was a member of that church or that he even attended it.[108]

Stanford was probably closer to Horatio Stebbins, the successor to Thomas Starr King as pastor of First Unitarian Church of San Francisco, than he was to most religionists. Stebbins delivered the sermon on November 22, 1885, commemorating the founding of Stanford University, gave the invocation at the laying of the cornerstone of the university on May 14, 1887, and, as noted, Stebbins delivered a eulogy as one of three ministers officiating at Stanford's funeral.[109]

---

[100]Ibid.   [101]UNC, SFS 10:70.   [102]*NY World*, Nov 27, 1890.

[103]Charles W. Hayes, *A New Parish Register* (15th ed., rev., NY: EPD, 1887), 6 and 122; Stanley Pearce, *Lift Up Your Hearts, a History of Trinity Parish, Menlo Park* (MP: TriP, 1974), 20–21.

[104]Robert Monzingo, *Thomas Starr King: Eminent Californian, Civil War Statesman, Unitarian Minister* (Pacific Grove: BP, 1991), 123.

[105]Charles Janeway Stillâe, *History of the United States Sanitary Commission* (Phil.: JBLC, 1866), 541–549.

[106]*Sac Union*, Sep 26, 1862.

[107]Regnery, "A Study of the Leland Stanford House in Sacramento, California," 144.

[108]Author inter. with Bruce Kleinsmith, church hist., St. Paul's Epis. Church, Sac, Feb 15, 2001.

[109]Charles A. Murdock, *Horatio Stebbins, His Ministry and His Personality* (Boston and NY: HMC, 1921), 76–77.

Stanford also served with Stebbins as regent of the University of California in late 1882 and early 1883.[110] It was no surprise when four years later Stanford appointed Stebbins to be a trustee of Stanford University, a position he filled from November 12, 1886, until his death on April 9, 1902.[111] Stebbins was, indeed, a trusted friend and consultant to the Stanfords.

Though Stanford was never a parishioner of First Unitarian Church, some members of his family were very active in this church. On occasion, his brothers Phil and Josiah paid pew rent there, Josiah for the years 1866 to 1870, and Phil from 1864 to 1865.[112] For a time Josiah's daughter Gertrude attended the First Unitarian Church's Pilgrim Sunday School.[113] On May 12, 1950, her funeral was held in the same church.[114] And Phil's son Jerome Bonaparte Stanford was married there to Lillian M. Clark on June 12, 1870, the service having been conducted by Horatio Stebbins.[115]

Certainly the nondogmatic, nondenominational stance of the Unitarian Church found a welcome place in Stanford's mind. David Starr Jordan underscored Stanford's "caring nothing for creed or ceremony," having yet a deeply religious nature.[116] Jordan added that Stanford's theological position, the result of clear thinking combined with warm feeling, might have been partially defined as "Unitarian Methodist."[117]

All of this testifies to the fact that Stanford was not indifferent to religious matters, but possessed no particular loyalty to any one doctrine or church. His religious position was aptly summarized by his wife, the woman who knew the workings of her husband's mind better than anyone else, who characterized the essence of his religion, or, perhaps better, his religious philosophy, as follows:

> If a firm belief in a beneficent Creator, a profound admiration for Jesus of Nazareth and his teaching, and the certainty of a personal life hereafter constitute religion then Leland Stanford was a religious man. The narrow walls of a creed could not confine him; therefore he was not a professed member of any church, for in each confession of faith he found something to which he could not subscribe. But for the principles of religion he had a profound veneration; in his heart were the true sentiments of Christianity, and he often said that in his opinion the Golden Rule was the corner stone of all true religion.[118]

Years afterward, in response to a query about the religion of her husband, Jane

---

[110]Minutes of the Regents of UC, Oct 7, 1882, IV, 353.

[111]LS to Horatio Stebbins, Nov 12, 1886, SMCR, Book 40 of Deeds, 588; "Chronological Listing of Board of Trustees 1885 to Present [1995]." SUA.

[112]First Unit. Church of SF, "Pew Account, 1864–1873." In church arch.

[113]Ibid., "Receiving Book for the Pilgrim Sunday School." In church arch.

[114]Ibid., "Christenings, Marriages, Funerals," 388. In church arch.

[115]Ibid., "Marriage Licenses, 1864–1889." In church arch.   [116]Jordan, *Days of a Man*, I, 483.

[117]This statement tells us more about DSJ, who was a Unit., than it does about LS.

[118]*SF Examiner*, Jun 24, 1893.

Stanford wrote, "I take pleasure in saying that he was not only a true believer in the simple religion of Jesus Christ, but he lived up to it in the truest and highest sense of his belief."[119] Continuing, she underscored his dislike for denominationalism in religion, "He was not a believer in creeds and disliked extremely the dogmatisms of the churches, and he frankly said it was the creeds and dogmatism that prevented men of this age, coming out and uniting themselves with churches." Just four days earlier, she had written to the secretary of the California Universalist Convention that both she and her late husband had resolved that no professor would ever be employed by the university who preached denominational theories of religion.[120]

AN ASSESSMENT OF LELAND STANFORD—MAN OF MANY CAREERS

Stanford was what a later generation would call a "mover and shaker." He was never satisfied—as Huntington was—with complete absorption in and dedication to one thing—either creating the greatest railroad empire or making and saving money. The Governor was, indeed, a man of many careers and interests. One writer summarized him as follows:

> In the early history of this state, no man held a more prominent place than Leland Stanford and the notable events that marked his active and energetic life—the energy, foresight, diplomatic skill, and administrative ability displayed by him entitled him to rank as one of the strongest characters of his time. Possessing a broad public spirit, he devoted the flower of his life to the development of the vast resources of this state, while the fortune his genius, enterprise, industry and energy accumulated, he devoted to the cause of philanthropy.[121]

Stanford, of course, had his detractors. Probably the single most spiteful attack on the Governor was made at the height of anti-railroad feeling in California by Charles Edward Pickett, editor of the San Francisco News Bureau. He wrote a fifteen-page pamphlet depicting Stanford as drunk—"as was his custom"—and as a consequence of his alcohol-induced tongue-loosening, he betrayed his "selfish, black, [sic] soul to the world."[122] Pickett's charge—against a man known to be moderate in his drinking habits—was so ridiculous that not even Stanford's enemies could give it any credence.

Only the clever and wicked pen of Ambrose Bierce could ridicule the dead over their fresh graves, and often in premature epitaphs composed even before their subjects were dead: "HERE LIES FRANK PIXLEY—AS USUAL."[123] Bierce renamed

---

[119]JLS to Samuel Colwood, Mar 19, 1896.   [120]JLS to S. Goodenough, Mar 15, 1896.
[121]Peter Fanning, "Early History of California," *Douglas 20, Police Journal* 1926 4 (3): 17.
[122]Charles Edward Pickett, *The California King: His Conquests, Crimes, Confederates, Counsellors, Courtiers and Vassals: Stanford's Post-prandial New-Year's Day Soliloquy* (SF: [n.p.], 1876), in *SPRR Pamphlets*.
[123]O'Connor, *Ambrose Bierce*, 139. In Jul 1889, Day Bierce, sixteen-year-old son of Ambrose, murdered a *(continued)*

his former boss, "Mr. Pigsley of the Hogonaut."[124] Whose pen other than Bierce's could coin the catchy "£eland $tanford,"[125] or "Stealand Landford?"[126] Like a pun, Bierce was at his best when he was at his worst—and no foe was spared his poisoned barbs:

> Here Stanford lies, who thought it odd
> That he should go to meet his God.
> He looked, until his eye grew dim,
> For God to hasten to meet him.[127]

Setting aside this web of adulation on the one hand, and the envy and jealousy evidenced by others, when all is said and done, Stanford was essentially a practical man, a builder, a doer—not a theoretical man, not basically a thinker, certainly not a philosopher. One of his secrets of success was reaching his potential, and he succeeded mightily in this. When something needed to be done, such as finding a way to capture a horse's stride on film, or planting a vineyard, Stanford almost always had a plan. His brain teemed with ideas, usually of a practical nature. But he was never impulsive.

Leland Stanford was not a gambler in the ordinary sense of the word, yet his self-confidence and ambition made him willing to risk all he had to improve his life, as when he went to Port Washington, and then, set back by a catastrophe, moved to California and began again. He challenged rather than gambled on railroads, mines, and a myriad of other business concerns and hobbies. At any time after his thirty-fifth year he could have retired with a comfortable fortune, yet he risked it all, not for a greater fortune, but for greater challenges. Achievement was the objective.

Stanford was many-faceted, but also simple and uncomplicated, and in his case, his simplicity was more baffling than subtlety or complexity. He had no secret or overpowering psychological drives that make for titillating biography, and no great, unrealized ambitions that sometimes explain peculiar character traits.

(continued) rival in a love-suit and then took his own life. This incident was the occasion for Frank Pixley's matchless revenge for all the attacks he and others had suffered from the man with the "burning pen." Pixley penned an ed. that was itself worthy of Bierce, concluding with the words: "Upon his tomb may be carved the inscription, 'He quarreled with God, and found nothing in His creations worthy of the commendation of Ambrose Bierce.'" Pub. in the *Argonaut*, Aug 5, 1889. This ed. is recommended for the careful perusal by all Bierce-haters. See also, Jerome Hart, *In Our Second Century, from an Editor's Note-Book* (SF: PiP, 1931), 168–170.

[124]Paul Fatout, *Ambrose Bierce: The Devil's Lexicographer* (Norman: UOP, 1951), 137.

[125]Ambrose Bierce, "A Railroad Lackey," in *The Collected Works of Ambrose Bierce*. Vol. 5, *Black Beetles in Amber* (NY: NPC, 1911), 102. [126]Fatout, *Ambrose Bierce*, 146.

[127]Ibid., 192. No one could deny the power of the very clever and at times painfully funny poetry—perhaps *doggerel* would better describe his lines of wit—of Bierce. We even the score with him by broadcasting to the world that his middle name was Gwinnett, a name he detested and concealed with an initial until a parody of his initials "Almighty God Bierce" caused him to drop even the initial from his signature. C. Hartley Grattan, *Bitter Bierce, A Mystery of American Letters* (Garden City: DDC, 1929), 10.

And, unfortunately for the biographer, he seems to have been guilty of no notable indiscretions. No scandals are attached to his name, though detractors tried their best. Just one "the public be damned" would have won him great notoriety. Even those unable to measure up to his standards or enjoy his successes, who would later denigrate him as a member of the "robber baron class," prejudged him largely on the basis of his business associates; he was certainly not in the same ethical league with the Jim Fisks, Daniel Drews, and Collis Huntingtons.

In his eulogy in the House of Representatives, Congressman Eugene F. Loud of San Francisco praised Stanford as "a great and good man—a benefactor of the human race."[128] The editor of the *Sacramento Bee* wrote of him, "Governor Stanford was a noble, great and good man. He was a public-spirited man and a friend to all mankind."[129]

What does it mean to say that a man is great? What is a great life other than a life of great achievements? When we view a few Stanford "firsts" we find that many of them *were* great achievements.

Stanford Firsts

First Republican governor of California.
First president of the Central Pacific Railroad.
First president of the Southern Pacific Company.
Owner of the world's largest vineyard.
First among the world's trotting horse breeders.
First in world champion trotter records.
Developer of the world's first motion picture.
First president (and builder) of the California Street Cablecar.
First president of Pacific Mutual Life Insurance Company.
First in wealth in the United States Senate for his day.
First president of the Bodie Mining Company.
First in size of nineteenth-century private university endowment.
Creator of the largest university in land area in the world.
First president and co-founder of the Occidental & Oriental Steamship Company.
First railroad president elected to the United States Senate.

STANFORD WAS A GREAT MAN

Was Stanford a great man, as many of his contemporaries believed? In his railroad projects, he ranks in the same bracket with James J. Hill and other great builders. His material accomplishments were among the most extensive in the nation. His wines, his farms, his homes, his political successes were all of the first

---

[128] *Memorial Addresses on the Life and Character of Leland Stanford,* 123.   [129] *Sac Bee,* Jun 21, 1893.

order, and his philanthropies were prodigious. He worked hard and constantly; one might almost say "grimly." The record shows very little sense of humor and *not a trace* of idleness or indolence.

Great people seem always to make the encyclopedias: Stanford is included in *Harper's Encyclopedia of United States History*, the highly-respected *Dictionary of American Biography*, and Michael Martin and Leonard Gelber's *New Dictionary of American History*. In the section of his book called "Four Hundred Notable Americans," in the *Encyclopedia of American History*, Richard Morris counts Leland Stanford one of the top four hundred Americans of all time. Stanford's sketch is also in the prestigious *Twentieth Century Biographical Dictionary of Notable Americans*.[130]

HISTORIAN ROCKWELL DENNIS HUNT'S
TWELVE APOSTLES OF CALIFORNIA
1. Junípero Serra
2. Jedediah Strong Smith
3. Mariano Guadalupe Vallejo
4. John Augustus Sutter
5. John Bidwell
6. Thomas Starr King
7. John Muir
8. Leland Stanford
9. David Starr Jordan
10. Hubert Howe Bancroft
11. Will Rogers
12. Frank Augustus Miller*

*Hunt, "Twelve Apostles of California," *HSSCQ* 1956 38 (4): 9–38.

After a quest for twelve Californians so "vital to the history and development of California as to merit the title 'Apostles of California'"—each one possessed of his own individuality and having his own distinctive mission, each having made his own unique contribution—historian Rockwell Dennis Hunt included Stanford on his list. Hunt adds the explanatory caveat:

> This is not to say that each "apostle" was of saintly character or consistent loyalty to exalted ideals: it is simply averring that each of them—in several cases without conscious design—did something different but significant to enrich the history and development of California, and that no record of the Golden State can be deemed complete if any of their names are omitted.[131]

Leland Stanford is today largely a forgotten man. Yet his is the quintessence of the great American legend: the farm boy who makes good through hard work and struggle—the embodiment of the Horatio Alger myth. Still, the twentieth century witnessed perhaps the creation of even more great men than did the nineteenth. What goes into greatness is not those circumstances that make success easy.

This is not to place Stanford on a pedestal—pedestals are made for statues, not men. A monument, perhaps, is more in order, and the university he founded is his greatest monument. However, some monuments that commemorate his achievements were made while he still lived.

---

[130]Rossiter Johnson, ed.-in-chief, *The Twentieth Century Biographical Dictionary of Notable Americans* (10 vols., Boston: BS, 1994), IX, 9 unnumbered).

[131]Rockwell Dennis Hunt, "Twelve Apostles of California," *HSSCQ* 1956 38 (4): 9–10.

Stanford was a great railroad builder, a great horsebreeder, a great moneymaker, and a great philanthropist. Stanford possessed the qualities of a hero. His life was the kind that could be held up as an example to youth, worthy of their emulation, yet he was not a paragon of moral perfection. He had his human passions and frailties. But muckrakers, progressives, and political reformers were—and are—anxious to debunk heroes. Simply because he was a member of a successful class, he became known as a robber baron, a selfish representative of the octopus-age of railroad growth. Yes, Stanford was ambitious for power, money, and influence, but not to the extent of being greedy or having no regard for others.

Even *before* Stanford died, one writer had expressed the feelings of many later mourners in his assessment of Stanford's place among great Americans:

> The man, the corner stone of whose grand monument was laid at Palo Alto today, will occupy a place in the history of California, which, when it is written, will be read with wonderment the world over. As the master mind of the great overland railway system, an undertaking that required the utmost courage, calculation, and foresight, he should be entitled to take foremost rank with the great men of the nation.[132]

Sen. John W. Daniel of Virginia in his memorial address to the Senate called Leland Stanford "a great man, and one of the most remarkable characters that this country has produced."[133]

Leland Stanford must be included in the list of great men of the world. Who can view the Governor's accomplishments without marveling at them? Who can look at his university without appreciating its greatness and the magnanimity of the man who created it? Yes, by the standards we use in judging men great, I think Leland Stanford must be included in that class.

Stanford lived a significant life, a life that made a difference. He was a colossus among men.

---

[132] *Sac Bee*, May 14, 1887.   [133] *Memorial Addresses on the Life and Character of Leland Stanford*, 50.

CHAPTER 26

EPILOGUE AND LEGACY

Si Monumentum Requiris Circumspice

"If you seek for my monument look around you," is literally translated, the inscription in Latin on the plain marble slab which marks in the great cathedral of which he was the artificer, the resting place of Sir Christopher Wren. And to our railroad artificer this epitaph would be no less appropriate, not only for the marvelous achievement which has linked in bands of iron the shores of earth's fairest continent, but for his efforts toward the industrial development of the state, for his farms and vineyards, his grain fields and his orchards, and above all for the noble institution of learning which, with each returning year, shall be more fully appreciated, shedding broadcast its benign and exalting influence on those now living, and on future generations to the end of time. This it is to be immortal in this world as well as in other worlds.
                                                                  —Hubert Howe Bancroft[1]

THE BURIAL OF LELAND, JR., IN THE FAMILY MAUSOLEUM—JUNE 29, 1893

On June 29, just a week after Governor Stanford's funeral, the casket of Leland, Jr., was moved quietly, quickly, and without ceremony from his temporary mausoleum near the family home and placed in the family mausoleum alongside his father.[2]

In 1898 Jane Stanford had her son's original mausoleum dismantled. She kept two large slabs of white marble that had been used on the top and front of the casket, and had a few words of the poem "Haunted Ground" engraved on them.[3] The slabs were then erected into a memorial that marked the place where young Leland's original mausoleum stood, where he had rested for nine years.

Jane Stanford attributed the poem "Haunted Ground" to Elizabeth Barrett Browning, but, as Bertha Berner points out, the poem was not to be found among

---

[1]HHB, *Stanford*, 206.   [2]*SF Chronicle*, Jun 29, 1893; BB, *Mrs. Stanford*, 89.
[3]PASF, 1898, Letter Book, SUA; Laura Jones, Elena Reese, and John W. Rick, "Is it not 'Haunted Ground?'—Archeological, Archival, and Architectural Investigations of the Stanford's Palo Alto Home," *S & T* 1996 20 (1): 12; NET and ELT, *But . . . It's Written in Stone! The Memorial Monument of Leland Stanford Jr.* (PA: CHP, 1999). The story of Felicia Dorothea (Browne) Hemans' work *Haunted Ground*, as inscribed on the monument of LSJ.

Browning's works.[4] Berner quotes in part (and inaccurately) this poem that Jane Stanford loved to read over and over again in the years following the untimely death of Leland, Jr.

It seemed an easy task to locate the poem in Browning's works, and, if not *there*, to track it to its correct provenance. As expected, it was not Browning's; rather, the words of this poem were penned, probably in 1824, by English-born Felicia Dorothea (Browne) Hemans.[5] Mrs. Hemans' maiden name is obviously the source of Jane's confusion as to the author. The entire poem reads as follows:

HAUNTED GROUND

Yes, it *is* haunted, this quiet scene,
Fair as it looks, and all softly green;
Yet fear thou not—for the spell is thrown,
And the might of the shadow, on me alone.

Are thy thoughts wandering to elves and fays,
And spirits that dwell where the water plays?
Oh! in the heart where there are stronger powers,
That sway, though viewless, this world of ours!

Have I not lived midst these lonely dells,
And loved, and sorrow'd, and heard farewells,
And learn'd in my own deep soul to look,
And tremble before that mysterious book?

Have I not, under these whispering leaves,
Woven such dreams as the young heart weaves?
Shadows—yet unto which life seem'd bound;
And is it not—is it not haunted ground?

Must I not hear what *thou* hearest not,
Troubling the air of the sunny spot?
Is there not something to rouse but me,
Told by the rustling of every tree?

Song hath been here, with its flow of thought;
Love, with its passionate visions fraught;
Death, breathing stillness and sadness round;
And is it not—is it not haunted ground?

Are there no phantoms, but such as come
By night from the darkness that wraps the tomb?
A sound, a scent, or a whispering breeze,
Can summon up mightier far than these!

But I may not linger amidst them here!
Lovely they are, and yet things to fear;
Passing and leaving a weight behind,
And a thrill on the chords of the stricken mind.

Away, away!—that my soul may soar
As a free bird of blue skies once more!
Here from its wing it may never cast
The chains by those spirits brought back from the past.

Doubt it not—smile not—but go thou, too,
Look on the scenes where thy childhood grew—
Where thou hast pray'd at thy mother's knee,
Where thou hast roved with thy brethren free;

Go thou, when life unto thee is changed,
Friends thou hast loved as thy soul, estranged;
When from the idols thy heart hath made,
Thou hast seen the colours of glory fade.

Oh! painfully then, by the wind's low sigh,
By the voice of the stream, by the flower-cup's dye,
By a thousand tokens of sight and sound,
Thou wilt feel thou art treading on haunted ground.[6]

---

[4] BB, *Mrs. Stanford*, 89, explains mistaken attribution by JLS.

[5] I am indebted to Sue Presnell and Perry Willett of the Lilly Library at IU for the diligent detective work that finally led to the identification of the correct poet.

[6] Felicia Dorothea (Browne) Hemans, *The Forest Sanctuary. De Chatillon. With Other Poems*. Edinburgh and London: WBS, [1825], 1854. This work has gone through several pubs. with various accompanying poems and titles.

Below are the words as quoted in the Berner biography and which—one might have thought—would have been inscribed on Leland, Jr.'s monument in 1898:

> Yes, it is haunted, this quiet scene—
> Fair as it looks and all softly green:
> Yet fear thou not, for the spell is thrown
> And the weight of the shadows on me alone.
>
> Have I not under these whispering leaves,
> Woven such dreams as young happy heart weaves?
> Shadows yet unto which life seemed bound;
> And is it not, is it not haunted ground?
>
> Must I not hear what thou hearest not,
> Troubling the air of this sunny spot?
> Is there not something to none but me
> Told by the rustling of every tree?
>
> Song hath been here with its flow of thought,
> Love with its passionate visions fraught,
> Death, breathing stillness and sadness round;
> And is it not, is it not haunted ground?

The poem on the monument, unlike the original *and* unlike that published in Berner's biography, reads as follows:

[Side one of the monument]
May 14, 1868[7]

YES IT IS HAUNTED THIS
QUIET SCENE,
FAIR AS IT LOOKS AND
ALL SOFTLY GREEN,
YET FEAR THOU NOT, FOR
THE SPELL IS THROWN
AND THE MIGHT OF THE
SHADOWS ON ME ALONE.

HAVE I NOT UNDER THESE
WHISPERING LEAVES,
WOVEN SUCH DREAMS AS
YOUNG HAPPY HEART WEAVES
SHADOWS YET UNTO WHICH
LIFE SEEMED BOUND,
AND IS IT NOT, IS IT NOT
HAUNTED GROUND?
1876[8]

[Side two of the monument]
March 13, 1884[9]

MUST I NOT HEAR WHAT
THOU HEAREST NOT?
TROUBLING THE AIR OF
THIS SUNNY SPOT?
IS THERE NOT SOMETHING
TO NONE BUT ME?
TOLD BY THE RUSTLING
OF EVERY TREE?

SONG HATH BEEN HEREWITH
ITS FLOW OF THOUGHT
LOVE WITH ITS PASSIONATE
VISIONS FRAUGHT,
DEATH BREATHING STILLNESS
AND SADNESS AROUND,
AND IS IT NOT, IS IT NOT
HAUNTED GROUND?

June 21, 1893[10]
J.L.S.

---

[7]LSJ's date of birth.   [8]Year the country home was purchased.
[9]Death date of LSJ.   [10]Death date of LS.

142. Leland Junior memorial, located until 1999
where his original mausoleum stood,
near the site of the Palo Alto Farm house.
Stanford University Archives.

It can be seen that the words and punctuation of Bertha's version and those chiseled into the memorial differ from one another and that neither version is true to the original; so, unfortunately, the wording and punctuation of the poem as inscribed on Leland, Jr.'s monument intended for the ages are incorrect.[11]

A memorial to Leland, Jr., standing on the site of the original mausoleum, was erected in 1898.[12] It was dissembled by the Stanford University "Development" Department in 1998 to make room for additional unneeded housing. Until the summer of that year those interested in the memorial could still view it, located near where the old Stanford house stood, on the banks of the San Francisquito Creek. The memorial was approximately 150 yards from the creek, 70 yards from what is now Sand Hill Road (near the intersection of Arboretum opposite the Nordstrom department store), and just short of a half-mile from County Road (now known as El Camino Real). But a housing development in the fall of 1999 necessitated removing the monument and crating it for "safe keeping" until its fate could be decided.[13]

The Bristol Hotel, where Leland, Jr., died, was located in the Piazza Goldoni, just a few feet from the Arno River.[14] On March 13, 1930, Samuel Schwabacher, secretary of the Stanford University class of 1907, unveiled a bronze memorial tablet under the windows of the room at the Bristol Hotel where Leland had died. On that day, Joseph Emerson Haven, American consul in Florence, reported the unveiling of the plaque in a report to Secretary of State Henry L. Stimson.[15] Those present for

---

[11]Moreover, the chameleon-like punctuation of this poem that refuses to remain the same from one transcription to another varies slightly from those cited above in the English Poetry Full-Text Database pub. by CHL.

[12]Reese, Jones, and Rick, "Haunted Ground," 13.

[13]Author inter. with an unidentified construction foreman on LSJU road-widening project, Feb 24, 2000.

[14]Luana Malloni, gen. manager's asst., Hotel Helvetia & Bristol, to the author, Apr 30, 1997.

[15]Amer. Consular Service, Subject: Unveiling of memorial tablet to LSJ. Joseph Emerson Haven, Amer. consul, to the sec. of state, Copy in SUA.

143. Hotel Bristol in Florence in 1907, the place of Leland Junior's death.
The corner of Via Montebello in front, Lungarno Amerigo Vespucci alongside.
The Arno is to the left. *Stanford University Archives.*

the occasion were Count della Gherardesca, mayor of Florence, along with the rector of the University of Florence, several civil officials, and a number of local American residents.[16] The inscription reads as follows:

ALLA MEMORIA

DI

LELAND STANFORD JR

CHE MORÌ IN QUESTA CASA IL 13 MARZO 1884

ED IN OMAGGIO ALL'UNIVERSITÀ CHE PORTA IL SUO NOME

I LAUREANDI DELL'ANNO 1907 PONGONO QUESTO RICORDO

TO THE MEMORY

OF

LELAND STANFORD JR

WHO DIED IN THIS BUILDING 13 MARCH 1884

AND IN HOMAGE OF THE UNIVERSITY WHICH BEARS HIS NAME

THE GRADUATES OF THE YEAR 1907 PLACE THIS MEMORIAL

---

[16]Ibid.

144. Memorial plaque near the window of the room where Leland Junior died.
Stanford University Archives.

The former Bristol Hotel has undergone many changes, including its name. It is now, simply, the Grand Hotel, though earlier its full name was the Continental Royal de la Paix, or Grand Royal de la Paix.[17]

Following World War II, the original name Bristol was incorporated into the Helvetia Hotel, forming the Hotel Helvetia & Bristol, which today is just a few blocks from the Grand Hotel.[18]

LELAND STANFORD'S LAST WILL AND TESTAMENT

Stanford drew up his Last Will and Testament on November 29, 1886, naming his wife as executrix; in the event that she predeceased him, Ariel Lathrop, his old friend Circuit Judge Lorenzo Sawyer, Stephen T. Gage, and Darius O. Mills would be named executors in her place.[19] A subsequent codicil dated December 3, 1888, added Charles F. Crocker, John W. Allyne, and Russell J. Wilson to this list.[20] Following the death of Lorenzo Sawyer, on September 7, 1891, Stanford named Samuel Mountford

---

[17]Luana Malloni to the author, Jun 10, 1997.
[19]LS Last Will and Testament, 3. LS papers, SUA.

[18]Luana Malloni to the author, Apr 30, 1997.
[20]Ibid., 4–5.

THE 1907 CLASS MEMORIAL TO LELAND STANFORD, JR.,
is still intact, on the side of the building along which runs the street
Lungarno Amerigo Vespucci near the corner of Via Montebello. A
historical pamphlet published in 1992 by the Grand Hotel contains
the following reference to the death of Leland, Jr.:

*O anche il giovane americano Leland Stanford Jr, morto nel 1884, alla
cui memoria i genitori fondarono in California l'Università che ancora
oggi porta il suo nome.* * (. . . the young American Leland Stanford Jr,
who died in 1884, to whose memory his parents founded in California the university that still today bears his name.)

*Grand Hotel, *Grand Hotel, Il più "storico" degli alberghi di Firenze* (Corsico/
Milano: Grafiche Francesco Ghezzi, 1992), 5.

Wilson to fill the vacancy.[21] Wilson died on June 4, 1892, and Ariel Lathrop, after
serving as the business manager for his brother-in-law for twelve years, in November
1892 ended his business relations with Stanford—including the possibility of acting
as the executor of Stanford's will—and returned to New York the following
month.[22] A codicil dated December 28, 1892, just six months before Stanford's own
death, named Joseph McKenna and Nick Smith to fill these two vacancies.[23]

The value of Stanford's estate had long been the subject of much speculation; it
had been estimated at times as being between $50 million and $100 million, but a
court inventory set it at less than $18 million (this, after many gifts to the univer-
sity), of which $12 million was in stocks, $4 million in bonds, $1 million in notes,
with cash on hand and household effects regarded as incidental.[24] (Stanford's
wealth does not seem nearly so impressive until we view it in terms of present value
with a constant dollar-value calculated in. A 1998 study by *Forbes* described the forty
wealthiest Americans of all time by rank, name, dates, source of wealth, and original and present value of wealth.[25] The conversions were made using a formula com-

---

[21]Ibid., 6. Sawyer's death notices, *SF Call*, Sep 8, 1891; *Sac Union*, Sep 8, 1891.

[22]Wilson's death notices, *SF Call*, Jun 5, 1892; *Sac Union*, Jun 6, 1892.

[23]Stanford's Last Will and Testament, 7. The will was repr. in the *SF Call*, Jul 1, 1893. Lathrop, in *SF Morning Call*,
Nov 19, 1892.

[24]His stocks were identified and enumerated in the "Decree of Settlement of Final Account and Final Distribution, in the Superior Court of the State of California, in and for the City and County of San Francisco," *in the Matter of
the Estate of Leland Stanford, Deceased* No. 13690, Dept. No. 9, pp. 23–25. They were also listed, with some differences in
detail, in the *SF Examiner*, Oct 3, 1893, and the *SF Chronicle*, Jan 18, 1894.

[25]Michael Klepper and Robert Gunther, comps., "The American Heritage 40," *AH* 1998 49 (Oct): 56–60, 62, 66,
68, 70, 72, and 74.

paring the original value of wealth to the size of the U.S. economy at the time. This conversion set the value of Stanford's wealth at $30 million when he died and $18.1 billion in 1998 dollars.[26]

Most of Stanford's estate was left to his widow to dispose of as she saw fit. Jane became the sole executrix of her husband's will, which left $2.5 million to the university, as discussed below. Much of the university's wealth came from lands given in 1885.

Stanford was generous with relatives and friends alike. He left $100,000 to each of his fifteen nieces and nephews on *both* sides of the family. And since brother Josiah had already died, his $100,000 was to be shared equally by his two children—Agnes Stanford Taylor (wife of Dr. Edward Robeson Taylor), and Josiah (III) Winslow Stanford, in addition to their own $100,000 legacy. Josiah's stepdaughter Gertrude ("Gertie") also received $100,000. Herbert Nash was remembered for his long and faithful services by a bequest of $15,000.[27]

The Governor left $100,000 to Phil and $300,000 to Thomas Welton. Welton had always been Leland's favorite brother, while Phil was as close to being a black sheep as any member of the Stanford family ever had been; this undoubtedly was the reason for the difference in legacies.

Asa Phillips (Phil) and Annie Stanford

Stanford's brother Phil was dissatisfied with his $100,000 legacy and it was rumored that he planned to contest his brother's will, but nothing came of it; Phil, of all people, knew he had no legitimate claim against Leland's estate.[28] He had a gift for wasting fortunes, and even though he received this inheritance, only $25,000 came to him in cash; the rest went to cancel notes he owed.[29]

Phil had moved to London in 1872, where he engaged in various aspects of the mining business with his partner, Irwin Davis.[30] But speculation by the company named Irwin Davis & Stanford swallowed his fortune and he was left with little more than that which Leland left him, less the debt retirement. One newspaper account mentions that Phil's son Jerome in San Francisco had borrowed half a million from his sister, Mary, which Phil felt compelled for some undisclosed reason to repay.[31] These and other bad investments left the man destitute.[32]

---

[26]Ibid., 72.   [27]LS Last Will and Testament, 3 and 7.

[28][LSJU] *Daily Palo Alto*, Jan 22, 1894.

[29]UNC, Norwich (state not identified) newspaper, May 7, 1903—headed "Once Rich, Died Poor"—on the death of APS. SFP. SUA. This lengthy art. describes in detail the personal, familial, and financial woes of APS during the last few years of his life.   [30]*NY Times*, May 7, 1903.   [31]Ibid.

[32]The APS predicament reminds one of CPH's earlier assessment of the business prowess of APS: "It is very uncertain about what a fellow like Phil Stanford would do with his—build a windmill or do some other foolish thing. . . ." CPH to MH, May 11, 1866.

Asa Phillips Stanford died in poverty in 1903, and one report had it that his sister-in-law Jane Stanford was called upon to pay his burial expenses.[33] Phil's first wife, fifty-five-year-old Mary Whitney Stanford, died in Tunbridge Wells, England, on March 20, 1879.[34] He later married Annie Cunningham, a widow from New Haven, Connecticut. Subsequently, Annie blamed Phil's children for the events leading up to his breakdown and death. She reported that three weeks before his death Phil experienced a final, crushing blow when a bank draft drawn on his son Jerome Bonaparte, who still lived and worked in San Francisco, was returned dishonored.[35] (Jerome was not as well-to-do as some people thought. On June 20, 1902, he had filed a bankruptcy petition in the United States District Court in San Francisco. He, like his father, had squandered his $100,000 legacy from Uncle Leland.[36])

An earlier blow had occurred when Phil's thirty-two-year-old son Philip Welton Stanford died on June 1, 1898, and apparently left $35,000 intended for his father but which was awarded by a judge to the younger man's widow.[37] While this case was in court, Phil caught sight of his daughter, Mary Elizabeth Stanford, and rushed up to her with outstretched arms, only to have her rebuff him by asking him not to speak to her. This was the last time the two ever saw each other.[38] She died the next year.[39]

Eighty-two-year-old Col. Phil Stanford died at his home at 409 West Forty-seventh Street in New York City on May 6, 1903.[40] Although family ties may have restrained him from challenging Leland's will, Annie sued to get $600,000 from the estate of Jane Stanford. Annie claimed that years earlier her husband had turned over 500,000 shares of Central Pacific stock in exchange for a lifetime annuity of $12,000, which, she said, had never been paid.[41] One of Phil's obituaries said that Jane Stanford agreed that the promise of $1,000 per month guaranteed to Philip for life had been made, but insisted that this meant *Leland's* life, not Phil's.[42] This report was sheer nonsense; according to this interpretation, if Leland had died the day after the agreement was made, Phil would have had no further claim to his own money. There was a far more substantial reason that Annie had no claim against the Leland Stanford estate, this being Phil's bankruptcy settlement, which he signed on September 10, 1878, cited earlier, and which stated categorically that Leland did not owe Phil anything. Annie may not have known about this agreement or, knowing, hoped perhaps that it would not come to light at this time.

[33]"ONCE RICH, DIED POOR."   [34]*SF Chronicle*, Mar 28, 1879; *SF Alta California*, Mar 29, 1879.

[35]"ONCE RICH, DIED POOR." JBS, in Stanford, *Stanford Genealogy*, 55.

[36]*SF Chronicle*, Jun 21, 1902.

[37]"ONCE RICH, DIED POOR." On Philip Welton Stanford's death, see Stanford, *Stanford Genealogy*, 55 (records his middle name in error as "Wilton"), and *NY Times*, Jun 4, 1898.   [38]"ONCE RICH, DIED POOR."

[39]*NY Times*, May 7, 1903.   [40]*Sac Union*, May 7, 1903; *SF Call*, May 7, 1903; *NY Times*, May 7, 1903.

[41][LSJU] *Daily Palo Alto*, Apr 7, 1908.   [42]"ONCE RICH, DIED POOR."

Annie Stanford lost her case. In August 1907 she appealed the verdict to the California Supreme Court, and she lost there, too. On April 6, 1908, her claim was denied by this court, not because it lacked legal merit, but that she had ignored the statute of limitations: she had failed to file her petition against Jane Stanford's estate within the prescribed six months as established by law.[43]

STANFORD'S FARMS AND RANCHES

Leland Stanford had sold innumerable parcels that he had owned at one time or another in California, but at his death in June of 1893, he still owned lots, farms, ranches, and vineyards in seventeen of the state's counties.[44]

Lands by County in the Estate of Leland Stanford

1. Siskiyou	7. Solano	13. San Mateo
2. Tehama	8. Sacramento	14. Santa Clara
3. Glenn	9. Marin	15. Madera
4. Colusa	10. Contra Costa	16. San Luis Obispo
5. Yolo	11. Alameda	17. San Bernardino
6. Napa	12. San Francisco	

After the death of Leland Stanford, Jane—as sole executrix—placed on the market more acreage spread across the state of California than most people ever *imagined* that the Stanfords owned. There is no date on the sales literature, but we know that they had "long been for sale" by September 24, 1897.[45] The McAfee Brothers, the San Francisco real estate brokerage and financial firm chosen by Jane, had a real estate brochure printed describing all these properties.[46]

The Copeland Ranch in Tehama County alone contained 2,238 acres of land used primarily for grazing and grain. It was located a mile and a half north of Vina and about eighteen and a half miles south of Red Bluff. The ranch and its buildings were to be used primarily as a horse farm. The property included a two-storey house, barns, training tracks, a colt kindergarten, paddocks, and various enclosures.

Stanford's Shafer Ranch, a 240-acre spread, lay about a mile and a half east of the Copeland Ranch. It had about 30 acres in vineyards and another 30 in peaches and prunes. There were two old buildings used by Chinese workers as a house and stables.

The Government Ranch, known also as the Gwin Ranch—the main house had

---

[43][LSJU] *Daily Palo Alto*, Apr 7, 1908.

[44]If LS ever consummated the negotiations for the 108,000-acre San Joaquin Rancho in Los Angeles County or the 45,000-acre Chino Ranch in San Bernardino, as reported in *LA Times* on June 18, 1887, he must have sold them before his death. *NY Times*, Jun 27, 1887.   [45]*SF Chronicle*, Sep 25, 1897.

[46]"Estate of Leland Stanford, Deceased. Unusual Offering of Ranch Property by Order of Jane L. Stanford, Executrix." SF: McAfee Brothers, [n.d.]. The brochure is in LS Lands files, SUA.

MAP
OF
THE STATE OF
CALIFORNIA
SHOWING
RELATIVE POSITION
OF LANDS
BELONGING TO THE ESTATE OF
Leland Stanford

1. Siskiyou
2. Tehama
3. Glenn
4. Colusa
5. Yolo
6. Napa
7. Solano
8. Sacramento
9. Marin
10. Contra Costa
11. Alameda
12. San Francisco
13. San Mateo
14. Santa Clara
15. Madera
16. San Luis Obispo
17. San Bernardino

145. Map of Stanford lands in California at the time of his death.
Author's Collection.

been the residence of United States senator William McKendree Gwin (1805–1885)—had nearly 2,958 acres, located on the southern shores of Suisun Bay in Contra Costa County, about forty miles northeast of San Francisco. The lowlands were used for pasture and the high grounds for grain, grazing, and hay. Surrounding the house were 35 acres of vineyards and 10 acres in fruit trees. The property contained more than a dozen different buildings. (The real estate brochure said of this property that similar land in the area had sold for as much as $150 per acre.)

Further evidence that Jane Stanford did not consider all lands contiguous to the university as being a part of the institution was her offering for sale the so-called "Coon and Felt" tracts.

McAfee Brothers Sales Prospectus
"Coon" and "Felt" Tracts
San Mateo and Santa Clara Counties, California.

"Adjoin Stanford University, and make one compact body of land of about 1,200 acres, of which 50 acres are in vineyard and a small orchard, and the remainder in grain. It is all gently rolling, and all good soil, to the top of the hills. It can be well divided into home and villa lots, giving good views and excellent location for each place, and all within convenient walking distance of the University.

"Each of the two tracts has a comfortable dwelling, stables, barns, outhouses, etc., and abundant water from the private reservoir on the property, or from mains of the local Water Company or of the great Spring Valley Water Company of San Francisco."*

*"Estate of Leland Stanford, Deceased. Unusual Offering of Ranch Property by Order of Jane L. Stanford, Executrix." SF: McAfee Brothers, [undated]. The brochure is in LS Lands files, SUA.

The brochure included colorful descriptions of Stanford's beautiful 100-acre McCoppin Ranch near the town of San Luis Obispo. The improvements consisted of a five-room cottage, a stable for sixteen horses, a hayloft, a granary, a tool house, a men's bunkhouse, and a chicken house.

McAfee Brothers also offered for sale the 282.5-acre Stillman ranch, in San Bernardino County, not far from the business center of Redlands. The property was surrounded by orange and olive groves and many splendid residences. Two local railroads came close to the property. The buildings consisted of a winery, a stillhouse, a packinghouse, and a small house for the foreman and his family. Adequate irrigation was available for agricultural purposes.

With the establishment of Stanford University, in 1885, the Stanfords had given a large portion of their real estate holdings to the university, but not all of them, by any means. When Stanford's estate was closed, on March 28, 1898, almost five years after his death, his remaining real estate and personal property were listed in the "Decree of Settlement of Final Account and Final Distribution."[47] The acreage of these properties was minor in size compared to the 78,540.14 acres given to the university in 1885, but the following accounting (which includes the acreage of the farms and ranches mentioned above) listed by county, shows that they were, nonetheless, considerable:

San Francisco		2.33
Santa Clara		1,285.78
San Mateo		145.82
Sacramento Lots 1 & 2 N and O,		.60[48]
8 and 9		
Tehama		3,362.26
(plus lots 1, 2, 11, 12 of Vina)[49]		

Napa

Page	Item	Acreage
14	1[50]	unk
14	2	4.00
14	3	.28
14	4	unk
15	5	43.50
15	6 calc.	6.00
15	7	5.00
15–16	8	45.00
16	9	.33
16	10	20.00
Total		124.11+

Alameda [County]	3,089.54
Contra Costa	3,047.74
Yolo	Unspecified acreage.
Solano	Unspecified acreage.

[47]In the Superior Court of the State of California, in and for the City and County of San Francisco, *In the Matter of the Estate of Leland Stanford, Deceased*. No. 13,690, Dept. 9, pp. 7–23.

[48]Calif. DPR, *Leland Stanford Mansion State Historic Park, Historic Structures Report* (Sac: DPR, Apr 1996), 1.

[49]In the "Decree of Settlement of Final Account and of Final Distribution" the size of the parcels is unspecified, p. 14, line 7.

[50]Items 1 and 4 can no longer be identified by the Napa County Assessor. He estimates items 2, 3, and 9 as shown. John Tuteur, Napa County assessor, to the author, Nov 1, 2001.

A second accounting of land, to relatives, breaks it down as follows, by county:

Contra Costa		1,300.00
		18.68
		750.62
		160.00
		324.40
	957−454.99 =	502.01
	total	13,055.71

Siskiyou	5,893.75
Colusa	208.00
Glenn	164.29
Madera	171.43
San Luis Obispo	240.00
San Bernardino	282.10

Alameda [City]
    Lots 1−12 in Block A
    Lots 1−18 in Block B
    Lots 1−14 in Block C
    Lots 1−14 in Block D
    Lots 1−18 in Block E
    Lots 1−16 in Block F
    Lots 1−14 in Block G
    Lots 2−8 in Block J
    Total   8.443[51]

Marin
    Berry Rancho   3,865.67

Alameda
    Tract of marsh land   8.75
    Lot 32, Section 13   3.00
    Portion of lot 25   3.1
    Section 18
    Lots 9−11 and part of lot 8
    Block 1   (size not disclosed)
    Lots 13−16, Block 13   (size not disclosed)
    Lots 1−6, Block 14   (size not disclosed)
    Half interest in Bray property,
        Lots 37−38, 45−46
      (with minor exceptions) (size not disclosed)
    Total   3,880.52+[52]

---

[51]The "Decree of Settlement of Final Account and of Final Distribution," 22.
[52]Ibid., 22−23.

Stanford University's lands are still largely intact. There have been sales, offset by other land purchases, and parcels seized under threat of condemnation by city, county, state, and federal agencies. In 1955, for example, federal authorities purchased 87 acres for a veterans' hospital. Still, in 1999, university lands contained 8,180 acres in unincorporated Santa Clara County, unincorporated San Mateo County, Palo Alto, Menlo Park, Woodside, and Portola Valley.[53]

Though Stanford acreage is intact, the university has permitted several social and legal incursions and encroachments by the city of Palo Alto. It

STANFORD UNIVERSITY'S FINANCIAL STATISTICS FOR FISCAL YEAR 2000–2001	
Income	
Cash gifts	$469 million
Cash pledges	481 million
Investment returns on endowment assets	2.9 billion
Revenue	2.0 billion
Plant facilities	3.76 billion
Net assets of endowment	8.2 billion
Stanford Hospital	not available
Stanford Shopping Center	228 million
University net assets	12.1 billion
Total investments	10.8 billion*

*LSJU, *2001 Annual Report* (Stanford University: Office of the Controller, 2001), 30–32.

has permitted the neighboring city to treat street development and the policing of the Stanford Shopping Center to make it appear that the university is a part of the city. The same can be said for lands made available on university grounds for Palo Alto City Schools. The university is not in the city of Palo Alto; it is in Santa Clara County, but Palo Alto and the university are both acting more and more as though it were part of the city.

Much of the land not used for university purposes is now leased for grazing, agriculture, an industrial park, the Stanford Shopping Center, office buildings, and rental housing.

JANE STANFORD AND HER DISAFFECTED LEGATEES

It was understandable that Jane sought respite from her nieces and nephews demanding their legacies in hard cash when her entire fortune was tied up in the courts. It was quite another matter, so thought some of them, that when two years after Jane won her case in the U.S. Supreme Court they still had not been paid.

As early as August 1893, barely two months after Leland Stanford died, Jane was pressured to pay a portion of Christine Lathrop's (brother Daniel Shields Lathrop's daughter) inheritance.[54] Her attorney, Joseph D. Baucus, sent a letter from Saratoga

---

[53]LSJU, Planning Dept., *Summary and Explanation. Stanford University Draft Community Plan and General Use Permit Application*. Submitted to SCC Nov 15, 1999 (Stanford: SPD, 1999), back cover.

[54]In the will of LS, three unidentified nieces of Jane were all daughters of Jane's brother Daniel: Jeannie (Lathrop) Lawton, Aimee (Lathrop) Hanson, and Christine (Lathrop) Gunning.

Springs, New York, explaining to Jane Stanford her niece's dire straits and demands for payment on several notes. He asked that part of the legacy be paid immediately to save Christine from legal levies against her estate and possibly from insanity because of her situation.[55]

When pressure to "pay up" continued to mount, Jane devised a plan (one hesitates to say scheme) of payment that did not satisfy the legatees, nor was the Superior Court of the State of California pleased by it. She decided to foist off on them large tracts of land in lieu of cash payments. Many of these were the tracts of land listed for sale by McAfee Brothers, which she had been unable to sell. The land values were set by Jane herself, with no evidence that professional land appraisals had been made or that the legatees had been consulted in the matter.

Jane Stanford's "Petition for the Final Distribution of Said Estate," signed on September 4, 1897, amounted to a major modification of the will left by Leland Stanford. The document now read, "Appropriation and distribution in kind of the assets of said estate in settlement of the cash bequests in favor of . . . [with several legatee names listed] according to the judgement of said Jane L. Stanford. . . ."[56]

The revised document presented to the court for its approval named six legatees and identified certain properties they were to take in lieu of cash:

> Charles Stanford (nephew of Leland) was offered lands in Napa, San Bernardino county, and lots in Menlo Park that Herbert Nash had once owned. In all, cash $32,000; land, by Jane's estimate, $82,312.54.[57]
>
> Jane (Jennie) Stanford Byington (daughter of Charles Stanford) was to receive certain lands in Contra Costa County. In all, cash $22,000; land, by Jane's estimate, $92,612.[58]
>
> Nora Stanford Wells (daughter of Charles Stanford) was to take lands in Tehama County. In all, cash $22,000; land, by Jane's estimate, $92,612.[59]
>
> Leland Stanford Lathrop (son of Jane's brother Charles Lathrop) was to receive lands in Alameda County as a major portion of his legacy. In all, cash $4,500; land, by Jane's estimate, $110,380.48.[60]
>
> Charles Stanford (as assignee of his deceased brother Winfield Scott Stanford, who had transferred his legacy to his mother, E[liza Page] Stanford, who died on April 11, 1896), was to accept certain tracts of land in Santa Clara and San Mateo counties. In all, cash $22,000; land, by Jane's estimate, $92,612.[61]
>
> Maud Stanford Kinmouth (daughter of Charles Stanford) was offered certain lands in San Mateo and Santa Clara counties. In all, cash $22,000; in land, by Jane's estimate, $92, 612.[62]

Five of these six were Stanfords, only one was a Lathrop.

---

[55]Joseph D. Baucus to JLS, Aug 23, 1893.

[56]This proposed modification of the last will and testament of LS is available for any interested party to examine. LS papers, SUA.   [57]Ibid., 12–14.   [58]Ibid., 14–16.

[59]Ibid., 16–17.   [60]Ibid., 17–18.   [61]Ibid., 19–22.

[62]Ibid., 22–24.

The "Decree of Settlement of Final Account and Distribution" of the Stanford estate carries the story to its legal conclusion.[63] Wilson & Wilson appeared as attorneys for Jane Stanford, and the court appointed Edward Robeson Taylor, Agnes Stanford's husband, to represent "all interested underrepresented parties," namely, almost all the legatees involved.[64]

On September 24, 1897, Superior Court judge James Vincent Coffey took less than three hours of deliberation to decide that the legatees had to be paid in cash.[65]

The demurrer to Mrs. Stanford's petition was filed on behalf of the Charles Stanford heirs and Leland Stanford Lathrop.

The core of the objection to her petition was presented by Dr. Taylor, representing the "unrepresented heirs," when he argued:

> In this petition the trustee makes compulsorily this distribution in kind, subject only to your honor's approval. She assumes the right to so distribute in kind. She puts her own valuation on these lands and she asserts her right to force them upon these legatees.
>
> We believe that this petitioner thought she had the right, but we deny that she had the right. In the first place what power does this petitioner have under the will? These legacies are all so much money. In several parts of the will they are called cash bequests. There is nothing in the will from one end to the other to show that the testator intended to settle for anything less than hard cash. If one of the legatees chose to settle for anything less than money then the executrix was authorized, very properly, to settle with land. The executrix is utterly without power to pay these legatees in anything but money, unless the legatee agrees. If Senator Stanford in the codicil permitting Mrs. Stanford to settle in kind, so much relied on by Mr. Wilson, had intended to revamp the whole cause relating to the legacies, he would have had the clauses rewritten. In order to prevent the throwing of all these stocks and bonds on the market, at a considerable loss to the estate, Mrs. Stanford was privileged to settle in kind, if the legatees were willing.
>
> A trustee cannot be permitted to dispose of lands, one-half of which are without the jurisdiction of the Court, as in this case, when there are plenty of assets. Over half this estate Senator Stanford never had any testamentary power. He could not have referred to these lands when he gave Mrs. Stanford power to settle in kind. He must have referred to other property. Such a settlement would be inequitable. It is not a matter of necessity. There is plenty for every one.
>
> This trustee was chosen for reasons of her own, to give this land, entirely unproductive, as the papers in the estate show. Much of it could only be profitable by the expenditure of a great deal of money. These legatees live in the far East and could not attend to it. Confidence has been measurably restored, business is improving. Eastern securities are much more valuable than they were when Senator Stanford died. Railroad securities are going up constantly. There is no reason why the trustee should unload these unproductive lands on these legatees.[66]

---

[63]The "Decree of Settlement of Final Account and Distribution" is also in the LS papers. SUA.

[65]SF Chronicle, Sep 25, 1897; SF Examiner, Sep 25, 1897.

[64]Ibid., 1.

[66]Ibid.

It must have embarrassed Charles Lathrop, loyal servant to his sister, when his son Leland Stanford Lathrop hired attorney Thomas Van Ness and joined the Leland Stanford heirs in their action against Aunt Jennie.[67]

The gist of the case argued by Van Ness was that there was more than enough money in the Stanford estate to settle the outstanding claims in cash. He cited a $1 million uncollected debt owed the estate by the Pacific Improvement Company, which had the assets to pay, and stock in the Market Street Railway Company worth $1 million.[68]

Van Ness then attacked the quality of the lands Jane Stanford was trying to palm off on the legatees. Regardless of her appraisal, he insisted, these lands had no saleable value. This is proven by the fact that they had long been on the market for sale and had attracted no buyers. He chided Jane Stanford, who in her petition offered no reason why the legatees "should have been selected upon whom to unload undesirable lands, while the cream of the estate is reserved for Mrs. Stanford and the other legatees."

THE LAW FIRM OF WILSON & WILSON

looms large in the life of the Stanfords in San Francisco. It was from the Wilsons that Leland and Jane rented their temporary home at 711 Pine Street just after moving to San Francisco.

The Wilsons handled a great deal of the Stanfords' legal matters and acted for years as attorneys for the Central Pacific Railroad. The guest lists of major social events at the Stanford mansion often included one or two of the Wilsons.

At the head of Wilson & Wilson stood Samuel Mountford Wilson, almost an exact contemporary of Leland Stanford; he was born in the same year and he died only one year earlier. In 1874 Wilson took his son Russell J. Wilson into partnership with him, and for years the firm continued without change until they took another son and brother, Mountford S. Wilson, into the firm.

Wilson & Wilson represented many millionaires and countless major corporations as clients. The elder Wilson was considered one of the leading lawyers of the United States. His law practice brought him the greatest income of any attorney in California. He personally was the attorney for scores of millionaires, Wells, Fargo and Company, the Bank of California, and the Central Pacific Railroad. When Gov. Henry Haight offered him a seat on the California Supreme Court, he declined the honor.*

*SF Call, Jun 5, 1892.

---

[67]Ibid. Not all Stanfords and Lathrops were at odds. On Aug 7, 1893, the *SF Argonaut* reported: "The engagement is announced of Miss Maude L. Stanford, eldest daughter of Mr. Jerome B. Stanford, and Mr. Leland S[tanford] Lathrop, son of Mr. Charles G. Lathrop." This wedding never took place. On April 30, 1900, Maud married J. Allen Parsons of Belvedere. One record has it that Maud(e) Lillian Stanford was born in SF on Aug 13, 1870, the oldest of JBS's five children, four of whom were daughters. Her mother was Lillian M. (Clark) Stanford, the first of JBS's three wives. Stanford, *Stanford Genealogy*, 95–96. Leland Stanford Lathrop (Dec 4, 1870–May 5, 1963), an insurance broker, married Lillian Watson (Aug 29, 1871–May 11, 1947). Broker: *SF Chronicle*, May 5, 1947. They had one son, Leland Stanford Lathrop, Jr. (Apr 7, 1897–Feb 28, 1969).   [68]*SF Chronicle*, Sep 25, 1897.

Van Ness concluded his argument with a series of questions not appreciated by Russell Wilson, questions that called into question Mrs. Stanford's fairness and good intentions: "Why should she want to reserve for other legatees and for herself, as residual legatee the better part of the estate? Is it fair, is it equitable? Does it show an equitable intention on the part of the trustee?"

Judge Coffey's conclusion was final. He said that his first impression had been that Mrs. Stanford had the power her petition claimed, but that on reading Stanford's will it was obvious that the senator intended the legatees to be paid in cash.[69]

STANFORD VINEYARDS

Warm Springs Vineyard and Winery

Warm Springs, at Mission San José, was the last of the Stanford wineries to stop producing wine. The nineteenth century saw the Warm Springs winery and vineyards survive a variety of catastrophes: fires, earthquakes, depressions, and numerous changes of ownership.[70]

In 1923 Frank Kelley, a former Chicago businessman then living in San José, purchased the Warm Springs property and rebuilt the winery into a modern racing stable. He put in a bricked-in exercising paddock and laid out a mile-long track. Kelley raised many prize-winning horses and cattle there.[71]

The death of Fred Kelley ended this stage of the ranch's history. The ownership of the property passed to his widow and then to his son, Lawrence A. Kelley. The son reported in 1927 that 1,200 acres of the old Stanford property had been sold to the Sisters of the Holy Names of Jesus and Mary for $150,000.[72] The Oakland Order, then conducting a school on Lake Merritt in Oakland, announced that it would spend $2 million to establish at Warm Springs college classrooms, pools, and other facilities for women's sports, and have a new college ready for classes in the fall of 1928.[73]

The Sisters' plans fell through. In 1944 Fred Goossen bought the property with the intention of building a dude ranch. He renamed it the "Hidden Valley Ranch."[74] In 1945 Goossen sold the vineyard lands to the Weibel Wine Company, which is still in operation, though no longer at the Mission San José site. For a number of years Weibel used three of the buildings erected by the Stanford brothers three-quarters of a century earlier.[75] In the late 1960s the Weibel Company had 97 acres in vines, which with its other holdings was producing 800,000 gallons of wine per year.[76] By then this company had won more than three hundred awards for its high-quality wines.[77]

[69]Ibid.
[71]PA Times, Sep 26, 1927.
[74]Oakland Tribune, Nov 14, 1954, and Aug 16, 1959.
[76]Author inter. with Fred Weibel, Jr., Jul 1, 1969.
[70]See Warm Springs art. in LA Times, Jun 17, 1966.
[72]Ibid.   [73]Ibid.
[75]Ibid., Aug 16, 1959.
[77]Fremont News Register, Oct 2, 1958.

In September 1958 a historical landmark was dedicated at the site of the old winery, paying tribute to Leland and Josiah Stanford for the part they played in the creation of high quality California table wines.

CALIFORNIA REGISTERED HISTORICAL LANDMARK NO. 642 ALAMEDA COUNTY
LELAND STANFORD WINERY

"This winery was founded in 1869 by Leland Stanford—railroad builder, Governor of California, United States Senator, and founder of Stanford University. The vineyard, planted by his brother Josiah Stanford, helped to prove that wines equal to any in the world could be produced in California. The restored buildings and winery are now occupied and operated by Weibel Champagne Vineyards."*

*California registered Historical Landmark No 642. Plaque placed by the CSPC in cooperation with R[udolf] E. and F[rederick] E. Weibel and Weibel, Inc., Sep 27, 1958, Survey of CRHL, Alameda County No 642, Mar 29, 1979, in CDPR, 3.

On April 20, 1961, a fire raged through the Weibel winery, popping the corks of more than 100,000 bottles of champagne and sounding like "a blazing munitions dump."[78] It destroyed the main building and caused more than a million dollars in damage.[79] It was speculated that sunlight magnified through an empty wine bottle may have ignited a wooden pallet.

On May 1, 1996, what remained of Josiah's vineyard at Mission San José—now a part of the city of Fremont—was uprooted and demolished. The beautiful vine-covered hillsides and the site of the winery buildings are now covered with condominiums. There remains a small corporate office in Fremont, with all Weibel vineyards and winemaking operations now located in the town of Lodi, between Stockton and Sacramento.[80]

The health resort on the Hidden Valley Ranch—its old lodge building, bar, restaurant, and dance hall—is now nothing more than memories. The ranch and the Josiah Stanford home—itself once a retreat for alcoholics—had no connection with the Weibel winery, then only a half-mile away. They, too, have been demolished and *their* lands covered by houses in a seventy-parcel development known as Hidden Valley Terrace. To visit the old site, one takes Mission Road between Milpitas and Fremont to Stanford Avenue and a half-mile up the hill to the single remaining building. The city of Fremont is renovating this brick structure—the old still—to be the center of a one-acre city park set aside to commemorate the Stan-

[78]*SJ Mercury*, Apr 21, 1961; *Stockton Record*, Apr 21, 1961.   [79]*SJ Mercury*, Apr 21, 1961.
[80]Author inter. with Rennie Kirchof, personnel director, Weibel Winery, Corporate Offices, Fremont, Calif., Apr 1, 1997.

146. Weibel Winery's
Governor Stanford Champagne,
1998. *Author's Collection.*

ford Winery.[81] Here, close to the street, stands the 1958 state monument. From this vantage point, on a clear day one can see the Hoover Tower on the Stanford campus.

Menlo Park (Palo Alto Stock Farm)

The Palo Alto farm vineyards had always been a problem for Jane Stanford and David Starr Jordan. In 1894, the year after Stanford's death, Mrs. Stanford ordered John F. Lewis, manager of the Stanford winery, to sell wine by the case only, and to see that the cases were shipped out. This was a precautionary move on her part to curtail small-quantity student purchases of wine. Everyone knew that students could show up at the winery, containers in hand, and walk off with the desired elixir.[82]

Gone now are the vineyards and winery at the Palo Alto farm, as is the farm itself.[83] The red brick winery on the Stanford campus survived the 1906 earthquake unscathed. For a time it served as a storage building, a dairy, and a breeder's service facility. The refurbished building was reopened in April 1984 as a combination office building and center for a variety of international restaurants.

---

[81] *Weibel Winery Historic Buildings / Park, Feasibility Analysis* (SF: ARG, 1996). Author inter. with Janice Stern, assoc. planner, City of Fremont, Apr 21, 1998.

[82] Dorothy F. Regnery, *An Enduring Heritage, Historic Buildings on the San Francisco Peninsula* (Stanford: SUP, 1976), 73.

[83] As late as 1902 the PA Winery was still producing Angelica, Muscatel, Port, Sherry, Claret, Mozelle, Dry Muscat, Riesling, Zinfandel, Chasselas, Johannisberg, and grape juice. Dec 19, 1902, inventory, in PASF papers, SUA.

DAVID STARR JORDAN ON ALCOHOLIC DRINKS

"The sole purpose of alcoholic drinks is to force the nervous system to lie, and thus to vitiate its power of recording the truth. Men use alcohol, weak or strong, to feel warm when they are really cold, to 'feel good' without warrant, to feel emancipated from those restraints and reserves which constitute the essence of character building. Alcohol is a depressant, not a stimulant, appearing as such only because it affects the highest nerve-operations first.

"Its influence impinges alike on the three chief mental functions, sensation, reason, motion. It leaves its subject uncertain as to what he sees or feels, hazy as to cause and effect, and unsteady as to resultant action. No man of high purpose can afford to endanger the validity of these nerve processes which register his contact with reality."*

*DSJ, *Days of a Man*, I, 48.

The Palo Alto winery was closed in 1915, perhaps because—as it has been argued—it was no longer profitable, but also because of growing prohibition sentiment in the country. Jordan had always been against the use of all alcoholic beverages. His description of the evils of the use of alcohol as a drink gives no quarter to those—like Leland Stanford—who praised wine for its beneficial medicinal value. With convictions as extreme and as uncompromising on the subject as Jordan's were, it is little wonder that he was willing—eager—to cooperate in the closing of the Stanford Winery.

At any rate, the vines on the Palo Alto Stock Farm were uprooted and the land was planted with hay or leased to farmers who planted it with strawberries or tomatoes. Plans to convert the winery into a dormitory were scrapped in favor of leasing the structure to the Carnation Milk Company to be used as a dairy.[84] From then until 1958 the old winery was used by a succession of companies as a cattle barn. The Stanford Hospital on Willow (now Sand Hill) Road and the new shopping center north of the winery prompted the American Breeders Association to move its prize bulls to Wisconsin in 1958.

The winery then stood vacant until 1961, when a group of investors had the building remodeled into two floors of shops, offices, a bank, and an international restaurant.

Vina Winery and Farm

Vina was easily Stanford's most extensive as well as expensive winery. When Peter Lassen in the mid-1840s planted the first vines on what was to become the Stanford Vina winery, little could he imagine that in the early twentieth century his vines would still be bearing fruit on the vast Stanford ranch.

When Stanford died there were more than 4,000 acres in vines, with 2,500 acres producing wine. The Vina inventory of a half-million dollars' worth of brandy was sold immediately after his death.

On November 11, 1885, Stanford deeded the Vina Ranch to the trustees of Stan-

[84]SUNS, Press Release, Dec 12, 1960; *PA Times*, Dec 13, 1960; *PL*, Dec 16, 1960.

ford University as a perpetual source of income, though he continued to run it through his managers until his death, at which time it fell under the control of his widow, with the welcome advice of "dry" Jordan, whose advice she readily accepted. They were disappointed with the Vina property, since the winery proved to be an unprofitable enterprise, as it always had been—but Stanford had never needed nor did he share in the university's profit motive.[85]

Many of the problems that arose at Vina were a result of Jane's actions, yet in all fairness to her it must be said that with her estate tied up in court, she had financial problems just keeping the university afloat. Within three months of her husband's death, she paid a visit to Vina and peremptorily dismissed 150 Vina employees and cut the salaries of most of those remaining.[86] James Stewart Copeland, superintendent of the farming department, was notified that his salary had been reduced by one-third.[87] Other salary reductions were even greater. Gradually, more and more of the unused land was leased out to neighboring farmers, with the ranch getting one-third the income from their crops.

From then on the Governor's widow visited the Vina establishment quarterly to supervise those changes she had decreed.[88] It was argued that even with her strictures in place, the ranch continued to lose more and more money; Jordan complained that the property was plunging the university into debt at the rate of $500 a day.[89]

In addition to the losses sustained, or at best the small profits made, during the early days of the Vina project, the new managers had to contend with the growing prohibition movement as the century drew to a close. It is difficult to sort out whether Jordan's complaint was more from an economic consideration or the result of his long career as a prohibitionist and advocate of "dry" legislation. This question had been raised even before Stanford died.[90] It is doubtful that Vina ever made a profit, but apparently by mid-1895 it was finally breaking even.[91]

Stanford himself regarded wine drinking as a sure enemy of intemperance. Moderation in drinking wine, he insisted, was the best guarantee against immoderate use of hard liquors: "If I thought wine-making injurious to the human family I would pull up every vine that I have. The habitual use of wine does away with liquors between meals. In the countries using food wines the people are the most temperate."[92]

Though the production of wines and brandy at Vina was cut back, Mrs. Stanford favored continuing the making of brandy for medicinal purposes.[93]

---

[85]*SF Chronicle*, Jun 27, 1893; *SF Examiner*, Jul 14, 1895.

[86]*Sac Record-Union*, Sep 23, 1891; *SF Chronicle*, Sep 2 and 7, 1893.

[87]*SF Chronicle*, Sep 2 and 7, 1893; Ruth Hughes Hitchcock, comp., *Leaves of the Past, 1828–1880: A Pioneer Register, including an overview of the history and events of early Tehama County* (Part I, Chico: ANCRR, [undated; post-1964]).

[88]McConnell, "Stanford Vina Ranch," 57.

[89]DSJ, *Days of a Man*, I, 497–498.

[90]*SF Examiner*, Apr 6, 1890.

[91]McConnell, "Stanford Vina Ranch," 61.

[92]*SF Examiner*, Nov 25, 1889, and Apr 6, 1890.

[93]Ibid., Jul 14, 1895.

147. Entrance gates to "Vina Winery."
Author's Collection.

Before Jane's death, however, management of the vineyards was placed in university hands. She even agreed—contrary to the terms of the original grant—to give the trustees the right to sell the Vina ranch if they deemed it wise or necessary.[94] Apparently the trustees had no plans to sell the winery at the time; in 1908 they allowed the planting of 600 acres of vines, bringing the vineyard back to its original 3,000 acres.[95]

In 1908 there were four hundred men employed full-time at the Vina ranch, two-thirds of them Japanese and Chinese. The white men worked in the winery; the field labor was left to the Chinese.[96] During the six-to-eight-week winemaking season, 1.5 million gallons of wine and brandy were produced. Port, sherry, angelica, and muscats were made in large quantities, most of it shipped to New York for sale. (In 1896, Jane Stanford sent President Cleveland a gift of Stanford wine to thank him for his help. Since he did not know at the time where she might be, he addressed his thank you letter to her to the Vina Distillery of California, 68 Broad Street, New York, N.Y.[97])

---

[94]Gregg, "The History of the Famous Stanford Ranch at Vina, California," 338.
[95]Ibid.   [96]Ibid.
[97]Pres. Cleveland's priv. sec. addressed his letter to P[hil] L. Crovat, gen. agent of the Vina Distiller's NY off., Mar 14, 1896. The signature is illegible, but Cleveland's priv. sec. was Henry T. Thurber. Copy in JLS papers, SUA.

148. One of the original winery buildings.
Author's Collection.

149. Plaque announcing new ownership.
Author's Collection.

On July 24, 1915, the central building of the Vina Ranch—the winery itself—
burned, prompting the trustees to rethink even more their commitment to the
wine business. A number of factors caused them to lean toward closure. These were
aptly synopsized by a later journalist who wrote: "The high cost of labor and materials during the inflationary days of the World War in Europe, the criticism of prohi-
bitionists and others that a university should not be run on money made from the
sale of alcoholic beverages, and the lack of profit from the sale of grape juice."[98]

In 1915 the trustees shipped grapes to Lodi for pressing, which was the last harvest of the land once cultivated by Lassen, Gerke, and Stanford. In gradual steps the
trustees were freed from the original responsibility of maintaining the Vina property, and in 1915–1916 the vineyard was uprooted, bringing to a close another of
Stanford's experiments.[99]

The former vineyard was planted in alfalfa and the dairy herd was increased so
that gradually Vina took on the aspect of its neighboring farms. In 1919 and the

[98]*RB News*, Aug 3, 1956.   [99]*Chico Record*, Sep 29, 1915.

150. Another original winery building. *Author's Collection.*

151. Derelict car on a nearby street in Vina. *Author's Collection.*

1920s the bulk of the property was divided and sold to a number of different people, bringing in almost $2 million for the cash-hungry university.[100] In 1950 much of the land was purchased by the Pacific Soap Company of Los Angeles, and five years later the 580 acres central to the old ranch were bought by Trappist monks from Kentucky.[101] Six priests and twenty-two brothers moved into their new monastery

---

[100]Ibid., Apr 5, 1919.   [101]*RB News*, Jul 5, 1955; *Sac Bee*, Jul 8, 1955.

after rechristening it Our Lady of New Clairvaux.[102] To this day, these monks raise fruits, nuts, alfalfa, wheat, barley, and tend a herd of Holstein cows. Missing, however, are most reminders of the farm's past as California's largest vineyard and winery. Of Stanford's peak of 4,000 acres of grapevines, just under a half-acre remains today as a source of fresh table grapes.[103]

THE YEARS HAVE BROUGHT MANY CHANGES TO VINA since Joaquin Miller wrote his unflattering description in 1886. Today it still has a post office (Vina 96092), a market and deli at the corner of Sixth and Rowles streets, about one hundred feet from the railroad tracks just across the street. There is Lydia's beauty salon, a fire station, and several abandoned commercial buildings. The town has several city blocks of modest workers' houses and a number of dilapidated and abandoned old automobiles.

Still surviving, although in poor condition, is the two-and-a-half-acre building that was once the wine shed and several brick buildings that were the center of the brandy operations.

STANFORD HOMES

Sacramento House

Except for periodic visits to the capital city, when they stayed in their old home, the Stanford mansion in Sacramento was unoccupied from 1880 until 1900, except for a sole caretaker.[104] On April 18, 1900, before leaving for an extended trip to Europe, Mrs. Stanford gave the house, along with a $75,000 endowment, to the Roman Catholic Diocese of Sacramento.[105] Ultimately, Mrs. Stanford gave all properties and lots in Sacramento to the Roman Catholic bishop of Sacramento.[106]

For a number of years the Stanford house was run by the Sisters of Mercy as an orphanage and afterward was converted into a home for girls, under the direction of the Sisters of Social Service.[107] These two orders refurnished the parlors and family dining rooms as they had been in the nineteenth century.[108]

---

[102]*SF Examiner*, Mar 4, 1956; *Chico Enterprise-Record*, Jun 1, 1955.

[103]Author inter. with Trappist Monk Brother Oscar, Jun 11, 1997.

[104]Wenzel, "Facts about the Stanfords," 254; the most complete hist. of the Sac House is found in Dorothy F. Regnery's "A Study of the Leland Stanford House in Sacramento, California," c1987 by Dorothy F. Regnery, a 284-page, bound, unpub. ms. in Dorothy F. Regnery papers, SUA.

[105]Baird, "Architectural Legacy," 204; *Sac Bee*, Apr 18 and 19, 1900. The deed was recorded on May 14, 1900, in SCR, Book 177 of Deeds, 430–431; *Sac Union*, Feb 27, 1938; *SF Argonaut*, Apr 13, 1900.

[106]Legal docs. pertaining to this gift are found in the file "History of the Founders, Properties and Residences," in SUA; another hist. sketch of the Sac House is found in Calif. DPR, *Stanford House. State Historic Park General Plan* (Sac: DPR, 1989).

[107]Wenzel, "Facts about the Stanfords," 245; Baird, "Architectural Legacy," 204; *Sac Bee*, Mar 13, 1860; several brochures and flyers sketch the hist. of the school, including Tim Comstock, "Stanford Home for Children, Our History," a 4-p. brochure; a flyer titled "Our Heritage, Stanford Home for Children;" and a 2-p. "Jane Lathrop School" flyer.

[108]Baird, "Architectural Legacy," 204.

RESOLUTION 94
To have the State of California purchase the Stanford Mansion

WHEREAS, In memory of Leland Stanford, Jr., who was born in 1868 and died in 1884, the Leland Stanford family founded the university which so proudly bears the Stanford name; and

WHEREAS, The Stanford Mansion in Sacramento, in which Leland Stanford, Jr. was born, faces an uncertain and perhaps a hazardous future; and

WHEREAS, The Stanfords' contribution to this state in its earlier history was generous and extraordinary; and

WHEREAS, The Stanford Alumni Association and the people of this state have a direct interest in preserving the place held in California history by the Leland Stanfords and their son, Leland Stanford, Jr.; and

WHEREAS, The Stanford Mansion has become, in its grand architecture, a cherished memento to all the people of this state; and

WHEREAS, The Stanford Mansion is rapidly deteriorating and falling into despair; now, therefore, be it further

Resolved by the Assembly of the State of California, That the Members direct the Department of Parks and Recreation to study the feasibility of including the Stanford Home in the State Park System as a historic monument; and be it further

Resolved, That the Department of Parks and Recreation report its findings and recommendations to the Assembly not later than the fifth calendar day of the 1971 Regular Session of the Legislature; and be it further

Resolved, That the Chief Clerk of the Assembly transmit a copy of this resolution to the Director of Parks and Recreation.

When St. Patrick's Orphanage was later built, the Stanford mansion was converted into Sacramento's first settlement house, a place to provide entertainment, rest, instruction, and social service to the men, women, and children of the neighborhood.[109] In 1939 it was restored and renovated as a part of the Golden Empire Centennial.[110]

During the 1950s the status of the Stanford house became a matter of concern to historically-minded Californians.[111] On May 12, 1957, the State of California designated the Stanford House State Landmark No. 614.[112] In the following year, the Department of Beaches and Parks (now the Department of Parks and Recreation) recommended that the state acquire title to the house.[113]

---

[109] *Sac Bee*, Sep 9, 1937, includes men among those served. [110] *PA Times*, Jun 13, 1940.

[111] Statement by Dorothy F. Regnery, SHS, chairman, Stanford House Project, for the Budget & Fiscal Review Committee, Subcommittee No. 2, May 6, 1985, in Room 112, State Capitol, Sac. In SUA.

[112] DPR, *Stanford House State Historic Park, General Plan*, 6.

[113] *Old Town* (Sac: DPR, Nov 1958), I, 15; Regnery, "A Study of the Leland Stanford House in Sacramento, California," 187–188.

152. Sacramento house, photograph by John T. Headlee, June 1999. *Author's Collection.*

In 1960 the California State Capitol Plan, adopted by the Capitol Building and Planning Commission, decreed that the house was to be preserved.[114] Three years later, Bishop Alden J. Bell of the Sacramento Diocese of the Roman Catholic Church—the legal owner of the house—concluded that the house was no longer a safe and suitable home for the girls who lived there and that the church operation should be relocated.[115] On June 4, 1963, Bell wrote to Governor Edmund "Pat" Brown proposing that the State of California purchase the house and preserve it as a historic monument.[116] Legislators, private citizens, and public groups all joined in seconding the proposal to buy the property.

Governor Brown's successor, Ronald Reagan, also spoke in favor of the project.[117] William Penn Mott, Jr., Reagan's director of Parks and Recreation, wrote in reply to one inquirer, "Governor Reagan has asked me to reply to your recent inquiry about the Stanford home . . . as a period residence of a great Californian, the

---

[114]Regnery, SHS, chairman, Stanford House Project, to James M. Doyle, supervisor, Environmental Review Section, Oct 24, 1988, in *Stanford House State Historic Park, General Plan*, 99–110, 101 cited.

[115]Regnery, "A Study of the Leland Stanford House in Sacramento, California," 196.

[116]Ibid., 197–198; *Old Town*, I, 15.

[117]Regnery, "A Study of the Leland Stanford House in Sacramento, California," 202.

Stanford home should be preserved and interpreted for public viewing."[118] On May 13, 1970, fifteen assemblymen and senators co-authored and introduced Resolution 94, a measure that called for the State of California to buy the Stanford house.[119] On June 12, 1970, the legislature adopted this measure by a unanimous vote.[120]

Also in 1970, Congressman John E. Moss (D) of Sacramento attempted to focus national interest on the Stanford house by urging the secretary of the interior to declare the house a national historical landmark.[121] The National Park Service conducted studies preliminary to such a declaration, but for some reason the initiative was dropped; however, on December 9, 1971, the historic value of the house *was* recognized when it was included on the National Register of Historic Places, still falling short of being granted landmark status.[122]

When the California Department of Parks and Recreation adopted its Comprehensive History Plan in 1973, it listed the acquisition of the Stanford house as one of its leading priorities. Assemblyman Edwin L. Z'berg (D) had bipartisan support when he presented Assembly Bill 183, authorizing $951,000 for the purchase and restoration of the house, contingent upon the passage of the Bond Act of 1974.[123] This bond specifically listed the Stanford house, describing it as one of the most notable buildings in the state. The Bond Act was passed.[124]

Following Z'Berg's death, on August 26, 1975, his successor, Assemblyman Vic Fazio (D), led the movement to preserve the Stanford mansion. Bishop Bell on July 21, 1976, rejected a State offer of $576,546.[125] Based on *his* appraisal of the house and an eight-tenths-acre lot, he set the price at $1.5 million. Fazio then persuaded the state legislature to proceed with "friendly condemnation."[126]

---

[118] William Penn Mott, Jr., to John K. McKelvey, Jun 17, 1970, in ibid., 223.

[119] Ibid., 205; *CAJ*, 1970 Reg. Sess., *HR 94*, Relating to Stanford Mansion, Vol. I of II, 3183 (May 13, 1970); *Sac Bee*, May 15, 1970.   [120] *CAJ*, 1970 Reg. Sess., 4555 (Jun 12, 1970).

[121] Central Records, State Parks and Recreation, in Dorothy Regnery, "A Study of the Leland Stanford House in Sacramento, California," 207 and 254–255.

[122] *National Register of Historic Places 1966–1991. Cumulative List Through Jun 30, 1991* (Nashville: AASLH; Wash.: NPS; Wash.: NCSHPO, 1991), 66.

[123] One can trace the hist. of *AB 183*, relating to the Stanford House, from chronological entries in the index of *CAJ*, 1973–74 Reg. Sess., all dates in 1973: Vol. I of XI, 162 (Jan 29), 171 (Jan 30), 744 (Mar 8), 793 (Mar 12), 819 (Mar 13); IV, 6158, 6188, and 6193 (Aug 9), 6256 (Aug 13), 6423 and 6441 (Aug 15), 6533 (Aug 16); V, 8412 (Sep 13), and 9155 (Oct 9).

[124] *Calif Stats*, 1972 Reg. Sess. (Jan 3, 1972–Jan 5, 1973), 1620–1629, Chap. 912, *An act to add Chapter 1.67 (commencing with Section 5096.71) to Division 5 of the Public Resources Code, relating to financing of a program of acquiring and developing state and municipal beach, park, recreational, and historical facilities by proving the funds necessary therefor [sic] through the issuance and sale of bonds of the State of California, and by providing for the handling and disposition of such funds, and providing for the submission of the measure to a vote of the people at a special election to be consolidated with the 1974 direct primary election, and making an appropriation therefor.* App. Aug 15, 1872, by Gov. Ronald Reagan. See Regnery, "A Study of the Leland Stanford House in Sacramento, California," 216–217. *Calif Stats*, 1973–74 Reg. Sess. (Jan 8, 1973–Nov 30, 1974), Vol. I of II, 1383–1384, Chap. 771, *An act relating to the state park system, and in this connection to amend the Budget Act of 1973 (Chapter 129, Statutes of 1973–1974) by amending Section 2.8 thereof, and declaring the urgency thereof, to take effect immediately.* App. Sep 25, 1973, by Gov. Ronald Reagan.

[125] Regnery, "A Study of the Leland Stanford House in Sacramento, California," 227–228.

[126] DPR, *Leland Stanford Mansion State Historic Park, Historic Structures Report*, 23.

On July 27, 1978, Judge Lloyd A. Phillips of the Sacramento County Superior Court ruled that the property should be purchased at replacement cost.[127] Bell and the State Public Works Board agreed with the court decision. The Catholic Church was allowed one year to phase out its operations in the Stanford house. Title to the property was acquired by the State on August 8, 1978, for $1,301,495.89.[128] However, because of leasing arrangements made with the Roman Catholic Church to continue to "lease" the house rent-free, the State did not get occupancy of the building until November 1987.[129] Gov. Jerry Brown, a Roman Catholic, extended the lease—at no cost—to the Catholic Church until July 1983.[130]

In July 1983, upon termination of the lease, the State Department of Parks and Recreation classified the house as the Stanford House State Historical Park.[131] The 1983 legislative budget directed that on or before June 30, 1984, the new park should be in operation and placed under the management of the Department of Parks and Recreation. In 1984 the state legislature directed this department to make the house available to the public at the earliest possible date.

Dorothy Regnery, a Stanford activist dedicated to preserving the Stanford house, wrote that she and other concerned citizens were dumbfounded when told in February 1984 that during the previous year, without any public hearing or even public notice, the Catholic Church's lease had been extended until July 1985 for the meager amount of $900 per month—less than costs of emergency repairs paid by the Department of Parks and Recreation needed to preserve the house from destruction.[132] Regnery, pointing out that for eight years public funds had been used without legal sanction to subsidize a private corporation, was assured that a foolproof clause in the lease protected against any renewal options after July 1, 1985.

The Stanford house was designated a National Historic Landmark on April 9, 1987.[133]

San Francisco House

On April 18, 1906, slightly more than a year after Jane Stanford died, most of what remained of her world collapsed as the great earthquake and fire reduced her San Francisco mansion to smoldering rubble, destroyed a wing of the Palo Alto residence, severely damaged her Memorial Church, and damaged or destroyed other structures built under her direction at the university.

The one-and-one-third-acre property on Nob Hill was surrounded by a thirty-foot-high retaining wall of basalt and granite in the style of railroad buttresses and

[127]Ibid., Regnery, "A Study of the Leland Stanford House in Sacramento, California," 237.
[128]Ibid., 238.   [129]Ibid.   [130]Ibid., 243–245.
[131]*Stanford House State Historic Park, General Plan*, 22.   [132]Statement by Dorothy F. Regnery, May 6, 1985, 3.
[133]William Penn Mott, Jr., dir. of the NPS, USDOI, to Donald Winbigler, Jun 2, 1987, announcing that the house had been declared a national landmark. NPS Doc. H34(418).

topped with a wrought-iron fence, but on that fateful day no security system yet created could protect the structure—one of the most elegant private residences in the nation—from the hands of Mother Nature. No one ever thought of rebuilding it.

A year later Alaska and San Francisco real estate investor Lucien Sly bought this prime piece of San Francisco real estate. In 1912 Sly built the fashionable Stanford Court Apartments on the site.

A limited partnership known as the Stanford Hotel Company was formed in 1969 to operate a hotel on the site where the apartment building stood. The apartment building was gutted, leaving only the structural shell intact, and at a cost of $17 million the present-day Stanford Court Hotel was built and furnished for about $43,000 a bedroom. The hotel opened for business in 1972 under the auspices of the Stanford Court Management Company. In May of 1989 the hotel was acquired by Stouffer Hotels and Resorts, and in May of 1993 Stouffer joined Renaissance Hotels International. The combined company is now called Renaissance Hotels and Resorts.[134]

The only remaining vestige of the original Stanford property is part of the original retaining wall and part of the fence on the western side of the building, which marks the boundary between the home of the Stanfords and that built next door by Mark Hopkins.[135]

The Mark Hopkins mansion burned in the earthquake along with the Stanfords' home—it was learned too late that the Hopkins structure had a half-million gallon reservoir of water located beneath it.

In 1910 mining engineer George D. Smith boasted that someday he would build a hotel on the site—and he did. The belated grand opening of this dream took place on December 3, 1926. In 1939 Smith converted the eleven-room penthouse on the nineteenth floor into the "Top of The Mark," a glass-walled cocktail lounge famous for its 360-degree view. In 1962 an aging Smith sold the Mark to Louis Lurie, and in 1973, Inter-Continental Hotels Corporation, which owned or managed 170 luxury hotels on six continents, assumed management of the property.[136] In 1986, Inter-Continental Hotels, a subsidiary of Bass Hotels & Resorts, purchased the leasehold for the Mark Hopkins.[137]

---

[134]Stanford Court Hotel, *Renaissance Stanford Court Hotel History*. A 2-p. hist. distributed by the managers of the Stanford Court Hotel, which now sits on the site of the SF Stanford mansion.

[135]After Frances Hopkins died in 1891, her widower, Edward Searles, donated the long-unoccupied mansion to the UC. The story of how the SF Art Assn. came to occupy the building is told in Stadtman, *The Centennial Record of the University of California*, 460. Details in a letter from Michelle Heston, PR manager, MHIC Hotel, to the writer, Jun 13, 2001.

[136]MHIC Hotel, *A Walk Back in Time . . . The Mark Hopkins Inter-Continental Hotel* (SF: MHIC, [n.d.]).

[137]Author inter. with Michelle Heston, PR manager, MHIC Hotel, Jun 13, 2001; letter from Michelle Heston to the writer, Jun 13, 2001; "The Mark Hopkins Inter-Continental Hotel: A Short History of its Long and Illustrious History," a 5-p. hist. statement distributed by the PR dept. of the MHIC. Also, author inter. with Maria Kuhn, PR manager, MHIC, Dec 14, 2000.

SAN FRANCISCO'S NOB HILL

seemed destined to be the site of famous hotels; on April sixth, just two weeks before the 1906 inferno, the newly built Fairmont Hotel—just across California Street from the Hopkins house—was sold. It was named for the builders and sellers, Tessie and Virginia Fair, daughters of silver king James Graham Fair, who decided that the monument to their father's memory was just too great a project for them. The buyers, Herbert and Hartland Law, were more fortunate than their neighboring residential owners: the Fairmont escaped with only minor damage to the interior. A year after the earthquake the Fairmont had its grand opening. In 1908 Tessie (Fair) Oelrichs returned to the city and bought the hotel. In 1924 the manager, Daniel Moon Linnard, bought controlling interest, which he sold in 1929 to George Smith, the owner of the Mark Hopkins. As Tessie had done earlier, in 1941 Linnard repurchased the Fairmont. At the end of the Second World War Benjamin Swig bought the famous hotel and gave it a much-needed facelift. In June 1994 the Fairmont was purchased by Saudi Prince Al Waleed Bin Talal Bin Abdulaziz Al Saud.*

*The Fairmont Hotel, *A Fairmont History* (SF: Fairmont Hotel, [undated]). A brief history of the Fairmont, designed for distribution to patrons and curious historians. On George Smith and the Mark Hopkins Hotel, see *SF Argonaut*, Jan 24, 1925. See also *Constructive Californians* (LA: SNPC, 1926), 159–164.

Palo Alto Farm House

After Leland Stanford's death on the Palo Alto farm, until her death twelve years later, Jane spent a great deal of her time there.[138] Apparently the Palo Alto house was unoccupied on the morning of April 18, 1906, when the earthquake struck.

Following the death of her husband, Jane Stanford decided to erect the church they had outlined in the Founding Grant. It was built in the center of the main quad, where ground was broken in May 1899.[139] When completed in 1903, Jane dedicated it to the memory of her husband. Mrs. Stanford's economies in construction did not pay off: she had the church built without structural steel, and in 1906, a year after she died, the earthquake caused severe damage to the structure, but spared many of the interior elements. Historian Orrin Elliott described the damage briefly, "The fall of the tower and the heavy flying buttresses wrecked the interior of

[138] About this time telephones were installed in the Stanford properties. On the farm JLS could be reached at Main 3. Charles C. Hoag, ed., *Our Society Blue Book, The Fashionable Private Address Directory, containing the Names, Addresses, Reception Days and Country Residences of Prominent Families* (SF: CCH, 1895), 103; *San Francisco Blue Book* (SF: ALBC, Pubs., 1904), XV, 121. The year after LS died, the SF mansion phone was listed as East 44, changed eleven years later to Main 15. *Directory of Palo Alto, Mayfield, Menlo Park, The Campus* (PA: TPC, Dec 1, 1904).

[139] See Dorothy F. Regnery, *An Enduring Heritage, Historic Buildings on the San Francisco Peninsula* (Stanford: SUP, 1976), 81ff. for a description of the architecture, the artwork, and the architects who laid out the church; see Elliott, *Stanford University, the First Twenty-five Years,* 137–141, for a sketch on the construction of the church. See also, Paul V. Turner and Marcia E. Vetrocq, *The Founders and the Architects, the Design of Stanford University* (Stanford: SDA, 1976), passim.

153. Stanford University front gates before and after the 1906 earthquake.
Stanford University Archives.

Memorial Church, and the concussion blew the north wall into the quadrangle court. Organ, chimes, clock, stained-glass windows, and carved pulpit were practically uninjured."[140] The church was rebuilt without its great spire.

A portion of the house suffered extensive damage and was subsequently razed. In 1920 the Stanford Home for Convalescent Children leased what remained of the house.[141] The building was occupied by this organization until 1965. In that year a university administration not particularly interested in the history of the Stanford family, and giving no thought to restoring the house as a Stanford family museum, demolished it. Its hallowed timbers were ignominiously consigned to the annual bonfire—a custom since discontinued—commemorating the "Big Game" between

---

[140]Elliott, *Stanford University, the First Twenty-Five Years*, 147.

[141]William Frederick Durand, "Stanford Home for Convalescent Children—Physical Plant," and "Articles of Incorporation of the Stanford Convalescent Home, Jun 18, 1924," in SUA.

154. Stanford University sidewalk in front of the Chemistry Building
after the 1906 earthquake. The jolt tumbled the statue of Louis Agassiz
from its pedestal. A faculty member was quoted as having quipped that
Agassiz was great in the abstract, but not in the concrete.
Stanford University Archives.

Stanford and Cal (the University of California at Berkeley). In 1966 what was left of
the building was carted away to make way for the Children's Hospital complex,
which was built nearby.

Of the various structures once part of the Stanford family residence on the Palo
Alto farm, only a carriage house and the original Leland Junior memorial remained
until the fall of 1999, when the building was razed to make way for commercial and
residential enterprises (a practice that has gained momentum with time) on land
that once was a winery, a young boy's small railroad, and the site of the only Stanford family residence "to which the term *home* was ever applied."

During the winter of 1994–1995, an archeological team spent several months
looking for remains of the Stanford house, which was located between what is now
known as Sand Hill Road and the San Francisquito Creek, about two hundred yards
from the Stanford Shopping Center. The story of the archeological finds of a build-

155. The Angel of Grief was a memorial
to Jane Stanford's brother Henry
Clay Lathrop, who died in her
Palo Alto farm home on April 3, 1899.
Erected next to the Stanford family
mausoleum. *Stanford University Archives.*

156. Stanford University Memorial
Church after the 1906 earthquake.
In San Francisco, Charley Field
bantered:
 If, as they say, God spanked the town,
 For being over-friskey—
 Why did he burn all the churches down
 And spare Hotaling's whiskey?
Stanford University Archives.

157. Palo Alto Farm residence after the 1906 earthquake.
Stanford University Archives.

158. Stanford students on an archeological dig in 1997, searching for the foundations
of the Stanford country house, demolished by the university in 1965.
Author's Collection.

ing destroyed a bare thirty years earlier is told with skill and scientific detachment in the journal of the Stanford Historical Society by the members of this archeological team, which included Stanford campus archeologist Laura Jones, Elena Reese, an archeologist native to neighboring Menlo Park, and Stanford Professor of Anthropology John W. Rick.[142]

The archeological dig began as a step preliminary to allowing the university to build another condominium project and a residential-care facility for the elderly. The university also widened Sand Hill Road in the fall of 1999 and spring of 2000 and enlarged the Stanford Shopping Center. This expansion will be the third major renovation since the center was opened in the spring of 1956. At that time it had 45 stores; today it has five anchor department store tenants and a total of 140 stores and shops, covering seventy-one acres where a Stanford vineyard once stood.

Palo Alto Stock Farm

After Stanford died, the Palo Alto Stock Farm went steadily downhill. In 1903 it was closed as a breeding farm, though old brood mares were allowed to live out their lives in the familiar pastures. In 1909 the last of Stanford's important horses was laid to rest in the horse cemetery, located near the original training stable now known as the Red Barn. The rest of the horses were buried near San Francisquito Creek, under what is now the Stanford golf course.

Though as late as 1945 a breeding farm was still maintained on what had been the Stanford Stock Farm, today all that remains of the farm's glorious past are a number of the original buildings—those which survived the 1906 earthquake—and a riding school, with about 120 horses in its stables, two dozen owned by the university, the rest privately owned and boarded there.[143]

As a boarding place, the Red Barn serves Stanford faculty, staff, and the surrounding community. The riding school teaches horsemanship and offers Stanford University credit courses in physical education. The barn is also the home of the Stanford University intercollegiate riding teams.[144]

Stanford would have been disappointed to know that his dream that the breeding establishment would long outlive him was to be denied. Other than for the large Red Barn, the horse barn, which was completely restored in the early 1980s, all remnants of his breeding and racing farm are a thing of the past.[145]

---

[142]Jones, Reese, and Rick, "Is it not 'Haunted Ground?'" 3–14.

[143]Tom Rust Underwood, ed., *Thoroughbred Racing and Breeding: The Story of the Sport and Background of the Horse Industry* (NY: CMC, 1945), 48.

[144]Inter. with Sara Saxe, dir., Stanford Equestrian Center, Jan 23, 2001.

[145]See Peter C. Allen, "The Red Barn Rides again," in *Stanford's Red Barn* (Stanford: SHS, 1984), 19–23, for a synopsis of the reconstruction of the Red Barn.

Stanford University

U.S. Government Lawsuit

The crowning work of Leland Stanford's life was the creation of the university that bears his son's name; if he had never built a railroad, governed the state of California, or sat in the U.S. Senate, this university alone would have won him immortality.[146] As one journalist so aptly phrased it: "Most Californians, if asked to tell the first thing which came to mind when given the word 'Stanford,' would probably reply, 'University.'"[147]

The university was one of the most magnificent philanthropic gifts ever made by a single American couple. At the time of its founding in 1885 it was the most richly endowed educational institution in the country.

Stanford had taken out a life insurance policy for $10,000 on May 9, 1868—Policy No. 1 of the Pacific Mutual Life Insurance Company—which proved very helpful when Stan-

Like the ancient Roman poet HORACE, in praise of his own works, LELAND STANFORD could say:

I've reared a monument, my own, more durable than brass,
Yea, kingly pyramids of stone in height it doth surpass.
Rains shall not fall nor storms descend to sap its settled base,
Nor countless ages rolling past, its symmetry deface.*

*Horace, To Melpomene, *Odes*, III, 30; *Memorial Addresses on the Life and Character of Leland Stanford,* 47.

ford's estate was in probate and the U.S. government was trying to seize money owed by the Central Pacific Railroad from his estate. On August 9, 1893, Jane's attorneys, the father-son team of [Samuel M.] Wilson & [Russell J.] Wilson sent her a letter with a check from Pacific Mutual for $11,784.[148] A Pacific Mutual historian recognized the value of this money coming when it did: "That check helped soothe the monetary financial distress and no doubt eased the plight of the strapped university professors. Small as it may seem today, it was hard, available cash—essential at a time when the future of Stanford University was in question."[149]

Stanford never used any of the dividends of the policy, and after it was paid up, he seems to have forgotten all about it. His wife never knew of its existence. Jane later related the following account to Dr. William Robert Cluness of Sacramento, one of the original subscribers of capital stock in Pacific Mutual and in the 1890s the company's Medical Officer, and several other people present:

---

[146]Since this is not a hist. of LSJU, I will outline only those events immediately after the death of LS—until it was certain that LSJU would remain open—and offer a brief summary of the high points in the career of LSJU and its present standing in the world of higher education. For anything beyond this, the reader is referred to various gen. works on the subject in the biblio. See in particular Elliott, *Stanford University, the First Twenty-five Years*; Edith Ronald Mirrielees, *Stanford, The Story of a University* (NY: G.P. Putnam's Sons, 1959), and Roxanne Nilan, "Jane Lathrop Stanford and the Domestication of Stanford University," *SJS* 1979 5 (1): 7–29.

[147]Allen A. Arthur, "A Flip of a Coin Put Stanford University Down on the Farm," *LA Times*, Jun 17, 1966, Part 5, 10.

[148]Wilson & Wilson to JLS, Aug 9, 1893. [149]Nunis, *Past is Prologue*, 15.

PACIFIC MUTUAL LIFE INSURANCE COMPANY

In 1881 Pacific Mutual moved its headquarters from Sacramento to San Francisco.[a] Following the earthquake of April 18, 1906, on May 18 the home office was transferred to Los Angeles.[b] Branches were later opened in Chicago, New York, San Francisco, and St. Louis.[c]

In the year 2000 the company had assets of more than $55 billion, additional funds under management of over $281 billion, a total equity of $3.3 billion, annual revenues of more than $4.4 billion, a net operating income in excess of $328 million, and an annual net investment income of more than $1.6 billion.[d] All this, plus it has almost a dozen subsidiary companies and affiliated enterprises. The Governor helped start it all.

Pacific Mutual—now called Pacific Life—never forgot the generosity of its benefactor. In the 1960s the company provided a board room and offices atop its eight-storey Pacific Mutual Building at the northwest corner of California and Kearney streets in San Francisco for use by the Stanford Board of Trustees. The university was to rent the quarters, beginning in October 1962.[e]

In the fall of 1998 Pacific Mutual made a grant of $100,000 toward the restoration of the Stanford Mansion in Sacramento.[f]

[a]Moore, *Pacific Mutual Life Insurance Company*, 77.   [b]Ibid., 286.
[c]Ibid., 286–288.   [d]*Pacific [Mutual] Life Annual Report, 2000* (Newport Beach: PMLICC), 2001.
[e]Alf E. Brandin, Stanford vice president for business affairs, to Eugene S. Cox, district manager, PMLICC, Jul 12, 1962.
[f]Russell G. Haskel, president, Pacific Life Foundation, to Peter McCuen, chairman, board of directors, Leland Stanford Mansion Foundation, Nov 10, 1998; Michele Myszka, community relations director, Pacific Life Foundation, to NET, Apr 28, 2000.

Do you not know, that my husband was its first President and held Policy No. 1? I desire to relate a bit of history that may interest you. My husband passed away on June 21, 1893, and as soon thereafter as practicable, Mr. Huntington (then president of the Southern Pacific Company) was asked to let me know what he could do for me, for I required considerable money for my personal necessities and for the needs of the University, whose current expenses had not been paid for several weeks, owing to inability to procure funds—and what do you think? Mr. Huntington sent me a message to the effect that he could do nothing at the time.

A day or two afterwards a couple of boxes full of papers were sent me from Mr. Stanford's office. While examining them, with the assistance of my secretary, we came across what appeared to be a policy of insurance upon the life of my husband. Examining this document more closely, Miss Berner, my secretary, remarked: "Why, this appears to be a life insurance policy." But never having heard my husband say that he had effected insurance on his life, I remarked that it must be someone else. A day or two afterwards, Mr. Wilson, my attorney, called at the office of the Pacific Mutual Life Insurance Company, and returned with a check for $10,000, the amount of the policy.[150]

---

[150]Moore, *Pacific Mutual Life Insurance Company*, 33–34; Cluness, *Sac Union*, Oct 31 and Nov 28, 1863.

(Mrs. Stanford was reminded that with interest the check was for even more than the face value.)

This story is, perhaps, more interesting for what it tells us about Huntington than about Leland, Jane, or the finances of the university.

With the death of Senator Stanford, Jane became the administrator of the university, an institution financially and legally insecure and organizationally incomplete.[151] As the surviving grantor, she had the right to exercise the functions, powers, and duties of the provisional Board of Trustees, and she chose to do so until she resigned from the board in 1903.

Jane immediately faced a nationwide financial depression, uncooperative business associates at the Southern Pacific and Pacific Improvement Company, and people pretending to have a legal claim to some of the Stanford money. During the settlement of her husband's estate, Tim Hopkins tried to find money for her, to no avail.[152] The future looked bleak, but Jane announced that the university would remain open.[153] Though the actual probate court records were destroyed in the 1906 fire, a newspaper editorial at the time reported that a probate court had set her monthly income at $10,000, from which she had to pay all Stanford salaries.[154] The monthly salary expenses at the university alone amounted to $9,700, leaving her $300 a month to live on. To make up the difference she had to sell bonds, use Vina and Palo Alto proceeds, and dip into her personal funds.[155] She described the personal funds she had access to in an address to the university trustees on June 1, 1897. In 1883 her husband had given her approximately $1 million in stocks and bonds to guarantee her financial comfort in the event he died unexpectedly. She explained that after her husband's death in 1893 the interest on her bonds had helped keep the university open.[156]

On May 26, 1894, the U.S. government filed a contingent claim against the Stanford estate for more than $15 million, followed on June 3 by a lawsuit to confirm its claim.[157] The purpose of the contingent suit was to assure that assets were not distributed before the claim was due.[158] The government argued that the amount sought was Stanford's share, with interest, of government loans made for the construction of the Central Pacific Railroad. This move was made despite the fact that these loans were not yet due and the fact that under California law the stockholders were no longer personally liable for this debt.

[151]Nilan, "Jane Lathrop Stanford and the Domestication of Stanford University," 7.
[152]TNH to JLS, Aug 18, 1893.   [153]In a message HCN handed a reporter of the *SF Examiner*, pub. Jun 6, 1894.
[154]*SF Call*, Jan 27, 1896; repr. in the *Daily Palo Alto*, Jan 27, 1896; Elliott, *Stanford University, the First Twenty-Five Years*, 265.
[155]*SF Call*, Jan 27, 1896.
[156]There are two transcripts of the JLS address to the trustees, in JLS papers; see also Karen E. Bartholomew and Claude S. Brinegar, "Old Chemistry, One of Jane Stanford's Noble Works," *S&T* 1999 23 (1): 3–10.
[157]*NY Times*, Jun 7, 1894; see Elliott, *Stanford University, the First Twenty-Five Years*, 259.
[158]*NY Times*, Jun 7, 1894. For other reports on this suit, see *NY Times*, Jun 8, 9, 10, Jul 25, and Aug 5, 1894.

968	THE GOVERNOR: LELAND STANFORD

At the hearing, the California Circuit Court and the Circuit Court of Appeals for the Ninth District found in favor of Mrs. Stanford.[159] The government then carried its case to the U.S. Supreme Court, where it tried again to seize $15,237,000 from the Stanford estate.[160] As the case dragged on, Jane Stanford complained, "As a woman I know little of law. I cannot understand these things—the long delay in court nor the court routine which makes the delay of one case postpone another."[161]

Frustrated by the delay and needing more money to operate the university, Jane Stanford arranged an interview with President Cleveland and asked him to use his influence to speed up the hearing in the high court. Cleveland responded to her plea by asking Attorney General Richard Olney to see her.[162] Her anguish about trying to keep the university open and her gratitude toward the president for his help are evident in the thank you letter she sent to President Cleveland.

After examining all federal laws pertinent to the construction of the Central Pacific Railroad and the arguments presented by both sides in the matter in lower courts, the justices of the U.S. Supreme Court handed down the following decision in favor of the Stanford estate on March 2, 1896: "We are of opinion that the bill filed by the United States was properly dismissed, and that the order of the Circuit Court of Appeals affirming such dismissal was correct."[163]

Mrs. Stanford was flooded by letters and telegrams of congratulations after the court decided in her favor. Perhaps the first news came from A. L. Clarke, who wired from Washington on March 2, 1896: "The Supreme Court has affirmed decision of lower court in your case."[164] A welcome telegram of congratulations came from Lucius A. Booth in Oakland, one of the early directors of the newly formed Central Pacific who had dropped out even before railroad construction began.[165]

Never did a man seem so happy to have lost a case as did United States Attorney Henry S. Foote. Pitted against the Stanford estate by his official position, his letter of congratulations to Jane Stanford, on Department of Justice letterhead, read as follows:

My Dear Mrs. Stanford—

Circumstances of course compeled [sic] me to appear for the govt against you, in your noble and heroic effort to preserve for yourself, and the State of California the University that bears the name of your dear son.

---

[159]USCC, *United States v.* [Jane L.] *Stanford*. No. 12,053. Circuit Court, Northern Dist. of Calif. 69 *FRep* 25–47. Jun 29, 1895. USCCA, Ninth Circuit. *United States v.* [Jane L.] *Stanford*. No 246. 70 *FRep* 346–364. Oct 12, 1895.

[160]*United States v. Stanford*, 161 USSCR, Oct Term, 1895, 412–434, 413 cited.

[161]*SF Call*, Jan 27, 1896; repr. in the [LSJU] *Daily Palo Alto*, Jan 27, 1896.

[162]Pres. Grover Cleveland to Att. Gen. Richard Olney, Apr 30, 1895. "Mrs. Stanford has told me her story and wants very much to see you. You will not find her at all unreasonable or troublesome. It will be a relief to her if you can see her and I hope you will give her the opportunity." In JLS papers.

[163]*United States v. Stanford*, 161 USSCR, 434.   [164]Telegram in JLS papers.

[165]Lucius A. Booth to JLS, Mar 3, 1896.

JANE STANFORD TO GROVER CLEVELAND

To the President of the United States
Hon. Grover Cleveland

I would not be true to myself were I to leave unsaid the deep gratitude that fills my heart that you accorded to me so gracious and courteous a reception.

You made easy a hard and most painful task, for I had to step far beyond my natural womanly reserve and timidity to reach you and then to lay before you the inner struggle of my life to sustain the work so dear to the heart of my husband.

Since my visit to Washington I have decided to keep the doors of the University open another year hoping and trusting in an all Wise God that it will go on as long as the State of California exists.

Your kind letter to Attorney General [Richard] Olney secured for me a very kind and patient hearing and he generously consented to do all in his power to hasten to a speedy termination the Government Suit against my husband's Estate. I have implicit confidence in his promises and leave for my home to day with the great burden somewhat lightened.

I shall never cease to be grateful to you my distinguished friend for your kindness, and if the suit should be decided adversely, I will ever feel that in time of deep loneliness and distress you befriended me.

> Yours gratefully   Mrs. Leland Stanford
>
> May 9th 1895
> Fifth Avenue Hotel
> New York City
> N.Y.*

*JLS to President Grover Cleveland, May 9, 1895, in JLS papers.

But not for one moment have I had any other feeling than that you ought and would succeed, in preserving to the young men and women now living, and to those yet unborn the blessings entailed by the preservation of the institution so beloved in this State.

You will stand as you deserve to be the great central heroic figure in all future time, the grief stricken widow and mother, forgetful of her own griefs, smothering her own sorrow, and laboring in season and out of season, with tear dimmed eyes and soft and tender heart, in the same spirit that our great martyrs in religion and patriotism, have shed glorious light on the pages of history.

. . . .

> I am your true friend
> Henry S. Foote[166]

---

[166]Henry S. Foote to JLS, Mar 8, 1896.

President Martin Kellogg of the University of California also wrote Jane Stanford a letter of congratulations in which he praised her for the energy and ability she displayed in the discharge of her great responsibilities in the name of higher education in the interests of California.[167]

Once again, the future of Stanford University looked bright.

A small gift that Jane gave the university in 1900 has escaped the attention of most Stanford writers. In June of 1900 she drew up what she called a scholarship paper, which she sent to attorney Mountford Wilson for polishing. In this letter she explained her purpose: Leland, Jr., had saved his spare cash over the years and now Jane wanted to create a Leland Stanford Junior Memorial Scholarship.[168] The young boy's first deposit of $100 was placed in the Security Savings Bank of San Francisco on February 6, 1877, when he was eight years old. From then on, out of his allowance of $10 per month and money he made working—paid at the rate of twenty-five cents per hour—he deposited between $1.50 and $12 per month into this account. When he died, the account had $1,146.79 in it. With interest, by June 9, 1900, it had grown to $2,236.52.[169] She decreed that the scholarship would last as long as the university lasted. She selected a choice room at Encina Hall which she called the Leland Stanford Junior Memorial Room, presumably, for the boy receiving the scholarship.

Jane Stanford Gives the University More than $11 Million and Limits the Number of Women Students to Five Hundred

On May 31, 1899, Jane Stanford handed to the university trustees a gift of more than $11 million in stocks and bonds—all her stock in the Southern Pacific Company, 139 bonds at $1,000 each in the Chesapeake, Ohio, & Southwestern Railroad, 13,000 shares in the Market Street Railway Company, 1,817 shares in the Rocky Mountain Coal & Iron Company, and 10,000 shares in the Occidental & Oriental Steamship Company.[170]

She then handed the trustees deeds to real estate all over California—land in San Francisco, San Mateo, Tehama, Colusa, and Santa Clara counties. Her stated purpose was to prevent hostile legislation over her estate after she died. It was a gift of measureless generosity. Trustee Samuel Leib was quoted as having said that this gift was worth $38 million and could have been converted into $15 million in cash.[171]

Jane Stanford then dropped the first of two bombshells. Acting as sole trustee following the Governor's death, she decided that the liberal admission policy

---

[167]Martin Kellogg to JLS, Mar 3, 1896.   [168]JLS to Mountford Wilson, Jun 9, 1900.

[169]LSJ Memorial Scholarship, Full Account of Fund 353S732, Jan 17, 2001, from LSJU Student Aid Office.

[170]SF Examiner, Jun 1, 1899; PA Times, Jun 2, 1899; the LSJU Trustees' Minutes for 1899 have been lost or possibly were destroyed by the 1906 earthquake. See Elliott, Stanford University, the First Twenty-five Years, "Mending the Charter," 309–325, for a discussion of the legal significance of the timing of this grant.

[171]Portland Oregonian, Jun 3, 1899.

insisted upon by the Governor would soon result in Stanford's having more women students than men. She argued that the university had been created as a memorial to their son, and that she did not wish it to appear to be a school for girls. She declared that the number of women students should never exceed five hundred. Bertha Berner gives a different reason for Jane Stanford's decision to limit the number of women: she wanted an institution in which serious higher education would be pursued, but with girls on campus, *diverting social activity* would develop!

In fact, after reports of distressing indiscretions on campus that led to the patrolling of the campus by mounted watchmen, Mrs. Stanford wondered if it might not be better after all to exclude women altogether. She decided against this, but proposed that the trustees have the power to do so should they feel the need.[172]

During the first year, the ratio of the sexes at Stanford University was about three men to one woman.[173] Jane Stanford *may* have been satisfied with this proportion, but she "watched with interest the large growth in the attendance of the female students."[174] Concern was changed to alarm as Mrs. Stanford listened to Robert L'Amy Donald, a member of the Pioneer Class (Class of 1895) and speaker at the Memorial Day exercises on May 14, 1895.[175] She gave the speaker her undivided attention as he said: "For every one hundred men there were thirty-three women the first year. This year there are fifty-one women for every one hundred men. This is a startling increase. The most logical assumption is that Stanford is better suited for ladies than other colleges. This would seem to point to the possibility that within twenty years Stanford may become the Vassar of the Pacific Coast."[176]

This is not the kind of thing a woman who considered herself—mistakenly, as it turned out—the cofounder of a university as a memorial to her son wanted to hear.[177]

Before long, a series of athletic victories by the University of California over Stanford led some people to speculate that there were so many attractive women students at Stanford that the male athletes found it difficult to focus their attention on athletics.[178] Orrin Elliott quoted a *Portland Oregonian* writer with saying that even President Jordan wanted to limit the number of women students so that the university could make a better showing in athletics.[179] This writer complained that women were voting themselves into leadership positions in all the university organizations—thus rendering the institution less attractive to male students: one woman edited the junior class annual, another published the weekly paper, and still

[172]Elliott, *Stanford University, the First Twenty-five Years*, 135. See George E. Crothers, *Founding of the Leland Stanford Junior University* (SF: AMRob, 1932), 35–36, for the hist. of this provocative incident.

[173]Elliott, *Stanford University, the First Twenty-five Years*, 133. [174]Ibid.

[175]On identification of the speaker, see *SQ* 1894, I, 56. [176][LSJU] *Daily Palo Alto*, May 29, 1895.

[177]See Elliott, *Stanford University, the First Twenty-Five Years, passim*, 325, for the reason that JLS was neither technically nor legally the cofounder of LSJU. [178]*SF Chronicle*, Jun 2, 1899.

[179]Elliott, *Stanford University, the First Twenty-five Years*, 133–134.

another led the inter-collegiate debates. He concluded, "Thus there is an alarming tendency apparent toward reducing the University to the level of a 'woman's seminary,' which"—he reminded his readers—"Mrs. Stanford very much dreads."

Then there was that "elastic clause" in the Articles of Endowment—containing the words "varied only as nature dictates"—that pertained to equality between the sexes at Stanford University. On May 31, 1899—after the number of women reached 40 percent of the total student body—Jane Stanford took matters into her own hands when she stipulated in a formal address to the Board of Trustees: "The number of women attending the University as students shall at no time exceed five hundred."[180] In an explanation that was deleted in the final revision of amendments made in 1902 of the student ratio, she made her reasons clear:

> I have watched with interest the large growth in the attendance of female students, and if this growth continues in the future at the same rate, the number of women students will before long greatly exceed the number of men, and thereby have it regarded by the public as a university for females instead of for males. This was not my husband's wish, nor is it mine, nor would it have been my son's.[181]

This she did without consulting President Jordan. Years later, after Jane Stanford was dead, Jordan wrote: "In this matter I was not consulted because, so she naïvely explained to the press, I 'would probably be opposed,' and she did 'not want to be argued out of it.'"[182] No press statement can be found in which Jane Stanford said she did not want to be "argued out" of her position; it seems very unlike her to betray publicly either a personal weakness or a rift in university counsels. What she *did* say was, "probably President Jordan and the members of his faculty may not agree with me in this respect. But my conscience tells me I am right in my present attitude."[183]

Despite Mrs. Stanford's remark about her husband's wishes, she did not consult the memory of his own words in 1889: "I am inclined to think that if the education of either is neglected, it had better be that of the man than the woman."[184]

The editor of the *San Francisco Examiner* echoed the feeling of thousands when he wrote: "The limitation of the number of women who may attend the University is one of the most radical and surprising changes advocated by Mrs. Stanford."[185] Many people at Stanford had looked upon just such a limitation as the only way to preserve "that Stanford spirit which is best maintained by typical college men who

---

[180]The LSJU Trustees' Minutes for 1899 are missing; *SF Examiner*, Jun 1, 1899; DSJ, *Days of a Man*, I, 422; Nellita N. Choate, "Why Only 500?" *SIR* 1917 2 (8): 243–244.

[181]Address to the Board of Trustees, May 31, 1899, explanation in Elliott, *Stanford University, the First Twenty-five Years*, 134.

[182]DSJ, *Days of a Man*, I, 422. One wonders whether DSJ would have suggested that JLS was naïve were she still alive at the time.   [183]*SF Examiner*, Jun 6, 1899.

[184]Ibid., Oct 20, 1889, quoted in full in Chap. 19, "The Birth of Leland Stanford Junior University."

[185]*SF Examiner*, Jun 1, 1899.

make the most of their undergraduate days by participating in all departments of college life."[186]

Mrs. Stanford never realized that with the increase of women students at Stanford she was observing a widespread American phenomenon, not just a Stanford trend. The percentage of women students at Berkeley had increased from 27 percent in 1891 to 44 percent in 1899; in the East, the statistics were skewered by a tendency to create separate schools for women and were therefore misleading. It was not unusual for coeducational schools to have more women than men students.[187] And a backlog of potential women students was growing apparent by the fact that more women than men were graduating from high school, though it was still true that fewer women than men were attending college or university.

Stanford men were reported as jubilant about the limitation of women in the Stanford student body.[188] An attempt was made to placate the disappointed women by casual allusion to their beauty, but the faint praise it contained was most likely taken as an insult.

One might ask: "How did those Berkeley boys manage to win?" They must have had as many if not more "queens" on campus.

President Jordan hastened to explain that Mrs. Stanford's actions were in no way a criticism of the scholarship or character of the women who had attended or would now be excluded from Stanford University.[189] It was just that she had always intended the university to be primarily for men.

The limit of five hundred women

"QUEENING" AT STANFORD

"Were Stanford women less attractive they would not have so many recruits to swell their ranks and they would not increase the growing custom of college 'queening.' The average male undergraduate cannot devote the proper time to his studies and go 'queening' and participate in college affairs too.

"The more attractive women at Stanford the more 'queening' there will be and the less active participation in those student enterprises that go to make college spirit and athletic and forensic victories. The last year's string of defeats after so many years of victories over the University of California would indicate that Stanford men were not maintaining the old standard established by the pioneer class."*

*SF Chronicle, Jun 2, 1899.

students was reached in 1903. In that year restrictions were placed upon the admission of women students. Various schemes were utilized to maintain the limit; others were employed to "modify the evils that were resulting from . . . enforcing the 500 limit."[190] By 1921 there were four times as many women applicants as could be admitted. It was argued and practiced to a certain degree that the five hundred limit did not apply to graduate and medical school students—particularly since the

[186]Ibid.
[188]SF Chronicle, Jun 2, 1899.
[190] "Change in Entrance Rules for Women," SA 1914 15 (5): 182.

[187]Elliott, Stanford University, the First Twenty-five Years, 134.
[189]Ibid., Jun 3, 1899.

medical school was in San Francisco, a "safe distance" from the main campus. In 1933 the five hundred limitation was superseded by one that allowed a registration percentage based on the registration ratios of 1899.[191]

As late as the early 1930s, the 1899 ratio of 40 percent was still on the books, but over the years the ratio was ignored, and without any concrete university action, it just disappeared.[192] Student admission in the fall of 1944 and 1945 of 450 men and 250 women was based on the classroom and dormitory availability.[193] For some time a tacit limitation was observed based on rules that undergraduate women were required to live on campus, in limited housing, so women's registration was based on available housing.[194] The restriction of women's matriculation based on the availability of campus housing ended in the 1960s with the introduction of coeducational dormitories and the lifting of the requirement that women live in campus housing. Demonstrating that what one Board of Trustees—in this case a sole trustee—can do, another board can undo, on September 12, 1972, the university trustees finally took long overdue action to reverse Jane Stanford's policy of restricting the number of women; they took the first step in striking down all vestiges of *de jure* restriction based on sex (*de facto* restrictions had long since been eliminated in practice).

The trustees petitioned the Santa Clara County Superior Court to modify the Founding Grant to eliminate Jane Stanford's limitation on women students. On

STANFORD BOARD OF TRUSTEES PETITION TO THE SANTA CLARA COUNTY SUPERIOR COURT

"This Committee recommends that the General Counsel to the Board of Trustees be authorized to institute a legal proceeding seeking elimination of the 1899 amendment to the Founding Grant which allots a maximum number of 500 places for women in the student body and that upon the successful conclusion of such a proceeding, the May 11, 1933, resolution on the proportions of men and women in the student body is rescinded."*

*Minutes of the Board of Trustees of the LSJU, Sep 12, 1972, Vol. 53, 493; [LSJU] *CR* 1972 5 (1): 2; *S &T* 1997 21 (2): 15.

March 14, 1973, acting on the petition from the trustees, Superior Court judge Stanley M. Evans changed the Founding Grant to make it "patently clear" that there would be no numerical limitations on women's admission to the university.[195]

The entering class in the fall of 1971 included approximately 900 men and 550 women; today the number of undergraduate men and women is almost equal.

During his tenure, President Jordan knew better than to disagree with Jane Stanford—the lady with an "Iron Will"

[191] Elliott, *Stanford University, the First Twenty-five Years,* 136.   [192] *SUR,* 1933–1934, 118–119.
[193] Ibid., 1944–1945, 157.
[194] Author inter. with Jonathan P. Reider, senior assoc. dir. of admissions, LSJU, Oct 28, 1997.
[195] "New Changes in Founding Grant," *CR* 1973 5 (25) 1.

—when her mind was made up, so he decided that her restriction on the number of women at the university was "sound as a policy."[196] He then explained why Stanford University had accepted so many women: Many subjects of study attractive to women required far less outlay in equipment; furthermore, because the university had not been able to handle the curricula requested by men students, many applicants in law had been advised to go to Harvard, medical students had been sent to Johns Hopkins, and those choosing engineering had been advised to apply to Cornell.[197]

Jordan may well have resented being shunted aside by Mrs. Stanford, who was still functioning as the university's sole trustee—the University Board of Trustees was only an advisory group until she stepped aside—but if he *did* it was a well-kept secret. He seemed always able to find reasons to support Jane Stanford's position in such cases. In his Founders' Day address on March 9, 1909, he said of Jane: "I am to tell you to-day the story of a noble life, of one of the bravest, wisest, most patient, most courageous and most devout of all the women who have ever lived."[198]

Jane Stanford Fires Two Stanford University Trustees and Tries to Fire a Third

The second bomb dropped by Jane Stanford at the May 31, 1899, trustees' meeting lacked the element of surprise contained in the first, for the reason that insiders already knew about it. In the same meeting in which the "sole" trustee gave the university close to $11 million and limited the number of Stanford women students to five hundred, Jane Stanford announced that over the past two years she had asked for and received resignations from the Board of Trustees of Irving M. Scott (a shipbuilder and one of the founders of the Union Iron Works),[199] Dr. Edward R. Taylor (husband of Agnes Stanford Taylor, the daughter of Jane's brother-in-law Josiah), and Josiah Winslow Stanford, Jane's nephew and Josiah's son. Leland Stanford had appointed Scott, one of the original trustees, on November 11, 1885, and Taylor on December 7, 1891.[200] Jane Stanford had appointed Josiah W. Stanford a trustee on April 29, 1896.

In no case was the firing of these men due to conduct inimical to the interests of

[196]DSJ, *Days of a Man*, I, 421. "Iron Will"—the term as applied to JLS is Gunther Nagel's, not mine: Nagel's rev. ed. of *Jane Stanford: Her Life and Letters* was pub. as *Iron Will: The Life and Letters of Jane Stanford* (Stanford: SAA, 1985).

[197]DSJ, *Days of a Man*, I, 421–422.

[198]DSJ, "Jane Lathrop Stanford, A Eulogy," *SA* 1909 10 (7): 257–267; *PSM*, Aug 19, 1909, 157.

[199]*Illustrated Fraternal Directory Including Educational Institutions of the Pacific Coast. Giving a Succinct Description of the aims and objects of beneficiary and fraternal societies and a brief synopsis of the leading colleges and private seminaries compiled from official records and society archives* (SF: ALBC, 1889), 50; "Irving M. Scott," in Phelps, *Contemporary Biography of California's Representative Men*, I, 160–174; Scott obit. in *SF Argonaut*, Apr 28, 1903.

[200]Kenneth M. Johnson, *The Life and Times of Edward Robeson Taylor* (SF: BCC, 1968), 13. A SUA bio. card says Taylor served as a trustee from Dec 4, 1891, to May 9, 1899. A SUA list of trustees sets his beginning date incorrectly as Dec 4, 1898, which is months after JLS requested his resignation.

the university, as she claimed: in all three cases, the reasons were entirely personal and spiteful.[201]

In a letter to Irving M. Scott, dated May 11, 1898, Mrs. Stanford referred to an unidentified Central Pacific "action" of which she disapproved. Apparently Scott was too close to someone Jane considered an enemy. She wrote: "I consider anyone who designedly links himself to an antagonist of my husband is not a friend of mine therefore undesirable as a trustee, and your resignation is requested." She added that it was her "sacred duty" to ask for his resignation.[202]

Two weeks later, after licking her wounds for eight months, she mustered the audacity to send an almost identical letter to Dr. Edward Taylor, demanding his resignation. In this letter she spelled out her reasons in considerable detail, without once coming near to the truth. Because this letter was sent almost verbatim to Josiah Winslow Stanford, and because it best reflects the personal pique behind her demands, I quote the Taylor letter at length. After explaining how hard it had been to pay the "bequeathments" her generous husband had left to relatives, she focused on the attitudes of some of the relatives, particularly Taylor's:

> To these difficulties, some of the legatees, not all I am thankful to say, very largely contributed. Your own attitude towards me as Agnes' representative during the four years that I was so distressed for the want of money to pay these obligations, was a painful and disappointing surprise. I had hoped for sympathy and encouragement from you, for you so well understood the painful circumstances under which I was laboring—understood them better than most of the legatees because of your free access to the books and accounts, and also your close contact in a business way with my attorney. I prayed that you would be merciful and considerate and give me time to liquidate the obligations which I considered so sacred towards your wife. And here let me add, that for every urgent and relentless appeal that was made for money by you, to it was added another as persistently and heartlessly made on the part of Joie [Josiah Winslow] Stanford. He always ending with the unblushing demand that for every dollar that was paid to Agnes he expected the equivalent to be given to him, let the circumstances or conditions be what they might.
>
> Had I been possessed of the money, how gladly I would have poured it forth to have saved the affection and love I had in my heart for both Agnes and Joie. I had many a sleepless night of tears, wails, and prayers that hearts that I relied on to stand by me and defend and help me were so callous, so unsympathetic.
>
> In the part which you took in this attitude mentioned of antagonism I still fondly hope that Agnes did not know all the circumstances. I would like to give her the benefit of this doubt, for I loved her.
>
> My husband and I in our selection of Trustees of the Leland Stanford, Jr. Univer-

---

[201] *SF Examiner*, Jun 1, 1899; though the resignations were demanded and received in 1898, the three were still listed as trustees until 1900. *SQ*, 1900, VI, 9.

[202] JLS to Irving M. Scott, May 11, 1898. It was her conviction that JLS and her deity worked together very closely in railroad matters.

sity chose the men whom we thought would stand loyally by us during our lives, and also be loyal to the work which we have instituted for the good of humanity.

My experiences have made me feel that you ought in honor to seek release from the responsibilities which we asked you to assume, and I as the trusted survivor request that your resignation as a Trustee be placed in my hands as soon as possible.[203]

Having dealt with sycophants like David Starr Jordan for so long, Mrs. Stanford was absolutely stunned when Taylor refused her request for his resignation. In a letter to the university's Board of Trustees she complained that although she "requested" (she did not say "demanded") Taylor's resignation, he "declined to tender" it.[204] Not to be thwarted by this, she wrote: "I now wish to declare to you that I decline to further accept his services as a Trustee." In a letter to one of the attorneys involved in the matter, she demanded that her authority be regarded as equal to that of her husband were he acting on the trustee matter.[205]

Jane had requested the opinion of John T. Doyle (an attorney who had been one of the executors of the Margaret T. Clark estate) on her plan to get rid of Dr. Taylor. Doyle had replied in a very closely and carefully worded letter as follows: "I have carefully examined the foundation deed, and am compelled to conclude that you have no power to displace Dr. Taylor as a trustee. It can be done by a court, but only for some serious cause that his conduct would justify."[206]

Tired of the unprofitable squabble with Jane Stanford, on May 9, 1899, Taylor resigned form the Board of Trustees to move on to better things.[207]

In her letter addressed to "Mr. Josiah Stanford," who on this occasion was no longer nephew Joie, Aunt Jennie, now stiffly and formally Jane L. Stanford, repeated her opening statement to Taylor and then went on to complain about his (Josiah's) attitude towards her for the four years following her husband's death.[208] She expected mercy and trust from him rather than the callousness and lack of sympathy that had cost her so many sleepless nights.[209] Repeating what she had told Irving and Taylor, that her obligation to get rid of them was a "sacred duty," she wrote: "You ought in honor to seek release," etc., "and I request your resignation as a Trustee be placed in my hands as soon as possible."[210]

---

[203]JLS to Dr. Edward R. Taylor, May 27, 1898.

[204]JLS to the Board of Trustees of the LSJU, Jun 13, 1898.

[205]JLS to att. [John Thomas] Doyle, Jun 17, 1898, disagreeing with what he had reported in his letter to her of Jun 14.

[206]John T. Doyle to JLS, Jun 15, 1898.   [207]Johnson, *The Life and Times of Edward Robeson Taylor*, 13.

[208]JLS to JWS, May 27, 1898.

[209]This reference is undoubtedly to pressure JWS brought to bear on Aunt Jane to pay him the legacy left him in Uncle Leland's will. This was not the only time legatees short on cash had brought pressure to bear on Aunt Jane to settle up sooner rather than later. Christine Lathrop, Ariel's daughter, retained an att. to write to JLS and explain his client's urgent need for payment of her legacy. Joseph D. Baucus to JLS, Aug 23, 1893. In JLS papers.

[210]JLS to Board of Trustees of the LSJ Kindergartens [*sic*], Jun 15, 1898, announced that the resignation of JWS had been requested and accepted.

Dr. Edward Robeson Taylor

was not a man to be intimidated easily by, or to follow, spiteful commands of his aunt-in-law Jane Stanford.

Taylor received his M.D. degree in 1865 from Tulane Medical College (nucleus of the medical department at the University of California). He served as secretary to Gov. Henry H. Haight from 1867 to 1871.

Born on September 24, 1838, in Springfield, Illinois, Taylor was thirty-one years old when he married Agnes Stanford on April 20, 1870 (he may have met Agnes while Haight was renting the Governor's office in the Sacramento house). Taylor then decided to pursue law as a career. He was admitted to the California Bar in 1872.

Edward Taylor practiced law in San Francisco from 1872, and served as president of the San Francisco Bar Association in 1890–1891 and 1894–1895.

Dr. Taylor served as a trustee for the San Francisco Public Library in 1886, and was a member of the San Francisco Board of Freeholders in 1886, 1887, and 1898, when it drew up a new San Francisco city charter to replace the old consolidation act.

It was, indeed, a mutual honor to the university and to Taylor when Leland Stanford in 1891 asked him to serve as a trustee: to Taylor that the position was offered, to Stanford University that he accepted it.

Taylor afterward served as dean of Hastings Law School from 1899 to 1919, when he retired because of failing health.

As a physician Taylor was president and vice president of Cooper Medical College for the thirty years preceding its incorporation into Stanford University. It later became today's Stanford Medical Center.

Edward Taylor was mayor of San Francisco from July 1907 to 1910, following the hectic days of earthquake and fire and Eugene Schmidt (a mayor who went to prison). In 1920 Dr. Taylor was decorated with the Cross of the Legion of Honor by France.

Taylor was also a recognized poet and student of literature, and published a number of articles. Many of his ideas were expressed in poetry, particularly those related to his deep love of San Francisco.[a]

Following Taylor's death, on July 5, 1923, Mayor James Roth of San Francisco praised him warmly: "Dr. Taylor's career was typical of all that is best in American life. He was a man of the broadest education, a man of letters, a deeply read student of the law . . . a man of the highest ideals in both public life and personal character."[b]

This, then, was the giant of a Renaissance man and Stanford family member whom Mrs. Stanford thought to dismiss peremptorily and insultingly from the Stanford University Board of Trustees for entirely personal reasons.

[a]*SF Chronicle*, Jul 6 and 7, 1923; Stanford, *Stanford Genealogy*, 53.   [b]*SF Chronicle*, Jul 6, 1923.

Having cleaned house by removing two of her husband's major appointees, along with Josiah Winslow Stanford, Jane Stanford lavished money and power on the last of her remaining brothers—Charles Lathrop.[211] He was retained on the Board of Trustees and was to be named upon her own death, chairman of the Executive and Finance Committee. Moreover, he was to retain his annual salary of $10,000, and remain a director of the Southern Pacific Company and the Pacific Improvement Company so long as she had any interest in these companies.[212]

Charles Gardner Lathrop's Burial at Cypress Lawn Memorial Park

It has been suggested that the dislike of Charles Lathrop by university officials was the reason he was buried at Cypress Lawn in Colma rather than in the campus cemetery at Stanford: "Lathrop served as the first treasurer of Stanford University and became much despised by university officials, including Senator Stanford. This may account for the fact that whereas most of the Stanford and Lathrop families were buried on the campus, the pompous Lathrop was interred at Cypress Lawn."[a]

The facts in the case are:

1. Other than Leland, Jane, and Leland, Jr., there were no Stanfords buried on campus.

2. Other than Jane's brother Henry Clay Lathrop, there were no Lathrops buried on campus.

3. There is no documentation offered to substantiate that Charles Lathrop was despised by university officials or by Leland Stanford.

4. In 1902, a dozen years before Charles Lathrop died, on May 24, 1914, Jane Stanford wrote to Stanford University attorney and trustee Samuel F. Leib stating that she wanted the cemetery closed immediately. Realizing that there would be no limit to the number of people who might be interred there, she wrote; "I have concluded the cemetery shall now be closed forever, and no further burials allowed."[b] And her prohibition extended to "any of the land belonging to the said university."

5. Indeed, burials in the campus cemetery had become a problem. A campus editorial pointed out that a new cemetery had already been built between the towns of Mayfield and Mountain View months before Jane Stanford died and a decade before Charles Lathrop died.[c]

[a]Michael Svanevik and Shirley Burgett, *Pillars of the Past: A Guide to Cypress Lawn Memorial Park, Colma, California* (SF: CLE, 1992), 50.   [b]JLS to Samuel F. Leib, Jul 9, 1902.
[c]*SA*, 1904 6 (1): 6.

---

[211]On Nov 11, 1893, TWS became a trustee. Josiah Winslow's term lasted from Apr 29, 1896, to May 31, 1898, "Chronological Listing of Board of Trustees 1885 to Present," in SUA.

[212]*SF Examiner*, Jun 1, 1899.

Jane Stanford's Ideas on Higher Education

Judge George Edward Crothers, a member of the Stanford Pioneer Class, had close contact with Mrs. Stanford and probably knew her mind on public and educational issues better than anyone else. Crothers was her personal friend and advisor and the only alumnus of the university appointed by her to the Board of Trustees.[213]

Crothers said that during the last years of her life Mrs. Stanford came to doubt the desirability of co-education. She thought seriously of having a separate off-campus site for women's classes and even considered using her own residence as a girls' dormitory.

Jane Stanford criticized the university for spending too much time with remedial studies and teaching preparatory subjects that were—properly speaking—the responsibility of high schools. As president of the board, she delivered an address on August 1, 1904, to the Board of Trustees saying that such work should be abolished from the university. As she saw it: "At present we are only a college of the Middle-Western type."[214] In her view, too, university studies should be primarily post-graduate work.

What bothered Mrs. Stanford even more was the lack of religious purpose at the university and in its curriculum. In separate letters to each trustee she told them: "I would be better satisfied to see every department of the University secondary to the church work, and the church influence stand out supreme in the future life of every student. In my own feeble way I began by building a temple which I prayed might be regarded as fit for Christ to dwell in."[215]

Her notion that religion was the heart of the university was made very clear in a letter to Jordan in which she admonished the president not to forget that "every boy and every girl in this institution [Stanford University] has a soul germ which needs developing."[216]

As mentioned earlier, in 1890 Stanford had affirmed that he and his wife were Episcopalians.[217] The following year Jane reaffirmed this: "I am an Episcopalian. . . . No, I am not a Catholic."[218] When an *Examiner* reporter asked Stanford about an Associated Press report that his wife had been converted to Catholicism, he answered, "It is not true."[219] But Mrs. Stanford was thought to be considering joining the Roman Catholic Church when she penned the words to Jordan about developing "soul germs." Rumors were spread in Washington that she had become a Roman Catholic, despite the fact that people there always believed her to be "one of the strongest pillars of the Methodist denomination."[220] This belief was based on

---

[213]George Edward Crothers, "The Educational Ideals of Jane Lathrop Stanford, Co-Founder of the Leland Stanford Junior University," *SJMH*, Aug 20–26, 1933; a 32-p. pam. having the same title and repr. from these issues of the *SJ Mercury* is cited here. On Crothers' relationship to JLS, see 13.   [214]Ibid., 19.

[215]JLS, separate letters to every trustee, Jul 6, 1904.   [216]JLS to DSJ, May 31, 1899.

[217]*NY World*, Nov 27, 1890.   [218]*SF Examiner*, Jul 22, 1891.

[219]Ibid., Nov 28, 1890.   [220]*SF Chronicle*, Nov 27, 1890.

the Stanfords' friendship with John Newman, himself a Methodist. In answer to the question whether his wife were still a Methodist, the surprised senator had replied, "Mrs. Stanford is not a sectarian. She has good will for all churches. She has not been converted."[221] Stanford went on to say that what gave rise to this latest rumor that his wife had become a Roman Catholic was undoubtedly her gift for the erection of a monument to Junípero Serra at Monterey.

These rumors reported in the *Examiner* and *Chronicle* that Jane Stanford had become a Roman Catholic had been denied by the *Argonaut*.[222] The *Argonaut* editor chided the other two papers for not correcting their mistaken reports, hoping, as they did, that this rumor would injure Stanford and "wound the feelings of Mrs. Stanford."

Dr. John Casper Branner, who served as university president from 1913 to 1915, reported that Jane Stanford once said to him regarding the Stanford church: "But, Mr. Branner, while my whole heart is in this university, my soul is in that church."[223] She complained that it was difficult to find a professor—other than the chaplain—who even mentioned moral or spiritual matters to his students. She strongly urged that students of bad moral character be turned away from the doors of the university. Religion in general was much more important on campus than was academics, she said, and then told the president: "That, Mr. Branner, is why I am so much more interested in the church on the campus than I am in your precious rocks."[224] She continued:

> For no amount of learning can take the place of decency, and no amount of science can take the place of backbone. And as the moral and spiritual life is more important than the life of our bodies, so moral and spiritual instruction is more important to young people than instruction of any other kind. That is why I think the church should be the heart and center of this university.

As early as 1892 Jane Stanford had written Jordan that since true religion was found in the church, there was "no excuse for students not attending."[225]

Stanford University's Position in the World of Higher Education

Stanford University has belied Huntington's quip about its being "Stanford's circus;" it has taken its place among the world's preeminent institutions of higher education. Three of its seven schools offer undergraduate degrees, and its 7.5:1 student-to-faculty ratio offers the student an effective interaction with faculty members. The class of 2002 had 1,750 entering freshman, chosen from among the

---

[221]Ibid. [222]*SF Argonaut*, Dec 1, 1890.

[223]Founders' Day Address, Mar 10, 1917, in *SA* 1917 18 (7): 216–238; Branner's remarks are on 216–222, 219 quoted here.

[224]See note on Branner in Catherine C. Peck, "[Stanford Through the Century/John Casper Branner]," *S & T* 1997 21 (1): 11–12. [225]JLS to DSJ, May 8, 1892.

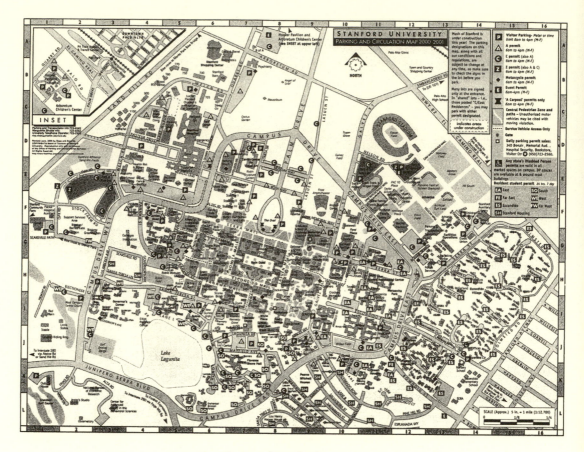

159. Aerial view of Stanford University, 2001.
Stanford Alumni Association.

17,919 applicants. Jane Stanford might be horrified to learn that 51 percent were females. And Leland Stanford, whose idea was to create a school that the children of California could attend, would be surprised to discover that the members of this class come from thirty-eight countries and forty-nine states. Only 40 percent of them come from California.

Stanford University's annual undergraduate costs per student at the time of writing total $37,026, which contrasts with Stanford's intention that his institution be a place where "poor boys and girls" could afford to go to school—unlike the more expensive University of California.[226] However, it must be said that Stanford

---

[226]Tuition in the amount of $25,917, plus another $8,304 for room and board, $1,125 for books and supplies, and $1,680 miscellaneous fees and personal expenses. *Stanford University—2002* (Stanford: OUA, 2001), 45.

University has a policy of never turning away a qualified student for lack of money, which is backed with more than $62 million in annual financial support for prospective students with a demonstrated need.

At the time of writing, there are more than 158,000 living Stanford degree holders. And Stanford's eighteen libraries contain more than seven million volumes and spend about $15 million a year on new acquisitions. Jordan's first faculty of fifteen men has grown to more than 1,660 tenure-track members. And since its founding, twenty-three Stanford faculty members have become Nobel Laureates. The present faculty boasts twelve Nobel Prizes, while three more are held by fellows at the Hoover Institution, the prestigious, affiliated policy research center.

There are now scores of articles on the national standing of Stanford University, pointing proudly to the positions of primacy it holds in the academic world.[227]

JANE STANFORD-BERTHA BERNER TRAVELS

Following the death of her husband, Mrs. Stanford spent the next dozen years assisting in the management of the university, disposing of her husband's prize stock farm and wineries, continuing her many philanthropies, and traveling.

Together, Jane and Bertha Berner made six trips abroad, though none of them entirely around the world.[228] Most of their travels had little to do directly with the life of Leland Stanford, but the first, when she hoped to sell her jewelry collection for the financial benefit of the university, the second, when they visited Larkin Goldsmith Mead, who was working on a family statuary commissioned earlier by Leland and Jane, the fourth trip, when Herbert Nash died, and the fifth, when they visited Stanford's brother Thomas Welton in Australia, do touch upon Stanford's life.

In early 1897 Jane Stanford decided to take about a three-month rest abroad—to be combined with business—by making a trip to England and Europe. While away, she would try to sell her jewelry collection in London, "where she hoped they would fetch a good sum during the glamour and excitement attendant to Queen Victoria's Diamond Jubilee."[229] The proceeds of her sale would, so she expected, put a sizeable amount of money in the university's library book fund.[230]

Thus it was that June 9, 1897, she and Bertha Berner boarded the American Line's steamship *Paris* in New York for the voyage to Southampton, rather than to the customary Liverpool.[231]

They arrived in Southampton on June 16, and were in London on June 22 for

[227]LS, File 0751/978, SUA.
[228]Gunther W. Nagel was wrong in thinking that Jane's 1903 trip carried her around the world, *Jane Stanford: Her Life and Letters* (Stanford: SAA, 1975), 156.   [229]Ibid., 99.
[230]BB, *Mrs. Stanford*, 105.   [231]*NY Times*, Jun 10, 1897; *SF Argonaut*, June 21, 1897.

Queen Victoria's large parade.[232] Their jewelry-peddling expedition in London was a flop.[233]

Jane then spent the summer in Europe, traveling widely in Switzerland and France.[234] They sailed from Liverpool on their return trip home on October 9, 1897, arriving in New York on the *Umbria* exactly one week later.[235]

A year and a half later Jane Stanford and party set out on her second trip abroad since her husband's death. Just before her planned departure, her ailing brother Henry Clay Lathrop, whom she had been nursing for several years, died at the Palo Alto farm on April 4, 1899.

On May 31 Jane Stanford notified the trustees that she was preparing to leave for about four months, and on June 14, 1899, the Stanford party boarded the *Teutonic* in New York and set sail for Liverpool, where they landed on June 22.[236]

They visited several towns and cities in England, then went on a tour of Belgium, Germany (six weeks in Kissingen and two weeks in Wiesbaden), and Switzerland. From Switzerland they traveled to various Italian cities, among them the Florence suburb of Villa Trollope, where they saw Vermont-born sculptor Larkin G. Mead, who was modeling a plaster cast for the bronze grouping of Leland, Jane, and Leland, Jr.[237]

The elder Stanfords had posed for the group piece, while young Leland's figure was modeled from photographs. Berner later said that Mrs. Stanford was never very happy with the work, because "no portraiture of Mr. Stanford or Leland ever appeared true or fine enough to satisfy her."[238]

From there they made a whirlwind tour of Rome, Genoa, and Paris, and then back to London. In Liverpool on October 21, they boarded the *Campania* for New York City, arriving there on October 28.[239]

They spent several weeks in New York and Thanksgiving Day in Albany. Railroad business detained her longer than expected, so she did not get home to California until December 5, 1899.[240]

As early as March 6, 1900, Jane had confirmed passage on the *Oceanic* for their next—extensive—trip abroad, and on July 11 she, with her niece Jennie S. Lathrop and Bertha Berner, sailed from New York to Liverpool, where they arrived on July

---

[232] Arrival in Southampton, *NY Times*, Jun 17, 1897.   [233] BB, *Mrs. Stanford*, 108.

[234] JLS to DSJ, Aug 30, 1897.

[235] *NY Times*, Oct 17, 1897. JLS had written to May Hopkins on Aug 5, 1897, that they were in Brighton and that she had taken a room on the *St. Paul* for Oct 4. It was unlike a Stanford to sail on any ship not of the White Star line, and, as it turned out, for some reason she had a change of plans and sailed on the *Umbria*. She checked into the Fifth Avenue Hotel in NY upon arrival. *NY Times*, Oct 17, 1897. Conclusive evidence that she did not sail on the *St. Paul* is the fact that this ship arrived in NY on Oct 22, almost a week after Jane checked into the Fifth Avenue Hotel. *NY Times*, October 22, 1897.   [236] *NY Times*, June 15 and 23, 1899; *NY Herald*, June 15, 1899; and *SF Argonaut*, June 19, 1899.

[237] BB, *Mrs. Stanford*, 115–124.   [238] Ibid., 125.

[239] *NY Times*, Oct 28, 1899.   [240] BB, *Mrs. Stanford*, 126.

18, 1900, beginning their third trip abroad.[241] After visiting London and Bad Kissingen, and then spending six weeks in Paris, they traveled to Switzerland and Italy.

On January 16, 1901, their party set sail for Egypt, where they spent a week in Cairo, toured various sites in Egypt, and then returned to Cairo for another two weeks.

THE MEAD STATUARY, KNOWN LATER AS THE STANFORD FAMILY GROUP, was placed in the Inner Quad in December of 1900.[a] In 1902 it was set onto a high pedestal of polished granite, approached from all sides by stone steps, in the Memorial Court.[b] It was later decided that the statuary was disintegrating in the weather and should be moved to the rotunda of the university museum.[c] This was done in March 1915.[d] An April 1973 letter to the editor of the *Stanford Daily* suggested that the family statue be given a more prominent place for display. William D. Andrews of the Central Microtext Staff complained: "For several years it has stood, hidden and almost forgotten, in the shadows of the veranda of the Stanford Art Gallery."[e] The places he suggested as more prominent included between the pillars at the entrance of the quad and the courtyard in front of the Stanford Memorial Church.

In 1975 art history professor Albert Elsen proposed that the peripatetic sculpture be moved from its position in the porch of the art gallery back to its prior location in Memorial Court.[f] In 1978 the bronze statue, then standing at the northeast corner of the art gallery, was damaged when vandals cut off the right thumb of Leland, Jr., with a hacksaw.[g]

The next report on the maintenance and protection of this Stanford family treasure appeared on March 22, 1978: "Following action by the Stanford Historical Society, the damaged statue of the Stanford family, which stands in the north porch of the Stanford Art Gallery, will be moved to a place of safekeeping until Leland Junior's thumb can be replaced."[h]

For years the statue stood all but abandoned in the maintenance yard of the university, completely devoid of protection from the elements, vandals, or the workers and trucks that provided a constant flow of traffic within inches of the piece of art. Though the environment would seem to be more conducive to the loss of a second thumb than to the reacquisition of the first, eventually Leland, Jr.'s missing thumb was restored.[i]

Following a campaign by Stanford alumni to find a permanent and protected home for the statuary, during the week of June 8–12, 1998, the university moved it to a site next to the Stanford family mausoleum.[j]

[a]*SA* 1900 2 (3): 41; see NET, "Stanfordians! Let us Preserve our Heritage." Eight-p. unpub. sketch of the hist. of the Mead Statuary.　　　　　　　　　　　　　　　　　　　　[b]*SA* 1902 4 (1): 5.
[c][LSJU]*Daily Palo Alto*, Feb 23, 1915; SA 1915 16 (6): 229–230; 16 (8): 292.
[d]Trustee Documents, Mar 1915.
[e]William D. Andrews to *Stanford Daily*, pub. in ed. of Apr 18, 1973.　　　　　　[f]*Sanford Daily*, Oct 10, 1975.
[g]Ibid., Mar 8, 1978.　　　　　　　　　　　　　　　　　　　　　　　　　[h][LSJU] *CR*, Mar 22, 1978.
[i]NET, "Stanfordians! Let Us Preserve our Heritage."
[j]Inter. with Michael A. Fox, special projects manager, LSJU, Apr 12, 2000; "A Home amid the Trees," *Stanford* Sep/Oct 1998, 29; *SF Chronicle*, Jun 20, 1998; and *SR*, Jul 1, 1998.

[241]Letter from White Star Line officer to JLS, Mar 7, 1900, in JLS papers. *NY Times*, Jul 11 and 12, 1900; *NY Herald*, Jul 11 and 12, 1900; *SF Argonaut*, Jul 9 and 23, 1900. *NY Herald*, Jul 19, 1900; *NY Times*, Jul 19, 1900.

Herbert Charles Nash

was born in Nice, France, on August 25, 1857.[a] He was educated in various French colleges and served as vice-consul of the United States at Nice from 1877 to 1881. He met Stanford in 1880 and Mrs. Stanford in May 1881 when she was visiting southern France.[b] Stanford recommended him to Jane, and she hired the twenty-four-year-old Nash as Leland's tutor.[c]

Nash served as Leland, Jr.'s tutor, then as the private secretary to his father, Senator Stanford.

He also served as secretary of the Stanford University Board of Trustees from 1886 until his death.[d] In 1893 he became Mrs. Stanford's secretary, and in 1896 was named the second librarian of Stanford University.

In 1892 Nash was trampled by a runaway horse in an attempt to save a woman. He had a lung torn, and the wound remained unhealed and was a contributing cause of his death.[e]

Thereafter, he never regained his health entirely. Jane Stanford once described a two-hour hemorrhage suffered by Nash.[f]

In 1900, Nash married Anna Louisa Brown, a graduate of Cornell University and an artist. They had no children. Anna Brown was the sister of Ellen Coit Elliott, who was the wife of Orrin Leslie Elliott, registrar of Stanford University and later author of *Stanford University, the First Twenty-Five Years*.[g] Mrs. Nash was the daughter of E. Woodward Brown, who had died in San Francisco just a week before on the ferry steamer *Berkeley*.[h]

Nash had been in poor health for some time, and was granted a leave of absence from his duties as librarian at Stanford University. He visited various sites in southern California and at the time of his death had been at the Hotel Keller in Pomona for six weeks with his wife.[i]

Forty-four-year-old Nash died in Pomona on June 7, 1902, of Bright's disease. Jane Stanford was on her way home from Japan when Nash died.

Nash's wife and brother-in-law were with him when he died, and they took his remains to Palo Alto. Arthur W. Roller Mortuary in Palo Alto officiated at his funeral and he was interred in the Cypress Lawn Memorial Park in Colma on August 15, 1902. A memorial service was held for him in the Stanford University chapel on October 8, 1902.[j] His widow was buried next to him on March 17, 1945, following her death six days earlier.[k]

[a]HCN, "Dictation by H. C. Nash on Leland Stanford, 9/14/89," 90. BL. *SF Chronicle*, Jun 8, 1902. HCN's burial record has him as a native of England, owing, no doubt, to the fact that his parents were English. Burial Record, Cypress Lawn Memorial Park, from Marilyn Calvey, tour and seminar director, Dec 29, 2000.

[b]HCN, "Dictation," 90. [c]Ibid. *SF Chronicle*, Jun 8, 1902.

[d]Elliott, *Stanford University, the First Twenty-five Years*, 23. [e]DSJ test., *SF Chronicle*, Jun 8, 1902.

[f]JLS to Tim and May Hopkins, Jun 10, 1892, from the Bristol Hotel, London, Burlington Gardens, London W. Jane added, "I am so very sorry his brother is not here." This is the first mention that Nash even had a brother.

[g]A notice of HCN's death and a bio. sketch were pub. in *SA* 1902 4 (1): 1.

[h]*SF Call*, Jun 8, 1902. [i]*SF Chronicle*, Jun 8, 1902.

[j]*SA* 1902 4 (2): 25. The Stanford Memorial Church was often known as the "Leland Stanford Jr. University Chapel," see *SS*, Dec 7, 1892, 170. [k]Cypress Lawn Memorial Park burial records.

On April 3 they left Port Said for Jerusalem, where they spent Easter, then went to Alexandria and from there sailed to Marseilles. They passed the month of April in Paris. Jane returned to Bad Kissingen for another six weeks, and then drifted from one European center to another for the entire summer of 1901.

Jane and her party set sail for home from Liverpool on August 28, 1901.[242] They arrived in New York on the *Majestic* on September 4, 1901, and checked into the Waldorf.[243]

The following spring, on April 10, 1902, Mrs. Stanford and Bertha Berner sailed from San Francisco to Honolulu, arriving on April 16 on the *Sierra*, on the first leg of their fourth trip abroad.[244] They spent two weeks visiting Hawaiian sites and then pushed on to Japan.

On April 23, 1902, the *China* sailed from San Francisco for Hong Kong via Honolulu and Yokohama.[245] It landed in Honolulu on April 29 and Jane and Bertha boarded the ship and sailed for Yokohama the next day, arriving there on May 11, 1902.[246] The Stanford party spent a month visiting a number of Japanese sites, including the cities of Tokyo and Kyoto.

On June 11, 1902, four days after the death of Herbert Nash, Jane and Bertha again boarded the *China* in Yokohama for the return trip to San Francisco, by way of Honolulu.[247] They arrived in San Francisco on June 28 and were back at the farm two days later.[248]

After two months in California, on August 6, 1903, Jane Stanford and party sailed from San Francisco on the *Ventura* for Sydney, New South Wales, Australia.[249] Their fifth trip abroad was to begin with an opportunity to visit Jane's brother-in-law, Thomas Welton Stanford, whom she had not seen in more than forty years.[250]

At 6 P.M. on August 24, 1903, the day before Jane Stanford's seventy-fifth birthday, she and Bertha landed in Auckland, New Zealand.[251] After four rough days at sea, on August 29, the Stanford party, consisting of "Mrs. Jane Stanford, maid, and manservant," landed at Sydney.[252] Thomas Welton lived in the "Stanford House," Clarendon Street, East Melbourne, Victoria, but he made the 520-nautical-mile trip to Sydney

[242] *SF Argonaut*, Sep 2, 1901.   [243] *NY Times*, Sep 4 and 5, 1901.

[244] *SF Call*, Apr 11, 1902; *SF Chronicle*, Apr 24, 1902.

[245] *SF Chronicle*, Apr 24, 1902.

[246] Ibid., May 8, 1902; see PMSC, Japan and China, Passenger List Souvenir, and OSC Passenger List, both docs. are in the JLS papers. Arrival in Yokohama, *SF Chronicle*, May 14, 1902.

[247] PMSC, Japan and China, Passenger List Souvenir, in JLS papers.

[248] *SF Chronicle*, Jun 28, 1902; *PA Times*, Jul 4, 1902.

[249] *SF Bulletin*, Aug 7, 1903; on Aug 3, the *SF Argonaut* had reported the Aug 6 sailing date.

[250] BB, *Mrs. Stanford*, 164ff. See PMSC, Japan and China, Passenger List Souvenir, in JLS papers.

[251] *SF Chronicle*, Aug 25, 1903. BB has them arriving on Aug 25, on Jane's birthday, *Mrs. Stanford*, 165.

[252] *Sydney Morning Herald*, Aug 29, 1903, and letter to the writer from Barbara Goldsmith, lib., SLNSW, May 14, 2001. The *SF Chronicle* and *SF Examiner* reported on Sep 3, 1903, only that the ship reached Sydney "prior to Sep 2."

Thomas Welton Stanford

arrived in Australia on March 13, 1860. Brother DeWitt died on April 18, 1862. Welton married Wilhelmina (Minnie) Watt on May 12, 1869, but she died within a year of their marriage, reportedly in childbirth.[a] Following her death, he moved to Clarendon Street, East Melbourne, "where he became known for his garden of rare plants, his aviaries of exotic birds, his fine collection of Australian Paintings, and, most of all, for his interest in spiritualism."[b] Welton later served as an American deputy consul general (sometimes called vice consul) for the United States.[c] He never once returned home.

[a]Test. of Dr. (Col.) Welton Joseph Crook, LSJU professor emeritus of metallurgy, godson of TWS, and son of TWS partner in Melbourne, Australia, where Professor Crook was born, on Feb 1, 1886. Jaques Cattell, ed., "Dr. Welton Joseph Crook," AMS, 10th ed., A–E. *The Physical and Biological Sciences* (Tempe, Ariz.: JCP, 1960), 817. For info. on the career of TWS and the statement that his wife died in childbirth, see inter. of Dr. Welton Crook in Jack Frasher, "Strange Legacy At Stanford—Endowed Chair for the Occult," *SJ Mercury-News*, Mar 29, 1964. Crook's colonelcy came from his being the officer in charge of engineering at the Rock Island, Illinois, arsenal during World War II, "Sixteen Professors Retire," *SR* 1952 53 (10): 13.
[b]E. Daniel Potts, "Thomas Welton Stanford," *ADB*, XII, 1890, 46–47.
[c]Stanford, *Stanford Genealogy*, 26; Lionel E. Fredman, "Thomas Welton Stanford," *VHM* 1962 33 (1): 247; Payson J. Treat, "Thomas Welton Stanford," *SS* 1907 17 (2): 44.

and met them there.[253] The disappointed sister-in-law was astonished to find her host quite different from what she expected. No matter what the topic of conversation, Welton, "one of the earliest and staunchest supporters of Spiritualism in Australia," did not wish to be diverted from the subject of "psychic research."[254]

The strained relationship was obvious when Welton invited Jane to stay in his home while in Australia only to have her say it might be better for both of them if she took rooms in a hotel, which she did. Berner says that the widow of the once robust and powerful Governor was disappointed to learn of the "deplorable condition" this "tall, very thin, and extremely nervous" relative was in; because of his fanatical and undivided concern with spiritualism, he had become almost a recluse.[255]

Welton pressured Jane to attend several "sittings" in his home and office, but this disturbed—almost provoked—his guest. She was frightened by what she saw in one of Welton's meetings; afterward, she suggested that he leave his present surroundings temporarily and go somewhere to recuperate.[256]

According to Bertha Berner's account, Jane's original plan had been to remain in Melbourne until sailing for India, but the experiences with her brother-in-law prompted her to leave early; she spent one week in Adelaide before boarding the steamer *Omrah* for Ceylon.[257]

Jane Stanford had been so shocked by what she heard about spiritualism while in Australia that she was cured once and for all of any interest in the subject—never again did she attend a séance. She "grieved" for Welton and for the condition into which his faith in spiritualism had led him.[258]

---

[253]Distance: inter. with International Tower Agent, Sydney Ports, Sydney, New South Wales, Australia, Aug 3, 2001. The complete address of TWS is in his will, dated Jun 2, 1911, in SFP, SUA.
[254]BB, *Mrs. Stanford*, 165; Fredman, "Thomas Welton Stanford," 247.   [255]BB, *Mrs. Stanford*, 166.
[256]Ibid., 167.   [257]Ibid.   [258]Ibid., 168.

160. Jane Stanford's last photograph, 1905.
Stanford University Archives

Despite the treatment received from his sister-in-law, Welton in 1912 embarrassed the university by making a gift in the amount of $526,000—in addition to approximately $1 million he left when he died in 1918—earmarked for pursuing research in psychic phenomena.[259] Unable to come up with a better solution, the university turned it over to the psychology department, a move often criticized for not being in keeping with Thomas Welton Stanford's intention.

Once in Ceylon Jane and her companion visited Colombo and Kandy. In November of 1903 they set sail for Calcutta, to Darjeeling, then returned to Calcutta, and visited the Taj Mahal, Delhi, and Bombay.

The pair then set sail for Egypt, where they retraced steps of an earlier trip. Jane Stanford changed her plans about visiting Europe again, and instead backtracked to Bombay, Madras, and Colombo, and then, sailing through the Straits of Malacca, they arrived in Singapore on about the 25th of March 1904.[260]

This was followed by a week-long trip to Hong Kong and Shanghai, and then Nagasaki, Yokohama, Tokyo, and back again to Yokohama. From there they set sail

[259]*SF Chronicle*, Aug 9 and 10, 1923. The TWS legacy of $1 million was the largest gift made to LSJU (other than that of Leland and JLS) at that time. Rixford K. Snyder, "Stanford and Australia," *S & T* 1989 13 (3): 8. The subject is Leland's brother TWS.   [260]*BB*, Mrs. Stanford, 191.

161. Bertha Berner, Jane Stanford's secretary and traveling companion from 1884 to 1905. *Stanford University Archives*

on the Pacific Mail's *China* for San Francisco, where they docked at First and Brannan streets late on the evening of May 2, 1904.[261] Jane was listed by name as one of the ship's 121 saloon (first class) passengers.[262]

JANE STANFORD'S DEATH

The cause of Jane Stanford's death has been a subject of speculation for writers, particularly those interested in the genres of mystery, the unknown, or even the occult. Articles continue to appear on the subject, recounting the details of how she thought she had been poisoned and at times speculating on who her murderer might have been. Was she killed by Toy Wing Toy, a man who said that she owed him $30,000, which he claimed he had in the Leland Stanford Junior University Trust Bank? There was, however, no such bank, and Toy himself had been committed to an insane asylum by the authorities who investigated his note of demand for payment.[263] "Did she die of a seizure, as university president Jordan claimed? Or was this an attempt by Jordan to hush up a murder by one of Mrs. Stanford's servants?

---

[261] *SF Call*, May 3, 1904; *PA Times*, May 3, 1904. In a letter from JLS to Mary Miller, Sep 10, 1904, she described their homecoming and said that BB had to go to her sick mother in May and was still away.

[262] *SF Chronicle*, May 3, 1904.

[263] Steve Gruber, "Who Killed Mrs. Stanford? Was it the butler? the maid? or was it a natural death? after 62 years, nobody knows," *SDM*, Friday, May 26, 1967 151A (1): 8.

Could it have been a suicide? Or was it a blunder by an incompetent druggist who filled a bicarbonate of soda bottle with strychnine?"[264] Missing from this list of suggestive questions is this: did the seventy-six-year-old-woman who had over-eaten the night before—contrary to her doctor's orders—simply die of natural causes, as many medical examiners concluded?

What is more important here than how Jane Stanford died was when she died. Jane Stanford had planned to live in the San Francisco house and spend every Sunday in Palo Alto so she could attend the university church there.[265] But on Saturday, January 14, 1905, Jane imagined a bitter taste in her drinking water, which was the beginning of her hallucination that someone was trying to poison her. Her bout with blood poisoning in 1883 probably had lingered in her memory so that every ailment she suffered from was somehow related to poison.[266] She decided to go to San José for a few days until she was feeling better. Afterward, her advisers suggested that a trip might be good for her nerves and Honolulu was decided upon. Thus it was that on February 15, 1905, she and Bertha Berner set sail on the *Korea* on their sixth and final voyage together, arriving in Honolulu on February 21.[267]

Following a lunch in Honolulu, in which Jane indulged herself in too much gingerbread and cream chocolates, contrary to Bertha's objections, the seventy-six-year-old woman had difficulty walking by herself. Bertha and a maid managed to get her back to her rooms. Late that night she screamed that she had been poisoned and demanded that the doctors pump her stomach. Yet before any medical action could be taken, she took faithful Bertha's hands in hers, leaned on her long-time companion for support, and, as Bertha later wrote: "I felt her body sink a little in the chair, and her soul had left her body."[268] It was a little after 11 P.M. on February 28, 1905. An autopsy, in which all her internal organs were examined, revealed enough evidence of poison to spark journalistic and conspiratorial speculations to the present day.[269]

Jane Stanford's remains were shipped from Honolulu on the *Alameda* on March 15, 1905, and reached San Francisco on March 21.[270]

Once her remains were back at the Palo Alto home, a nonsectarian memorial service was planned, to be directed by a Presbyterian minister and an Episcopalian priest.[271] The names of some of Mrs. Stanford's favorite hymns, provided by Bertha Berner, were sung at the service. Future Stanford president Ray Lyman Wilbur

---

[264]Ibid.

[265]BB, *Mrs. Stanford*, 200.

[266]LSJ to Aunt Kate Lathrop, Aug 2, 1883, from Paris.

[267]*SF Chronicle*, Feb 22, 1905; see BB, *Mrs. Stanford*, 203ff. BB's test., [Honolulu] *Pacific Commercial Advertiser*, Mar 7, 1905.

[268]BB, *Mrs. Stanford*, 207.

[269]Island of Oahu, Att. Gen.'s Files, Case No. 361. Coroner's Inquest. *In re Death of Jane Lathrop Stanford*, Feb 28, 1905. Original file in State Archives, Iolani Palace Grounds, Honolulu, Hawaii. Copy in JLS papers. See BB, *Mrs. Stanford*, 208–210, and Nagel, *Jane Stanford*, 173–175.

[270][Honolulu] *Pacific Commercial Advertiser*, Mar 16, 1905; *SF Call*, Mar 22, 1905.

[271]TNH to May Hopkins, Mar 4 and 9, 1905.

TIM HOPKINS AND DAVID STARR JORDAN

arrived in Honolulu on March 10, 1905.[a] A funeral service was held at Honolulu's Central Union Church on March 15, presided over by Episcopal bishop Henry B. Restarick and Pastor William Morris Kincaid of the Central Union Church. After this service, thousands of spectators lined the road from the church to the dock, and the pallbearers, honor guard, and mounted police joined a procession to the Oceanic Wharf, where Mrs. Stanford's remains were laid in the treasure room on the steamship *Alameda* to be taken to California, that same day.

Most of the flags in the harbor was flown at half-mast.

Mrs. Stanford's pallbearers were Gov. George R. Carter and U.S. judge Sanford B. Dole, representing the Territory of Hawaii; President David Starr Jordan and Trustee Timothy Hopkins representing Stanford University; Charles Dole, Abram Lewis, Carl S. Smith, and D[elos] L[ewis] Van Dine, representing Stanford alumni in Hawaii; and J. F. Hackfeld and C. M. Cooke, representing the Stanford estate.[b]

[a][Honolulu] *Pacific Commercial Advertiser*, Mar 11, 1905.
[b]Ibid., Mar 16, 1905.

JANE STANFORD'S AND BERTHA BERNER'S SIX TRIPS ABROAD

Trip	Date	Left	Ship	Arrived	Date
1.	Jun 9, 1897	New York	*Paris*	Southampton	Jun 16, 1897
	Oct 9, 1897	Liverpool	*Umbria*	New York	Oct 16, 1897
2.	Jun 14, 1899	New York	*Teutonic*	Liverpool	Jun 22, 1899
	Oct 21, 1899	Liverpool	*Campania*	New York	Oct 28, 1899
3.	Jul 11, 1900	New York	*Oceanic*	Liverpool	Jul 18, 1900
	Aug 28, 1901	Liverpool	*Majestic*	New York	Sep 4, 1901
4.	Apr 10, 1902	San Francisco	*Sierra*	Honolulu	Apr 16, 1902
	Apr 30, 1902	Honolulu	*China*	Yokohama	May 11, 1902
	Jun 11, 1902	Yokohama	*China*	San Francisco	Jun 28, 1902
5.	Aug 6, 1903	San Francisco	*Ventura*	Sydney	Aug 29, 1903
	Apr 15, 1904*	Yokohama	*China*	San Francisco	May 2, 1904
6.	Feb 15, 1905	San Francisco	*Korea*	Honolulu	Feb 21, 1905
	Mar 15, 1905	Honolulu	*Alameda*	San Francisco	Mar 21, 1905

*Calculated by number of days at sea.

contributed the following remarks on Jane Stanford's funeral, "Eloquent of her ideal universality for the Memorial Church was the presence of an Episcopalian bishop, a Jewish rabbi [sic], two Presbyterian preachers, and a Congregationalist, a Baptist, and a Methodist clergyman."[272] The funeral services were held at the Stan-

[272]Edgar Eugene Robinson and Paul Carroll Edwards, eds., *The Memoirs of Ray Lyman Wilbur, 1875–1949* (Stanford: SUP, 1960), 125; the seven were John W. Dinsmore, retired Presbyterian minister in San José; Episcopal bishop William F. Nichols; William Kirk Guthrie, pastor of the First Presb. Church of SF; Rabbi Jacob Voorsanger *(continued)*

Bertha Berner

was born on July 12, 1861, making her almost exactly thirty-three years younger than Jane Stanford. She was Jane's private secretary, friend, and traveling companion from late 1884 until Jane's death in 1905. (Jane referred to her on occasion as her "maid."[a])

Berner later wrote that sometime in the late 1890s she and Jane Stanford were sitting in their workroom—a beautiful sitting room on the upper floor of the San Francisco mansion—when Mrs. Stanford first broached the subject of her biography. Reminiscing about something that happened when she was twelve years old, she remarked to Bertha, "When you write about me when I am gone, that time will be a good beginning." Henry Clay Lathrop, Jane's brother, who was living with them at the time, underscored this suggestion.[b]

It was not until 1931, when speaking at the opening of the new Women's Gymnasium at Stanford, that Berner was shocked by the students' ignorance about the Stanfords. Questions about whether Mrs. Stanford had ever lived on campus or whether Leland, Jr., was born in San Francisco or Palo Alto led her to begin writing the life story of her long-time friend.

Bertha Berner lived in the house Jane Stanford had given her behind the Stanford campus, at the southwest corner of the Alameda de las Pulgas (now called Santa Cruz Avenue) and Sand Hill Road (the former Mayfield-Searsville Road). In 1934 she published her biography of Jane Stanford, written, from all appearances, more from memory than notes. Despite its many factual errors, used in a judicious and critical manner Berner's volume is still a valuable contribution to Stanford literature.

The Berner papers have never been found. In her will she established an August Berner Scholarship Fund (which is still active) for two $300 scholarships per year to two promising male students, one in the Mechanical Engineering Department and the other in the Mining Engineering Department.[c]

Berner's brother August was living with her at the time of his death, on November 11, 1943.[d] Bertha died at her Menlo Park home on March 11, 1945.[e]

[a]JLS to Mary Miller, Sep 10, 1904.   [b]BB, *Mrs. Stanford*, 1–2.
[c]This fund that began with a modest sum of approx. $70,000 has a present value of almost $421,932 and earned $22,425 in 2003, paying from its earnings $11,400 to earth sciences and $11,147 to mechanical engineering. Inter. with Mary K. Morrison, senior associate director, Financial Aid, LSJU, Feb 25, 2003. Apparently, JLS had a close personal relationship with August Berner. In 1898 she provided him with a railroad pass good for a year, from Oroville to SF and back. JLS to Mr. Julius Kruttschmitt of the SPC, May 14, 1898.
[d]Funeral Record, signed by Willis Roller of Roller & Hapgood, PA [now Roller & Hapgood & Tinney].
[e]She was cremated at the Alta Mesa Memorial Park in Los Altos, and her ashes were sent to the PA funeral home of Roller & Hapgood, where all trace of them has been lost. Funeral Record of Roller & Hapgood, Mar 11, 1945; *SF Chronicle*, Mar 12, 1945.

ford Memorial Church, after which students conveyed Jane Stanford's body to the family mausoleum to be placed along side those of her husband and son.[273] It was reported that five thousand mourners were there.[274]

(*continued*) of Temple Emanu-El of SF; Elbert R. Dille, pastor of the First Meth. Epis. Church of Oakland; Claiborne Milton Hill, pres. of the Berkeley Baptist Divinity School; and Dr. Charles R. Brown, pastor of the First Cong. Church of Oakland. See *SF Call*, Mar 25, 1905.   [273]BB, *Mrs. Stanford*, 208.
[274]*SF Call*, Mar 25, 1905.

MURDER, THEY WROTE

Murder has always been more interesting than accidental or natural death—at least to journalists, for it sells vastly more newspapers. And murders are so simple, at least in the old days before drive-by shootings and the killing of total strangers just to see them die. There was a motive, a victim, and a perpetrator. In these latter-day murders, there is frequently lacking a viable suspect, and motives are a thing of the past that investigative authorities can ignore; all that is needed is innuendo—and screaming headlines to manufacture money.

Nor have the writers of historical fiction failed to notice this motif for attracting the gullible, conspiracy-thesis advocates to their writings and to the cashiers' stands. In the history of California, journalists and sensationalists have not failed to capitalize on this income-producing theme.

(Many times I have been warned that the main element lacking in my biography of Stanford is sex and violence, each a *sine qua non* of good marketing—hence the story of Eadweard, Flora, and Harry.)

The account of the simple but tragic death of David Colton was many years after the fact converted into a murder mystery. No motive, no evidence, not even a good old-fashioned corpse.[a]

It was all a mystery.

Not even the corpse of President Warren G. Harding could make its way out of San Francisco without death by ptomaine poisoning being transmogrified into first-degree murder.

It, too, was all a mystery.

The most unlikely, and almost comical in its absurdity, of all the manufactured California murder cases has been the death of Jane Stanford. No motive, no viable suspect, just headlines and gullible readers. But what else is needed?

This murder farce has now been playing to a dwindling audience for ninety-nine years, and every third of a century or so someone rediscovers it, and, thinking he has something new, writes a newspaper editorial, an article, or a book on this "new" story. After all, any story that one has not read is a new story.

But, it is all a mystery.

Jane Stanford was a woman obsessed with illness, death, and going to Heaven. Like so many true believers, she wanted to go to Heaven without dying, but found that pathway barred. Her letters by the scores are centered on her illnesses, the death of her loved ones, and her fanatical desire to see them again.

The following excerpts are quoted as written from a number Jane Stanford's outgoing letters, cited here to show how often these themes intrude into her letter writing.[b] Each paragraph is from a different letter.

Leland [Junior] was not well the entire time sore throat hoarseness and a little malaria fever he was not out but four or five times while there. I gave him small doses of quinine and some homeopathic remedies for the hoarseness and sore throat.

But I dare not stay here; there is so much typhoid fever among the visitors.

I have been sick the entire time.

Today I expected to leave Rome for Florence . . . but have been prevented by the sickness of Leland . . . but I thought with love and my old homeopathic remedies he would be all right in a few days, but Thursday night he had so much fever I sent for Dr. Valerie. I have had such a dread

of Bonn . . . but I argued with myself that it was only a morbid condition of my mind in consequence of not being well.

(Leland Jr.: Mama is ill she has had a very inflamed eye she is in a dark room all the time. The Doctor says it is quite serious and she must keep very quiet and that it comes from weakness and inaction of the heart. It is very painful she sleeps very little.)

I have no one other than myself to talk to.

All these festive days bring added sorrowful remembrances of the dear past. When your gift came this time I said to think they should remember poor broken hearted me.

I cannot but contrast the present with the loneliness of house, the vacant chairs at our hearth, and at our table with the gladness that used to pervade our home. I have been particularly depressed this season because of the very sad and unexpected relations in which we have been thrown. We went as helpers to others with heavier woe and I constantly said to myself who will God call next to the higher life . . . the beautiful remembrance that was sent to poor me . . . you and Tim [Hopkins] to remember us with our stricken sorrow still upon us.

The world seems very full of sorrow, I hope dear May [Hopkins] you will keep cheerful, you have no reason to fear for yourself. The case is very rare where one is called from life when performing the laws nature and God requires from carrying out the requirements to give birth to a child.

I have a thousand fears for your [her husband's] safety——and will scarcely be able to sleep from anxiety till [sic] you are safely on this side.

I get very tired but I make it a rule to be in bed at nine and I never rise till [sic] nine.

I had expected to go to Menlo long ere this but I have been confined to the house and to my bed by sickness.

I was always sorry for her lonely condition and her delicate state of health. . . . But felt as I did that it was asking too much of that frail body to sing often.

Had we known she was soon to be called to Grace Paridise [sic] . . . I would have asked her to deliver loving messages to my dear ones.

My sick sore heart.

I am sorry I can not write in person, but for the past two weeks my eyes have been so painful, so much so that I have even been obliged to stop reading my precious book—Thomas à Kempis. I have on my desk a photo. just received from Jennie Flood and her father. Mr. Flood does not look as badly as one would expect, although he is greatly changed from what he was when you last saw him. This photo was taken in October, since then he has failed very much, so Jennie writes me, and they are expecting his departure from earthlife at any hour. I am suffering from extreme nervous exhaustion.

I had a sudden attack of La Grippe.

I have had quite a severe attack of the Grippe it came upon me very severely and closely confined me to room and bed for one week—in fact, I am not yet over its effects and nearly two weeks have passed. The Doctor advised me to go into another climate for a while to rid myself of its after effects.

I am overpowered with distress.

Thanks for the bon bons.

Thanks for the bon bons.

I opened the wrappers, and finally came to the beautiful basket filled (*continued on next page*)

with the choicest bon bons and candied fruits. . . . Ever since our arrival it has been very cold, and to day it is dark and rain is falling. I was this morning as soon as I could get away to see Dora Miller, poor child she has passed through great trials, her baby had to be taken from her, at eight months to save her life, kidney troubles had come upon her and without it had been taken by instruments she could not have lived, if it had been delayed till the nine months had elapsed, her Mother has been very ill ever since they left Cal. The baby is only three weeks old to day, and Dora had not been permitted to know her Mother was critically ill 'till three days ago, then the Dr's thought she was dying and told Dora.

We are feeling sad over the painful news that reached us yesterday of the passing from life here on earth of Mr. Charles Crocker, before we left New York last May, we knew of his severe illness, and feared a fatal result, but since then have constantly heard of an improved condition and the sudden termination of life here gave us a severe shock. God only separates them for a very short time they are fast journeying towards the same country, to be reunited never to suffer sickness and death again.

I cannot let a longer time elapse without writing and learning from yourself how your health is at present. Now in this season of epidemic when many are falling like leaves from the forest trees it is so very much to be thankful for if our loved ones keep well. The epidemic is rageing [sic] all around us here, and I notice by telegraph news in the papers of to day, that S. Francisco is suffering and the death rate very much increased there. The Doctor in N.Y. advised my going to a clear cold climate for awhile, as I did not feel at all well after being here a few weeks.

The Doctor said my extreme nervous exhaustion, and the local difficulty from which I was suffering made it absolutely necessary for me to keep entirely quiet mentally and physically. To day I am feeling much better and I am sitting up as I did also yesterday and if I have not set back I hope to go to dear Menlo Saturday. Tomorrow will be two weeks since I have been confined to my room.

I wrote a letter to your [Tim Hopkins'] Mother telling her I felt May was threatened I thought mentally and physically with something, she was so entirely unlike her old self, while writing the letter the telephone message came from Mr. Nash that she was at Monterey and threatened with typhoid fever. I want to urge upon you that great caution should be practiced by May, for that disease is so insidious and all traces should be so thoroughly eradicated before she takes up her old life.

The flowers and the bon bons that brighten the route over the [text missing]. Fires almost out entirely and all the family are complaining of inertness weakness and irritability.

I know it will interest you both [Tim and May Hopkins] to hear from us and know while around us there has been sickness we with God's protection have escaped even the entire household. I hope May will occasionally go and see my sister and plainly tell me what she thinks of her condition I feel anxious all the time about her.

I feel better than I have in three days, and think I am nearly over the attack of illness.

While so very many here have been so seriously ill he has by Gods mercy escaped. Mr. Blaine is very ill now with the Gripp [sic]. I am greatly relieved about my sister, although I never for one moment thought there was anything malignant the matter with her. She had really become diseased in mind and it is just as bad as reality, to become a slave to the imagination.

I can assure you for the Doctor was kind in his effort to tell me he did not look forward to the cure as being much benefit to my dear husband I read it in his manner as well in words on Leland's health.

Never in all my travels from home have I ever felt so joyless so very depressed, ever helpless as I do at present. My thoughts travel back to my very sick sister who does not appear to advance since my departure. I fear it depressed her and she cannot rebound.

My sister is no better and failing I fear, from the cables I get she is on my heart and never off and I fear I may never see her again in this life, I am praying for strength to be *brave* and to be able to do my duty to all I love.

I am not well and we have been delayed by it here as I had to have a doctor again and now I am so eager to get away from the dampness and in the mountains.

On the illness of sister Anna.

Mr. Nash was taken at eleven last eve with a bad hemorrhage. He thinks he would like to go [*sic*] the Hospital but I do not favor it I am sick at heart over this for I am very fond of him and can't bear to leave him. Henry [her brother] was taken ill on our arrival here, but felt better when we retired, he is not up yet but I hope he is all right this morning.

[Writes about Leland's health.]

[Tells of her fear of not again seeing her sister alive.]

We are not well.

I think there has been a gradual improvement in my husband's health but I do not approve this second cure—it is too weakening, but Dr. Blanch approved it.

Yesterday, my dear sister has been in the life eternal one month, and I said to my dear husband how much more she knows than she did a month ago. My boy may be her teacher.

My bleeding heart.

I feel so utterly powerless to make things different. I am glad to hear cholera is dying out in Europe you can then make your trip without anxiety. I have heard of nothing special that would interest you. I have seen no one to tell me anything. I remain here for the quiet and rest—the house in the city with its stillness its vacant rooms where I left my sister are very depressing and I must be brave and courageous.

My heart is too full for utterance. I ask myself each day how it can be I live with this great, overwhelming sorrow upon me, never for any time away from my thoughts—only when I sleep and the awakening is so dreadful. At first I say, is it not a dreadful dream, but no, it is too true and again I face the truth.

I think there has been a gradual improvement in my husband's health. I then stepped closer to the side of his bed and said he [Leland Junior] has opened the gates of Heaven to us.

The dear letters received from various sources seems [*sic*] to be the "only connecting link with the world."

I have been quite ill with the Grippe. I dislike to be away from here and I feel as if this was home in the truest sense for here lies all that [*sic*] dearest that is left to me in earth life of my loved ones.

[Writes to a Mrs. Harvey regarding her [Jane's] own "sick hungry heart."]

[Writes to Tim Hopkins on illness of May and death of their son.]

[Writes about her bowel troubles.]

[On the severity of the grip [*sic*] in New York City.]

[Mr. Stanford began the "Salisbury Cure" under the direction of the doctor while in New York.]

[On illness and death.]

[On Herbert Nash's health.]   (*continued on next page*)

[Every boy and girl at LSJU has a "soul germ" that needs developing.]

[She had not had a "funny" time when a surgeon removed seven cysts from her scalp and the wounds were slow in healing.]

[After staying at a hotel in Montreal, she wrote:] "I seemed to have been under a spell and not equel [sic] to taking a pen I [sic] hand to write—I really believed those rooms poisoned my system through and through for I have no [sic] been well since—first I had bowel trouble and then bronchites [sic] and when I arrived here I sent for a doctor, he has helped me, and now I am very anxious to be home—really I am afflicted with severe home sickness."

To know this institution [Stanford University] is on such a low plane has actually made me sick.

[On her overtaxed nerves.]

[On her days and nights of tears and anguish.]

Sick sore heart, weary waiting for better days.

[Her son died twelve years ago.]

These few citations—few when compared to the number of letters Jane Stanford wrote about illness, misery, fear of death, the joyful anticipation of going to Heaven, etc.—are offered to give an inkling into the frame of Jane Stanford's mind long before and just before she died.

There is no attempt at Stanford University to cover up the imaginary murder of Jane Stanford. All archival records are open to all researchers. And is it not odd that if these stories were given much credit, or that David Starr Jordan's reputation were about to be besmirched by those pointing the finger of guilt at him or at least impugning his veracity and honesty, that it is the university history journals and the Stanford University Press that year after year publishes these scurrilous diatribes?[c]

In summary, by 1905 Jane Stanford's life had become one of hysteria about illness and death, and, on the other side, the constant thought of seeing her son and husband again.

Many of the so-called "true" accounts of the death of Jane Stanford insist on pointing to murder, not to overeating or old age, not even to heart trouble or her overwhelming desire to die and join her loved ones in some other life, or even to accidental poisoning as a result of having too much strychnine in her ever-present bicarbonate of soda—all of which may have contributed to the final collapse of a frail body and not too strong a mind.

[a]Lewis, *The Big Four*, 302: "Rumors persisted that the General had been murdered, but details of the mystery—if it was a mystery—never reached the public." For the results of the autopsy on Colton, see Charles C. Keeney, "Case of General Colton, and the Causes of his Death," *PMSJ* 1878 21 (7): 309–316.

[b]The few letters quoted above and a few bibliographical entries are placed here to acknowledge the presence of the controversy and as a harbinger of a book on the life, illnesses, and death of Jane Stanford now in preparation by the author of this biography of Leland Stanford. Complete quotations will be given in that work, within context and with addressees identified and dates given.

[c]See Berner, *Mrs. Stanford*, 201–207, for an account of the last days and death of Jane Stanford told by her close friend and traveling companion and an eyewitness to her death; DSJ, *The Days of a Man*, II, 156–157; Island of Oahu, Attorney General's Files, Case No. 361. Coroner's Inquest. *In re Death of Jane Lathrop Stanford*, February 28, 1905; Gruber, "Who Killed Mrs. Stanford? Was it the butler? the maid? or was it a natural death? after 62 years, nobody knows," *SDM*, Friday, May 26, 1967 151 A (1): 8–9; and Robert W. P. Cutler, *The Mysterious Death of Jane Stanford* (Stanford: Stanford General Books, SUP, 2003). Stanford General Books is the popular, non-scholarly imprint of the Stanford University Press. This interesting little book is the latest in the growing list of accounts purporting to tell once and for all the truth about the death of Jane Stanford.

Railroad Affairs

End of the Line for Car Stanford—June 27, 1911

Following the death of Leland Stanford, Jane used *Car Stanford* for the rest of her life. Reportedly, it was passed free over every railroad in the country out of respect for her esteemed husband.[275] Although it was a privately owned car, *Car Stanford* was listed on the first Central Pacific roster as a Central Pacific officer's car. Leland Stanford's private horse car, the *Palo Alto*, was also listed on this register.[276] Stanford's car was first listed on the register as a Southern Pacific Company director's car in July 1894, a year after he died.[277]

On August 20, 1896, Jane sent *Car Stanford* to the Sacramento Southern Pacific shops for refurbishing, including a new paint job. Victor Lemay, superintendent of Motive Power and Machinery, notified the shop personnel: "Car Stanford will be put through shops for general overhauling and painting. It is the desire of Mrs. Stanford that the car be painted yellow, same as now. Charge all labor and material direct to car [*sic*] 'Stanford.'"[278] On the following day Lemay added instructions received from Newton H. Foster at the San Francisco headquarters of the Southern Pacific: "Further in regards to Mrs. Stanford's Car: she desires that new outside curtains be furnished, same as the old ones, and wants the same color and the monogram. Please arrange for this with the other work."[279]

Car Stanford was no longer carried on the register as a director's car after August 1900.[280] Perhaps executive changes at the Southern Pacific Company as a result of Huntington's death in the same month were responsible.

Bertha Berner's last specific mention of Jane's use of *Car Stanford* was for a long trip they made to New York in October 1904, arriving back home in California on December 21. On December 24 they went home to Palo Alto and on Christmas Day returned to San Francisco, then back to Palo Alto on New Year's Day. Thereafter, they made almost weekly jaunts between San Francisco and Palo Alto, so Jane could go to church at Stanford every Sunday. There is no doubt that Jane used her private car on these trips, though not specifically mentioned by Bertha. The next-to-the-last-use by Jane Stanford of *Car Stanford* was on a trip to the Hotel Vendome in San José on January 15, 1905. Jane Stanford's final use of *Car Stanford* was on or about

---

[275]Lucius Morris Beebe, *Mansions on Rails: The Folklore of the Private Railway Cars* (Berkeley: HNB, 1959), 22.

[276] "Southern Pacific Company," *OIREGR* [title varies] Jun 1885 1 (Jul): 65.

[277]Ibid., 1894 10 (2): 122–128, citation on 123.

[278][Victor] Lemay, supt. of Motive Power and Machinery (Pacific System), to "All Concerned," in CSRML, Ms. 10, Letters, 1890–1900. 1896 folder; *SCD*, 1900, 310.

[279]N[ewton] H. Foster to H[enry] J. Small, supt., Motive Power and Machinery (Pacific System), in CSRML, Ms. 10, Letters, 1890–1900. 1896 folder. See also John Steven McGroarty, "Newton H. Foster," in *California of the South—A History* (5 vols., Chicago: SJCPC, 1933), IV, 475–476, and (on Small) *SCD*, 1900, 425.

[280]*OREGR*, 1900 16 (3): 148–151. Had it been listed, it would have appeared on 150.

January 27 or 28 for the return trip to San Francisco. On February 10, 1905, she left
for Honolulu, where she died two weeks later.[281]

What became of *Car Stanford* after the death of Jane Stanford? The very long probate of Jane Stanford's estate was not discharged until May 3, 1959, but those
records provide the first clue as to how *Car Stanford* left the Stanford estate after
twenty-four years.[282] On May 25, 1905, the value of *Car Stanford* was set by court-
appointed appraisers at $10,000—a small portion of Mrs. Stanford's total estate,
appraised at $3,391,871.32.[283] On November 30, 1906, three of the executors of the
estate, Charles G. Lathrop, Timothy Hopkins, and Joseph Grant, signed an agreement selling the car to a W. L. Stevenson for the appraised value.[284]

Promoter William L. Stevenson—proud owner of what had once been the
costliest and most spectacular private railroad car ever built—had incorporated
the Nevada Railroad Company on March 10, 1906, and the Nevada Consolidated
Mining and Milling Company on May 9. He arrived on the scene of speculative railroad building and mining activities near Olinghouse, Nevada, in the spring of
1907.[285] Stevenson apparently had the financial backing of a number of Reno capitalists, among them Judge Charles E. Mack and his wife, Mary J. Mack (who seems
to have been the one who put up the money), and Richard Kirman, president of the
Farmers and Merchants Bank and mayor of Reno.[286]

On May 27, Stevenson sent his private railroad car *Sunland*—his new name for
Car Stanford—to Reno to pick up Gov. John Sparks and bring him to a big barbecue
the next day.[287]

For Stevenson's purposes, the *Sunland* proved to be a disappointment at Olinghouse, owing to its sixty-foot length—seventy with the platforms at both ends—
since the curves at the upper end of the line near Olinghouse were too tight to

[281]BB, *Mrs. Stanford*, 195, 199–200, and 202–203.

[282]SCC, SupC Probate Index, Vol. 2, 1903–1917, Register M, 587, identifies JLS probate case no. as 5802. Her probate records are on Mfilms 159 and 160. The trustee for her estate was the Union Trust Co. of SF, which, on Dec 31,
1923, was merged into the Wells Fargo Bank and Union and Trust Co.

[283]SupC "Inventory and Appraisal," ibid., Reel 159; reported in the *SF Call*, Sep 19, 1906. An inventory of the separate estate of JLS, filed on Sep 18, 1906, by the appraisers of the estate, set the value of *Car Stanford* at $10,000. The total
estate was listed as $3,391,871.32, broken down as follows: cash $27,056.32, wardrobe $1,000, household linen $1,500,
silver plate $250, pearl necklace $1,293, jewelry $10,000, *Car Stanford* $10,000, horses and harness $900, and the bal-
ance in bonds of various railroad companies.

[284]SCC, SupC "Order Confirming Sale of Personal Property," Probate Records for Case No. 5802, Reel 160;
reported in the *SF Call*, Dec 3, 1907, in its report on the second ann. account of the disposition of the JLS estate.

[285]Some of the mining activities of the short-lived Olinghouse boom are described in the *Reno Evening Gazette*,
Nov 24, 1906.

[286]David F. Myrick, *Railroads of Nevada and Eastern California*. Vol. 1 of 2, *The Northern Roads* (Reno: UNvP, 1990,
c1962), 54; elected to the state assembly in 1899, at age twenty-one Richard Kirman was the youngest person ever to
serve in the Nev. leg. In 1934 he was elected gov. of Nev. and served from 1935 to 1939. *Sierra Sage*, Oct 1998, 2; inter.
with Mona Reno, Head of Federal Pubs., NSLA, Mar 18, 1999.

[287]*Comstock Chronicle*, Sep 30, 1988; Sparks was a Silver-Democrat gov. from 1903 until his death on May 22, 1908.
John Koontz, *Political History of Nevada* (Carson City: SPO, 1960), 43.

allow the car to be brought into town. On the main lines of other railroads, however, it served its purpose admirably by helping Stevenson impress "the investing public and disengage hesitant investors from their money."[288]

The Nevada Railroad operated from February 4 to December 31, 1907, when it went bankrupt.[289] After the Nevada Consolidated Mill went broke in 1907 and closed near the end of the year, the rails of the Nevada Railroad (all ten miles of them!) were torn up. So thorough was the demolition that no trace of the railroad was left.[290]

To continue the saga of *Car Stanford*, when Stevenson later fell upon hard times and was unable to pay moneys owned to Richard Kirman, the Reno banker brought suit against Stevenson in the Superior Court of California in the County of Sacramento and on June 30, 1909, secured a judgment against him for $6,253.33.[291]

Meanwhile, the Nevada Railroad Company had ordered work done on the *Sunland* at the Sacramento Southern Pacific shops for the owner, Stevenson, which he never paid for. The Southern Pacific retained possession of the car under a claim of lien in the amount of $976.74. Kirman then paid this lien and on July 30, 1909, the Southern Pacific Company turned over to Kirman clear title to the *Sunland*.[292]

On February 2, 1911, Kirman sold the *Sunland* to the Southern Pacific Company.[293] Taken again to the Southern Pacific shops in Sacramento, the *Sunland* was refurbished and then assigned to Joseph Henry Dyer, Southern Pacific general manager at Tucson, Arizona Territory, to serve as his private car.[294] It was renamed the *Tucson*, to reflect its new ownership and new assignment.

The end finally came for *Car Stanford / Sunland / Tucson*, with its new conditioning and its new name, on the twenty-seventh day of June in the year 1911—far, far from its original home, and just as far from the loving care of the Stanfords—on the

---

[288]*Comstock Chronicle*, Sep 30, 1988; Myrick, *Railroads of Nevada and Eastern California*, I, 54.

[289]See Donald B. Robertson, *Encyclopedia of Western Railroad History, The Desert States: Arizona, Nevada, New Mexico, Utah* (Vol. 1 of 4, Caldwell, Idaho: CP, 1986), I, 154, for detailed entry, including map, on this railroad.

[290]The railroad was reported as abandoned in 1909; William D. Edson, comp., *Railroad Names: A Directory of Common Carrier Railroads Operating in the United States, 1826–1989* (Potomac, Maryland: WDE, 1989), 85.

[291]In the SupC, of the State of Calif., in and for the County of Sac, Case No. 12955. Richard Kirman, Plaintiff, W[illiam] L. Stevenson, Defendant. Sheriff's Sale of Personal Property. Judgment Rendered on the 30th day of Jun 1909, Decree No. 85132; John G. Hoffa, independent hist. researcher, NHS, to the writer, Mar 30, 2000.

[292]In the SupC of the State of Calif., in and for the County of Sac. Richard Kirman, Plaintiff, W[illiam] L. Stevenson, Defendant. Certificate of Sale of Personal Property. David Reese, sheriff, to Richard Kirman, Jul 30, 1909. The complete court record, including sheriff's notices, writs, attachments, case records, and final decree, are in the SCA & MCC.   [293]Myrick, *Railroads of Nevada and Eastern California*, I, 56.

[294]Joseph Henry Dyer enjoyed a long and successful career with the SPC; beginning in 1889 as a laborer, he rose on Sep 1, 1918, to the position of gen. man. of the Pacific System. He retired on Apr 1, 1942, as vice pres. of operations, after working for the SPRR and SPC for fifty-four years. *Biographical Directory of the Railroad Officials of America* (NY: S-B, 1900–1985). Various years were ed. and comp. by different people: e.g., vols. used in this work, 1913 (163 cited here) by Harold Francis Lane, and 1922 (186–187 cited here) by Elmer T. Howson. Dyer died at the SPC Hospital in SF on Jun 14, 1947, at age seventy-five. *SF Chronicle*, Jun 15, 1947.

deserts of Arizona. Just "two months after its release from the shops," writes railroad historian David Myrick, "it was destroyed by fire."[295]

Lucius Beebe, whose oft-quoted, self-proclaimed historical research *modus operandi* of "never let the facts stand in the way of a good story," was sure that Dyer's young son Joseph Junior, later art commissioner of San Francisco, smuggled into his stateroom a supply of rockets, Roman candles, and other explosives to celebrate the coming Fourth of July and that when the explosives detonated prematurely the car went up in "a blaze of glory," in Yuma, Arizona.[296] Beebe may not have been far from the truth, except for his fanciful speculation about the origins of the explosion and his mistake in the location of the train when the fire broke out.

> ## PRIVATE CAR DESTROYED
> ### HOT BOX SETS FIRE TO $8,000 COACH ON THE ARIZONA DESERT
>
> "The private car of Superintendent J. H. Dyer of the Southern Pacific at Tucson, Ariz., caught fire last Tuesday afternoon while running as part of a train on special time at thirty miles an hour and was totally destroyed.
>
> "The car was valued at $8,000 and the contents at $750. The officials here have ordered the appointment of a board of inquiry to ascertain the cause of the unusual fire.
>
> "At Mescal, Ariz., the conductor of the train, which was a special, consisting of the private cars of the officials of the Southern Pacific Company, which officials were just returning here after a three-weeks' educational trip over the lines of several eastern railroads, passed through the car. He saw the rear brakeman in the observation end of the car and the porter in his room. At that time everything was all right. Passing Amole smoke was noticed coming from the car, and while everything was done to extinguish the flames, the attempt was unsuccessful."*
>
> *SF Examiner, Jun 29, 1911.

Thus, in Amole, Arizona—not Yuma—about thirty-three miles east of Tucson, the car burned completely.[297] A board of inquiry was assembled to investigate the fire.[298] On July 1, 1911, the *Tucson Citizen* reported the findings of the board of inquiry assigned to ascertain the cause of the fire that destroyed Dyer's car. Contrary to the report published by the *Examiner* on June 29, quoted above, on June 30, the board concluded that in some undetermined manner a bundle of fuses had been left in a locker under the washstand in one of the car's staterooms. The smell of the fuses was noticeable after the car had been on fire. Whether the fuses were ignited accidentally or by spontaneous combustion was never resolved.[299]

[295]Myrick, *Railroads of Nevada and Eastern California,* I, 56.   [296]Beebe, *Mansions on Rails,* 22.

[297]*Tucson Citizen,* Jul 1, 1911; *Yuma Daily Examiner,* Jul 3, 1911; Riva Dean, arch. dir., AHS, to author, May 1, 1998; author inter. with Frank Love, hist. researcher, Yuma, Ariz., Apr 10, 1998.

[298]*SF Examiner,* Jun 29, 1911.   [299]*Tucson Citizen,* Jun 1, 1911, repr. in the *Yuma Daily Examiner,* Jul 3, 1911.

The long and glorious career of the *Stanford/Sunland/Tucson*, like so many of Stanford's possessions, came to a fiery end.

End of the Line for the Central Pacific Railway—June 30, 1959

Part of the Central Pacific track was destroyed during a World War II scrap drive, when 120.8 miles of the original track was dismantled, including the ten-mile stretch where Charlie Crocker's workers set the all-time record for laying ten miles of rails in one day. On September 8, 1942, "unspiking" ceremonies were held near Promontory as the U.S. government requisitioned the tracks at that historic site for use by the Navy, some to be reused as railroad tracks in Navy yards, others to be melted down and converted into weapons of war. One San Francisco newspaper announced:

> Golden Spike Ceremonies
> Are Done in Reverse[300]

Another pointed out the mirror-image parallels of the events of May 10, 1869, and September 8, 1942:

> Governor Pulls Last Spike
> On 1st Cross-U.S. Railroad[301]

The last spike driven was pulled out of the track base by Gov. Herbert B. Maw of Utah while two giant engines faced each other as they had seventy-three years earlier. A military exigency during the Civil War was an impetus to *lay* the rails connecting the eastern states with California; now, another military crisis caused those same rails to be torn up.

The lease of the Central Pacific Railroad—modified to about seventy-five years rather than the original ninety-nine—expired in 1959. As a result of this, on June 30, 1959, the Central Pacific Railway Company lost its separate identity and existence by being merged into the Southern Pacific Company.[302] This merger had been approved by the Interstate Commerce Commission on May 28, 1959.[303] The Central Pacific had $106,789,941.40 in combined common and preferred stocks canceled.[304] The Southern Pacific Company assumed all stock and bond liability.[305]

So ended the separate existence—though not the romance and history—of the once glorious Central Pacific Railroad.

---

[300]*SF Chronicle*, Sep 9, 1942.

[301]*SF Examiner*, Sep 9, 1942; *Sac Bee*, Mag. Sect., 4–5, Sep 26, 1942.

[302]SPC, *Statistical Supplement to the 76th Annual Report, 1959*, 9, note (a). The separate existence of the CPRR's sister line, the SPRR, terminated on Sep 30, 1955, by merger with the SPC, a Del Corp. #220752. File 1004, CSA.

[303]Ibid., Finance Docket No. 20445.

[304]Ibid., 11, note (a).

[305]Ibid., 14, note (a).

End of the Line for the Southern Pacific Company
(Southern Pacific Lines)—September 11, 1996

Years of discussions of how best to assure payment to the federal government of the Central Pacific's debt came to an end in 1899. On February 1 the total indebtedness of the Central Pacific and Western Pacific railroads was determined to be $58,812,715.48.[306] The U.S. government decided that the Central Pacific debt should be retired in full, not discounted. This was done by a series of complicated moves whereby the Central Pacific was reorganized, subsidy bonds were issued, and the Southern Pacific Company became the guarantor of its debts.

On July 7, 1898, Congress passed an act appointing the secretary of the treasury, the secretary of the interior, and the attorney general as a commission of three with full power to settle the question of the Central Pacific's indebtedness to the government.[307]

The results of this commission's work were summarized by railroad historian Stuart Daggett:

In carrying out the proposed plan the commission named in the Act of July 7, 1897, reported to Congress under date of February 15, 1899, that an agreement had been reached, and that the subsidy bonds were to be refunded into twenty notes of $2,940,635.78 each. On March 3, 1899, Congress authorized the Secretary of the Treasury to sell the first four notes in order that the agreement with Speyer and Company might be carried out. These notes were already in the Secretary's hands. They were duly purchased by the bankers named on March 10 of the same year. During the summer of 1899, the Central Pacific Railway was incorporated to succeed the former railroad company, and the various issues called for by the reorganization plan were put forth. On February 1, 1909, the last of the refunding notes matured and was duly paid. The divorce of the Central and Western Pacific companies from the government was complete.[308]

Edward Henry Harriman of the Union Pacific had long wanted to control the Southern Pacific, but Huntington continued to refuse to sell him any interest in the road. Harriman's prospects brightened with the death of Huntington on August 13, 1900, but Huntington had willed so many shares of his stock to his widow and his

---

[306]*HMD* 238, 55th Cong., 3rd, Sess., 9 pages, 1 cited (Feb 15, 1899), *Indebtedness of Central Pacific and Western Pacific Railroads.* SSN 3812; *USCR*, 55th Cong., 3rd Sess., Sen., 2082, House, 2121 (Feb 20, 1899).

[307]30 *US Stats*, 55th Cong., 2nd Sess. (Dec 6, 1897–Jul 8, 1898), 652–659, Chap. 571, "An Act Making appropriations to supply deficiencies in the appropriations for the fiscal year ending June thirtieth, eighteen hundred and ninety-eight, and for prior years, and for other purposes." App. Jul 5, 1898. The terms applying to the CPRR and WPRR are on 659.

[308]Daggett, *Chapters on the History of the Southern Pacific*, 422–423; 30 *US Stats*, 55th Cong., 2nd Sess., 1214–1250, Chap. 427, "An Act Making appropriations to supply deficiencies in the appropriations for the fiscal year ending June thirtieth, eighteen hundred and ninety-nine, and for prior years, and for other purposes." App. Mar 3, 1899. Speyer and Co. was an investment banking institution with German affiliations. Through this house, CPH had been able to place CPRR bonds on the German market, Grodinsky, *Transcontinental Railroad Strategy, 1869–1893*, 4.

nephew Henry E. Huntington that Harrison's intentions were long frustrated. In 1901 Harriman was finally able to gain control of 38 percent of the Southern Pacific stock and with this he declared himself in control of the Southern Pacific.[309] On September 26, 1901, he made himself president of the Southern Pacific Company. One of his first goals was to repair and rebuild the Central Pacific so that it could carry as much freight from Ogden to San Francisco as the Union Pacific did from Council Bluffs to Ogden.[310]

The fact that the Union Pacific and Southern Pacific railroads had competed with each other before their merger but ceased to after the merger was all it took to persuade the U.S. Supreme Court that the new holding company was in violation of the Sherman Anti-trust Act. On December 12, 1912, the U.S. Supreme Court dissolved the merger.[311]

In 1915, when the Woodrow Wilson administration attempted to strip the Central Pacific from the Southern Pacific, nationwide protest against this move was overwhelming. On March 10, 1917, the government lost its suit and the half-century alliance of the two roads was maintained.[312]

Battles between the Southern Pacific and Union Pacific for control of the Central Pacific continued in railroad legal offices, in the press and in the courts, includ-

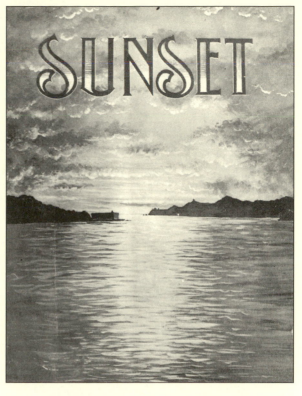

162. First *Sunset Magazine* issue, May 1898.
Sunset was founded by the Southern Pacific Company to attract tourists and colonists to California. The magazine was sold to private interests in 1914.
Union Pacific Collection.

---

[309]Don L. Hofsommer, *The Southern Pacific, 1901–1985* (College Station: TA & MUP, 1986), 9.

[310]David F. Myrick, *Refinancing and Building the Central Pacific: 1899–1915*. Prepared for the Golden Spike Symposium, UU, 1969. Pub. and Distributed by the SPC.

[311]USSCR, Vol. 226, *Cases Adjudged in the Supreme Court at October Term, 1912, United States v. Union Pacific Railroad Company*. Appeal from the Circuit Court of the United States for the District of Utah. No. 446, pp. 61–98 and 470–477. Argued Apr 19, 22, and 23, 1912. Decided Dec 2, 1912.

[312]239 *FR*, 998–1009; *SF Examiner*, Mar 11, 1917; Hofsommer, *Southern Pacific*, 78ff.

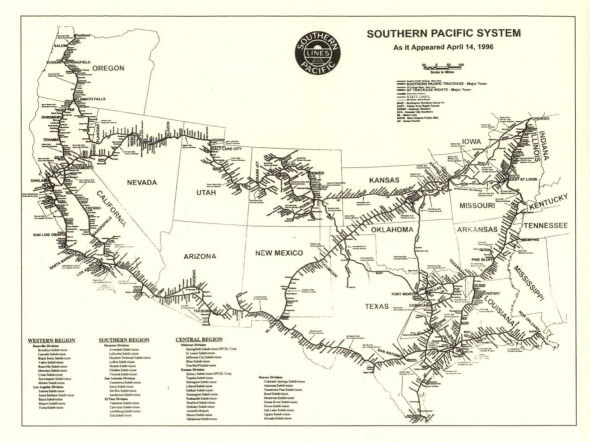

163. Map of the Southern Pacific System on April 14, 1996,
before it was sold to the Union Pacific. *Union Pacific Collection.*

ing the Supreme Court of the United States. Finally, on February 6, 1923, the Interstate Commerce Commission agreed—with a number of favorable provisions for
the Union Pacific—to the continuation of lease and control of the Central Pacific
by the Southern Pacific.[313]

In 1994 an economic comparison of the Union Pacific and Southern Pacific
showed, respectively: operating revenues of $6.44 billion and $3.1 billion; operating incomes of $1.4 billion and $346 million; 35,000 and 18,010 employees; 22,600
and 14,500 miles of track; 23 and 15 states served; 3,922 and 2,413 locomotives;
97,600 and 44,629 freight cars; and 1,397 and 750 trains operating daily.[314]

[313]ICC Reports. Decisions of the ICC of the U.S. (Finance Reports). Nov 1922–Mar 1923, LXXVI, 508–531.
Finance Docket No. 2613. *Control of Central Pacific by Southern Pacific.*

[314]UPRR, PR Dept., *Fast Facts*, Oct 17, 1997.

On November 30, 1996, the Union Pacific Corporation filed an application with the Interstate Commerce Commission (ICC) to acquire the Southern Pacific Rail Corporation.[315] For the time it was the most extensive railway merger in history: the application alone filled 8,100 pages bound in fourteen volumes. The reason given was the effect on the Southern Pacific of the merger of the Burlington Northern and Santa Fe in 1995. The merger of the Union Pacific and Southern Pacific took place on September 11, 1996; it was a $5.4 billion transaction creating North America's largest railroad, a 31,000-mile network operating in twenty-five states, Mexico, and Canada.[316]

And so ended the separate existence—though not the romance and history—of the Southern Pacific Company.

Tributes Paid to Leland Stanford

Statuary Hall Resolutions

In November 1884 the members of the California Commandery of the Military Order of the Loyal Legion of the United States had honored Leland Stanford in life by making him an honorary member of their organization. The recorder of the organization wrote later: "His great services in behalf of the Union during the war were recognized by the Military Order of the Loyal Legion, and he was elected by the Commandery of the State of California, November 19, 1884, to its most honored membership, as a Companion of the Third Class (No. 349), Insignia No. 3,993."[317]

The California Press Association was joined by others in adopting the following resolution:

Resolved:—That since California is entitled to fill two places in the Statuary Hall at the National Capitol with statues of distinguished citizens, it would be eminently fitting and do honor to the State to have one of such places filled by the statue of Leland Stanford.[318]

While it is obvious from the accolades highlighted in "The End of the Line," the previous chapter, Stanford was almost universally regarded as California's favorite son; yet when it came time to fill these two positions of honor, Stanford and worthies like John Muir and Hiram Johnson were passed over for the choice of Junípero Serra and Thomas Starr King, whose combined influence for the good of California was little compared to that of those mentioned and others who could be mentioned. King spent only four years of his life in California: he arrived in 1860 and

[315]UPRR News Release, Nov 30, 1996.　　　　　　　[316]UPRR, *Chronological History*, 1998, 8.

[317]Smedberg, *In Memoriam Leland Stanford*.

[318]LS Division #283, Brotherhood of Locomotive Engineers; repr. in *SF Chronicle*, Jun 25, 1893.

died in 1864.[319] Most of his brief California career was spent combating the imaginary specter of secessionism. Serra spent fifteen years in Spanish California, having died in 1784, and was about as far from being a resident of the American state of California as anyone could have been. Serra was one of only about a half-dozen men in the country being neither an American nor a resident of an American state who was so honored.[320]

Recognition of Stanford for his Contributions to
Motion Picture Research and Development

On Tuesday and Wednesday, May 7 and 8, 1929, a number of people gathered at Stanford University to celebrate the motion picture research conducted by Leland Stanford from 1878 to 1879.[321] The celebrants included several official delegates from the Academy of Motion Picture Arts and Sciences. On Tuesday evening Louis H. Tolhurst, a motion picture technical expert and member of the Academy of Motion Picture Arts and Sciences, delivered a lecture titled the "Evolution of the Motion Picture."

The following morning, with acting president of Stanford University Robert E. Swain presiding (Stanford President Ray Lyman Wilbur, though present, was on leave from his Stanford post from 1929 to 1933 while serving as secretary of the interior in the Herbert Hoover cabinet), Walter R. Miles, professor of experimental psychology, gave a talk that dealt with "The Stanford-Muybridge Research on the Portrayal of Motion." Louis B. Mayer, vice president of Metro-Goldwyn-Mayer, remembered Stanford's role in the origins of motion pictures in his talk titled "The Debt of Motion Pictures to the Early Researcher." Following other talks titled "The Cost and Value of Research," "Technique and Results of the Palo Alto Experiments," and "The Modern Movie Camera and its Performance," two commemorative tablets were unveiled. One was placed in the Memorial Court, where-Alex B. Frances, representing the Academy of Motion Picture Arts and Sciences; the second was placed at the stock farm site, about one hundred yards southwest of the Red Barn, where the Muybridge Studio once stood. Stanford comptroller Almon E. Roth made the concluding remarks.[322]

The celebration ended with dinner given by the Stanford University Board of Trustees honoring the representatives of the Academy of Motion Picture Arts and

[319]Harris Elwood Starr, "Thomas Starr King," *DAB*, V, Part 2, 403–405; *SD* 102, 72nd Cong., 1st Sess., *Acceptance and Unveiling of the Statues of Junipero Serra and Thomas Starr King. Presented by the State of California. Proceedings in the Congress and in Statuary Hall. United States Capitol. Mar 1, 1931.* SSN 9515, 1–63.

[320]A complete listing of the NSHC sorted by names is available on the Internet.

[321]LSJU Board of Trustees, the program read: "Semi-Centennial Celebration in Commemoration of the Motion Picture Research Conducted by Leland Stanford 1878–1879, with the Assistance of Edweard J. Muybridge, John D. Isaacs, J.D.B. Stillman." LSJU, May 8, 1928. Participated in by Official Delegates from Academy of Motion Picture Arts and Sciences.   [322]Ibid.; on Wilbur, see Elliott, *Stanford University, the First Twenty-Five Years,* 579.

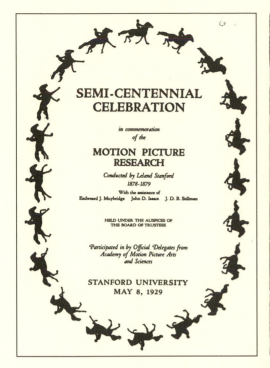

(clockwise from top left)

164. Program cover of the semi-centennial celebration of Leland Stanford's motion picture research, May 8, 1929. *Stanford University Archives.*

165. Bronze plaque in the Memorial Court and near the Red Barn commemorating Leland Stanford's photographic experiments in motion pictures, May 8, 1929. *Stanford University Archives.*

166. California Registered Historical Landmark 834, for the development of motion pictures—commemorative plaque, near the Red Barn on campus. *Stanford University Archives.*

Sciences and with remarks by William C. DeMille and Stanford president Ray Lyman Wilbur.

A pantheon of luminaries remembered the Governor for his ideas and support in making the world's first motion picture.

On April 30, 1983, a third plaque was placed at Stanford University on Campus Drive West, across from the Stanford Golf Course Driving Range, this one by the California Department of Parks and Recreation in cooperation with the Stanford Historical Society, Stanford E Clampus Vitus Alumni, and the Mountain Charlie Chapter 1850 of E Clampus Vitus, commemorating the motion picture research conducted by Eadweard Muybridge and Leland Stanford at the Palo Alto Stock Farm.[323]

Mountain of a Man

The people of California have named several natural landmarks for Leland Stanford to honor him for his service and gifts to the state. Four of them were mountains.

The first mountain named for Stanford was an 8,473-foot mountain in Placer County, about three miles west of Lake Tahoe and halfway between Tahoe City and Homewood. It was given the name Stanford Peak or Stanford Rock, and is known also as Stanford Mountain.[324]

On August 1, 1896, Stanford professor of fine arts Bolton Coit Brown climbed a prominent mountain in northeastern Tulare County towering 13,963 feet above sea level, higher than both the celebrated Jungfrau of Switzerland at only 13,642 feet and the Eiger at 13,025.[325] Bolton's peak was just west of the Sierra Crest where he and his wife, Lucy, earlier the same day had made the first ascent of Mount Davidson, in the Kings-Kern Divide. This was the first time since the Whitney survey party of 1864 that any reliable witness had investigated this mountainous region. Brown left behind on the summit a monument bearing the inscription "Mt. Stanford."[326]

When Brown later discovered that the name Stanford had already been given to the peak in Placer County, he suggested that if "his mountain" were disqualified

[323]Kenneth M. Castro and Eugene L. "Gino" Fambrini, comps., *E Clampus Vitus Plaques. A Compilation of historical Plaques with Photographs dedicated by the Ancient and Honorable Order of E Clampus Vitus, 1930–1995* (Oakland: ECV, 1995), 138.

[324]This promontory is situated at lat. 39' 07" 27° north and long. 120' 12" 10° west, in Frank R. Abate, ed., *Omni Gazetteer of the United States of America, Providing Name, Location, and Identification for Nearly 1,500,000 Populated Places, Structures, Facilities, Locales, Historic Places; and Geographic Features in the Fifty States, the District of Columbia, Puerto Rico, and U.S. Territories* (Vol. 9 of 11, Detroit: Omnigraphics, 1991), 388; and PC Transportation Planning Agency, "Placer County Bike Map," 1999.

[325]David L. Durham, *California's Geographic Names, A Gazetteer of Historic and Modern Names of the State* (Clovis, Calif.: WDP, 1998), 1078, gives Mt. Stanford in Tulare County as 13,963; Edward M. Douglas, comp., *Gazetteer of the Mountains of the State of California* (Preliminary [incomplete] ed.) (Wash.: [Federal Bureau of Surveys and Maps], 1929), 54, gives the elevation as 13,983. It is not unusual for the elevation of mountains or their geographic coordinates to vary from one source to another; they vary with climactic conditions, places from which measurements are made, and the technological differences in equipment.

[326]Hal Roth, *Pathway in the Sky: The Story of the John Muir Trail* (Berkeley: HNB, 1965), 36–37; Francis P. Farquhar, "Exploration of the Sierra Nevada," *CHSQ* 1925 4 (1): 47.

from bearing the Stanford name because of the former use of the name, then his be renamed Stanford University Peak.[327] Since there was no objection to having more than one peak named for a man, this was never done.[328]

The third mountain named for Leland Stanford—sometimes designated Stanford Point—is considerably lower than the others, rising only 6,659 feet above sea level. It is in Mariposa County, in the extreme southwestern corner of Yosemite National Park.[329] This peak appeared on the first Yosemite Valley map made by the U.S. Geological Survey in July 1907.[330] There is a Crocker Point, named for Charles Crocker, jutting 7,090 feet above sea level about a half-mile to the east.[331]

When the geological survey mapped the region of the Fresno and Mono county line in 1907–1909, Chief U.S. Geological Survey Geographer Richard Bradford Marshall (1869–1949) named four peaks surrounding the Pioneer Basin in memory of the four major Associates of the Central Pacific Railroad. Since then they have been known as the Pioneer Peaks.[332]

In 1911 one of the summits was named Stanford Peak by the U.S. Board on Geographic Names (BGN). In 1982 the BGN renamed it Mount Stanford.[333] At 12,826 feet, Mount Stanford is the highest of the four Pioneer Peaks, followed by Mount Crocker at 12,448, Mount Huntington at 12,393, and Mount Hopkins at 12,300.[334]

About a half-mile east of Mount Stanford is Stanford Lake, elevation 11,436 feet.[335] As the proverbial crow flies, Mount Crocker is about three miles southwest of Mount Stanford; Mount Hopkins lies about two miles southeast of Mount Crocker; and Mount Huntington is about two and a half miles west of Hopkins. Mounts Crocker and Hopkins also have lakes sharing the names of the mountains and Hopkins has a creek named for him.[336]

---

[327] Phil Townsend Hanna, comp., *The Dictionary of California Land Names* (LA: ACSC, 1946), 288.

[328] Brown's suggestion led Francis P. Farquhar to the mistaken conclusion that this mountain was named for LSJU, "Place Names of the High Sierra [Part III]," *SCB* 1925 12 (2): 126–147, 135 cited. The geographical coordinates of *this* Mt. Stanford are lat. 36' 42" 14° north, long. 118' 23" 41° west, in Abate, *Omni Gazetteer,* 388. Durham, *California's Geographic Names,* 1078, gives its coordinates as lat. 36' 42" 10° north and long. 118' 23" 40° west, as does the ACSC map titled "Eastern Sierra," 1997. Douglas, *Gazetteer,* 54, sets the coordinates at lat. 36' 42" 30° north and long. 118' 23" 30° west.

[329] Douglas, *Gazetteer,* 54; Peter Browning, *Place Names of the Sierra Nevada, From Abbot to Zumwalt* (Berkeley: WPr, 1986), 207.

[330] "Map of Yosemite Valley," Yosemite National Park, Calif., Mariposa County. DOI, USGS, Jul 1907 (surveyed in 1905–1906); see Browning, *Place Names of the Sierra Nevada,* 207; see also, Richard J. Hartesveldt, "Yosemite Valley Place Names," *YNN* 1955 34 (1): 17.

[331] ACSC map titled "Yosemite," 1988. The lat. of Stanford Point is 37' 42" 30° north and long. 119' 39" 55° west, in Abate, *Omni Gazetteer,* 388; Douglas, *Gazetteer,* 54, rounds off the long. at 119' 40".

[332] Erwin G. Gudde, *California Place Names: The Origin and Etymology of Current Geographical Names* (Berkeley: UCP, 1960 and 1969), 76.   [333] Nancy Dukes, Geographic Names Officer, USBGN, to the author, Apr 11, 2000.

[334] Hanna, *Dictionary of California Land Names,* 69, 126, 129, and 287–288; also, Douglas, *Gazetteer,* 54, agrees with Hanna's statistics on Mt. Stanford.   [335] Browning, *Place Names of the Sierra Nevada,* 207.

[336] The coordinates of the Pioneer Peaks according to Durham, *California's Geographic Names* (1076, 1077, and 1078) are as follows: Crocker, lat. 37' 29" 00° north, long. 118' 49" 30° west; Hopkins, lat. 37' 27" 50° north, long. 118' 48" 45° west; Huntington, lat. 37' 28" 10° north, long. 118' 46" 35° west; and Stanford, lat. 37' 29" 25° north, long. 118' 47" 45° west. See also U.S. DOI, Geological Survey, map of Mt. Abbot California Quadrangle, 1982.

September 30, 1990

Greetings!

I write you on the eve of Stanford's 100th year — the first-day-of-issue of this postal card which the United States Postal Service created in honor of Stanford's centennial.

This anniversary year offers a range of memorable programs, from the San Francisco Symphony to academic symposia. I personally invite you to return to campus for **Centennial Weekend September 28 – October 1, 1991**, the 100th anniversary of Opening Day. This will be an exceptional occasion, and registration materials will arrive in the Spring issue of *Stanford Magazine*.

For news of this card, and other Centennial events, please read the Stanford *Observer*, or contact the Centennial Year Office at **(415) 725-1991**.

Donald Kennedy
President

(*above*) 167. A 1944 postage stamp commemorating the seventy-fifth anniversary of the completion of the first transcontinental railroad. *Author's Collection.*

(*left*) 168. A 1990 fifteen-cent postcard (with verso text) commemorating the centennial of the opening of Stanford University. *Author's Collection.*

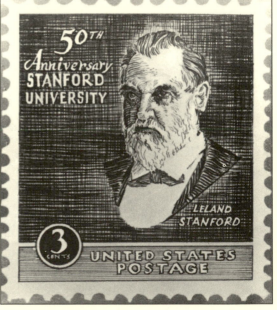

(*above*) 169. Three-cent stamp celebrating the fiftieth anniversary of the opening of Stanford University (founded in 1885). Not adopted. *Author's Collection.*

(*right*) 170. Three-cent stamp celebrating the fiftieth anniversary of the opening of Stanford University. Not adopted. *Author's Collection.*

United States Postage Stamps

Several attempts have been made to honor Stanford's work by the issuance of special commemorative postage stamps; some were issued, while others failed to win approval.

Liberty Ship S.S. Leland Stanford *and the Barkentine* Jane L. Stanford

Another honor accorded Stanford was the naming of one of 2,751 World War II Liberty ships the *S.S. Leland Stanford.* The keel of this 10,500-ton ship was laid by the California Shipbuilding Corporation in Wilmington, California, on June 23, 1942. Forty-two days later, on August 2, Mrs. Vera Thomas Petree, a Stanford alumna of the class of 1918 and secretary of the Stanford Women's Club of Los Angeles, christened the ship. It was the fifty-third Liberty ship launched by the shipyard, which sent its first ship, the *S.S. John C. Fremont*, down the ways on September 27, 1941, after 126 days in the making.[337]

After twenty-five years of service, the *S.S. Leland Stanford* was scrapped in Oakland, California, in August 1967.[338]

Jane Stanford was also honored by having a ship named for her. On December 20, 1892, the largest sailing vessel ever built in California was launched from the Bendixsen Shipyard at Fairhaven, on the Humboldt Peninsula.[339] Named the *Jane L. Stanford*, this barkentine had a lumber capacity of 1,250,000 board feet. The ship was owned by John J. Smith, a prominent San Francisco shipowner, but there is no indication of why it was named for Jane Stanford.[340]

At one time the *Jane L. Stanford* was ranked as "the proudest member of the American Merchant Fleet to China and the South Seas."[341] Sailors who manned this ship could tell blood-curdling tales of her adventures and escapades, including being attacked by pirates on the Yellow Sea. The *Jane L. Stanford* was known for her speed. She made passage in 1920 from Chin-wang-tao, North China, to Royal Roads, Victoria, in only forty-two days.[342] Her last trip, with Capt. Patrick Alexander McDonald in command, was to North China with lumber for the Robert Dollar Company.[343]

---

[337] "Commemorating Stanford's Founder," *SAR* 1942 44 (1): 13; "Ship Named for Founder," ibid., 1943 44 (8): 1.

[338] Inter. with Richard Hill, volunteer oiler on the *Jeremiah O'Brien*, Mar 11, 1999.

[339] *Humboldt Standard*, Dec 20, 1892; *Daily Humboldt Times*, Dec 21, 1892; John Mathewson Eddy, *In the Redwoods Realm* (SF: S & C, 1893, repr. 1987), 47. There is a photo of the ship on p. 49. A photograph taken on launching day is in Jim Gibbs, *West Coast Windjammers In Story and Pictures* (NY: BoB, 1968), 83. For a detailed description of the ship and of her launching, see Wallace E. Martin, comp., *Sail & Steam on the California Coast* (SF: NMMA, 1983), 221.

[340] *Daily Humboldt Times*, Dec 21, 1892; *SFCD*, 1892, 1275.

[341] Gordon L'Allemand, "The Luck of the Jane L. Stanford," *LA Times Sunday Magazine*, Jun 5, 1927.

[342] Capt. Patrick Alexander McDonald, "Some interesting details concerning the fate of once-famous ships," *SPSNCM* Jul 1929 12 (116): 181–182. [343] L'Allemand, "The Luck of the Jane L. Stanford."

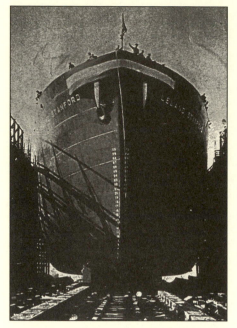

171. Liberty ship *S.S. Leland Stanford. California Shipbuilding Corporation.*

172. Barkentine *Jane L. Stanford. Capt. Patrick Alexander McDonald.*

This ship was rated at a Paris International Exposition as the finest American-built cargo vessel. It was reported that she sailed around the world eleven times during her thirty-seven-year life and touched at every port of call "under the sun."[344] In 1926 the elderly *Jane L. Stanford* became a fishing barge. While anchored in Santa Barbara, at 3:30 A.M. on the morning of August 30, 1929, the ship was run down by the White Flyer Line steam passenger-freighter *Humboldt*, named, ironically, for the bay where the *Jane L. Stanford* was built. (The captain of the *Humboldt* insisted that the *Jane L. Stanford* had no lights on at the time of impact.[345]) The Coast Guard cutter *Tamaroa* towed the badly damaged ship to Skunk Point on Santa Rosa Island and there blew it up with wrecking mines on September 19, though partly submerged pieces of the wreckage were reported still visible the next day.[346] Remains of the ship are still to be found scattered in the water and along the beach, now part of Channel Island National Marine Sanctuary and Channel Island National Park.[347]

[344]Ibid.   ·   [345]*SBar Morning Press*, Aug 31, 1929.

[346]Inter. with Robert Schwemmer, cultural resources coordinator, CINMS/CINP, Mar 1, 2000; for a hist. of the *Jane L. Stanford*, see Robert Schwemmer, "Seventy Year Search for Jane, 1929–1999," *SBBMMC* 1999 (Sep): 1–4. See U.S.C.G. log of the *Tamaroa* and other CG records for details of the towing and the destruction of the wreckage, NARA, Pacific Region (San Miguel, Calif.). See also U.S. Pacific Coast Shipwreck Database. This database is owned by Fred Gamble, Channel Crossings Marine Education, and Robert Schwemmer. John Lyman, "Pacific Coast-Built Sailors," *MD*, May 17, 1941, p. 2.

[347]There is a painting of the *Jane L. Stanford* at the CRMM, Astoria, Ore. Bob Schwemmer inter.

173. Thomas Welton Stanford.
Stanford University Archives.

Albany, New York, Hall of Fame

In 1946 Leland Stanford was honored by the capital city of the state of his birth with election to the Albany Hall of Fame, where he was designated an "Empire Builder."[348] At the time of this election, there was a total of only eighteen New Yorkers so honored, so we find Leland Stanford associated with many of the luminaries of New York history, among them Bret Harte, Philip Livingston, Philip Schuyler, and Stephen van Rensselaer.[349]

A Tribute by Leland Stanford's Favorite Brother

Eighty-six-year-old Thomas Welton, the youngest and last to die of the six Stanford brothers, died in Melbourne on August 28, 1918.[350] He paid a touching tribute to the Governor in choosing the following words for the headstone shared with his wife, Minnie, in the Methodist section of the Melbourne General Cemetery:

> Youngest brother of the late Senator LELAND STANFORD Founder of
> the Leland Stanford Junior University of California U.S.A.

No greater tribute was ever paid the Governor than wanting to be remembered for nothing other than being *his* brother.

---

[348]Hatch, John Davis, Jr. [LS election to Albany, NY Hall of Fame], *ACHAR* 1948 7 (2): 1.
[349]Ibid.
[350]Potts and Potts, "Thomas Welton Stanford," 196 and 208; Stanford, *Stanford Genealogy*, 26.

In Memoriam

Prominent Personalities in the Life of Leland Stanford

[Listed Chronologically by Date of Death]

Elvira Stanford, Leland's sister (July 3, 1815–April 16, 1816), age 9 months.

Anna Maria Lathrop [I], Jane's sister (December 2, 1826–January 21, 1830), age 3.

Jerome Bonaparte Stanford, brother of Leland (June 21, 1829–November 8, 1838), age 9.

Dyer Lathrop, Jane Stanford's father (May 14, 1788–April 19, 1855), age 67.

DeWitt Clinton Stanford, Leland's brother (May 15, 1826–April 18, 1862), age 35.

Josiah Stanford, father of Leland (February 28, 1795–April 19, 1862), age 67.

Theodore DeHone Judah (March 4, 1826–November 2, 1863), age 37.

Abraham Lincoln (February 12, 1809–April 15, 1865), age 56.

Elizabeth (Phillips) Stanford, mother of Leland (April 14, 1791–February 25, 1873), age 81.

Edwin Bryant Crocker (April 26, 1818–June 24, 1875), age 57.

Mark Hopkins (September 1, 1813–March 29, 1878), age 64.

David Douty Colton (July 17, 1832–October 9, 1878), age 46.

Jane Ann (Shields) Lathrop, Jane's mother (May 16, 1803–September 4, 1882), age 79.

Daniel Shields Lathrop, Jane's brother (April 13, 1825–February 13, 1883), age 57.

Leland [DeWitt] Stanford, Jr. (May 14, 1868–March 13, 1884), age 15.

Hiram Ulysses Simpson Grant (April 27, 1822–July 23, 1885), age 63.

Charles Stanford, brother of Leland (April 26, 1819–August 24, 1885), age 66.

Jennie M. (Easton) Crocker, wife of Fred Crocker (June 25, 1858–February 25, 1887), age 28.

Aaron Augustus Sargent (October 28, 1827–August 14, 1887), age 59.

Charles Crocker (September 16, 1822–August 14, 1888), age 65.

Henry Vrooman (July 25, 1844–April 8, 1889), age 44.

Florence Eliza "Lizzie" (Hull) Grant (August 10, 1862–August 8, 1889), age 26.

Mary Ann (Deming) Crocker, Charles Crocker's wife (November 26, 1827–October 27, 1889), age 61.

Josiah Stanford, brother of Leland (March 5, 1817–May 14, 1890), age 73.

Wilson "Wilsie" Grissim Taylor (February 17, 1865–December 28, 1890), age 25.

George Hearst (September 3, 1820–February 28, 1891), age 70.

Mary Frances (Sherwood) Hopkins Searles (March 8, 1818–July 25, 1891), age 73.

Lorenzo Sawyer (May 23, 1820–September 7, 1891), age 71.

Moses Hopkins (January 19, 1817–February 2, 1892), age 75.

Anna Maria (Lathrop) [II] Hewes, Jane's sister (September 22, 1832–August 3, 1892), age 59.

Joseph Augustine Benton (May 7, 1818–April 8, 1892), age 73.

Creed Haymond (April 22, 1836–January 13, 1893), age 56.

Rutherford Birchard Hayes (October 4, 1822–January 17, 1893), age 70.

James Gillespie Blaine (January 31, 1830–January 27, 1893), age 62.

Amasa Leland Stanford (March 9, 1824–June 20/21, 1893), age 69.

Frederick Ferdinand Low (January 30, 1828–July 21, 1894), age 66.

Frank Morrison Pixley (January 31, 1825–August 11, 1895), age 70.

Alban Nelson Towne (May 26, 1829–July 16, 1895), age 66.

Marcus Derckheim Boruck (May 29, 1834–June 26, 1895), age 61.

Charles Frederick Crocker (December 26, 1854–July 17, 1897), age 42.

Henry Clay Lathrop, Jane's brother (May 20, 1844–April 3, 1899), age 54.

Stephen Johnson Field (November 4, 1816–April 9, 1899), age 82.

Lloyd Tevis (March 20, 1824–July 24, 1899), age 75.

Collis Potter Huntington (October 22, 1821–August 13, 1900), age 78.

Benjamin Harrison (August 20, 1833–March 13, 1901), 67.

Harvey Willson Harkness (May 25, 1821–July 10, 1901), age 80.

Margaret Eleanor (Rhodes) Crocker, wife of Edwin Crocker (February 25, 1822–December 1, 1901), age 79.

Herbert Charles Nash (August 25, 1857–June 7, 1902), age 44.

Julia Boggs (Dent) Grant (January 26, 1826–December 14, 1902), age 76.

James Madison Bassett (November 9, 1830–April 24, 1903), age 72.

Asa Phillips Stanford, brother of Leland (January 16, 1821–May 6, 1903), age 82.

Adam Grant (December 27, 1828–March 21, 1904), age 75.

Eadweard Muybridge (Edward James Muggeridge) (April 9, 1830–May 8, 1904), age 74.

Ellen M. (White) Colton (June 10, 1836–February 10, 1905), age 68.

Jane Eliza[beth] (Lathrop) Stanford (August 25, 1828–February 28, 1905), age 76.

Nicholas T. Smith (November 19, 1829–April 23, 1907), age 77.

Stephen Grover Cleveland (March 18, 1837–June 24, 1908), age 71.

Ariel Lathrop, Jane's brother (December 30, 1830–October 11, 1908), age 77.

William Morris Stewart (August 9, 1827–April 23, 1909), age 81.

Darius Ogden Mills (September 25, 1825–January 3, 1910), age 84.

Charles Gardner Lathrop, Jane's brother (March 11, 1849–May 24, 1914), age 65.

David Hewes (May 16, 1822–July 23, 1915), age 93.

Stephen Thornton Gage (March 7, 1831–September 30, 1916), age 85.

Thomas Welton Stanford, Leland's brother (March 11, 1832–August 28, 1918), age 86.

Edward Francis Searles (July 4, 1841–August 6, 1920), age 79.

James Harvey Strobridge (April 23, 1827–July 27, 1921), age 94.

Edward Robeson Taylor (September 24, 1838–July 5, 1923), age 84.

Cornelius Cole (September 17, 1822–November 3, 1924), age 102.

Jerome Bonaparte Stanford, Philip's son (October 8, 1846–April 18, 1929), age 82.

David Starr Jordan (January 19, 1851–September 19, 1931), age 80.

Timothy Nolan Hopkins (March 2, 1859–January 1, 1936), age 76.

Josiah Winslow Stanford (August 24, 1864–September 10, 1937), age 73.

Frank Shay (November 8, 1855–December 21, 1940), age 85.

Mary "May" Kellogg (Crittenden) Hopkins (June 6, 1863–October 14, 1941), age 78.

Joseph Donohoe Grant (March 29, 1858–February 19, 1942), age 83.

Bertha Berner (July 12, 1861–March 11, 1945), age 83.

Lydia Kellogg Hopkins (March 27, 1887–January 8, 1965), age 77.

Douglas Grant (August 7, 1887–March 17, 1966), age 78.

A SELECT BIBLIOGRAPHY
OF WORKS CITED

He who shall hereafter write the biography of Governor Stanford will find his best material for gauging the mind of Stanford in his written papers and speeches in the Leland Stanford University.
— Frank Pixley, *San Francisco Argonaut,* June 26, 1893

OUTLINE OF CONTENTS

Among the obstacles to writing a biography of Leland Stanford is that many essential documents have been lost or destroyed. Jane Stanford did posterity and history an unforgivable disservice by burning most of her personal letters from her husband, letters that would have filled many of the gaps in our understanding of him. She had two bundles of letters written by him between 1852 and 1855 when he was in California and she in New York, all numbered and kept safe in an attic in her house. Shortly after the Governor died, she had her secretary, Bertha Berner, burn all of them. Jane explained—in the words of her biographer—that she could not endure the thought of strangers ever reading them—"the outpourings of two young hearts." Largely because of Jane, not a single Stanford letter now survives regarding his first three years in California.

Jane Stanford's second incidence of record-burning was even worse. She had kept a journal from 1881 until 1897, when she destroyed all but two entries, which she turned over to David Starr Jordan.

It is believed, erroneously, that all the Central Pacific Railroad files were burned in the San Francisco conflagration of 1906. Many valuable records of the Pacific Improvement Company and other companies owned and controlled by the Central/Southern Pacific Associates are still safely stored in the Stanford University Libraries and in the Union Pacific Railroad archives. Many Union Pacific records, and—after its merger into the Union Pacific in 1996—Southern Pacific Company records (with the records of all its railroads) have been deposited at the Nebraska State Historical Society.

There are, however, scores of Stanford's letters to a variety of recipients preserved in the various collections in the Stanford University Archives and elsewhere. Many of the letters from Huntington to Hopkins, along with other railroad records, were being used by Timothy Hopkins at his Menlo Park home and there escaped the 1906 fire in San Francisco.

George Thomas Clark's 1931 life of Stanford is incomplete as a biography. The author knew nothing of men like the accomplished engineer Henry Root; he hardly touched upon the various railroad-owned construction companies; and he barely recognized Stanford's position in the Occidental & Oriental Steamship Company. Nor did he have access to the material contained in Bertha Berner's biography of Mrs. Stanford—other than information gleaned from a few interviews with Berner—which was published three years after Clark's work. Yet he did give us a useful source book. He quotes in their entirety a number of letters that Stanford wrote during his school days, many of them never seen again after Clark used them. These letters have been used in the present work.

An almost untapped source of information is a series of over thirty bound volumes of family scrapbooks, filled with newspaper clippings from all over the country on a wide variety of subjects. The collectors were selective, so most of the clippings treat their subject favorably. From the hundreds of editorials in this collection one can retrace many of Stanford's steps and reconstruct a number of controversies surrounding his political career.

The only thoroughly anti-Stanford diatribe found was published in 1876 by Charles Edward Pickett, editor of the San Francisco News Bureau. This is a fifteen-page pamphlet titled *The California King: His Conquests, Crimes, Confederates, Counsellors, Courtiers, and Vassals. Stanford's Post-Prandial New-Year's Day Soliloquy*. It is now found in a collection of Southern Pacific Railroad pamphlets at the Stanford Library. Other criticisms of Stanford—not taken seriously by students of his life—are found in the "poetry" of Ambrose Gwinett Bierce, not just Stanford's foe, but—so say many—the enemy of all mankind!

As in the life of any prominent public man, the act of judging evidence in order to separate fact from fiction is a challenging undertaking. The historian's role as detective is taxed to the limit by Hubert Howe Bancroft's puzzling *History of the Life of Leland Stanford:A Character Study*—a romanticized sketch of the life of Stanford—which he left in manuscript form in the Bancroft Library and which was not published until 1952. This impressionistic and adulatory sketch of Stanford's career was unworthy of Bancroft and his "history factory." Two decades later, in his *Retrospection, Political and Personal* (New York: The Bancroft Company, 1912), 238–239, Bancroft evened the score over a grievance against Stanford, presumably over the latter's cancellation of his subscription to Bancroft's *Chronicles of the Builders of the Commonwealth*. In his later work Bancroft described the California senator as pure "pose and piety." His "Asiatic eyes" were placed too close together and "rolled heavenward in hypocritical ecstasy whenever he wished to be impressive." In his earlier work, Bancroft felt that Stanford's founding of his university was enough in itself to make his life worth recording, but in the latter piece he said that in default of an heir, Stanford gave his money to found a university so as to make high crime respectable. Most eulogists inclined toward Bancroft's earlier view of Stanford; unlike Bancroft, they had no loss of revenue to prompt a later reevaluation.

Bancroft's *History of the Life of Leland Stanford* included among its contributors a half-dozen of Stanford's closest associates, as well as Stanford himself. This manuscript mixes fact, adulation, and sheer nonsense in a way that leaves the historian-detective unsure of its reliability. A judicious use of the data contained in it, however, does provide some insight into the life of Stanford.

1. Manuscript Collections
(Collections and Guides to Collections)

Allyne, John D. Manuscript 43. California Historical Society. 11 folders. Folder 1 used.

Bancroft, Hubert Howe. Papers. Bancroft Library, University of California, Berkeley.

California Academy of Sciences. *Minute Books,* January 15, 1872–July 20, 1874.

California State Railroad Museum Library. Manuscript 1.92. Central Pacific Railroad. Chinese Payroll, 1865.

California State Railroad Museum Library. Manuscript 10. Superintendent of Motive Power and Machinery (Pacific System) Letters, 1890–1900. 1896 folder used.

Casement, John S. and Frances J. "The John Stephen and Frances Jennings Casement Papers, 1857–1928." Accession Number 308, American Heritage Center, University of Wyoming.

Catlin, Amos Parmalee. Manuscript Collection. California State Library.

Clark, George Thomas. Papers. Stanford University Archives.

Cole, Cornelius. Papers. Department of Special Collections, University of California, Los Angeles.

Colton, David Douty. Manuscript Collection. Bancroft Library.

Crocker, Charles. Papers. Bancroft Library. The main biographical record in these papers is the account of a Bancroft researcher's interview with Crocker. The collection contains several versions of notes compiled for Bancroft's *Chronicles of the Builders of the Commonwealth*.

Curry, John. Manuscript. "Political History of California," California State Library.

Davidson, George. Papers. Bancroft Library.

Edwards, Mrs. Orville DeForest. Collection. Dobbs Ferry, New York, containing Esther Osborne's "Notebook of Reminiscences."

Ellis, Henry H. Papers. Bancroft Library.

Fisher, Helen Dwight. Manuscript. "Leland Stanford, 1824–1893."

Hefting, Eugene. Papers. Sacramento City Archives and Museum Collection Center.

Hill, Roscoe R. Papers. Roy W. Hebard. *The Story of the First Transcontinental Railroad*. The Panama Railroad, 1855–1955. Bancroft Library.

Hill, Thomas. *History of the "Spike Picture," and why it is still in my Possession*. [San Francisco]: R.R. Hill, [1905?].

Hopkins, Moses. Interviews of Moses Hopkins, much of them dealing with his brother Mark Hopkins, March 24 and 28, April 4 and 18, June 9 and 15, 1891, and some undated. Bancroft Library.

Hopkins, Timothy Nolan. Papers. "Timothy Hopkins Chronological Record Book, June 15, 1889, to April 28, 1928." Stanford University Archives.

Huneker, James G. Manuscripts, 1860–1921. "Estate of Leland Stanford." Stanford University Archives.

Huntington, Collis Potter. Autobiography: a dictation. 1889? Recorded by David R. Sessions. Bancroft Library.

Huntington, Collis Potter. Papers. Bancroft Library.

Index to the Abraham Lincoln Papers. Washington: Manuscript Division, Library of Congress, 1960. References to Leland Stanford in the microfilm series are found in reels 17 (1861), 20 (1861), 29 (1861), 33 (1862), 37 (1862), 41 (1862), 42 (1862), 58 (1863), and 62 (1863).

Judah, Anna Ferona (Mrs. Theodore D.). Manuscript C–D 800:3, December 14, 1889. Seventeen pages of correspondence with Amos Parmalee Catlin and David R. Sessions concerning her husband, for Hubert Howe Bancroft's History Company publication. Bancroft Library.

Lincoln, Abraham. Papers. Brown University Library.

Lincoln, Robert Todd. Collection of the Papers of Abraham Lincoln. Library of Congress.

Low, Frederick F. Papers. Bancroft Library.

McKinley, William. *Index to the William McKinley Papers*. Washington: Library of Congress, 1963.

McKinley, William. *William McKinley Papers*. References to Justice Stephen Johnson Field in Series 2, reels 17 and 18 (1897).

Muybridge, Eadweard. Muybridge Manuscripts. Bancroft Library.

Nash, Herbert C. "Dictation by H. C. Nash on Leland Stanford, 9/14/89." Bancroft Library.

Ross, Edward P. Papers. *Guide to a Microfilm Edition*. Harold L. Miller and Lynn Buckley Aber, eds. Madison: State Historical Society of Wisconsin, 1986.

Selected Papers of the South Aurora Silver Mining Company, Limited. Companies Registration Office, Bush House, London; *The South Aurora Silver Mining Company, Limited. Prospectus*. London: Wertheimer, Lea and Co., 1870.

Shay, Frank. "A Lifetime in California 1860–1939. People. Events. Politics. The First Overland Railroad and its Builders. Brief Historical Review." Stanford University Archives. Contains a great deal of material on Leland Stanford, written by one of Stanford's private secretaries.

Stanford, Jane Lathrop. Papers. Stanford University Archives.

Stanford, Josiah. Papers. John Miller interview of Josiah Stanford, July 18, 1889, for Hubert H. Bancroft. Bancroft Library.

Stanford, Leland. Manuscript. Bancroft Library.

Stanford, Leland. Papers. Stanford University Archives.

Stanford, Leland, Junior. Papers. Stanford University Archives.

Stanford, Thomas Welton. Papers. Stanford University Archives.

Treat, Archibald J. Papers. Stanford University Archives.

Vrooman, Henry. Manuscript. "Honorable Leland Stanford." In Hubert Howe Bancroft Papers. Bancroft Library.

2. REFERENCE WORKS

(*Archival and Research Guides, Rosters, and Indices*)

A. Books

Administrative Office of the U.S. Courts. *Judges of the United States*. Washington: Bicentennial Committee of the Judicial Conference of the United States, 1978.

Attinger, Victor, ed. *Dictionnaire Historique & Biographique de la Suisse*. Neuchtel: Administration du Dictionnaire Historique et Biographique de la Suisse, 1928 and 1932.

Bailey, Liberty Hyde, and Ethel Zoe Bailey, comps. *Hortus Third, A Concise Dictionary of Plants Cultivated in the United States and Canada*. New York: Macmillan Publishing Co., [1934], 1976.

California. Historical Records Survey. *Guide to Depositories of Manuscript Collections in the United States: California*. Los Angeles: Southern California Historical Records Survey Project [Work Projects Administration], 1941.

Cohen, Saul B., ed. *Columbia Gazetteer of the World*. 3 vols., New York: Columbia University Press, 1998.

Coy, Owen Cochran. *Guide to the County Archives of California*. Sacramento: California Historical Survey Commission, 1919.

Directory of Palo Alto, Mayfield, Menlo Park, The Campus. Palo Alto: The Times Publishing Co., December 1, 1904.

Heitman, Francis B. comp. *Historical Register and Dictionary of the United States Army, from its Organization, September 29, 1789, to March 2, 1903*. 2 vols., Washington: Government Printing Office, 1903.

Kiple, Kenneth F., ed. *The Cambridge World History of Human Disease*. Cambridge: Cambridge University Press, [1992], 1993.

Landau, Sidney L., ed.-in-chief. *International Dictionary of Medicine and Biology*. 3 vols., New York: John Wiley & Sons, 1986.

Lewis, Abraham, Jr., ed.-in-chief. *The Stanford Quad*. Vol. 1. San Francisco: H[enry] S[mith] Crocker, 1894. This issue was edited by the junior class at Stanford University.

Little, Elbert L. *The Audubon Society Field Guide to North American Trees. Western Region*. 2 vols., New York: Alfred A. Knopf, 1980.

McGraw-Hill Dictionary of Scientific and Technical Terms. 5th ed., New York: McGraw-Hill, 1994.

National Register of Historic Places 1966–1991. Cumulative List Through June 30, 1991. Nashville: American Association for State and Local History; Washington: National Park Service, 1991; Washington: National Conference of State Historic Preservation Officers, 1991.

Regnery, Dorothy. "French Bronze Horse Statue and the Palo Alto Stock Farm Horse Cemetery," April 24, 1984. One-page bibliography. Stanford University Archives.

Rocq, Margaret Miller, ed. *California Local History: A Bibliography and Union List of Library Holdings*. 2nd ed., Stanford: Stanford University Press, 1970.

Sibley, Robert, ed. *The Golden Book of California*. Berkeley: California Alumni Association, 1937.

Smith, Benjamin E., ed. *The Century Cyclopedia of Names, A Pronouncing and Etymological Dictionary of Names in Geography, Biography, Mythology, History, Ethnology, Art, Archaeology, Fiction, Etc., Etc., Etc.* New York: The Century History Co., 1894.

Spofford, Ainsworth R., ed. *American Almanac and Treasury of Facts, Statistical, Financial, and Political, for the Year 1879*. New York: The American News Co., 1879.

Teggart, Frederick John. *Catalogue of the Hopkins Railway Library*. Palo Alto: [no publisher given], 1895. Printed by the Commercial Publishing Co. of San Francisco. In Stanford University Archives. The *Railroad Gazette*, January 18, 1895, describes the collection's 3,000 books and about the same number of pamphlets. According to Teggart's *Catalogue*, the collection had more than 9,200 books and pamphlets. In March 1892 Timothy Hopkins presented to the Stanford Library his railroad library consisting of 667 bound volumes and about 1,000 pamphlets. *The* [Stanford] *Sequoia*, September 10, 1893.

The Official Railway Equipment Guide (Register). A Monthly Register of Rolling Stock Equipment of the Railways and Car Companies of North America. New York: The Railway Equipment and Publication Co., 1885–present.

Thrush, Paul W., ed. *A Dictionary of Mining, Mineral, and Related Terms*. Washington: U.S. Department of the Interior, 1968.

B. Periodicals

Baker, Hugh S. "'Rational Amusement in Our Midst,' Public Libraries in California, 1849–1859," *California Historical Society Quarterly* 1959 38 (4): 295–320.

Brayer, Herbert O. "Preliminary Guide to Indexed Newspapers in the United States, 1850–1900," *Mississippi Valley Historical Review* 1946 33 (2): 237–258.

Davis, William N. Newell, Jr. "Research Uses of County Court Records, 1850–1879, And Incidental Intimate Glimpses of California Life and Society," Part I, *California Historical Quarterly* 1973 52 (3): 241–263.

Hammond, George P. "Manuscript Collections in the Bancroft Library," *American Archivist* 1950 13 (1): 15–26.

Wenzel, Caroline. "Finding Facts about the Stanfords in the California State Library," *California Historical Society Quarterly* 1940 19 (3): 245–255.

Williams, Dawson, ed. "Obituary, Sir William Jenner," *The British Medical Journal* 1898 2 (October–December): 249–252.

3. COLLECTED WORKS
(Anthologies, Records, Minutes, Literature, and Poetry)

Angle, Paul M., comp. *New Letters and Papers of Lincoln*. Boston and New York: Houghton Mifflin Co., 1930.

Basler, Roy P., ed. *The Collected Works of Abraham Lincoln*. 8 vols., New Brunswick: Rutgers University Press, 1953.

Bierce, Ambrose. *The Collected Works of Ambrose Bierce*. Vol. 5, *Black Beetles in Amber*. New York: The Neale Publishing Co., 1911.

Boggs, Mae Hélène Bacon, comp. *My Playhouse was a Concord Coach, An Anthology of Newspaper Clippings and Documents Relating to Those Who Made California History During the Years 1822–1888*. Oakland: Howell-North Press, 1942.

Bürger, Gottfried August. *Le(o)nore*. 1813 ballad.

Emerson, Ralph Waldo. "History," in *The Selected Writings of Ralph Waldo Emerson*. Brooks Atkinson, ed. New York: The Modern Library, 1950.

Harte, Francis "Frank" Bret. *The Complete Poetical Works of Bret Harte*. Cabinet Edition. Boston: Houghton Mifflin Co., [1870], 1901.

Hemans, Felicia Dorothea (Browne). *The Forest Sanctuary. De Chatillon. With Other Poems*. Edinburgh and London: William Blackwood and Sons, [1825], 1854. This work has gone through several publications with varying accompanying poems and titles.

Homer [translated by Alexander Pope]. *The Iliad and Odyssey of Homer*. London: Frederick Warne and Co., 1894 (?).

Kipling, Rudyard. "How I got to San Francisco and took Tea with the Natives There," Chapter 13 of *From Sea to Sea, Letters of Travel, American Notes*. Garden City: Doubleday, Page & Co., 1914.

Miller, Joaquin [Cincinnatus Heine(r) Miller]. *Joaquin Miller's Poems*. 6 vols., San Francisco: Harr Wagner Publishing Co., 1917. "An Introduction," and Vol. I, Chapter 1, "Camps and Cabins."

Minutes of the Regents of the University of California, October 7, 1882. Office of the President, University of California, Oakland, California.

Occidental & Oriental Steamship Company Record. Minutes of the Board of Directors, 1874 to 1908. The Huntington Library.

Pacific Improvement Company Records. Stanford University Archives.

Shakespeare, William. *Merchant of Venice*.

Society of California Pioneers. Archives Records.

Society of California Pioneers. Marshal's Records.

4. UNITED STATES GOVERNMENT DOCUMENTS
(Executive, Legislative, and Judicial)
A. Executive

Department of Commerce. *Annual Report of the Commissioner of Patents for the Year 1858*. Washington: Government Printing Office, 1865.

Department of Commerce. *Annual Report of the Commissioner of Patents for the Year 1865*. 3 vols., Washington: Government Printing Office, 1865.

Department of Commerce. *Annual Report of the Commissioner of Patents for the Year 1868*. Washington: Government Printing Office, 1869.

Department of Commerce. *Annual Report of the Commissioner of Patents for the Year 1869.* Washington: Government Printing Office, 1871.

Department of Commerce. *Annual Report of the Commissioner of Patents for the Year 1879.* Washington: Government Printing Office, 1880.

Department of Commerce. *Official Gazette of the United States Patent Office* 1879 15 (9): 310.

Department of the Interior. *Population of the United States in 1860: Compiled from the Original Returns of the Eighth Census.* Washington: Government Printing Office, 1864.

Department of the Interior. *A Compendium of the Ninth Census (June 1, 1870).* Francis A. Walker, Superintendent of Census. Washington: Government Printing Office, 1872.

Department of the Interior. *Population of the United States in 1860; Compiled from the Original Returns of the Eighth Census, under the Direction of the Secretary of the Interior.* Joseph C. G. Kennedy, Superintendent of Census. Washington: Government Printing Office, 1864.

Treasury Department. Bureau of Customs. Collector of Customs of the Collection District of New York, Port of New York. Passenger List of the *Illinois*, arrival from Aspinwall, March 28, 1856.

Treasury Department. (Endorsement) No. 2. Report of Commissioners. Sept. 8th, 1864. "A" 1 to 31. Correspondence on determining the western boundary of the Sierra Nevada Mountains.

Treasury Department. Record Group 36, Bureau of Customs. Port of San Francisco. "Record of Arrival of Vessels Under and Over 20 Tons, March 26, 1849–December 30, 1851," National Archives and Records Administration, Federal Archives and Records Center, San Bruno, California.

Treasury Department. United States Coast Guard. Official records on the role of the Coast Guard in the demolition of the *Jane L. Stanford* in 1929. In National Archives and Records Administration, Pacific Region, San Miguel, California.

War Department. *United States Military Reservations, National Cemeteries, Military Parks, Title, Jurisdiction, Etc.* Washington: Government Printing Office, 1916.

B. Legislative
1. Congress

Congressional Globe, Thirty-fourth Congress, First Session (December 3, 1855, to August 18, 1856).

Congressional Globe, Thirty-seventh Congress, Second Session (December 12, 1861, to July 17, 1862).

Congressional Globe, Forty-second Congress, Second Session (December 4, 1871, to June 10, 1872).

Congressional Record, Forty-fourth Congress, First Session. *Senate Miscellaneous Document 85*, "Letter from C. P. Huntington, Vice-President of the Central Pacific Railroad Company, to Hon. George F. Edmunds, United States Senate, in Relation to a Bill to create a sinking-fund for the liquidation of the Government bonds advanced to the Central and Western Pacific Railroad Companies," April 3, 1876, 1–4.

Congressional Record, Forty-fourth Congress, First Session, Appendix (July 29, 1876), 235–245. Gilbert C. Walker of Georgia introduced a resolution (House Resolution 748) to apply the proceeds of all public land sales to education. On July 29, 1876, Congressman Henry William Blair of New Hampshire spoke in favor of this measure. Similar bills introduced by Blair passed the Senate on three occasions only to be killed in the House of Representatives.

Congressional Record, Forty-fourth Congress, Second Session (December 4, 1876, to March 3, 1877).

Congressional Record, Forty-ninth Congress, First Session (February 9, 1886), 1237. Stanford's first speech in the Senate, on the need of a new post office in San Francisco.

Congressional Record, Forty-ninth Congress, Second Session (February 16, 1887), 1804–1805. Leland Stanford speech on cooperative associations.

Congressional Record, Fiftieth Congress, First Session (May 25, 1888), 4615. Sen. Henry William Blair of New Hampshire proposed a constitutional amendment (Senate Resolution 86) requiring states to maintain free, non-sectarian schools for all children.

Congressional Record, Fifty-first Congress, First Session (February 25, 1890), 1687–1688. Stanford speech in favor of the Blair education bill.

Congressional Record, Fifty-first Congress, First Session (March 10, 1890), 2068. Stanford submitted a resolution to the Senate requesting that the committee on finance inquire into the possibility of making loans directly to farmers, with their real estate as security.

Congressional Record, Fifty-first Congress, First Session (May 23, 1890), 5169–5170. Stanford presented a bill to direct the Secretary of the Treasury to print $100 million in paper money secured by land at no more than 50 percent of the land value.

Congressional Record, Fifty-first Congress, First Session (June 11, 1890), 5922. On June 11, 1890, the Senate Committee on Finance postponed Stanford's money bill.

Congressional Record, Fifty-first Congress, Second Session (December 1, 1890), 667–668. Stanford introduced another money bill.

Congressional Record, Fifty-second Congress, First Session (December 7, 1891, to August 5, 1892).

Congressional Record, Fifty-third Congress, Special Session (March 4 to April 15, 1893).

2. House of Representatives

Campbell, Douglas, *Closing Argument of Douglas Campbell, Esq. in reply to Gov. John C. Brown, J. A. Davenport, Esq., and Major James Turner, before the Judiciary Committee of the House of Representatives, in regard to the title of the Texas and Pacific Railway Company to the property of the Memphis, El Paso and Pacific Railroad Company. April 24, 1878* (Washington: Thomas McGill & Co., 1878), 3. Committee on the Judiciary, Forty-fifth Congress, Second Session. This document was not published in the Serial Set.

"Contracts between Southern Pacific Railroad [*sic*] and other Companies," *House Executive Document 60,* Forty-ninth Congress, First Session (December 7, 1885, to August 5, 1886), February 4, 1886, 14 pp. Serial Set No. 2398.

"Indebtedness of Central Pacific and Western Pacific Railroads," *House Executive Document 238,* Fifty-fifth Congress, Third Session (December 5, 1898, to March 3, 1899), February 15, 1899, 9 pp. Serial Set No. 3812.

"Memorial of the Texas and Pacific Railway Company and the Atlantic and Pacific Railroad Company," *House Miscellaneous Document 6,* Forty-third Congress, Second Session (December 7, 1874, to March 3, 1875), December 8, 1874. Serial Set No. 1653.

Nimmo, Joseph, Jr., Chief, Bureau of Statistics, "Treasury Department, Report on the Internal Commerce of the United States, December 31, 1884," 1–63. "Description of Transcontinental Railroads, 37–63," *House Executive Document 7,* Part 2, Forty-eighth Congress, Second Session (December 1, 1884, to March 3, 1885). Serial Set No. 2295.

"Pacific Railroad Memorial of the Central Pacific Railroad Company of California," *House Miscellaneous Document 12,* Thirty-seventh Congress, Second Session (December 2, 1861, to July 17, 1862).

"Report of the Commissioner of the General Land Office, November 1, 1869," in 406-page "Report of the Secretary of the Interior," *House Executive Document 1,* Part 3, Forty-first Congress, Second Session. Serial Set No. 1414.

"Report of the Select Committee of the House of Representatives, appointed under the resolution

of January 6, 1873, to make inquiry in relation to the affairs of the Union Pacific Railroad Company, the Credit Mobilier of America, and other matters specific in said resolution and in other
resolutions referred to said Committee." Select Committee on Credit Mobilier and Union
Pacific Railroad, *House Report 78*, Forty-second Congress, Third Session. Published separately as
a 770-page book. Washington: Government Printing Office, 1873.

"Report on the Sinking Fund for the Several Pacific Railroad Companies; together with the Acts of
Congress, Decisions of Courts, and Documents relating to said Railroad Companies," Committee on the Judiciary, *House Report 440*, Forty-fourth Congress, First Session.

"Whitney's Railroad to the Pacific" (March 13, 1850), 2 vols. (1849–1850), I, 117 pp. *House Report
140*, Thirty-first Congress, First Session. Serial Set No. 583.

"Whitney's Railroad to the Pacific" (January 20, 1852), 10 pp. *House Report 101*, Thirty-second Congress, First Session. Serial Set No. 656.

3. Senate

"Acceptance and Unveiling of the Statues of Junipero Serra and Thomas Starr King. Presented by the
State of California. Proceedings in the Congress and in Statuary Hall. United States Capitol"
(March 1, 1931), 1–63. *Senate Document 102*, Seventy-second Congress, First Session (December
7, 1931, to July 16, 1932). Serial Set No. 9515.

"Arguments before the Committee on Military Affairs of the Senate for and against the bill (House
Resolution 1553) to lease Goat Island for a railway terminus, February 17, 1873" (January 18 and
19, 1873), *Senate Miscellaneous Document 75*, Forty-second Congress, Third Session (December 2,
1872, to March 3, 1873), 1–139. Serial Set No. 1546.

"Letter of the Secretary of the Interior, communicating, In compliance with a resolution of the Senate of the 5th instant, the annual reports of the several Pacific railroad companies." No. 2:
"Annual Report of the Central Pacific Railroad Company, of California, to the Secretary of the
Interior of the United States, for the Year Ending June 30, 1868." Includes names and residences
of stockholders. No. 6: "Annual Report of the Western Pacific Railroad Company, of California,
to the Secretary of the Interior, for the six months ending June 30, 1868" (January 7, 1869). *Senate
Executive Document 10*, Fortieth Congress, Third Session (December 7, 1868, to March 3, 1869).
Serial Set No. 1360.

"Memorial Addresses on the Life and Character of George Hearst, [*sic*] (A Senator from California,)
[*sic*] Delivered in the Senate and House of Representatives, March 25, 1892, and February 24,
1894," *Senate Miscellaneous Document 65*, 52nd Congress, 2nd Session (December 5, 1892, to
March 3, 1893), Vol. V. Serial Set *Senate Executive Document 10*, Fortieth Congress, Third Session
(December 7, 1868, to March 3, 1869). Serial Set No. 3068.

"Memorial Addresses on the Life and Character of Leland Stanford, A Senator from California,
Delivered in the Senate and House of Representatives, September 16, 1893, and February 12,
1894," *Senate Miscellaneous Document 122*, Fifty-third Congress, Second Session (December 4,
1893, to August 28, 1894), VI, 5–126. Serial Set No. 3172.

"Memorial of Asa Whitney, of the City of New York" (January 28, 1845), III, 1–4, *Senate Document
69*, 28th Congress, 2nd Session (December 2, 1844, to March 3, 1845). Serial Set No. 451; *Senate
Executive Document 10*, Fortieth Congress, Third Session, 1–47 (December 7, 1868, to March 3,
1869). Serial Set No. 1360.

"Memorial of the Chamber of Commerce of San Francisco, Remonstrating against The Passage of the
bill granting a part of Goat Island, in the harbor of San Francisco, to the Central Pacific Railroad
Company" (March 8, 1872), prepared by Robert B. Swain, President of the Chamber of Com-

merce, and Washington Bartlett, Secretary, on March 7, 1872. *Senate Miscellaneous Document 108*, Forty-second Congress, Second Session (December 4, 1871, to June 10, 1872). Serial Set No. 1482.

Pacific Railway Commission. "Testimony Taken by the United States Pacific Railway Commission, Appointed under the Act of Congress Approved March 3, 1887, Entitled 'An Act Authorizing an Investigation of the Books, Accounts, and Methods of Railroads Which Have Received Aid from the United States, and for Other Purposes,'" *Senate Executive Document 51*, Part 2. Fiftieth Congress, First Session (December 5, 1887, to October 20, 1888).

The nine volumes of testimony were bound in five, with the *Report* as Part 1, Vol. 2. The Serial Set numbers listed correspond to the five bound volumes. The following table identifies the nine volumes, parts, pages, and Serial Set numbers of all United States Pacific Railway Commission (USPRC) Records of the entire set:

USPRC Presidential Message and Commissioners' Report, Part 1, pp. 1–217. Serial Set No. 2505.

USPRC, Testimony, Vol. 1, Part 2, pp. 1–597. Serial Set No. 2505.

USPRC, Testimony, Vol. 2, Part 3, pp. 595–1011. Serial Set No. 2505.

USPRC, Testimony, Vol. 3, Part 4, pp. 1013–1716. Serial Set No. 2506.

USPRC, Testimony, Vol. 4, Part 5, pp. 1717–2330. Serial Set No. 2506.

USPRC, Testimony, Vol. 5, Part 6, pp. 2331–3088. Serial Set No. 2507.

USPRC, Testimony, Vol. 6, Part 7, pp. 3089–3629. Serial Set No. 2507.

USPRC, Testimony, Vol. 7, Part 8, pp. 3631–4431. Serial Set No. 2508.

USPRC, Testimony, Vol. 8, Part 9, pp. 4433–5394. Serial Set No. 2509.

USPRC, Testimony, Vol. 9, Index, pp. 5395–5561. Serial Set No. 2509.

The pagination in all volumes is continuous; to facilitate the location of material I have included volume numbers in note citations. All citations in the annotations after the first are abbreviated to the initial letters as in the following parentheses: *U.S. Pacific Railway Commission (USPRC)*, or *Report, U.S. Pacific Railway Commission (RUSPRC)*, with page numbers.

"Reimbursement of the State of California" [for Civil War expenditures]. Includes a ten-page reprint (5–14) of *House Report 1162* (June 10, 1935), Seventy-fourth Congress, First Session. *Senate Report 2446*, August 25 (legislative day, July 20), 1950, 1–3, Eighty-first Congress, Second Session (January 3, 1950, to January 2, 1951). Serial Set Nos. 11372 and 9888.

Report No. 778 by the Senate Committee on Pacific Railroads to accompany Senate Bill 2894, Vol. 4, Part 2 (February 20, 1896), 298 pp. Contains testimony by Collis P. Huntington on why "rich men" refused to invest with him and his Associates in the building of the transcontinental railroad. Fifty-fourth Congress, First Session (December 2, 1895, to June 11, 1896). Serial Set No. 3365.

"Resolutions of the Legislature of Pennsylvania, in favor of Whitney's plan for a railroad from Lake Michigan to the Pacific" (January 21, 1850), *Senate Miscellaneous Document 29*, Thirty-first Congress, First Session (December 3, 1849, to September 30, 1850), 2 vols. (1849–1850), I, 1–2. Serial Set No. 563.

4. Statutes-at-Large

The Pacific Railroad Acts of Congress, and Amendments, Carefully compiled from authenticated Copies for the Central Pacific Railroad Co. New York: Evening Post Steam Presses, 1876. A compilation of the Railroad Acts of 1862, 1863, 1864, 1865, 1866, 1868, 1869, 1870, 1873, and 1874.

10 *U.S. Statutes* 244–248. Thirty-second Congress, Second Session (December 6, 1852, to March 3, 1853), Chapter 145, *An Act to provide for the Survey of the Public Lands in California, the granting of Preemption Rights therein, and for other purposes*. Approved March 3, 1853.

11 *U.S. Statutes* 27. Thirty-fourth Congress, First Session (December 3, 1855, to August 18, 1856). Chapter 65, *An Act for the Construction of a Road from Fort Ridgley in the Territory of Minnesota, to the South Pass of the Rocky Mountains, in the Territory of Nebraska.* Approved July 22, 1856.

11 *U.S. Statutes* 162–163. Thirty-fourth Congress, Third Session (December 1, 1856, to March 3, 1857). Chapter 50, *An Act for the Construction of a Wagon Road from Fort Kearney via the South Pass of the Rocky Mountains and Great Salt Lake Valley, to the eastern Portion of the State of California, and for other Purposes.* Approved February 17, 1857.

12 *U.S. Statutes* 276. Thirty-seventh Congress, First Session (July 4, 1861, to August 6, 1861). Chapter 21, *An Act to Indemnify the States for Expenses incurred by them in Defence* [sic] *of the United States.* Approved July 27, 1861.

12 *U.S. Statutes* 489–498. Thirty-seventh Congress, Second Session (December 2, 1861, to July 17, 1862). Chapter 120, *An Act to Aid in the Construction of a Railroad and Telegraph Line from the Missouri River to the Pacific Ocean, and to secure to the Government the Use of the same for Postal, Military, and Other Purposes.* Approved July 1, 1862.

13 *U.S. Statutes* 356–365. Thirty-eighth Congress, First Session (December 7, 1863, to July 4, 1864). Chapter 216, *An Act to Amend an Act entitled "An Act to aid in the Construction of a Railroad and Telegraph Line from the Missouri River to the Pacific Ocean, and to secure to the Government the Use of the same for Postal, Military, and Other Purposes," approved July 1, 1862.* Approved July 2, 1864.

13 *U.S. Statutes* 504. Thirty-eighth Congress, Second Session (December 5, 1864, to March 3, 1865). Chapter 88, Section 2. *An Act to Amend an Act entitled "An Act to aid in the Construction of a Railroad and Telegraph Line from the Missouri River to the Pacific Ocean, and to secure to the Government the Use of the same for postal, military, and other Purposes," approved July first, eighteen hundred and sixty-two, and to amend an Act amendatory thereof, approved July 2, eighteen hundred and sixty-four.* Approved March 3, 1865.

14 *U.S. Statutes* 79–80. Thirty-ninth Congress, First Session (December 4, 1865, to July 28, 1866). Chapter 159, *An Act to amend An Act entitled "An Act to amend an Act entitled 'An Act to aid in the Construction of a Railroad and Telegraph Line from the Missouri River to the Pacific Ocean, and to secure to the Government the Use of the same for Postal, Military, and Other Purposes, approved July 1, 1862,' approved July 2, 1864."* Approved July 3, 1866.

14 *U.S. Statutes* 239–242. Thirty-ninth Congress, First Session (December 4, 1865, to July 28, 1866). Chapter 242, *An Act granting Lands to aid in the Construction of a Railroad and Telegraph Line from the Central Pacific Railroad, in California, to Portland, in Oregon.* Approved July 25, 1866.

14 *U.S. Statutes* 292–299. Thirty-ninth Congress, First Session (December 4, 1865, to July 28, 1866). Chapter 278, *An Act granting Lands to aid in the Construction of a Railroad and Telegraph Line from the States of Missouri and Arkansas to the Pacific Coast.* Approved July 27, 1866.

14 *U.S. Statutes* 356. Thirty-ninth Congress, First Session (December 4, 1865, to July 28, 1866). No. 40. *A [Joint] Resolution to extend the Time for the Construction of the first Section of the Western Pacific Railroad.* Approved May 21, 1866.

16 *U.S. Statutes* 56–57. Forty-first Congress, First Session (March 4, 1869, to April 10, 1869). No. 19. *Joint Resolution for the Protection of the Interests of the United States in the Union Pacific Railroad Company, the Central Pacific Railroad Company, and for other Purposes.* Approved April 10, 1869.

16 *U.S. Statutes* 573–579. Forty-first Congress, Third Session (December 5, 1870, to March 3, 1871). Chapter 122. *An Act to incorporate the Texas Pacific Railroad Company, and to aid in the Construction of its Road, and for other Purposes.* Approved March 3, 1871.

17 *U.S. Statutes* 485–509. Forty-second Congress, Third Session (December 2, 1872, to March 4, 1874). Chapter 226, *An Act making Appropriations for the legislative, executive and judicial Expenses of the Government for the Year ending June thirtieth, eighteen hundred and seventy-four, and for other Pur-*

poses. "War Department," 500–501. Discusses claims to be paid to states for "collecting, drilling, and organizing volunteers for the war of the rebellion." Approved March 3, 1873.

20 *U.S. Statutes* 56–61. Forty-fifth Congress, Second Session (December 3, 1877, to June 20, 1878). Chapter 96, *An Act to alter and amend the act entitled "An act to aid in the construction of a railroad and telegraph line from the Missouri River to the Pacific Ocean, and to secure to the Government the use of the same for postal, military and other purposes",* [sic] *approved July first, eighteen hundred and sixty-two, and also to alter and amend the act of Congress approved July second, eighteen hundred and sixty-four, in amendment of said first-named act.* Approved May 7, 1878.

24 *U.S. Statutes* 488–492. Forty-ninth Congress, Second Session (December 6, 1886, to March 3, 1887). Chapter 345, *An act authorizing an investigation of the books, accounts, and methods of railroads which have received aid from the United States, and for other purposes.* Approved March 3, 1887.

30 *U.S. Statutes* 652–714. Fifty-fifth Congress, Second Session (December 6, 1897, to July 8, 1898). Chapter 571, *An Act Making appropriations to supply deficiencies in the appropriations for the fiscal year ending June thirtieth, eighteen hundred and ninety-eight, and for prior years, and for other purposes.* Approved July 7, 1898. The Central Pacific settlement of its debt with the federal government is treated on 652.

C. Judicial
1. Federal Court Cases

Circuit Court of Appeals, Ninth Circuit. *United States v.* [Jane L.] *Stanford.* No. 246. 70 *Federal Reporter* 346–364, October 12, 1895. United States suit against the Stanford estate.

Circuit Court of the United States. District of California. *Southern Pacific v.* [Pierpont] *Orton.* 32 *Federal Reporter* 457–480, December 15, 1879. Deals with disputed land claims in the Mussel Slough matter.

Circuit Court of the United States. Northern District of California. Proceedings in the matter of the *Application of the United States Pacific Railway Commission to Compel Leland Stanford to answer certain interrogatories to him propounded by said Commission.* August 13–29, 1887. Bound in *United States Pacific Railway Commission,* VII, 4164–4250.

Circuit Court of the United States. Northern District of California. *United States v.* [Jane L.] *Stanford.* No. 12,053. Circuit Court, Northern District of California. 69 *Federal Reporter* 25–47. June 29, 1895. United States suit against Stanford estate.

District Court of the United States of America for the Northern District of California. *U.S. District Court vs. Robert Waterman and James Douglass.* Criminal Case Files, 1851–1912. Cases 1–21 (December 8, 1851 to January 1852). In Record Group 21, Federal Archives and Records Center, San Bruno, California.

District Court, District of Utah. *United States of America versus Southern Pacific Company, Central Pacific Railroad, and Union Trust Company of New York,* Case No. 3575 (Equity Case 420), Entry 3, "Combined Bankruptcy, Civil, and Criminal Case Files, 1880–1931," Boxes 362–372, in Record Group 21, National Archives and Records Administration, Rocky Mountain Region, Denver. The testimony is from a case brought in 1914 under the antitrust law of 1890 to compel the separation of the Central Pacific Railroad from the Southern Pacific Company. In the course of the testimony the history of the Southern Pacific Company was discussed in considerable detail. This case is generally known as the 1914–1915 Unmerger Case, synopsized in *Brief of Defendants.*

District Court. Certificate of Final Discharge of Bankruptcy. A. P. Stanford, February 18, 1879. Federal Archives and Records Center, San Bruno, California.

District Court. Certificate of Final Discharge of Bankruptcy. Josiah Stanford, May 14, 1878, filed January 14, 1879. In Federal Archives and Records Center, San Bruno, California.

District Court. District of California, in Bankruptcy. Docket Case No. 2449, in the Matter of Josiah Stanford, May 14, 1878. Federal Archives and Records Center, San Bruno, California.

District Court. District of California, in Bankruptcy. Docket Case No. 2694, in the Matter of A. P. Stanford, August 31, 1878. Federal Archives and Records Center, San Bruno, California.

District Court. Fourteenth District, Placer County. *Butterfield v. Central Pacific Railroad Co. of Cal.*, 14th District Court, Placer County, in "Transcript on Appeal," CSC No. 1837 (15683), 16–17. Reprinted in Sacramento Historical Society *Golden Notes* July 1969 15 (4): 1–9.

United States Court of Claims. *State of California v. United States*. No. 49912. *119 Federal Supplement*, 174–186 (March 2 to June 7, 1954). California case against the United States for reimbursement of money spent during the Civil War.

2. Supreme Court Cases

Supreme Court. Reports. Vol. 99. Cases Argued and Adjudged in the Supreme Court of the United States. October Term, 1878. Sinking-Fund Cases. *Union Pacific Railroad Company v. United States and Central Pacific Railroad Company v. Gallatin*. Cases to test the constitutionality of the Thurman Act (99 *U.S. Statutes* 700–769, May 5, 1879).

Supreme Court. Reports. Vol. 135. Cases Adjudged in the Supreme Court at October Term, 1889. Docket title *Thomas Cunningham, Sheriff of the County of San Joaquin, California, Appellant, v. David Neagle, Petitioner* (135 *U.S. Statutes* 1–99). Argued March 4 and 5, 1890. Decided April 14, 1890.

Supreme Court. Reports. Vol. 144. Cases Adjudged in the Supreme Court at October Term, 1891. Docket title *Logan v. United States* (144 *U.S. Statutes* 263–310). Argued January 26 and 27, 1892. Decided April 4, 1892.

Supreme Court. Reports. Vol. 161. Cases Adjudged in the Supreme Court at October Term, 1895. *United States v. [Jane L.] Stanford*. Appeal from the Circuit Court of Appeals for the Ninth Circuit. No. 783. Argued January 28 and 29, 1896. Decided March 2, 1896.

Supreme Court. Reports. Vol. 226. Cases Adjudged in the Supreme Court at October Term 1912. *United States v. Union Pacific Railroad Company*. Appeal from the Circuit Court of the United States for the District of Utah. No. 446, pp. 61–98 and 470–477. Argued April 19, 22, and 23, 1912. Decided December 2, 1912.

5. CALIFORNIA STATE GOVERNMENT DOCUMENTS
(*Executive, Legislative, and Judicial*)

A. Executive

Adjutant General. *Annual Report of the Adjutant-General of the State of California*, May 1, 1864–November 30, 1865.

Board of Railroad Commissioners. *Report of the Board of Railroad Commissioners of the State of California*. Beginning in 1880. Annual or biennial. Used reports from 1880 to 1900.

Department of Parks and Recreation. *California Historical Landmarks*. Sacramento: California Department of Parks and Recreation, 1979.

Department of Parks and Recreation. *Leland Stanford Mansion State Historic Park, Historic Structures Report*. Sacramento: Department of Parks and Recreation, April 1966.

Department of Parks and Recreation. *Leland Stanford Mansion State Historic Park: Historic Structures Report*. Sacramento: Department of Parks and Recreation, 1996.

Department of Parks and Recreation. *Stanford House State Historic Park, General Plan*. Sacramento: State Park and Recreation Commission, 1989.

Department of Parks and Recreation. *Stanford House State Historic Park, Interpretive Plan*. Sacramento: Department of Parks and Recreation, 1989.

Division of Beaches and Parks. Carroll Douglas Hall (Part 1), Carroll Douglas Hall and Hero E. Rensch (Part 2), Jack R. Dyson and Norman L. Wilson (Part 3), eds. *Old Sacramento, A Report on its Significance to the City, State, and Nation, with recommendations for the preservation and use of its principal historical structures and sites*. 3 vols., Sacramento: California Division of Beaches and Parks, 1958–1960.

Executive Records. California State Mining Bureau. *Annual Reports of the State Mineralogist*.

Executive Records. Governor's appointments, Vol. 1058. California State Archives.

Executive Records. Official Record, Executive Department, Administration of Governor [George C.] Perkins. Register of Official Transactions, 1880–1883. California State Archives, File F3639-10.

Governor's Office. Governor Leland Stanford Daily Journals and Diaries. 1862 F3637:4; 1863 F3637:5.

Secretary of State. Agreement of merger, on September 30, 1955, of the Southern Pacific Railroad with the Southern Pacific Company, a Delaware Corporation. #220752. File 1004, California State Archives.

Secretary of State. Amended Articles of Association of the Pacific and Atlantic Rail Road Company, dated September 6, filed September 14, 1853. File 144, California State Archives.

Secretary of State. Amended Articles of Association, Incorporation, Amalgamation and Consolidation of the Southern Pacific Railroad Company, dated October 31, filed November 3, 1892. File 821, California State Archives.

Secretary of State. Articles of Association and Consolidation of the California Southern Railroad Company and California Southern Extension Railroad Company, dated December 28, 1881, filed January 10, 1882. File 380, California State Archives.

Secretary of State. Articles of Association of the California Central Rail Road Co., signed April 4, filed April 5, 1857. File 67, California State Archives.

Secretary of State. Articles of Association of the California Central Rail Road Co., signed December 28, filed December 29, 1870. File 60, California State Archives.

Secretary of State. Articles of Association of the California Pacific Rail Road Co., Consolidation of San Francisco & Marysville Rail Road Co. & Sacramento & San Francisco Rail Road Co., signed January 6, filed January 10, 1865. File 37, California State Archives.

Secretary of State. Articles of Association of the California Southern Railroad Co., signed January 21, filed January 22, 1870. File 54, California State Archives.

Secretary of State. Articles of Association of the Central Pacific Rail Road, signed and filed June 28, 1861. This file is missing from the California State Archives. Sometimes designated Articles of Incorporation.

Secretary of State. Articles of Association of the Contract and Finance Company Incorporation Papers, signed and filed October 28, 1867. File 2024, California State Archives.

Secretary of State. Articles of Association of the Marysville Railroad Co., signed November 23, filed November 29, 1867. File 120, California State Archives.

Secretary of State. Articles of Association of the Pacific and Atlantic Rail Road Co., dated October 24, filed October 25, 1851. File 144, California State Archives.

Secretary of State. Articles of Association of the Pajaro Valley Rail Road Co., signed December 31, 1867, filed January 2, 1868. File 194, California State Archives.

Secretary of State. Articles of Association of the Placerville and Sacramento Valley Rail Road Co., signed December 16, filed December 18, 1869. File 146, California State Archives.

Secretary of State. Articles of Association of the Sacramento Valley Rail Road Co., signed August 14, filed August 16, 1852. File 186, California State Archives. This document was published as Articles of Association of the Sacramento Valley Rail Road Co., signed August 14, filed August 16, 1852, in pamphlet titled *Articles of Association and By-Laws of the Sacramento Valley Railroad Co., Together with an Estimate of the Gross Receipts of the Road when in Operation.* New York: Baker, Godwin & Co., 1853, 3–5. This sixteen-page pamphlet is bound as Pamphlet 6 in Volume 7 of 10 volumes of Pamphlets on California Railroads. Bancroft Library.

Secretary of State. Articles of Association of the San Francisco and Alameda Railroad Co., signed March 14, filed March 25, 1863. File 204, California State Archives.

Secretary of State. Articles of Association of the San Francisco and Oakland Rail Road Co., signed October 18, filed October 21, 1861. File 219, California State Archives.

Secretary of State. Articles of Association of the San Francisco Bay Railroad Co., signed and filed September 25, 1868. File 221, California State Archives.

Secretary of State. Articles of Association of the San Francisco, Alameda and Stockton Rail-Road Co., signed October 7, filed December 8, 1863. File 220, California State Archives.

Secretary of State. Articles of Association of the San Joaquin Valley Rail Road Co., signed February 4, filed February 5, 1868. File 241, California State Archives.

Secretary of State. Articles of Association of the Southern Pacific Branch Railroad Co., signed December 20, filed December 23, 1872. File 257, California State Archives.

Secretary of State. Articles of Association of the Southern Pacific Branch Railway Co., signed April 9, recorded April 10, and filed April 12, 1886. File 483, California State Archives.

Secretary of State. Articles of Association of the Southern Pacific Railroad Company, signed November 29, filed December 2, 1865. File 256, California State Archives.

Secretary of State. Articles of Association of the Terminal Central Pacific Railway Company, signed January 29, filed January 30, 1867. File 293, California State Archives.

Secretary of State. Articles of Association of the Western Pacific Railroad Company, signed December 11, filed December 13, 1862. File 304, Recorded in San Francisco City and County Recorder's Office, Book C, 752–754.

Secretary of State. Articles of Association, Amalgamation and Consolidation. "Made and executed on this the eleventh day of October A.D. 1870 by and between the San Francisco and San Jose Railroad Company of the first part, the Santa Clara and Pajaro Valley Railroad Company of the second part, the Southern Pacific Railroad Company of the third part and the California Southern Railroad Company of the fourth part. . . . Said parties do hereby amalgamate and consolidate themselves into a new corporation under the name and style of the Southern Pacific Railroad Company." This is part of Amended Certificate of Incorporation of the Southern Pacific Railroad Company, dated April 11, filed April 15, 1871. File 266, California State Archives.

Secretary of State. Articles of Association, Amalgamation, and Consolidation of the Los Angeles and San Pedro Railroad and the Southern Pacific Railroad, signed December 17, filed December 18, 1874. File 380, California State Archives.

Secretary of State. Articles of Association, Amalgamation, and Consolidation of the San Francisco and Alameda Rail Road Company and the San Francisco, Alameda and Stockton Rail Road Company, signed October 14, and filed October 15, 1864. File 217, California State Archives.

Secretary of State. Articles of Association, Amalgamation, and Consolidation of the Southern Pacific Railroad Company of the first part and the Southern Pacific Branch Railroad Company of the second part into a new Southern Pacific Railroad Company, signed August 12, filed August 19, 1873. File 258, California State Archives.

Secretary of State. Articles of Association, California Pacific Rail Road Company, Consolidation of the California Pacific Railroad Company and the California Pacific Extension Railroad Company, signed December 24, filed December 29, 1869. File 35, California State Archives.

Secretary of State. Articles of Association, California Pacific Rail Road Eastern Extension Company, signed May 22, filed May 23, 1871. File 57, California State Archives.

Secretary of State. Articles of Association, Incorporation, Amalgamation and Consolidation of the Southern Pacific Railroad Company, the San Jose and Almaden Railroad Company, the Pajaro and Santa Cruz Railroad Company, the Monterey Railroad Company, the Monterey Extension Railroad Company, the Southern Pacific Branch Railway Company, the San Pablo and Tulare Railroad Company, the San Pablo and Tulare Extension Railroad Company, the San Ramon Valley Railroad Co., the Stockton and Copperopolis Railroad Co., the Stockton and Tulare Railroad Co., the San Joaquin Valley and Yosemite Railroad Co., the Los Angeles and San Diego Railroad Co., the Los Angeles and Independence Railroad Co., the Long Beach, Whittier and Los Angeles County Railroad Co., the Long Beach Railroad Co., the Southern Pacific Railroad Extension Co., and the Ramona and San Bernardino Railroad Co., dated May 4, filed May 12, 1888. File 651, California State Archives.

Secretary of State. Articles of Association, of Amalgamation and Consolidation of The Western Pacific Railroad Co. and the San Francisco Bay Railroad Co., dated October 28, filed November 2, 1869. File 305, California State Archives.

Secretary of State. Articles of Association, of Amalgamation and Consolidation between the Central Pacific Railroad Co. of California and the Western Pacific Railroad Co., signed June 22, filed June 23, 1870. File 40, California State Archives.

Secretary of State. Articles of Association, of Amalgamation and Consolidation of the California and Oregon Railroad Co. and the Marysville Railroad Co., signed December 10, 1867, filed January 16, 1868. File 51, California State Archives.

Secretary of State. Articles of Association, of Amalgamation and Consolidation of the California and Oregon Railroad Co. and the Yuba Railroad Co., signed December 15, filed December 18, 1869. File 50, California State Archives.

Secretary of State. Articles of Association, of the California and Oregon Rail Road Co., signed June 29, filed June 30, 1865. File 52, California State Archives.

Secretary of State. Articles of Consolidation of the Central Pacific Railroad Company, and the (1) California and Oregon Railroad Company, (2) San Francisco, Oakland, and Alameda Railroad Company, and (3) the San Joaquin Valley Railroad Company, incorporated August 20, filed August 22, 1870. File 41, California State Archives.

Secretary of State. Articles of Consolidation of the Central Pacific Railroad Company of California with the Western Pacific Railroad Company, consolidated and filed June 22, 1870. File 40, California State Archives.

Secretary of State. Articles of Consolidation of the Southern Pacific Railroad Company and the Southern Pacific Branch Railroad Company, signed August 12, filed August 19, 1873. File 258, California State Archives.

Secretary of State. Articles of Incorporation and Affidavit of Treasurer of Market Street Cable Railway Company, signed and filed May 19, 1882. File 389, California State Archives.

Secretary of State. Articles of Incorporation of the California Southern Rail Road Company, signed October 19, filed October 23, 1880. File 331, California State Archives.

Secretary of State. Articles of Incorporation of the Ione Coal and Iron Company, signed January 25, filed February 1, 1877. File 4654, California State Archives.

Secretary of State. Articles of Incorporation of the Mayfield Bank & Trust Co., signed October 27, filed December 30, 1904. File A41756, California State Archives.

Secretary of State. Articles of Incorporation of the Northern Railway Company, signed and filed July 19, 1871. File 21, California State Archives.

Secretary of State. Articles of Incorporation of the Occidental and Oriental Steamship Company, signed November 25, filed November 28, 1874. File 6953, California State Archives.

Secretary of State. Articles of Incorporation of the Occidental and Oriental Steamship Company, dated April 30, filed May 8, 1917. File 84451, California State Archives.

Secretary of State. Articles of Incorporation of the Southern Development Company, dated and notarized January 31, endorsed with the Clerk of the City and County of San Francisco February 1, and filed February 3, 1881. File 12626, California State Archives.

Secretary of State. Articles of Incorporation of the Union Quartz Mining Company, dated April 11, filed April 19, 1855. File 10191, California State Archives.

Secretary of State. Articles of Incorporation of the Western Development Company, dated December 15, filed December 16, 1874. Recorded in City and County of San Francisco, Book 9, page 337. File 10729, California State Archives.

Secretary of State. Articles of Incorporation of the Western Development Company, signed Feb 11, filed Feb 16, 1911. File 64367, California State Archives.

Secretary of State. Articles of Incorporation of the Western Development Company, signed April 28, filed June 17, 1933. File 154404, California State Archives.

Secretary of State. Articles of [Reincorporation] of the Placerville and Sacramento Valley Railroad Co., signed June 4, filed June 12, 1862. File 156, California State Archives.

Secretary of State. Central Pacific Railroad Company of California extension from Sacramento to Goat Island, signed March 14, filed March 21, 1867. File 77, California State Archives.

Secretary of State. Certificate of Incorporation of the Oakland Water Front Company, signed March 28, filed April 1, 1868. File 6894, California State Archives.

Secretary of State. Certificate of the Governor Stanford Gold and Silver Mining Company, signed April 16, recorded in San Francisco, April 17, and filed April 18, 1863. File 5086, California State Archives.

Secretary of State. Designation of Agent for the State of California, relating to the Rocky Mountain Coal and Iron Company of Wyoming, signed October 3, filed October 4, 1906. File 47686, California State Archives.

Secretary of State. In the Matter of the State License Tax against Rocky Mountain Coal and Iron Company, signed by company president Charles G. Lathrop, on November 17, filed November 19, 1913. File 47686, California State Archives.

Secretary of State. New Articles of Association of the Sacramento Valley Railroad Company, signed October 21, filed October 25, 1853. File 174, California State Archives. This document was also published as Articles of Association of the Sacramento Valley Railroad Company, signed October 21, filed October 25, 1853, in a pamphlet titled *Articles of Association and By-Laws of the Sacramento Valley Railroad Co., Together with an Estimate of the Gross Receipts of the Road when in Operation*. New York: Baker, Godwin & Co., 1853, 5–7. This sixteen-page pamphlet is bound as Pamphlet 6 in Volume 7 of 10 volumes of Pamphlets on California Railroads. Bancroft Library.

Secretary of State. New Articles of Incorporation of the Western Development Company, signed and filed May 19, 1909. File 57371, California State Archives.

The Adjutant-General of the State of California, 1880. Vol. 3, 1872–1884, Table G, "Roster of Officers of the National Guard of California, July 31st, 1880."

Treasurer Reports, Vol. 2, 1861–92. *Annual Report of the State Treasurer for the Year 1862*. California State Library.

B. Legislative
1. Assembly

Assembly Journal. Fourth Session (January 3 to May 19, 1853), 344 (March 28, 1853). On the incorporation of California railroads and railroad rate structures.

Assembly Journal. Eleventh Session (January 2 to April 13, 1860), 40–74 (January 7, 1860). Governor John B. Weller's Annual Message, dated only by month and year.

Assembly Journal. Twelfth Session (January 7 to May 20, 1861), 6 (January 7, 1861), 782 (April 29, 1861). Charles Crocker in the California Assembly.

Assembly Journal. Fourteenth Session (January 5 to April 27, 1863), 34–56 (January 7, 1863). Governor Stanford's First Annual Message.

Assembly Journal. Fourteenth Session (January 5 to April 27, 1863), 83–84 (January 10, 1863). Discussion of and vote on President Abraham Lincoln's "Proclamation of Freedom."

Assembly Journal. Fifteenth Session (December 7, 1863, to April 4, 1864), 47–67 (December 9, 1863). Governor Stanford's Second Annual Message.

Assembly Journal. Sixteenth Session (December 4, 1865, to April 2, 1866), 608–609 (March 19, 1866), 665 (March 23, 1866), and 769 (March 30, 1866). Discussions of and votes on bills pertaining to the incorporation of railroads and railroad fares.

Assembly Journal. Nineteenth Session (December 4, 1871, to April 1, 1872), 114 (December 7, 1871). The introduction of an act to amend the May 20, 1861, state law on the incorporation and management of railroad companies.

Assembly Journal. Twentieth Session (December 1, 1873, to March 30, 1874), 394 (January 10, 1874), approval of the need for a committee to report on the need for a new state constitution; 413 (January 13, 1874), adoption of a resolution upon the need for a new state constitution, and 506 (January 29, 1874), vote on and adoption of an act to regulate fares and freights on the state's railroads.

Assembly Journal. Twenty-first Session (December 6, 1875, to April 3, 1876), 133–134 (January 11, 1876), introduction of the Archer bill to regulate freight and passenger rates on the state's railroads; 381 (February 29, 1876), passage of a modified Archer bill; 636 (March 30, 1876), note that the Senate had adopted a modified bill to provide for a state board of commissioners of transportation.

Assembly Journal. Twenty-second Session (December 3, 1877, to April 1, 1878), 102 (December 11, 1877), an abstract of the vote for and against holding a constitutional convention; 240 (January 22, 1878), results of the election to hold a constitutional convention; 340 (February 11, 1878), introduction of Assembly Bill 436, to implement the Constitutional referendum passed by the people of California; 416 (February 21, 1878), the bill passed the Assembly; 510 (March 5, 1878), it passed the Senate.

Assembly Journal. Twenty-fourth Session (January 3 to March 4, 1881), 195–204 (February 2, 1881), resolution requesting a presidential pardon for the Mussel Slough prisoners.

Assembly Journal. Twenty-sixth Session (January 5 to March 11, 1885), 102 (January 26, 1885), introduction of Assembly Bill 290, the "Stanford University" bill; 318 (February 17, 1885), adoption of the "Stanford University" bill; 586 (March 5, 1885), report that the Senate had passed the "Stanford University" bill.

Assembly Journal. 1970 Regular Session (January 5 to September 23, 1970). House Resolution 94, relating to the Stanford House in Sacramento, May 13, 1970.

Assembly Journal. 1973–74 Regular Session (January 8, 1973, to November 30, 1974), I, 162 (January 29, 1973). Introduction of Assembly Bill 183, relating to the Stanford House in Sacramento. The history of the bill until signed by the governor is listed on 209.

2. Senate

Senate Journal. Fourth Session (January 3, to May 19, 1853), 118 (February 16, 1853), the introduction of "An Act to Provide for the Incorporation of Railroad Companies," 329 (April 9, 1853), the bill was passed by the Assembly; 401 (April 23, 1853), the bill providing for the incorporation of California railroads and rate structures of the railroads was passed by the Senate and signed by the governor on April 22.

Senate Journal. Fifth Session (January 2, to May 15, 1854), 573 (May 9, 1854), introduction of a bill to amend the 1853 railroad law; 614 (May 13, 1854), the bill modifying the 1853 railroad law and lowering fares was passed by the Senate.

Senate Journal. Eleventh Session (January 2 to April 13, 1860), 36–70 (dated only January 1860). Gov. John B. Weller's Annual Message, received in the Senate on January 9.

Senate Journal. Thirteenth Session (January 6 to May 15, 1862), 523 (April 9, 1862), letters from Gov. Leland Stanford to Secretary of State William H. Steward and others regarding the defenses of the harbor of San Francisco.

Senate Journal. Fourteenth Session (January 5 to April 27, 1853), 27–48 (January 7, 1863), Governor Stanford's First Annual Message.

Senate Journal. Fifteenth Session (December 7, 1863, to April 4, 1864), 21–41 (December 9, 1863). Governor Stanford's Second Annual Message.

Senate Journal. Sixteenth Session (December 4, 1865, to April 2, 1866), 152 (January 12, 1866), deals with Senate Bill 103, to amend the statute of May 2, 1861, pertaining to the incorporation and management of California railroads.

Senate Journal. Twentieth Session (December 1, 1873, to March 30, 1874), 301–302 (January 12, 1874), Senate concurrence in Joint Resolution 18 calling for a seven-man committee—three from the Senate and four from the Assembly—to study the need for a constitutional convention to bring about a thorough revision of the state's constitution.

Senate Journal. Twenty-first Session (December 6, 1875, to April 3, 1876), 85–633 (January 4–April 3, 1876), various bills to regulate California railroads.

Senate Journal. Twenty-second Session (December 3, 1877, to April 1, 1878), 510 (March 5, 1878), bill to implement the state constitutional referendum.

Senate Journal. Twenty-fourth Session (January 3 to March 4, 1881), 157–158 (January 29, 1881), passage of concurrent resolution to request presidential pardon of Mussel Slough prisoners.

Senate Journal. Twenty-fifth Session (January 8 to March 13, 1883), 39–41 (January 17, 1883), N. Greene Curtis not confirmed as a University of California regent; 256 (February 26, 1883), at his request, Leland Stanford's name is withdrawn from regent confirmation list.

Senate Journal. Twenty-sixth Session (January 5, to March 11, 1885), 151–170 (January 27, 1885), California legislature elects Stanford to the U.S. Senate.

Senate. *Preliminary Report of the Committee on Corporations*, 3–20 (1874). Printed in Business Regulation Pamphlets, VII, Pamphlet 4, Robert Crown Law Library, Stanford University—CN H7. On the Freeman Bill.

3. Senate and Assembly Journal Appendices

Appendix to Journals of Senate and Assembly. Fourteenth Session (January 5 to April 27, 1863), 3–7 (January 8, 1863), Correspondence on payment to the U.S. Treasury Department.

Appendix to Journals of Senate and Assembly. Fourteenth Session (January 5 to April 27, 1863), 1–12 (March 30, 1863), *Message of the Governor to the Legislature of California transmitting Report of Commissioner to Nevada Territory, with Correspondence, etc.*, including Report of Sheriff Elisha H. Pierce of Plumas County to Governor Stanford, March 2, 1863, and various documents pertaining to California-Nevada differences over disputed territories.

Appendix to Journals of Senate and Assembly. Nineteenth Session (December 4, 1871, to April 1, 1872). Volume IV of 4 volumes (January 1872), *Appendix to the Report of the Committee on Corporations of the Assembly, upon Railroad Freights and Fares*. Published as an Appendix to Pamphlet 7 of *Business Regulation Pamphlets*, in Crown Law Library collection, Stanford University—CN H7.

Appendix to Journals of Senate and Assembly. Twentieth Session (December 1, 1873, to March 30, 1874), IV. 3–5 (undated), *Petitions of Citizens of San Francisco relative to Arbitrary Exactions and Injustices of Railroad Companies*.

Appendix to Journals of Senate and Assembly. Twentieth Session (December 1, 1873, to March 30, 1874), IV, Document 12, 9–161. Leland Stanford testimony, 9–55 (February 9, 1874). Committee on Corporations, *Report of the Testimony and Proceedings had before the Senate Committee on Corporations having under Consideration the subject of Fares and Freights*. Freeman Bill.

Appendix to Journals of Senate and Assembly. Twentieth Session (December 1, 1873, to March 30, 1874), V, 2–4 (undated), *Remonstrance from Citizens and Residents of the City of Sacramento against the Passage of Freeman's Freight and Fare Bill*; V, 1–3 (February 25, 1874), *Report of Joint Committee on propriety of calling a Constitutional Convention*; VI, 1–39 (March 5, 1874), "Testimony taken by the Special Committee on Central Pacific Railroad Matters."

Appendix to Journals of Senate and Assembly. Twenty-first Session (December 6, 1875, to April 3, 1876), V, Document 1, 1–13 (undated), Committee on Corporations, "Railroad Fares and Freights. Report of the Senate Committee on Corporations on Senate Bills Nos. 332, 319, and 334, and Assembly Bill No. 182." Also published in Pamphlet 9, Business Regulation Pamphlets, in Crown Law Library collection, Stanford University—CN H7. Reprinted as Pamphlet 6, *In the District Court of the Fourth Judicial District of the State of California*.

Appendix to Journals of Senate and Assembly. Twenty-fifth Session (January 8 to March 13, 1883), Hearings (January 17 to February 9, 1883), III, Document 4, 1–176, Committee on Corporations. *Report on the Committee on Corporations of the Assembly of California dealing with an investigation of three state railroad commissioners*.

4. Statutes

Statutes of California. Fourth Session (January 3 to May 19, 1853), 99–114, Chapter 72, *An Act to Provide for the Incorporation of Railroad Companies*. Approved April 19, 1853.

Statutes of California. Fifth Session (January 2 to May 15, 1854), 224, Joint Resolutions in Relation to the Pacific Railroad. Passed May 13, 1854.

Statutes of California. Fifth Session (January 2 to May 15, 1854), 170–176, Chapter 105, *Amendatory of an Act entitled "An Act to Provide for the Incorporation of Railroad Companies," approved April twenty-second, eighteen hundred and fifty-three*. Approved May 15, 1854.

Statutes of California. Fifth Session, 266 and 276 (January 2 to May 15, 1854), "Concurrent Resolution concerning the Pacific Railroad." Passed February 25, 1854.

Statutes of California. Sixth Session (January 1 to May 2, 1855), 180–181, Chapter 145, *An Act to provide for the Survey and Construction of a Wagon Road over the Sierra Nevada Mountains*. Approved April 28, 1855.

Statutes of California. Eighth Session (January 5 to April 13, 1857), 272–273, Chapter 235, *Submitting to the People of El Dorado and Sacramento Counties a Proposition to appropriate Money for the Construction of a Wagon Road*. Approved April 27, 1857.

Statutes of California. Tenth Session (January 3 to April 19, 1859), 391, *Current Resolution* No. 25, Calling for a convention to meet in San Francisco on September 20, 1859, to consider refusal of the U.S. government to build a transcontinental railroad. Passed April 5, 1859.

Statutes of California. Thirteenth Session (January 6 to May 15, 1862), 415–419, Chapter 302, *An Act for the Encouragement of Agriculture and Manufactures in California.* Approved April 25, 1862.

Statutes of California. Thirteenth Session (January 6 to May 15, 1862), 434–435, Chapter 317, *An Act to provide for the submission of the proposed Amendments to the Constitution of the State, as proposed by the Legislature of eighteen hundred and sixty-one, and adopted by the Legislature of eighteen hundred and sixty-two, to the votes of the qualified electors at the next General Election.* Approved April 25, 1862. See also, "Amendments to the Constitution. Proposed at the Twelfth Session of the Legislature, and Adopted at the Thirteenth Session," 581–586 (adopted by the Assembly on April 4, 1862, and by the Senate on April 8, 1862). These state constitutional amendments were passed by the voters of California on September 3, 1862.

Statutes of California. Thirteenth Session (January 6 to May 15, 1862), 462–465, Chapter 339, *An Act to protect Free White Labor against competition with Chinese Coolie Labor, and to discourage the Immigration of the Chinese into the State of California.* Approved April 26, 1862.

Statutes of California. Fourteenth Session (January 5 to April 27, 1863), 60, Chapter 68, *An Act to amend an Act entitled an Act to Regulate proceedings in Civil Cases in the Courts of Justice in this State, passed April twenty-ninth, eighteen hundred and fifty-one.* Approved March 16, 1863.

Statutes of California. Fourteenth Session (January 5 to April 27, 1863), 69, Chapter 70, *An Act to amend an Act entitled an Act concerning Crimes and Punishments, passed April sixteenth, eighteen hundred and fifty.* Approved March 18, 1863.

Statutes of California. Fourteenth Session (January 5 to April 27, 1863), 80–87, Chapter 77, *An Act to authorize the Board of Supervisors of the County of San Joaquin to take and subscribe Two Hundred and Fifty Thousand Dollars to the Capital Stock of "The Western Pacific Railroad Company," and to provide for the payment of the same, and other matters relating thereto.* Approved March 21, 1863.

Statutes of California. Fourteenth Session (January 5 to April 27, 1863), 145–150, Chapter 125, *An Act to authorize the County of Placer to subscribe to the Capital Stock of the Central Pacific Railroad Company of California, and to provide for the payment of the same, and other matters relating thereto.* Approved April 2, 1863.

Statutes of California. Thirteenth Session (January 6 to May 13, 1862), 199–205, Chapter 187, "An Act to provide for the Formation of Corporations for the Accumulation and Investment of Funds and Savings." Approved April 11, 1862.

Statutes of California. Fifth Session (January 6 to May 15, 1854), 257–261, Chapter 171, "An Act Concerning the Office of Secretary of State." Approved May 15, 1854.

Statutes of California. Fourteenth Session (January 5 to April 27, 1863), 350, 490–491, 566–567, 727, and 755, Chapter 264, "An Act supplementary to an Act entitled an Act concerning Crimes and Punishment, passed April 16, one thousand eight hundred and fifty." Approved April 20, 1863.

Statutes of California. Fourteenth Session (January 5 to April 27, 1863), 350, 490–491, 566–567, 727, and 755, Chapter 327, "An Act to prevent the Arming and Equipping, within the jurisdiction of this State, of Vehicles for Privateering purposes, and other treasonable conduct." Approved April 25, 1863.

Statutes of California. Fourteenth Session (January 5 to April 27, 1863), 350, 490–491, 566–567, 727, and 755, Chapter 365, "An Act to exclude Traitors and Alien Enemies from the Courts of Justice in Civil Cases." Approved April 25, 1863.

Statutes of California. Fourteenth Session (January 5 to April 27, 1863), 350, 490–491, 566–567, 727, and 755, Chapter 450, "An Act concerning Teachers of Common Schools in this State." Approved April 27, 1863.

Statutes of California. Fourteenth Session (January 5 to April 27, 1863), 350, 490–491, 566–567, 727, and 755, Chapter 498, "An Act to punish Offences against the Peace of the State." Approved April 27, 1863.

Statutes of California. Fourteenth Session (January 5 to April 27, 1863), 186–187, Chapter 155, *An Act to protect certain parties in and to a Railroad Survey, to connect Portland, Oregon, with Marysville, California.* Approved April 6, 1863.

Statutes of California. Fourteenth Session (January 5 to April 27, 1863), 276–281, Chapter 207, *An Act to authorize the Board of Supervisors of the County of Santa Clara to take and subscribe one hundred and fifty thousand dollars to the Capital Stock of the Western Pacific Railroad Company, and to provide for the payment of the same, and other matters relating thereto.* Approved April 14, 1863.

Statutes of California. Fourteenth Session (January 5 to April 27, 1863), 288–290, Chapter 209, *An Act granting certain rights to the Central Pacific Railroad Company of California, and for other purposes.* Approved April 14, 1863.

Statutes of California. Fourteenth Session (January 5 to April 27, 1863), 320–321, Chapter 244, *An Act to authorize the re-location of the Route of the Central Pacific Railroad Company of California, and for other matters relating thereto.* Approved April 17, 1863.

Statutes of California. Fourteenth Session (January 5 to April 27, 1863), 380–385, Chapter 291, *An Act to authorize the Board of Supervisors of the City and County of San Francisco to take and subscribe One Million Dollars to the Capital Stock of "The Western Pacific Railroad Company," and "The Central Pacific Railroad Company of California," and to provide for the payment of the same, and other matters relating thereto.* Approved April 22, 1863.

Statutes of California. Fourteenth Session (January 5 to April 27, 1863), 447–451, Chapter 310, *An Act to authorize the City and County of Sacramento to subscribe to the Capital Stock of "The Central Pacific Railroad Company of California," and providing for the payment of the same, and other matters relating thereto.* Approved April 25, 1863.

Statutes of California. Fourteenth Session (January 5 to April 27, 1863), 465–467, Chapter 314, *An Act to aid the Construction of the Central Pacific Railroad in the State of California, and other matters relating thereto.* Approved April 25, 1863.

Statutes of California. Fourteenth Session (January 5 to April 27, 1863), 749, Chapter 486, *An Act to authorize the Sacramento, Placer, and Nevada Railroad Company to sell and convey their Road, and other matters relating thereto.* Approved April 27, 1863.

Statutes of California. Fourteenth Session (January 5 to April 27, 1863), 793, No. I, Concurrent Resolution on President Abraham Lincoln's "Proclamation of Freedom." Approved January 26, 1863.

Statutes of California. Fifteenth Session (December 7, 1863, to April 4, 1864), 344–346, Chapter 320, *An Act to aid the construction of the Central Pacific Railroad, and to secure the use of the same to this State for Military and other purposes, and other matters relating thereto.* Approved April 4, 1864.

Statutes of California. Fifteenth Session (December 7, 1863, to April 4, 1864), 388, Chapter 344, *An Act to confer additional powers upon the Board of Supervisors of the City and County of San Francisco, and upon the Auditor and Treasurer thereof, and to authorize the appropriation of money by said Board.* Approved April 4, 1864.

Statutes of California. Fifteenth Session (December 7, 1863, to April 4, 1864), 542, No. III—Concurrent Resolution, *Resolved,* "By the Assembly, the Senate concurring, that the thanks of the people are merited, and are hereby tendered to Leland Stanford, for the able, upright, and faithful manner in which he has discharged the duties of the office of Governor of the State of California for the past two years." Adopted December 15, 1863.

Statutes of California. Sixteenth Session (December 4, 1865, to April 2, 1866), 157–158, Chapter 176, *An Act to legalize and confirm a certain contract made between the County of Santa Clara, by the Board of Supervisors thereof, and the Western Pacific Railroad Company, bearing date the twentieth-eighth day of March,* A.D. *eighteen hundred and sixty-five.* Approved March 3, 1866.

Statutes of California. Seventeenth Session (December 2, 1867, to March 13, 1868), 473–475, Chapter 386, *An Act to provide depot grounds for the Terminal Central Pacific Railway Company.* Approved March 28, 1868.

Statutes of California and Amendments to the Codes. Twenty-first Session (December 6, 1875, to April 3, 1876), 783–791, Chapter 515, *An Act to provide for the appointment of Commissioners of Transportation, to fix the maximum charges for freights and fares, and to prevent extortion and discrimination on railroads in this State.* Approved April 3, 1876.

Statutes of California and Amendments to the Codes. Twenty-second Session (December 3, 1877, to April 1, 1878), 759–765, Chapter 489, *An Act to Provide for a Convention to frame a new Constitution for the State of California.* Approved March 30, 1878.

Statutes of California and Amendments to the Codes. Twenty-second Session (December 3, 1877, to April 1, 1878), 969–986, Chapter 641, *Act to create the office of Commissioner of Transportation, and to define its powers and duties; to fix the maximum charges for transporting passengers and freights on certain railroads, and to prevent extortion and unjust discrimination thereon.* Approved April 1, 1878.

Statutes of California and Amendments to the Codes. Twenty-sixth Session (January 5 to March 11, 1885), 49–53, Chapter 47, *An Act to advance learning, the arts and sciences, and to promote the public welfare by providing for the conveyance, holding, and protection of property, and the Creation of trusts for the founding, endowment, erection, and maintenance within this State of universities, colleges, schools, seminaries of learning, mechanical institutes, museums, and galleries of art.* Approved March 9, 1885.

Statutes of California. 1972 Regular Session (January 3, 1972, to January 5, 1973), 1620–1629, Chapter 912, *An act to add Chapter 1.67 (commencing with Section 5096.71) to Division 5 of the Public Resources Code, relating to financing of a program of acquiring and developing state and municipal beach, park, recreational, and historical facilities by proving the funds necessary therefor* [sic] *through the issuance and sale of bonds of the State of California, and by providing for the handling and disposition of such funds, and providing for the submission of the measure to a vote of the people at a special election to be consolidated with the 1974 direct primary election, and making an appropriation therefor.* Approved August 15, 1872.

Statutes of California. 1973–74 Regular Session (January 8, 1973, to November 30, 1974), Vol. I of II, 1383–1384, Chapter 771, *An act relating to the state park system, and in this connection to amend the Budget Act of 1973 (Chapter 129, Statutes of 1973–1974) by amending Section 2.8 thereof, and declaring the urgency thereof, to take effect immediately.* Approved September 25, 1973.

The Political Code of the State of California, annotated by Creed Haymond and John C. Burch, of the California Code Commission. 2 vols., Sacramento: H[enry] S[mith] Crocker & Co., 1872.

C. Judicial
1. Superior Courts

District Court of the Fourth Judicial District of the State of California. Reprinted in Pamphlet 2, Silas Woodruff Sanderson, *An Argument against the Power of the Legislature of the State of California to regulate Fares and Freights on the Central Pacific Railroad.* Sacramento: H[enry] S[mith] Crocker & Co., 1872.

District Court of the Fourth Judicial District of the State of California. Published in Pamphlet 3, *Extracts from Report of the Committee appointed November 11, 1873, by the Chamber of Commerce of San*

Francisco, to Prepare Bills for Legislative Action on the Subject of Fares and Freights. San Francisco: [no publisher given], 1874.

Superior Court. State of California, City and County of San Francisco. In the Matter of the Estate of Leland Stanford, Deceased. Decree of Settlement of Final Account and of Final Distribution. No. 13,690. Department No. 9. December 28, 1898. Stanford University Archives.

Superior Court. State of California, County of Sacramento. *Complaint. Richard Kirman, Plaintiff vs. W[illiam] L. Stevenson, Defendant,* April 26, 1909.

Superior Court. State of California, County of Sacramento. Department 2, Case No. 12955. *Richard Kirman vs. W[illiam] L. Stevenson.* Filed November 12, 1908.

Superior Court. State of California, County of Sacramento. Richard Kirman, Plaintiff, W[illiam] L. Stevenson, Defendant. Sheriff's Sale of Personal Property. Judgment Rendered on the 30th day of June 1909.

Superior Court. State of California, County of Sacramento. Richard Kirman, Plaintiff, W[illiam] L. Stevenson, Defendant. Certificate of Sale of Personal Property. David Reese, Sheriff, to Richard Kirman. July 30, 1909.

Superior Court. State of California, County of Sacramento. Sheriff's Office. Return on Attachment (Garnishment). November 13, 1908. A Writ of Attachment against the *Sunland* [former *Car Stanford*], held by the Southern Pacific Company.

Superior Court. State of California, County of Sacramento. Writ of Attachment, levied against W[illiam] L. Stevenson, November 12, 1908.

Superior Court. State of California, County of Santa Clara. In the matter of the Estate of Samuel J. Crosby, Parts 1 and 2 of Case No. 74-15812. These court records are now in the San José Historical Museum.

Superior Court. State of California, County of Santa Clara. Probate Court #146, regarding the estate of David Adams. His widow, Nancy Adams, was the administratrix of the estate. These court records are now in the San José Historical Museum.

Superior Court. State of California, County of Santa Clara. Probate Index, Vol. 1, 1850–1902, Registry C, Case 946, Probate of John James Clark's estate.

Superior Court. State of California, County of Santa Clara. Index to Proceedings in Probate Court, Book A, 1860–1880.

Superior Court. State of California, County of Santa Clara. Probate Index, Vol. 2, 1903–1917, Register M, 587, identifies Jane L. Stanford's probate case number as 5802. Her probate records are on Microfilms 159 and 160.

Superior Court. State of California, County of Sonoma, 1883. *Colton Case Depositions.* Vol. 1. *Depostition of the Defendant, C. P. Hintington, taken in New York, September 1883, before Wm. Shillaber, Esq.* New York: E. Wells Sackett & Rankin, Printers, 1883).

Superior Court. State of California, County of Sonoma, 1883. *Colton Case Depositions.* Vol. 2. *Depositions of Leland Stanford, C. P. Huntington, Charles Crocker, and Wells, Fargo & Company.* San Francisco: Bacon & Co., 1883.

Superior Court. State of California, County of Sonoma, 1883. *Ellen M. Colton vs. Leland Stanford, C.P. Huntington, Charles Crocker, and Wells, Fargo & Company,* 1883. Contains eighteen volumes plus three volumes of depositions.

Superior Court. State of California, County of Sonoma, Department No. 2. *Ellen M. Colton, Plaintiff, vs. Leland Stanford, et al, Defendants.* Findings. San Francisco: H[enry] S[mith] Crocker & Co., 1886. 123-page decision in the *Colton Case.* In *Colton Case Depositions,* II, Document 5.

2. Supreme Court

Reports of Cases determined in the Supreme Court of the State of California. Vol. XX, 534–586 and 730 (July Term, 1862), *Lin Sing v. Washburn*.

Reports of Cases determined in the Supreme Court of the State of California. Vol. VI, 499–506 (October Term, 1856), *The People v. J. Neely Johnson*, et al. The Supreme Court upheld the decision of a San Francisco judge who ruled that the Wagon Road law of April 28, 1855, was unconstitutional.

Reports of Cases determined in the Supreme Court of the State of California. Vol. XXII (1863).

Reports of Cases determined in the Supreme Court of the State of California. Vol. XXIV, 518–560 (April Term, 1864), *Wheeler N. French v. Henry F. Teschemaker et als*. On the refusal of the San Francisco Board of Supervisors to pay the Central Pacific Railroad a subsidy as mandated by state law and popular vote.

Reports of Cases determined in the Supreme Court of the State of California. Vol. XXIV, 616–633 (October Term, 1864), *Soledad Ortega de Argüello, José Ramon Argüello, and S. M. Mezes v. John Greer, Maria Louisa Greer, Manuela Coppinger, James Morrison, Joseph B. Crockett, Alexander P. Crittenden, and Dennis Martin*.

Reports of Cases determined in the Supreme Court of the State of California. Vol. XXV, 635–653 (July Term, 1864), *The People of the State of California on the relation of the Central Pacific Railroad of California, vs. Henry P. Coon, Mayor of the City and County of San Francisco*, et als. Brief on Behalf of Defendants. Published as Case 391, San Francisco: Towne & Bacon, 1864.

Reports of Cases determined in the Supreme Court of the State of California. Vol. XXVII, 175–228 (October Term, 1864, and January Term, 1865), *The People of the State of California* ex. rel. J[ohn] *G. McCullough, Attorney-General v. Romualdo Pacheco*, Treasurer of said State, and the Central Pacific Railroad Company of California.

Reports of Cases determined in the Supreme Court of the State of California. No. 1192. Vol. LXXXII, 351–412 (January 2, 1890), *Ellen M. Colton v. Leland Stanford*, et al. No. 11903.

Reports of Cases Determined in the Supreme Court of the State of California. Vol. CXVIII, 160–233 and 234–254 (September 13, 1897), for exact case names and numbers, *City of Oakland (A Municipal Corporation). Plaintiff and Respondent Vs. The Oakland Water Front Company (A Corporation). Defendant and Appellant. Vs. The City of Oakland. No. 109485*. Transcription on Appeal. Vol. I, i–xxxv, 1–996; Vol. II, 997–2010. 2 vols. Nos. 389 and 527.

6. MISCELLANEOUS STATE AND TERRITORIAL PUBLICATIONS

A. Arizona Territory

No. 33. "An Act To secure the construction and operation of certain railroad and telegraph lines, and to provide for other matters relating thereto." Approved February 7, 1877, by the Legislative Assembly of the Territory of Arizona.

B. California

Final Report of the California World's Fair Commission, including a Description of All Exhibits from the State of California, Collected and Maintained under the Legislative Enactments, at the World's Columbian Exposition. Sacramento: Alfred J. Johnston, Superintendent of State Printing, 1894.

Report on the Fifth Annual Viticultural Convention. San Francisco: [no publisher given], 1887.

Report of the Sixth Annual Viticultural Convention. Sacramento: [no publisher given], 1888.

Willis, Evander Berry, and Philip Keagy Stockton, official stenographers. *Debates and Proceedings of the Constitutional Convention of the State of California, convened at the City of Sacramento, Saturday, September 28, 1878*. 3 vols., Sacramento: John D. Young, Superintendent of State Printing, 1880. This set has continuous pagination, I, 1–640; II, 641–1152; III, 1153–1578.

C. Hawaii

Island of Oahu. Attorney General's Files, Case No. 361. Coroner's Inquest. *In re Death of Jane Lathrop Stanford*, February 28, 1905. Original file in the State Archives, Iolani Palace Grounds, Honolulu, Hawaii. Copy in Jane Stanford Papers, Stanford University Archives.

D. Kentucky

Chapter 403, "An Act to incorporate the Southern Pacific Company," *Acts of the General Assembly of the Commonwealth of Kentucky, Passed at the Regular Session of the General Assembly, which was begun and held in the City of Frankfort on Monday, the thirty-first Day of December, Eighteen Hundred and eighty-three*. Frankfort: Kentucky Yeoman Office, 1884.

E. Massachusetts

Circuit Court of Massachusetts, *Muybridge vs. Osgood*, September 14, 1882.

Commonwealth of Massachusetts, *Edward [sic] J. Muybridge vs. Leland Stanford*, 1883.

Secretary of the Commonwealth. Massachusetts State Archives. *Soldiers and Sailors in the American Revolution*. 17 vols., Boston: Wright and Potter Printing Co., 1896.

Suffolk S.S. [sworn statement], Superior Court, *Edward [sic] J. Muybridge vs. Leland Stanford*, 1883, Stanford University Archives.

Suffolk S.S. [sworn statement], Superior Court, *Edward [sic] J. Muybridge vs. Leland Stanford*, 1883. Deposition of Arthur Brown, July 18, 1883. Stanford University Archives.

Suffolk S.S. [sworn statement], Superior Court, *Edward [sic] J. Muybridge vs. Leland Stanford*, 1883. Deposition of John D[ove] Isaacs, July 18, 1883. Stanford University Archives.

Suffolk S.S. [sworn statement], Superior Court, *Edward [sic] J. Muybridge vs. Leland Stanford*, 1883. Deposition of Frank Shay, July 23 and 24, 1883. Copy in Stanford University Archives.

Suffolk S.S. [sworn statement], Superior Court, *Edward [sic] J. Muybridge vs. Leland Stanford*, 1883. Deposition of Leland Stanford [undated], 1883. Stanford University Archives.

Suffolk S.S. [sworn statement], Superior Court, *Edward [sic] J. Muybridge vs. Leland Stanford*, 1883. Deposition of J[acob] D[avis] B[abcock] Stillman, August 7, 1883. Stanford University Archives.

F. Nevada

Department of Business and Industry. Division of Minerals, Bulletin 85, *Geology and Mineral Resources of White Pine County, Nevada*. Reno: Mackay School of Mines, University of Nevada, 1976.

Incorporations Certificate, Eberhardt and Aurora Mining Company of Nevada, signed September 4, filed September 13, and recorded October 10, 1877. File I-583, Book 1 of Incorporations, 583–584, Nevada State Library and Archives.

Journal of the Senate during the Fourth Session of the Legislature of the State of Nevada, 1873 (January 6 to March 6, 1873). Appendix, Biennial Report of the State Mineralogist of the State of Nevada for the Years 1871 and 1872.

Journal of the Senate during the Sixth Session of the Legislature of the State of Nevada, 1869 (January 4 to March 4, 1869). Appendix, Nevada State Mineralogist's Report for the Years 1867 and 1869.

Official Report of the Debates and Proceedings in the Constitutional Convention of the State of Nevada, Assembled at Carson City, July 4th 1864, to form a Constitution and State Government (Andrew J. Marsh, Official Reporter). San Francisco: [State of Nevada], 1866.

Report of the State Mineralogist of Nevada for the Years 1867 and 1868. Carson City: Henry R. Miguels, State Printer, 1869.

Report of the State Mineralogist of Nevada for the Years 1869 and 1870. Carson City: Henry R. Miguels, State Printer, 1871.

Senate Committee on Railroads. "Evidence Concerning Projected Railroads across the Sierra Nevada Mountains." Statement made to the Nevada Senate Committee by Leland Stanford (53–71). Sacramento: [no publisher given], 1865.

Senate Committee on Railroads. *Evidence Concerning Projected Railways across the Sierra Nevada Mountains, from Pacific Tide Waters in California: and the Resources, Promises and Action of Companies organized to construct the same: together with Statements concerning present and prospective Railroad Enterprises in the State of Nevada procured by the Committee on Railroads of the First Nevada Legislature.* Carson City: John Church, State Printer, 1865, Bound as Vol. IV, Pamphlets on California Railroads. Bancroft Library.

Statutes of the State of Nevada passed at the First Session of the Legislature, 1864–5 (December 12, 1864, to March 11, 1865), 180–183, Chapter 59, *An Act authorizing the Construction of a Railroad from Virginia City to the Truckee River.* Approved over the Governor's veto, March 2, 1865.

Statutes of the State of Nevada passed at the First Session of the Legislature, 1864–5 (December 12, 1864, to March 11, 1865). No. VIII, Concurrent Resolution. Passed February 28, 1865, 453. A resolution instructing the state's U.S. senators and congressmen to press Congress for the passage of a law providing $10 million in United States bonds to that railroad completing the first line between the Sacramento River and the Nevada border with California.

G. New York

Laws of the State of New York, passed at the Eighty-seventh Session of the Legislature (January 5 to April 23, 1864), viii. Charles Stanford, Assemblyman from Schenectady.

Laws of the State of New York, passed at the Eighty-eighth Session of the Legislature (January 3 to April 29, 1865), viii. Charles Stanford, Assemblyman from Schenectady.

Laws of the State of New York, passed at the Eighty-ninth Session of the Legislature (January 2 to April 20, 1866), v. Charles Stanford, Senator from Schenectady.

Laws of the State of New York, passed at the Ninetieth Session of the Legislature (January 1 to April 20, 1867), v. Charles Stanford, Senator from Schenectady.

Laws of the State of New York, passed at the Ninety-first Session of the Legislature (January 7 to May 6, 1868), v. Charles Stanford, Senator from Schenectady.

Laws of the State of New York, passed at the Ninety-second Session of the Legislature (January 5 to May 10, 1869), v. Charles Stanford, Senator from Schenectady.

Stephen Van Rensselaer Manor. Ledger A2, Folio 820 in the New York State Library. The deed was recorded May 28, 1840, in *Albany County Book of Deeds.*

Supreme Court. State of New York, City and County of New York. *David Stewart, vs. Collis P. Huntington, Leland Stanford, Charles Crocker, &c. Lloyd Aspinwall, and o[the]rs Ex'rs, &c., vs. The Same. William Paton, vs. The Same. Elizabeth S. Paton, Ex'r'x, &c., vs. The Same. John T. Agnew, et al., Sur'g Part'rs, &c., vs. The Same,* New York: Charles S. Hamilton & Co., 1982. Bound in Volume 7, Pamphlet 1, of Central Pacific Railroad Pamphlets.

H. Oregon

Oregon. *Acts and Resolutions of the Legislative Assembly of the State of Oregon, passed at the Fourth Regular Session, 1866. With an Appendix.* House Joint Resolution No. 13, Relating to the railroad land grant from the Central Pacific Railroad in California to Portland, Oregon. Salem: W. & A. McPherson, State Printer, 1866.

I. Wisconsin

Wisconsin. Legislative Manual, State of Wisconsin, 1871 and 1872.

7. City and County Government Documents and Maps
(*Listed by County*)

Alameda County. *Great Register of the County of Alameda*. Oakland: Tribune Publishing Co., 1882.

Alameda County. Recorder's Office, Book 319 of Deeds, Deed from Leland Stanford to Josiah Stanford on the Warm Springs Ranch, 239–242, November 24, 1886.

Amador County Maps. Compiled from Official and Private Surveys by Revilo Frederick Morton, C.E., published in San Francisco, in 1910.

Amador County Maps. Drawn by W. E. Proctor, published by the *Amador Record*, "Map of a Portion of Amador County, Cal. Showing the Mother Lode and Adjacent Mines." This map identifies names, locations, owners, and superintendents of ninety-four Mother Lode mines. On file at the Amador County Recorder's Office, Jackson, California; and in the Earth Sciences Library at Stanford University.

Amador County Maps. Nurse and Reaves, Surveyors, drawn by G. L. Nusbaumer, 1871, "Map of the Town of Sutter Creek Amador Co. Cal."

Amador County Maps. "Ten Miles of the Mother Lode, Amador County, California." Published November 1, 1933. On file at the Amador County Recorder's Office, Jackson, California.

Amador County. Recorder's Office, Books D, H, M, and N of Deeds, Grantors and Grantees, August 4, 1854, to August 7, 1899.

El Dorado County. Dungan, J. S[hade(?)]. *California Census of 1852—County of El Dorado*. Vol. 2. No city given: Copied under the direction of the Genealogical Records Committee of the Daughters of the American Revolution, 1934.

El Dorado County. *Great Register of El Dorado County*, 1867. Placerville: Courier Print, 1867. Bancroft Library.

Placer County. [Tax] Assessment Books, 1853–1857, in Placer County Archives.

Placer County. Board of Supervisors [Majority] Report on the Central Pacific Railroad. Bound in Vol. IV, Pamphlet 5, California Railroad Documents. Bancroft Library.

Placer County. Board of Supervisors Minutes, 1852–1859. In Placer County Archives, identified as A1852–1859.

Placer County. Board of Supervisors Report on the Central Pacific Railroad.

Placer County. Recorder's Office, Index to Deeds, 1851–1872.

Placer County. Recorder's Office. Books B, D, G, H, and K of Deeds, Grantor-Grantee.

Placer County. Recorder's Office. Placer County Records, I and IV.

Sacramento City Archives. Sacramento City Council Minutes, November 16, 1854, to September 3, 1855, 144–153.

Sacramento County. *Great Register, California, Sacramento County 1896*. Sacramento: D[avid] Johnston and Co., 1896.

Sacramento County. Recorder's Office, Assessment Rolls and Map Books, 1849–1862. Grantees.

Sacramento County. Recorder's Office, Books of Grantors and Grantees, 1852–1855.

San Bernardino County. Luther A. Ingersoll, ed. *Ingersoll's Century Annals of San Bernardino County, 1769 to 1904, prefaced with a Brief History of the State of California*. Los Angeles: L.A. Ingersoll, 1904.

San Francisco City and County. J[ulius] C. Henkenius, cartographer, "Map of the City and County of San Francisco." San Francisco: Warren Holt, 1884. History Room, San Francisco Public Library.

San Mateo County. Recorder's Office, Books 29, 33, 35, 36, 39, 40, 41, 52, 56, 64, and 143 of Deeds.

San Mateo County. Recorder's Office, Deed from William M. Bevins and Wife to George Gordon, January 12, 1863.

San Mateo and Santa Clara Counties Maps. Adolph T. Herrmann, and Frank A. Herrmann Bros., Surveyors. Map of the Lands of the Leland Stanford Junior University, at and Near the Site of the University, and in the Counties of Santa Clara and San Mateo, California. Surveyed at the Request of the Board of Trustees. July and November 1908.

San Mateo and Santa Clara Counties Map. Coombs Map. "Map of Land Situated in Santa Clara & San Mateo Counties. The Property of Leland Stanford surveyed at the request of Ariel Lathrop under the supervision of James C. Gould. 1883–85." Stanford University Archives Map File.

Santa Barbara County. Recorder's Office. Deed from Rogers M. Fullerton to A. P. Stanford, March 9, 1865, recorded March 16, 1865.

Santa Clara County. *Great Register, containing the names and registration of the domiciled inhabitants of the County of Santa Clara; who by virtue of citizenship, lawful age, and other qualifications prescribed by the Constitution, are qualified electors and legal voters.* 1876.

Santa Clara County. Office of the Clerk, Records Section, 1869. George Gordon Probate, Case 492.

Santa Clara County. Office of the Clerk, Records Section, 1874. Elizabeth A. Gordon Probate, Case 805.

Santa Clara County. Recorder's Office, Books G, H, K, 17, 27, 40, 45, 47, 51, 55, 66, 80, 85, 90, 94, and 95 of Deeds.

Santa Clara County. Recorder's Office, Deed from Delavan Hoag *et al* to Thomas J. Wilson, February 21, 1859.

Santa Clara. Recorder's Office, Deed from Delavan Hoag to Leland Stanford, August 9, 1876.

Santa Clara. Recorder's Office, Deed from Delavan Hoag and Elizabeth Hoag to Leland Stanford, April 6, 1877. 909.72 acres, from San Francisquito Rancho 619.72 acres and Rincon de San Francisquito 290 acres.

Santa Clara County. Recorder's Office, Deed from Thomas J. Wilson *et al* to A[ndrew] J[ackson] Pitman, April 14, 1857.

Santa Clara County. Recorder's Office. Quitclaim Deed from Nancy Adams (widow) to Leland Stanford, August 9, 1876. Two parcels of land, amounting to 909.72 acres, consisted of 619.72 acres from the San Francisquito Palo Alto Rancho, and 290 acres of the Rincon de San Francisquito Rancho. All for one dollar in gold coin. Nancy Adams' mark "X" was notarized with the testimony of witnesses, on April 6, 1877, and the deed was recorded on August 9, 1877.

Tehama County. Recorder's Office, Book 1 of Deeds. Henry Gerke loan on land.

Tehama County. Recorder's Office, Book C of Deeds. U.S. government confirmation of Peter Lassen land grant by deed to Henry Gerke.

Tehama County. Recorder's Office, Book P of Deeds. Joseph S. Cone purchase of Henry Gerke property.

Tehama County. Recorder's Office, Book Q of Deeds. Nick Smith purchases land from Joseph S. Cone.

Tehama County. Recorder's Office, Book R of Deeds. Nick Smith deeds land purchased from Joseph S. Cone to Stanford.

Tehama County. Recorder's Office, Index to Deeds, Grantor and Grantee, 1880–1889.

Tehama County. Recorder's Office, Probate File 52.

Yuba County. Marysville City Council Minutes, 1884. On microfilm in the John Q. Packard Library of Yuba County.

Yuba County. Yuba County Cemetery Book, May 7, 1998, in John Q. Packard Library of Yuba County.

8. CORRESPONDENCE
(*Miscellaneous and Collected Letters*)
A. Miscellaneous Letters

Brotherhood of Locomotive Engineers, Leland Stanford Division, No. 238. Ten-page letter addressed to Messrs Editors—"Eulogy of Leland Stanford." 1893. Stanford Papers.

Browne, J[ohn] Ross. Letter to Congressman—later President—James A. Garfield when California's wines were threatened by a federal tax, June 20, 1866, in Joseph Henry Jackson, ed. *The Vine in Early California*. San Francisco: Book Club of California, 1955. Folder 1 of a 10-folder Keepsake Series.

Burbank, G. W. Assistant Grand Chief Engineer, Brotherhood of Locomotive Engineers, letter to Con M. Buckley, November 1, 1949. Stanford Papers. Statement on "Eulogy of Leland Stanford."

Clark, George Thomas, ed. "Letters from Leland Stanford to Mark Hopkins," *California Historical Society Quarterly* 1926 5 (2): 178–183.

Coit, Daniel Wadsworth [edited, with introduction by George P. Hammond]. *Digging for Gold—Without a Shovel*. Denver: Fred Rosenstock, 1967. Coit describes the Mexican side of the war with the United States and later, when he was in San Francisco, writes about the Gold Rush. His sketches include views of San Francisco and Benicia.

Hammond, [Henry B.]-[Edward Henry] Rollins Correspondence, Ms. 3761, SG 8, Series 2, Outgoing Correspondence, October 23, 1868–August 31, 1869, I, 86–89, Nebraska State Historical Society, Nebraska State Archives.

Hart, A[lbert]. [Private secretary to Governor George Perkins]. Letter to J. H[armon] S. Bonté [Secretary, University of California Board of Regents], September 23, 1882, announcing the appointment of Leland Stanford to the University of California Board of Regents on September 14, 1882. Note on reverse side says the appointment was announced to the Board of Regents on October 7, 1882. Bancroft Library.

Judah, Anna. "Early Pacific Railroad History," Sacramento *Themis* 1889 I (43): 1–8. Contains a letter (2–3) that is an abridgement of Anna Judah's manuscript C–D 800:3, Bancroft Library. Deals with her husband Theodore Dehone Judah.

Moore, Joseph H. *An Open Letter. A Protest and a Petition. From a Citizen of California to the United States Congress*. San Francisco: James H. Barry, Printer, [1876(?)].

Moreland, William Walter [Private secretary to Governor George Stoneman]. Letter to J. H[armon] S. Bonté [Secretary, University of California Board of Regents], March 30, 1883. Announces the resignation of Leland Stanford from the Board of Regents of the University of California. His successor, George T. Marye, was appointed on March 12, 1883. Bancroft Library.

Mott, T[homas] D., and B[enjamin Davis] Wilson, two prominent southern Californians, to Leland Stanford, May 5, 1872, in Maj. Ben C. Truman's monthly magazine, the *Del Monte Wave*, June, 1886, 4.

Poor, Henry Varnum. *The Pacific Railroads and the Relations existing between them and the Government of the United States*. New York: [no publisher given], 1879. Sixteen-page pamphlet—a letter from

Henry V. Poor to John A. Dix, March 6, 1879. Poor argues that the Thurmond Bill of May 8, 1878, deliberately undertook to override the 1875 decision of the U.S. Supreme Court in relation to a sinking fund guaranteeing that the Pacific railroads would be able to retire their bonds at maturity. U.S. Supreme Court. Reports. Vol. 25, Cases Adjudged in the Supreme Court at October Term, 1875, 72–91, *The United States v. Union Pacific Railroad Company.*

Robinson, L[ester] L. [Civil Engineer]. Letter to Charles B. Sumner and Henry Epstein, Chairmen, Committees on Railroads, Legislature of Nevada, February 3, 1865. *Railroad Pamphlets*, Vol. I, Pamphlet 5, 121–127, in *The Railroad System of California. Oakland and Vicinity*. San Francisco: John H. Carmany & Co., Printers, 1871. Argues that the railroad proposed by the Central Pacific Associates was not buildable.

Stalder, Walter. Letters to the Stanford University [Special Collections Department], April 27 and 28, 1938. Walter Stalder was an oil geologist. These letters of transmittal accompanied his gift to the Stanford Archives of two books used by Josiah Stanford in connection with his San Francisco oil refinery. They were given to Stalder by Josiah's children Gertrude and Josiah W. Stanford. See works by Abraham Gesner and Thomas Antisell.

Stanford, Leland. Letter to Charles B. Sumner and Henry Epstein, February 14, 1865. Published as Central Pacific Railroad. Reply to the Letter of L.L. Robinson. Bound in *Railroad Pamphlets*, Vol. I, Pamphlet 5, 129–139, in *The Railroad System of California. Oakland and Vicinity*. San Francisco: J.H. Carmany & Co., Printers, 1871. This is a reply to L[ester] L. Robinson's February 3, 1865, letter to Sumner and Epstein.

Taylor, John. "A Notable Voyage of the Days of '49" [A letter given to the Society of California Pioneers on June 15, 1901, describing the voyage of the *Orpheus* from New York to San Francisco, from January 30 to July 8, 1849]. Now in the National Archives and Records Administration Archives, San Bruno, California.

B. Collected Letters

Boerner, Arthur R., ed. "Early Letters of Dr. Theodore E. F. Hartwig, Cedarburg's Physician and Surgeon," *Wisconsin Magazine of History* 1946 29 (3): 347–356.

Clark, George Thomas, ed. "Letters of Leland Stanford to Mark Hopkins," *California Historical Society Quarterly* 1926 5 (2): 178–183.

Evans, Elliot, ed. "Some Letters of William S. Jewett, California Artist," *California Historical Society Quarterly* 1944 23 (3), 227–246.

Jackson, W[illiam] Turrentine. *Twenty Years on the Pacific Slope, Letters of Henry Eno from California and Nevada, 1848–1871*. New Haven: Yale University Press, 1965.

Kipling, Rudyard [Thomas Pinney, ed.]. *The Letters of Rudyard Kipling*. London: Macmillan, 1990.

Letters from Collis P. Huntington to Mark Hopkins, Leland Stanford, Charles Crocker, E. B. Crocker, Charles F. Crocker, and D. D. Colton, from August 20, 1867, to August 5, 1869. New York: John C. Rankin Co., 1892.

Letters from Collis P. Huntington to Mark Hopkins, Leland Stanford, Charles Crocker, and E. B. Crocker, from August 5, 1869, to March 26, 1873. New York: John C. Rankin Co., 1892.

Letters from Collis P. Huntington to Mark Hopkins, Leland Stanford, Charles Crocker, and D. D. Colton, from April 2, 1873, to March 31, 1876. New York: John C. Rankin Co., 1892.

Letters from Mark Hopkins, Leland Stanford, Charles Crocker, Charles F. Crocker, and David D. Colton, to Collis P. Huntington, from August 27th, 1869, to December 30th, 1879. New York: John C. Rankin Co., 1891.

Nagel, Gunther W. *Jane Stanford: Her Life and Letters*. Stanford: Stanford Alumni Association, 1975. Deals more with her correspondence than with her life story. Rev. ed. published as *Iron Will: The Life and Letters of Jane Stanford*. Stanford: Stanford Alumni Association, 1985.

Ramírez, Salvador A., ed. *The Octopus Speaks: The Colton Letters*. Carlsbad: The Tentacled Press, 1982.

The Collis P. Huntington Papers, 1856–1901. A Guide to the Microfilm Collection. New York: Microfilming Corporation of America, 1979. Contains 115 microfilm reels of Huntington papers.

Whitman, Walt. *Passage to India*. Washington: [no publisher given], 1871.

Williams, Charles Richard, ed. *Diary and Letters of Rutherford Birchard Hayes, Nineteenth President of the United States*. 4 vols., Columbus: Ohio State Archeological and Historical Society, 1925.

9. PERSONAL NARRATIVES
(*Interviews, Speeches, Talks, and Statements*)

Alway, Robert H. "Senator Stanford was a Pioneer California Vintner," *Stanford Historical Society Newsletter* 1980 5 (1): 2, 3, and 8.

Bacon, Rosamond Clarke. "Remarks at the Founders' Day Ceremonies at the Stanford Mausoleum." March 9, 1977. An eight-page historical sketch of the building of the Stanford family mausoleum at Stanford University.

Becker, Robert, ed. *Some Reflections on an Early California Governor contained in a short dictated Memoir by Frederick F. Low, Ninth Governor of California, and Notes from an Interview between Governor Low and Hubert Howe Bancroft in 1883*. Sacramento: Sacramento Book Collectors Club, 1959.

Black, Chauncey F., ed. *Essays and Speeches of Jeremiah S[ullivan] Black. With a Biographical Sketch*. New York: D. Appleton & Co., 1885.

Cohen, Alfred Andrew. *An Address on the Railroad Evil and its Remedy*. San Francisco: Francis, Valentine & Co., 1879. Twenty-three-page brochure on an address delivered at San Francisco's Platt's Hall on August 2, 1879.

Crothers, George Edward. "The Educational Ideals of Jane Lathrop Stanford, Co-Founder of the Leland Stanford Junior University." *San José Mercury Herald*, August 20–26, 1933. An address delivered to the California State Conference of the Daughters of the American Revolution, reprinted as a thirty-two-page pamphlet bearing the same title and reprinted from the *San José Mercury*.

Dodge, Grenville Mellen. *How We Built the Union Pacific Railway, and other Railway Addresses*. [No city given]: [Maj. Gen. Grenville M. Dodge, Chief Engineer, Union Pacific Railway], 1866–1870. Contains "Fortieth Anniversary of Driving the Last Spike of the Union Pacific and Central Pacific Railway," 5–50.

Hazard, Rowland G. *The Crédit Mobilier of America*. A forty-two-page paper read before the Rhode Island Historical Society, February 22, 1881. Providence: Sidney S. Rider, 1881. Ann Arbor: University Microfilms, 1971.

Ouellette, Eugene G. "J.D.B.," a talk given at the Fortnightly Club of Redlands, California, on February 17, 2000. Copy at the A[lbert K[eith] Smiley Public Library, Redlands, California. The subject is Dr. Jacob Davis Babcock Stillman.

Regnery, Dorothy. Statement by Dorothy F. Regnery, Stanford Historical Society, Chairman, Stanford House Project, for the Budget & Fiscal Review Committee, Subcommittee No. 2, May 6, 1995, in Room 112, State Capitol, Sacramento.

Silliman, Benjamin. *Remarks Made on a Short Tour Between Hartford and Quebec in the Autumn of 1819*. 2nd ed., New-Haven: S. Converse, [1820], 1824.

Stanford, Leland. "Address of Leland Stanford at the Opening of the Tenth Annual Fair of the State Agricultural Society, at Sacramento [September 26, 1863]," *Transactions of the California State Agricultural Society During the Year 1863*. Sacramento: Orlando M. Clayes, State Printer, 1864, 43–51.

Stanford, Leland. *Speech of Honorable Leland Stanford in the Constitutional Convention of the State of Nevada, on Wednesday, July 13, 1864.* San Francisco: Francis, Valentine & Co., 1865. Bound as a twelve-page pamphlet in Pamphlets on California Railroads, Vol. III, Pamphlet 9. Bancroft Library.

Stanford, Leland. *Statement Made to Senate Committee of Nevada Legislature*, January 12, 1865. Sacramento: [no city given], 1865, bound in Vol. 3, Pamphlet 4, in Pamphlets on California Railroads. Bancroft Library.

Wozencraft, Oliver M. *Address Delivered before the Mechanics' Institute on the Subject of the Atlantic and Pacific Rail-road, the Policy of our Government in Reference to Internal Improvements.* San Francisco: Agnew & Deffebach, 1856.

10. AUTOBIOGRAPHICAL WORKS
(*Autobiographies, Diaries, Journals, Memoirs, and Reminiscences*)
A. Books

Ayers, James Joseph. *Gold and Sunshine: Reminiscences of Early California.* Boston: R.G. Badger, 1922.

Bancroft, Hubert Howe. *Retrospection, Political and Personal.* New York: The Bancroft Co., 1912.

Bell, Horace. *Reminiscences of a Ranger.* Los Angeles: Yarnell, Caystile & Mathes, Printers, 1881.

Benton, Joseph Augustine. "Record of Preaching," Book 1, Pacific School of Religion Archives, Berkeley, California.

Bosqui, Edward. *Memoirs of Edward Bosqui.* Oakland: Holmes Book Co., 1952.

Browning, Orville Freeman. *The Diary of Orville Freeman Browning. Vol. II, 1865–1881* [James G. Randall, ed.]. 2 vols., Springfield: Illinois State Historical Library, 1932.

Buffum, Edward Gould. *Six Months in the Gold Mines: From a Journal of Three Years' Residence in* Upper and Lower *California. 1847–8–9.* Philadelphia: Lea and Blanchard, 1850.

Cole, Cornelius. *Memoirs of Cornelius Cole, Ex-senator of the United States from California.* New York: McLoughlin Brothers, 1908.

Cool, Peter Y. Diary, May 13, 1850–July 3, 1852. Cool was a twenty-year-old Amador County preacher who participated in a revival in Cold Springs and commented on the camp there. Bancroft Library.

Dodge, Grenville Mellen. *Personal Recollections of President Abraham Lincoln, General Ulysses S. Grant and General William T. Sherman.* Council Bluffs: The Monarch Printing Co., 1914.

Doten, Alfred [Walter Van Tilburg Clark, ed.]. *The Journals of Alfred Doten, 1849–1903.* 3 vols., Reno: University of Nevada Press, 1973.

Frémont, John Charles. *Memoirs of My Life, including in the Narrative five Journeys of Western Exploration, during the Years 1842, 1843–4, 1845–6–7, 1848–9, 1853–4. Together with a sketch of the Life of Senator Benton...by Jessie Benton.* Chicago: Belford, Clarke, 1887.

Grant, Joseph Donohoe. *Redwoods and Reminiscences. "The World went very well then." A Chronicle of Traffics and Excursions, of Work and Play, of Ups and Downs, During More Than Half a Century Happily Spent in California and Elsewhere.* San Francisco: Save-the-Redwoods League and the Menninger Tradition, 1973.

Greeley, Horace. *An Overland Journey from New York to San Francisco in the Summer of 1859.* New York: C.M. Saxton, Barker & Co., 1860; New York: Alfred A. Knopf, 1964.

Jordan, David Starr. *The Days of a Man, being Memoirs of a Naturalist, Teacher, and Minor Prophet of Democracy.* 2 vols., Yonkers on Hudson, New York: World Book Co., 1922.

Leach, Frank Aleamon. *Recollections of a Newspaperman, A Record of Life and Events in California.* San Francisco: S. Levinson, 1917.

Newmark, Maurice H. and Marco R., editors. *Sixty Years in Southern California, 1853–1913, Containing the Reminiscences of Harris Newmark*. Boston: Houghton Mifflin Co., [1916], 1930.

Robinson, Edgar Eugene, and Paul Carroll Edwards, eds. *The Memoirs of Ray Lyman Wilbur, 1875–1949*. Stanford: Stanford University Press, 1960.

Root, Henry. *Henry Root: Surveyor, Engineer, and Inventor, Personal History and Reminiscences, with Personal Opinions on Contemporary Events, 1845–1921*. San Francisco: [privately printed], 1921.

Stewart, William Morris [George Rothwell Brown, ed.]. *Reminiscences of Senator William M. Stewart of Nevada*. New York: The Neale Publishing Co., 1908.

White, Andrew Dickson. *Autobiography of Andrew Dickson White*. 2 vols., New York: The Century History Co., 1922.

Yount, George C. *George C. Yount and his Chronicles of the West, Comprising Extracts from his Memoirs and from the Orange Clark Narrative*. Edited by Charles L. Camp, Denver: Old West Publishing Co., 1966.

B. Periodicals

Hopkins, Caspar T. "California Recollections of Caspar T. Hopkins," *California Historical Society Quarterly* 1947 26 (1): 63–75; 26 (2): 175–183; 26 (3): 253–266; 1948 27 (2): 165–174; 27 (3): 267–274; 27 (4): 339–351.

Nash, Herbert Charles. "Personal Reminiscences of Senator Stanford," *Stanford Sequoia* 1893 3 (September 3): 3–4.

Stanford, Thomas Welton, "Mr. Thomas Welton Stanford of Melbourne (VIC., A.C.)—Some Reminiscences," *The Bankers' Magazine of Australasia*, August 8, 1901, 27–33.

Taggart, Harold F., ed. "The Journal of David Jackson Staples," *California Historical Society Quarterly* 1943 22 (2): 110–150.

Wheat, Carl I. "'California's Bantam Cock'—The Journals of Charles E. De Long, 1854–1863," *California Historical Society Quarterly* 1931 10 (1): 40–78; 10 (4): 355–395.

11. BIOGRAPHICAL WORKS
(Biographies, Family Histories, and Genealogies)
A. Books and Pamphlets

A Memorial & Biographical History of Northern California. Chicago: The Lewis Publishing Co., 1880.

Anderson, Frederick Lincoln. *Galusha Anderson: Preacher and Educator, 1832–1918*. Wenham, Massachusetts: Edwin Raymond Anderson, 1933. The author was Galusha Anderson's son.

Anderson, Nancy K., and Linda S. Ferber. *Albert Bierstadt: Art & Enterprise*. New York: Brooklyn Museum in Association with Hudson Hills, [1990], 1991.

Bancroft, Hubert Howe. *Chronicles of the Builders of the Commonwealth*. 7 vols., San Francisco: The History Co., 1891.

Bancroft, Hubert Howe. *History of the Life of Leland Stanford: A Character Study*. Oakland: Biobooks, 1952.

Berner, Bertha. *Mrs. Leland Stanford: An Intimate Account*. Stanford: Stanford University Press, 1934.

Binheim, Max, comp. and ed. *Women of the West: A Series of Biographical Sketches of Living Eminent Women in the Eleven Western States of the United States of America*. Los Angeles: Publishers Press, 1928.

Birkenhead, Lord. *Rudyard Kipling*. London: Weidenfield and Nicolson, 1978.

Blair, Harry C., and Rebecca Tarshis. *Lincoln's Constant Ally: The Life of Colonel Edward D. Baker*. Portland: Oregon Historical Society, 1960.

Bradley, Erwin Stanley. *Simon Cameron, Lincoln's Secretary of War: A Political Biography*. Philadelphia: University of Pennsylvania Press, 1966.

Brigance, William Norwood. *Jeremiah Sullivan Black, A Defender of the Constitution and the Ten Commandments*. Philadelphia: University of Pennsylvania Press, 1934.

Brown, Louise S., and Mallissa R. Doolittle. *The Doolittle Family in America* (Part VIII). Dallas: Oak Cliff Typesetting, 1967.

Busbey, T. Addison, ed. and comp. *Biographical Directory of the Railroad Officials of America*. Chicago: The Railway Age, 1901.

Campbell, Fred M. "Senator Stanford! To My Fellow Republicans of California." Oakland: Fred M. Campbell, October 16, 1890. Four-page anti-Stanford broadside that inveighs against Stanford's reelection to the U.S. Senate.

Carrington, Charles. *Rudyard Kipling, His Life and Work*. London: Macmillan, [1955], 1978.

Cate, Wirt Armistead. *Lucius Q[uintus] C[incinnatus] Lamar, Secession and Reunion*. Chapel Hill: University of North Carolina Press, 1935.

Clark, George Thomas. *Leland Stanford, War Governor of California, Railroad Builder, and Founder of Stanford University*. Stanford: Stanford University Press, 1931.

Clarke, Dwight L. *William Tecumseh Sherman: Gold Rush Banker*. San Francisco: California Historical Society, 1969.

Constructive Californians. Los Angeles: Saturday Night Publishing Co., 1926.

[Crocker, James Russell]. *Crocker Genealogy*. [San Diego: James Russell Crocker, 1967]. No author or publication information given in the book. A note at the end identifies the printer as A-1 Bindery, 918 Industrial Blvd., Chula Vista, California.

Curtis, Edward. *Two California Sketches: William Watt and Leland Stanford*. San Francisco: Thomas' Steam Printing House, 1880.

Davis, Margo, and Roxanne Nilan. *The Family Album: A Photographic History of Stanford*. Stanford: Stanford University Press, 1989.

Deming, Judson Keith, comp. and ed. *Genealogy of the Descendants of John Deming of Wethersfield, Connecticut, with Historical Notes*. Dubuque, Iowa: Mathis-Mets Co., 1904.

Dickson, Samuel. *San Francisco is Your Home*. Stanford: Stanford University Press, 1947. Chapter 24, "Jane Stanford," 196–203.

Die Centenar—Feier der Geburt des König Ludwigs I. Von Bayern. Program der Festlichkeiten während der Tage vom 29.–31. Juli 1888 in München. Nach Mittheilungen der Festausschüsse im Auftrage des Central-Comité's herausgegeben von Preßausschusse [sic]. From the collection of Wolfgang Hasselmann, with an Introduction by Richard Bauer. Reprint, Munich: Süddeutscher Verlag, 1986.

Driscoll, James D., and Darryl R. White. *List of Constitutional Officers, Congressional Representatives, Members of the California State Legislature and Members of the Supreme Court—1849–1985*. [Sacramento (?)]: James D. Driscoll and Darryl R. White, 1985.

Ellington, Charles G. *The Trial of U.S. Grant: The Pacific Coast Years, 1852–1854*. Glendale: The Arthur H. Clark Co., 1987.

Evans, Cerinda W. *Collis Potter Huntington*. 2 vols., Newport News: Mariners' Museum, 1954.

Fatout, Paul. *Ambrose Bierce: The Devil's Lexicographer*. Norman: University of Oklahoma Press, 1951.

Foote, Henry Stuart. *Pan Pictures from the Garden of the World or Santa Clara County, California. Containing a History of the County of Santa Clara from the Earliest Period of its Occupancy to the Present Time*. Chicago: Lewis Publishing Co., 1888.

Friis, Leo J. *David Hewes: More Than the Golden Spike*. Santa Ana: Friis-Pioneer Press, 1974.

Grant, Joseph Donohoe. *The Stanfords*. Stanford: Stanford University Press, 1938.

Grattan, C. Hartley. *Bitter Bierce, A Mystery of American Letters*. Garden City: Doubleday, Doran & Co., 1929.

Gréard, C.O. [Valéry-Clément-Octave Gréard], *Jean-Louis-Ernest Meissonier. Ses Souvenirs—Ses Entretiens. Précédés d'une Étude sur sa Vie et son Oeuvre*. Paris: Hachette et Cie, 1897.

Gréard, Vallery [sic] C.O. [Valéry-Clément-Octave Gréard], *Meissonier: His Life and His Art, with Extracts from his Note-Books, and his Opinions and Impressions on Art and Artists, Collected by his Wife*. New York: A.C. Armstrong and Son, 1897. English translation of the above.

Haas, Robert Bartlett. *Muybridge: Man in Motion*. Berkeley: University of California Press, 1976.

Halasz, Nicholas. *Nobel*. New York: Orion Press, 1959.

Harpending, Asbury [James H. Wilkins, ed.]. *The Great Diamond Hoax and other Stirring Incidents in the Life of Asbury Harpending*. San Francisco: The James H. Barry Co., 1913.

Hart, James D. *A Companion to California*. Berkeley: University of California Press, 1987.

Haskins, Charles Warren. *The Argonauts of California, Being the Reminiscences of Scenes and Incidents that occurred in California in early Mining Days. By a Pioneer*. New York: Fords, Howard & Hulbert, 1890. The very descriptive subtitle continues: "And believing that it will be of some historical value as well as of interest generally to know the names of those who were the first to venture forth in the search of gold, and by whose energy and labor the foundations of a great state were laid, and also a general prosperity created throughout the entire country, I have therefore prefixed to the work the names of those that I have been able to obtain, numbering about 35,000, and including among them the names of several thousand who are now living in the various States of the Union."

Haslip, Joan. *The Sultan: The Life of Abdul Hamid II*. New York: Holt, Rinehart and Winston, [1958], 1973.

Headley, Joel Tyler. *The Life and Travels of General Grant*. Philadelphia: Hubbard Brothers, 1879.

Heintz, William F. *San Francisco's Mayors, 1850–1880*. Woodside, California: Gilbert Richards Publications, 1975.

Hendricks, Gordon. *Albert Bierstadt; Painter of the American West*. New York: Harry N. Abrams, [1973], 1974.

Hermann, Ruth. *Gold and Silver Colossus William Morris Stewart and his Southern Bride*. Sparks, Nevada: Dave's Printing and Publishing, 1975.

Hitchcock, Ruth Hughes, comp. *Leaves of the Past, 1828–1880: A Pioneer Register, including an overview of the history and events of early Tehama County*. Part I. Chico: Association of Northern California Records and Research, [no date given; post 1964].

Hopkins, Timothy, comp. *The Kelloggs in the Old World and the New*. 3 vols., San Francisco: Sunset Press and Photo Engraving Co., 1903.

Hopwood, Henry V. *Living Pictures, Their History, Photo-Production and Practical Working*. New York: Arno Press, 1970.

Howard, Louise Narjot. *California's Pioneer Artist, Ernest Narjot: A Brief Resume of the Career of a Versatile Genius*. San Francisco: Albert Dressler, 1936.

Hunt, Rockwell Dennis. *California's Stately Hall of Fame*. Stockton: College of the Pacific, 1950.

Hunt, Rockwell Dennis. *John Bidwell, Prince of California Pioneers*. Caldwell, Idaho: The Caxton Printers, 1942.

Huntington, Elijah Baldwin. *A Genealogical Memoir of the Lo-Lathrop Family in this Country Embracing the Descendants, as far as known, of the Rev. John Lothropp of Scituate and Barnstable, Mass., and Mark Lothropp, of Salem and Bridgewater, Mass., and the First Generation of Descendants of other Names*. Ridgefield, Connecticut: [Julia M. Huntington], 1884.

Hutchinson, William Henry. *Oil, Land and Politics, The California Career of Thomas Robert Bard*. Norman: University of Oklahoma Press, 1965.

Ingersoll, Lurton Dunham. *The Life of Horace Greeley*. Chicago: Union Publishing Co., 1873; reprinted, New York: Beekman Publishers, 1974.

Jackson, Donald, and, Mary Lee Spence, eds. *The Expeditions of John Charles Frémont*. Vol. 2, *The Bear Flag Revolt and the Court-Martial*. Urbana: University of Illinois Press, 1973.

James, George Wharton. *Heroes of California: The Story of the Founders of the Golden State as Narrated by Themselves or Gleaned from other Sources*. Boston: Little, Brown, and Co., 1910.

Johnson, J. Edward. *History of the California Supreme Court, 1850–1900*. 3 vols., San Francisco: Bender-Moss Co., 1963. "Edwin Bryant Crocker," I, 86–88.

Johnson, Kenneth M. *The Life and Times of Edward Robeson Taylor*. San Francisco: Book Club of California, 1968.

Jones, Francis Arthur. *Thomas Alva Edison*. New York: Thomas Y. Crowell & Co., [1907], 1908.

Jones, Helen (Hinckley). *Rails from the West: A Biography of Theodore D. Judah*. San Marino: Golden West Books, 1969.

Kens, Paul. *Justice Stephen Field: Shaping Liberty from the Gold Rush to the Gilded Age*. Lawrence: University of Kansas Press, 1996.

Kincaid, Helen H. *Kellogg Research, Incorporated Presents The Hopkins Hoax*. Williamston, North Carolina: Kellogg Research, 1973.

Latta, Estelle. *Controversial Mark Hopkins: The Great Swindle of American History*. New York: Greenburg, 1953.

Lavender, David Sievert. *Nothing Seemed Impossible, William C. Ralston and Early San Francisco*. Palo Alto: American West Publishing Co., 1975.

Lavender, David Sievert. *The Great Persuader*. Garden City: Doubleday & Co., 1970.

Levinsohn, John L. *Frank Morrison Pixley of the Argonaut*. San Francisco: Book Club of California, 1989.

Lewis, Oscar. *Silver Kings: The Lives and Times of Mackay, Fair, Flood, and O'Brien, Lords of the Nevada Comstock Lode*. New York: Alfred A. Knopf, 1947.

Lewis, Oscar. *The Big Four: The Story of Huntington, Stanford, Hopkins, and Crocker, and the Building of the Central Pacific*. New York: Alfred A. Knopf, [1938], 1962.

Loughead, Flora H., ed. *Life, Diary, and Letters of Oscar Lovell Shafter*. San Francisco: Blair-Murdock Co., 1915.

MacDonnell, Kevin. *Eadweard Muybridge: The Man who invented the Moving Picture*. Boston: Little, Brown, and Co., 1972.

Master Hands in the Affairs of the Pacific Coast: Historical, Biographical and Descriptive: a Resume of the Builders of our Material Progress. San Francisco: Western Historical and Publishing. Co., 1892.

Mayes, Edward. *Lucius Q.C. Lamar: His Life, Times, and Speeches*. Nashville: Publishing House of the Methodist Episcopal Church, South, 1896.

McComish, Charles Davis, and Rebecca T. Lambert. *History of Colusa and Glenn Counties, California, with Biographical Sketches of the Leading Men and Women of the Counties Who have been Identified with their Growth and Development from the Early Days to the Present*. Los Angeles: Historic Record Co., 1918.

McGroarty, John Steven. *California of the South—A History*. 5 vols., Chicago: S.J. Clarke Publishing Co., 1933.

Melendy, Howard Brett, and Benjamin Franklin Gilbert. *The Governors of California: Peter H. Burnett to Edmund G. Brown*. Georgetown, California: Talisman Press, 1965.

Memorial Address on the Life and Character of Mrs. David Hewes, with The Funeral Services Held at the Residence of Her Sister, Mrs. Leland Stanford, San Francisco, Cal., August 6, 1892. 42-page brochure. Much on the Lathrop family.

Men of California. San Francisco: Pacific Art Co., 1901. Contains hundreds of portraits and one- or two-line identification sketches.

Monzingo, Robert. *Thomas Starr King: Eminent Californian, Civil War Statesman, Unitarian Minister*. Pacific Grove: The Boxwood Press, 1991.

Munroe, James Phinney. *A Life of Francis Amasa Walker*. New York: Henry Holt & Co., 1923.

Murdock, Charles A. *Horatio Stebbins, His Ministry and His Personality*. Boston and New York: Houghton Mifflin Co., 1921.

[Nash, Herbert Charles]. *In Memoriam. Leland Stanford, Jr.* The book entry at the California State Library, History Section, identifies Nash as the writer and editor. This beautiful 249-page bound volume contains no publication data. It contains a lengthy sketch of the life of Leland, Jr., copies of letters he wrote home to various correspondents while on his last European trip, scores of letters and telegrams sent to the parents following his death, and scores of poems written in memory of him, and several pages of existing poems sent to the parents in remembrance of him.

Nevins, Allan. *Grover Cleveland, A Study in Courage*. New York: Dodd, Mead & Co., 1932.

O'Connor, Richard. *Ambrose Bierce, A Biography*. Boston: Little, Brown and Co., 1967.

O'Day, Edward F. *Varied Types*. San Francisco: Town Talk Press, 1915.

Official Register of Physicians and Surgeons in the State of California, January 31, 1891. 5th ed., San Francisco: Board of Examiners of the Medical Society of the State of California, 1891.

Official Register of Physicians and Surgeons in the State of California, January 1, 1893. 6th ed., San Francisco: Board of Examiners of the Medical Society of the State of California, 1893.

Older, Mr. and Mrs. Fremont. *George Hearst, California Pioneer*. Los Angeles: Westernlore, 1966.

Parton, James, et al. *Sketches of Men of Progress*. [no city given]: New York and Hartford Publishing Co., 1870–1871; Cincinnati: Greer, 1870–1871.

Phelps, Alonzo. *Contemporary Biography of California's Representative Men, with Contributions from Distinguished Scholars and Scientists*. 2 vols., San Francisco: A[lbert] L[ittle] Bancroft and Co., 1881–1882.

Phillips, Catherine Coffin. *Cornelius Cole, California Pioneer and United States Senator: A Study in Personality and Achievements bearing upon the Growth of a Commonwealth*. San Francisco: John Henry Nash, 1929.

Pickett, Charles Edward. *The California King: His Conquests, Crimes, Confederates, Counsellors, Courtiers and Vassals: Stanford's Post-prandial New-Year's Day Soliloquy*. San Francisco: San Francisco News Co., 1876.

Putnam, Eben, ed. and comp. *Lieutenant Joshua Hewes, A New England Pioneer and Some of His Descendants*. [no city given]: [privately printed], 1913. Includes David Hewes, "Hewes, An Autobiography," 223–264.

Ralli, Augustus. *Guide to Carlyle*. London: George, Allen & Unwin, 1920.

Records of the Families of California Pioneers. [San Francisco]: Daughters of the American Revolution, 1942, "Josiah Sessions," XII, 468–471.

Redding, Benjamin B. *A Sketch of the Life of Mark Hopkins of California*. San Francisco: A.L. Bancroft & Co., 1881.

Register of the Commissioned and Warrant Officers of the Navy of the United States, and the Marine Corps, to January 1, 1893. Washington: Government Printing Office, 1893.

Roper, Laura Wood. F.L.O., *A Biography of Frederick Law Olmsted*. Baltimore: The Johns Hopkins University Press, 1971.

Sandburg, Carl. *Abraham Lincoln, The Prairie Years and the War Years*. 3 vols., New York: Dell Publishing Co., 1963.

Scherer, James Augustin Brown. *The Lion of the Vigilantes: William T. Coleman and the Life of Old San Francisco*. Indianapolis & New York: The Bobbs-Merrill Co., 1939.

Schneider, Kurt O., comp. *Centennial—Ozaukee Lodge No. 17, F.&A.M. 1847–1947*. Port Washington: [no publisher given], November 29, 1947.

Scott, Edward B. *A Time for Recollection. A Tribute to Samuel F.B. Morse, Whose Dedicated Purpose for more than Half-a-Century Has Been the Preservation of Del Monte Forest*. Crystal Bay, Tahoe, Nevada: Sierra-Tahoe Publishing Co., 1969.

Scribner's Concise Dictionary of American Biography. New York: Scribner & Sons, 1964.

Shuck, Oscar Tully, ed. *Representative and Leading Men of the Pacific: being Original Sketches of the Lives and Characters of the Principal Men living and deceased, of the Pacific States and Territories—Pioneers, Politicians, Lawyers, Doctors, Merchants, Orators, and Divines—to which are added their Speeches, Addresses, Orations, Eulogies, Lectures, and Poems, upon a Variety of Subjects, including the happiest forensic Efforts of Baker, Randolph, McDougall, T. Starr King, and other popular Orators*. San Francisco: Bacon and Co., 1870.

Shumate, Albert. *The California of George Gordon, and the 1849 Sea Voyages of his California Association: A San Francisco Pioneer rescued from the Legend of the First Novel of Gertrude Atherton*. Glendale: The Arthur H. Clark Co., 1976; republished with slightly altered title and contents as *A San Francisco Scandal: The California of George Gordon, '49er, Pioneer, and Builder of South Park in San Francisco*. Spokane: The Arthur H. Clark Co., 1994.

Skiles, Jack. *Judge Roy Bean Country*. Lubbock: Texas Tech University Press, 1996.

Smedberg, William R., Bvt. Lt. Col., U.S. Army [Recorder]. Military Order of the Loyal Legion of the United States. Headquarters Commandery of the State of California. *In Memoriam Leland Stanford. A Companion of the third Class died at Palo Alto, Cal. Wednesday, June 21, 1893*. San Francisco: California Commandery, 1904. Circular No. 20, Series 1893, Whole Number 335. July 3, 1893. Stanford University Archives.

Smedberg, William R., Bvt. Lt. Col., U.S. Army [Recorder]. Military Order of the Loyal Legion of the United States. Headquarters Commandery of the State of California. San Francisco: California Commandery, *In Memoriam Lorenzo Dow Mason*. Died in Oakland, October 28, 1893. Circular No. 7, Series of 1893. Whole No. 342. Vol. II, No. 24.

Smith, Lois Remington, comp. *Moses Stanford, Minuteman, A Stanford Family History, with Connections to other Colonial Massachusetts Families*. San José: [no publisher given], 1978.

Society of California Pioneers. *Constitution and By-Laws of the Society of California Pioneers as revised December 1912 and List of Members since its Organization*. San Francisco: Society of California Pioneers, 1912.

Society of California Pioneers. *Constitution and By-Laws of the Sacramento Society of California Pioneers*. Sacramento: Jefferis, 1872.

Spinazze, Libera Martina, et al., comps. *The Index of People, Ships, Immigration and Mining Companies Mentioned in C[harles] W[arren] Haskins' "The Argonauts of California."* New Orleans: Polyanthos, 1975.

Stanford, Arthur Willis. *Stanford Genealogy, Comprising the Descendants of Abner Stanford, the Revolutionary Soldier*. Yokohama: The Fukuin Printing Co., 1906.

Starrett, Vincent. *Ambrose Bierce: A Bibliography*. Philadelphia: The Centaur Book Shop, 1929.

Stevenson, Elizabeth. *Park Maker: Frederick Law Olmsted*. New York: Macmillan, 1977.

Stoddard, William O. *Men of Achievement. Men of Business*. New York: Charles Scribner's Sons. 1893. Chapter 16, "Leland Stanford," 295–317. There is hardly a paragraph without a mistake.

Swasey, William F. *The Early Days and Men of California*. Oakland: Pacific Press Publishing Co., 1891, "Frank M. Pixley," 311–317.

Swisher, Carl Brent. *Stephen J. Field: Craftsman of the Law*. Washington: The Brookings Institution, 1930.

The Bay of San Francisco. The Metropolis of the Pacific Coast and its Suburban Cities. A History. 2 vols., Chicago: The Lewis Publishing Co., 1892. A series of biographical sketches.

Thompson, Gerald. *Edward F. Beale & the American West*. Albuquerque: University of New Mexico Press, 1983.

Tilton, Cecil Gage. *William Chapman Ralston, Courageous Builder*. Boston: Christopher Publishing House, 1935.

"Tour of the President, to the Pacific Coast, April 14th to May 16th, 1891." The complete itinerary of President Benjamin Harrison's trip to the Pacific Coast, with tables and maps. Stanford Papers.

Tutorow, Norman Eugene. *James Gillespie Blaine and the Presidency: A Documentary Study and Source Book*. New York: Peter Lang Publishing, 1989.

Tutorow, Norman Eugene. *Leland Stanford: Man of Many Careers*. Menlo Park: Pacific Coast Publishers, 1970.

Tutorow, Norman Eugene. *The Early Years of Leland Stanford. New Yorker Who Built the Central Pacific Railroad*. Pamphlet, Ithaca, New York: Historical Society of Tompkins County, 1969.

Tutorow, Norman Eugene, and Evelyn "Evie" LaNora Tutorow. *But . . . It's Written in Stone! The Memorial Monument of Leland Stanford, Jr*. Palo Alto: Chadwick House Publishers, 1999.

United States Naval Academy. *Register of Alumni: Graduates and former Naval Cadets and Midshipmen*. Annapolis: United States Naval Academy Alumni Association, 1972.

The War of the Rebellion: A Compilation of the Official Records of the Union and Confederation Armies. 4 series. 70 "vols.," 128 books. Washington: Government Printing Office, 1880–1901. Roman numerals are used for Series, Vols., and Parts (if any); pages are in Arabic numerals.

Williams, David A. *David C. Broderick, A Political Portrait*. San Marino: The Huntington Library, 1969.

Wood, Ellen Lamont. *George Yount, The Kindly Host of Caymus Rancho*. San Francisco: Grabhorn Press, 1941.

B. Periodicals, Biographical Reference Works, and Sections of Books

"Aaron Augustus Sargent," *Biographical Directory of the American Congress 1774–1961*. Washington: Government Printing Office, 1961. Also printed as *House Document 442*, Eighty-fifth Congress, Second Session.

"Adolf Kussmaul, obituary," *Directory of Deceased American Physicians 1804–1929*, I.

"Alfred Bernhard Nobel," *New Columbia Encyclopedia*, 1975, p. 1948.

Bach, Christian A., and Frederic Logan Paxson [Allen Johnson and Dumas Malone, eds.]. "Ulysses Simpson Grant," *Dictionary of American Biography*. New York: Charles Scribner's Sons, [1930], 1959, IV, Part 1, 492–501.

"Baker, Edward Dickinson," *Biographical Directory of the American Congress 1774–1961*. Washington: Government Printing Office, 1961. Printed as *House Document 442*, Eighty-fifth Congress, Second Session.

Bakken, Gordon Morris. "Postscript: The Retirement of Stephen Field," *The California Supreme Court Historical Society Yearbook* 1996–1997 3 (annual): 138–145.

Barker, Charles A. "Elisha Oscar Crosby, A California Lawyer in the Eighteen-Fifties," *California Historical Society Quarterly* 1948 27 (2): 133–140.

Bateman, Newton, and Paul Selby. "Littler, David T.," *Historical Encyclopedia of Illinois*, I, 341.

"Beard, Augustus Field," *Who Was Who Among North American Authors, 1921–1939*, Vol. 1. A–J. Detroit: Gale Research Co., 1976.

"Beard, Augustus Field," *Who Was Who in America, Vol. 1, 1897–1942*. Chicago: Marquis Who's Who, 1960.

Bieber, Ralph Paul. "Samuel Brannan," *Dictionary of American Biography*, Allen Johnson and Dumas Malone, eds. New York: Charles Scribner's Sons, [1930] 1959, I, Part 2, 601–602.

Biographical Directory of the Railroad Officials of America. New York: Simmons-Boardman, 1900–1985. Various years were edited and compiled by different people: volumes used in this work include one in 1913 by Harold Francis Lane, and another in 1922 by Elmer T. Howson.

"Bonner, Robert," *The National Cyclopedia of American Biography* 1900, X, 298–299.

Bridgman, Louis W. "Leland Stanford of Port Washington," *Wisconsin Freemason* 1955 12 (-): 5–6.

Brown, Leon B., and Raymond M. Kay, copywriters. "Traditions," *Stanford Quad* 1925, 41–49.

Brownson, Carleton L. [Allen Johnson and Dumas Malone, eds.]. "Sidney Edward Mezes," *Dictionary of American Biography*. New York: Charles Scribner's Sons, [1930], 1959, VI, Part 2, 588–589.

Burch, George W., Jr. "A California Giant, Leland Stanford as a Freemason," *California Freemason* 1964 11 (1): 19–29.

Camp, Charles L. "William Alexander Trubody and the Overland Pioneers of 1847," *California Historical Society Quarterly* 1937 16 (2): 122–143.

"Captain Nicholas T. Smith," *San Francisco: Its Builders Past and Recent, Pictorial and Biographical*. Chicago and San Francisco: The S. J. Clarke Publishing Co., 1913, I, 398–401.

Cattell, Jaques, ed. "Dr. Welton Joseph Crook," *American Men of Science*, tenth ed., A–E. *The Physical and Biological Sciences*. Tempe, Arizona: Jaques Cattell Press, 1960.

Clark, George Thomas. "Leland Stanford and H. H. Bancroft's 'History,' A Bibliographical Curiosity," *The Papers of the Bibliographical Society of America* 1933 27 (Part 1): 12–23.

Coman, Edwin Truman, Jr. "Sidelights on the Investment Policies of Stanford, Huntington, Hopkins, and Crocker," *Bulletin of the Business Historical Society* 1942 16 (November): 85–89.

"Commemorating Stanford's Founder," *Stanford Alumni Review* 1942 44 (1): 13.

Corwin, Edward S. [Allen Johnson and Dumas Malone, eds.]. "Stephen Johnson Field," *Dictionary of American Biography*. New York: Charles Scribner's Sons, [1930], 1959, III, Part 2, 372–376.

Cutter, Charles H. "Parsimonious Patron of the University of California [Michael Reese]," *California Historical Society Quarterly* 1963 42 (2): 127–144.

Daggett, Stuart [Allen Johnson and Dumas Malone, eds.]. "Theodore DeHone Judah," *Dictionary of American Biography*. New York: Charles Scribner's Sons, [1930], 1959, V, Part 2, 229.

"David Douty Colton," *Records of the Families of California Pioneers*. [San Francisco]: Daughters of the American Revolution, 1941, IX, 73–76.

Dinsmore, Charles Allen [Allen Johnson and Dumas Malone, eds.]. "Phillips Brooks," *Dictionary of American Biography*. New York: Charles Scribner's Sons, [1930], 1959, VII, Part 1, 83–88.

Drury, Clifford M. "John White Geary and his Brother Edward," *California Historical Society Quarterly* 1941 20 (1): 12–25.

"Drusilla O. Montz [James Otterson's granddaughter]," *Wagon Wheels* 1967 17 (1): 41.

Dunlap, Boutwell. "Some Facts Concerning Leland Stanford and His Contemporaries in Placer County," *California Historical Society Quarterly* 1923 2 (3): 203–210.

"Elisha Oscar Crosby," *The Bay of San Francisco. The Metropolis of the Pacific Coast and its Suburban Cities. A History*. 3 vols., Chicago: The Lewis Publishing Co., 1892, II, 108–112.

"Erastus Sauren Holden," *Records of the Families of California Pioneers*. [San Francisco]: Daughters of the American Revolution, 1941, X, 367–370.

"ETC," *Overland Monthly* 1893 22 (128): 219–220.

Fanning, Peter. "Early History of California," *Douglas 20, Police Journal* 1926 4 (3): 17, 42–43. Biographical sketch of Leland Stanford.

Ferris, Joel E. "Hiram Gano Ferris of Illinois and California," *California Historical Society Quarterly* 1947 26 (3): 289–307.

Fish, Carl Russell [Allen Johnson and Dumas Malone, eds.]. "George Ticknor Curtis," *Dictionary of American Biography*. New York: Charles Scribner's Sons, [1930], 1959, II, Part 2, 613–614.

"Foote, Henry Stuart," *Biographical Directory of the American Congress 1774–1961*. Washington: Government Printing Office, 1961.

Ford, Miriam Allen de. "Palo Alto's Mysterious Frenchman," *California Historical Society Quarterly* 1954 33 (2): 169–174.

"F[rançois] L[ouis] A[lfred] Pioche," *California Mail Bag*, May 1872, i–viii.

Frederick, John H. [Allen Johnson and Dumas Malone, eds.]. "Charles Crocker," *Dictionary of American Biography*. New York: Charles Scribner's Sons, [1930], 1959, II, Part 2, 552.

Frederick, John H. [Allen Johnson and Dumas Malone, eds.]. "Robert Emory Pattison," *Dictionary of American Biography*. New York: Charles Scribner's Sons, [1930], 1959, VII, Part 2, 313–314.

Fredman, Lionel E. "Thomas Welton Stanford: An American in Exile," *The Victorian Historical Magazine* 1962 33 (1): 244–250.

Freeman, Christine. "1827—Aaron Augustus Sargent—1887, Nevada County's International Citizen," *Nevada County Historical Society Bulletin* 1978 32 (3): 13–21.

Fuess, Claude M. [Allen Johnson and Dumas Malone, eds.]. "Wendell Phillips," *Dictionary of American Biography*. New York: Charles Scribner's Sons, [1930], 1959, VII, Part 2, 546–547.

Gruber, Steve. "Who Killed Mrs. Stanford? Was it the butler? the maid? or was it a natural death? after 62 years, nobody knows," *Stanford Daily Magazine*, Friday, May 26, 1967 151A (1): 8–9.

Hafner, Arthur W., ed. *Directory of Deceased American Physicians 1804–1929; a Genealogical Guide to over 149,000 Medical Practitioners providing brief biographical Sketches drawn from the American Medical Association's Deceased Physician Masterfile*. 2 vols., Chicago: American Medical Association, 1993.

Hafner, Arthur W., ed. "William Jenner," *Directory of Deceased American Physicians 1804–1929*, I, 798;

Hagar, Horace H. [Allen Johnson and Dumas Malone, eds.]. "David Smith Terry," *Dictionary of American Biography*. New York: Charles Scribner's Sons, [1930], 1959, IX, Part 2, 379–380.

Harlow, Alvin F. [Allen Johnson and Dumas Malone, eds.]. "Lloyd Tevis," *Dictionary of American Biography*. New York: Charles Scribner's Sons, [1930], 1959, IX, Part 2, 384–385.

Harlow, Alvin F. [Allen Johnson and Dumas Malone, eds.]. "Alexander Turney Stewart," *Dictionary of American Biography*. New York: Charles Scribner's Sons, [1930], 1959, IX, Part 2, 3–5.

Harlow, Alvin F. [Allen Johnson and Dumas Malone, eds.]. "William Marcy Tweed," *Dictionary of American Biography*. New York: Charles Scribner's Sons, [1930], 1959, X, Part 1, 79–82.

"Harry Pratt Judson," *The National Cyclopedia of American Biography*, Vol. 20. New York: James T. White & Co., 1929.

"Hastings, Serranus Clinton," *Biographical Directory of the American Congress 1774–1961*. Washington: Government Printing Office, 1961, 1022. Also printed as *House Document 442*, Eighty-fifth Congress, Second Session.

Hatch, John Davis, Jr. [Stanford's election to New York Hall of Fame], *Albany County Historical Association Record* 1948 7 (2): 1–4.

Hubert, Mme E. "Gréard, Valéry-Clément-Octave," in Roman D'Amat, ed. *Dictionnaire de Biographie Française*. Vol. 16, p. 1126. Paris: Librairie Letouzey et Ané, 1975.

Hunt, Rockwell Dennis. "Twelve Apostles of California," *Historical Society of Southern California Quarterly* 1956 38 (4): 9–38.

"James Harvey Strobridge," in James Miller Guinn, *History of the State of California*, 739–740. See full book title.

Johnson, Rossiter, ed.-in-chief. *The Twentieth Century Biographical Dictionary of Notable Americans*. 10 vols., Boston: The Biographical Society, 1994.

Johnston, Theresa. "About a Boy," *Stanford* July/August 2003 31 (4) 38–43.

Jordan, David Starr. "Jane Lathrop Stanford, A Eulogy," *Stanford Alumnus* 1909 10 (7): 257–267; *Popular Science Monthly*, August 19, 1909, 157–171. Founders' Day Address, March 9, 1909.

Jordan, David Starr. "ON THE NORTH FORK (The Keeper of the Toll Gate Speaks of Leland Stanford.)," first published in the *Stanford Sequoia* March 1918 27 (5): 161–162; reprinted in part in "The First Stanford Home," *Stanford Illustrated Review* 1923 24 (June): 477 and 495.

Keeney, Charles C. "Case of General Colton, and the Causes of his Death," *Pacific Medical and Surgical Journal* 1878 21 (7): 309–316.

Kennedy, Donald. "Kennedy Assesses the Jordan Years," *Sandstone & Tile* 1981 5 (2): 8–9.

Klepper, Michael, and Robert Gunther, comps. Biographical sketches by Jeanette Baik, Linda Barth, and Christine Gibson. "The American Heritage 40," *American Heritage* 1998 49 (October): 56–60, 62, 66, 68, 70, 72, and 74. A ranking of the forty wealthiest Americans of all time.

Knott, H. W. Howard. [Allen Johnson and Dumas Malone, eds.]. "Delphin Michael Delmas," *Dictionary of American Biography*. New York: Charles Scribner's Sons, [1930], 1959, III, Part 1, 226.

"Leland Stanford," *California Mail Bag* 1871 1 (3): 1–4.

"Leland Stanford," *California Mail Bag* 1874 5 (4): i–xxiv. Contains a biographical sketch of Leland Stanford and a copy of "Leland Stanford's Speech to the Men who Work in the Rail Shops at Sacramento," made on March 10, 1873.

"Leland Stanford," *The Centennial Spirit of the Times*. San Francisco: California Spirit of the Times and Fireman's Journal, July 4, 1876, 2 (40-page special ed.).

"Leland Stanford," *Harper's Encyclopaedia of United States History, from 458 A.D. to 1905.* 10 vols., New York: Harper & Brothers Publishers, 1906.

"Leland Stanford," in Richard B. Morris, ed., *Encyclopedia of American History*. New York: Harper & Row, Publishers, [1953], 1965.

"Leland Stanford," *San Francisco: Its Builders Past and Recent, Pictorial and Biographical*. Chicago and San Francisco: The S. J. Clarke Publishing Co., 1913, II, 18–26. It is a challenge to find a single accurate statement in this oft-used sketch, but with great perseverance it can be done.

"Lincoln, Abraham," *Biographical Directory of the American Congress 1774–1961*. Washington: Government Printing Office, 1961.

Long, Linda J. "The Stanfords as Parents," *Sandstone & Tile* 1991 15 (1): 10–13.

Lowney, Barbara. "Lady Bountiful: Margaret Crocker of Sacramento," *California Historical Society Quarterly* 1968 47 (2): 99–112.

Luck, J. Murray. "Cooperation—An Aspect of the Social Philosophy of Leland Stanford," *Co-Op News*, April 13, 27, May 11, 1950.

Lummis, Charles F., ed. "A Jason of the Coast [Frank Pixley obituary]," *The Land of Sunshine, A Southwestern Magazine* 1895 3 (June to November): 237.

"Mark Hopkins," *The New Encyclopedia Britannica* (Micropaedia), 15th ed., VI, 55.

"Mark Twain," *Encyclopedia Americana*, 1998, XXVII, 291a–291d.

"Mark Twain," *The New Encyclopedia Britannica*, 1998, XII, 75–77.

May, Ernest R. "Benjamin Parke Avery," *California Historical Society Quarterly* 1951 30 (2): 125–149.

McDowell, Kate. "The Stanfords' Sacramento Years," *Sandstone & Tile* 1991 15 (1): 1–9.

McKee, Irving. "Three Wine-Growing Senators," *California Magazine of the Pacific* 1947 37 (9): 15, 28–29.

Meneely, A. Howard [Allen Johnson and Dumas Malone, eds.]. "Edwin McMasters Stanton," *Dictionary of American Biography*. New York: Charles Scribner's Sons, [1930], 1959, IX, Part 1, 517–521.

Meneely, A. Howard [Allen Johnson and Dumas Malone, eds.]. "Simon Cameron," *Dictionary of American Biography*. New York: Charles Scribner's Sons, [1930], 1959, II, Part 1, 437–439.

Mighels, "Aunt" Ella Sterling (Clark) Cummins (pseudonyms, Aurora Esmeralda and "Uncle" Adley Sterling). "A Memory of the Governor," *The Grizzly Bear* (Official Organ of the Native Sons of the Golden West, and the Native Daughters of the Golden West) 1912 10 (4): 4–5.

Morrow, William W. "The Founders of the University," *Leland Stanford Junior University Publications, Trustees' Series* 1914 25 (annual): 11–31. Founders' Day address, March 9, 1914.

"Mott, George Newell," *Biographical Directory of the American Congress 1774–1961*. Washington: Government Printing Office, 1961. Printed as *House Document 442*, Eighty-fifth Congress, Second Session.

Nagel, Gunther. "Boy in a Gilded Age," *California History* 1978/79 57 (4): 320–331.

Nevins, Allan [Allen Johnson and Dumas Malone, eds.]. "Horace Greeley," *Dictionary of American Biography*. New York: Charles Scribner's Sons, [1930], 1959, IV, Part 1, 528–534.

Nevins, Allan [Allen Johnson and Dumas Malone, eds.]. "Jay Gould," *Dictionary of American Biography*. New York: Charles Scribner's Sons, [1930], 1959, IV, Part 1, 454–455.

Nevins, Allan [Allen Johnson and Dumas Malone, eds.]. "Rutherford Birchard Hayes," *Dictionary of American Biography*. New York: Charles Scribner's Sons, [1930], 1959, IV, Part 2, 446–451.

"Nicholas T. Smith," *The National Cyclopedia of American Biography*, 1922, XVIII, 158.

Nichols, Jeannette P. [Allen Johnson and Dumas Malone, eds.]. "Francis Amasa Walker," *Dictionary of American Biography*. New York: Charles Scribner's Sons, [1930], 1959, X, Part 1, 342–344.

Nichols, Roy F. [Allen Johnson and Dumas Malone, eds.]. "Jeremiah Sullivan Black," *Dictionary of American Biography*. New York: Charles Scribner's Sons, [1930], 1959, I, Part 2, 310–313.

Nichols, Roy F. [Allen Johnson and Dumas Malone, eds.]. "John White Geary," *Dictionary of American Biography*. New York: Charles Scribner's Sons, [1930], 1959, IV, Part 1, 203–204.

Nilan, Roxanne. "Jane Lathrop Stanford and the Domestication of Stanford University," *San Jose Studies* 1979 5 (1): 7–29.

Nilan, Roxanne. "Josiah Home in Oakland Restored," *Stanford Historical Society Newsletter* 1978 3 (4): 7.

Nilan, Roxanne. "The Life and Times of a Victorian Lady: Jane Lathrop Stanford," *Sandstone & Tile* 1997 21 (3): 3–14.

Nilan, Roxanne. "The Tenacious and Courageous Jane L. Stanford," *Stanford Historical Society Newsletter* 1984 9 (1): 2–13.

Oberholtzer, Ellis Paxon. "Jay Cooke," *Dictionary of American Biography*, Allen Johnson and Dumas Malone, eds. New York: Charles Scribner's Sons, [1930], 1959, II, Part 2, 383–384.

Pallette, Edward M. "Peter the Frenchman," *Stanford Illustrated Review* 1925 4 (1): 131–132.

Park, Helen Van Cleave, ed., and Elinor Burt, assistant ed. "Remembering Frank Morrison Pixley," *Marin County Historical Society Bulletin* 1967 1 (2): 3.

Parker, J. Carlyle. *An Index to the Biographees [sic] in 19th Century California County Histories*. Detroit: Gail Research Co., 1977.

Pease, Otis A. "The Man, the Time, the Risk: Leland Stanford's last Extraordinary Enterprise in Founding the University," *Stanford Magazine* 1974 2 (1): 14–19.

Peck, Catherine C. "[Stanford Through the Century/John Casper Branner]," *Sandstone & Tile* 1997 21 (1): 11–12.

Potts, E. Daniel. "Thomas Welton Stanford," *Australian Dictionary of Biography*. 12 vols., Melbourne: Melbourne University Press, 1990.

Potts, E. Daniel, and Annette Potts. "Thomas Welton Stanford (1832–1918) and American-Australian Business and Cultural Relations," *Historical Studies* [University of Melbourne] 1976 17 (67): 193–209.

Randall, James G. [Allen Johnson and Dumas Malone, eds.]. "Lincoln, Abraham," *Dictionary of American Biography*. New York: Charles Scribner's Sons, [1930], 1959, VI, Part 1, 242–259.

Ray, Perley Orman [Allen Johnson and Dumas Malone, eds.]. "Aaron Augustus Sargent," *Dictionary of American Biography.* New York: Charles Scribner's Sons, [1930], 1959, VIII, Part 2, 353–354.

Ray, Perley Orman [Allen Johnson and Dumas Malone, eds.]. "Denis Kearney," *Dictionary of American Biography.* New York: Charles Scribner's Sons, [1930], 1959, V, Part 2, 268–269.

Ray, Perley Orman [Allen Johnson and Dumas Malone, eds.]. "John Franklin Swift," *Dictionary of American Biography.* New York: Charles Scribner's Sons, [1930], 1959, IX, Part 2, 246–247.

Ray, Perley Orman [Allen Johnson and Dumas Malone, eds.]. "Louis Sloss," *Dictionary of American Biography.* New York: Charles Scribner's Sons, [1930], 1959, IX, Part 1, 219–220.

Regnery, Dorothy. "Coutts was no Eccentric, Study Shows," *Stanford Historical Society Newsletter* 1981 5 (3): 3–6.

Regnery, Dorothy. "Researcher Finds final resting [*sic*] for Peter Coutts," *Stanford Historical Society Newsletter* 1982 6 (2): 15–16.

Robson, Katherine Pixley. "Frank Morrison Pixley," *Marin County Historical Society Bulletin* 1967 1 (2): 4–5.

"Salisbury, James Henry," *The National Cyclopedia of American Biography*, VIII, 469–470.

"Samuel Langhorne Clemens," *Encyclopedia Britannica*, 1895, V, 477.

Sewell, Alfred L. "Reward of Honest Industry" [Sketch of the life of Alban Nelson Towne], *The National Car-Builder* 1880 11 (1): 1–2.

Shaw, Albert. "Leland Stanford: Some Notes on the Career of a Successful Man," *Review of Reviews* 1893 8 (43): 154–168.

"Ship Named for Founder," *Stanford Alumni Review* 1943 44 (8): 1.

"Sir William Jenner," *Journal of the American Medical Association* 1970 214 (5): 907–908.

Smith, Gerald Birney [Allen Johnson and Dumas Malone, eds.]. "Galusha Anderson," *Dictionary of American Biography.* New York: Charles Scribner's Sons, [1930], 1959, I, Part 1, 264–265.

Snyder, Rixford K. "Stanford and Australia," *Sandstone & Tile* 1989 13 (3): 7–8. The subject is Leland's brother Welton.

Sobel, Robert, ed.-in-chief. *Biographical Directory of the United States Executive Branch 1774–1971.* Westport: Greenwood Publishing Company, 1971.

Spaulding, Oliver L., Jr. [Allen Johnson and Dumas Malone, eds.]. "George Stoneman," *Dictionary of American Biography.* New York: Charles Scribner's Sons, [1930], 1959, XI, Part 2, 92–93.

Staniford, Edward. "Horace W. Carpentier—King of Controversy," *Berkeley Independent and Gazette*, June 15, 1980.

Starr, Harris Elwood [Allen Johnson and Dumas Malone, eds.]. "Thomas Starr King," *Dictionary of American Biography.* New York: Charles Scribner's Sons, [1930], 1959, V, Part 2, 403–405.

Stewart, George R., Jr. [Allen Johnson and Dumas Malone, eds.]. "Francis Brett Harte," *Dictionary of American Biography.* New York: Charles Scribner's Sons, [1930], 1959, IV, Part 2, 362–365.

Svanevik, Michael, and Shirley Burgett. "One Man's Family," *Gentry Magazine* 1993 1 (3): 39–40.

Taggart, Harold F., ed. "The Journal of David Jackson Staples," *California Historical Society Quarterly* 1943 22 (2): 110–150.

Taylor, Katherine Ames. "New Light on Mrs. Stanford," *Stanford Illustrated Review* 1935 37 (1): 28–29. Remarks on Bertha Berner and her biography of Jane Stanford.

"The Strobridge Family," *Adobe Trails* 1970 6 (4): 8–12.

"Timothy Guy Phelps," *Biographical Directory of the American Congress 1774–1961.* Washington: Government Printing Office, 1961. Printed as *House Document 442*, Eighty-fifth Congress, Second Session.

Treat, Payson J. "Thomas Welton Stanford," *Stanford Sequoia* 1907 17 (2): 43–46. An oft-quoted work almost every "factual" statement of which is incorrect.

Tutorow, Norman Eugene. "Charles Crocker," *Encyclopedia USA: The Encyclopedia of the United States of America—Past and Present* 1992, XVII, 126–129.

Tutorow, Norman Eugene. "Leland Stanford: Civil War Governor of California," *California and the Civil War 1861–1865.* Robert J. Chandler, ed. San Francisco: Book Club of California, 1993. Keepsake Series.

Tutorow, Norman Eugene. "Leland Stanford, President of the Occidental and Oriental Steamship Co.," *American Neptune* 1971 31 (2): 120–129.

Tutorow, Norman Eugene. "Leland Stanford's Wisconsin Years," *Wisconsin Then and Now* 1969 15 (10): 1–4.

Tutorow, Norman Eugene. "Leland Stanford, 1824–1893," *Read More about It: An Encyclopedia of Information on Historical Figures and Events.* Ann Arbor: The Pierian Press, 1989. III, 653–655.

Tutorow, Norman Eugene. "Stanford's Response to Competition: Rhetoric versus Reality," *Southern California Quarterly* 1970 52 (3): 231–247.

Tutorow, Norman Eugene, and Evelyn "Evie" LaNora Tutorow. "Captain Nicholas T. Smith, from Schodack to San Carlos," *La Peninsula* [The Journal of the San Mateo County (California) Historical Society] 1998 31 (2): 3–28.

Wagner, Henry R. "Edward Bosqui, Printer and Man of Affairs," *California Historical Society Quarterly* 1941 21 (4): 321–332.

"Washburn, Charles Ames," *National Cyclopedia of American Biography,* V, 255–256.

Weber, David C. "Pixley of Pixley: An Artesian Spring in the Valley," *The Book Club of California Quarterly News-Letter* 1997 62 (1): 15–20.

Wheat, Carl I. "A Sketch of the Life of Theodore D. Judah," *California Historical Society Quarterly* 1925 4 (3): 219–271.

Wheat, Carl I. "'California's Bantam Cock'—The Journals of Charles E. De Long, 1854–1863," *California Historical Society Quarterly* 1931 10 (1): 40–78; 10 (4): 355–395.

Whitwell, Gertrude Howard (the subject's granddaughter). "William Davis Merry Howard," *California Historical Society Quarterly* 1948 27 (2): 105–112; (3): 249–255; (4): 319–332.

"William H. Sharp," *The Bay of San Francisco. The Metropolis of the Pacific Coast and its Suburban Cities. A History.* 3 vols., Chicago: The Lewis Publishing Co., 1892, II, 269–270.

"William W. Morrow," *Biographical Directory of the American Congress 1774–1961.* Washington: Government Printing Office, 1961.

Williams, David A. "The Forgery of the Broderick Will," *California Historical Society Quarterly* 1961 40 (3): 203–214.

Winn, William W. "Joaquin Miller's 'Real Name,'" *California Historical Society Quarterly* 1954 33 (2): 143–146.

Winn, William W. "The Joaquin Miller Foundation," *California Historical Society Quarterly* 1953 32 (3): 231–241.

12. Stanford University Studies

A. Books

Allen, Peter C. *Stanford from the Beginning.* Stanford: Office of Public Affairs, [1962], 1984. This seventy-three-page pamphlet contains an overview of the founding of Stanford University.

Allen, Peter C. *Stanford: from the Foothills to the Bay.* Palo Alto: Stanford Alumni Association & Stanford Historical Society, 1980.

Bartholomew, Karen, Claude S. Brinegar, and Roxanne Nilan. *A Chronology of Stanford University and its Founders: 1824–2000.* Stanford: Stanford Historical Society, 2001.

Crothers, George E. *Founding of the Leland Stanford Junior University*. San Francisco: A.M. Robertson, 1932.

Davis, Horace. *The Meaning of the University. An Address at Leland Stanford Junior University on Founder's Day, March 9, 1894*. San Francisco: [no publisher given], 1895.

Elliott, Orrin Leslie. *Stanford University, the First Twenty-five Years*. Stanford: Stanford University Press, 1937.

Hofstadter, Richard, and Walter P. Metzger. *The Development of Academic Freedom in the United States*. New York: Columbia University Press, 1955.

Hutten, Ulrich von [Eduard Böcking, ed.]. *Ulrichi Hutteni equities germani opera quæ reperiri potuerunt omnia*. Edidit Eduardus Böcking. Lipsiæ: Teubnerianis, 1859–1870. [*The Works of Ulrich von Hutten*]. 7 vols., Leipzig: B[enedikt] G[otthelf] Teubner, 1859–1862, II.

Illustrated Fraternal Directory including Educational Institutions of the Pacific Coast, giving a Succinct Description of the Aims and Objects of Beneficiary and Fraternal Societies and a Brief Synopsis of the Leading Colleges and Private Seminaries compiled from Official Records and Society Archives. San Francisco: Bancroft and Co., 1889.

Jordan, David Starr. *Leland Stanford's Views on Higher Education*. Stanford: Stanford University Press, 1901.

Jordan, David Starr. *Ulrich von Hutten* (Knight of the Order of Poets). Boston: American Unitarian Association, 1910; Yonkers-on-Hudson, New York: World Book, 1922.

The Leland Stanford Junior University First Annual Register 1891–1892. Palo Alto: Stanford University, 1892.

The Leland Stanford Junior University. Includes "Senator Stanford's Plan for its Organization," "The Grant Founding and Endowing the University," "Description of the Property Embraced in Grant," and "Portraits of the Trustees." San Francisco: The Bancroft Co., 1888.

Mirrielees, Edith Ronald. *Stanford, The Story of a University*. New York: G. P. Putnam's Sons, 1959.

Osborne, Carol Margot. *Museum Builders of the West: The Stanfords as Collectors and Patrons of Art 1870–1906*. Stanford: Stanford University Museum of Art, 1986.

Simpson, Fronia W. *The Stanford Museum Centennial Handbook. 100 Years. 100 Works of Art*. Stanford: Stanford University Museum of Art, 1991.

Stanford: A man, a woman, and a University. Stanford: Stanford Publications Service, 1962.

Stanford University. *2000 Annual Report*. Stanford: Stanford Publications Service. Office of the Controller, 2000.

Stanford University—2002. Stanford: Office of Undergraduate Admission, 2001.

Stanford University. *The Founding Grant With Amendments, Legislation, and Court Decrees Published by the University 1971*. [Stanford: Stanford University, 1971].

Summary and Explanation. Stanford University Draft Community Plan and General Use Permit Application. Stanford: Stanford Planning Department, 1999. Submitted to Santa Clara County, November 15, 1999.

Turner, Paul V., and Marcia E. Vetrocq. *The Founders and the Architects, the Design of Stanford University*. Stanford: Stanford Department of Art, 1976.

B. Periodicals

Allen, Peter C. "Quad-Angles . . . with the editor," *Stanford Review* 1947 48 (5): 14.

Altenberg, Lee. "Beyond Capitalism: Leland Stanford's Forgotten Vision," *Sandstone & Tile* 1990 14 (1): 8–20. This has been published in varying forms, including one on Internet.

Arthur, Allen A. "A Flip of a Coin Put Stanford University Down on the Farm," *Los Angeles Times*, June 17, 1966, Part 5, 10.

Barclay, Thomas S. "Genesis of a Great University," *Stanford Review* 1962 63 (6): 16–19.

Bartholomew, Karen E. "The Bad Boys of Encina Hall," *Stanford* September/October 1998, 80–82.

Bartholomew, Karen E., and Claude S. Brinegar. "Old Chemistry, One of Jane Stanford's Noble Works," *Sandstone & Tile* 1999 23 (1): 3–10.

Casper, Gerhard. "Die Luft der Freiheit weht—on and off," *Sandstone & Tile* 1995 19 (4): 13–23. On the origins and history of a Stanford motto.

"Change in Entrance Rules for Women," *Stanford Alumnus* 1914 15 (5): 182.

Choate, Nellita N. "Why Only 500?" *Stanford Illustrated Review* 1917 2 (8): 243–244.

Clark, George Thomas. "The Romance that Founded Stanford," *Stanford Illustrated Review* 1929 30 (June): 461–467.

Cole, John Y. *Book Collectors at Stanford: An Eclectic Eight Who Shaped the Stanford University Libraries*. Sacramento: California State Library Foundation, 1991. Particularly "Thomas Welton Stanford, A Friend in Australia," 36–42.

Crothers, George E. "Historical Outline of the Founding of Stanford," *Stanford Illustrated Review* 1931 33 (1): 14–15, 26–34, 36, 38, and 40.

Crothers, Thomas G. "In the matter of the Petition of Leland Stanford, Jr. University and of Timothy Hopkins, Horace Davis, et al." In the Superior Court of the County of Santa Clara, State of California. No. 14912, Department 2. This document is now in the Stanford Law Library, "Golden" Collection.

Elliott, Orrin Leslie. "Stanford University," *California Commerce* 1897 1 (4): 2–3.

"The First Founders' Day," *Stanford Review* 1952 53 (6): 14–15.

"The Founders' Day Addresses," *Stanford Alumnus* 1917 18 (7): 216–230; David Starr Jordan discusses "Foundation Ideals," 224–226. Founders' Day, March 10, 1917.

"The Founding of Stanford University: An Exhibit in Celebration," *Stanford Historical Society Newsletter* 1985 10 (1): 1–11.

"A Home amid the Trees," *Stanford* September/October 1998, 29.

Johnston, Theresa. "Mrs. Stanford and the Netherworld," *Stanford Magazine* 2000 (May/June): 68–73.

Jordan, David Starr. "The Educational Ideas of Leland Stanford," *The Sequoia* 1893 3 (2): 19–22.

Jordan, David Starr. "The Foundation Ideals of Stanford University," *Leland Stanford Junior University Publications*, Trustees' Series No. 27, 1915, 3–22. Founders' Day Address, March 9, 1915.

Jordan, David Starr. "The Wind of Freedom," *Stanford Illustrated Review* 1918 19 (8): 297.

Mohr, James C. "Academic Turmoil and Public Opinion: The Ross Case at Stanford," *Pacific Historical Review* 1970 39 (1): 39–61.

Morgan, B[ayard] Q[uincy]. "How Stanford Selected that 'Winds of Freedom' Slogan," *Stanford Illustrated Review* 1937 39 (9): 22–23.

Nagel, Gunther W. "The Legacy of Ulrich von Hutten," *Stanford Review* 1962 63 (6): 12–15.

Osborne, Carol Margot. "Stanford Family Portraits by Bonnat, Carolus-Duran, Meissonier, and other French Artists of the 1880s," *Stanford Museum* 1980–1981 10 and 11 (-): 2–12.

Press, Harry. "Stanford Celebrates its Founding," *Sandstone & Tile* 1986 10 (2): 3–12.

"Resignation of Dr. E. A. Ross," *Stanford Alumnus* 1900 2 (3): 33–37.

Shinn, Milicent W. "The Leland Stanford, Junior University," *Overland Monthly* 1891 18 (106): 337–355.

"Sixteen Professors Retire," *Stanford Review* 1952 53 (10): 13.

Strauss, David Friederich. *Ulrich von Hutten*. Two vols. published as one, Leipzig: F. A. Brockhaus, 1858, II.

Turner, Paul V. "The Stanfords' Vision of Their University: Was It Appropriate?" *Sandstone & Tile* 2000 24 (2–3): 1–7. First delivered as a Stanford University Founder's Day Talk, April 9, 2000.

Tutorow, Norman Eugene. "Four Universities: Founders' Visions and Today's Reality: Stanford University," *Academic Questions* 1998 11 (2): 70–73.

13. VINEYARDS AND STOCK FARM
A. Books, Brochures, and Pamphlets

Adams, Burton Warren. *Wente Bros.* Folder 9 of James D. Hart, ed. *The Vine in Early California*. San Francisco: Book Club of California, 1955. Keepsake Series.

Adams, Leon D. *Inglenook*. Folder 1 of Joseph Henry Jackson, ed. *The Vine in Early California*. San Francisco: Book Club of California, 1955. Keepsake Series.

Beard, James E. *Charles Krug*. Folder 8 of James D. Hart, ed. *The Vine in Early California*. San Francisco: Book Club of California, 1955. Keepsake Series.

Brown, Philip S. *El Aliso*. Folder 6 of Joseph Henry Jackson, ed. *The Vine in Early California*. San Francisco: Book Club of California, 1955. Keepsake Series.

Bundschu, Charles. *The Vineyards in Alameda County, The Report of Charles Bundschu, Commissioner for the San Francisco District, to the Board of State Viticultural Commissioners of California*. Sacramento: [no publisher given], 1893.

Bynum, Lindley. *San Gabriel*. Folder 4 of Joseph Henry Jackson, ed. *The Vine in Early California*. San Francisco: Book Club of California, 1955. Keepsake Series.

Carosso, Vincent P. *The California Wine Industry, A Study of the Formative Years, 1830–1895*. Berkeley: University of California Press, 1951.

Castro, Kenneth M., and Eugene L. "Gino" Fambrini, comps. *E Clampus Vitus Plaques. A Compilation of historical Plaques with Photographs dedicated by the Ancient and Honorable Order of E Clampus Vitus, 1930–1995*. Oakland: E Clampus Vitus, 1995.

Colburn, Frona Eunice Wait (Smith). *Wines and Vines of California, A Treatise on the Ethics of Wine-Drinking*. San Francisco: Bancroft, 1889.

Goodlett, Joan. *Korbel*. Folder 11 of James D. Hart, ed. *The Vine in Early California*. San Francisco: Book Club of California, 1955. Keepsake Series.

Hart, James D., ed. Folders 8–13 of 12-folder (13 with Contents) series *The Vine in Early California*. San Francisco: Book Club of California, 1955. Keepsake Series.

Jackson, Joseph Henry. *The Mammoth Vine*. Folder 7 of Joseph Henry Jackson, ed. *The Vine in Early California*. San Francisco: Book Club of California, 1955. Keepsake Series.

Jackson, Joseph Henry. *Nouveau Medoc*. Folder 3 of Joseph Henry Jackson, ed. *The Vine in Early California*. San Francisco: Book Club of California, 1955. Keepsake Series.

Jackson, Joseph Henry, ed. Table of Contents and the first 8 in the 12-folder (13 with Contents) series *The Vine in Early California*. San Francisco: Book Club of California, 1955. Keepsake Series.

Jones, Idwal. *Vines in the Sun: A Journey through the California Vineyards*. New York: Ballantine Books, [1949], 1972.

Lachman, Henry. See entry under Wiley, Harvey Washington.

Leggett, Herbert B. *Early History of Wine Production in California*. San Francisco: Wine Institute, April 2, 1941.

Marvin, Charles. *Training the Trotting Horse: A Natural and Improved Method of Educating Trotting Colts and Horses*. 4th ed., New York: Marvin Publishing Co., 1892.

Melville, John. *Paul Masson*. Folder 2 of Joseph Henry Jackson, ed. *The Vine in Early California*. San Francisco: Book Club of California, 1955. Keepsake Series.

Norris, Frank. *Italian Swiss Colony*. Folder 12 of James D. Hart, ed. *The Vine in Early California*. San Francisco: Book Club of California, 1955. Keepsake Series.

Palo Alto Stock Farm Eleventh Annual Catalogue. San Francisco: [no publisher given], 1894.

Peninou, Ernest P., comp. *Leland Stanford's Great Vina Ranch, 1881–1919, A Research Paper: The History of Senator Stanford's Vina Vineyard and the World's Largest Winery formerly the Site of Peter Lassen's Bosquejo and Henry Gerke's Ranch*. San Francisco: Yolo Hills Viticultural Society, 1991.

Price, Harold H. *Buena Vista*. Folder 5 of Joseph Henry Jackson, ed. *The Vine in Early California*. San Francisco: Book Club of California, 1955. Keepsake Series.

Regnery, Dorothy. *The History of Jasper Ridge: From Searsville Pioneers to Stanford Scientists*. Stanford: Stanford Historical Society, 1991.

Robson, Francis Thurston. *Stanford—Vina*. Folder 10 of James D. Hart, ed. *The Vine in Early California*. San Francisco: Book Club of California, 1955. Keepsake Series.

Stanford Historical Society. *Stanford's Red Barn*. Stanford: Stanford Historical Society, 1984.

Underwood, Thomas Rust, ed. *Thoroughbred Racing and Breeding: The Story of the Sport and Background of the Horse Industry*. New York: Coward-McCann, 1945.

Wallace, John Hankins, ed. *Wallace's Year-Book of Trotting and Racing*. New York: Wallace's Monthly, 1886–1926.

Wetmore, Charles Augustus. *Treatise on Wine Production and Special Reports on Wine Examinations, the Tariff and Internal Revenue Taxes, and Chemical Analyses, Appendix B, The Report of the Board of State Viticultural Commissioners for 1893–1894*. Sacramento: Alfred J. Johnston, Superintendent of State Printing, 1894.

Wiley, Harvey Washington. *American Wines at the Paris Exposition of 1900: Their Composition and Character*. With a monograph on the manufacture of wines in California, by Henry Lachman. Washington: Government Printing Office, 1903.

B. Periodicals and Sections of Books

Allen, Peter C. "The Red Barn Rides again," *Stanford's Red Barn*. Stanford: Stanford Historical Society, 1984.

Alway, Robert H. "A History of Stanford Vineyards and Wineries," *Bulletin of the Society of Medical Friends of Wine* 1977 19 (2): 5–7.

Arbuckle, Helen. "The Heyday of the Palo Alto Stock Farm," *Hoof Beats* May 1986, 118, 120. Text varies only slightly from following entry.

Arbuckle, Helen. "The Heyday of the Palo Alto Stock Farm," *The Western Horseman* 1973 38 (3): 76–77, 142–145.

Bartholomew, Karen. "The Farm a Century Ago," *Campus Report* 1983 15 (21): 1–4. On Palo Alto Stock Farm and its horses, twelve illustrations. Adapted and reprinted in the Stanford Historical Society's *Stanford's Red Barn*. Stanford: Stanford Historical Society, 1984.

"Electioneer's Honor Roll," in *Palo Alto Stock Farm Eleventh Annual Catalogue*. San Francisco: [no publisher given], 1894, 4–8.

"Estate of Leland Stanford, Deceased. Unusual Offering of Ranch Property by Order of Jane L. Stanford, Executrix." San Francisco: McAfee Brothers, [undated].

Gregg, Elizabeth. "The History of the Famous Stanford Ranch at Vina, California," *Overland Monthly* 1908 52 (4): 334–338.

Hansen, Ralph W. "One Hundred Years Down on the Farm," *The Imprint of the Stanford Library Associates* 1976 2 (1): 14–17.

McKee, Irving. "Historic Alameda County Wine Growers," *California Magazine of the Pacific* 1953 43 (9): 20–23.

Mosher, Francis W. "The Stanford Vina Ranch," *Stanford Illustrated Review* 1933 34 (6): 182.

"Palo Alto Stock Farm," *California Commerce* 1897 1 (4): 26–31.

Simpson, Joseph Cairn. "Horses of California. From the Days of the Missions to the Present. Fourth Paper—The Horses of Palo Alto," *Sunset Magazine* 1901 7 (1): 9–23.

Stoll, Horatio Francis. "The Wineries of Northern California," *Wines and Vines* 1937 18 (6): 3–5.

"The Residence of Leland Stanford," *The Centennial Spirit of the Times*. San Francisco: California Spirit of the Times and Fireman's Journal, July 4, 1876, 31 (40-page special edition).

Tutorow, Norman Eugene. "Leland Stanford, the Successful Failure," *Wines and Vines* 1970 51 (6): 61–62.

14. STANFORD AND MUYBRIDGE MOTION PICTURE RESEARCH

A. Books, Brochures, and Pamphlets

Board of Trustees, Stanford University. "Semi-Centennial Celebration in Commemoration of the Motion Picture Research Conducted by Leland Stanford 1878–1879, with the Assistance of Edweard [*sic*] J. Muybridge, John D. Isaacs, Jacob Davis Babcock Stillman." Stanford University, May 8, 1928. Official Delegates from the Academy of Motion Pictures Arts and Sciences participated in the celebration.

Brown, Travis. *Historical First Patents, The First United States Patent for Many Everyday Things*. Metuchen, N.J.: Scarecrow Press, 1994.

Burns, E. Bradford. *Eadweard Muybridge in Guatemala: the Photographer as Social Recorder*. Berkeley: University of California Press, 1986. The eighty-three Muybridge photographs reprinted here are copies of pictures in two albums, both titled *The Pacific Coast of Central America and Mexico; The Isthmus of Panama; Guatemala; and the Cultivation and Shipment of Coffee, Illustrated by Muybridge*. San Francisco: [Edward Bosqui & Co.], 1876. Muybridge's work does not identify the publisher, but a box in the California State Library containing this work has a business card in the book and miscellaneous Muybridge correspondence to Janet Pendegast Leigh identifying Bosqui & Co. as "Fine Arts Publishers."

Duhousset, Émile. *Le Cheval; études sur les allures, l'exterieur et les proportions du cheval; analyse de tableaux*. Paris: Charles, 1874; reprinted, Paris: Morel, 1881. It appeared in English as *The Gaits, Exterior and Proportions of the Horse*. London: P. Young, 1896.

Duval, Mathias Marie. *Artistic anatomy*. London and New York: Cassell & Co., 1884.

Gale Research Company, comp. *Currier & Ives, A Catalogue Raisonné. A Comprehensive Catalogue of the Lithographs of Nathaniel Currier, James Merritt Ives and Charles Currier, including Ephemera Associated with the Firm*. Detroit: Gale Research Co., 1984.

Gernsheim, Helmut, in collaboration with Alison Gernsheim. *The History of Photography: From the Earliest Use of the Camera Obscura in the Eleventh Century up to 1914*. London: Oxford University Press, 1955.

Haas, Robert Bartlett. "Eadweard Muybridge, 1830–1904," in Stanford Department of Art, *Eadweard Muybridge, the Stanford Years 1872–1882*. Stanford: Stanford Department of Art, 1972.

Harris, David, with Eric Sandweiss. *Eadweard Muybridge and the Photographic Panorama of San Francisco, 1850–1880*. Montreal: Centre Canadien d'Architecture, 1993.

Hendricks, Gordon. *Eadweard Muybridge: the Father of the Motion Picture*. New York: Grossman Publishers, 1975.

Hendricks, Gordon. *The Edison Motion Picture Myth*. Berkeley: University of California Press, 1961.

Hungerford, Constance Cain. *Ernest Meissonier: Master in his Genre*. Cambridge: Cambridge University Press, 1999.

MacDonnell, Kevin. *Eadweard Muybridge: The Man who invented the Moving Picture*. Boston: Little, Brown, and Co., 1972.

Marek, Kurt W. [C.W. Ceram, pseudonym]. [Eine] *Archäologie des Kinos*. London: Thames and Hudson, 1965; [Reinbek bei Hamburg]: Rowohlt, [1965]; published in English as *Archaeology of the Cinema*. New York: Harcourt, Brace & World, [1965].

Marey, Étienne-Jules. *Développement de la méthode graphique par l'emploi de la photographie. Supplement à la méthode graphique*. Paris: G. Masson, [1884].

Marey, Étienne-Jules. *La Chronophotographie*. Paris: 1899. Cited in Library of Congress entry as *Chronophotographie appliquée à l'étude des actes musculaires dans la locomotion*. Paris: [no publisher given], 1898.

Marey, Étienne-Jules. *La Machine animale, locomotion terrestre et aérienne*. Paris: Ancienne Librairie Germer Bailliére, 1873; redone, Paris: Librairie F. Alcan [éditeur], 1886. Published in English as *Animal Mechanism, a Treatise on Terrestrial and Aërial Locomotion*. London and New York: D. Appleton & Co., 1874. The 1890 English edition is used here.

Marey, Étienne-Jules. *Le mouvement*. Nîmes: Éditions Jacqueline Chambon, 1994, based on the 1884 edition of the work.

Muybridge, Eadweard. *Animal Locomotion. An Electro-photographic Investigation of Consecutive Phases of Animal Movements, 1872–1885*. Philadelphia: University of Pennsylvania Press, 1887.

Muybridge, Eadweard. *Animal Locomotion: Muybridge's Complete Human and Animal Locomotion: all 781 Plates from the 1887 Animal Locomotion*. New York: Dover Publications, 1979.

Muybridge, Eadweard [Lewis S. Brown, ed.]. *Animals in Motion*. New York: Dover Publications, 1957.

Muybridge, Eadweard. *Descriptive Zoöpraxography*. Chicago: R.R. Donnelley & Sons, 1893. The subtitle reads: *or the Science of Animal Locomotion made Popular by Eadweard Muybridge, with Selected Outline Tracings from some of the Illustrations of "Animal Locomotion," an Electro-photographic Investigation of Consecutive Phases of Animal Movements, Commenced 1872, Completed 1885, and Published 1887, under the Auspices of the University of Pennsylvania*. Additional publication information given: "Published As a Memento of a Series of Lectures Given by the Author under the Auspices of the United States Government Bureau of Education at the World's Columbian Exposition, in Zoopraxographical Hall, 1893."

Muybridge, Eadweard. *The Human Figure in Motion*. London: Chapman & Hall, 1901; New York: Dover Publications, 1955.

Pettigrew, J. Bell. *Animal Locomotion, or Walking, Swimming, and Flying, with a Dissertation on Aerodynamics*. New York: D. Appleton & Co., [1874], 1891.

Quigley, Martin, Jr. *Magic Shadows: The Story of the Origins of Motion Pictures*. Washington: Georgetown University Press, 1948.

Ramsaye, Terry. *A Million and One Nights, A History of the Motion Picture*. New York: Simon and Schuster, [1926], 1964.

Stillman, Jacob Davis Babcock. *The Horse in Motion as shown by instantaneous Photography, with a Study on Animal Mechanics founded on Anatomy and the Revelations of the Camera, in which is demonstrated the Theory of Quadrupedal Locomotion*. Boston: J[ames] R. Osgood and Co., 1882.

Taylor, Deems, Marcelene Peterson, and Bryant Hale. *A Pictorial History of the Movies*. New York: Simon and Schuster, 1943.

Van Zile, Edward Sims. *That Marvel—the Movie: A Glance at its reckless Past, its promising Present, and its significant Future*. New York and London: G.P. Putnam's Sons, 1923.

Wood, Leslie. *The Miracle of the Movies*. London: Burke Publishing Co., 1947.

B. Periodicals and Sections of Books

"A Horse's Motion Scientifically Determined," *Scientific American* October 19, 1878 39 (16) [New Series]: 239 (Front Cover) and 241.

Dalton, Susan. "Moving Images: Conservation and Preservation," 61–72 of Kathryn Luther Henderson and William T. Henderson, eds., *Conserving and Preserving Materials in Nonbook Formats* (Proceedings of the Allerton Park Institute, November 6–9, 1988). Urbana-Champaign, Illinois: University of Illinois, Graduate School of Library and Information Science, 1991.

"Edweard [sic] Muybridge Produced World's First Movie," *Stanford Historical Society Newsletter* 1980 5 (12): 1–2.

Forster-Hahn, Françoise. "Marey, Muybridge and Meissonier, The Study of Movement in Science and Art," in Mozley, ed., *Eadweard Muybridge, the Stanford Years 1872–1882*.

Haack, Ray. "Eadweard Muybridge: Pioneer of Motion Pictures: Eccentric Photographer," *American West* 1987 24 (1): 38–45.

Hood, Mary V. Jessup, and Robert Bartlett Haas. "Eadweard Muybridge's Yosemite Valley Photographs, 1867–1872," *California Historical Society Quarterly* 1963 42 (1): 5–26.

Lesser, Julian Bud. "Occident Trotting—A Strange Title," *American Cinematographer* 1988 69 (3): 34–40; published under the same title in *Sandstone & Tile* 1988 13 (1): 12–19.

Miles, Walter B. "Leland Stanford and the Motion Pictures," *Stanford Illustrated Review* 1929 30 (June): 469–472.

Mozley, Anita Ventura, ed. "Introduction." *Eadweard Muybridge, the Stanford Years 1872–1882*. Stanford: Stanford Department of Art, 1972.

Mozley, Anita Ventura, ed. "Photographs by Muybridge, 1872–1880. Catalogue and Notes on the Work," *Eadweard Muybridge, the Stanford Years 1872–1882*. Stanford: Stanford Department of Art, 1972.

"Mr. Muybridge's Photograph of Animals in Motion," *Scientific American Supplement* January 28, 1882 13 (317): 5058–5059.

Newhall, Beaumont. "Photography and the development of Kinetic Visualization," *Journal of the Warburg and Courtauld Institute* 1944 7 (1–2): 40–45.

Peterson, Harry C. "The Birthplace of the Motion Picture," *Sunset Magazine* November 1915, 909–915.

Tutorow, Norman Eugene. "Leland Stanford, Midwife of the Movies," *Pacific Historian* 1970 14 (2): 85–96.

15. STATE HISTORY
A. Books

Abate, Frank R., ed. *Omni Gazetteer of the United States of America, Providing Name, Location, and Identification for Nearly 1,500,000 Populated Places, Structures, Facilities, Locales, Historic Places, and Geographic Features in the Fifty States, the District of Columbia, Puerto Rico, and U.S. Territories*. Vol. 9 of 11, Detroit: Omnigraphics, 1991.

Angel, Myron. *History of Nevada: With Illustrations and Biographical Sketches of its Prominent Men and Pioneers*. Oakland: [Thomas Hinckley] Thompson & [Albert Augustus] West, 1881; reprinted, Berkeley: Howell-North, 1958.

Ashbaugh, Don. *Nevada's Turbulent Yesterday; a Study of Ghost Towns*. Los Angeles: Westernlore Press, 1963.

Bancroft, Hubert Howe. *History of California*. 7 vols., San Francisco: The History Co., 1886–1890.

Bancroft, Hubert Howe. *History of Nevada, Colorado, and Wyoming, 1540–1888*. San Francisco: The History Co., 1890.

Barber, John W., and Henry Howe. *Historical Collections of the State of New York*. New York: S. Tuttle, 1842.

Bates, Joseph Clement, ed. *History of the Bench and Bar of California*. San Francisco: Bench and Bar Publishing Co., 1912.

Bean, Walton. *California: An Interpretive History*. New York: McGraw-Hill, 1968.

Blumann, Ethel, and Mabel W. Thomas, eds. *California Local History, A Centennial Bibliography, compiled by the California Library Association, Committee on Local History*. Stanford: Stanford University Press, 1950.

Browne, John Ross, ed. and comp. *Report of the Debates in the Convention of California, on the Formation of the State Constitution, in September and October, 1840*. Washington: John T. Towers, Printer, 1850.

Browning, Peter. *Place Names of the Sierra Nevada, From Abbot to Zumwalt*. Berkeley: Wilderness Press, 1986.

Carlson, Helen S. *Nevada Place Names, A Geographical Dictionary*. Reno: University of Nevada Press, 1974.

Carr, John. *Pioneer Days in California*. Eureka: Times Publishing Co., 1891.

Davis, John Francis. *Index to the Laws of California, 1850–1907, including the statutes, the codes, and the constitution of 1879, together with amendments thereto; also a list of sections of the codes added, amended or repealed since their adoption; a list of statutes repealed by the codes; a list of the statutes remaining in force; and code commissioner's notes, sessions of 1905 and 1907*. Prepared in accordance with Acts of the Legislature approved March 15 and 18, 1907. Sacramento: W. W. Shannon, 1908.

Davis, Winfield J. *History of Political Conventions in California, 1849–1892*. Sacramento: California State Library, 1893.

Delgado, James P. *To California by Sea: A Maritime History of the California Gold Rush*. Columbia: University of South Carolina Press, 1990.

Dilts, Bryan Lee, comp. *1860 California Census Index. Heads of Households and Other Surnames in Household Index*. Salt Lake City: Index Publishing, 1984. Though similar in form and contents, this is not a state document.

Douglas, Edward M., comp. *Gazetteer of the Mountains of the State of California*. Preliminary (incomplete) ed. Washington: [Federal Bureau of Surveys and Maps], 1929.

Durham, David L. *California's Geographic Names, A Gazetteer of Historic and Modern Names of the State*. Clovis, California: Word Dancer Press, 1998.

Eddy, John Mathewson. *In the Redwoods Realm*. San Francisco: Stanley & Co., 2nd ed., 1893; reprinted 1987.

Eldredge, Zoeth Skinner, ed. *History of California*. 5 vols., New York: The Century History Co., 1915.

Evans, Albert S. *White Pine: Its Geographical Location, Topography, Geological Formation; Mining Laws; Mineral Resources; Towns; Surroundings; Climate, population, Altitude, and General Characteristics; Conditions of Society; How to Reach There; What it Costs to Get There and Life There; When to Go There, etc., etc*. San Francisco: Alta California Printing House, 1869.

Fay, James S., ed. *California Almanac*. 7th ed., Santa Barbara: Pacific Data Resources, 1995.

Fitzgerald, Oscar Penn. *California Sketches, New and Old*. Nashville: Publishing House of the Methodist Episcopal Church, South, 1897.

Fowler, Harland Davey. *Camels to California*. Stanford: Stanford University Press, 1950.

Franks, Kenny A., and Paul F. Lambert. *Early California Oil, A Photographic History, 1865–1940*. College Station: Texas A & M University Press, 1985.

Frickstad, Walter Nettleton. *A Century of California Post Offices, 1848–1954*. Oakland: Walter N. Frickstad, 1955.

Fritz, Christian G. *Federal Justice in California: The Court of Ogden Hoffman, 1851–1891*. Lincoln: University of Nebraska Press, 1991.

Gudde, Erwin Gustav [Elisabeth K. Gudde, ed.]. *California Gold Camps, A Geographical Historical Dictionary of Camps, Towns, and Localities Where Gold Was Found and Mined; Wayside Stations and Trading Centers*. Berkeley: University of California Press, 1975.

Gudde, Erwin Gustav. *California Place Names: The Origin and Etymology of Current Geographical Names*. Berkeley: University of California Press, 1960 and 1969.

Guinn, James Miller. *History of the State of California and Biographical Record of Coast Counties, California*. Chicago: Chapman Publishing Co., 1904.

Guinn, James Miller. *History of the State of California and Biographical Record of Oakland and its Environs also Containing Biographies of Well-Known Citizens of the Past and Present*. 2 vols., Los Angeles: Historic Record Co., 1907, II, 596–597.

Guinn, James Miller. *History of the State of California and Biographical Record of the San Joaquin Valley, California. An [sic] Historical Story of the State's marvelous Growth from its earliest Settlement to the present Time. Also Containing Biographies of Well-Known Citizens of the Past and Present*. 2 vols., Chicago: Chapman Publishing Co., 1905.

Hanna, Phil Townsend, comp. *The Dictionary of California Land Names*. Los Angeles: Automobile Club of Southern California, 1946.

Higgs, Gerald B. *Lost Legends of the Silver State*. Salt Lake City: Western Epics, 1976.

Hittell, Theodore Henry. *History of California*. 4 vols., San Francisco: Vols. 1–2, Pacific Press Publishing House and Occidental Publishing Co., 1885; Vols. 3–4, San Francisco: N[athan] J. Stone & Co., 1885–1897.

Hoover, Mildred Brooke, and Hero Eugene & Ethel Grace Rensch, rev. by Ruth Teiser. *Historic Spots in California*. Stanford: Stanford University Press, [1932], 1948; rev. again by Douglas E. Kyle in 1990.

Hulse, James W. *The Nevada Adventure, A History*. Reno: University of Nevada Press, 1966.

Hunt, Rockwell Dennis. *California Firsts*. San Francisco: Fearon Publishers, 1957.

Jackson, Joseph Henry. *Anybody's Gold: The Story of California's Mining Towns*. San Francisco: Chronicle Books, 1970.

Kennedy, Elijah R. *The Contest for California: How Colonel E. D. Baker Saved the Pacific States to the Union*. Boston: Houghton Mifflin Co., 1912.

Koontz, John. *Political History of Nevada*. Carson City: State Printing Office, 1960.

Lapp, Rudolph M. *Blacks in Gold Rush California*. New Haven: Yale University Press, 1977.

Lord, Eliot. *Comstock Miners and Mining*. Berkeley: Howell-North, [1883], 1959.

Marcosson, Isaac F. *Anaconda*. New York: Dodd, Mead & Co., 1957.

Martin, Wallace E., comp. *Sail & Steam on the Northern California Coast, 1850–1900*. San Francisco: National Maritime Museum Association, 1983.

Nevada State Historical Society Papers, 1923–1924. Reno: Nevada State Historical Society, 1924.

New Handbook of Texas. Austin: Texas State Historical Association, 1996.

Nordhoff, Charles. *Northern California, Oregon, and the Sandwich Islands*. New York: Harper & Brothers, 1874.

Norris, Benjamin Franklin ("Frank"). *The Octopus: A Story of California*. New York: New American Library, [1901], 1964.

Orton, Richard H., comp. *Records of California Men in the War of the Rebellion, 1861–1867*. Sacramento: State Office, 1890; reprinted, Salem, Mass.: Higginson Book Co., 2000.

Paher, Stanley W. *Nevada Ghost Towns & Mining Camps*. San Diego: Howell-North Books, 1970.

Patera, Edward L., and Harold E. Salley, eds. *History of California Post Offices, 1849–1990*. 2nd ed., [Lake Grove, Oregon]: The Depot, 1991.

Paul, Rodman Wilson. *California Gold: The Beginning of Mining in the Far West*. Cambridge: Harvard University Press, 1947; Lincoln: University of Nebraska Press, 1965.

Pomeroy, Earl. *The Pacific Slope: A History of California, Oregon, Washington, Idaho, Utah, and Nevada*. New York: Alfred A. Knopf, 1965.

Ransom, Leander, and A[lonzo] J. Doolittle Map. San Francisco: Warren Holt, 1866.

Roster of Military Forces of State of California. Officer Lists, 1863. Military Series, Vol. IX, 1855–1867. Pomona: Pomona Valley Genealogical Society, 1991.

Roth, Hal. *Pathway in the Sky: The Story of the John Muir Trail*. Berkeley: Howell-North Books, 1965.

Royce, Josiah. *California from the Conquest in 1846 to the Second Vigilance Committee in San Francisco* [1856]. Boston: Houghton Mifflin Co., 1886; New York: Alfred A. Knopf, 1948; Santa Barbara: Peregrin Publishers, 1970.

Royce, Josiah. *The Feud of Oldfield Creek: A Novel of California Life*. Boston: Houghton Mifflin Co., 1887.

Schwenke, Karl, and Thomas Winnett. *Sierra North*. Berkeley: Wilderness Press, [1967], 1969.

Shuck, Oscar Tully, ed. *History of the Bench and Bar of California: being biographies of many remarkable men, a store of humorous and pathetic recollections, accounts of important legislation and extraordinary cases, comprehending the judicial history of the state*. Los Angeles: Commercial Printing House, 1891.

Smith, Alice E. *The History of Wisconsin*. Vol. I, *From Exploration to Statehood*. Madison: State Historical Society of Wisconsin, 1973.

Stadtman, Verne A., ed. and comp. *The Centennial Record of the University of California*. Berkeley: University of California, 1968.

Stadtman, Verne A. *The University of California 1868–1968*. New York: McGraw-Hill Book Co., 1970.

Stillman, Jacob Davis Babcock. *Around the Horn to California*. Palo Alto: Lewis Osborne, 1967.

The State Register and Year Book of Facts for the Year 1859. San Francisco: [Henry G.] Langley and [Samuel A.] Morison, 1859. This is a two-page chart, "Official Vote of the State of California—1857."

Thompson, [Thomas Hinckley], and [Albert Augustus] West. *History of Nevada, 1881. With Illustrations. And Biographical Sketches of its Prominent Men and Pioneers*. Repr., Berkeley: Howell-North, 1958.

Uzes, Francois D. *Chaining the Land; a History of Surveying in California*. Sacramento: Landmark Enterprises, 1977.

Whicher, John. *Masonic Beginnings in California and Hawaii*. [San Francisco (?)]: published by order of the Grand Master, 1931.

White, Gerald Taylor. *Formative Years in the Far West, A History of the Standard Oil Company of California and its Predecessors through 1919*. New York: Appleton-Century-Crofts, 1962.

Winther, Oscar Osburn. *Express and Stagecoach Days in California, from the Gold Rush to the Civil War*. Stanford: Stanford University Press, 1936. Based on "The Express and Stage-coach Business in California, 1848–1860." Ph.D. dissertation (Stanford University, 1934).

Winther, Oscar Osburn. *The Transportation Frontier: Trans-Mississippi West, 1865–1890*. New York: Holt, Rinehart and Winston, 1964.

B. Periodicals

Bakken, Gordon Morris. "Looking Back: the Court and California Law in 1897," *The California Supreme Court Historical Society Yearbook* 1996–1997 3 (annual): 121–139.

Chandler, Robert Joseph. "Democratic Turmoil: California During the Civil War Years," *Dogtown Territorial Quarterly* 1997 Issue 31: 32–46.

Chandler, Robert Joseph. "Private Feelings: Californians View the Civil War," *Dogtown Territorial Quarterly* 1997 Issue 31: 47–53.

Clendenen, Clarence C. "A Confederate Spy in California: A Curious Incident of the Civil War," *Southern California Quarterly* 1963 45 (3): 219–233.

Dyer, Brainerd. "California's Civil War Claims," *Southern California Quarterly* 1963 45 (1): 1–24.

Ellison, Joseph Waldo. "The Sentiment for a Pacific Republic, 1843–1862," *Proceedings of the Pacific Coast Branch of the American Historical Association* 1929 (annual): 94–118.

Farquhar, Francis Peloubet. "Exploration of the Sierra Nevada," *California Historical Society Quarterly* 1925 4 (1): 3–58.

Farquhar, Francis Peloubet. "Place Names of the High Sierra [Part III], *Sierra Club Bulletin* 1925 12 (2): 126–147.

Gilbert, Benjamin Franklin. "California and the Civil War: A Bibliographical Essay," *California Historical Society Quarterly* 1961 40 (4): 289–307.

Gilbert, Benjamin Franklin. "The Confederate Minority in California," *California Historical Society Quarterly* 1941 20 (2): 154–170.

Goldman, Henry H. "Southern Sympathy in Southern California, 1860–1865," *Journal of the West* 1965 4 (4): 577–586.

Hichborn, Franklin. "The Party, the Machine, and the Vote: The Story of Crossfiling in California Politics," *California Historical Society Quarterly* 1959 38 (4): 349–357.

Hunt, Rockwell Dennis. "Significant Events in the History of California," *Publications of the Historical Society of Southern California* 1909–1910 8 (annual): 24–30.

Hurt, Peyton. "The Rise and Fall of the 'Know Nothings' in California," *California Historical Society Quarterly* 1930 9 (2): 99–128.

Kibby, Leo P. "California, the Civil War, and the Indian Problem: An Account of California's Participation in the Great Conflict," *Journal of the West* 1965 4 (2): 183–209; 4 (3): 377–410.

Kibby, Leo P. "Union Loyalty of California's Civil War Governors," *California Historical Society Quarterly* 1965 44 (4): 311–321.

Military Order of the Loyal Legion of the United States. Headquarters Commandery of the State of California. Circular No. 38, Series of 1904, Whole No. 776. San Francisco, November 29, 1904. Commander and Toastmaster: Maj.-Gen. Arthur MacArthur. Speakers: Sen. George C. Pardee, "The effects of the ultimate success of the Union cause upon the destinies of our State." Sen. George C. Perkins, "The condition of affairs in our State at the outbreak of the War in 1861; how California was kept in the Union; and what California did for the Union cause." Acting President John M. Stillman of Stanford University, "What a Companion of our Commandery has done for our State in war and in peace." Brig-Gen. Charles A. Woodruff, "A few crude ideas about the present war in the East as contrasted with ours of 1861 to 1865."

Nuttail, Donald A. "The Gobernantes of Spanish Upper California: A Profile," *California Historical Quarterly* 1972 60 (3): 253–280.

Pomeroy, Earl. "California, 1846–1860: Politics of a Representative Frontier State," *California Historical Society Quarterly* 1953 32 (4): 291–302.

Poole, William. "Shasta," *Via* 1998 (July/August): 40–45.

"Rensselaer Polytechnic Institute," *Encyclopedia America*, 1998, XXIII, 406.

Rodecape, Lois. "Celestial Drama in the Golden Hills: The Chinese Theatre in California, 1849–1869," *California Historical Society Quarterly* 1944 23 (2): 97–116.

Shutes, Milton H. "Republican Nominating Convention of 1860: A California Report," *California Historical Society Quarterly* 1948 27 (2): 97–103.

Stalder, Walter. "New Light on California's Early Days," *Petroleum World* 1931 28 (12) 32–34, 40.

Stanley, Gerald. "Racism and the Early Republican Party: The 1856 Presidential Election in California," *Pacific Historical Review* 1974 43 (2): 171–187. Based on "The Politics of Race: California Republicans in the Election of 1860," a paper delivered at the Pacific Coast Branch, American Historical Association Meeting, August 1974.

Stanley, Gerald. "The Politics of the Antebellum Far West: The Impact of the Slavery and Race Issues in California," *Journal of the West* 1977 16 (4): 19–25.

Tutorow, Norman Eugene. "Consolidated Virginia and California Mines (1869–1878)," *Encyclopedia USA: The Encyclopedia of the United States of America—Past and Present* 1991 Vol. 15, pp. 168–170.

16. COUNTY AND REGIONAL HISTORY
A. Books

[Angel, Myron, comp.]. *A Memorial and Biographical History of the Counties of Fresno, Tulare, and Kern, California. Illustrated. Containing a history of this important section of the Pacific coast from the earliest period . . . and biographical mention of many of its pioneers, and also of prominent citizens of to-day.* Chicago: The Lewis Publishing Co., [1892].

[Angel, Myron, and Mahlon Dickerson Fairchild]. *History of Placer County, California, with Illustrations and Biographical Sketches of its Prominent Men and Pioneers.* Oakland: [Thomas Hinckley] Thompson and [Albert Augustus] West, 1882. The authors were cousins.

An Illustrated History of Los Angeles County, California. Containing a History of Los Angeles County from the Earliest Period of its Occupancy to the Present Time, together with Glimpses of its Prospective Future; with Profuse Illustrations of its Beautiful Scenery, Full-Page Portraits of Some of its most Eminent Men, and Biographical Mention of Many of its Pioneers and also of Prominent Citizens of To-day. Chicago: The Lewis Publishing Co., 1889.

An Illustrated History of Sonoma County, California. Containing a History of the County of Sonoma from the Earliest Period of its Occupancy to the Present Time, together with Glimpses of its Prospective Future; with Profuse Illustrations of its Beautiful Scenery, Full-Page Portraits of some of its most Eminent Men, and Biographical Mention of Many of its Pioneers and also of Prominent Citizens of To-day. Chicago: Lewis Publishing Co., 1889.

Bowman, Amos. *Report on the Properties and Domain of the California Water Company, situated on Georgetown Divide; embracing the Mining, Water and Landed Resources of the Country, between the South and Middle Forks of the American River, in El Dorado County, California.* San Francisco: A[lbert] L[ittle] Bancroft & Co., 1874.

Browne, John Ross. *Report of J. Ross Browne on the Mineral Resources of the States and Territories West of the Rocky Mountains.* Washington: Government Printing Office, 1868.

Burton, George Ward. *Men of Achievement in the Great Southwest. Illustrated. A Story of Pioneer Struggles, During Early Days in Los Angeles and Southern California, with Biographies, Heretofore Unpublished Facts, Anecdotes and Incidents in the Lives of the Builders.* [Los Angeles]: Los Angeles Times, 1904.

Butterfield, Consul Wilshire. *History of Washington and Ozaukee Counties, Wisconsin, containing an account of its settlement, growth, development and resources . . . Biographical Sketches, portraits of prominent*

men and early settlers; the whole preceded by a history of Wisconsin . . . and an abstract of its laws and constitution . . . Chicago: Western Historical Co., 1881.

Carnall-Hopkins Company. *California Illustrated, A Guide for Tourists and Settlers*. San Francisco: Carnall-Hopkins Co., 1891.

Chapman, Charles C. *The History of St. Joseph County, Indiana; together with sketches of its cities, villages
and townships, educational, religious, civil, military, and political history, and biographies of representative
citizens. History of Indiana, embracing accounts of the pre-historic races, aborigines, French, English and
American conquests, and a general review of its civil, political and military history*. Chicago: Charles C.
Chapman Co., 1880.

Colquhoun, Joseph Alex, comp. *Illustrated Album of Alameda County, California, its Early History and
Progress—Agriculture, Viticulture and Horticulture—Educational, Manufacturing and Railroad Advantages—Oakland Environs—Interior Townships—Statistics, Etc., Etc*. Oakland: Pacific Press Publishing Co., 1893.

Comstock, David Allan. *Greenbacks and Copperheads*. Grass Valley: Comstock Bonanza Press, 1995.

Cook, Fred S., ed. *Legends of Western El Dorado County, and Discovery of Gold*. Volcano, California: California Traveler, 1970.

Davis, William Newell, Jr. *Sagebrush Corner: The Opening of California's Northeast*. New York: Garland
Publishing, 1974. Vol. 5 of 6 of the California Indians in the Garland American Indian Ethnohis-
tory Series.

Davis, Winfield J. *An Illustrated History of Sacramento County, California. Containing a History of Sacra-
mento County from the Earliest Period of its Occupancy to the Present Time, together with Glimpses of its
Prospective Future; with Profuse Illustrations of its Beautiful Scenery, Full-Page Portraits of Some of its most
Eminent Men, and Biographical Mention of Many of its Pioneers and also of Prominent Citizens of To-day*.
Chicago: The Lewis Publishing Co., 1890. "Hon. Newton Booth," pp. 287–289.

Ellis, George Merle, ed. *Gold Rush Desert Trails to San Diego and Los Angeles in 1849*. San Diego: San
Diego Corral of Westerners [Brand Book Number Nine], 1995.

*Great Register, containing the Names and Registration of the Domiciled Inhabitants of the County of Santa
Clara, who by virtue of Citizenship, Lawful Age, and other qualifications prescribed by the Constitution, are
qualified Electors and Legal Voters thereof*. San Jose: Cottle & Wright, 1879.

Halley, William. *The Centennial Year Book of Alameda County, California, containing a Summary of the Discovery and Settlement of California; a Description of the Contra Costa under Spanish, Mexican and American Rule; an Account of the Organization and Settlement of Alameda County, with a Yearly Synopsis of
important Events, down to the Centennial Year of American Independence, together with the important Events
of the Year 1876. Also, a Gazetteer of each Township, useful local and general statistical Information, appropriate for the present Time. To which are added Biographical Sketches of Prominent Pioneers and Public Men*.
Oakland: William Halley, 1876.

Howell, George Rogers, and John H. Munsell, eds. Assisted by local writers. *History of the County of
Schenectady, New York, from 1662 to 1886*. New York: W. W. Munsell & Co., 1886.

Howell, George Rogers, and Jonathan Tenney, eds. Assisted by local writers. *Bi-centennial of Albany.
History of the County of Albany, New York, from 1609 to 1886*. New York: W. W. Munsell & Co., 1886.

Hunt, Aurora. *The Army of the Pacific: Its operations in California, Texas, Arizona, New Mexico, Utah, Nevada,
Oregon, Washington, plains region, Mexico, etc. 1860–1866*. Glendale: The Arthur H. Clark Co., 1951.

Illustrated History of Plumas, Lassen & Sierra Counties: with California from 1513 to 1850. San Francisco:
Fariss and [Clarence L.] Smith, 1882. Frank T. Gilbert wrote the section *California from 1513 to
1850*. This contribution by Wright was also published in *The Illustrated Atlas and History of Yolo
County, Cal., containing a History of California from 1513 to 1850, a History of Yolo County from 1825 to*

1880, with Statistics . . . Lithographic Views . . . Portraits of well-known Citizens, and the official County Map. San Francisco: De Pue & Company, 1879. The 1882 work was reprinted as *Reproduction of Fariss and Smith's History of Plumas, Lassen & Sierra Counties, California, 1882: and Biographical Sketches of their prominent Men and Pioneers.* Berkeley: Howell-North Books, 1971.

Kelm, Mrs. Arthur [Dorothy], Mrs. James S. [Violet] McCray, and Mrs. Arnold [Jeanette] Barr. *Early Ozaukee County Historical Sketches.* Port Washington: Ozaukee County Historical Society, 1967.

Lardner, William Branson, and Michael John Brock. *History of Placer and Nevada Counties, California, with Biographical Sketches of the Leading Men and Women of the Counties Who Have Been Identified with Their Growth and Development from the Early Days to the Present.* Los Angeles: Historic Record Co., 1924.

Mason, Jesse D. *History of Amador County, California, with Illustrations and Biographical Sketches of its Prominent Men and Pioneers.* Oakland: [Thomas Hinckley] Thompson and [Albert Augustus] West, 1881.

Merritt, Frank Clinton. *History of Alameda County, California.* Chicago: S. J. Clarke Publishing Co., 1928.

Millard, Bailey. *History of the San Francisco Bay Region.* 3 vols., Chicago: American Historical Society, 1924.

Moore, [Edwin S.] & [George M.] *DePue's illustrated History of San Mateo County, California, 1878.* San Francisco: Grafton Tyler Brown & Co., 1878; reprinted, Woodside: Gilbert Richards Publications, 1974.

Munro-Fraser, J. P., and Myron W. Wood. *History of Alameda County, California: including its Geology, Topography, Soil, and Productions: together with a full and particular record of the Spanish grants . . . separate histories of each of the Townships . . . also Incidents of Pioneer Life.* Oakland: M[yron] W. Wood, 1883. The preface is signed by Wood and Munro-Fraser.

[Munro-Fraser, J. P.]. *History of Santa Clara County, California; including its Geography, Geology, Topography, Climatology and Description, together with A Record of the Mexican Grants; Its Mines and Natural Springs; The Early History and Settlements, Compiled from the Most Authentic Sources; The Names of Original Spanish and American Pioneers; Full Legislative History of the County; Separate Histories of each Township, Showing the Advance in Population and Agriculture. Also Incidents of Public Life; The Mexican War; and Biographical Sketches of Early and Prominent Settlers and Representative Men; and of its Cities, Towns, Churches, Colleges, Secret Societies, Etc., Etc.* San Francisco: Alley, Bowen & Co., 1881.

Nadeau, Remi. *Ghost Towns and Mining Camps of California.* Los Angeles: Ward Ritchie Press, 1965.

Palmer, Lyman L. *History of Napa and Lake Counties, California, comprising their Geography, Geology, Topography, Climatography, Springs and Timber, also, extended Sketches of their Milling, Mining, Pisciculture and Wine Interests; together with a Full and Particular Record of the Mexican Grants; Early History and Settlement, compiled from the most Authentic Sources; Names of Original Spanish and American Pioneers; a Full Record of their Organization and Segregation; a Complete Political History, including a Tabular Statement of Officeholders since the Organization of the Counties. Also, separate Histories of all the Townships in both Counties, including Towns, Churches, Societies, etc., Incidents of Pioneer Life, and Biographical Sketches of Early Settlers and Representative Men.* San Francisco: Slocum, Bowen, & Co., 1881.

Reed, G. Walter, ed. *History of Sacramento County, California: with Biographical Sketches of The Leading Men and Women of the County Who Have Been Identified with its Growth and Development from the Early Days to the Present.* Los Angeles: Historic Record Co., 1921.

Sawyer, Eugene Taylor. *History of Santa Clara County, California, with Biographical Sketches of the Leading Men and Women of the County Who Have Been Identified With Its Growth and Development From the Early Days to the Present.* Los Angeles: Historic Record Co., 1922.

Scott, Edward B. *The Saga of Lake Tahoe, A Complete Documentation of Lake Tahoe's Development over the last One Hundred Years.* Crystal Bay, Nevada: Sierra-Tahoe Publishing Co., 1957.

Sioli, Paolo. *Historical Souvenir of El Dorado County, California, with Illustrations and Biographical Sketches of its Prominent Men & Pioneers*. Oakland: Paolo Sioli, 1883.

Smith, A. McCall, ed. [Annie Rosalind Mitchell, writer]. *A Modern History of Tulare County*. Visalia: Limited Editions of Visalia, [1974].

Smith, Wallace. *Garden of the Sun: A History of the San Joaquin Valley, 1772–1939*. Los Angeles: Lymanhouse, 1939.

Storke, (Mrs.) Yda Addis. *A Memorial and Biographical History of Santa Barbara, San Luis Obispo and Ventura, California*. Chicago: Lewis Publishing Co., 1891.

Thompson, [Thomas Hinckley], and [Albert Augustus] West. *History of Nevada County, California: with Illustrations descriptive of its scenery, residences, public buildings, fine blocks, and manufactories*. Oakland: [Thomas Hinckley] Thompson & [Albert Augustus] West, 1880; reprinted by Henry Laurentz Wells. Berkeley: Howell-North Books, 1970.

Wells, Henry Laurenz. *History of Siskiyou County, California, Illustrated with Views of Residences, Business Buildings and Natural Scenery, and containing Portraits and Biographies of its Leading Citizens*. Oakland: D. J. Stewart & Co., 1881.

Willis, William Ladd. *History of Sacramento County, California, with Sketches of The Leading Men and Women of the County Who Have Been Identified With Its Growth and Development From the Early Days to the Present*. Los Angeles: Historic Record Co., 1913.

Woolridge, Jesse Walton. *History of the Sacramento Valley California*. 3 vols., Chicago: Pioneer Historical Publishing Co., 1931.

Wright, George F., ed. *History of Sacramento County, California: with Illustrations descriptive of its Scenery, Residences, Public Buildings, fine Blocks, and Manufactories from original Sketches by Artists of the highest Ability*. Oakland: [Thomas H.] Thompson & [Albert A.] West, 1880; reprinted, Berkeley: Howell-North, 1960.

B. Periodicals

Aiken, Charles Curry. "The Sagebrush War: The California-Nevada Boundary Dispute on the 120th Meridian," *Journal of the Shaw Historical Library* 1991 5 (1 and 2): 45–112.

Hartesveldt, Richard J. "Yosemite Valley Place Names," *Yosemite Nature Notes* 1955 34 (1): 17. Stanford Point in Yosemite.

Miller, Robert Cunningham. "The California Academy of Sciences and the Early History of Science in the West," *California Historical Society Quarterly* 1942 21 (4): 363–371.

Ringler, Donald. "Hillsborough-San Mateo Mansions," *La Peninsula* [The Journal of the San Mateo County (California) Historical Society] 1976 18 (3): 3–31.

C. Maps

"Map of Yosemite Valley," Yosemite National Park, California, Mariposa County. Department of the Interior, U.S. Geological Survey, July 1907 (surveyed in 1905–1906).

Metsker, Charles Frederick. Map of Santa Clara County (Flat Map).

Thompson, [Thomas Hinckley], and [Albert Augustus] West. *Historical Atlas Map of Santa Clara County, California: Compiled, Drawn and Published from Personal Examinations and Surveys*. Oakland and San Francisco: [Thomas Hinckley] Thompson & [Albert Augustus] West, 1876; reprinted, San Jose: Smith & McKay Printing, c1973.

Thompson, Thomas Hinckley. *Official Historical Site Map of Tulare County, Compiled, Drawn and Published from Personal Examinations and Surveys*. Tulare: Thomas Hinckley Thompson, 1892.

Trask, John Boardman. "Topographical Map of the Mineral Districts of California. Being the First Map ever published from Actual Survey." San Francisco: Britton & Rey, 1853.

17. TOWN AND CITY HISTORY
(Catalogues, Directories, and Buildings)
A. Books

Albany Female Academy. *Catalogue for Year Ending May 1, 1845*. Albany: Joel Munsell, 1845.

Albany Female Academy. *Catalogue for Year Ending January 1, 1848*. Albany: Joel Munsell, 1848.

Allan, Morton. *Directory of European Passenger Steamship Arrivals for the Years 1890 to 1930 at the Port of New York and for the Years 1904 to 1926 at the Ports of New York, Philadelphia, Boston, and Baltimore*. Baltimore: Genealogical Publishing Co., 1979.

Altrocchi, Julia Cooley. *The Spectacular San Franciscans*. New York: E. P. Dutton, 1949.

Arbuckle, Clyde. *Clyde Arbuckle's History of San José*. San José: Smith & McKay, 1985.

Aron, Joseph. *History of a Great Work and of an Honest Miner*. Paris: Printed by E. Régnault, 1892. One of several pamphlets in the Bancroft Library on the history of the Sutro tunnel. Almost identical to the following entry.

Aron, Joseph. *History of the Sutro Tunnel* [Paris?: no publisher given, 1891?]. One of several pamphlets in the Bancroft Library on the history of the Sutro tunnel. Almost identical to the previous entry.

Asbury, Herbert. *The Barbary Coast: An Informal History of the San Francisco Underworld*. New York: Alfred A. Knopf, 1933.

Bagwell, Beth. *Oakland, The Story of a City*. Novato: Presidio Press, 1982.

Beautiful Menlo Park, Ringwood Park, Baywood Field, Subdivision of the Town of Menlo. San Francisco: Hoag & Lansdale, [no date]. In Menlo Park Historical Association Collection.

Block, Eugene B. *The Immortal San Franciscans for whom the Streets were Named*. San Francisco: Chronicle Books, [1971].

Bulwer-Lytton, Edward. *Last Days of Pompeii*. Paris: Baudry, 1834.

Burns, John, ed. *Sacramento Gold Rush Legacy, Metropolitan Destiny*. Sacramento: Sacramento County Historical Society and Heritage Media Corporation, 1999.

Cain, Ella M. *The Story of Bodie*. San Francisco: Fearon Publishers, 1956.

Carr, Peter E. *San Francisco Passenger Departure Lists*. San Bernardino: The Cuban Index, 1991, 1992, 1993. Vol. 1 (September 30 to December 31, 1850), Vol. 2 (January 3 to June 14, 1851), Vol. 3 (July 15 to December 31, 1851).

Catalogue of the Officers and Students of Clinton Liberal Institute. Utica, New York: Clinton Liberal Institute, 1844.

Circular and Catalogue of the Albany Female Academy. 1839. Albany: Packard, Van Benthuysen and Co., Printers, 1839.

Circular and Catalogue of the Albany Female Academy. 1843. Albany: Packard, Van Benthuysen and Co., Printers, 1843.

Cleese, John Irving. *Tales of Old Menlo*. Menlo Park: Menlo Park Historical Association, 1994.

Cooke, Reginald B., and [Joshua J.] LeCount. *A "Pile," or A Glance at the Wealth of the Monied Men of San Francisco and Sacramento City: also, an accurate List of the lawyers, their former places of residence and date of arrival in San Francisco*. San Francisco: Cooke & LeCount, Booksellers, 1851.

Cravens, Jean, and Judith Schulte. *Eleven Decades of a Pioneer Church, 1834–1944. A History of the First United Presbyterian Church of Mishawaka, Indiana*. Mishawaka: The Bicentennial Committee of Sessions, 1976 (1940–1976 update).

Davis, Leonard M. *Rocklin, Past, Present, Future: An Illustrated History of Rocklin, Placer County, California, From 1864 To 1981*. Roseville: Rocklin Friends of the Library, 1981.

Drury, Wells. *An Editor on the Comstock Lode*. New York: Farrar & Rinehart, 1936.

Flenner, Jessie Boudinot. *Vital Statistics from Records in Trinity Episcopal Church of San Francisco, California*. [San Francisco (?)]: Daughters of the American Revolution, [1936]. Contains baptism, marriage, and burial records of the Trinity Episcopal Church San Francisco, California, from 1849 to July 1, 1906.

Grand Hotel. *Grand Hotel, Il più "storico" degli alberghi di Firenze*. Corsico/Milano: Grafiche Francesco Ghezzi, 1992.

Gritschneder, Otto. *Weitere Randbemerkungen*. München: Otto Gritschneder, 1986.

Gullard, Pamela, and Nancy Lund. *History of Palo Alto: The Early Years*. San Francisco: Scottwall Associates, 1989.

Hall, Frederic. *The History of San Jose and Surroundings, with Biographical Sketches of Early Settlers*. San Francisco: A[lbert] L[ittle] Bancroft and Co., 1871.

Hansen, Gladys. *San Francisco Almanac: Everything you want to know about the City*. San Francisco: Chronicle Books, 1975.

Hollweck, Ludwig. *In München vor hundert Jahren*. München: Mosaik Verlag, 1988.

Jackson, W[illiam] Turrentine. *Treasure Hill: Portrait of a Mining Camp*. Tucson: University of Arizona Press, 1963.

Kemble, John Haskell. *San Francisco Bay: A Pictorial Maritime History*. New York: Bonanza Books, [1957], 1972.

Kibbey, Mead B., ed. *Facsimile Reproduction of the California State Library Copy of Samuel Colville's Sacramento Directory for the Year 1853–1854*. Sacramento: California State Library Foundation, 1997.

Kreuz, Charmayne. *A Tradition of New Horizons: The Story of Menlo Park*. Menlo Park: The City of Menlo Park, 1974.

Lassagne, Art. *California Pioneer Towns*. Alamo: Gold Bug Books, 1968.

Liggett, John H. *The Industries of San Francisco, California: A Review of the Manufacturing, Mercantile and Business Interests of the Bay City: together with a Historical Sketch of her Rise and Progress*. San Francisco: Cosmopolitan Publishing Co., 1889.

Lloyd, Benjamin E. *Lights and Shades in San Francisco*. San Francisco: A[lbert] L[ittle] Bancroft & Co., 1876.

Loewenstein, Louis K. *Streets of San Francisco. The Origins of Street and Place Names*. Berkeley: Wilderness Press, 1996.

Mahany, Effie C. *Though the Years in San Carlos (A Narrative)*. San Carlos, California: [no publisher or date given].

Mark Hopkins Inter-Continental Hotel. *A Walk Back in Time . . . The Mark Hopkins Inter-Continental Hotel*. San Francisco: Mark Hopkins Inter-Continental, [no date]. A brief history of the Hopkins house and its successor structures.

Mark Hopkins Inter-Continental Hotel. *The Mark Hopkins Inter-Continental Hotel: A Short History of its Long and Illustrious History*. San Francisco: Mark Hopkins Inter-Continental, [no date]. A five-page historical statement distributed by the Public Relations Department of the Mark Hopkins Hotel.

Muscatine, Doris. *Old San Francisco: The Biography of a City, from Early Days to the Earthquake*. New York: G. P. Putnam's Sons, 1975.

Oakland Military Academy. *General Average of Cadets*. Oakland: Oakland Military Academy, 1872.

O'Brien, Robert. *This is San Francisco*. New York: Whittlesey, [1948].

O'Day Edward F. *San Francisco Past and Present*. San Francisco: Adobe Press, 1935.

Pearce, Stanley. *Lift Up Your Hearts, a History of Trinity Parish, Menlo Park*. Menlo Park: Trinity Parish, 1974.

Rasmussen, Louis James. *Railway Passenger Lists of overland Trains to San Francisco and the West*. 2 vols., Vol. 1, Baltimore: Deford, [1966]; Vol. 2, Chicago: Adams Press, [1968]. Incomplete contents, Vol. 1 (July 28, 1870, to December 13, 1871); Vol. 2 (November 14, 1871, to April 23, 1873).

Rasmussen, Louis James. *San Francisco Ship Passenger Lists*. 4 vols., Colma: San Francisco Historical Records, 1965–1970. Vol. 1, 1965 (1850–1875); Vol. 2, 1966 (April 1850 to November 1851); Vol. 3, 1967 (November 7, 1851, to June 6, 1852); Vol. 4, 1970 (June 17, 1852 to January 6, 1853).

Rather, Lois. *Oakland's Image, A History of Oakland, California*. Oakland: The Rather Press, 1972.

Regnery, Dorothy F. *An Enduring Heritage, Historic Buildings on the San Francisco Peninsula*. Stanford: Stanford University Press, 1976. With photographs by Jack E. Boucher.

Reinstadt, Randall A. *Incredible Ghosts of old Monterey's Hotel Del Monte*. Carmel: Ghost Town Publications, 1980.

Rice, William B. *The Los Angeles Star, 1851–1864*. Berkeley and Los Angeles: University of California Press, 1947.

Rudd, Helen Neilson. *A Century of Schools in Clinton*. Clinton, New York: Clinton Historical Society, 1964.

Schimmel, Jerry F. *The Old Streets of San Francisco. Early Street Names on Some Brass Tokens*. San Francisco: Pacific Coast Numismatic Society, 1993.

Severson, Thor. *Sacramento, An Illustrated History: 1839 to 1874, from Sutter's Fort to Capital City*. San Francisco: California Historical Society, 1973.

Smith, Eugene W. *Passenger Ships of the World—Past and Present*. Boston: George H. Dean Co., 1978.

Soulé, Frank, John H. Gihon, and James Nisbet. *The Annals of San Francisco*. New York: D. Appleton & Co., 1855. Facsimile of the original work, Berkeley: Berkeley Hills Books, 1998.

Stanford Court Hotel. *Renaissance Stanford Court Hotel History*. San Francisco: Stanford Court Hotel, [no date]. A two-page history distributed by the managers of the Stanford Court Hotel, which now sits on the site of the San Francisco Stanford mansion.

Svanevik, Michael, and Shirley Burgett. *Pillars of the Past: A Guide to Cypress Lawn Memorial Park, Colma, California*. San Francisco: Custom & Limited Eds., 1992.

The Fairmont Hotel. *A Fairmont History*. San Francisco: Fairmont Hotel, [no date]. A brief history of the Fairmont Hotel, designed for distribution to patrons and curious historians.

Weibel Winery Historic Buildings/Park, Feasibility Analysis. San Francisco: Architectural Resources Group, 1996.

West, Richard Vincent, ed. *Crocker Art Museum, Handbook of Paintings*. Sacramento: Crocker Art Museum, 1979.

[Wilson, Ruth, Lucy Evans, and Dorothy Regnery]. *The Story of Mayfield, 1850–1925, A Lost Town which is now Part of South Palo Alto*. Palo Alto: Palo Alto Historical Association, [1990].

Winkler, Jack R. *Old Hangtown: A History of Placerville, California from 1848 through 1856*. Placerville: JRW Press, 2000.

Wood, Dallas England, ed.-in-chief (Norris Edward James, associate ed. and comp.). *History of Palo Alto*. Palo Alto: A[rthur] H[amilton] Cawston, 1939.

B. Periodicals

Baird, Joseph Armstrong. "Architectural Legacy of Sacramento, A Study of 19th Century Style," *California Historical Society Quarterly* 1960 39 (3): 193–207.

Bartholomew, Karen, and Roxanne Nilan. "State Still Planning Restoration of Stanford's Sacramento Home," *Stanford Historical Society Newsletter* 1984 8 (3): 1–4.

Copeland, Peter F., and Marko Zlatich. "Imperial Russian Navy, 1863–1864," *Military Collector & Historian* 1964 16 (1): 18–19.

"The First Stanford Home," *Stanford Illustrated Review* 1923 24 (June): 477 and 495.

Gilbert, Benjamin Franklin. "Welcome to the Czar's Fleet, An Incident of Civil War Days in San Francisco," *California Historical Society Quarterly* 1947 26 (1): 13–19.

Golder, Frank A. "The Russian Fleet and the Civil War," *American Historical Review* 1915 20 (4): 800–812.

Jones, Laura, Elena Reese, and John W. Rick. "Is it not 'Haunted Ground?'—Archeological, Archival, and Architectural Investigations of the Stanfords' Palo Alto Home," *Sandstone & Tile* 1996 20 (1): 3–14.

Keagle, Cora L. "Pixley's History, 1886–1922," in unidentified newspaper account [post 1922], in Vertical File, Pixley Branch of the Tulare County Library.

Lagorio, Elmer. "Burning Questions: Mysteries Revealed as a Man Stands Trial for Hotel Del Monte Fire," *Alta Vista Magazine*, July 26, 1992, 7–11.

Mathes, Wayne A., and Frances Hayden Rhodes. "The Camron-Stanford House in Oakland, California," *Antiques* 1984 125 (2): 880–885.

McGuckin, Andrew J. "Golden Bonanza Lost in the Courts," *Frontier Times* 1965 (October–November): 10–13.

Netz, Joseph. "The Great Los Angeles Real Estate Boom of 1887," *Historical Society of Southern California, Annual Publications*, 1915 10 (Annual): 54–68.

Pattiani, Evelyn Craig. "Silk in Piedmont," *California Historical Society Quarterly* 1952 31 (4): 335–342.

Pomeroy, Earl. "The Visit of the Russian Fleet in 1863," *New York History* 1943 24 (4): 512–517.

Smith, Grant H. "Bodie; The Last of the Old-Time Mining Camps," *California Historical Society Quarterly* 1925 4 (1): 64–80.

"Stanford's Palace, the Finest Private Residence in America," *San Francisco Chronicle*, April 2, 1876.

Strazdes, Diana. "The Millionaire's Palace: Leland Stanford's Commission for Pottier and Stymus in San Francisco," *Winterthur Portfolio* 2001 36 (4): 213–246.

Strazdes, Diana. "The Visual Rhetoric of the Leland Stanford Mansion in Sacramento," *Stanford University Museum of Art Journal*. Biennial publication for the years 1994–1995, combined volumes 24–25, pages 12–24. Contains eighteen photographs, most of them interior views and works of art.

"The Nob Hill Home of the Stanford Family," *Stanford Historical Society Newsletter* 1984 9 (1): 10.

"There has to be a better Solution," *The* [Fremont, California] *Argus*, October 10, 1991. Editorial on the destruction of and real estate development of the Stanford historic site at Warm Springs.

Tutorow, Norman Eugene. "San Francisco over the Rocks: The Sitka [Ice Company] and the City," in Robert F. Schoeppner and Robert Joseph Chandler, eds. *California Vignettes* [San Francisco Corral of the Westerners Brand Book]. San Francisco: Great West Books, 1996, 87–105.

C. City, County, and Territorial Directories and Registers

Albany [New York] *City Directory*, 1846–1847, 1847–1848.

Austin [Nevada] *City Directory*, 1865–1868.

Child, Edmund B., comp. *Child's Albany Directory, and City Register, for the Years 1833–4*. Albany: E. B. Child, 1833.

City and County Directory of San Joaquin, Stanislaus, Merced, and Tuolumne. San Francisco: L. M. McKenny & Co., Publishers, 1881.

Directory of Nevada Territory, 1863. Nevada State Library and Archives.

General List of Citizens of the United States, Resident in the City and County of San Francisco, also Registered in the Great Register of said City and County. San Francisco: Towne and Bacon, Printers for the City, July 1867. Contains a diagram of city wards.

Great Register of the City and County of San Francisco. General List of Resident Voters existing on Great Register of said City and County, up to August 1, 1873. San Francisco: A. L. Bancroft and Co., 1873.

Hayes, Charles Wells. *A New Parish Register.* 15th ed., rev., New York: E. P. Dutton & Co., 1887.

Hoag, Charles C., ed. *Our Society Blue Book, The Fashionable Private Address Directory, containing the Names, Addresses, Reception Days and Country Residences of Prominent Families.* San Francisco: Charles C. Hoag, 1895. Later, *San Francisco Blue Book [and Elite Directory].* San Francisco: Bancroft and Co., 1888–1890; Hoag & Irving, c1891–c1903; Charles C. Hoag, c1904–.

Langley, Henry G. *San Francisco City Directory, 1850–present.*

Los Angeles City Directory, 1876–1890.

Marysville Directory, 1894–1895.

Masonic Cemetery File, History Room, San Francisco Public Library.

Milwaukee City Directory, 1890–1910.

Oakland City Directory, 1868–1900.

Philadelphia City Directory, 1869–1909.

Placerville City Directory, 1862.

Sacramento City Directory, 1851–1975.

San Francisco Ward Register. *1st Ward of the City and County of San Francisco. List of Resident Voters of the First Ward existing on the Great Register of said City and County, up to August 1, 1877.* San Francisco: Frank Eastman, 1877.

St. Louis City Directory, 1870–1900.

18. Railroad History
(*General History, Documents, and Reports*)
A. Books and Pamphlets

Appeal to the California Delegation in Congress Upon the Goat Island Grant to the Central Pacific Railroad Company, with accompanying military and scientific reports, correspondence of Mayor Alvord, veto by Governor Booth of Terminal R.R. bill, etc. San Francisco: Alta California Printing House, 1872.

Athearn, Fred G. *The Separation of The Central Pacific and The Southern Pacific Railroads: A Plain Statement of the Facts.* San Francisco: Union Pacific Railroad Co., 1922.

Bain, David Haward. *Empire Express: Building the first Transcontinental Railroad.* New York: Viking Books, 1999.

Bain, William E. *Frisco Folks: Stories and Pictures of the great Steam Days of the Frisco Road (St. Louis-San Francisco Railway Company).* Denver: Sage Books, 1961.

Baughman, James P. *Charles Morgan and the Development of Southern Transportation.* Nashville: Vanderbilt University Press, 1968.

Beebe, Lucius Morris. *Mansions on Rails: The Folklore of the Private Railway Cars.* Berkeley: Howell-North, 1959.

Beebe, Lucius Morris. *The Central Pacific & the Southern Pacific Railroads.* Berkeley: Howell-North, 1963.

Brown, Dee. *Hear that Lonesome Whistle Blow: Railroads in the West.* New York: Holt, Rinehart and Winston, 1977.

Brown, James Lorin. *The Mussel Slough Tragedy.* Fresno: [no publisher given], 1958.

Bryant, Keith L., Jr. *History of the Atchison, Topeka and Santa Fe Railway.* New York: Macmillan, 1974.

Campbell, Douglas. *Closing Argument of Douglas Campbell, Esq., in reply to Gov. John C. Brown, J.A. Davenport, Esq., and Major James Turner, before the Judiciary Committee of the House of Representatives, in regard* to the title of the Texas and Pacific Railway Company to the property of the Memphis, El Paso and Pacific Railroad Company. April 24, 1878. Washington City: Thomas McGill & Co., 1878. This document was not published in the Serial Set.

Central Pacific Railroad Company. "A Friend to the Pacific Railroad." The Pacific Railroad. A Defense Against its Enemies, with a Report of the Supervisors of Placer County, and a Report of Mr. Montanya, made to the Supervisors of the City and County of San Francisco. San Francisco: [no publisher given], December 1864. This work is bound in Pamphlets on California Railroads, Vol. 4, Pamphlet 5. Bancroft Library.

Central Pacific Railroad Company. Annual Report of the Board of Directors of the Central Pacific Railroad Co. to the Stockholders for the Year Ending December 31st, 1878. San Francisco: H[enry] S[mith] Crocker & Co. 1879.

Conkling, Roscoe. An Opinion as to the Power of the Railroad Commissioners of the State of California to Regulate Fares and Freights on the Central and Southern Pacific Railroads. San Francisco: H[enry] S[mith] Crocker & Co., 1882.

Crump, Spender. Western Pacific: The Railroad that was built too Late. Los Angeles: Trans-Anglo Books, 1962.

Daggett, Stuart. Chapters on the History of the Southern Pacific. New York: The Ronald Press Co., 1922.

Davis, John Patterson. The Union Pacific Railway, A Study in Railway Politics, History, and Economics. Chicago: S. C. Griggs and Co., 1894.

[Dawes, Horace(?)]. The Great Dutch Flat Swindle: The City of San Francisco Demands Justice; the matter in controversy, and the present state of the question; an address to the Board of Supervisors officers, and people of San Francisco. San Francisco: [no publisher given], 1864.

Delano, Alonzo (pseudonym, "Old Block"). The Central Pacific Railroad, or '49 and '69. San Francisco: White & Bauer, 1869.

Dumke, Glenn. The Boom of the Eighties in Southern California. San Marino: Huntington Library, 1944.

Dunscomb, Guy L. A Century of Southern Pacific Steam Locomotives, 1862–1962. Modesto: Guy L. Dunscomb, 1963.

Eargle, Dolan, Jr. Tickets Please: All about California Railroads. San Francisco: California Living Books, 1979.

Edson, William D., comp. Railroad Names: A Directory of Common Carrier Railroads Operating in the United States, 1826–1989. Potomac, Maryland: William D. Edson, 1989.

First Mortgage of the Southern Pacific Branch Railway Company (of California). San Francisco: [no publisher given], 1887, II, 13; this 17-page pamphlet was published in Vol. 2, Document 8, of Southern Pacific Railroad Pamphlets.

Galloway, John Debo. The First Transcontinental Railroad: The Central Pacific and Union Pacific, 1863–1869. New York: Simmons-Boardman, 1950; Dorset Press, 1989.

Goen, Steve Allen. Texas & Pacific—Color Pictorial. [No city or publisher given], [1997].

Gray, George E. Central Pacific Railroad of California: Report of George E. Gray upon the Constructed Road and the Located Route, made July 31, 1865. Sacramento: H[enry] S[mith] Crocker & Co., 1865.

Greever, William S. Arid Domain, The Santa Fe Railway and Its Western Land Grant. Stanford: Stanford University Press, 1954.

Griswold, Wesley S. A Work of Giants: Building the First Transcontinental Railroad. New York: McGraw-Hill, 1962.

Grodinsky, Julius. Transcontinental Railway Strategy, 1869–1893: A Study of Businessmen. Philadelphia: University of Pennsylvania Press, 1962.

Gross, Joseph, comp. *Railroads of North America: A Complete Listing of all North America Railroads, 1827 to 1986*. Spencerport, New York: Joseph Gross, 1986.

Haney, Lewis Henry. *A Congressional History of Railways* in the United States to 1850. Madison: [no publisher given], 1908. This work was a Ph.D. dissertation at the University of Wisconsin in 1906, first published in the *Bulletin of the University of Wisconsin*, No. 342, Economics and Political Science Series. 1908 3 (2): 167–439.

Haney, Lewis Henry. *A Congressional History of Railways in the United States, 1850 to 1887*. Madison: Democrat Printing Co., 1910. An extension of the previous entry.

Haymond, Creed. *The Central Pacific Railroad Co. Its Relations to the Government. It Has Performed Every Obligation*. San Francisco: H[enry] S[mith] Crocker & Co., 1888.

Hofsommer, Don L. *The Southern Pacific, 1901–1985*. College Station: Texas A & M University Press, 1986. Vol. 2 of a corporate history.

Holbrook, Stewart H. *The Story of American Railroads*. New York: Crown Publishers, 1947.

Howard, Robert West. *The Great Iron Trail: the Story of the First Transcontinental Railroad*. New York: Putnam, 1962.

Jensen, Larry. *The Movie Railroads*. Burbank: Darwin Publications, 1981.

Johnson, Enid. *Rails Across the Continent: The story of the First Transcontinental Railroad*. New York: J. Messner, 1965.

Jones, Eliot. *Principles of Railway Transportation*. New York: Macmillan, 1924. Contains a history of state and federal railroad regulation.

Jones, J. Roy. *The Old Central Pacific Hospital*. Sacramento: Western Association of Railway Surgeons, 1960.

Judah, Theodore Dehone. *A Practical Plan for Building the Pacific Railroad*. Washington: H. Polkinhorn, 1857, in *Pamphlets on California Railroads*, VII, No. 6, Bancroft Library.

Judah, Theodore Dehone. *Central Pacific Railroad Company of California*. November 1, 1860. San Francisco: Towne and Bacon, Printers, 1860.

Judah, Theodore Dehone. *Report of the Chief Engineer of the Central Pacific Railroad Company of California on his operations in the Atlantic States*. Sacramento: H[enry] S[mith] Crocker & Co., 1862.

Judah, Theodore Dehone. *Report of the Chief Engineer on the Preliminary Survey and Cost of Construction of the Central Pacific Railroad of California, across the Sierra Nevada Mountains from Sacramento to the eastern Boundary of California*. Sacramento: [no publisher given], October 1, 1861.

Judah, Theodore Dehone. *Report of the Chief Engineer on the Preliminary Surveys and Future Business of the Sacramento Valley Railroad. May 30, 1854*. Sacramento: Democratic State Journal Office, 1854. This twenty-four-page pamphlet is also found in *Pamphlets on California Railroads*, VII, No. 3, Bancroft Library.

Judah, Theodore Dehone. *Report of the Chief Engineer on the Preliminary Survey, Cost of Construction, and estimated Revenue of the Central Pacific Railroad of California across the Sierra Nevada Mountains, from Sacramento to the eastern Boundary of California. October 22, 1862*. Sacramento: H[enry] S[mith] Crocker & Co., 1862.

Judah, Theodore Dehone. *Report of the Chief Engineer upon recent Surveys, Progress of Construction, and an Approximate Estimate of Cost of First Division of Fifty Miles of the Central Pacific Railroad of Cal., July 1st, 1863*. Sacramento: James Anthony & Co., 1863.

Judah, Theodore Dehone. *Report to the Executive Committee of the Pacific Railroad Convention of 1859*. Sacramento: [no publisher given], 1860.

Kahn, Edgar M. *Cable Car Days in San Francisco*. Stanford: Stanford University Press, 1940.

Kibbey, Mead B. (Peter E. Palmquist, ed.). *The Railroad Photographs of Alfred A. Hart, Artist*. Sacramento: The California State Library Foundation, 1996.

Klein, Maury. *Union Pacific: Birth of a Railroad, 1862–1893*. New York: Doubleday & Co., 1987.

Klein, Maury. *Union Pacific: The Rebirth, 1894–1969*. New York: Doubleday & Co., 1989.

Kneiss, Gilbert H. *Bonanza Railroads*. Stanford: Stanford University Press, [1941] 1963.

Kraus, George. *High Road to Promontory: Building the Central Pacific (now the Southern Pacific) across the High Sierra*. Palo Alto: American West Publishing Co., 1969.

Lansing, Gerrit Livingston. *Relations Between the Central Pacific Railroad Company and the U.S. Government. Summary of Facts*. San Francisco: H[enry] S[mith] Crocker & Co., 1889.

MacMullen, Jerry. *Paddle-Wheel Days in California*. Stanford: Stanford University Press, 1944.

Madden, Jerome. *The Lands of the Southern Pacific Railroad Company of California*. San Francisco: Southern Pacific Railroad Journal, 1877.

McAfee, Ward Merner. *California's Railroad Era 1850–1911*. San Marino: Golden West Books, 1973. Revised and enlarged edition of "Local Interests and Railroad Regulation in Nineteenth Century California." Ph.D. dissertation (Stanford, 1965).

McCague, James. *Moguls and Iron Men: The Story of the First Transcontinental Railroad*. New York: Harper & Row, 1964.

Meyer, Hugo Richard. *Government Regulation of Railroad Rates; A Study of the Experience of the United States, Germany, France, Austria-Hungary, Russia and Australia*. New York: Macmillan, 1905.

Miller, David E., ed. *The Golden Spike*. Salt Lake City: University of Utah Press, 1974.

Miller, Louis Richard. *The History of the San Francisco and San Jose Railroad*. Berkeley: [no publisher given], 1948? Copies in University of California, Berkeley, Library and California State Library. Based on a term paper written at the San Mateo Junior College, June 1941. San Mateo County Historical Society.

Miner, H. Craig. *The St. Louis-San Francisco Transcontinental Railroad, the Thirty-fifth Parallel Project, 1853–1890*. Lawrence: University Press of Kansas, 1972.

Myrick, David F. *Railroads of Nevada and Eastern California*. Vol. 1 of 2, *The Northern Roads*. Reno: University of Nevada Press, [1962], 1990.

Myrick, David F. *Refinancing and Building the Central Pacific: 1899–1915*. Prepared for the Golden Spike Symposium, University of Utah, May 6–9, 1969. Published and distributed by the Southern Pacific.

Nordhoff, Charles. *California for Health, Pleasure, and Residence: a Book for Travellers and Settlers*. New York: Harper & Brothers, c1872, 1874, 1875, and 1882. Reprinted as *California: For Health, Pleasure, and Residence, a Book for Travellers and Settlers*. [Berkeley]: Ten Speed Press, 1973. Chapter III, "The Central Pacific Railroad," 45–60, reprinted in 32 pages as *C.P.R.R.—The Central Pacific Railroad*. Golden, Colorado: Outlooks, 1976; and, in 48 pages, by VistaBooks, Silverthorne, Colorado, 1996.

Otis, Fessenden Nott. *Illustrated History of the Panama Railroad, Together with a Traveler's Guide and Businessman's Handbook for the Panama Railroad and Its Connections*. New York: Harper and Brothers, 1861.

Poor, Henry Varnum. *Manual of the Railroads of the United States, for 1868–1869, Showing Their Mileage, Stocks, Bonds, Cost, Earnings, Expenses, and Organizations, with a Sketch of their Rise, Progress, Influence, &c. Together with an Appendix, containing A Full Analysis of the Debts of the United States, and of the several States*. New York: H[enry] V[arnum] Poor and H[enry] W[illiam] Poor, 1868.

Poor, Henry Varnum. *Poor's Manual of the Railroads of the United States for 1869–1870*. New York: Henry Varnum Poor and Henry William Poor, 1869.

Poor, Henry Varnum, and Henry William Poor. *Poor's Directory of Railway Officials and Manual of American Street Railways*. New York: American Bank Note Co., 1892, 1893.

Redding, Benjamin B. [Pacific Coast Land Bureau, compiler]. *California Guide Book, The Lands of the Central Pacific and Southern Pacific Railroad Companies in California, Nevada, and Utah*. San Francisco: Pacific Coast Land Bureau, 1875.

Riegel, Robert Edgar. *The Story of the Western Railroads, from 1852 Through the Reign of the Giants*. New York: Macmillan, 1926; Lincoln: University of Nebraska Press, 1926. Contains an excellent though dated bibliographical essay on all aspects of western railroad development.

Robertson, Donald B. *Encyclopedia of Western Railroad History, The Desert States: Arizona, Nevada, New Mexico, Utah*. Vol. 1 of 4. Caldwell, Idaho: Caxton Printers, 1986.

Robertson, Donald B. *Encyclopedia of Western Railroad History*. Vol. 4 of 4, *California*. Caldwell, Idaho: Caxton Printers, 1998.

Robinson, John W. *Southern California's First Railroad. The Los Angeles & San Pedro Railroad, 1869–1873*. Los Angeles: Dawson's Book Shop, 1978.

Russel, Robert Royal. *Improvement of Communication with the Pacific Coast as an Issue in American Politics, 1783–1864*. Cedar Rapids: Torch Press, 1948.

Sabin, Edward Legrand. *Building the Pacific Railway: The Construction-story of America's First Iron Thoroughfare between the Missouri River and California, from the Inception of the Idea to the Day, May 10, 1869, when the Union Pacific and the Central Pacific joined Tracks at Promontory Point [sic], Utah, to form the Nation's Transcontinental*. Philadelphia: J. B. Lippincott Co., 1919.

Settlers Committee of the Mussel Slough Company. *The Struggle of the Mussel Slough Settlers for their Homes. An Appeal to the People. History of the Land Troubles in Tulare and Fresno Counties. The Grasping Greed of the Railroad Monopoly*. Visalia: Delta Printing Establishment, 1880. A 32-page pamphlet.

Smallwood, Charles A. *The White Front Cars of San Francisco*. South Gate, Calif.: Ira L. Swett, 1970.

Southern Pacific Company. *Annual Report of the Southern Pacific Company, Its Proprietary Companies, and Leased Lines. For the Years Ending* [1885–1901, 1959]. Reports of the Southern Pacific Company Hospital were included in the annual reports; for example, December 31, 1891, Hospital Report, p. 20; December 31, 1892, Hospital Report, p. 21.

Southern Pacific Company. Bureau of News, Development Department. *Historical Outline, Southern Pacific Company*. San Francisco: Southern Pacific Co., 1933.

Southern Pacific Company. *Statistical Supplement to the 76th Annual Report*, 1959.

Southern Pacific Company. Valuation Department, comp. *Corporate History of Southern Pacific Company Lines (Pacific System) as of June 30, 1916*. San Francisco: Southern Pacific Co., 1919.

Southern Pacific Railroad Company [submitted by Chief Engineer George E. Gray]. *Annual Report of the Board of Directors of the Southern Pacific Railroad Co., to the Stockholders. For the Eighteen Months Ending December 31st, 1878*. San Francisco: H[enry] S[mith] Crocker & Co., 1879.

Southern Pacific Railroad Company. *Annual Report of the Board of Directors of the Southern Pacific Railroad Co., to the Stockholders. For the Year Ending June 30th, 1876 and 1877*. San Francisco: H[enry] S[mith] Crocker & Co., 1877.

Southern Pacific Railroad Company. *Annual Report of the Board of Directors of the Southern Pacific Railroad Co., to the Stockholders. For the Year Ending December 31st, 1880*. San Francisco: H[enry] S[mith] Crocker & Co., 1880.

Southern Pacific Railroad Company. *Annual Report of the Southern Pacific Railroad Company, year ending December 31, 1869* [also years 1876–1888]. California State Archives.

Southern Pacific Railroad Company. *Organization. Articles of Association and Consolidation, and Acts of Congress and of the Legislature of the State of California relative thereto*. New York: Evening Post Steam Presses, 1873.

Southern Pacific Railroad Company. *Organization. Articles of Association and Consolidation, and Acts of Congress and of the Legislature of the State of California relative thereto.* New York: Evening Post Steam Presses, 1875.

Southern Pacific Railroad Company. *The Lands of the Southern Pacific Railroad Company of California; their situation, soil, climate, vegetation, present and prospective values, price, and the terms under which they are offered for Sale.* San Francisco: Southern Pacific Railroad , 1876 (?).

Stanford, Leland. *Central Pacific Railroad. Statement Made to the President of the United States, and Secretary of the Interior, of the Progress of the Work, October 10th, 1865.* Sacramento: H[enry] S[mith] Crocker & Co., 1865.

Stanford, Leland. *Report from the Hon. Leland Stanford, President of the Central Pacific Railroad Company, to His Excellency, Frederick F. Low, Governor of California.* Sacramento: Orlando M. Clayes, 1865, published as Pamphlet 8, a 5-page document bound in Business Regulation Pamphlets, Crown Law Library, Stanford University—CN H7.

Starr, John W., Jr. *Lincoln and the Railroads, A Biographical Study.* New York: Dodd, Mead & Co., 1927.

Strobridge, Edson Turner. *The Central Pacific Railroad and the Legend of Cape Horn.* San Luis Obispo: Edson T. Strobridge, 2001.

Trafzer, Clifford Earl. *The Yuma Crossing: A Short History of a Southwestern Crossing.* Yuma: Yuma County Historical Society, 1974.

Trottman, Nelson. *History of the Union Pacific: A Financial and Economic Survey.* New York: The Ronald Press, 1923.

Waters, Lawrence Leslie. *Steel Trails to Santa Fe.* Lawrence: University of Kansas Press, 1950.

Williams, John Hoyt. *A Great and Shining Road.* New York: Times Books, 1988.

Wilson, Neill Compton, and Frank J. Taylor. *Southern Pacific, the Roaring Story of a Fighting Railroad.* New York: McGraw-Hill, 1952.

B. Periodicals and Ephemera

Anderson, Chuck, and Karen E. Bartholomew. "The Governor Stanford: It's No. 1," *Sandstone & Tile* 1978 2 (3): 1–7.

Arrington, Leonard J. "The Transcontinental Railroad and the Development of the West," *Utah Historical Quarterly* 1969 37 (1): 3–15.

Athearn, Robert G. "Contracting for the Union Pacific," *Utah Historical Quarterly* 1969 37 (1): 16–40.

"Atlantic and Pacific Railroad," *California Mail Bag* 1872 2 (2): 30–32.

Bailey, William Frances, "The Story of the Central Pacific: The Rise of the Big Four: Huntington, Stanford, Crocker and Hopkins," *The Pacific Monthly: A Magazine of Education and Progress* 1908 19 (1) 12–27; (2): 200–214.

Best, Gerald M. "Rendezvous at Promontory: The 'Jupiter' and No. 119," *Utah Historical Quarterly* 1969 37 (1): 69–75.

Bowman, Jacob Nebert. "Driving the Last Spike at Promontory, 1869," *California Historical Society Quarterly* 1957 36 (2): 97–106; 36 (3): 263–274; reprinted in *Utah Historical Quarterly* 1969 37 (1): 76–101.

Brown, James L. "More Fictional Memorials to Mussel Slough," *Pacific Historical Review* 1957 26 (4): 373–377.

Brown, Margaret L. "Asa Whitney and His Pacific Railroad Publicity Campaign," *Mississippi Valley Historical Review* 1933 20 (2): 209–224.

Carman, Harry J., and Charles H. Mueller. "The Contract and Finance Company and the Central Pacific Railroad," *Mississippi Valley Historical Review* 1927 14 (2): 326–341.

Carranco, Lynwood, and Mrs. Eugene Fountain. "California's First Railroad: The Union Plank Walk, Rail Track, and Wharf Company Railroad," *Journal of the West* 1964 3 (2): 243–256.

"Central Pacific Railroad Company's Hospital" [in Sacramento], *The Centennial Spirit of the Times*. San Francisco: California Spirit of the Times and Fireman's Journal, July 4, 1876, 9 (40-page special edition).

Cotterill, Robert Spencer. "Early Agitation for a Pacific Railroad, 1845–1850," *Mississippi Valley Historical Review* 1919 5 (4): 396–414.

Curtis, Edward. "What the Locomotive has Done for California," *California Mail Bag* 1874 4 (March): 97.

Daggett, Stuart. "Southern Pacific Unmerger: Judicial Proceedings for the Separation of the Central Pacific and Southern Pacific Railroad Lines," *University of California Chronicle*. October 22, 1922 24 (4): 465–496.

Due, John F. "The San Francisco and Alameda Railroad," *Pacific Railway Journal* 1956 1 (11): 2–8.

Farnham, Wallace D. "The Pacific Railroad Act of 1862," *Nebraska History* 1962 43 (3): 141–167.

"From Trail to Rail—The Story of Beginning of Southern Pacific," *Southern Pacific Bulletin* 1926–1931 volumes 14–19. Forty-four chapters, covering all aspects of Central Pacific/Southern Pacific history.

George, Henry. "What the Railroad Will Bring Us," *Overland Monthly* 1868 1 (4): 297–306.

Gilliss, John R. "Tunnels of the Pacific Railroad," *American Society of Civil Engineers. Transactions* 1872 1 (13): 153–171. A paper read before the society, January 5, 1870.

Grosvenor, William Mason. "The Railroads and the Farms," *Atlantic Monthly* 1873 32 (193): 591–610.

Heath, Erle. "A Railroad Record that Defies Defeat," *Southern Pacific Bulletin* 1928 16 (5): 3–5.

Hoffman, Elwyn. "The Old Dutch Flat Road," *Sunset Magazine*, February 1905, 373–376.

Huffman, Wendell W. "Iron Horse along the Truckee: The Central Pacific Reaches Nevada," *Nevada Historical Society Quarterly* 1995 38 (1): 19–36.

Kemble, John Haskell. "The Transpacific Railroads, 1869–1915," *Pacific Historical Review* 1949 18 (3): 331–343.

Ketterson, Francis A., Jr. "Golden Spike National Historic Site: Development of an Historical Reconstruction," *Utah Historical Quarterly* 1969 37 (1): 58–68.

Kotter, Richard E. "The Transcontinental Railroad and Ogden City Politics," *Utah Historical Quarterly* 1974 42 (3): 278–284.

Kraus, George. "Chinese Laborers and the Construction of the Central Pacific," *Utah Historical Quarterly* 1969 37 (1): 41–57.

Lamb, Blaine Peterson, and Ellen Halteman Schwartz. "The Paper Trail of the Iron Horse: The California State Railroad Museum Library," *California History* 1991 70 (1): 94–113.

Leonard, Levi O., and Jack T. Johnson. *A Railroad to the Sea*. Iowa City: Midland House Publishers, 1939.

Lesley, Lewis B. "A Southern Transcontinental Railroad into California: Texas and Pacific versus Southern Pacific, 1865–1885," *Pacific Historical Review* 1936 5 (1): 52–60.

Lesley, Lewis B. "The Entrance of the Santa Fé Railroad into California," *Pacific Historical Review* 1939 8 (1): 89–96.

Loomis, Nelson H. "Asa Whitney: Father of Pacific Railroads," *Mississippi Valley Historical Association Proceedings* 1912–1913 6 (annual): 166–175.

Mann, David H. "The Undriving of the Golden Spike," *Utah Historical Quarterly* 1969 37 (1): 124–134.

McKee, Irving. "Notable Memorials to Mussel Slough," *Pacific Historical Review* 1948 17 (1): 19–27.

Morgan, Richard Price, Jr., Inspecting Engineer for the United States Pacific Railway Commission. "Report on the Union Pacific Railway and its Branches; the Central Pacific Railway and its Branches; the Central Branch of the Union Pacific Railroad; also on Auxiliary and Leased Lines, October 15, 1887," *United States Pacific Railway Commission*, VIII, 4439–4465.

O'Meara, James. "The Union or the Dominion?" *Overland Monthly* 1889 14 (82): 414–428.

Orsi, Richard J. "The Octopus Reconsidered: The Southern Pacific and Agricultural Modernization in California, 1865–1915," *California Historical Quarterly* 1975 54 (3): 196–220.

Putnam, Frank B. "Serape to Levi . . . Southern Pacific [this is the complete title]," *Historical Society of Southern California Quarterly* 1956 38 (3): 211–224.

Sandoval, John. "Transcontinental Railroad comes to the East Bay," *The Western Railroader* 1969 32 (9): 3–10.

Saxton, Alexander. "The Army of Canton in the High Sierra," *Pacific Historical Review* 1966 35 (2): 141–152.

Southern Development Company. Document on Board of Directors meeting, June 10, 1881.

Traxler, Ralph N., Jr. "Collis P. Huntington and the Texas and Pacific Railroad Land Grant," *New Mexico Historical Review* 1959 34 (2): 117–133.

Union Pacific Railroad. *Chronological History*, 1998.

Union Pacific Railroad. News Release, November 30, 1996.

Union Pacific Railroad. Public Relations Department. *Fast Facts*, October 17, 1997.

White, Chester Lee. "Surmounting the Sierras [*sic*]: The Campaign for a Wagon Road," *California Historical Society Quarterly* 1928 7 (1): 3–19.

Winther, Oscar Osburn. "The Story of San Jose, 1777–1869—California's First Pueblo," Chapter V, "The Railroad Comes to San Jose, the Early Sixties," *California Historical Society Quarterly* 1935 14 (2): 164–167 and 174.

Wyatt, Kyle. "From the Gold Spike to the Silver State," *Sagebrush Headlight* 1998 19 (2): 4–7.

19. General Works
A. Books

Antisell, Thomas. *The Manufacture of Photogenic or Hydro-Carbon Oils*. New York: D. Appleton and Co., 1865.

Beard, Augustus Field. *A Crusade of Brotherhood: A History of the American Missionary Association*. Boston: The Pilgrim Press, 1909.

Berthold, Victor Maximilian. *The Pioneer Steamer* California *1848–1849*. Cambridge: Riverside Press, 1932.

Böckli, Peter. *Bis zum Tod der Gräfin: Das Drama um den Hotelpalast des Grafen de Renesse in Maloja*. Zürich: Neue Zürcher Zeitung, 1998.

Brown, George Ingham. *The Big Bang: A History of Explosives*. Stroud, Gloucestershire: Sutton Publishing, 1998.

Bunker, John Gorley. *Liberty Ships*. Salem, New Hampshire: Ayer Co., Publishers, [1972], 1985.

Carman, Harry J., and Reinhold H. Luthin. *Lincoln and the Patronage*. New York: Columbia University Press, 1943.

Drinker, Henry Sturgis. *A Treatise on Explosive Compounds, Machine Rock Drills and Blasting*. New York: John Wiley & Sons, 1883.

Gesner, Abraham. *A Practical Treatise on Coal, Petroleum and Other Distilled Oils*. New York: Balliere Press, 1865. Used by Josiah Stanford in connection with the San Francisco oil refinery.

Gibbs, James. *West Coast Windjammers In Story and Pictures*. New York: Bonanza Books, 1968.

Goodwin, Charles Carroll. *As I Remember Them*. Salt Lake City: Salt Lake Commercial Club, 1913.

Greeley, Horace, and John Fitch Cleveland, comps. *A Political Text-Book for 1860: Comprising a Brief View of Presidential Nominations and Elections, including all the national platforms ever yet adopted, also a history of the struggle respecting slavery in the territories, and of the action of Congress as to the freedom of the public lands, with the most notable speeches and letters of Messrs. Lincoln, Douglas, Bell, Cass, Seward, Everett, Breckinridge, H. V. Johnson, etc., etc., touching the questions of the day, and returns of all presidential elections since 1836*. New York: Tribune Association, 1860.

Hague, James D. *Mining Industry*. Washington: Government Printing Office, 1870. Vol. III of Clarence King. *United States Geological Exploration of the Fortieth Parallel*. Papers of the Engineer Department, U.S. Army, No. 18.

Halstead, Murat. *Caucuses of 1860. A History of the National Political Conventions of the Current Presidential Campaign: being a Complete Record of the Conventions; with sketches of distinguished men in attendance upon them, and descriptions of the most characteristic scenes and memorable events*. Columbus, Ohio: Follett, Foster and Co., 1860.

Hart, Jerome. *In Our Second Century, from an Editor's Note-Book*. San Francisco: The Pioneer Press, 1931.

Hatcher, James B., ed.-in-chief. *Scott's Standard Postage Stamp Catalogue. The Encyclopedia of Philately, 1972*. 3 vols., New York: Scott Publishing Co., 1972.

Hawgood, John Arkas. *America's Western Frontiers, the Exploration and Settlement of the Trans-Mississippi West*. New York: Alfred A. Knopf, 1967.

Herodotus [David Grene, translator]. *The History*. Chicago: University of Chicago Press, 1987.

Herodotus [J. Enoch Powell, ed.]. *Herodotus*. Oxford: Clarendon Press, 1949.

Herodotus [Walter Blanco and Jennifer Tolbert Roberts, eds.; Walter Blanco, translator]. *The Histories*. New York: W. W. Norton, 1992.

Hesseltine, William B., ed. *Three Against Lincoln, Murat Halstead Reports the Caucuses of 1860*. Baton Rouge: Louisiana State University, 1960.

Hittell, John Shertzer. *The Commerce and Industries of the Pacific Coast of North America*. San Francisco: A[lbert] L[ittle] Bancroft & Co., 1882.

Homer (Alexander Pope, translator). *The Iliad and the Odyssey*. "Albion Edition." London: Frederick Warne and Co., 1894.

Jackson, W[illiam] Turrentine. *Wagon Roads West: A Study of Federal Land Surveys and Construction in the Trans-Mississippi West, 1846–1869*. Berkeley: University of California Press, 1952.

Jane, Fred T. *The Imperial Russian Navy, Its Past, Present, and Future*. London: W. Thacker & Co., 1899.

Josephson, Matthew. *The Robber Barons. The Great American Capitalists, 1861–1901*. New York: Harcourt, Brace & World, 1934.

Kemble, John Haskell. *A Hundred Years of Pacific Mail*. Newport News: Mariners' Museum, 1950.

Kemble, John Haskell. *The Panama Route, 1848–1869*. Berkeley: University of California Press, 1943.

King, Clarence. *United States Geological Exploration of the Fortieth Parallel*. Vol. III, *Mining Industry*, by James D. Hague. Washington: Government Printing Office, 1870.

Knoles, George Harmon. *The Presidential Campaign and Election of 1892*. Stanford University Publications, University Series. *History Economics, and Political Science*, Vol. V, No. 1. Stanford: Stanford University Press, 1942.

Lawson, Will. *Pacific Steamers*. Glasgow: Brown, Son & Ferguson Co., 1927.

Lovejoy, Amos J., Jr. *The Rise and Decline of the American Cut Nail Industry: A Study of the Interrelationships of Technology, Business Organization, and Management Techniques*. Westport: Greenwood Press, 1983.

Macesich, George. *Political Economy of Money: emerging fiat monetary regime*. London: Praeger, 1999.

Moore, Charles Irwin Douglas. *The Pacific Mutual Life Insurance Company of California: A History of the Company and the Development of its Organization*. Los Angeles: The Pacific Mutual Life Insurance Company of California, 1928.

Morgan, H[oward] Wayne. *The Gilded Age: A Reappraisal*. Syracuse, New York: Syracuse University Press, 1963.

Mowbray, George M. *Tri-Nitro Glycerin, as Applied in the Hoosac Tunnel, etc., etc., etc.* Rev. ed., New York: D. Van Nostrand; 2nd edition, North Adams, Mass.: James T. Robinson & Son, 1874. The hard-to-find original ed., published by Robinson & Son in 1872, has different pagination.

Myers, Gustavus. *History of the Great American Fortunes*. Chicago: C. H. Kerr & Co., 1910; New York: Modern Library, 1936.

Nunis, Doyce Blackman, Jr. *Past is Prologue: A Centennial Profile of Pacific Mutual Life Insurance Company*. [Los Angeles]: Pacific Mutual Life Insurance Co., [1967].

Pacific Coast Annual Mining Review and Stock Ledger, containing Detailed Official Reports of the Principal Gold and Silver Mines of Nevada, California, Arizona, Utah, New Mexico, and Idaho; A History and Description of Mining and Stock Dealing on this Coast, with Biographical Sketches of 100 of the Principal Men Engaged Therein; and a Series of Finance Articles by Col. Henry S. Fitch. San Francisco: Francis & Valentine, 1878.

Pacific [Mutual] Life Annual Report, 2000. Newport Beach: Pacific [Mutual] Life Insurance Co., 2001.

Parrington, Vernon Louis. *Main Currents in American Thought: An Interpretation of American Literature from the Beginning to 1920*. New York: Harcourt, Brace and Co., 1927–1930; three volumes in one. Vol. 3: *The Beginnings of Critical Realism in America: 1860–1920*.

Porter, Kirk H., and Donald Bruce Johnson. *National Party Platforms, 1840–1964*. Urbana: University of Illinois Press, 1966.

Reddy, William. *First Fifty Years of Cazenovia Seminary, 1825–1875*. Cazenovia: Nelson and Phillips, 1877.

Republican Party. *Official Proceedings of the Republican National Convention held at Chicago, June 3, 4, 5, and 6, 1884*. Minneapolis: Charles W. Johnson, 1903.

Rodell, Fred. *Nine Men: A Political History of the Supreme Court from 1790 to 1955*. New York: Random House, 1955.

Salisbury, James Henry. *Microscopic Examinations of Blood; and Vegetations found in Variola, Vaccina, and Typhoid Fever*. New York: Moorhead, Bond & Co., 1868.

Sawyer, Leonard Arthur, and William Harry Mitchell. *The Liberty Ships: The History of the "Emergency" Type Cargo Ships Constructed during World War II*. Cambridge, Maryland: Cornell Maritime Press, 1970.

Smith, Eugene Waldo. *Passenger Ships of the World, Past and Present*. 2nd ed., Boston: G. H. Dean Co., [1947], 1978.

Spratt, Hereward Philip. *Transatlantic Paddle Steamers*. Glasgow: Brown, Son & Ferguson, 1951.

Stanwood, Edward. *A History of the Presidency, from 1788–1897*. 2 vols., rev. ed., Boston and New York: Houghton Mifflin Co., [1898] 1928.

Stedman, Thomas Lathrop. *Stedman's Medical Dictionary*. 25th ed., Baltimore and London: Williams & Wilkins, 1990.

Stillâe, Charles Janeway. *History of the United States Sanitary Commission*. Philadelphia: J. B. Lippincott & Co., 1866.

Thayer, William Makepiece. *Marvels of the New West. A Vivid Portrayal of the unparalleled Marvels in the vast Wonderland West of the Missouri River. Graphically and truthfully described by William M. Thayer … Illustrated with three hundred and seventy-nine fine Engravings and Maps*. Norwich, Conn.: The Henry Bill Publishing Co., 1888.

Thoreau, Henry David. "Sounds," *Walden, or Life in the Woods*. New York: Heritage Press, [1854], 1939.

Twain, Mark, and Charles Dudley Moore. *The Gilded Age A Tale of Today*. Reprinted in 2 volumes, Vol. 2, New York: P. F. Collier & Son, [1873], 1915.

Van Gelder, Arthur Pine, and Hugo Schlatter. *History of the Explosives Industry in America*. New York: Columbia University Press, 1927.

Whitman, Walt. *Passage to India*. Washington: [no publisher given], 1871.

B. Periodicals and Newspaper Articles

Betts, John Rickards. "The Technological Revolution and the Rise of Sport, 1850–1900," *Mississippi Valley Historical Review* 1953 40 (2): 231–256.

Chester, Stephen. "Nitro-Glycerin: Its Manufacture and Use," *American Society of Civil Engineers. Transactions*. 1872 1 (11): 117–134. A paper read before the society, June 2, 1869.

Kemble, John Haskell. "The Big Four at Sea, the History of the Occidental and Oriental Steamship Company," *Huntington Library Quarterly* 1940 3 (3): 339–357.

Kemble, John Haskell. "The Genesis of the Pacific Mail Steamship Company—Part I," Chapter I, "The Pacific Mail Steamship Company" (240–247); Chapter II, "Three Ships" (247–254), *California Historical Society Quarterly* 1934 13 (3): 240–254; 13 (4), "The Genesis of the Pacific Mail Steamship Company (Concluded)," Chapter III, "Getting Under Way," 386–406.

L'Allemand, Gordon. "The Luck of the *Jane L. Stanford*," *Los Angeles Times Sunday Magazine*, June 5, 1927.

Lyman, John. "Pacific Coast-Built Sailors," *The Marine Digest*, May 17, 1941, p. 2.

McDonald, Patrick Alexander. "Ships and Record Pacific Passages, Part I," *Nautical Research Journal* 1967 14 (1): 17–22.

McDonald, Patrick Alexander. "Some interesting details concerning the fate of once-famous ships," *Seabreezes, the P*[acific] *S*[hip] *N*[avigation] *C*[ompany] *Magazine* July 1929 12 (116): 181–182.

Miller, Robert Ryal. "The *Camanche*: First Monitor of the Pacific," *California Historical Society Quarterly* 1996 45 (2): 113–124.

Millis, Walter, "The Iron Sea Elephants," *The American Neptune* 1950 10 (1): 15–32.

North, Edward P. "Blasting with Nitro-Glycerine," *American Society of Civil Engineers. Transactions*. 1872 1 (2): 13–21. A paper read before the society, March 4, 1868.

Schwemmer, Robert. "Seventy Year Search for Jane, 30 August 1929–1999," *Santa Barbara Maritime Museum Currents* 1999 (September): 3–4.

Tegeder, Vincent G. "Lincoln and the Territorial Patronage: The Ascendancy of the Radicals in the West," *Mississippi Valley Historical Review* 1948 35 (1): 77–90.

20. UNPUBLISHED AND EPHEMERAL WORKS

Ball, Donald Clyde. "A History of the E. B. Crocker Art Gallery and its Founder." M.A. thesis (College of the Pacific, 1955).

Ballard, Roy Page. "History of the Stanford Campus, of 1894." Stanford University Archives, Roy Page Ballard Collection. Part of this work was published as the "San Francisquito Rancho," in the *Stanford Sequoia* 1895 4 (32, May 24), 381–384.

Best, Gerald M. "Story of the Golden Spike at Lang Station," from the Golden Spike Centennial Souvenir Program, September 5, 1976, distributed by the Santa Clarita Valley Historical Society in its Santa Clarita Valley History in Pictures series.

Biography File. History Room, California State Library.

Bracewell, Ron. "Trees on the Stanford Campus," 1984. Stanford University Archives.

Caratzas, Michael D. "Leland Stanford: War Governor of California, Railroad Builder, and Watervliet Native." Term paper (Rensselaer Polytechnic Institute, Troy, New York, Fall, 1991).

"Chronological Listing of Board of Trustees 1885 to Present [1995]." Stanford University Archives.

"Claridge's, A Brief History." Claridge's Hotel, London, undated.

Clark, George Thomas. "Record" book, Spring 1907, containing notes compiled and interviews made by Clark for his biography of Leland Stanford.

Dayton, Dello Grimmett. "The California Militia, 1859–1866." Ph.D. dissertation (University of California, Berkeley, 1951).

"Directory [of Members]," Unitarian Church of Palo Alto, 1919.

Elliott, Russell Richard. "The Early History of White Pine County, Nevada, 1865–1867." M.A. thesis (University of Washington, 1938).

Fahey, Frank M. "The Legislative Background of the Constitutional Convention of 1879." M.A. thesis (Stanford University, 1947).

First Unitarian Church of San Francisco. "Christenings, Marriages, Funerals." In church archives.

First Unitarian Church of San Francisco. "Marriage Licenses, 1864–1889." In church archives.

First Unitarian Church of San Francisco. "Pew Account, 1864–1873." In church archives.

First Unitarian Church of San Francisco. "Receiving Book for the Pilgrim Sunday School." In church archives.

Foss, Werner C., Jr. "The History of Ravenswood." A term paper by a student at San Mateo Junior College, 1942, San Mateo County Historical Society.

Gundelfinger, Edward R. "The Pacific Mail Steamship Company, 1847–1917: Its Relations with the Railroads." B.A. thesis (University of California, Berkeley, 1917).

Harrington, Marie. "A Golden Spike: The Beginning," *Santa Clarita Valley in Pictures*. Newhall: Santa Clarita Valley Historical Society, September 5, 1976. Distributed by the society in its Santa Clarita Valley History in Pictures series.

Hemsing, Peter. "The Stanfords in Europe." 1968. A 30-page study of the Stanfords' European travels, with maps of their trip from June to September 1888. Stanford University Archives.

"History of the Oakland Water Front, with Map of Oakland Water Front." Oakland, 1879. A collection of hundreds of pages of newspaper articles dealing with the company. Oakland History Room, Oakland Public Library.

Hoyt, Franklin. "Railroad Development in Southern California, 1868 to 1900." Ph.D. dissertation (University of Southern California, 1951).

Johnson, William D. "Inland Steam Navigation in California." M.A. thesis (Stanford University, 1952).

Kincaid, E.A. "The Federal Land Grants of the Central Pacific Railroad." Ph.D. dissertation (University of California, 1922).

Lesley, Lewis B. "The Struggle of San Diego for a Southern Transcontinental Railroad Connection, 1854–1891." Ph.D. dissertation (University of California, Berkeley, 1933).

Lucas, Arel. "Annotated Bibliography of Sources at Stanford on Eadweard Muybridge." Nine-page finding aid for Muybridge sources in the Stanford University Archives.

McConnell, John A. "The Stanford Vina Ranch." M.A. thesis (Stanford University, 1961).

McKinney, William Clyde. "The Mussel Slough Episode, A Chapter in the Settlement of the San Joaquin Valley, 1865–1880." M.A. thesis (University of California, Berkeley, 1948).

Mosher, Clelia Duel, comp. "Notes Concerning Jane E. Lathrop (Mrs. Leland Stanford) who attended the Albany Female Academy in the 1840's [sic]." Stanford University, 1939, in Jane Stanford papers. Stanford University Archives.

Mudgett, Margaret Holt. "The Political Career of Leland Stanford." M.A. thesis (University of Southern California, 1933).

Native Sons of the Golden West, Sutter's Fort Committee. "Memorandum Book used at Sacramento by Eugene J. Gregory and Frank D. Ryan for the Listing of Subscriptions to the Fund for the Purchase of the Sutter Fort Property, etc." [Sacramento: no publisher given, 1890].

Quinlan, Tim. "The Success of Leland Stanford: a Different Perspective," December 9, 1977. Seminar paper that deals with Leland Stanford as a great American in the Mason Weems tradition. Stanford University Archives.

Regnery, Dorothy. "A Study of the Leland Stanford House in Sacramento, California," c1987 by Dorothy Regnery, a 284-page, bound manuscript in Dorothy Regnery papers. Stanford University Archives.

Robinson, Edward I. "California Historical Events and Reminiscences." Los Angeles, June 1915.

Roth, Arnold. "The California Supreme Court, 1860–1879," Ph.D. dissertation (University of Southern California, 1973).

Ruhkala, Roy. "History of Rocklin, California," 1975. Stanford University Archives.

Sawyer, Otis V. [Rossiter Preston Johnson Memorial Pamphlet]. San Francisco, June 7, 1862. Obituary presented to the Society of California Pioneers, in History Room, California State Library.

Schneider, Lynn. "Leland Stanford, Businessman and Politician," Term Paper (Wells College, Aurora, New York, January 31, 1979). Copy in Stanford Archives.

Sheaff, Carolyn. "Cameron-Stanford House, Chain of Title," "Resident Families at 1218 Oak Street, Oakland, California." Four-page manuscript, in Stanford Archives.

Spoehr, Luther William. "Progress' Pilgrim: David Starr Jordan and the Circle of Reform, 1891–1931," Ph.D. dissertation (Stanford University, 1975).

Stalder, Walter. "Stanford Brothers as California Oil Pioneers" (December 9, 1935), originally intended as a chapter in a book by Emory Evans Smith that was never published. Stanford University Archives.

Stockton Savings and Loan Association. "Manteca Memories, Photographic Recollections of the Manteca Area." Stockton: unpublished pamphlet, no date. In the Cesar Chavez Central Library, Stockton, California.

Treat, Archibald. "The Stanfords and their Golden Key." Unpublished manuscript. San Francisco, 1937. Stanford papers.

Tutorow, Norman Eugene. "Stanfordians! Let Us Preserve our Heritage." Eight-page unpublished sketch of the history of the Mead Statuary.

Tutorow, Norman Eugene, and Evelyn "Evie" LaNora Tutorow. "Friends of Leland Stanford Jr: Lizzie Hull and Wilsie Taylor."

Tutorow, Norman Eugene, and Evelyn "Evie" LaNora Tutorow. "The Family of Miss Lizzie Hull," unpublished manuscript.

Yen, Tzu-Kuei. "Chinese Workers and the First Transcontinental Railroad of the United States of America." Ph.D. dissertation (St. John's University, New York), 1976.

21. NEWSPAPERS CITED OR QUOTED

A. California

[Auburn] *Placer Herald*

[Bakersfield] *Kern County Californian*

[Oakland] *Alameda County*

[Pacific Grove] *Del Monte Wave*

[Placerville] *Mountain Democrat-Times*

[Redwood City] [San Mateo] *Times and Gazette*

[Sacramento] *Daily California Times*

[Sacramento] *Democratic State Journal*

[San Francisco] *Arthur McEwen's Letter*

Alameda County Gazette

Alameda Star

Alameda Telegram

Berkeley Independent and Gazette

Butte Record

Chico Chronicle

Chico Enterprise-Record

Chico Northern Enterprise

Chico Record

Colfax Weekly Record

Colusa Morning Gazette

Colusa Sun

Downieville Mountain Messenger

Dutch Flat Enquirer

Eureka Times

Folsom Telegraph

Fremont News-Register and Gazette

Granite Journal

Hollister Free Lance

Humboldt Standard

Humboldt Times

Los Angeles Daily Express

Los Angeles Semi-Weekly Southern News

Los Angeles Southern Californian

Los Angeles Star

Los Angeles Times

Marysville Appeal

Menlo-Atherton Recorder

Merced Star

Monterey Herald

Monterey Monitor

Napa County Reporter

Napa Daily Register

Nevada [City] *Journal*

Nevada City Transcript

Oakland Enquirer

Oakland Morning Times

Oakland Tribune

Pacific Life

Palo Alto Times

Petaluma Argus

Petaluma Daily Imprint

Petaluma Daily Sentinel

Pixley Enterprise

Placerville News

Red Bluff News

Red Bluff People's Cause

Red Bluff Semi-Weekly Independent

Red Bluff Sentinel

Red Bluff Tri-Weekly Independent

Redding Republican Free Press

Redlands Daily Facts

Redwood City Tribune

Sacramento Bee

Sacramento Placer Times

Sacramento Record

Sacramento Record-Union

Sacramento State Capital Reporter

Sacramento State Journal

Sacramento Union

San Diego Seaport News

San Francisco Alta California

San Francisco Argonaut

San Francisco Bulletin

*San Francisco California Spirit of the Times and
    Underwriters' Journal*

San Francisco Call

San Francisco Chronicle

San Francisco City Argus

San Francisco Commercial Record

San Francisco Daily Report

San Francisco Daily Times

San Francisco Examiner

San Francisco Herald

San Francisco News-Letter and California Advertiser

San Francisco Post

San Francisco Real Estate Circular

San Francisco Wasp

San Francisco Wave

San Joaquin Valley Argus

San José Mercury

San José Telegraph

San José Times

San José Tribune

Santa Barbara Morning Press

Santa Barbara News-Press

Santa Cruz Sentinel

Saucelito [sic] *Weekly Herald*

Shasta Courier

Stanford [University] *Daily*

Stockton Independent

Terra Bella News

The Encinal of Alameda

Truckee Republican

Vallejo Chronicle

B. Other States and Territories

[Austin, Nevada] *Reese River Reveille*

[Hamilton, Nevada] *Inland Empire*

[Honolulu] *Pacific Commercial Advertiser* (*Honolulu Advertiser* after 1921)

[Juneau] *Alaska Free Press*

[Salem] *Willamette Farmer*

[Yuma] *Arizona Sentinel*

Albany Journal

Albany Press

Albany Telegram

Albany Times-Union

Atlanta Journal

Bloomington [Illinois] *Pantograph*

Boston Courier

Boston Evening Transcript

Buffalo Illustrated Express

Cedarburg [Wisconsin] *News*

Chicago Examiner

Chicago Post

Chicago Tribune

Cincinnati Enquirer

Cincinnati Tribune

Comstock [Nevada] *Chronicle*

Daily Elko Independent

El Paso Lone Star

Ely Record

Financial Chronicle and Hunt's Merchant's Magazine

Galveston Daily News

Gardnerville [Nevada] *Record-Courier*

Indianapolis Journal

Jerseyville [Illinois] *Republican-Examiner*

Juneau [Alaska] *City Mining Record*

Lander [Nevada] *Free Press*

Las Vegas Sun

Lewisburg [Pennsylvania] *News*

Louisville Post

Malden [Mass.] *Evening News*

Milwaukee Journal

Milwaukee Sentinel

Minneapolis Tribune

New Orleans Times-Democrat

New York Commercial Advertiser

New York Evangelist

New York Herald

New York Press

New York Recorder

New York Spirit of the Times

New York Star

New York Times

New York World

Omaha Bee

Omaha Herald

Philadelphia Inquirer

Philadelphia Record

Philadelphia Times

Phoenix Herald

Pittsburgh Times

Port Washington Democrat

Port Washington Pilot

Portland [Maine] *Argus*

Portland [Oregon] *Mercury*

Portland Oregonian

Reno Evening Gazette

Salt Lake Daily Reporter

San Antonio Daily Express

Schenectady Gazette

Sheboygan Press

Sierra [Nevada] *Sage*

Sitka [Alaska] *North Star*

Sitka Alaskan

St Louis Democrat

The World (city not identified)

Tucson Citizen

Twin Falls [Idaho] *Citizen*
Washington [D.C.] *Critic*
Washington National Republican
Washington National View
Washington News
Washington Post

Washington Star
Washington Sun
White Pine [Nevada] *Evening Telegram*
White Pine [Nevada] *News*
Yuma Daily Examiner

C. Other Countries

[*München*] *Süddeutsche Zeitung*
Le Figaro (Paris)
Le Globe (Paris)
Münchner Fremdenblatt

Münchner Neueste Nachrichten
Panama Star (*Panama Star and Herald*)
Sydney Morning Herald
Times (of London)

22. AUTHOR INTERVIEWS

(*Listed in Chronological Order*)

Unidentified resident of Michigan Bluff, California, February 22, 1997.

Shirley McChesney, Pacific-Union Club, San Francisco, March 7, 1997.

Karen Iversen, Education and External Projects Administrator, Heald Colleges, San Francisco, March 14, 1997.

Susan Haas, Registrar, Society of California Pioneers, San Francisco, March 25, 1997.

Stephanie Paulson, Receptionist, Stanford-Lathrop Memorial Home for Friendless Children, Sacramento, California, March 26, 1997.

Rennie Kirchof, Personnel Director, Weibel Winery, Corporate Offices, Fremont, California, April 1, 1997.

Ernest P. Peninou, San Francisco author of a book on the Stanford Vina Ranch, April 3, 1997.

John Rick, Archaeologist and Professor of Anthropological Archaeology, Stanford University, April 8 and 12, 1997.

Zita Eastman, Wine Librarian, Sonoma County Wine Library, April 9, 1997.

Gerhard Casper, President of Stanford University, April 13, 1997.

Anne Shaw, Associate Secretary, Office of the Secretary, The Regents of the University of California, Oakland, California, April 16 and May 3, 1997.

Virginia B. Bowers, Historian, City of Albany, New York, May 24, 1997.

Brother Francis, Monk, Public Relations contact, Vina Trappist Monastery, June 1, 1997.

Brother Oscar, Monk at Vina Trappist Monastery, June 4, 1997.

John Baudendistel, Cold Springs, California, February 22 and June 14, 1997.

Amy Lee, Customer Services Representative, Mountain View Cemetery, Oakland, California, June 18, 1997.

Don Hofsommer, Railroad Historian, St. Cloud, Minnesota, September 29, 1997.

Ken Longe, Union Pacific Railroad, Public Relations Department, October 17, 1997.

Diana Weibel, owner, Weibel Winery, Lodi, California, November 26, 1997.

John W. Buszta, Registrar, Albany, New York, Rural Cemetery, December 3, 1997, and October 27, 1999.

Bill Sturm, Oakland History Room, Oakland Public Library, January 9, 1998.

Bill Jones, Meriam Library, Chico State University, January 9, 1998.

Joan Howard, Archivist, National Archives and Records Administration, Rocky Mountain Region, Denver, Colorado, February 4, 19, and 24, 1998.

Louise York, Chief Deputy Clerk, United States District Court for the District of Utah, February 4 and 19, 1998.

Judith Amsbaugh, Stanford University Museum Docent, February 4, 1998.

Marisol Rodriquez, Tulare County Branch Librarian, Pixley, California, March 13, 1998.

Robert Zerkowitz, Research Assistant, San Francisco Wine Institute, March 27, 1998.

Sarah Logue, Assistant Librarian, California State Railroad Museum, Sacramento, April 1, 1998.

Marilyn D. Sommerdorf, Exhibits, California State Railroad Museum, Sacramento, April 1, 1998.

Lois Warren, Substitute Librarian, St. Joseph County [Indiana] Library, April 3, 1998.

David Eisen, Library Director, Mishawaka-Penn Public Library, Mishawaka, Indiana, April 3, 1998.

Frank Love, Historical Researcher, Yuma, Arizona, April 10, 1998.

Bill Panum, Western Americana Bibliographer, Denver Public Library, Denver, Colorado, April 21, 1998.

Janice Stern, Associate Planner, City of Fremont, California, April 21, 1998.

Ann Billesbach, Head of Reference Services, Nebraska State Historical Society, April 29, 1998.

Mary Robertson, Library Technician, John Q. Packard Library of Yuba County, April 30 and May 5, 1998.

Doreen Herburger, Mountain View Cemetery, Oakland, California, May 5, 1998.

Ambrose Mayer, Port Washington, Wisconsin, Historian, May 12, 1998 (since deceased).

Lowell A. Tainter, Secretary, Ozaukee Masonic Lodge, May [undated], 1998.

James L. Hansen, Newspaper Specialist, State Historical Society of Wisconsin, May 12, 1998.

Susan Roberts-Manganelli, Head of Registration and Conservation, Stanford Museum of Art, May 15, 1998.

Melissa O'Grady, Library Assistant, Cleveland Heights Library, Cleveland, Ohio, May 20, 1998.

Doris Muscatine, Author of a history of San Francisco, May 25, 1998.

Karrie L. Dvorak, Reference Assistant, Nebraska State Historical Society, May 27, 1998.

Ronald K. Inouye, Research Librarian, University of Alaska, May 29, 1998.

Madelleine Banfield, Woodlawn Memorial Park, Colma, California, June 4, 1998.

Richard T. Mangold, Historical Researcher, Madison, Wisconsin, June 15, 1998.

Ellen R. Halteman, Librarian, California State Railroad Museum and Library, September 2, 1998.

Sheldon D. Johnson, Amador County Recorder, September 2 and 18, 1998.

Robert A. Pecotich, Railroad Historian, Saratoga, California, September 4 and 18, 1998.

Dave Mirtoni, Placer County Building Department, September 9, 1998.

David Myrick, Railroad Historian, Santa Barbara, California, September 29, 1997, and October 11, 1998.

Kyle Wyatt, Curator of History, Nevada State Railroad Museum, October 1, 1998.

Richard W. "Dusty" Rhodes, Superior Court Judge, descendant of William Henry Rhodes (pen name "Caxton"), October 14 and 15, 1998.

Ian Campbell, Reference Librarian, Washoe County Library, October 28, 1998.

Guy Rocha, Nevada State Archivist, October 29, 1998.

G. J. "Chris" Graves, Central Pacific Railroad Collector and Researcher, Newcastle, California, January 27, 1999, July 7, 2001, et al.

Lynn Dale Farrar, Southern Pacific Company Valuations Engineer, January 27, 1999, et al.

Deidre Routt, Archivist, Union Pacific Railroad Company, February 9, 1999.

Helmut Kuen, Owner and manager of Hotel La Staila, Silvaplana, Switzerland, February 9 and December 15, 1999.

Peter Böckli, Author of Bis zum Tod der Gräfin, February 9 and March 5, 1999

Peter Hansen, Summer Manager, Hotel Maloja Palace, February 12 and 19, 1999.

Richard Hill, *Jeremiah O'Brien* Oiler, March 11, 1999.

Mona Reno, Head of Federal Publications, Nevada State Library and Archives, March 18, 1999.

Carol Teval, Library Assistant, Cesar Chavez Central Library, Stockton, California, March 25, 1999.

Dale Stickney, Information Geologist, California Department of Conservation, Division of Mines and Geology, Sacramento, September 1 and October 8, 1999.

Cindy Stark, Reference Librarian, Cultural Education Center, New York State Library, October 19 and 20, 1999.

Mead B. Kibbey, Sacramento Historian, December 18, 1999.

Jane Ingalls, Operations Manager, Earth Sciences Library, Stanford University, December 28, 1999.

Mary K. Morrison, Senior Associate Director, Financial Aid, Stanford University, January 3, 2000.

Unidentified construction foreman on Stanford road widening project, February 24, 2000.

Robert Schwemmer, Cultural Resources Coordinator, Channel Island National Marine Sanctuary and Channel Island National Park, March 1, 2000.

Gail Redmann, Reference Librarian, Washington, D.C., Historical Society, April 6, 2000.

Michael A. Fox, Special Projects Manager, Stanford University, April 12, 2000.

Patricia J. Johnson, Assistant Archivist, Sacramento Archives and Museum Collection Center, City of Sacramento, April 19, 2000.

Peter Bissoo, Foyer Manager, Claridge's [Hotel], London, May 28, 2000.

Wendy Dowling, Reservation Manager, Claridge's [Hotel], London, May 28, 2000.

Susan Scott, Archivist, The Savoy Group [of hotels], London, May 30, 2000.

Mary Colleen Brower, Archivist, First Unitarian-Universalist Church of San Francisco, June 23, 2000.

William Russ, Church Historian, Menlo Park Presbyterian Church, June 28, 2000.

Kristina P. Smith, Secretary, Unitarian-Universalist Church of Palo Alto, June 28, 2000.

David Kazen, User Education Assistant, Alderman, Library University of Virginia, September 15, 2000.

Janice Braun, Archivist, Mills College, September 29, 2000.

Laura Waterhouse, Director of Alumnae Relations, Albany Academy for Girls, Albany, New York, November 28, 2000.

Pat Keats, Library Director, Society of California Pioneers, San Francisco, December 8 and 11, 2000.

Lucinda GlennRand, Archivist, Graduate Theological Union, Berkeley, California, December 11 and 13, 2000.

Charlotte Flanagan, Curatorial Assistant, Stanford University Museum, January 17, 2001.

Betty Smart, Chief Curator of the California State Museum Resource Center, January 23, 2001.

Sara Sax, Director, Stanford Equestrian Center, January 23, 2001.

Maureen Miller, Library Specialist, A[lbert] K[eith] Smiley Public Library, Redlands, California, January 24, 2001.

Bruce Kleinsmith, Church Historian, St. Paul's Episcopal Church, Sacramento, February 15, 2001.

John Gonzales, Reference Librarian, California State Library History Room, February, 15, 2001.

Brother Guire Cleary, S.S.F., Curator, Mission Dolores, San Francisco, February 27, 2001.

Sally Childs-Helton, Archivist, Butler University, February 28, 2001.

Carmel Barry-Schweyer, Curator of Archives, Placer County Archives, Auburn, California, April 24, 2001.

Norma Hungerford, Family Service Counselor, Catholic Cemeteries & Mausoleum, Diocese of Sacramento, April 25, 2001.

Ruth Ellis, Sacramento Room Librarian, Sacramento Central Library, May 31, 2001.

Michelle Heston, Public Relations Manager, Mark Hopkins Inter-Continental Hotel, June 13, 2001.

Chuck Swete, Fireman, Promontory National Historic Site, Promontory, Utah, July 7, 2001.

Otis A. Pease, Professor of History, University of Washington, and former Professor of History at Stanford, July 11, 2001.

Edson Turner Strobridge, Central Pacific Railroad researcher and distant relative of James Harvey Strobridge, July 19 and August 25, 2001.

Bill Green, Archivist, Federal Archives and Records Center, San Bruno, California, August 1, 12001.

International Tower Agent, Sydney Ports, Sydney, New South Wales, Australia, August 3, 2001.

Linda Johnson, Archivist, California State Archives, August 14, 2001.

Aaron Purcell, University Archivist, University of Tennessee, September 14, 2001.

Wendell Huffman, Carson City Librarian, November 6, 2001, *et al.*

Alisa Austin, Assistant Librarian, Doris Foley Library for Historical Research, Nevada City, California, December 8, 2001.

Ron Verstraeten, Postmaster, Foresthill, California, January 14, 2002.

Carol Parris, Law Librarian, University of Kentucky, January 30, 2002.

James Winter, Central Pacific Railroad Photographic History Museum, April 17, 2002.

Robert LaPerriere, April 25 and 26, 2002.

Larry Cenotto, Amador County Archivist, April 24, 2002.

Lynn Dale Farrar, Southern Pacific Company Evaluations Engineer, July 3, 2002, *et al.*

Dennis Hyatt, Director of the Law Library, University of Oregon, September 20, 2002.

Elmer Lagorio, Teacher and Researcher, Carmel, California, October 24, 2002.

John Dojka, Institute Archivist, Rensselaer Polytechnic Institute, December 30, 2002.

Joel K. Thiele, Special Collections Librarian, Malden [Mass.] Public Library, January 15, 2003.

Thomas Carey, Reference Library, San Francisco Public Library History Room. January 15, 2003.

David Kravitz, Reference Librarian, California Room, San José Public Library, January 31, 2003.

Sally Childs-Helton, Archivist, Butler University, February 19, 2003.

Kristen Sanders , Assistant Archivist, Indiana University, February 21, 2003.

Robert J. Chandler, Wells Fargo Bank Historian, San Francisco, March 12, 2003.

23. AUTHOR CORRESPONDENCE

(Listed in Chronological Order)

Cazenovia Librarian to author, October 25, 1996.

Librarian, Port Washington, Wisconsin, Historical Society, October 25, 1996.

Patricia J. Johnson, Assistant Archivist, Sacramento Archives and Museum Collection Center, City of Sacramento, January 22, 1997, April 2, 1998, and April 16, 2001.

Diana Strazdes, Stanford University Museum Curator of American Art, February 19, 1997.

Virginia B. Bowers, Historian, City of Albany, New York, March 26, May 26 and November 23, 1997.

Anne Shaw, Associate Secretary, Office of the Secretary, Regents of the University of California, April 17, 1997.

Paul Miner, Chief Deputy Director of Planning and Research for Gov. Pete Wilson, Sacramento, May 10, 1997.

Ruth Bayliss, Reference Librarian, Alexander Mackie Curriculum Resources Library, University of Sydney, Australia, April 24 and 29, May 5, July 18, November 13 and 20, 1997.

Barry Nunn, Librarian, State Library of New South Wales, Australia, May 21, 1997.

Irene Saganich, Historian, Town of Schodack, New York, May 23, 1997.

Luana Malloni, Assistant Manager, Hotel Helvetia & Bristol, Florence, Italy, April 10 and 30, and June 6, 1997.

Jonathan P. Reider, Senior Associate Director of Admissions, Stanford University, October 28, 1997.

Patricia Turse, California Park Ranger, Stanford Mansion, Sacramento, January 22, 1998.

Peggy Tilley, Reference Librarian, Merced County Library, January 30, 1998.

Judith Amsbaugh, Stanford University Museum Docent, February 4, 1998.

George W. Peabody, El Dorado County Museum, Placerville, California, March 5, 1998.

David Eisen, Director, Mishawaka-Penn Public Library, Mishawaka, Indiana, April 23, 1998.

Mary Robertson, Library Technician, John Q. Packard Library of Yuba County, California, May 7, 1998.

Karrie L. Dvorak, Reference Assistant, Nebraska State Historical Society, May 15 and 27, 1998.

Rosie Ramirez, Historical Records Researcher, Sacramento Archives and Museum Collection Center, Sacramento, June 19, 1998.

Richard T. Mangold, Historical Researcher, Madison, Wisconsin, June 20, 1998.

Charles J. Ansbach, President, Ansbach & Associates, Sacramento, and fundraiser for the Sacramento Stanford house, July 30 and 31, 1998.

George Deukmejian, former Governor of California, August 11 and 19, 1998.

Guy L. Dunscomb, Railroad Historian, August 27, 1998.

Kyle Wyatt, Curator of History, Nevada State Railroad Museum, October 1, 1998.

Walter Schivo, resident of Michigan Bluff, California, October 1998.

Helmut Kuen, Owner and manager of Hotel La Staila, Silvaplana, Switzerland, January 28, 1999.

Arnie Weiss, Virginia historical researcher, February 10, 1999.

Edward Howes, Professor of History, California State University at Sacramento, May 15, 1999.

Mrs. Elspeth Bobbs, Granddaughter of Lizzie (Hull) Grant, September 3, 1999.

Imtraud Stockinger, Leiterin der Monacensia Bibliothek, Munich, November 16, 1999.

Connie Johnston, Mishawaka-Penn Public Library, Mishawaka, Indiana, December 13, 1999.

Kathleen Brewster, Library Services, Santa Barbara Historical Society, March 1, 2000.

Robert Schwemmer, Cultural Resources Coordinator, Channel Island National Marine Sanctuary and Channel Island National Park, March 22, 2000.

Eric N. Moody, Curator of Manuscripts, Nevada Historical Society, March 23, 2000.

John G. Hoffa, Historical Researcher, Nevada Historical Society, March 30, 2000.

Nancy Dukes, Geographic Names Officer, U.S. Board on Geographic Names, April 11, 2000.

Karen E. Bartholomew, April 22 and November 29, 2000.

Michele Myszka, Community Relations Director, Pacific Life Foundation, April 28, 2000.

Charlene Duval, Reference Librarian, California Room, San José Public Library, May 6, 2000.

David Melrose, General Manager, Holiday Inn, Garden Court, London, June 19, 2000.

Kristina P. Smith, Secretary, Unitarian-Universalist Church of Palo Alto, June 28, 2000.

Anita V. Mozley, former Curator of the Stanford Museum, July 16, 2000.

Kathleen Leles DiGiovanni, Librarian, Oakland History Room, Oakland Public Library, November 28, 2000.

Chad Wall, Reference librarian, Nebraska State Historical Society, December 12, 2000.

Jeff Edwards, Edwards Studio, Private Historical Researcher, Porterville, California, December 19, 2000.

Marilyn Calvey, Tour and Seminar Director, Cypress Lawn Memorial Cemetery, Colma, California, June 4, 1998, and December 29, 2000.

G. J. "Chris" Graves, Newcastle, California, Independent Central Pacific Researcher, January 14, 2001, and January 16, 2002.

Joseph Angier, Thomas Lennon Films, February 6, 2002.

Lee Altenberg, Adjunct Assistant Professor of History, University of Hawaii at Manoa, February 25, 2001.

Theresa La Bianca, Archivist, Green-Wood Cemetery, Brooklyn, New York, April 19, 2001.

Richard Cottle, Professor of Management Science & Engineering, Stanford University, May 2, 2001.

Barbara Goldsmith, Librarian, State Library of New South Wales, Australia, May 14, 2001.

Nancy Lealas, Government Information Secretary, Albany Law School, May 24, 2001.

Wendell W. Huffman, Librarian, Carson City Public Library, June 9, 2001.

Michelle Heston, Public Relations Manager, Mark Hopkins Inter-Continental Hotel, June 13, 2001.

John Tuteur, Napa County Assessor/Recorder, Napa, California, August 8 and November 1, 2001.

Miriam Biro, Director of Museums, North Lake Tahoe Historical Society, September 14, 2001.

Diane Norman, Reference Librarian, Otis Library, Norwich, Connecticut, September 14, 2001.

Susan Sneeringer, Volunteer, Archives of Albany Academy for Girls, September 17, 2001.

Edson Turner Strobridge, Independent Researcher on the life of James Harvey Strobridge, January 16, June 13, and October 25, 2002.

Nancy Lyon, Office Manager, St. John's Episcopal Church, Bridgeport, Connecticut, January 28, 2002.

John Rawlinson Hayes, Archivist of the Episcopal Diocese of California, February 14, 2002.

Beth Janopaul, former Business and Facilities Manager, Menlo Park Trinity Episcopal Church, February 15, 2002.

Bob Johnson, Reference Librarian, California Room, San José Public Library, March 16, 2002.

James Winter, Central Pacific Railroad Photographic History Museum, April 17, 2002.

Larry Cenotto, Amador County Archivist, April 24, 2002.

Lynn Dale Farrar, Southern Pacific Company Valuations Engineer, May 4, 2002.

Stephen E. Drew, Chief Curator, California State Railroad Museum, July 26, 2002.

Charles P. Zlatkovich, Associate Dean, College of Business Administration, University of Texas at El Paso, July 31, 2002.

Susan Snyder, Reference Librarian, Bancroft Library, August 13, 2002.

Dennis Hyatt, Director of the Law Library, University of Oregon, September 20, 2002.

Carol Harrison, Reference Librarian, El Dorado County Library, September 25, 2002.

George C. Werner, Texas Railroad Historian, September 28 and October 26, 2002, and February 13, 2003.

Sarah R. Terrill, Circulation Services Librarian, SUL Ross State University, October 11, 2002.

Elmer Lagorio, Teacher and Researcher, October 26, 2002.

Salvador A. Ramírez, Historical Researcher and Writer, biographer of Mark Hopkins, April 18 and October 30, 2002.

Graml, Josh, Reference Researcher, Mariners' Museum, Newport News, Virginia, November 5, 2002.

Ian Ferguson, of Redwood City, California, nephew of James Harvey Strobridge's adopted daughter Carrie Ferguson, November 8, 2002.

Rebecca L. Wendt, Archivist, California State Archives, December 18, 2002.

John Dojka, Institute Archivist, Rensselaer Polytechnic Institute, December 31, 2002, and January 2, 2003.

Joel K. Thiele, Special Collections Librarian, Malden [Mass.] Public Library, January 15, 2003.

Lynn D. Farrar, Southern Pacific Company Valuations Engineer, February 13, 2003.

Tom Carey, Librarian, San Francisco Public Library, March 28, 2003.

Linda Emond, Advertising and Public Relations Specialist, Pacific Life Insurance Co., September 8, 2003.

Deborah Dalton, Librarian, Sacramento Public Library, September 23, 2003.

Index

Stoneman, George B., governor of Calif., 674; on
   railroad commission, 550-555; at Lang Station,
   354; signs LSJU bill into law, 710
Stony Ford Stud Farm, 442
Storey, William Benson, 286, 588
Story, Joseph, 566
Story, Mary Oliver, 566
Stow, William W., 826, 832, 837; Stanford honorary
   pallbearer, 910
Stowe, Harriet Beecher, 693
Strauss, David Friederick, 716
Strobridge, Edson Turner, 244, 271, 295
Strobridge, James Harvey, CPRR and SPRR
   superintendent of construction, 589; family of,
   244; on employment of Chinese, 244-245, 247-
   249, 300; biographical information, 244; loss of
   right eye at Bloomer Cut, 244; rejects use of
   steam-drilling machines, 250-251; completes
   the railroad from Niles to Oakland, 306; independent contractor, 306; takes a brief hiatus in
   railroad work, 351; at Lang Station celebration,
   351-352, 354; president of the Pacific Improvement Co., 586; progress in Ariz., 594; on engineering decisions, 589; pronounced
   "Strawbridge" in Texas, 610; retirement from
   railroad construction, 629; in memoriam, 1018
Strobridge, Maria (Keating), first wife of J. H.
   Strobridge, 244
Strobridge, Tullius W., 94
Strong, Daniel, works with Judah on Pacific railroad route, 187; and the Pacific Railroad, 188,
   191; as director of the CPRR, 191-193; on the
   beginning of the Sierra foothills, 211; Judah
   complains to him about CPRR management,
   221; ownership in Dutch Flat & Donner Lake
   Wagon Road Co., 230; photograph of, 218
Stubbs, David D., brother of John Christian Spayd
   Stubbs, 640, 647
Stubbs, John Christian Spayd, 756; in N.Y. for rail-
   road meeting, 616; opinion of railroad control
   622; biographical information, 623; in New
   Orleans, 756; USPRC testimony, 625; director
   of Southern Pacific Co., 810
Stumpf, Thomas Jefferson, 468
Stymus, William Pierre, 370
Suez Canal, 635-636
Sullivan, Elizabeth Ann (Yount), 390
Sullivan, Eugene L., 115, 143, 324-326

Sullivan, Frank J., 671
Sullivan, Mike, 286
Sultan Abdülhâmid II, 687-690
Summit tunnel (No. 6), use of nitroglycerin on, 251
Sumner, Charles B., 258
Sumner, Edwin V., 153
Sunland, 1000-1003. *See also Car Stanford*
Sunset Magazine, 630; photograph of first cover,
   1005
Sunset Route, 623-625
Sutro, Adolph, 83
Sutter, John Augustus, 925
Sutter's Fort, 364
Swain, Oliver, 870
Swain, Robert E., 1008
Swann, Mrs. J. Thompson, 773
Swett, Leonard, 141
Swig, Benjamin, 959
Syracuse University, 12

Taggert, [Deputy], 873
Taylor, Agnes (Stanford), daughter of Josiah, 978;
   at Leland, Jr., funeral, 701; one of the first to
   arrive at Stanford's deathbed, 908; in Stanford
   funeral cortège, 909; legacy from Stanford, 934
Taylor, Clay W., 671
Taylor, Edward Robeson, in Stanford funeral
   cortège, 909; Josiah Stanford's son-in-law, 934;
   defends "disaffected" legatees in suit against
   Aunt Jane, 943-944; asked to resign from LSJU
   trustees, 975-977; biographical sidebar, 978; in
   memoriam, 1018
Taylor, Emma, F., mother of Wilsie, 884
Taylor, Frank, 185
Taylor, John G., father of Wilsie, 884
Taylor, John, 384
Taylor, Willson "Wilsie" Grissim, 660, 682; friend
   of Leland, Jr., 652, 682-683; copy of *In
   Memoriam*, 693; death of, 883-885; in memo-
   riam, 1017
Taylor, Zachary, 88-89
Teas and kettledrums, 668
Teller, Henry M., 677
Temple, Jackson, 573
Terry, David Smith, chief justice of Calif., 87-88;
   duel with Broderick, 349; death of, 872-876
Tevis, Lloyd, banker, 268, 394, 573; and the SPRR,
   263-264, 319; secretary of the Oakland Water

The Governor: The Life and Legacy of Leland Stanford—A California Colossus
by Norman E. Tutorow
has been produced in an edition of 1,550 copies,
50 of which were bound in leather, signed by the author, and numbered.

The typeface used is Perpetua.
Designed by Ariane C. Smith under the direction of Robert A. Clark.
Printing by Sheridan Books, Inc., of Ann Arbor, Michigan.